AN INDEX TO

Changes of Name

*Under Authority of Act of Parliament or Royal Licence
and including Irregular Changes from*
1 GEORGE III to 64 VICTORIA,
1760 to 1901,

COMPILED BY
W. P. W. PHILLIMORE & EDW. ALEX. FRY,

With an Introduction on the
Law of Change of Name
BY
W. P. W. PHILLIMORE.

LONDON: PHILLIMORE & CO, 124, CHANCERY LANE.
1905

Note to the Reader.

THE compilation of the present index was commenced several years ago, and has proved a longer and more tedious task than at the outset was anticipated. It was at first intended to include only changes of name effected under the royal sign manual, or by the authority of a private act of parliament But so many changes have been effected irregularly within the last half century, that it was thought it would be a matter of some practical utility if they also could be included, even though they were without authority, and this accordingly has been done, though it has somewhat delayed the completion of the index, and added in no small degree to the labour of compiling it. But if it adds to the utility of the index, the compilers will be fully satisfied.

The sources from which this index has been compiled are several. Primarily it is based on the Changes of Name by Royal licence. For this purpose the volumes of the London Gazette, and also the Dublin Gazette from 1760 to 1901 were examined, but it must be remembered that not all Royal licences are advertised in the Gazettes, though the vast majority are so advertised for obvious reasons of convenience, and often also in the "Times" and other newspapers Registration at Heralds' College only, is a sufficient compliance with the Royal licence granted

Next, this list comprises those names changed under the authority of Private Acts of Parliament, a method now but little resorted to In this list they, as a rule, are indicated simply by the usual references of year of the reign and chapter by which such Acts are usually referred to, but occasionally also the reference to the Index to Private Acts of Parliament is also quoted

The next class are those changes made, *suo motu*, without any licence or Act of Parliament, and these, which are usually evidenced by deeds poll and simple advertisement, have been taken chiefly from the columns of the "Times," though, as this method of irregular change did not become frequent till somewhat less than 50 years ago, it was not thought necessary to search the "Times" before the year 1861 These changes are indicated by the word "Times," and the date of issue, and when accompanied by a deed poll, that fact is indicated by the initials d p Some changes are not advertised in the "Times," and these it has not been found practical to include with any degree of completeness, but when they have come under notice, they have always been inserted, though unfortunately, as in some cases they are taken from small collections of

Note to the Reader.

change of name advertisements, in which the source was not always given, it has not been found possible to indicate in every case the newspaper in which the advertisement appeared

Some few also are included which have not even been advertised, and the authority for these rests on information given to the Editors though they have not included any such, unless satisfied that they have been in permanent use.

With these irregular changes it has been thought well, for the sake of identification, to give nearly all particulars which are stated in the advertisements. So much more information than could be given in an Index like this is, may be obtained from the Heralds' Office, that in the cases of Royal licence changes, it has been thought best merely to supply the reference and the initials of the Christian names

Besides the changes just referred to, there are those Scottish ones recorded in the Registers of the Lord Lyon, in Edinburgh, and the Irish changes noted in Ulsters Office in Dublin The latter are advertised in the Dublin Gazette, just as in England they appear in the London Gazette In some cases they appear in both Gazettes In addition to the regular changes entered in Ulster Office, there is there a short list of various irregular changes noted by a former Ulster, W. Betham, and distinguished in this Index under his name.

It may be noted that very considerable help may be derived by the genealogist from changes of name made in pursuance of a Royal licence. By the terms of the licence such changes have to be entered at Heralds' College. In the greater number of cases it will be found that pedigrees have been consequently recorded there, and in the majority of cases, a grant of Arms has been made to the person effecting a change of name. Often, too, in the London Gazette, and also in the Dublin Gazette, the advertisements themselves contain a short recital of the pedigree, or the reason for the change. Less information is obtainable from irregular changes, and in not a few cases the advertiser does not even trouble to supply his address, or gives merely a temporary one

In consulting this Index the following points must be noted :—
It is primarily an Index to names *adopted* thus
    Smith : Jones, A 6 June, 1810 (1461)
means Smith, adopted by A. Jones, under a Royal licence dated 6 June, 1810, advertised on page 1461 of the London Gazette for 1810

The name *discarded* is also indexed with a cross reference thus :
    Jones *see* Smith.

Note to the Reader. vii.

No particulars are given under the entry of the discarded name. Cases in which the Christian name, or its equivalent is altered, are indexed only once, and that under the surname.

When merely a date appears, the reader will understand that such an entry relates to an irregular change, for which the compilers are unable to give precise authority, though they are satisfied that such a change did actually take place. In most cases this lack of authority arises from their having been obtained from some newspaper cutting to which the reference has not been attached.

The figures within parenthesis following a simple date relate to the London Gazette. Before the year 1785, the figures indicate the several *numbers* of the Gazette itself; from that date onwards the Gazette is paged consecutively for each year, and thenceforward these figures indicate the *page* of the Gazette.

The *dates* following names indicate, as a general rule, the date of the Royal licence; in irregular cases they refer to the date of the "Times" in which the advertisement was first published. occasionally it may be found that they indicate the date of the deed poll.

The following contractions have been made use of :—

Betham   = a list made by W. Betham, Ulster, about 1810.
con.   = continue the name of
com.   = commonly.
D.C.   = Dublin Castle.
D.G.   = Dublin Gazette.
d. p.   = deed poll.
Lyon   = Lyon Register, Edinburgh.
L G.   = London Gazette.
R.L.   = Royal Licence.
St. J.   = St. James.
W. Wll. or Whll. = Whitehall.

Various other contractions have also been adopted which will cause the reader no difficulty.

Finally, it is requisite to express our obligations for help given in the compilation of this index, without which it would have been still less complete than it is.

The late Garter King of Arms, Sir Albert Woods, K C B., had formed a large collection of irregular changes of name which he courteously placed at the Compilers' service, and aided in the work by his advice, whilst his colleague, Mr. G. E. Cokayne, Clarenceux King of Arms, also allowed

Note to the Reader.

his collection of changes to be made use of for this index. Sir James Balfour Paul, Lord Lyon, supplied the references in Lyon's Register, and Sir Arthur Vicars, Ulster King of Arms, supplied a list of Irish changes, whilst both the last-named scanned many of the proof sheets as regards other changes with which they are officially concerned. In Ireland too, the help of Mr. Burtchael, of Ulster's Office, must be acknowledged; and thanks are due to others who have occasionally added some changes which would otherwise have escaped notice.

This list of changes of name, large as it is, and it has proved far larger than the Editors ever anticipated, is by no means complete. Not only is it certain that many changes, regular and irregular, are not recorded, but no attempt has been made to deal with those made before the first year of George III.

The Compilers' having in view the issue hereafter of a supplement, will be glad to have note of any changes made before 1760, whether regular or informal. In the latter case the fullest particulars should be given, and the authority should be carefully stated. And in these changes may be included the cases of *aliases* which are found in wills of the sixteenth and seventeenth centuries, many of which seem to have been the ancient equivalent of our modern "double-barrelled" names.

Lastly, as it is certain that in an index now for the first time compiled, and dealing with so large a number of facts, there must of necessity be *errors* and *omissions*, any corrections will be specially valued, and when received will be carefully noted for inclusion in the proposed supplement.

W. P. W. P.
E. A. F.

THE LAW AND PRACTICE OF CHANGE OF NAME.

From early times various persons have found it necessary or desirable to change the name or names by which they have been known. Of recent years, that is during the past half-century, the practice of thus altering the personal designation appears to have much increased. Obviously for this there is more than one cause. Some are directed to change their names on succeeding to property under a will or a settlement with the view of perpetuating the memory of some family which has become extinct in the male line, and for them it is compulsory. Others assume a fresh surname on their own initiative for a similar reason or as a mark of respect to some distinguished or favourite ancestor. Yet another class adopt the same course in order to escape the disadvantage of some frequent* or it may be offensive appellation, while others effect such changes from mere whim. Lastly there are those whose past history has been so evil that a change of name becomes a necessity, either to enable them to effect a reformation in their life's history, or, it may be more frequently, to allow them to continue their evil course with less risk of detection. With this last class it is unnecessary to deal and further they do not willingly leave any record of their change of name, and such record as there may be is preserved only in the law courts.

It will be seen that changes of name, unless brought about by mere whim or worse, are usually made for motives which can only be regarded as praiseworthy, and it is perhaps to a consciousness of this that the number of such changes has in recent years somewhat increased.

During the last one hundred and fifty years several thousands of families, principally in the upper and well-to-do classes of society, have by one way or another changed their names, so that the subject is obviously of very considerable importance from a genealogical point of view. These changes indicate the existence in very many cases of a pedigree registered at Heralds' College, and not infrequently the grant of a coat of arms.

---

* Sometimes, as in Wales is very noticeable, an insufficient number and variety of surnames may be a considerable inconvenience. This, in Denmark, was so obvious that the Government of that country in 1903 proposed a law empowering Danes to change their names. It was stated that in Copenhagen one person in ten bore the name Hansen, while Petersen and Sorensen are almost as common. In one commune it was alleged that there are only twenty different surnames amongst some 20,000 inhabitants.

Changes of name were formerly almost, if not entirely, confined to the surname, but of recent years there have been very many instances of attempting the change also of the Christian or personal name. How such changes should be effected, if it is possible to effect them, is a subject which has been very hotly debated, but before considering the legality of any particular view it may be as well to consider very briefly the origin and nature of personal nomenclature in this Kingdom.

Anciently, but at very early date, individuals were distinguished merely by the single name given to them in their baptism, and to the present day the Church, in its catechism and marriage service, entirely ignores the surname and recognizes merely the name acquired in baptism. The inconvenience of a single name and the obvious difficulty of distinguishing individuals early led to the adoption of some surname or soubriquet by which one man might be known from another. How early such surnames were adopted it is not easy to say, nor can we precisely fix the time when they became hereditary. The convenience of the practice was obvious and for a very long period surnames, in this country, have been universal, with the sole exception of the present Royal family, which possesses no permanent general family surname and uses the name of baptism only.

It would be out of place here to enter into a long dissertation of the etymology and origin of surnames. It will suffice to indicate the principal classes into which they may be divided. These are:—

1. *Patronymics.*—Derived from the personal name of some remote ancestor. These again may be sub-divided into:—

    (a) *Paleo-patronymics.*—Derived from personal names chiefly in use before the Norman Conquest, *e.g.*, Wigg, Froude, Orme, Finn, etc. They are mostly monosyllabic in form.

    (b) *Neo-patronymics.*—These are later than the Conquest. They are distinguished in England by the suffix *son*, often contracted into *s*, such as Johnson and Jones, Williamson and Williams, or represented in Norman-French by the prefix *Fitz* as in FitzGerald, FitzRoy, in Wales by *ap* or *P* as in ap Rice and ap Owen, which become Price and Bowen, in Scotland by the prefix *Mac* as in MacDonald, also variously written as McDonald, M'Donald, or Macdonald, and in Ireland by the prefix *O* as in O'Brien.

2. *Topographical.*—Dividing into :—

    (*a*) Surnames from villages, towns and districts, as Clifton, Buckingham, Wiltshire

    (*b*) Surnames from local features, as Wood, Hill, Dale, Combe, Atwood, Athill, Agate, Twells, Bythesea.

3. *Occupational.*—Such as Smith, Archdeacon, Priest, Carpenter, Draper.

4. *Nicknames.*—Such as Blount, Whitlock, Gifford, Strong-ith'arm, Armstrong.

And contractions, diminutives and misspellings have further produced an infinite variety of surnames, many of which even by the experienced can scarcely be traced to their origin.

The nature of the change effected varies very considerably. As regards those by Royal Licence there appear to be but three forms. In the simplest the name taken is "in lieu and instead of" the original patronymic. Thus John Brown, who adopts the name of Smith "*in lieu and instead of*" being John Brown, becomes simply John Smith. In many of the earlier notices in the *London Gazette* the license is simply expressed " to assume the name of," thus leaving it uncertain whether it is in addition to or in lieu of the original surname. If the license permits him to adopt Smith *in addition* to and after his own he becomes John Brown-Smith : if it be as a *prefix* then in such an instance he is John Smith-Brown. It is usual when two names are adopted to connect them by a hyphen, though for this custom there does not appear to be any distinct authority. When the surnames thus conjoined are more than monosyllables the result is inconvenient, and obviously in many cases it becomes impossible to address the individuals by their composite names, and in such cases the last name to all practical purposes becomes the surname, and indeed in heraldic practice becomes the principal surname, for when a person bearing a double surname is entitled to arms in respect of both names the arms of the last are always put in the first or principal quarter of his shield. Sometimes the owner of a double name assumes a third and even a fourth name, when the result may become almost grotesque. Thus the Thurlow family first became Hovell-Thurlow and afterwards adopted two more names, thus acquiring the cumbrous designation of Hovell-Thurlow-Cumming-Bruce.

The fact that some surnames are so frequent as in some cases to almost cease to be a means of identification is a very great inducement to alter or add to a surname for distinction's sake, and very often a man's neighbour will do this for him if he possesses a distinctive Christian name which readily blends with his surname. Thus John Stanley Brown will be addressed as Mr. Stanley-Brown. Indeed some such change becomes from reasons of convenience almost a necessity. Even on the judicial bench the newspapers have made us familiar with Mr. Justice Gorell Barnes and Mr. Justice Swinfen Eady, though neither of those learned judges appear to be entitled to the distinction, if such it be, of a " double-barrelled " name.

Thus again the possession of a grotesque or even offensive surname is another inducement to change, as may be seen by glancing through this index, for of such names there are unfortunately too many. Such names are often a positive detriment to their bearers and a man may well be excused for effecting a change by the best means available, even though the formal and preferable method of a Royal licence for one reason or another may not be open to him.

There are also name changes which are dictated by a mere vanity and sometimes by vanity coupled with ignorance. Of these the most common examples are the assumption of the prefix *de* or *le*, or the sanctification of a name by prefixing to it *St*. Except in the case of foreigners recently settled in England the use of *de* as a prefix can only be regarded as a foolish affectation. The assumption of *de* was perhaps more frequent in the first half of last century and was no doubt a consequence of the so-called medieval revival. Often too a change is effected by adopting some obsolete or fanciful spelling of a name. Perhaps the most remarkable instance of this is to be found amongst the Smiths. An Essex baronet of that name adopted the grotesque form of Smijth, presumably in ignorance of the fact that what he took to be " ij " in old documents was merely the letter " y," which at one time was written with two dots. A little knowledge of paleography would have saved him from rendering his family name permanently ridiculous. Of a similar nature is the odd use of " ff " instead of the capital " F," on which some people appear to pride themselves, in ignorance of the fact that double " ff " is merely an obsolete form of writing the capital. Such trivialities are much to be deprecated; they are inaccurate and what is worse give needless trouble to other people, who fear that they may cause offence if they address a letter to Mrs. Foulkes instead of Mrs. ffoulkes.

It will be of interest to note the number of those who assume or discard some of the more frequent surnames. Thus of those bearing the surname Smith, some 73 entirely discarded it, while 93 modified it by affixing or prefixing some other surname to that patronymic. A prefix seems to be the more popular method of differencing, as we find some 57 adopting prefixes as against 36 who added other names. The total of those who discarded or modified Smith is 166. In the case of the next most common name, Jones—115 discarded or modified it, while only 6 assumed it, which may indicate that Smith, though the commoner, is the more popular name. The proportions in the case of Brown or Browne, which it is needless to distinguish here, are very different; 83, exactly half that of the Smiths, discard or modify it, but in 19 instances it is assumed, though if the proportion found with the Smiths were followed there would be but eight. Of Taylors, 37 discard or modify the name, whilst nine assume it. In the case of the two Welsh names of frequent occurrence, Davies or Davis and Williams, there are 40 in each instance who discard their patronymic, whilst there are but three instances of assumption of Davis and five of Williams. It is thus plain that the desire of getting rid of common surnames leads to such being discarded with a greater frequency than they are adopted.

The simple canons adopted for changes by license are by no means adhered to in irregular changes. Persons making these irregular changes will without hesitation convert one of their Christian names into the new surname, merely dropping their proper surname, or conjoin them with a hyphen; they will wholly alter their Christian name, or it may be, add a new Christian name or change their positions; occasionally a new name is constructed out of the same letters as the old one consists of.

A few examples may now be given :—

Sir Henry Hoghton becomes Sir Henry de Hoghton, 1863.

John Ely Fisher became St. John Ely Viviane, 1863

Philip Lybbe Powys became Philip Lybbe Powys Lybbe, 1863.

David Richard Jones became David Richard St Paul, 1862.

Abraham Solomans became Alfred Phillips, 1862.

Shirt became Hirst, 1820.

Henry Hollingworth Wells Beman became Henry Beman Wells, 1862.

> This gentleman advertized that he took the surname of Wells in lieu of Beman, but made no remark as to his Christian names, though it will be seen that he dropped two of them and adopted his late surname as a Christian one

Nathan Norton Laventhall became Norton Nathan Laventhal Lonsdale, 1863.

> Here the first names were transposed and a new surname added but not hyphened. It may be assumed that this family, presumably a foreign one, is now known as Lonsdale only.

Vere Jones became Vere Jones Vere, 1863.

> This was a singular case as Vere Jones was the infant son of Thomas J. Jones, who apparently did not change his own name.

John Joseph Deadman became John Joseph Dedman, 1864.

> This is a change of spelling made for obvious reason.

Albert Henry Benson O'Fflahertie became Albert Henry Benson de Vere, 1864.

Robert William Scoble became Robert William Scobell, 1864.

> Here is a change of spelling in order to cast the accent on the last syllable, for that method of pronunciation by many is regarded as the more fashionable one.

Edward FitzGerald Galaher became Edward Fitzgerald, 1864.

> Here the surname is simply dropped and the Christian name became the new surname.

Henry Perkins Wolrige became Henry Gordon Wolrige, 1864.

> Here, "by reason of succession to an estate," he drops Perkins and assumes instead the surname of Gordon —apparently he does not treat it as a "double" name. He afterwards became Henry Wolrige Gordon by Royal licence in 1873.

Charles Reed Driver became Charles Reed de la Bere, 1864.

> He "resumes" his "ancient family surname"—a strange misuse of the the word "resume." It might be imagined that he formerly bore the name de la Bere, but such was not the case. It is evidently the name of some remote (presumed) ancestor.

A desire to conceal racial origin produces many changes. The motive in these cases doubtless varies Some may be ashamed of their origin, others find it merely inconvenient in business to appear as foreigners, or do not desire to appear singular amongst their neighbours By a few the process is reversed for obvious purpose of deception, as when the Irish singer Foley called himself Signor Foli with the evident object of inducing the public to think that he was an Italian vocalist.

Jews, Germans, Russians and Irish* are especially prone to this weakness, but it may be remarked that this is not so much the case with Frenchmen and Italians. Genealogically it may be noted that a certain prestige appears to attach to surnames of French origin, which is not the case with others Doubtless this is due to the still existing influence of the Norman Conquest upon our family history.

If we take as an example the distinctively Jewish name of Moses we find that fourteen discarded the name entirely while three others added English surnames as hyphened additions. It might have been thought that those who possess names of the antiquity of the Jewish patriarchs would have been proud thereof and would have been reluctant to replace them by others of comparatively modern origin, but such does not appear to be the case

What is perhaps the best known change of name is that of Bug to Howard. In the *Times* of 26 June, 1862, appeared the following advertisement :—

> I, NORFOLK HOWARD, heretofore called and known by the name of Joshua Bug, late of Epsom in the County of Surrey, now of Wakefield in the County of York and Landlord of the Swan Tavern in the same County, do hereby give notice that on the 20th day of this present day of June, for and on behalf of myself and my heirs lawfully begotten, I did wholly ABANDON the use of the SURNAME of BUG and ASSUMED, took and used, and am determined at all times hereafter in all writings, actions, dealings, matters and things, and upon all other occasions whatsoever to be distinguished, to subscribe, to be called and known by the name of NORFOLK HOWARD only. I further refer all whom it may concern to the deed poll under my hand and seal declaring that I choose to renounce the use of the surname of Bug and that I assume in lieu thereof the above surname of Norfolk Howard, and also declaring my determination upon all occasions whatsoever to be called and distinguished exclusively by the said surname of Norfolk Howard, duly enrolled by me in the High Court of Chancery. Dated this 23rd day of June, 1862
>
> NORFOLK HOWARD, late Joshua Bug.

Some uncertainty, however, is attached to the example for it has been alleged that the advertisement was merely a *jeu d'esprit* of a well-known genealogist who wished to cast ridicule upon the method, then coming into fashion, of attempting to effect a change of surname by means of a deed poll, coupled with a newspaper advertisement

---

* The recrudescence of local national feeling has tended to arrest a change that some years ago was silently taking effect with names possessing the distinctively Irish prefix O. This was in process of disuse, and so O'Donovan became simply Donovan At the present time the tendency is to resume the use of this prefix.

The most familiar change of name is that which daily takes place on marriage, when the newly-married wife wholly discards her maiden surname and assumes that of her husband. So complete is this change in England, so completely is the wife's individuality absorbed by the husband's family, that in genealogical inquiries it frequently proves to be a matter of extreme difficulty, often an impossibility, to identify the wives in a pedigree. This obliteration of the wife's identity is the natural outcome of the old theory of English law that her personality by marriage became absorbed or merged in that of her husband. The inconvenience of this obliteration of the woman's maiden surname has become very evident in modern times, especially with women who become authors or engage in business or professional life. Literary women have sought to obviate the inconvenience in a variety of ways. One is that of adopting the husband's surname as an addition, as in the case of the famous American writer, Harriet Beecher, who after her marriage became known as Mrs. Harriet Beecher Stowe, a useful innovation, to which the only objection is that it is not always clear that the second name may not be merely a baptismal or given name. This difficulty, however, might be and often is obviated to some extent by the use of a hyphen, as Mrs. Harriet Beecher-Stowe. Other feminine authors retain for literary purposes their maiden name on a title page, adding their married description in brackets or smaller type below. By others the process is reversed. They appear on the title as Mrs. John Smith, while their maiden name follows in brackets. On the stage the reverse is the case and the actress as a rule, even though married, prefers to retain her original or adopted name in preference to using that of her husband. Both actors and actresses as a rule, it may be said, adopt a stage name, a custom arising doubtless from the disrepute long attaching to the occupation of the play actor.

The obliteration of the maiden name has the great inconvenience in genealogical inquiries of rendering it almost impossible to trace for any long period ancestry in the female line. Logically, it would seem reasonable in working out a pedigree to trace not merely the paternal line, *i.e.*, the father's father or grandfather, and so on, but also the maternal line, *i.e.*, the mother, grandmother, and so on in the female line. What, however, a man usually means when he tells one that he has worked out his wife's pedigree or his mother's is that he has traced their *paternal* ancestry in the male line, and indeed the obstacles to tracing out a true maternal line are in England almost insurmountable, as obviously the surname must change with each generation that the pedigree is carried back.

This difficulty is not felt to the same degree in Scotland, where, owing to the reasonable practice of women retaining for all legal purposes their own original name but adding that of their husband as an *alias*, the history of the wife's family may be traced back with a fulness which is rarely feasible in England. Miss Jean MacNabb on her marriage to Donald Douglas becomes for legal purposes Mrs. Jean MacNabb or Douglas, though socially, as in England, she is addressed as Mrs. Douglas. On her tombstone she will be described as " Jean MacNabb spouse of Donald Douglas " It cannot be doubted that in the way of dealing with the surnames of women the Scotch practice is better than that which obtains in England. In Ireland the practice as to women's surnames after marriage varies or has varied from both the English and Scottish practice. Thus a post-nuptial settlement of 1751, relating to a Wicklow family, describes the lady as Catherine Finnemore, *alias* Ussher, the last being her maiden surname. Though this practice is clearer than the English style, yet it must be regarded as inferior in convenience to the method followed in Scotland. It is akin to the custom at one time observed in the Prerogative Court of Canterbury, which, in its calendars of wills, adds a woman's maiden name as an *alias* to her married style.

It is a matter for surprise that this question does not appear to have been touched on by those who have interested themselves in removing the various artificial disabilities to which women have been, and still are, in many respects, subjected.

That the identity of the wife should disappear so completely as it does in England must be regarded not merely as a petty grievance but as a serious inconvenience, and it would be no small advantage were the right of a woman to retain her own name through life for all legal purposes definitely recognised and established. Such a practice would not interefere with the convenient social practice by which a married woman is addressed by her husband's name. That name she would adopt, as a matter of course, during the continuance of the marriage bond and also during widowhood as an addition or suffix to her own. Thus Miss Mary Brown on her marriage to Mr. John Smith would become, formally, Mrs. Brown-Smith, though she would be colloquially addressed as Mrs. Smith.

It would be a further advantageous reform, though it may, to some, seem a most revolutionary proposal, if it became customary for the daughters of a family to use their mother's maiden name as their own principal surname, which they could differentiate by prefixing to it their father's surname. Thus the

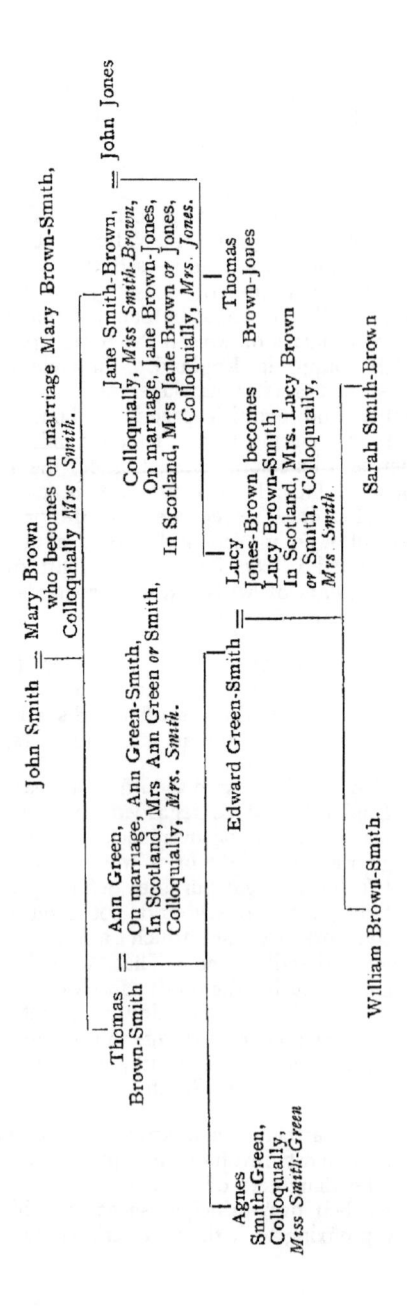

```
                    John Smith = Mary Brown
                                 who becomes on marriage Mary Brown-Smith,
                                 Colloquially Mrs Smith.
        |                                    |
        |                                    |
   Thomas            Ann Green,         Jane Smith-Brown,              = John Jones
   Brown-Smith =     On marriage, Ann Green-Smith,   Colloquially, Miss Smith-Brown,
                     In Scotland, Mrs Ann Green or Smith,  On marriage, Jane Brown-Jones,
                     Colloquially, Mrs. Smith.            In Scotland, Mrs Jane Brown or Jones,
                                                          Colloquially, Mrs. Jones.
                     |                              |
           Edward Green-Smith =  Lucy              Thomas
                                 Jones-Brown becomes   Brown-Jones
                                 Lucy Brown-Smith,
                                 In Scotland, Mrs. Lucy Brown
                                 or Smith, Colloquially,
                                 Mrs. Smith
                     |
           William Brown-Smith.     Sarah Smith-Brown

   Agnes
   Smith-Green,
   Colloquially,
   Miss Smith-Green
```

daughter of Mrs Brown-Smith would be styled Miss Jane Smith-Brown, just as the son might be styled Mr. Thomas Brown-Smith. On her marriage to Mr. John Jones, Miss Smith-Brown would become Mrs Brown-Jones, thus dropping her paternal surname and emphasizing, as is suitable for a woman, the female line instead of, as at present, absolutely ignoring her mother's family.

Such a scheme of family nomenclature is outlined in the pedigree opposite, which gives the suggested legal name of each individual with the social style added in italics.

Whether a hyphen should be used or the alternative *or* or *alias* is obviously a point of minor importance. By a system of conjoined names the identity of individuals and families would be preserved and without the slightest difficulty it would be possible to trace maternal ancestry. At the present time, as we have seen, owing to the imperfection of our system of nomenclature this, save in very rare cases, unfortunately cannot be done. The female ancestry is as full of interest and as worthy of investigation as is the paternal line, which unfortunately, as a rule, alone attracts the attention of the genealogist.

But to the rule that women change their name on marriage or re-marriage there appears to be one exception, which if it does not receive formal acknowledgment is tacitly acquiesced in by "society." when the exception is claimed by the lady making it. The exception occurs in the case when a lady has acquired a title by marriage and subsequently makes a second marriage with a commoner. Legally, of course, she loses the precedence obtained from her first husband and, logically, she should discard the title and name acquired from him.

Too frequently a foolish feminine vanity prevents the adoption of a course which every consideration of propriety and commonsense would dictate, and she prefers to retain a style to which she is no longer entitled and which in some cases should be even distasteful to her. This subject underwent considerable discussion in the Cowley case in 1901.[*] Earl Cowley had been divorced on the petition of his wife who, after she had obtained a dissolution of the marriage, continued to style herself Countess Cowley. It is difficult to understand the state of mind of any lady who would wish to continue a style derived from a guilty husband whom she had divorced, but in the uncertainty that attaches to the status and style of a divorced lady its use by her may be excused. But on her re-marriage such an excuse no longer exists, as she then by custom becomes entitled to her new

---

[*] 85 L.T Rep. 254, P. 1900, 118, A.C. 1901, 450.

husband's name. Nevertheless the ex-Countess Cowley insisted upon the retention of that title and continued so to describe herself after she had re-married and become the wife of a commoner. Thereupon her former husband, Earl Cowley, gave notice of motion to restrain her from using the style or title of "Countess Cowley." This motion was made in the Probate Divorce and Admiralty Division and purported to be in the Divorce proceedings, but it was treated, at the suggestion of the judge, Barnes, J., as a motion in an action in the High Court to restrain the respondent from the use of the title. The application was granted by Barnes, J. Countess Cowley then appealed and the Court of Appeal reversed that decision, Earl Cowley thereupon appealed to the House of Lords, sitting as Court of Appeal, the Lords present being the Lord Chancellor, Lord MacNaughten, Lord James of Hereford, Lord Brampton, and Lord Lindley. Considered judgments were delivered by four of those peers. The substance of these judgments was that being a matter of a dignity it was not a case for a court of law but for a committee of privileges of the House of Lords, and that the Divorce Court had no jurisdiction to deal with it. Lord Lindley pointed out that the controversy between the parties was reduced to a dispute about the use of a name as distinguished from a dignity, and he laid down the proposition that "speaking generally the law of this country allows any person to assume and use any name, provided its use is not calculated to deceive and to inflict pecuniary loss."

In the result the House of Lords dismissed the appeal, thus confirming the view of the Court of Appeal which had reversed the decision of Barnes, J. The judgments appear to have admitted that the lady, at any rate after her re-marriage to a commoner, lost any right she had in the title, though it would seem that till that event she retained all of the peculiar rights and privileges attaching to the wife of a peer. The headnote of the case runs thus: "When the marriage of a peer has been dissolved by decree at the instance of the wife, and she afterwards on marrying a commoner, continues to use the title she acquired by her first marriage, she does not thereby, though having no legal right to the user, commit such a legal wrong against her former husband, or so affect his enjoyment of the incorporeal hereditaments he possesses in his title, as to entitle him in the absence of malice to an injunction to restrain her use of the title. Only the House of Lords can try questions of right in matters of peerage or questions concerned therewith."

But it must be noted that these judgments make it quite clear that the lady had no legal right to the style of Countess Cowley after her re-marriage.

As to changes of Christian name, it is laid down very positively in the various text books that no means exist whereby a name given at baptism can be varied save, it is usual to add, at confirmation by the Bishop. This latter method, at any rate in the Anglican Church, is practically obsolete, though a few years ago the late Bishop of Liverpool confirmed a lady adding her mother's surname as an additional Christian name. But the Roman Church still retains the custom of giving a new name at confirmation.

It does not appear to have been considered what is the position of persons not members of a Christian church who obviously have no Christian names, or even what is the position of a Baptist, who acquires his first name without any ceremony. Indeed there does not appear to be any obligation upon a parent to give his child any name at all. A Jew or Mahomedan British subject who may de domiciled in England is, clearly, as regards his names, to be considered from another standpoint than that of a Christian, and it may be presumed that there is no reason why he should not change both his name and his surname, or whatever may be the equivalent of a man's personal appellation.*

Under the Registration Act of 1837 the birth of a child may be registered without the entry of any personal name, the sex only being indicated, though it is open to the parents to record it subsequently in the books of the Registrar General. Evidently a child could grow to adult age without having had any personal name formally conferred, and thus it would seem evident that any name afterwards used by such a person would be one of repute only and could be altered at will. Indeed any question as to the name of such an individual would be a question of fact. There would appear to be nothing to hinder such a person from having any indefinite number of *aliases*.

In cases of illegitimacy a person has no surname except that which he acquires by use or reputation. In England it is usual for such to adopt the mother's name, but the Crown will, with the assent of the putative father, grant a license for assuming his name. In Ireland the custom is different and there a child takes his father's surname, a course which may render it difficult to distinguish the legitimate and illegitimate lines of a pedigree, though it has the advantage that it does not punish the children for the parents' fault.

In 1862 very considerable discussion took place both in and out of Parliament on the subject of changes of name in connec-

---

* Presumably the same reasoning must apply to the first names of Baptist children, at least so long as they remain unbaptized.

tion with the Jones-Herbert case. There was settled in the county of Monmouth at Llanarth and Clytha a family of the name of Jones whose ancestors, it would appear, had once used the surname of Herbert and were descended from the same stock as the Herberts, Earls of Pembroke and Carnarvon. In 1848 Mr John Jones of Llanarth, who was afterwards sheriff of his county, obtained the Royal License for changing his name to Herbert. It may be presumed that he was chiefly moved thereto by a natural desire to discard a somewhat homely and frequent surname in favour of one more euphonious and infrequent, and probably to emphasize his undoubted, though very remote, kinship to the various ennobled families of Herbert. The pedigree which Mr. William (Jones) Herbert published in justification of the change shows that his paternal ancestors had borne the name of Jones for eight generations and that some four or five hundred years had passed by since any of them were known by the name of Herbert. Both Herbert and Jones are merely patronymics and in origin the one is no more distinguished than the other. This Mr Herbert had married the only child of the late Lord Llanover, better known as Benjamin Hall, M.P. for Marylebone, who in his capacity of Lord-Lieutenant of his county afterwards raised the discussion by his refusal to recognise the change from Jones to Herbert made without Royal License by another member of the family of Jones. It was in 1861 that Mr. William Jones of Clytha, uncle of Mr. John Herbert, late Jones, of Llanarth, actuated it may be assumed, by the same reasons as had in 1848 moved his nephew, adopted the ancestral name of Herbert in lieu of the obnoxious one of Jones. Mr. William Herbert late Jones, of Clytha, like his nephew, applied for a Royal License. It was indeed suggested at a later date that the application to the Home Office had been refused but he appears to have gone no further in his application than to consult one of the heralds, and that as the opinion was somewhat hostile to his proposal he dropped that procedure and ultimately effected the change without obtaining the accustomed permission for the purpose. Probably this unauthorized change, of local and personal interest only, would have passed unnoticed had not Lord Llanover, as Lord-Lieutenant of Monmouthshire, declined to permit Mr Herbert of Clytha to qualify for the magistracy in his new name or to grant a Commission in the Militia to the son in any name but that of Jones. It might have been thought that Lord Llanover in such a matter would have preferred to see the near relatives of his son-in-law bearing the same name and would have assisted them as far as lay in his power. It is evident that he held strong views to the contrary. Whether it was due to any personal feeling or to an exaggerated view of his duties as Lord-

Change of Name.

Lieutenant it is perhaps not very material now to inquire. However, it was Lord Llanover who raised the question of Mr. Herbert of Clytha's right to change his name in the way he did, he corresponded upon the matter with various officials, including the Home Secretary and the Chancellor, and took the course of publishing the letter in the newspapers in order to defend, despite the annoyance it would cause to a near connexion, the view he enunciated—"that it was his duty as Lord-Lieutenant of the "County to preserve intact the prerogative of the Queen, who "can alone sanction and legalize a change of name."

In consequence of his persistent refusal to recognise Mr. William Herbert or his son under any other than their "real" name of Jones, or to recommend the son for a commission in the Militia, the subject was at last brought to the notice of the House of Commons, by Mr. Roebuck, in the form of an address for a return from the Home Office of the names of all persons who had applied for licences to change their names since 1850; "of the instances in which such licences have been granted during that period, together with a statement of the names of the successful applicants and of the names which they have been permitted to assume by Royal Licence, of the names of the persons so applying who have been refused during the same period, with the reasons assigned in each case for the refusal; of the principles by which the Home Office is guided in granting and refusing such licences, and of the amount of fees demanded for such licences since 1850, and the manner in which the moneys received have been applied." To this motion, which was seconded by Col. Clifford, the Secretary of State, Sir George Grey, replied After stating that Mr. Jones of Clytha had not applied for a Royal Licence, he said "The hon and learned gentleman (Mr. Roebuck) says there is no doubt that any person may assume any name he choses without Royal Licence Now I am not going to dispute the legal question. I believe there is no legal right to a name Any person may take any name he pleases, but it does not follow that everybody else will at once recognise him by that name It is by no means a matter of course, because a gentleman who has hitherto been known as Jones suddenly calls himself Herbert or any other name that whim may direct, that all the world will immediately acquiesce to the alteration In short, this is rather a question of fact than of law. A man's name is that by which he is generally known How he may have acquired it does not matter It is his name and he has the right to be called by it if it is the name which he usually receives amongst his friends and acquaintances . . As to the principle by which the Home Office has been guided in dealing with these applications I have to inform my hon. and learned friend that there is no written law on the subject.

About 200 years ago the practice of applying for permission to change names arose, and in 1783, in consequence of the frequency of these requests, it was deemed necessary to put some check on them. A regulation was therefore made that all cases should be referred to the College of Arms. That reference, however, is not necessarily decisive, as it is intended only for the information of the department. That usage has been universally adopted subject to the modification introduced by Sir Robert Peel that when there are no plausible grounds for an application, and it is obviously the result of mere whim or caprice, it should be at once declined without any reference to the College of Arms, leaving it to the applicant to exercise the right which the hon. and learned gentleman said all possessed of changing his name on his own responsibility."

The Home Secretary further stated that he was willing to make returns of the number of applications which have been made and the number which have been rejected, and to give every information as to the fees which are paid over to the fee fund. This was, under protest, agreed to by Mr. Roebuck.

The Solicitor General (Sir Roundell Palmer) added that to the best of his belief there was no positive law on the subject. The fact was that surnames grew up mostly as nicknames. That very origin showed that there was no positive law on the subject. It was a matter of usage and reputation from the beginning, the name clung to the man and the law permitted him to shuffle it off if he could. There was no law forbidding a man to change his name, but there was also no law which compelled his neighbours to acknowledge him under the name he might assume . . . . When, however, by usage a man had acquired a name by reputation those persons in public authority were obliged to acknowledge this new surname. There was, however, no principle of law that any person occupying an official position was bound to recognise a capricious or arbitrary assumption of names by persons who had no right to them either by descent or by the requirements of property.

In 1862 Mr. Thomas Falconer, a County Court Judge, brother-in-law to Mr. Roebuck, published a pamphlet "On Surnames and the Rules of Law affecting their Change," and a second edition of it in the same year with comments on the Jones-Herbert case. This last extended to 88 pages, and the following year, 1863, appeared a "Supplement with Appendix," filling 42 pages more. In reply to this was issued in the same year, anonymously "An Answer to Mr. Falconer on the Assumption of Surnames without Royal Licence." This contained some 90 pages and dealt with "The Gradual Establishment of English Surnames." "The Clytha Case," Mr. Falconer's "Conclusions and Suggestions" while the correspondence and other papers in the Clytha case, were issued as a Parliamentary paper, and also reprinted as a pamphlet of 40 pages. Mr. William Herbert, late Jones, also issued a short statement, with pedigree and arms, in explanation of his action; an article appeared on "The Law of Proper Names" in the *Herald and Genealogist*, also another in the same magazine on "Changes of Surname *proprio motu*," while the *Cornhill* printed a paper on "Surnames and Arms," which also was the outcome of the Clytha case. Added to this was a considerable correspondence in the newspapers, all illustrating the interest which is invariably taken in any subject which is in any way of a personal nature. Recently the subject has been subjected to fresh consideration in the pages of the *Genealogical Magazine* in 1901, in which the view that any change is illegal, except with the licence of the Crown, is put forth, and much learning on the subject is there collected together.

To summarize the subject of change of surnames. There are two opposing views. The advocates of the one aver that change of name without the Royal Licence or Act of Parliament is "illegal," and they point to an undeviating custom or practice for nearly 250 years by which the more authentic changes have been effected by one or other of these ways, and allege that a change in other mode is merely an *alias*, which no one is compelled to recognize, and they seek to prove that it is now part of the Common Law that changes by Royal Licences are the only lawful means by which alteration of name can be effected. The other view is that a man is at liberty to change his name when and as often as he pleases, that what a man's name may be is but a question of fact. Further, that it is "lawful" for anyone to do any act which is not explicitly forbidden by Statute or Common Law, and that a practice arising within the last two or three hundred years cannot create a Common Law prerogative of the Crown, restraining and making illegal what certainly was a common practice in ancient times.

The courts will not restrain the use of another name, unless in such cases as those in which fraud is intended or commercial loss will be caused to the person whose name is assumed, and those cases belonging rather to matters of commercial law. This point was decided in the case of Du Boulay v. Du Boulay (L R., 2 P.C., p. 430). The plaintiff was the son of a mulatto slave woman known only as Rose, who, on being emancipated, assumed her master's surname, as did her son, who started business in the isle of St. Lucia in that name. In 1867 the Du Boulay family took proceedings in St. Lucia to restrain the defendant, who was not related to them, from using their name. The matter went on appeal to the Privy Council, when, on dismissing the appeal, Lord Chelmsford said :—

"The mere assumption of a name which is the patronymic of a family, by a stranger who had never before been called by that name, whatever cause of annoyance it may be to the family, is a grievance for which our law affords no remedy."

And this may, in principle, be regarded as confirmed in Lady Cowley's case, already referred to, although that related rather to the assumption of a title than a surname.

The practice of obtaining a Royal Licence has been in existence since the reign of Charles II, and the necessity of obtaining the Royal assent is specifically referred to in the King's warrant, dated 6 July, 1679, which empowered the Earl of Ogle, who was the son and heir of the Duke of Newcastle, upon his marriage, to assume and take the surname of Percie and to bear the arms of Percie quarterly with his own paternal arms, "neither of which may regularly be done, according to the law of armes, without the special dispensacon and licence of Us, as We are by Our supream power and prerogative the onely Fountain of Honour."

This prerogative of the Crown has been continuously asserted to the present time. It is an advantage that there should exist some authority dealing with the question of changes of name and a guarantee that the change made is effected for a sufficient reason and not a matter of passing whim, and those who wish to change their surnames will be well advised if they adopt the formal and regular process instead of a mere advertisement or deed poll.

The disadvantage of a mere voluntary change is that there exists no means by which its recognition by others can be enforced, while in certain official circles it will be entirely ignored. The better course to follow where a change has to be effected is to adopt the more effectual, if more expensive, method of a Royal Licence, under which no question can arise as to the legality of the change so made.

The following is the procedure usually adopted upon making a change of name by means of a Royal Licence. A petition to the Crown is prepared and presented through the Heralds' Office, and, as the terms of this petition, if granted, will govern the terms of the Royal Licence, the solicitor of the applicant should prepare it in conference with the Officer of Arms. This is especially important in cases of voluntary application, as the Officer will be able to advise whether it is one likely to be granted.

When granted, the Royal Licence is given under the actual Sign Manual and Privy Seal of the Sovereign, and is countersigned by the Secretary of State for the Home Department. For a voluntary application the Stamp Duty is £10. For a change made by direction of a will or settlement the Stamp Duty is increased to £50. This large extra charge of £40 may in some cases be avoided if the person who expects to have to change his name does so under a *voluntary* application before the time at which it becomes compulsory to do so under the will or settlement. There is, however, no obligation on the Home Office, to whom the Office of Arms refers such petition, to advise the Sovereign to grant the prayer of the petition.

When the petition is made pursuant to some will or settlement the practice is for a licence to be granted as a matter of course. In other cases the applicant must show good and sufficient reasons for the proposed change. It is not possible in what is a matter of grace to set out any definite rule as to what constitutes good and sufficient reason. When the applicant has no connection with the family whose name he proposes to assume and wishes to do so from mere whim or caprice, his application will almost certainly be refused.

The petition will usually be granted if the applicant is the representative of a male of that family or when he can show that some ancestor through whom he claims similarly represented the family whose name he wishes to take.

A ward will be permitted to take his guardian's name if the application be made in the latter's lifetime. And a licence will be given to assume some obsolete spelling or the use of a prefix such as *de*, provided descent be proved from an ancestor thus writing his name. And a natural child will be allowed to assume his father's surname, provided it be done with his consent.

The petition will be couched in the following words and should be engrossed upon foolscap paper :—

To the King's most excellent Majesty.

The humble petition of [John Smith, of Blackacre, in the county of Blank, gentleman.]
Sheweth

That your petitioner is [*then set out the facts of the pedigree or other reasons justifying the application for a licence.*]

xxviii.   *The Law and Practice of*

Your Petitioner therefore most humbly prays your Majesty's Royal Licence and Authority that he and his issue may take and henceforth use the surname of [Brown in lieu and instead of Smith.]

And your Majesty's petitioner shall [etc.].

(Signed)   JOHN SMITH.

The above represents a petition of the simplest class, but it is obvious that as the circumstances and facts of every case vary, the document will have to be prepared by the petitioner's solicitor in conjunction with the Officer of Arms, who forwards it to the Home Office.

It may, however, be noted that the prayer of the petition must be carefully worded as the Licence to be subsequently granted will follow its terms with precision. If therefore in the case above the petitioner desires to be known as Smith-Brown he will ask that " he may take and henceforth use the surname of Brown in addition to and after that of Smith."

The petition may also ask to use arms for the adopted name, but this part of the subject concerns the subject of the law of grants of arms rather than changes of name. It may be noted that if the applicant is in a position of life to use arms and does not already possess that distinction, such an occasion is a suitable one for obtaining a grant of arms.

The licence, if granted, will be prepared at the Home Office and will be in the following form :—

(Signed) VICTORIA R.

[Seal.]

[Stamp, £10.]

Victoria, by the Grace of God of the United Kingdom of Great Britain and Ireland, Queen, Defender of the Faith, To Our Right Trusty and Right Entirely Beloved Cousin Henry, Duke of Norfolk, Earl Marshal of England and Hereditary Marshal of England. Greeting! Whereas John Smith, of Blackacre, in the County of Blank, Gentleman, hath by his petition humbly represented to Us that [*here are set out the reasons justifying the change*].

The Petitioner therefore most humbly prays Our Royal Licence and Authority that he and his issue may take and henceforth use the surname of Brown in lieu and instead of that of Smith. Know ye that We of Our Princely Grace and Special favour have given and Granted and do by these presents give and grant unto him the said John Smith Our Royal Licence and Authority that he and his issue may take and henceforth use the surname of Brown in lieu and instead of that of Smith, Provided that this Our Concession and Declaration be recorded in Our College of Arms, otherwise this Our Licence and Permission to be void and of none effect.

Our Will and Pleasure therefore is that you, Henry Duke of Norfolk, to whom the cognizance of matters of this nature doth properly belong, do require and command that this Our Concession and Declaration be recorded in Our College of Arms to the end that Our Officers of Arms and all others upon occasion may take full notice and have full knowledge thereof And for so doing this shall be your Warrant

Given at our Court of Saint James the Twenty-first day of May, 1873. in the Thirty-sixth year of Our Reign.

By Her Majesty's Command.

(Signed) H. A. BRUCE.

Recorded in the College of Arms, London, pursuant to a Warrant from the Earl Marshal of England.

(Signed) GEORGE HARRISON,
Windsor Herald

At the foot of the first page will be the following note :—

John Smith, Licence that he and his issue may take and use the surname of Brown in lieu and instead of that of Smith

The *London Gazette* advertisement will be in the following form and that in the *Dublin Gazette* will be similar. It is not requisite to advertize the change in either Gazette though such is the usual practice. In the case of Irish changes the fact is sometimes notified in both Gazettes :—

Whitehall, 1 January, 1905.

The King has been pleased to grant unto John Smith, of Blackacre, in the county of Blank, Gentleman, his Royal Licence and Authority that he and his issue may henceforth use the name [and arms] of Brown in lieu and instead of that of Smith.

And to Command that the said Royal Licence and Authority be recorded in his Majesty's College of Arms, otherwise to be void and of none effect.

Certain fees and stamp duty must be paid by the applicant in advance and these are fixed according to the following invariable scales :—

These fees in England are :— £ s. d.

To the Heralds' Office for preparing and presenting Petition.

Reporting officially on the case to the Home Secretary, obtaining the Earl Marshall's Warrant, and recording the Royal Licence in the books of the College 34 10 6

Stamp Duty payable to the Inland Revenue:
If a voluntary application 10 0 0

If a compulsory one under a clause in a will or settlement ... 50 0 0

Exchequer fee 10 2 6

If a grant of arms be made at the same time, fees to Heralds' College* 66 10 0

If the change of name be advertized in the *London Gazette*, as usually is done, a fee varying with length of the advertisement, including copies of the *Gazette*, about ... 2 2 0

The fees taken in Ireland upon a change of name are :—

Change of name by Royal Licence on a Voluntary application, together with a grant of arms 120 0 0

The like under a will or settlement 160 0 0

Change of name upon a voluntary application 60 0 0

Further, as the applicant will rarely carry through the business himself, but will find it requisite to obtain the aid of a solicitor experienced in such matters, there will usually be certain legal charges in addition to the official fees mentioned above.

It may be noted that a Royal Licence to change or to assume a surname is merely permissive. The change must be made by the licensee himself. It is perhaps a matter for surprise that the Crown instead of granting a mere licence has not adopted the method of making an actual grant of the name, just as it does

---

* On a grant of arms being made independently of any change of name the Inland Revenue exacts a duty of £10, making the total fees £76 10s 0d.

in the case of granting a coat of arms. This process was actually adopted in the case of the Ross family, one of whom had distinguished himself at the battle of Bladensberg, and in 1816 the Crown granted and ordained that the widow of General Ross and his descendants should thenceforth be called "Ross of Bladensberg," and this family has since been known by the unusual style of Ross of Bladensberg.

The Lyon Office Act in Scotland, 1672, declares "that it is only allowed for noblemen and bishops to subscribe by their titles. And that all others shall subscribe their christened names or the initial letter thereof with their surnames, and may if they please adject the designation of their lands, prefixing the word 'Of' to the saids designations." From this is derived the practice, well known in Scotland, of landowners adding the name of the property of which they chance to be "laird." Thus John Graham, who *owns* Redford, will be known as John Graham *of* Redford; his *tenant* will be known as John Williamson *in* Redford. And this distinction is still carefully observed in Scottish legal documents.

The practice of Peers signing themselves by their titles only seems in England to rest upon custom and it may be noted that anciently it was not unusual for peers to prefix their Christian name to their signatures, though when that practice fell wholly into disuse it would not be easy to say. English Bishops still sign with the initial of their Christian name, though they are in Scotland, by the Act just referred to, on an equality with the hereditary peers in that respect.

The practice of change by Royal Licence has never obtained to any extent in Scotland, as in that country it has always been held sufficient to register arms under the new name.

Changes of name purporting to be made by deed poll or advertisement derive no additional force or validity from the adoption of either of these methods. The advertisements in such cases need not follow any particular form and indeed they vary so much that it seems scarcely worth while to give an example, but should it be thought well to attempt to effect a change in this way the advertisement may adopt some such form as this:—

I, John Smith, of Blank, in the County of Blank, gentleman, do hereby give notice that I have assumed and intend henceforth upon all occasions to sign and use and to be called and known by the surname of Green only, in lieu of my present surname of Smith, and that such intended change of name is formally declared and evidenced by a deed poll under my hand and seal bearing date this day and intended to be forthwith enrolled in the Central Office of the Supreme Court of Judicature. In witness whereof I do hereby sign and subscribe myself by my said intended future name.

    Dated, etc.

       (Signed) JOHN GREEN.

Witness: John Thompson,
   of Blank, Solicitor's Clerk.

The deed poll may follow the wording of the advertisement and can then be enrolled in the Central Office. The change thus made derives no validity from either the advertisement or the deed poll, whether enrolled or not, and the only result gained is that of giving publicity to the intended alteration of name.

124, Chancery Lane,
 June, 1905.

# AN INDEX

TO

CHANGES OF NAME,

1760 to 1901

A

Aaron *see* Arnold.
Aarons *see* Miller.
Aaronson *see* Harrison.
Abarbanel *see* Lindo-Abarbanel
Abbey Williams Williams, L. R., of Jesus Coll, Oxon Times, d p, 8 Aug., 1873
Abbott-Dunbar : Abbott, J. S _2 Oct 1802 (4887)
Abbott-Fullwood : Abbott, D, of 75, Haberdasher St., Hoxton, Middlesex. Times, 12 June, 1889
Abbs *see* Stafford
Abdy : Rutherforth, T. A   3 June, 1775 (11566)
à Beckett à Beckett-Turner, W. Times, 11 May, 1896
Abel *see* Knill-Abel.
Abel-Knapton : Abel, J K. 9 July 1887 (2537)
Abeltshauser *see* D'Arenberg.
Abercrombie *see* Mumford
Aberdeen *see* Harvey
Aberigh-Mackay : Mackay, Rev. J., Senior Military Chaplain of the Bengal Estab. at Meerut, Bengal, India, late of Penang in the Straits of Malacca Times, 2 Dec., 1869.
Abney-Hastings : Hastings, Sir C   1 Dec., 1823 (2072)
   : Clifton, C F   Index pub and priv Statutes
          p. 502   22 Vict. c l.
Abraham *see* Adams
         ., Clifton
         ,, Willis
Abrahams *see* Allingham
         ., Miller
         ,. Paine
Abrey *see* Aubrey

Ackers - Smith, W. 5 Aug., 1853 (2137).
Ackland see Fuller-Ackland-Hood
Ackroyd see Rawson-Ackroyd.
Acland see Fuller-Palmer-Acland
Acland-Troyte. Troyte, Rev. R. H. D., of Porlock, Somerset, and J E, Lieut 4th Reg. at Gibralter. Times, d p., 7 Aug., 1876.
à Court-Holmes : à Court, W H A 14 Oct 1833 (1869)
    see Holmes à Court.
à Court-Repington : à Court, E H. 24 Sept 1847 (3405).
Acres see Little
Acton see Ball-Acton.
    Barrar, E. 31 George III. 1791
    see Dalberg-Acton
    ,, Lee-Acton.
    ,, Wood-Acton
Adair : Jones, Wm. D G, 27 May, 1782 (4298).
Adams, A L : Abraham, A. S. L., but carrying on business as Robt. Abraham, of Aldersgate St., London, and Stratford, Essex, photographic material warehouseman Times, d p, 22 July, 1890.
    Cuff, A. and T 22 Aug., 1842 (2278)
    Cuff, E A. 22 Aug. 1842 (2278)
    see Anson
    ,, Cokayne
    ,, Franklin-Adams
    ,, Hamilton
    ,, Hyett
    ,, Rawson
    ,, Sidney
    ,, Stanley-Adams.
    ,, Timms.
    ,, Woollcombe-Adams
Adams-Robinson : Adams, S, clerk, incumbent of Derrylane, Cavan. Times, 15 May, 1874
Adams-Wylie : Adams, C. H. B. of Hythe, Southants Times, 22 Mar, 1899
Adamson see Lilburn.
Adcock see Halford-Adcock
    ,, Hall.
Addams see Altham
Addenbrooke : Homfray, J. A 3 Mar, 1792 (141).
Adderley see Cradock.
    ,, Broughton-Adderley
Addison-Fountaine : Addison, W 25 June, 1800 (730)
Ade-Murray : Ade, J., of Sheffield, Yorks, spinster. Times, 16 Jan., 1872.

A'Deane : Tucker, J and M. 23 Oct, 1865 (4987 and 5140).
Adey *see* Adye.
Adye *see* Willett
    Adey, Rev. F. W., of Markyate Cell, Hertfordshire Times, 18 Nov, 1869
    Adey, G., Sub-Lieut 12th Foot, C. G. Sub-Lieut 1st Warwicks Mil and A., Royal Military Coll., Sandhurst. Times, 20 Aug, 1874
Affleck *see* Danby
Agar : Preston, B. 2 Sept, 1786 (407).
Agar-Hutton : Cohen, L., of King William St., London Times, 24 Sept, 1898
Agar-Robartes : Agar, T. J. 9 Apr, 1822 (598)
Agg-Gardner : Agg, J. 13 Sept., 1836 (1602).
Aglionby . Cooper, A. S. 11 Aug, 1885 (3701).
Agor *see* Turner.
Agutter *see* Hughes-Agutter
Aiken *see* Chetwood-Aiken
Aikman-Gresham : Aikman, John. Times, 11 Feb, 1870.
Ainley-Walker . Walker, E. W., of Christ Church, Oxford Times, 23 Sept, 1895
Ainslie *see* Rutherfurd-Ainslie
    Rutherford, J. 11 July, 1786 (311).
Ainsworth : Figg, T., of Bexley, Kent, gent. Times, d.p., 31 Dec, 1875
Airey *see* Gelderd.
Aitchison-Denman · Denman, Lord Times, 20 Nov, 1876 (7143)
Aked *see* Watson
Akers-Douglas of Baads . Akers, A. 24 May, 1875 (2773)
Akerman *see* Dowell-Akerman
Alcock *see* Alston.
  ,, Henshall.
Alcock-Beck . Towers, W. 13 May, 1856 (1942)
Alcock-Stawell · Alcock, W. St. Leger 21 Nov, 1845 (92)
    · Alcock, W. St. L. Dublin, 28 Oct., 1845
Alcock-Stawell-Riversdale Alcock-Stawell, W. T. J. 28 Feb., 9 Mar, 1871 (D.G 194).
Aldam Pease, J. 19 Oct., 1807 (1409).
    Pease, W 25 Jan, 1810 (138)
    see Warde-Aldam.
Alder-Smith Smith, H., of Christ's Hospital, London Times, 25 Nov. 1891
Alderman . New, B. P., of Seymour Place, Staines Road, Hounslow, Middlesex, gent Times, 23 May, 1867
Alderson · Alderson-Lloyd, C. 16 June, 1812 (1175).
Aldrich-Blake : Aldrich, F. I. 13 Jan, 1863 (496 and 574)

Aldridge *see* Bliss
  „ Frostick Aldridge
Aldridge-Busby Aldridge, R 24 Oct., 1820 (1997)
Aldworth *see* Neville.
  „ Sentleger
Alers-Hankey Alers, W 30 Dec, 1816 (4)
Alewood *see* Aylwood.
Alexander, W Lindsay : Alexander, W., sometime of Calcutta, now of London, merchant Times, 9 Mar., 1886
  Alexander-Shaw, W 4 July, 1876 (D.G 409)
  Alexander-Shaw, G W., of 11, Brunswick St, Liverpool, corn merchant. Times, d.p., 2 July, 1889.
  Gibb-Samson, G., of Park Row, Albert Gate, Middlesex Times, d.p., 29 Jan, 1889.
  see Humphrys-Alexander
  : McTurk, J. Times, d p, 4 May, 1896
  see Shaw
Alexander-Prior : Alexander, R C 16 April, 1859 (1726)
Alexander-Sinclair : Alexander, E. S, Lieut R N Times, 8 May, 1894 Lyon, Vol XV., 76, 31 Jan, 1900.
Alexander-Shaw *see* Alexander.
Algernon *see* Greville
Alington *see* Pye
Allan *see* Havelock-Allan.
Allan . Murray, T 18 Mar, 1800 (1030)
Allan-Fraser Allan, P 28 Mar, 1851 (860) Lyon, V., 30, 27 Apr., 1882
Allard-Kemeys Allard, R J 20 July, 1810 (1081)
Allardyce *see* Barclay-Allardyce
Allason *see* Bannatine-Allason
Allcard Courtin H J 15 May, 1863 (2570)
Allen *see* Alleyn
  „ Ellacott.
  Eric Baker, Ellen Annie, of Dover, Kent, gentleman Times d.p. 3 Dec. 1895
  see Greenley
  „ Hogge-Allen
  „ Jalfon
  McMaster-Allen, W A G, of Greenwich, Kent, gent Times, d p, 17 Aug, 1880
  see Rayne.
  „ Temple-Allen
  „ Tournay
Allen-Faulkner Allen, C F 14 Aug, 1843 (2745)
Allen-Jeffreys · Allen, J C, of Gatchell House. Taunton, Somerset, barrister, J.P Times, d.p., 14 June, 1889
Allen-Olney · Allen, H 11 April, 1831 (693)

Allen-Philipps · Allen, C   22 Aug., 1799 (858).
Allen-Smith : Smith, C. R., of 4, Edgar Buildings, Bath, dental surgeon   Times, d p   11 Aug, 1893
Allen-Wilkie   Allen, J   14 July, 1810 (1022 and 2021)
Allenby, R.   Bean, R Allenby, jun. of 15, Park Cres, York, gent.   Times, 31 May. 1889
    see Montgomery
Alleyn : Allen, E G , of Tottenham, Middlesex   Times, d p , 21 Aug., 1889
Allibone   Langton : Allibone, J., of Millmorton, Warwicks   Times, d p , 7 Aug., 1876
Allingham, John Ellis   Abrahams, Joel Ellis.   Times, d.p., 18 Mar, 1896
Alley-Jones see Galmoye.
Allison see Ireland
Allman see Higginson
Allnatt see Surtees-Allnatt
Allsebrook   Cupit, W. C   of Burton-on-Trent, Staffs , medical botanist   Times, d p., 16 May, 1891
Allsopp-Lowdham   Allsopp, L   26 Feb , 1825 (372)
Allsup see Richardson-Allsup.
Allwright see Speers
Alsager : Williams, A   21 Mar , 1796 (278)
Alston   Alcock, G H   Times, d.p , 12 Dec., 1889
Alston-Stewart   Alston   Major James   Lyon, Vol III , 16 April, 1830
Altham   Cook, W. S and Addams, A   8 Feb   1862 (891)
    : Scott, T , of 48, Parson Lane, Clitheroe.   Times, 6 June, 1877
Alvarenga see Howard.
Alwyn · Crowther, A M , of 166, Earl's Court Road, London, spinster   Times, d.p , 3 July, 1883
    Davies, S A , of 9, Scarsdale Terrace, Kensington, Middlesex, gent   Times, d p , 16 Jan , 1891
Ambrose : O Ferrall Jas., Major-General in Austrian Army   13 April, 1811
Amcotts   Cracroft, Sir W   11 July, 1854 (2160)
    Cracroft, W   24 July, 1857 (2551)
    see Cracroft
    ,, Cracroft-Amcotts
    ,, Ingilby-Amcotts
        Emerson W.   17 May, 1777 (11770)
Amcotts-Ingilby   Ingilby, Sir W. A.   April, 1822 (1179)
Ames-Lyde   Ames, L N. F.   12 May, 1874 (2674)
Amherst see Tyssen-Amherst
Amhurst see Tyssen-Amhurst
        ,, Tyssen-Daniel-Amhurst.

Amor *see* Barnes Amor
Amory *see* Heathcoate-Amory
Amphlett · Dunne. C. 19 Mar, 1855 (1182)
Amyand *see* Cornewall
Amyatt : Brown, A. E., late Capt. 5th Lancers. Times, d.p., 23 Jan., 1878.
Amyatt-Burney · Burney, E. K. A., C. M. A. and H. A., all children of Rev. E. Burney, of Gosport. Times, d.p. 26 Dec., 1873
: Burney, E. A., of Gosport, Southampton, esq. Times, d.p., 18 Dec., 1873
Ancketill Anketell, W. R., now of Quinton Castle, co. Down, Ireland, esq. Times, 18 June, 1874.
Anketell, F. M., of Spa House, Box, Wilts, gent. Times, 18 June, 1874
Anketell, M. A., esq., 2nd Capt. R.A., retired, now at Spa House, Box, Wilts. Times, 18 June, 1874
Ancketell, W., of Ancketill's Grove, Monaghan, Ireland. Times, 19 June, 1874.
Anderdon *see* Murray-Anderdon
Anderson-Campbell Lewis Gonville Anderson, Charles Lewis Gonville. Times, 16 Nov., 1871.
J. Chapman . Anderson, J., of Beulah Spa, Upper Norwood, and of Blairgowrie, N.B., barrister-at-law. Times, d.p., 23 Jan., 1890
Charles L. G. *see* Anderson, Campbell L. G.
see Bewicke
: Evan, R. R., formerly of Carmarthenshire, but now of Paris. Times, 6 Nov., 1871
see Groome-Anderson
: Hurker, C. A. 15 Feb., 1811 (381).
see Macaulay-Anderson.
„ Scott.
„ Seton
„ Wright-Anderson.
Young. Charles 5 Aug., 1797 (733)
Anderson-Berry *see* Berry, D., of 117, Goldhawk Rd., Shepherd's Bush, Middlesex, surgeon. Times, 14 Oct., 1893
Anderson-Morshead Anderson, H. 22 Jan., 1805 (93)
Anderton *see* Gill-Anderton
Smith, G. F., of Charlcombe, Saltram Crescent, Paddington, Midlesex, gent. Times, d.p. 19 Nov., 1892.
André : Calcas, P. C. 26 Jan., 1804 (113).
Andrew *see* Harrison-Andrew.
Andrewes *see* Uthwatt
Andrews *see* Baker.
: Hunt, E. A. 1 April, 1822 (558)

Andrews : Surridge, W. N. (Rev.), of Tring, Herts Times, d p
    20 Sept., 1882.
  see Uthwatt.
  ,, Woodward.
Angell : Brown, B. J. A. 5 July, 1800 (762).
von Angern : von Zedlitz, M. H. R., of 25, Craven Street, Strand.
    Times, 17 Dec., 1887
Anichini-Rolfes Anichini, J. W., of Thurlow Lodge, Lower
    Norwood, Surrey Times, d.p., 1 Oct., 1867
Anketell see Ancketill
Anne : Charleton, L. S. 31 May, 1883 (3037)
  see Tasburgh
Annesley see Joynt-Annesley.
    Levy, A 25 April, 1801 (445)
    see Lyttleton-Annesley
    MacLeod, A. L. 31 Oct., 1844 (3875)
Anson : Adams, G 1 May, 1773 (11348)
Anson-Cartwright : Cartwright, H., late of Ford House, Devon.
    now of Heavitree, Devon, esq., J.P., son of William, of
    Brimley House, W Teignmouth, Devon Times, d p., 15
    Aug., 1871
Anson-Horton Anson, A. T. 8 May, 1883 (2828).
Anstey-Calvert Anstey, A 15 Dec., 1819 (2282)
Anstis see Du Santoy Anstis
Anstruther see Courtenay-Anstruther
    ,, Lloyd-Anstruther
    ,, Locke-Anstruther.
Anstruther-Duncan Duncan, Lt.-Col. Alexr Wm., R.A Lyon
    Vol. XIV, 17 May, 1897
Anthony see Verney
Anthony-Wilson Anthony G. L 13 Aug., 1858 (3935)
Anwyl-Passingham : Passingham R. T., of Bala, Merioneth,
    Wales, Hon. Major. Times, d p, 19 Oct., 1888
Appelbee-Fisher Appelbee, W. J., and H his wife, of 34,
    Tavistock Terrace, Upper Holloway Middlesex Times
    d.p, 14 Dec., 1874
Applebee-Eaton : Applebee, E. J., of 3, Cornwall Residences,
    Regent's Park. Times, d.p., 24 Nov., 1880.
Appleby Johnson, W. 28 Sept., 1830 (2186)
Applegate : Neale. C. M., of The Square, Palmerston N 7
    Times, 23 May, 1895
ap Ellis-Eyton : Eyton, A., of Camberwell Times 5 March, 1869
Appleton see Searles-Wood.
    · Harland. 13 Aug., 1814 (1829)
Apsley see Griffith-Apsley.
Arathoon see Lambe
Arbuthnott see Capel-Carnegy-Arbuthnott

Arbuckle *see* Vaughan Arbuckle.
Arcedeckne-Butler Butler, J H E.   St James's, 4 Nov. (D G. 1399 and 1415), Whitehall, 18 Nov., 1867.
Archbold *see* Pears-Archbold.
Archer-Snelling   Archer, J. S., of Upton St Leonard's, co Gloucester Times, 24 Feb., 1870.
Archdall *see* Porter.
  „   Gray-Archdall.
Archdall-Gratwicke : Archdall, Geo., and Jemima E., his wife. 28 April, 1863 (D.G. 503).
Archer, T. Searancke : Archer, T., of 2 Gt Winchester Buildings, Lond., architect. Times, d p., 6 Dec., 1875.
Archer-Hind : Archer, Eliz.   10 Oct., 1835 (2020)
Archer-Houblon   Eyre, G. B.   17 Dec., 1891 (7165).
Archer-Burton : South, L   4 Nov., 1835 (2075)
Arden *see* Baillie-Arden.
Arden-Gorwyn : Arden, J L   14 May, 1824 (827).
Arderne : Jones, D. D   6 Dec., 1887 (6994)
Arding : Wells, A. C.   25 Jan., 1890 (955)
Argles *see* Venables.
Arlington *see* Gapp-Arlington.
Arlosh   Losh, J., of Ponsonby, co Cumberland   Times, d p., 30 June, 1870
Armelle . Greene, H. P., esq. son of Rev H. A. Greene, of Cowsden Hall, Worcesters. Times, 1 Jan., 1877
Armfield-Marrow · Marrow, E A.   16 Feb., 1897 (1097)
Armitage *see* Wormald
Armour Roberts, Alfred Edward of Bridgwater Somerset Times, 24 Aug., 1899
Armstrong *see* Hedley-Armstrong
   „   Heaton-Armstrong
   „   Lushington-Tulloch.
   „   Watson-Armstrong
Armstrong-Martinez : Armstrong, W H   24 Sept., 1838 (2145)
Armstrong-MacDonnell : Armstrong, W E. St J., 18 May, D Castle, 27 May, 1858 (D G. 1113 and 1149)
Armstrong *see* Wright-Armstrong
Armstrong-Lamb · Armstrong, W. L., of Victoria Colliery, near Wakefield, York, gent Times, 15 May, 1891.
Armstrong-Lambe . Armstrong, H   14 April, 1881 (1957)
Armytage *see* Green-Armytage
   „   Wentworth
Arnall *see* Thompson.
Arnall Thompson · Arnall H. T., of Knighton, Leic., and of Brasenose Coll., Oxford, esq Times 7 Dec., 1885.
Arno *see* Hayward

Arnold : Aaron, H. L , articled clerk, of 35, Bloomsbury Square,
Middlesex. Times, d p , 20 Oct., 1871
  Coape-Arnold, H. F. J , of Wolvey Hall, Wolvey, Warw ,
  and Goldhanger, Essex Times, 18 Feb., 1898
    see Coape-Arnold
    ,, Haughton
    ,, Kerchever-Arnold.
  E. Carrington : Hart, E Montague, of London, late of
  Leicester Times, 13 July, 1886
  Sargent, G. A   1 March, 1777 (11748)
    see Wallinger
    ,, Willson-Arnold
Arnold-Bainbrigge   Arnold, W. 8 Aug., 1845 (2386)
Arnold-Forster: Arnold, E P., of Burley-in-Wharfedale, York
  and also by Florence M. Arnold,   ,,   ,,
                 H O Arnold,   ,,   ,
                 F E. Arnold,   ,,   ,,
                              d.p., 9 June, 1879
Arnold-Wallinger   Wallinger, R (incorrectly described as) of Kitts
  Croft, Writtle, Essex, L R C P., M R C S   Times, d p.,
  18 Dec., 1893
Arnot see Rae-Arnot
Arthur : Cohen, A C , of Johannesburgh, S Africa, commission
  agent Times, d p , 2 Nov , 1894
    see Fane
Arundale : Kay, F. R., of 10, Chenie Street, Tottenham Court
  Road. Times, d.p , 4 April, 1896
Arundel Brazier, Sir J. 20 Feb , 1801 (202)
    see Harris-Arundel
    ,, Jago-Arundel
    ,, Tagg-Arundel
Arundell : Galway, Right Hon. W , Viscount   22 Dec , 1769
  (11005)
    see Hunter-Arundell
    ,, Monckton-Arundell
    ,, Saunders
  Tagg, E W , B A. London, of Chipping Barnet, Herts.
  Times, 8 March, 1871
    see Tagg Arundell
Aschkenasi see Hunter.
Ashburner : Wilson, E   16 Dec , 1839 (2677)
  . Mathews, H. J , now residing at Horsham, Sussex
  Times, 19 Aug., 1872
Ashburnham-Clement· Ashburnham, A, P, and E A , his wife
  10 May, 1899 (3103)
Ashby : Hermann, N and A   24 June, 1808
  : Latham. E   23 June, 1808 (8)

Ashby : Maddock, G A   21 Aug, 1857 (2885)
    see Mayer Ashby.
Ashe see Hargood-Ashe
    „ Hoadly-Ashe.
Ashe-a'Court-Repington   Ashe-a'Court, C   25 Oct, 1855 (3994)
Asheton see Smith
Ashfordby-Trenchard : Ashfordby, J   1 April 1802 (374).
Ashman : Green, T A. A. of 4, Belgrave Terrace, Torquay, Devon, esq.   Times, d.p , 19 May, 1893
Ashpinshaw see Staunton.
Asheton see Duff-Asheton-Smith
Ashton, Albert Rossi : Ashton, Albert Isaac   Times d p , 25 April, 1891
    see Burchardt-Ashton
    „ Mackenzie-Ashton
    „ Shorrock.
    Walford, T W. H   21 April, 1886 (2058)
    White, M. N D, of Tremaine, W. Dulwich, Surrey, formerly of Weston-super-Mare, widow   Times, d p, 23 May, 1885
Ashton-Gwatkin : Gwatkin, Rev W H T, of Laurel Lodge, Twickenham, Middlesex.   Times, d p , 24 Feb , 1888
Ashworth, Geo H.: Ashworth G H. Barker, of Oxton, Chester, and Liverpool, merchant   Times, d.p , 16 Nov., 1875
    see Hoyle
Askew-Bell : Bell, J . of The Chapel, Bassenthwaite. Cumb , gent   Times, 3 Sep , 1874
Askew-Robertson : Askew W   20 Sept , 1890 (5267)
Aspinall-Dudley   Aspinall, W. L. C   28 Apr., 1857 (1536)
Assheton-Smith see Duff-Assheton-Smith.
Assey see Dacre-Assey.
Astell : Thornton, W.   9 June, 1807 (794)
Astle see Astley.
    „ Hills.
Astley see Frankland-Russell-Astley
    „ Gough
    · Astle, D G , surgeon, of Newcastle-under-Lyme   Times, d p, 4 May, 1871.
    see Ludford-Astley
Astley-Corbett. Astley, F E G   11 Dec., 1889 (733).
Astley-Sparke · Sparke, J F . Captain and Adjutant of Oxford Militia, residing in Oxford   Times, 1 Jan , 1873
Aston-Pudsey   Aston, G. P   27 Jan , 1862 (447).
Aston see Magill-Aston
    „ Pudsey
    „ Webb-Aston.

Atcheler *see* Bury
Atcherley : Jones, D F. 21 March, 1834 (510)
Atherton . Gwillym, Rev V A 8 March, 1779 (11950)
Athorpe : Blanchard, R A 13th Geo. III, 1773
      : Middleton, J C. 3 Aug, 1821 (1617)
Atkin *see* Roberts
Atkins *see* Burnaby-Atkins
Atkins-Bowyer : Atkins, W 16 Nov., 1835 (2155)
Atkins - Bowyer, W 16 Dec , 1820 (2457)
    : Martin, E 24 March, 1792 (189)
     Kelsey, J 17 Jan , 1797 (44)
   see Newell-Atkins
   ,, Woodward
Atkinson Bradford, J. H H 10 March, 1840 (597)
     Bradford, R. 12 Feb., 1872 (713)
   see Farmer-Atkinson
   ,, Harle.
   ,, Honey-Atkinson
   ., Lacon.
   ,, Owst-Atkinson
    - Procter, H 23 Sept , 1872 (4451)
     Purvis, R A 26 June, 1828 (1246)
     Rutherford, A 3 Dec , 1827 (2489)
   see Savile
   ., Simmons-Atkinson
    Wilkinson, J J 22 May, 1861 (2263)
    Wilson, G C. 23 Nov , 1860 (4959)
   see Wilson-Atkinson
Atkinson-Grimshaw Atkinson, R 15 Sept , 1877 (5287)
Atkinson-Jowett. Atkinson, N 15 June, 1855 (2309)
Atkyins-Wright: Atkyins, J. 28 March, 1797 (290)
Atwell-Smith Smith, M W, of The Cedars, Worsley Road, Southsea, Hants, late of Warleigh House, Southsea, spinster Times, 21 Aug , 1872
        Smith, H S., of The Cedars, Worsley Road. Southsea Hants, late of Warleigh House, Southsea, spinster Times, 21 Aug., 1872
Attwood *see* Bridgen.
Attwood-Mathews *see* Mathews
       Mathews, B. St. J., of Pontrilas, Hereford Times, d p., 30 Aug , 1881
Aubrey : Abrey, G H., of Springfield, Essex, gent Times, d p., 28 Dec., 1876
   see Griffiths-Aubrey
   : Ricketts, C A 7 March, 1874 (1644)
   see Tozer-Aubrey
   ,, Windsor-Aubrey

Aubrey *see* Wynne-Aubrey.
Aughe *see* Hawe.
Augier *see* McVane
Aukdall-Gratwicke : Auckdall, G 28 April, 1863 (2245)
Aulton : Dew, Emily L, of Bradford Street, Walsall, Staffs. Times, 13 Nov, 1877.
Austen *see* Godwin-Austen
    „ Knight
    „ Puddicombe
  : Roberts, W. C 19 Sep, 1885 (4598)
    Stoffold, H. 33rd Geo II., 1760
    Stoffold, R 33rd Geo II., 1760
  see Treffry.
Austen-Leigh : Austen, J. E. 31 Jan, 1837 (263)
Austen-Cartmell Cartmell, J. 30 Aug, 1886 (4225)
Austin *see* Brocas
    „ Hicks-Austin
    Smith, T. G and S C Smith, now or late of Luton, Bedford. Times, d p, 27 April, 1866
    Westcott, S. T G A, of South Vale, Blackheath Times, 3 Dec, 1888
Aveland, Lady *see* Heathcote-Drummond
Aveling *see* Nairn.
Averill *see* Griffiths-Averill.
Avery-Grimes · Leon-Avery, L A, of South Kensington, London Times, 19 Oct, 1899
Avigdor *see* Verona-Avigdor.
Awe *see* Hawe.
Ayerst . De Lasaux, R G. 23 Oct, 1812 (2118)
Aylesbury *see* Walker Aylesbury
Aylmer *see* Hendrick-Aylemer
    „ Lintott-Aylmer
Aylmer-Whitworth : Aylmer, Right Hon. M. 4 July, 1825 (1295)
Aylon *see* Tyrrell
Aylward-Kearney Aylward, J D. G., 12 April, 1876 (233 and 225)
Aylward *see* Toler-Aylward
Aylwood : Alewood, A., of Crofton Court, Orpington, Kent, esq Times, 27 Aug, 1869.
Aynsley Mitford, A 17 July, 1792 (553)
    Murray, Lord C 15 June, 1793 (491)
  see Taylor
Ayrton *see* Wadsworth
Ayscough *see* Perry Ayscough
    : Smith, Rev. T. A., of The Vicarage, Tenby, Worcester. Times, d p, 24 May, 1890
Ayton *see* Lee

Ayton—Lee, E. C., of 30, Great James Street, Bedford Row, and of St. Mary's, Teddington, Middlesex, architect. d.p., 14 Sept., 1887.
: Lee, E. C. A., of Bedford Row and Teddington, Middlesex, architect. Times, d.p., 17 Sept., 1887
— Lee, F. C., of The Rookery, Shooter's Hill, Kent, esq., no occupation. Times, d.p., 17 Sept. 1887

B

Bache see Booth.
Bacon · Bushby, A. B. 28 Sept., 1792 (753)
    : Forster, W. B. 1 Feb., 1802 (115)
    · Williams, C. 25 Aug., 1802 (929)
    : McCausland, R., of Dublin, barrister. Dublin, 25 March, 1829.
Bacon-Grey : Bacon, C. 11 July, 1823 (1175)
Bacon-Hickman : Bacon. H. 27 April, 1826 (1095)
Badcock see Elliot.
    „ Bentley.
    „ Frampton.
    „ Harris.
    „ Lovell.
Badger-Eastwood Badger, T S., of Lincoln's Inn, Middlesex, barrister-at-law Times. 7 Oct., 1863.
Badgley see Weeding
Baeda Thom, Patrick : Thom. Peter (son of Wm.) Times, 20 Oct., 1880
Bagenal : Newton, P., jun., of Dunleckny, co. Carlow. D G. 6 March, 1832
Baggalley see Weeding.
Bagge see Lee-Warner
Baghott · Wathen, P. 20 May, 1812 (954)
Baghot de la Bere : Edwards, J. 31 May, 1879 (3906)
Bagnall Wild Kirkby, R. B. D.G., 23 Nov., 1868 (1326)
Bagnall-Wilde Kirkby. R B 1868 (6403)
Bagot see Howard
    „ Neville-Bagot.
Bagshaw : Darling, W C 19 Dec., 1801 (1487)
    see Greaves-Bagshaw
Bagster Wilson : Wilson, A., of 15, Wells Road, Sydenham, Kent Times, 15 June, 1892

Bagwell-Purefoy : Bagwell, E. D.G., 5 April, 24 April, 1847 (621 and 630)
Baikie : Cowan, A., of Croydon. Times, 19 Dec., 1898
   see Simpson-Baikie
Bailey *see* Page-Bailey.
   : Bishop, G. J., of Langley Burrell, Wilts, gent. Times 17 Dec., 1870
   . Tinson, G. F. R., spinster, residing at The Terrace, Oaken, Staffs. Times, 2 Oct., 1888.
   Wilson, G., of Thorney Hills, Kendal, Westmorland Times, 21 June, 1881.
Bailie *see* Crookshanks-Bailie.
Baillie *see* Cochran-Wisheart-Baillie
   „ Gordon Baillie
   „ Kennedy-Baillie
   Reid, J. 31 July, 1792 (596).
Baillie-Arden · Baillie, G. 31 Dec., 1858 (39)
Baillie-Gage : Gage, T. R. D.G., 8 Aug., 1876 (473)
Baillie-Hamilton : (Earl of Haddington) Baillie, G. 24 March, 1859 (1369).
Baillie-Hamilton : Baillie, Hamilton George, of Jerviswood, Earl of Haddington. Lyon, Vol. VI., 4 May, 1859.
Baily-Browne : Browne, A. B., 13, Park Terrace, Nottingham Times, d.p., 27 Nov., 1886
Baily-Neale : Baily, R. N., of Nunne, nr. Frome, Somerset Times, d.p., 23 Oct., 1895.
Bainbridge *see* Daniell-Bainbridge.
   : O'Brien, J. B., of 1, Alfred Place, Thurloe Square. S. Kensington gent. Times, d.p., 23 April, 1886
   : Martin, C. B. 21 April, 1886 (5054).
Bainbridge-Bell : Bell, H. W. 13 Nov., 1895 (7300).
   . Bell, L. M. and A. M., of The Rectory, Cheltenham, spinsters ; W. D., of The Vicarage Micheldever, F. C., of Balham ; and B. W., of The Rectory, Cheltenham. Times, d.p., 20 Aug., 1895
Bainbrigge *see* Arnold-Bainbrigge
Bainbrigge-Le Hunt · Bainbrigge, P. 7 May, 1832 (1221)
Baines Beanes, F. E. V., of Walsingham House, Piccadilly, Middlesex, esq. Times, d.p., 8 March, 1892.
   see Emmitt
   . Raines
   „ Sikes.
'Baird : Forster, J. and W. 30 Jan., 1821 (368).
   see Maturin-Baird.
Baird-Carter Carter, A., of 49, Russell Square, London, printseller, &c. Times, d.p., 6 Dec., 1894

Baird-Hay, of Belton . Hay, Jas. Geo   Lyon, Vol. IX., 6 May, 1874
Baker *see* Allen
   „ Baker-Gothard
   „ Baker-Wilbraham
   „ Bere.
   „ Bethune-Baker
   „ Bruce
   .. Budd-Budd
   „ Bykur.
   „ De Wynter.
   „ Pullman-Baker.
   „ Tathwell.
   „ Watson.
   : Andrews, J 19 April, 1768 (10825)
   : Cresswell, A J 59 Geo. III., c. 72 (503).
   : Elsley, T. B. 29 Oct., 1793 (951).
   Littlehales, Sir E B 17 Jan., 1817 (263)
   see Milles-Baker
   : Pearson, F 9 Jan 1888 (423).
   : Tower, J H B. 29 Jan., 1844 (309)
   · Wingfield, W. 29 Dec., 1849 (2)
Baker Carr : Baker, R. J, of Lanteglos, Camelford, Cornwall. clk in h.o. Times, 5 May, 1885
Baker-Cresswell : Cresswell-Baker, A. J. 25 Aug., 1840 (1945
Baker Gothard . Baker, Arth Gothard, of Buenos Ayres   Times, 15 Aug 1899
Baker-Stallard-Penoyre · Baker, Rev S , and A. F., his wife, of Landbourne, Worcester; The Moor, Hereford, and 2, Berkeley Villas. Cheltenham. Times, d p, 8 Jan., 1890
   : Baker, S. R. (Rev.), of The Moor, Hereford, etc Times, d.p., 18 April, 1893
Balack *see* Hanway.
Balcarras *see* Thomson-Balcarras
Baldomero Hyacinth de Bertodano Baldomero Hyacinth de Bertodano Lopez, of 22, Chester Terrace, Regent's Park, Middlesex. M. Post, 12 Oct., 1897
Baldrey *see* Stow-Baldrey
Baldwin *see* Biggs-Baldwin
   „ Rigbye.
Baldwyn-Childe · Childe, E. G., of Kyre Park, Worces Times, d p, 12 Feb, 1881
Balfour *see* Stewart-Balfour
   „ Paterson-Balfour-Hay

Balfour-Melville, of Pilrig : Balfour, John Mackintosh Lyon, Vol. XI., 28 Jan., 1884.
Balfour-Stewart, of Arbigland : Stewart, Robt Lyon, Vol. VIII, 3 May, 1869.
Balfour-Kinnear, of Birstane : Kinnear, Geo. Thomas. Lyon, Vol. XI., 22 Feb., 1888.
Balguy : Haverfield. Evelina, of Marsh Court, Sherborne Times, 3 Aug., 1899
Ball *see* Tannas
Ballantine-Dykes Ballantine, J D 29 Jan, 1800 (141).
De Balinhard Carnegy, J. A. of Dublin. Dublin, 17 Aug., 1832.
Ballantine : Dykes, L. 23 Jan., 1773 (11320)
Baller *see* Longworth.
Ball-Acton Acton, C., Major and Brev. Lieut.-Col. 51st Light Infantry, at Dalhousie, India. Times, 2 June, 1875.
Ball-Hughes : Ball, E. H. 7 Aug., 1819 (1426).
Balls-Headley Balls, W., of 5, Tavistock Place, Tavistock Square, Middlesex, esquire, M B Times. 14 June, 1886.
Balls Woolby : Balls, J., L.R.C.P. Eng. of Holton Halesworth, Suffolk. Times, d.p., 4 Oct. 1879
Balme *see* Wheatley-Balme
Bamford . Hesketh, R. 22 April, 1806 (511)
Bamford-Hesketh Bamford, R 15 Jan., 1810 (87)
Bamford-Taylor : Bamford, E. and Elizth., his wife W., 26 Nov., 1857 (D.G. 1178)
Bancroft : Butterfield, Squire B., of 3, Eaton Terrace, St. John's Wood, Marylebone, Middlesex, gent Times, d.p., 14 Dec., 1876
Bankes *see* Goring-Bankes.
 . Holme, M. 6 Sept. 1803 (1824)
  Murray 30 May. 1882 (2590)
 : Murray, E. S. L., of Winstanley Hall, Lancs Times, 12 June, 1882
Banks Cleaver, J 15 March, 1788 (121).
 see Davies.
  Sharpe. R. J 17 Feb., 1854 (680)
Bannatine-Allason : Bannatine, R. A., of Ayrshire, Scotland, Capt. R A Times, d.p., 1 April 1886
Banner *see* Harmood Banner
Bannerman *see* Campbell-Bannerman
   Le French, H d p, 12 Oct., 1883
   see Smith-Bannerman
Bannerman-Phillips . Phillips, H., Capt. 1st Batt. Welsh Reg. Times, d.p., 6 July, 1894.
Banning *see* Greaves-Banning
Banson *see* Barlee

Barbaro *see* Zimmermann-Barbaro
Barber *see* Garlick
— : Windebank, C H , of Bishopsgate St , E C , and of Portslade, Sussex, gent Times, d.p , 19 Dec , 1887
Barber-Starkey   Barber, W T S   28 March, 1873 (1775)
Barclay *see* Robertson-Barclay
Barclay-Allardice   Ritchie, Margaret , Robt Barclay, Allardice, David Stuart Barclay   Lyon Vol. XI., 2 July, 1883
Barclay-Brown   Brown, Sophia A., of Lindores, Upper Richmond Road, Putney, widow   Times, d p , 27 June, 1895
Barclay-Harvey   Harvey, J C , J P , of 5, De Vere Gardens, Middlesex   Times, d p , 2 March, 1889
Barclay-Smith   Smith, Woltera Mercy   Times, 31 July, 1899
Barfoot *see* Parham.
Barfoot-Saunt   Gatty, W H , of Market Harborough, Leicesters., gent. Times, d p., 4 Jan , 1899
Bargate, G · Moses, G Bellas, of Greystone, Lancs , gent. Times, d p , 27 May, 1874
Bargrave *see* Tournay-Bargrave
Baring *see* Bence-Baring
Baring-Gould : Baring, W. 14 July, 1795 (746).
Barker   Carnaby· Johnson : Barker, Johnson (Rev), of Wilton, Wilts. Times, 25 Sept., 1888
   see Bullock-Barker
   — Copeman. G R   5 July, 1889 (3695)   Times, 3 June, 1889
   · Cragg, R. B — Sept . 1833 (1748)
   see Darling-Barker
   ,, Hethersett
   ., Purvis
   · Jones, G C , of 10. Leinster Square, Middlesex, esq Times, d p , 13 Oct , 1876
   Ponsonby   Chambre Brabazon, of Belmont, Queen's Co 9 Nov 1818 (R L 12)
   Raymond, J   2 June, 1789 (409)
   Smith, G M., of Waterloo St , Brighton, esq   Times, d.p, 16 Feb , 1875
Barker-Mill   Barker, J   8 May, 1835 (964)
Barlee · Buckle, C   11 Dec , 1811 (27)
— Banson C B   1 June, 1779 (11983)
see Davy.
Barley *see* Fearon.
Barlow   Bredall, T A. J   30 Nov., 1799 (1294)
   see Fogg
   ,. Hoy
   ,, Lazarus-Barlow
   ,. Masterman

B

Barlow · Owen, H   24 March, 1789 (149).
Barlow-Massicks . Massicks, T , of The Oaks, Millom, Cumberland, ironmaster. Times, 6 Dec , 1883
Barnard : Bolders, L   5 Dec , 1769 (10997)
    see Tyrrell.
    ,, Verney
Barneby *see* Higginson.
Barneby Lutley   Barneby. J. H   29 Nov., 1864 (6083).
Barned *see* Lewis-Barned
Barnes *see* Douglas.
    ,, Pemberton-Barnes.
    ,, Slacke-Barnes
Barnes Amor · Barnes, J., of Evans Hotel, Covent Garden, Midx. Times, d p , 28 Nov , 1876.
Barnes Lawrence : Barnes, Rev H F , of Birkin, Yorks   Times, d.p., 10 Nov., 1877.
Barnes-Williams · Williams, T , late of Old Jewry, now of 11, Clements Lane, Lombard Street, architect and surveyor   Times, d p , 30 Dec , 1887, 2 Jan , 1888
Barnet *see* Phillips.
Barnett *see* Hastings.
Barnewall   M'Loughlin, N   8 Oct , 1785 (461)
Barnwell · Herring, C B   14 Oct , 1825 (1864)
    see Turnor-Barnwell.
Barraclough *see* Slingsby
Barrar *see* Acton
Barratt *see* Layland-Barratt.
Barrett, Chas   Vaux, of 19, Winson Green Road, Birmingham. life assur agent. Times. d.p , 6 June, 1889
    see Brydges-Barrett.
    ,, Buchanan-Boyd
    ,, Moulton, E. B. and S B   6 Jan., 1798 (11)
Barreto   Bliss, Baron, of Brandon Park, Suffolk   3 Jan , 1867
Barret Lennard, of Belhouse, Sir Thos   R L , Lyon Vol II., 1 Aug , 1812   The R-L was dated 30 March, 1786
Barrett-Hamilton : Barrett, S   31 Aug , 1887 (D G. 1073).
Barrett-Lennard   Thomas T and B   18 March, 1786 (113)
Barrington   Kennett, Vis Hunter Barrington   24 Feb., 1885 (858)
Barrington-Kennett   Kennett, V. H B.   12 July, 1878 (4367)
Barrington White · White, J , of Wellington Park, Belfast, of 53, Sloane Street, and 37, Mark Lane, London. Times, d p , 27 Nov., 1893
Barrs-Haden · Barrs, A H   24 Nov , 1876 (6683)
Barrow *see* Temple-Barrow
Barry *see* Bury-Barry; Otter-Barry
    « Neale, P   20 Nov , 1811 (69)
    see Smith-Barry

Barrymore   Bews, W.   28 Aug., 1802 (899).
Bartelot : Bartlett, R. G., Corfe Castle, Dorset   Times, 5 Dec., 1898
Bartlett-Burdett-Coutts   Burdett-Coutts-Bartlett-Coutts   W. L. A.   19 May, 1882 (2475)
Bartlett *see* Burdett-Coutts-Bartlett
   „   Stuckey-Bartlett
   „   Wathen-Bartlett
Barton   Beyfus, Jane, of 3, Duke Street, Portland Place, London, widow.   Times, d.p., 29 April, 1893.
   · Buggs, S., corn and coal merchant, of Epsom, Surrey   Times, 21 Jan., 1868
   : Dumpleton, R., now of Luton.   Times, 30 April, 1874.
   : Metcalfe, H.   22 Aug., 1795 (863)
   see Perrins.
   : Shirt, W. H., of 79, Monmouth Street and 151, Broomhall Street, Sheffield, grocer, and Sarah E., his wife   Times, d.p., 18 Feb., 1890
Barton-Wright   Wright, E. W., of 158, Cromwell Road, South Kensington, Middlesex, engineer.   Times, d.p., 2 June, 1892.
Baruchson *see* De Beer
Barwell-Ewins : Bennett, William John Ewins, of Marston Trussell Hall, Market Harborough.   Times, 21 Jan., 1898
Baseley *see* Wade
Baseley-Tooke · Baseley, J.   19 Oct., 1802 (1105)
Basil *see* Fleck-Basil
Baskerville *see* Mynors-Baskerville
   . Viveash, H.   5 March 1838 (578).
Bass-Eltham · Bass, James, of Goswell Street, Middlesex, now residing at Woodward Cottage, North End, Portsea, Southampton   Times, 7 April, 1870.
Basset : Bruce, W. W. J.   22 Dec., 1865 (6806)
   see Davie-Basset
   · Williams, C. H.   11 Oct., 1880 (5283 and 5325)
Bassett · Popkin. T. P.   9 Nov., 1820 (2135)
Bassett-Smith · Smith, W., of 10, John Street, Adelphi, architect   Times, d.p., 14 April, 1881.
Batard *see* Bearda-Batard
Batchelor *see* Kendall
Batchelor-Taylor · Batchelor, W. B.   Times, 14 Dec., 1893
Bateman   Buckley, J.   17 Oct., 1827 (2218)
   Caudle, W. A. F., of The Old Palace, Richmond, Surrey, medical student of King's College, London   Times, 5 Feb, 1863
   · Hudson T.   8 Sept., 1818 (1932) (*see* 1981)
   see Jones-Bateman
   „   La Trobe-Bateman.

Bateman-Champain : Champain, J U., of Halton Park, Lancaster, Major R E., Director-General of Gov Indo-European Telegraphs Times, 7 Oct., 1870
Bateman-Hanbury-Kincaid Lennox, of Woodhead and Kincard: Bateman-Hanbury, C. S. 28 Jan , 1862
Bateman-Hanbury Hanbury, W (Lord Bateman) 4 Feb., 1837 (723)
Bateman-Robson Holland, R. 26 Nov., 1791 (649)
Bates *see* Elliot-Bates
Bateson *see* Harvey.
Bateson de Yarburgh : Bateson, G. W. and M E. 24 April, 1876 (2613)
Bateson Wood Wood, Mary E., of Fallowfield, Lancs , spinster Times, d p , 24 Dec 1889
Batey *see* Holroyd.
Bath *see* De Bathe
Bathurst · Bragge, Rt Hon C 11 May, 1804 (639)
    see Hervey-Bathurst.
    Hervey. F E 19 Jan , 1802 (61)
Batley *see* Beynon
  ,, Harrison-Batley
Batstone-Stone : Batstone, G. B , of Hornsey, London Times, 7 Feb , 1899
Batten *see* Chisholm-Batten
Battersby · Harford, A 55th Geo III , 1815
Battersby-Harford Harford-Battersby. J 12 Feb , 1850 (397)
Battersby-Wybrants · Battersby, G M B. (widow). 11 Jan , 1876 (D G 17)
Battie-Wrightson Thomas, W H 26 Dec , 1891 (255)
Battye-Trevor Trevor Battye. C E A T . Capt 3rd Batt East Lancashire Reg , of 8, Duke Street, St James Times 31 Aug , 1894.
Baumberg *see* Bernard.
Baumgartner *see* Champion.
Bax Ironside Bax, J H 18 Oct., 1866 (5527)
Baxter Morley, R. M , wine and spirit merchant, of The Irongate, Derby Times, d.p., 22 June, 1870.
Bayley *see* Laurie
Bayley-Worthington Bayley, Gibbon. W., 5 Dec , 1863 (D.G. 1451)
Baylis *see* Clarke Baylis
Bayly · Dark, W H 5 Sept., 1809 (1421).
    see Sparvel-Bayly
Bayly-Wallis Bayly, L. 17 Sept.. 1800 (1086)
Baynes *see* Farrer-Baynes
  ,, Jago
Bayntun-Sandys Sandys, E. B. 9 May, 1807 (614).

Beach *see* De la Bêche.
    : Hicks-Beach, W. 24 Jan , 1838 (234).
    : Hicks, M. 3 July, 1790 (405)
Beadle *see* Bedolpe.
Beadle-Bedolpe : Beadle, W V., formerly of Tewkesbury and Bristol, now of Boulevard d'Italie 29. Paris. Times, d.p., 25 May, 1866
Beal *see* Bonnell
Beale-Browne : Browne, G W B , of Salperton Park, Gloucester, esq Times, 18 Dec., 1876.
Beale-Brown : Browne, J of Salperton Park, Gloucester, and Crotta House. Kerry. Times, d p., 2 Aug , 1867
Bean *see* Allenby
   „ Rodbard
   „ Whitaker-Bean
Beanes *see* Baines.
Bear *see* Mason.
Beard de Beauchamp : Beard, T A , late of St James' Road. Surbiton, Surrey, now of 4, Rue de Marignan, Champs Elysées, Paris. Times, 23 Nov., 1865.
Bearda-Batard : Bearda, T. 15 Feb , 1811 (335)
Beaty-Pownall : Beaty, C C. 16 Jan., 1835 (102)
Beauchamp *see* Farthing-Beauchamp
    : Tucker, E. B , of Trevinee, Cornwall, esq Times, d p , 15 May, 1874
    see Proctor-Beauchamp
Beauchamp-Proctor *see* Proctor-Beauchamp
Beauchant *see* Nowell-Usticke.
Beauclerk : Cronmire, S. H., of 2 Camden Gardens, Shepherd's Bush, agent Times, d p , 25 April, 1888
Beaudesert, Baron of *see* Paget
Beaumont : Hunt, J 18 March, 1775 (11544)
    : McCumming. R. H J B 5 June. 1857 (1975)
Beavan *see* Dixon Beavan.
Beavis : Hartnell, E H. 9 June, 1892 (3588)
Bebb : Lawrell, H 7 June, 1850 (1599)
Beck *see* Alcock-Beck
   „ Hyde.
   „ Church
Becher : Wrixon, W , of Ballygibbin, co Cork Dublin, 29 Sep , 1831.
à Beckett *see* Turner
Beckett Denison. Sir E 9 Dec , 1872 (43)
    see Denison
   „ Turner
Beckford *see* Pitt-Rivers.

Beddington   Moses, H L , of 3, Cornwall Terrace, Regent's Park and 34, Monkwell Street, London, merchant, Times, d.p., 11 Dec., 1868
   Moses, S. H., of 29, Oakley Square, St Pancras, Middlesex, and 14, Cannon Street West, London, formerly of 13, Talbot Square, Hyde Park Times, d p., 24 July, 1866
   Moses, M., of Hyde House, Thornton Road, Clapham Park, Surrey, and 34, Monkwell Street, London, merchant. Times, d p., 7 Aug., 1868
   Moses, A H., of 11, York Gate, Regent's Park, Middlesex Times, 4 Nov, 1868
   Moses, J H., of 20, Ulster Place, Regent's Park, and 4, Moorgate Buildings, London, wool-broker Times, d.p, 29 Oct, 1868.
   Moses, E H , of 98, Lancaster Gate, Hyde Park, Middlesex and of 61 (late 14), Cannon Street West, London, merchant; lately residing at Fern Lodge, Atkins Road, Clapham Park, Surrey Times. d p , 30 Jan, 1868.
Bedell-Sivwright, of Southhouse and Meggetland   Beddell, Wm Henry Revell   Lyon Vol IX., 6 Feb., 1874
Beddoes   Weale, J. 20 May, 1844 (1764)
Beddow · Beddow-Green, J J , of Aldridge, Stafford, brick and tile manufacturer   Times, d p. 2 Aug, 1887
   Beddow-Green, J. B.. of Aldridge, Stafford, brick and tile manufacturer   d p., 26 July, 1887.
Bedford *see* Edwards
   : Jubb, J. 21 May, 1785 (241)
   see Kenyon
Bedingfeld *see* Paston-Bisshopp-Bedingfeld
   ,, Paston-Bedingfeld.
Bedolfe : Beadle, J C., Pastor of the Independent Church at Falmouth, Cornwall   Times, d p , 16 Nov., 1868
   see Beadle-Bedolfe.
Bedwardine *see* Wilmot
Beer · Conybeare H. of 21 Higher Union Street Torquay. Devon painter and glazier Times, d p, 26 June 1867
   Parkin, J. 18 July, 1827 (1591).
Beers *see* Leslie.
Beesley · North, J S. K., of 103. Boundary Road, St John's Wood, Middlesex, tailor   Times, 2 July, 1884
Beete *see* Picton
Beevor *see* Hare
   ,, Lombe
Beilby *see* Herbert.
Belcher *see* Stringer

Belches *see* Stuart.
Belcombe : Bulcock, W. 15 Aug., 1789 (541)
Beldam-Johns : Nash-Woodham. F. M. 10 May, 1867 (2929)
 (D.G 677)
  Beldam, E. 5 Dec., 1804 (113)
Beldams-Johns : Nash-Woodhouse, F. M.
Belgrave *see* Grubb Belgrave
Bell *see* Bainbridge-Bell.
 Joseph Askew : Bell, J., of The Chapel, Bassenthwaite, Cumberland, gent. Times, 3 Sept., 1874
  see Bowdler.
  „ Carlyle-Bell
   : Grubb, C. R E Times, d.p., 8 Dec., 1880
  see Lawson-Bell
  „ Livesey.
   · Macbean, F. 27 Jan., 1852 (291)
  see Martin
   Robson, E. 17 March, 1868 (1976)
   : Robson Ed. Whll., 17 Mar., 1868 (D G 371).
   : Robson, J. B 7 Jan., 1867 (100) (D G 65)
  see Senhouse.
   : Smith, R. 6 Aug., 1877 (51)
  see Spencer Bell.
  „ Towerson
Bellairs *see* Stevenson.
Bellamy : Frey, Mrs. Mary Ann, of Lordship Road, Stoke Newington. N. Times, d.p., 10 Feb., 1892.
Bellas *see* Greenhough
Bellasis *see* Dalglish-Bellasis
  , Oliver-Bellasis
Bellasyse *see* Lee-Bellasyse
  „ Wynn-Bellasye
Bellenden *see* Ker Bellenden
Bellew *see* Bryan : Grattan-Bellew.
Bellwood Garfit, F. H. D B 12 Feb., 1870 (1026) (D.G. 252)
Belward *see* Moyse-Belward.
Beman, H. H. W. *see* Wells, H B.
Bempde *see* Johnstone
  „ Venden-Bempde
Bence : Sparrow B. 12 May, 1804 (590).
Bence-Baring : Bence, Edward, 2, Montpelier Terrace, Cheltenham. Times, 17 Jan., 1898.
Bence Lambert Lambert, G. L., of Claremorris, co. Mayo, esq., Times, d.p., 29 Jan., 1885.
Bence-Pembroke . Pembroke-Jones. F. C., Bude. Cornwall. Times, 25 June, 1898.

Bence Trower · Trower, P., of St. Mary-at-Hill and Hyde Park,
    London, esq. Times, d p., 26 May, 1877
Benet *see* Pye-Benet.
Benett *see* Stanford.
Benett-Stanford Benett, Vere.   11 Dec., 1868 (6705) (D G. 1421)
Benison *see* Worsley-Benison
Benjamin *see* Bevan.
    ,, Bertram.
    ., Greyham
    ,, Henry-Benjamin.
    ,, Liebmann.
    ,, Neville.
Benn *see* Walsh.
Bennet, Robt Ottiwell Gifford : Bennet, Robt , of Buxton, Derby,
    M.D. Times, d.p., 12 April, 1889
    see Barwell Ewins
    ., Coffin
    Richards, F B   9 Oct , 1867 (5605) (D.G. 1305)
Bennett : Jackson, Joseph Henry. of Ballymore, co Cork   Ir.
    R.L., 22 Oct., 1811.
    see Fletcher-Bennett.
    : Jackson, J C. 1 Jan and 12 Jan , 1874 (D G 25)
    see Luckman-Bennett.
    : Pobgee, E. B., of Carlton Cottage, Cowper Road, Stoke
        Newington, Middlesex, and 11, Staple Inn
        Times, d.p., 4 Jan , 1865
    : Tuck, S., Palmerston Buildings, London. Times, 19
        March, 1898.
Bennett Goldney : Evans, F , of Langley Burrell, Chippenham,
    Wilts , gent. Times, d p , 25 April, 1892.
Bennett-Poe : Poe, J. T., of Riverston, Nenagh, Tipperary, esq
    Times, d p., 14 May, 1889
Benson-Brown : Brown, W. H., of 4, Market Place, Horncastle,
    Lincoln, and of Durham, student Times, 21 June, 1889
Benson Griffiths . Griffiths, T , of Neath Abbey, Neath, Glamorgan-
    shire, land and min. surveyor   Times, 30 Jan., 1892
Bentinck-Scott : Bentinck, W. H C (com called Marquis of
    Titchfield). 19 Sept., 1795 (954).
Bentley : Badcock, H., of 7, Densham Terrace, Plymouth.
    Times, 19 Dec., 1872.
    see Forbes-Bentley.
    : Gordon, B 17 May, 1777 (11770)
Bentley-Innes : Bentley, F S Times, d.p., 21 March, 1864.
Bentley-Taylor . Bentley, Rev. R., of Pudleston Rectory,
    Leominster, Hereford, and Maria A. W., his wife. Times,
    d.p., 23 May, 1893.
Benwell *see* de Courcy-Benwell.

Benyon — Fellowes, R. 10 Jan., 1855 (135)
    see Powlett-Wright
Benyon-De Beauvoir : Powlett-Wrighte-Benyon, R 24 April, 1822 (717)
Benyon-Winsor — Winsor, W. 5 March, 1867 (1660) (D G 365)
Berdmore *see* Fowler-Berdmore
Berdoe-Wilkinson, E · Wilkinson, E Geo A., now at Dusseldorf, Germany, merchant Times, 3 June, 1876
Bere — Baker, M B 16 Dec., 1775 (11622).
Berens — McLaughlin, Rev. R. H., of Keston, Kent. Times, d p, 10 Jan., 1877
    McLaughlin, R H 15 July, 1885 (3373)
Beresford : Berisford, T, of 4. Garfield Terr., Cann-Hall Road, Leytonstone, Essex. exam. office of customs Times, 26 Sept., 1892
    . Brown, G F, formerly of Poole, Dorset, now of Kennington Park, Surrey, med. stud. Times, d.p., 10 Nov., 1884.
    : Smyly, J. B., Col. and Hon. Major (retired), of Portrush, co Antrim Times, d p., 21 Feb., 1888.
Beresford-Drummond . Drummond, Francis Colebrook, Lieut. 7th Dragoon Guards. Lyon Vol IX., 19 Nov., 1875
Beresford-Hope : Hope, A. J B 30 May, 1854 (1729)
Beresford-Massy Massy, J. M 4 May, 18 May, 1871 (D G 389)
    see Massy-Beresford
Beresford-Peirse Beresford. H W de La Poer 29 Sept., 1851 (2645)
Berger *see* Steigenberger.
Bergne-Coupland . Bergne. R. C. 24 Feb., 1868 (1364) (D.G. 235)
Beridge — Sparrow 21 June, 1895 (3658)
Berisford *see* Beresford
Berkeley, T — Hardtman. T B. Times. 27 Dec., 1872.
    Tomkins. R (Tomkyns) 9 Oct., 1832 (2324) (2394).
Berkeley-Calcott Berkeley G 18 Sept., 1826 (2330).
Berkin-Meackham Berkin, W 14 Feb., 1795 (144)
Berliner-Goodman Berliner, M, of Luton Road and High Street. Chatham, Kent. pawnbroker Times, d p, 25 Feb., 1888
Bernal *see* Osborne
Bernard — Baumberg. B. of 14. Lansdowne Gardens, South Lambeth. Surrey. journalist Times. d p., 24 Jan., 1893
    : Camplin, J 14 Dec., 1881 (2374)
    see Morland
Bernard Dent O'Brien, J, of 189. Blackfriar's Road. London Times, 27 Feb., 1894

Berrie · Denness, A. K , of Packington, Ashby-de-la-Zouche, spinster. Times, d.p., 3 Dec., 1881
Berrill *see* Downes
Berrington *see* Davies-Berrington
Berry *see* Anderson-Berry
    ,, De Berry
    ,, Ferguson
    : Haley, J., of Bollington, nr. Macclesfield. Times, 9 Jan., 1890.
    : Thomas, J. 4th and 5th Will. IV., 1834
Bertie . Codwise, E. 21 May, 1832 (1222).
    : Hoar, T. 20 May, 1788 (237)
    : Lichigaray, M. 3 March, 1823 (499)
    : Taliacarne, A J., of Trin Coll , Oxford, and 10, Bury St., Middlesex, and of New Zealand, esq. Times, 1 Feb., 1882.
Bertie-Greatheed : Greatheed, B. 20 May, 1819 (906).
Bertie-Mathew : Mathew, B. 5 May, 1819 (842)
Bertrand . D'Anglebermes, E. R 3 Oct., 1820 (1897)
Besly *see* Finch-Hatton-Besly
  ,, Wood-Besly.
Best *see* Haden-Best
Beswick *see* Myers-Beswick.
Beswicke Royds : Royds, C. R N 19 July, 1867 (4287) (D G 997)
Betenson . Slyman, W. B , W. D., C. H. P., and F. R., all of 26, Caversham Rd , Kentish Town, Middlesex, gent Times, d.p , 8 Jan., 1891
Bethell : Codrington, W J. 7 April, 1798 (283).
Bethune of Kilconguhal : Lindsay, Sir Henry. Lyon Vol IV., 20 Feb., 1836
    Patton, W D. P. 30 Aug. 1882 (4175)
    see Patton-Bethune.
    . Sharpe, A. 23 Aug, 1815 (1945)
Bethune-Baker : Baker. J F , of Edgbaston, Warwick. and of Pembroke Coll , Cambs. Times, 21 Jan., 1885.
    : Baker, A. A., and G. T., eldest and second sons of A Baker, of Edgbaston, Warwick, gent. Times, d.p., 17 Dec., 1891.
Bettesworth-Trevanion : Bettesworth, J. T. P 18 Dec., 1801 (1505).
Betton *see* Bright Betton
Betts *see* Burton
Betty *see* Kemmis-Betty.
  ,, Shattock.
Bevan . Benjamin, J., of 80, Kings Rd.. Brighton. dealer in works of art Times, d.p., 22 Mar, 1886.

Bevan : Evans, F., of Newport, Monmouths. Times, 3 Jan., 1885
Beveridge see Lock-Beveridge.
Beveridge-Duncan : Beveridge, J. 8 Dec., 1798 (1166).
Beverly : Collard, A B., of 78, Hamilton Terr., Middlesex, esq.
    Times, d.p., 6 Sept., 1886.
Bewicke : Bewicke-Anderson, C. 30 Dec., 1816 (5)
    Robt Calverly Bewicke : Bewicke, Robt. Calverly, of
        Coulby Manor, York. Times, 21 Oct., 1865.
Bewicke-Copley : Bewicke, R. C. A. 5 April, 1892 (2166).
Bews see Barrymore.
Beyfus see Barton.
    ,, Ferguson
Beynon : Batley, E. T. 1 Nov., 1805 (1343).
    see Crowther-Beynon.
Beynon Williams : Williams, Muriel, of Dukes Road, Euston
    Road, Middlesex. Times, 29 Nov., 1899.
Bibby-Hesketh : Bibby, C. H. 6 Feb., 1899 (866)
Bickerstaffe see Drew
Bickersteth see Harley.
Bickford Smith : Smith, W., Esq., M.P., of Trevarno, Helston.
    Cornwall. Times, d.p., 23 Dec., 1885.
Biddulph see Middleton-Biddulph.
    ,, Wright-Biddulph.
Biddulph-Colclough : Biddulph, F. D. 17 July, 1886 (D.G 615)
Biddulph-Parker : Parker, J. Times, 24 June, 1868
Bidgood : Sloane, H. F. 5 Nov., 1822 (1850)
Biedermann see Von Skala.
Bigg see Wither
Bigge see Selby-Bigge.
Biggs see Isaac-Biggs
    ,, Lesingham.
    ,, Yeatman-Biggs.
Biggs-Baldwin : Biggs, W. H. 13 March, 1879 (D.G 201).
Bigot : Godin, J. 20th Geo III., 1780.
Billinghurst see Woodroffe
Binden Marcus, C. G. : Muller, C. G., engineer of H.M.S.
    Audacious, China Station. Times 13 June, 1877
Bindon see Goodliffe.
Bingham see Smith-Bingham.
Bingham-Copestake : Bingham. 10 Dec., 1819 (284).
Bingham-Cox : Cox, W. H. 3 Dec., 1889 (7201).
Binks-Urquahart : Binks, W. U., Sunny-side, Westgate-on-Sea,
    Kent. Times, 5 Sept., 1898.
Binns see Lambert.
Binsteed see Farrant.
Binswanger see Byng.

Birch see Bosvile
,, Caccia Birch.
,, Newell-Birch.
,, Wyrley Birch
— : New, S 15 Jan., 1800 (62)
Birch-Jones . Jones, M. R., of Ebley Court, Stroud, Glos. Times. 18 Feb., 1898
Birch-Reynardson · Birch, T. 25 Nov., 1811 (48).
Birch-Wolf Birch, T. 28 Oct., 1864 (5118)
— · Birch, W. 1 Sept., 1859 (3358)
—: Birch, R. 19 July, 1827 (1562)
Bircham see Halsey Bircham
Birchill : Diprose, B. H. H. 12 June, 1858 (2963)
Bird see Byrde.
,, Golding-Bird.
,, Lewis-Bird
,, Peniston-Bird.
Bird Lindeman : Bird, F. P., of Wentworth Lodge, Anerley, Kent, spinster. Times, d p., 30 Oct., 1890
Bird Mortimer : Bird, J. H. C., of Gravesend, Kent. Times, d.p., 21 Aug., 1877.
Birket see Higgin-Birket.
Birkley-Forrester Birkley, R 12 May, 1849 (1649).
Birnie see Hamilton
Birt Davis : Davis, W. E., of 10, Clement Street, Birmingham. merchant Times, d p., 20 March, 1880.
Birt-Davies : Davies, S. M., of Areley Cottage, Edgbaston, Warwicks. Times, 15 Jan., 1881.
Biscoe : Earle. 20 March, 1830 (783).
— : Tyndale, W. E. 6 July, 1866(3872) (D G 1077)
see Tyndale-Biscoe
Bishop see Bailey
Bishop-Culpeper . Bishop, J. 16 Aug., 1839 (1605)
Bishopp see Paston-Bisshopp-Bedingfield
Bisse-Challoner : Bisse, T. C. 22 Jan., 1829 (130)
Bisset see Fenwick-Bisset
— : Elrington, Janet E., Charles E., Maurice E., Mordaunt E. Lyon Vol. XI. 17 July, 1885.
Bisset-Snell : Snell, W., of Onslow Gardens, Middlesex, dep. surg. gen Times, d p., 31 Oct., 1883
Bisson see de Carteret Bisson.
Bisshopp see Paston-Bisshopp-Bedingfield.
— Streeter, J 26 Sept., 1812 (2018).
Bizouard de la Courtine de Montille : de Montille, J. B. A., of Paris, gent. Times, d p., 23 Mar., 1895.
Black-Hawkins : Hawkins, E. B., of Speen, Berks, gent. Times, d p., 27 March and 16 April, 1879

Blackburne-Maze : Blackburne, W. I. 1 Dec., 1855 (4712).
Blacker *see* Douglass.
Blackett Crofts *see* Crofts.
Blackett-Ord : Blackett, J. A. 7 Dec., 1855 (4675)
Blackler : Burnell, W. B., of Broadhempston, Devon, gent.
 Times, d.p., 6 Aug., 1879.
Blackman *see* Harnage.
Blackwall *see* Evans-Blackwall.
Blackwell · Harwood, W 10th Geo. III. 1770.
Blackwood *see* Price.
Blagrove *see* Bradshaw.
   : Bradshaw, H. 22 Dec., 1840 (3046).
    Coore, H. J 30 Nov., 1842 (3566).
Blair *see* Stopford-Blair
Blake *see* Aldrich-Blake
  : Crockford, E. B., now residing at Rue du Four à Chaux,
   nr. Boulogne-sur-Mer, France Times, 8 Jan., 1870
  see Daly
  · Foster, R. B. D. Castle, March (no date given), 1847
   (D.G. 418 and 427).
  see Harward.
  . Hodge, T. D. P. 24 May, 1866 (3256).
  see Jex-Blake
  ·· Norman, S. W. 20 Oct., 1832 (2419)
  : Van Braam, H. 10 May, 1837 (1222)
Blake-Campbell : Campbell, J. F. 8 Aug., 1891 (4437).
    St. John Frank : Campbell, John Francis, late of
     Kingstown, Dublin, but now at Victoria
     Hotel, Liverpool, L.R C.S. Times, 13 Aug,
     1890.
Blake-Forster : Foster H. W., of The Cedars, Beckington,
 Somerset, esq. Times. d.p., 3 June, 1890
Blake-Humfrey · Blake, R 9 Aug., 1847 (2923)
  see Humfrey-Mason.
Blake-Kent : Blake, Henry, of 169, High Street, Southampton,
 ironmonger Times, d.p., 16 Feb., 1870
Blakelock : Smith, P., of Herringthorpe, near Rotherham, West
  Riding, Yorks, esq., J.P., Chairman of the
  Sheffield Water Works at Sheffield; and
  C. O. Smith, M.A., Clerk in Holy Orders, and Rector
   of Shelfanger, near Diss, Norfolk; and
  Charlotte E. B Smith, Rosamond M. Smith and A.
   Smith, all of Bent's Green Lodge, Sheffield,
   Yorks Times, 21 April, 1882
Blakemore *see* Booker-Blakemore.
Blakeney-Lyon-Stewart : Stewart, Thos. St James', 23 June,
 Dublin Castle, 13 July, 1855 (D.G 1005 and 1033)

Blakiston-Houston : Blakiston, R B , of Orangefield, co Down.
Dublin, 12 Apr., 1843.
Blanchard *see* Athorpe
Bland Crumpe N 21 Oct., 1811 (2054)
Davison, T. 31 July 1786 (337).
Blandy · Walker, J 28 April, 1792 (258)
Blandy-Jenkins Blandy, C. A 14 Oct , 1856 (3508)
Blatch : Smythies, J 14 March, 1772 (11235)
Blathwayt Crane, W. 26 March, 1817 (1002).
Blayds *see* Calverley
Calverley, J 23 Feb , 1807 (260)
Blencowe-Shuckburgh Blencowe, C 30 Sept., 1848 (3585)
(D.G 1063)
Blennerhassett Tincler, C L , late of Kingstown, Dublin, esq.
Times, d p , 25 Oct., 1882
Tincler, E B., of 4. George Place, Guernsey,
Chan Isds , Lieut Times, d p , 30 April.
1885
Tincler, B M , late of Aldershot, Hants, Army
surgeon. Times. d p , 18 Nov . 1879
Bletsoe *see* Morgan-Bletsoe
Bliss Aldridge, H 2 April, 1845 (1081)
see Barreto.
Blomefield Jenyns, L 27 Sept 1871 (4165)
Mason, G 13 Oct , 1836 (2069).
Mayes, G , of Monzie, Perth, now at Edenhall,
Cumberland, gent Times, d.p . 10 July, 1879
Blondeau *see* Hart
Bloodworth *see* Broughton
Blossett Peckwell, R. H 4 May, 1811 (800)
Blossett-Maule Maule F B , of S Kensington, London
Times, d.p , 15 July, 1895.
Blount Coffin, A B , now at Granville Square, Middlesex.
physician and surgeon Times. 19 Dec., 1881.
see Darell
Blowers *see* Vivian
Bluett-Duncan Bluett, J D Times, d p., 11 July, 1896
Blundell Pippard, N B 7 April, 1772 (11237).
see Weld-Blundell
Blundell-Hollinshead Blundell H 9 Sept , 1802 (953)
Blundell-Hollinshead-Blundell Blundell-Hollinshead R B 26
Aug., 1836 (1535)
Blunt *see* Dalby
Blyth *see* Kerslake
Blyth Browne · Browne, Margaret Constance, of Kensington,
London Times, Aug 10, 1898

Blythe *see* Burn-Blythe.
· Gibbons, E C, of 52, Sinclair Road, Kensington, gent Times, 16 Aug. 1892
Boardman *see* Haydock
Bockett-Pugh . Bockett, H. P. of Hyde-End House. Shinfield. Reading, Berks Times, d p., 23 April. 1868
Boddam-Whetham Boddam. M. A 1884 (2234)
. Boddam, A , of Thirklington, Nottingham, Lieut.-Col. of Royal Sherwood Foresters
J. W. Boddam, Lieut. 73rd Foot.
A. R. Boddam, Lieut 60th Rifles
A. T. Boddam, Ensign 23rd R Fusiliers , and
C Boddam, spinster Times, d p., 4 April, 1870.
Boggers *see* Hay Burgess
Boggis Rolfe Boggis, J. E 16 April. 1866 (2568)
Boggs *see* Brenton.
Boghurst-Fisher Boghurst, H. 6 March 1879 (2241)
Bogie *see* Greig Rutherford Elliot
Boheim *see* Von Roemer.
Bohun : Browne, Le G. 28 March, 1787 (153).
Boileau-Pollen Boileau, G P 25 June, 1821 (1493)
Bold-Hoghton : Hoghton, H 26 Feb., 1825 (371).
Bolden : Leonard, J. 8 Feb., 1800 (115)
Bolders *see* Barnard.
Bolesworth *see* Wood
Bolney Brown, E W. V, of Stretty, Glamorgan, 2nd s. of Alexander Rozel, and grandson of late Wm., Rear-Admiral of the Red Times, d p , 1868
Bolster *see* Smith.
Bolton *see* Mann
Bolton-Massy · Bolton, J. M , of Brazil, co Dublin, and Ballywire. co Tipperary. Dublin, 17 Sep , 1842.
Bomford *see* Jessop
Bomford-North : North. I . of Ferrans. co Meath Dublin. 10 Nov., 1837 ·
Bompass *see* Cox.
Bonaparte, Louis Clovis · Richard, L C C , of Palace Chambers. Westminster, London, engineer Times, d.p . 22 Oct . 1891
Bond W. H. B. *see* Hodgson, W.
 see Hopkins
 ., MacGeough-Bond-Shelton.
Bond-Cabbell Cabbell, J , of Cromer, Bognor and Middlesex, esq Times, d p., 18 March. 1875.
Bond Shelton *see* Mac Geough Bond Shelton.
Bone *see* Egerton-Bone.

Bone Hawkesford : Bone, J., of 122, Bridge Rd., Battersea, S W. Times, 22 Dec, 1880
Bones *see* Churchill
   ., Goodwin
   .. Lewis
Bonham-Carter : Carter, J 19 March, 1827 (666)
Bonn *see* Collard
Bonnell *see* Harvey-Bonnell
    Beal, J. 16 Aug, 1774 (11483)
Bonnor *see* Warwick.
Bonnor-Maurice : Bonner, R M. 21 Dec., 1829 (2398).
Bonsell *see* Hughes-Bonsell
Bontein *see* Stanley
Bontein-Stanley : Bontein, Mary A. 6 April, 1835 (750)
Booker *see* Gregor.
Booker-Blakemore Booker, T. W 21 Aug., 1855 (3324)
Boomer *see* Chesmer.
Boone *see* Tatnall-Boone
Booth *see* Gore-Booth.
    Bache, W. C 17 Dec., 1811 (2413).
    Calvert, T. 26 Nov. 1782 (12391).
    Calvert, Thos. W., 17 Sept., 1782 (D G 4190).
    Griffith, W. 7 April, 1792 (220).
    see Haworth-Booth
    Jackson A A N 7 Aug, 1878 (4714).
    see Sclater-Booth.
Booth-Clibborn : Clibborn, A S, of Paris, Officer in Salvation Army Times, d p, 4 Feb, 1887
Booth-Hellberg : Hellberg, E. D., of 15, Lordship Lane, Woodgreen, Middlesex Times, d p. 16 Oct, 1894
Booth-Smith Smith, M L, late of Huxley, Edmonton, Middlesex, spinster. Times, d p, 7 Sept, 1888
Booth-Tucker : Tucker, F. S L, of 101, Queen Victoria Street, Officer in Salvation Army Times d.p., 7 April, 1888
Boothby Heathcote Heathcote, C S and I. G, of Round Coppice, Uxbridge, Middlesex Times, d p., 24 Dec 1894
Bootle-Wilbraham Bootle, E. W. 8 Dec., 1814 (2508)
Borgnis *see* Hammond-Chambers-Borgnis
Borlase *see* Eady-Borlase
Borlase-Warren-Venables-Vernon Venables Vernon, W J. 4 Jan, 1856 (112)
                                Venables Vernon W J 4 Jan,. 1856 (D G. 53).
Borough *see* Roberts-Gawen.
Bosanquet *see* Smith-Bosanquet.
Boscawen *see* Griffith Boscawen.
Bostock *see* Rich.

Bosvile : Birch, T. J. 22 May, 1824 (851)
 " Lee, T. B. 28 July, 1829 (1414).
Bosville Macdonald, D.
           Macdonald, E. D.
         : Macdonald, J.
           Macdonald, J. W.
           Macdonald, L.
           Macdonald, S. H.
           Macdonald, Hon. G. 11 April, 1814 (835).
Bosville-Macdonald : Bosville, Rt. Hon. G. (Baron Macdonald)
    16 Sept., 1824 (1535)
Boswall *see* Houston-Boswall
    " Houstoun-Boswall-Preston
Boswell of Balmuto : Syme, Jno. Thos. Irvine Boswell. Lyon Vol. X., 28 May 1875
Boteler *see* Casberd-Boteler.
Botfield *see* Garnett-Botfield
Bothwick-Gilchrist : Gilchrist, J. 29 March, 1806 (388).
Bottom *see* Radford
Bottom Downs : Bottom, W., of Southwark and Kennington Park, Surrey, builder. Times, d.p., 27 July, 1875
Bottomley *see* Drury
Bottomley-Firth : Bottomley, J. F. 20 Feb., 1873 (782)
Bouch *see* Carey-Bouch
Bouch-Tremayne : Bouch, T. J., of Hurst View, St Leonards-on-Sea, Sussex, and of "Brock Hill," Bracknell, Berks, esq. Times, d.p., 4 March, 1884, and 5 April, 1884.
Boucher : Crabb, J. G. 30 Aug., 1837 (2309)
Boughey : Fletcher, J. F. 21 May, 1805 (683)
Boughton : Brathwaite, G. C. 14 Aug., 1798 (757)
    see Ward-Boughton-Leigh
    "   Rouse-Boughton-Knight
Boulderson : Holmes, C. E., late of Wargrave, Berks, now of Reading, Berks. Times, 12 Sept., 1883
Boulier-Yorke : Boulier, P., of 3 Sylvester Row, Hackney, Middx., gent. d.p., 10 Aug., 1882
Boulton : Crabb, R. 30 Oct., 1773 (11400)
Bourke *see* De Burgh
Bourman *see* Davison.
Bourne *see* Sturges-Bourne
    "   May-Bourne
Bourne-May : May-Bourne, J. W. S. 19 Feb., 1897 (1166)
Bouverie *see* Pleydell-Bouverie-Campbell-Wyndham
Bouverie-Campbell-Wyndham : Bouverie-Campbell, P. A. P. 13 Dec., 1890 (3).
Bouverie-Campbell of Dunoon : Bouverie, Philip Arthur Pleydell. Lyon Vol. VIII., 28 June, 1869

Bowcher Butcher, W. H., of Stroud Green Road, Hornsey, and of 154, Fleet Street, City   Times, 7 March, 1873
Bowden *see* Cornish-Bowden
  „ Fullarton
Bowdler : Bell, C. W. 15 July, 1892 (4248).
Bowdon *see* Butler-Bowdon.
Bowen Elwood, Anthony, of Armefield, co. Mayo 12 R L., 10 Feb., 1813
  · Jones. J. B , formerly of Brecon, but now of 3, Torrington Square, Middlesex Times, d p , 1 Sept 1883
  see Watson
  : Webb, H 3 Nov., 1801 (1339).
Bowen-Colthurst : Bowen, R. W. T. 26 Dec., 1882 (D.G. 1390).
Bower : Dunn, J. B. M. 3 Feb., 1881 (607)
  see Jodrell.
Bower-St Clair : Bower, A. 24 July, 1854 (2325).
Bowes *see* Foord-Bowes.
  Saml. : Bowes, Saml. Dunn, of Elham, Canterbury, farmer. d.p., 14 Jan., 1895.
  : Stoney, A. R. 11 Feb., 1777 (11743).
  see Strathmore
Bowker *see* Jebb.
Bowles *see* Shakespear.
  : Treacher, H. C. B. 20 May, 1852 (1436)
Bowling Trevanion Bowling, H. P., of 26, Essex Street, Strand, and of Hampton Hill, Middlesex, solicitor. Times, 14 Jan , 1891.
Bowlt *see* Sharp.
Bowman : Coates, *als.* Boardman, C 24 July, 1798 (701).
  see Davison.
Bowman-Vaughan : Bowman, C., of The Strand, Middlesex, silversmith. Times, 9 May, 1866
Bown *see* Winston.
Bowyer *see* Atkins
  „ Atkins-Bowyer.
Bowyer-Smijth : Smijth, Sir E 15 June, 1839 (1207)
Boxall *see* Brown.
Boycott *see* Digby
  „ Morse-Boycott
  „ Wight-Boycott.
Boycott-Wight : Wight, C. B., of Rudge Hall, Salop 10 May, 1886 (1028).
Boyd *see* Buchanan-Boyd.
  Keown, Anne B., of Summerhill, co. Down Dublin, 1 June, 1836
  : Porter, W. H. 26 May, 1891 (D.G. 1077).
  see Raworth.

Boyd see Rochfort-Boyd
  „   Wallis
Boyd-Carpenter   Carpenter, Rev. A. B., of 1, Montague Place,
    Middlesex   Times, d.p., 14 Dec., 1888
Boyd-Rochfort   Rochfort-Boyd, R H   Times, 6 Feb., 1888
Boyd-Wallis : Wallis, Albert Wm., of Brentwood, Essex   Times,
    4 Sep., 1899
Boyman   Boyman-Pizzey, R.   25 May, 1819 (1023)
Boys-Tombs : Tombs, E. S. B., of Brixton Hill, Surrey, and of 12,
    Red Cross Street, London, manufacturer   Times, d.p., 10
    July, 1886
Boyse see Hunt-Boyse
Brabazon see Colthurst-Brabazon
            · Higgins, Hugh Brabazon.   15 Sep., 9 Oct., 1852
              (D G. 789 and 797)
            see Moore-Brabazon
            Sharpe, H   23 April, 1841 (1056)
            Sharpe, H. B   9 Aug., 1847 (2293)
Brack see Clayton
Bracken see Hirst-Bracken
Brackenridge   Trimble, G C   D Castle, 12 Mar., 1846 (D G
    321)
Bradbury   Cliffe, C, of Crumpsall House, nr. Manchester,
            Lancs. merchant   Times, 18 Oct., 1875
    see Norton
Braddyll   Gale. W   17 Aug., 1776 (11692)
    see Richmond-Gale-Braddyll
Bradfield see Sanders-Bradfield
Bradford see Atkinson
        „   Campbell Bradford
Bradish see Bradish-Ellames
Bradley see Courtail
    · Dyne, A H   26 Aug., 1800 (961).
Bradley-Dyne   Bradley, F   29 July, 1844 (2632)
Bradney Marsh   Evans, Rev J., of Penn, Staffs, and Penn Grove,
    Hereford   Times, d p., 26 July, 1881
Bradshaw   Blagrove, H   3 Nov., 1856 (3609)
           Blagrove, Hy, heretofore Bradshaw   W, 3 Nov.
              1856 (D G 1363)
    see Blagrove
        Cavendish, A   5 Jan., 1790 (9)
        · Fletcher, B   18 Sept., 1781 (12225)
    see Greaves
        „   Hathornthwaite
Bradshaw-Peirson · Repinder. L   22 Jan., 1774 (11424)
Bradshaw Taylor   Bradshaw, P. B   2 Jan., 1864

Brady *see* Browne.
,, Geale-Brady
Bragg *see* Lucock-Bragg
Bragge *see* Bathurst
Braham   Meadows, W S H.   10 July, 1851 (1808)
Braikenridge : Smith, W B, of Sydenham Kent member of London Stock Exchange   Times, d.p 29 Nov., 1877
Braine-Hartnell   Braine, Rev. G T., of Liskeard, Cornwall, M A., and G M P. of the Asylum, Powick, Worces, M.R C S., L R C P   Times, d p, 11 Sept, 1888
Braithwaite *see* Boughton
          Lucas, G V   6 June, 1846 (2141)
          see Oxley
Bramall Wall · Bramall, E F, of Sproatley Rectory, Sproatley, Yorks, spinster   Times, d p, 27 May, 1887
Bramley *see* Jennings
Bramley-Moore   Moore, J   7 April, 1841 (944)
Bramston *see* Stane
Brand *see* Trevor
Brander *see* Dunbar-Brander
          Spieker, J   20 Feb, 1787 (85)
Brandreth *see* Gandy
          Gibbs, H.   27 Oct, 1804 (3767)
Branfill *see* Russell
Brannagan *see* Ponsonby.
Branton-Day · Branton, T D   17 April, 1827 (942)
Bravo . Turner, C D, of 20, Lancaster Gate, Hyde Park, Middlesex.   Times, 25 Aug, 1868
Brawne-Lindon   Lindon, H V   17 Dec, 1887 (7064)
Braxton Hicks : Hicks, E E, of 24, George Street, Hanover Square, spinster   Times, d p., 7 Oct, 1887
Brayley-Brayley   Brayley, G, of The Cotmeau, Bideford, Devon, gentleman.   Times, 7 March, 1871
Braysher Deighton, C, formerly of Cambridge, now of Shanghai, China   Times, 24 Oct., 1864
Brazier *see* Arundel
Breach *see* Raymond.
Breakell *see* Moss-Breakell-Moss
Brealey, John Howard   Brealey, J, of Costa Rica, and of Eltham, Kent, merchant   Times, d p, 3 Sept, 1873
Bredall *see* Barlow
Bree *see* Stapylton
Breedon   Symonds, J   15 Feb, 1783 (12414)
Brent Coopy, J   33rd Geo II. 1760
       Coopy, H B.   33rd Geo II, 1760
Brenton : Boggs, M, F G., H. S, and E D, all of 36, Argyll Street, Kensington.   Times, d.p., 6 April, 1883.

Brereton : Trelawney, C 12 June, 1800 (646).
    see Westfailing.
Bretherton : Stapleton-Bretherton, F 23 June, 1884 (2795).
    see Stapleton-Bretherton.
Breton see Wolstenholme.
Brettargh Leeming : Leeming, R.. junr., of Greaves House, Lancaster Times, d p., 15 Oct., 1884
Brettell : Hall, G. 24 May, 1796 (508)
Brettell-Vaughan see Shipley Hewett Edwards Brettell-Vaughan.
Brettrell see Edwards-Brettell-Vaughan.
Brewerton see Hirons.
Brewster see French-Brewster
Brice see Bruce
    „ Kingsmill.
    „ Montefiore Brice
Brickdale see Fortescue-Brickdale
Bridgman see Simpson.
Bridgeman : Simpson, G. A. B. B., of Hill Ridgware House, Rugeley, Staffs Times, d p, 9 Nov, 1896.
    : Simpson, F. C. B., Capt. R.N., and E. C. B., of Copgrove, nr. Leeds. Times, d p , 9 Nov., 1896.
Bridger see Mugeridge
Bridgman-Mansfield : Bridgman, C. L , of 88, High Street, Ilfracombe. Times, d p , 8 Sept., 1896
Brietzske see Dean
Bridgen : Attwood, T. B 21 Sept , 1790 (581)
Brigg see Gulston
Briggs see Broun.
Briggs-Bury : Briggs, R. 19 May, 1871 (2695).
Bright : Betton, J. 12 Oct , 1807 (1379).
Bright-Betton : Bright, Rev. E. A , of Lydbury North, Salop, and of Narborough, Norfolk. Times, 8 Apl., 1886.
    : Bright, R. B., of 16. Albert Road, Brighton Times, d p , 11 Jan., 1893.
Bright-Smith : Smith. Rev G. A., of Buscot Lodge, Warwick Road, Maida Hill, Middlesex Times. d p., 3 Oct., 1871.
Brinckman : Broadhead, Sir T. H. L. 8 July, 1842 (1869)
Brind see Taylor.
Brine see Knapton
Bringhurst see Farmar-Bringhurst
Brisbane see Makdougall-Brisbane
Briscoe Ironside : Briscoe, H., of Wanstead, Essex Times, 26 Feb., 1884.
Bristow see Collyer-Bristow
Britten : Johnson, W. 18 June. 1830 (1620)
    : Wilcox, J 2 April, 1811 (603)
Britton see Carlyon-Britton

Broadbent *see* Stidston-Broadbent
Broade (Philip) *see* Stanier
    see Stanier-Broade
    „ Stanier-Philip-Broade
Broadhead *see* Brinckman
Broadhurst : Nichols, T. 10 Aug., 1809 (1258 and 1384).
Broadley *see* Harrison-Broadley.
Brocas : Austin, B. 21 June, 1794 (578)
Brock *see* Clutton-Brock
  „ Hollinshead
Brock-Jones : Brock, B, W, 8 Feb. 1847 (D.G. 278)
Brockbank, Bertie Sadler Brockbank, Herbert Wm, of Thornehome, Withington. Lancs., gent Times, d.p., 3 Apl., 1886
Brockholes *see* Fitzherbert-Brockholes
Brockhurst : Sumner, J. B. 24 Oct., 1800 (1207)
Brocklebank Fisher, T. 11 Dec. 1845 (7171)
Brockman Drake, R. 8th Geo III., 1768
Brodbelt-Stallard-Penoyre Brodbelt, F. R. 24 Mar, 1824 (523).
Brodhurst . Whitley, G. 18 Jan., 1813 (138)
Brodrick Ick. C. C. of Beaulieu House, Jersey, esq, Paymaster R N. Times, d p., 15 June, 1877
    Ick, Rev W R, of The Vicarage, Peasmarsh, Sussex. B D. Times, d.p., 15 June, 1877
    Ick, E G. Mac D, of Birkenhead, Chester, esq., Capt and Adjut 1st Cheshire Rifle Volunteers Times, d.p., 15 June, 1877
Brodrick-Smith-Brodrick Brodrick-Smith, G., of 85, London Road, Liverpool and H. G. Brodrick-Smith, of Christ Church Oxon Times, d p., 11 Aug., 1894.
Brograve Rye, G A. 10 Aug., 1831 (1631)
Broke-Middleton Broke Sir Geo. N, W, 17 July, 1860 (D.G. 853)
Broke-Vere Broke, Sir C. 23 July, 1822 (1276).
Bromet. Albert : Bromet, Abraham, of Goswell Rd., London, and of Leytonstone Essex, merchant Times, d p., 17 June, 1892
Bromfield *see* Worthington
Bromley *see* Davenport-Bromley
  „ Pauncefote.
  „ Potts Bromley
    Smith Sir G. 10 Feb., 1778 (11847)
Bromley-Davenport Davenport-Bromley, Wm. 27 Dec. 1867 (D G. 19)
Bromley-Smith *see* Mackintosh
Bromley-Wilson Bromley, M. 4 Feb., 1897 (985)
Bromwich-Ryder : Bromwich, W, of 48, Plymouth Grove, Manchester, Lancaster. Times, d p., 31 Oct., 1865.

Brooke Cozens, H , late of Walsall, now of Bristol Road,
	Birmingham, gent Times, d p., 20 Mar , 1884
	see De Capell-Brooke
	Grove, Thos , of Castle Grove, Donegal 25 Feb ,
	1808
	see Hamilton Gyll-Brooke
	„ Howard-Brooke
	„ Johnson-Brooke
	„ Langford-Brooke
	„ Luxmoore
	Luxmoore, C 5 April, 1844 (1665).
	Osbaldestone, T 30 May, 1836 (1029)
	Reeve, J. 13 Feb . 1840 (302)
	Robson R S 13 Aug , 1850 (2247)
	see Shaw-Brooke
	Young, T , of Lough Esk, co Donegal, and Dublin.
	16 July, 1830
	Townshend, G B 25 March, 1797 (275)
Brooke-Hunt Hunt, C G , of Ford House, Ulverston, Lancaster,
	esq , e. s. of Charles Brooke, of Upton St
	Leonards, Gloucester, esq ,
	A. E Hunt and
	M H L , spinsters. both of Upton Times, d p ,
	12 July, 1872
	Hunt, R H , Lieut 72nd Highlanders, 2nd s of
	Charles Brooke, of Upton St Leonards,
	Gloucester Times, d.p., 17 May, 1872
Brooke-Jones Brooke, R 26 Jan . 1833 (222).
Brooke-Smith Smith, E , of Port Elizabeth, S Africa, merchant.
	Times, 17 July, 1880
Brookes see Osbaldeston
Brookes-Kemp : Brookes. G 7 Nov 1839 (2191)
Brooks see Burd Brooks
	„ Close-Brooks.
Brooks Hill Brooks, F A , of Weymouth. Dorset, esq Times,
	d p , 11 July, 1876
Brooksbank Reyner, J — Nov , 1827 (2412)
Brooksbank-James James Geo T , of Carlisle Mansions,
	Westminster, M R C S Times, d p , 17
	Dec , 1896
Broomhead see Colton-Fox
Broomhead-Colton-Fox Broomhead, B P 4 Sept , 1890 (4997)
Brough see Watson
Brougham see Lamplugh
Broughton Bloodworth J , of Waterloo, nr Liverpool, formerly
	of Manchester. gent , and M A , his wife
	Times, d p., 1 Sept., 1874

Broughton : Broughton-Strey, P. 25 Nov., 1836 (2429)
  see Delves
  : Smith, F. D. B , Assistant Paymaster H.M S. Hector.
    Times, d.p., 25 June, 1868
    see Walthall.
Broughton-Adderley : Broughton, H. J. 22 Sept., 1886 (5055).
Broughton-Strey : Broughton, P. 29 Oct., 1827 (2219)
Broun : Briggs, W. H., of 13, Bury Street, Westminster, Surgeon
  Lieut.-Col. R. A Times, d.p., 11 Oct., 1894.
Broun-Morison of Finderlie . Brown, Jno. Brown Lyon Reg.
  VII , 20 April, 1866.
          . Brown-Brown-Morison, John Lyon
               Reg XI., 17 July, 1885
Brown *see* Amyatt.
  ,, Angell.
  ,, Barclay-Brown
  ,, Benson-Brown
  ,, Beresford.
  ,, Bolney.
  : Boxall, J. B. 1 Sept . 1835 (1662).
  see Browne.
  ,, Candler-Brown
  ,, Cavis-Brown
  ,, Cheviot
  ,, Cooper-Brown.
  ,, Cornish-Brown.
  ,, Corsbie.
  ,, Crompton-Brown
  ,, Crosbie.
  ,, Darell-Brown
  : de Moulin, N. S 13 Oct , 1885 (4786).
  see Deans-Brown.
  ,, Dixon.
  ,, Dixon-Brown
  ,, Drewett
  ,, Edon-Brown
    Fearon, J. 24 Feb 1821 (530).
  see Ficklin
  ,, Forster-Brown
  ,, Forsyth-Brown.
  ,, Gage-Brown
  ,, Gilpin-Brown.
  ,, Goodwin-Brown.
  ,, Grant-Browne-Sheridan
  ,, Graver-Brown.
  : Greenwood, W J, of Hacconby, Lincoln, farmer.
    Times, d p , 20 April, 1876.

Brown *see* Grieve.
    . Hamilton, C H. 29 March, 1865 (2044)
    see Hamilton
    „ Helsham-Brown.
    : Hull, R. P. 15 May, 1848 (1895).
    see Hunt
    „ Langridge Brown.
    „ Laurie
    „ Laurie-Brown
    „ Losh
    „ McKerrell-Brown.
    „ Maxwell
    : Maxwell, E. 14 Oct., 1786 (486).
    : Mayor, P 21 Sept., 1841 (2349)
    see Ogden.
    „ Ogilvie.
    „ Oswald-Brown.
    : Piercy, J., formerly of Horncliff, now of Sydney, Australia, farmer's assistant. Times, 14 Apl., 1875.
    · Pigg, G. A, of 16, Percy Park Road, Tynemouth, gent. Times, 27 Sept., 1887.
    Pigg. H N. D, of Tynemouth, Northumberland, banker's clerk. Times, 1 June, 1892
    see Radford.
    : Robinson, W. 2 May, 1810 (641).
    see Selby.
    „ Southam
    „ Sparrow.
    „ Stallard-Penoyre
    „ Tabberer-Brown
    „ Trotter
    „ Verling-Brown.
Brown-Constable : Brown, C. 27 Jan., 1853 (229).
Brown-Fairlie Brown, J. D., M.R.C.S., of 53. St. Oswald Road, S. Kensington. Times, 14 Mar., 1893.
Brown Greaves : Brown. R. E 21 April. 1877 (2882)
Brown-Laurie : Brown. J. L., gent. Times. d.p., 4 April 1874
Brown-Westhead : Westhead, J. P. 31 Jan., 1850 (397)
Browne *see* Beale-Browne.
    „ Baily-Browne.
    „ Blythe-Browne.
    „ Bohun.
    : Brady, W. St. James's, 3 Jan., 15 Jan, 1866 (D.G. 70 and 99).
    . Brady, T B 5 April, 1877 (D.G. 249).
    Chas Milner : Brown, Wm. Chas., of Sydenham, Kent, M.B. Times. 31 May, 1889.

Browne : Collins, G F 24 Sept , 1799 (995)
   see Davies-Browne
      „ de Beauvoir.
      · Eaton, R 13 Aug , 1798 (792)
      : Eaton, R 29 Jan., 1845 (601)
   see Guthrie of Mount
      „ Heitland-Browne
      : Jones, P. 5 Sept , 1823 (1590)
   see Knox-Browne
      „ Lecky-Browne.
      „ Murray-Browne
      „ Orde-Browne.
      „ Paige-Browne
      „ Staples-Browne.
      „ William-Browne
      . Wylde, R. B 28th Geo III., 1788
Browne-Clarke : Murray, Sir R. L 1 April, 1802 (335)
Browne-Clayton : Browne, R 30 Sept , 1829 (1968 and 1989)
            Browne, W C 14 March, 1889 (D G 281)
Browne-Davies : Davies, T A , of Neuadd Llanbedr, Brecon
      Times 11 June, 1898.
Browne-Greive Brown J T 14 Oct., 1872 (4938)
Browne-Lecky . Browne R S. 4 Mar., 9 Mar , 1871 (D.G 194)
Browne-Mill Browne, G. G 6 April, 1803 (434)
Browne-Mason : Mason, J. T., of 6, Southernhay, Exeter, L C D S
      Times, d.p., 26 May, 1880
Browning *see* Button Browning.
         „ Dansey Browning.
Brownjohn *see* Glynton
Brownlow (Earl) *see* Egerton Cust.
Brownsmith · Hipper, R 7 Oct , 1816 (2205).
Bruce, Edgar Baker, Edwd. Geo Times, d p , 6 June, 1890
   see Basset
      · Brice, E., of Kilroot, co Antrim Dublin, 11 May, 1831
      . Brice, F. W, late Capt., now an officer Bechuanaland
         Border Police, S. Africa Times, d p , 31 Oct , 1887
      : Brice, A. A. 1 Oct , 1825 (1795).
      . Brice. E A, Lieut 19th Foot, and H M Lieut. 54th
         Foot Times, d p , 20 Aug., 1875.
   see Cumming-Bruce
      „ Hamilton-Tyndall-Bruce.
      „ Hovell-Thurlow-Cumming-Bruce
      : Knight, J B. 25 Nov , 1805 (1468)
   see Knight-Bruce.
      „ Pryce.
      „ Tyndall-Bruce.
      „ Wright Bruce.

Bruce Rae : Rae, G., of 26, Queen's Road, Liverpool, bank clerk.
    Times, d p., 16 June, 1875
Bruce-Simson   Simson, H , of Eastern House, Anglesey,
            S'hampton, spinster   Times, d p , 24 May, 1880
            Simson, C. A., of Eastern House, Anglesey,
            S'hampton, spinster   Times, d p , 24 May, 1880
          : Simson, E., of Eastern House, Anglesey,
            S hampton, spinster. Times, d p , 24 May, 1880
Bruges see Ludlow-Bruges.
Brunel-Norman : Harris, R. B., of Westerham, Kent, solicitor.
    Times, 20 Sept , 1888
Brunning Maddison : Chappell, F , of Harley Street, London, and
    Brasenose Coll., Oxon   Times, d.p., 5 Feb , 1873.
Brunton see Dunbar-Brunton.
Brunyce see Hill.
Bruxner-Randall : Randall, R. G , of Thurlaston Holt, Leicester-
    shire. now of 25, Silver St , Bury, Lancs., Major   Times,
    d.p , 4 May, 1893.
Bryan : Bellew, G. L   28 Oct , 1880 (D.G 922 and 934)
      : George. A. E.   18 June, 1844 (2132).
Brydges see Jones-Brydges.
        Munn. J   21 March, 1812 (519).
Brydges-Barrett . Brydges, T. B   6 May, 1811 (831).
Bubb see Dangerfield.
Buchan see Fordyce-Buchan.
Buchanan see Fergusson-Buchanan
        ,, Macallum
      : Riddell, Sir J   30th Geo. III., 1790
Buchanan-Boyd · Barrett, E. N B , of Accra, Gold Coast Colony.
    Times, d p., 10 Feb., 1893.
Buchanan-Dunlop   Dunlop, C. G., now at 56, Oxford Terrace,
    Hyde Park. Middlesex, merchant   Times, d.p , 17 Dec ,
    1889.
Buchanan-Hamilton . Hamilton, C. W , esq , surgeon R N , and
    Helen M , of Trent Valley House, Lichfield, wife of above.
    Times, d.p , 9 May. 1890
Buck see Cromey Buck.
    ,, Dauntesey
    ,, Stucley.
Buckhurst see Sackville-West.
Buckle see Barlee.
Buckley see Bateman.
      ,, Ellis
Buckley-Bateman see McLean Buckley.
Buckley-Mathew · Mathew, G. B   9 May, 1865 (2476)
Bucknall see Dyot
        Estcourt, T G   1 May, 1823 (730).

Bucknall : Grimston, W. 21 Jan , 1797 (49).
: Grimston, Hon H 9 July, 1814 (1390)
Bucknall-Estcourt *see* Sotheron-Estcourt.
  „ Sotheron.
Bucknell : Cosway, R., of Witheridge, Devon, yeoman Times, 25 May, 1872
Buckworth-Herne-Soame : Buckworth-Herne, Sir E 13 Dec., 1806 (1613).
Buckworth *see* Shakerley
Budd-Budd : Baker, F. J , of Restlands, nr. E. Grinstead, Sussex steward Times, d p , 28 April, 1890
Baker, L. A. (lately L A Cathala) of Auteuil, Paris, wife of E, P A Cathala. Times, 13 Mar., 1891
Baker, M. C , of Restlands, nr. E Grinstead, Sussex, spinster. Times, d p., 27 Feb , 1891.
: Baker, M E , of Restlands, nr. E Grinstead, Sussex, spinster. Times, d p., 27 Feb , 1891
: Baker, F. W., of The Mansion, Twickenham, Middlesex, marine insur clerk Times. d.p , 18 May, 1891
: Baker, Edith A., of Restlands, E Grinstead, Sussex, spinster. Times, d p., Oct , 1894.
Budworth *see* Palmer.
Bug *see* Norfolk-Howard
Bugg *see* Burg.
  „ Coaks
  „ Compton.
  „ Durrant
  „ Wilson
Buggin *see* Underwood
Buggs *see* Barton
Buist Buist-Sparks, F B , Major, Army Service Corps, D A Q M G , of Ladbroke House, Redhill, Surrey, formerly of New Scone, Perth d p., — Mar.. 1897.
see Gray-Murray
Buist-Sparks : Buist, F , 2nd Lieut 48th Foot Reg , residing at Tybryn Renoldstone, Glamorgan Times, d p , 13 Sep . 1880.
Bulcock *see* Belcombe
  „ Colthurst
Bulkeley *see* Williams-Bulkeley.
  „ Warren Bulkeley.
Bulkeley Johnson Johnson, F 4 Dec , 1884 (5720)
: Johnson, J 5 July, 1836 (1226).
Johnson, H. H., of Beulah Villa, Upper Norwood Times, 1 Oct , 1873

Bull *see* Cooke.
　　„ Hemment.
　　„ Kirk.
Bull-Shaw : Bull, E., spinster. Times, 27 Mar., 1896
Bullen *see* Symes-Bullen.
　　„ Tatchell.
　　„ Tatchell-Bullen
Buller *see* Dunbar-Buller.
　　„ Drummond-Buller-Elphinstone
　　: Hughes, H. W. 5 Oct., 1883 (6312).
　　see Manningham-Buller.
　　„ Wentworth Buller.
Buller-Hippesley-Cox : Buller, J. F. 23 April, 1796 (402).
Buller-Yarde-Buller (Lord Churston) . Yarde-Buller, J. 6 March, 1860 (943).
Bullin *see* Leyland.
Bullock *see* Hall.
　　: Thompson, B. 5 March, 1845 (744).
　　: Thompson, R. 27 Nov., 1821 (3).
　　: Thompson, T. 7 Oct., 1797 (955).
　　see Troyte.
　　„ Troyte-Chafyn-Grove
　　: Watson, J. J. C. 10 Feb., 1810 (219).
Bullock-Barker : Barker, W. G. B., of Walsingham House, Piccadilly, Middlesex. and of Shipdham, Norfolk. Times, d.p., 14 Mar., 1894.
Bullock-Featherstonhaugh : Bullock, F. 8 Sept., 1874 (4533).
Bullock-Webster · Bullock, E. W. 12 Nov., 1808 (1519)
Bulmer *see* Morgan-Bulmer
Bulwer-Lytton · Bulwer, B. 14 May, 1811 (874).
　　Bulwer, Sir G. E. E. L. 20 Feb., 1844 (580).
Bunbury : Bunbury-Isaac, C. T. and V. T. 15 Sept., 1858 (4249).
　　see Richardson-Bunbury.
　　„ Tighe-Bunbury.
Bunbury Thompson : Thompson, Lieut.-Gen. A., and Charlotte, his wife, of Northfield, Maidenhead, Berks. Times, d.p., 19 June, 1891.
Bunce *see* Thurgood.
Buncombe *see* Thomson-Buncome-Poulett.
Buncombe-Poulett-Scrope · Buncombe-Poulett-Thompson, G. J. 22 March, 1821 (870).
Bund *see* Willis-Bund
Bunning : Gaudet, G. H., esq., lately officer 4th Hussars. Times, d.p., 18 May, 1888
Bunney *see* Hartopp

Bundock-Mackinnon Bundock, W J., adopted by his uncle. Mr
    L Mackinnon, of Elfordleigh, Devon. 1 Jan., 1879.
Bunny see St. John
Bunton : Topp, A, of Springfield, Bognor, Sussex, gent Times,
    d p., 2 Sept., 1893.
        Topp, Margaret C, of Springfield, Bognor, Sussex, wife
            of A Bunton. Times, d p., 2 Sept, 1893
Burbidge-Hambly Burbidge, C H 21 Dec., 1853 (3785).
Burchardt-Ashton : Burchardt, A G 23 Aug, 1890 (4831).
          . Burchardt, F 23 Aug., 1890 (4831)
Burchell-Herne Burchell, H H 17 July, 1854 (2231).
Burd-Brooks Burd, S 14 Feb., 189 (1026)
        . Burd, S, of Beckenham, Kent, banker. Times
            d p., 4 Jan. 1889
Burdett see Jones
    ,, Ness, W. E., of Ringstead Lodge, nr King's Lynn
        Norfolk, Capt (Reserves) Times. d.p., 4 Oct..
        1884
    Ness, R. 24 March, 1788 (141).
    · Pritchard, T F 31 July, 1781 (12210)
Burdett-Coutts-Bartlett-Coutts see Bartlett-Burdett-Coutts
Burdett-Coutts Burdett A G 19 Sept. 1837 (2447)
Burdett-Coutts-Bartlett . Bartlett, W L A 11 Feb., 1881 (656).
Burdett-Coutts-Bartlett-Coutts Burdett-Coutts-Bartlett, W L A,
    of 80, Piccadilly, Middlesex, esq Times, 29 July, 1881
Burdon D'Audebert, A E 29 March, 1871 (1742)
    see Sanderson
Burford-Hancock Hancock, H. J. B 23 April. 1881 (2554).
Burg Bugg. J. H., of Spalding, Lincoln, common brewer
    Times, d p., 2 Feb., 1877
Burge see Burgess
Burges see Lamb
    Smith, J 17 April, 1790 (225).
Burgess : Burge, W., late of Dulverton, Somerset, now of Bury
        Lodge, Malvern Wells, Worcester, patentee of
        alarm guns d p, 10 Oct., 1882.
    see Hay Burgess
    ,, Hitchcock Burgess
    ,, Sheepshanks-Burgess
Burgess-Henville Burgess, Ellen, of Brockley, Kent Times, 20
    Nov, 1889.
Burgh Coppinger, F 10 April, 1779 (11968)
    see De Burgh
Burghardt-Hardcastle Burghardt, C J D and C A L, of
    Munich, and F. E, Officer in Indian Army Times, d p,
    2 Jan., 1888
Burgin : Roby, W 17 May, 1803 (569)

Burgin *see* Roby-Burgin
Burgoyne : Murphy, M., of 4, Argyle Terrace, Southsea, Hants, clerk. Times, d.p., 5 May, 1888
Burke *see* Haviland-Burke
Burke-Smythe : Burke, O. 5 Oct., 1793 (876)
Burland *see* Harris-Burland
Burn : Teasdale, J. 11 March, 1802 (270)
Burn-Blythe : Burn, R. 12 Jan., 1874 (135)
Burnaby *see* Dyott
Burnaby-Atkins : Burnaby, T. F. 3 Jan., 1873 (43)
Burnam-Pateshall : Pateshall, E. 1 March, 1820 (493)
Barnard *see* Chichester.
Burnell *see* Blacker.
    „ Jones
    „ Pegge-Burnell.
    „ Smith, A. B., of 14, Denbigh Place, Middlesex, architect. Times, d.p., 30 Jan., 1882.
Burnell-Jeffery : Jeffery, J., of Maiden Lane, St. Pancras, coal merchant. Times, d p., 17 Oct., 1894
Burnes-Floyer : Jones, T. O. 19 Dec., 1818 (2277).
Burnett *see* Ramsay
    „ Ramsay, of Balmain.
    „ Turner-Burnett.
Burney *see* Amyatt-Burney
Burnley-Campbell, of Ormidale : Burnley, Lt.-Col Hardin (also Mrs. Margaret Jane Campbell Burnley-Campbell, his wife). Lyon XIII., 15 July, 1895.
Burns-Hartopp : Burnes, J. 6 July, 1894 (4213).
Burns-Lindow : Lindow, J. S. 21 March, 1871 (1542)
Burnsall : Ellard, J. 2 Nov., 1793 (974)
Burr *see* Higford
Burra *see* Pomfret.
Burrall *see* Porter-Burrall.
Burrard *see* Neale
Burrell : Hadgley, G. B. 27 Sep., 1805 (1245)
Burroughs : Salusbury, L. 11 July, 1804 (853)
Burroughs-Paulet : Paulet, Most Hon C. I. (Marquess of Winchester) 16 Aug., 1839 (1605)
Burrows *see* Robson-Burrows
Burrowes : Kilborn, W. 17th Geo III., 1777
    : Taylor, W., of 14, University Street, Tottenham Court Road. Times, 25 Dec., 1868.
Burt. J. Thornton : Burt, J. Thomas of Shepherd's Bush, Midx., gent. Times, d p., 7 Aug., 1873
  see Champneys
Burt-Marshall, of Luncarty : Burt, James Lyon Vol. IX., 27 Mar., 1872

Burton see Archer-Burton.
: Betts, A , of Hill Farm, Norfolk, farmer   Times, d.p.,
    10 March, 1888
  see Christie-Burton
   ,, Conyngham
   ,, North
   ,, Phillipson
  . Kingsford, Mrs C. S , wife of Rev A G Kingsford (née
    Cleaveland), formerly Mrs. R L Burton   27
    April, 1898 (2890)
    Kingsford, A. G., and Catherine Sophia, his wife, of
    Longner Hall, Salop. Times, 13 April, 1898
  . Robinson, D   19 Aug , 1828 (1575)
  : Rayner, W B   24 Feb., 1815 (454)
Burton-Fanning : Burton, F. W., of Weybridge, Surrey, and late
  of Addenbrooke's Hospital, Cambs., M.B   Times, d p ,
  2 May, 1891
Burton-Mackenzie, of Kilcoy : Burton, Lt.-Col. John Edward
  Lyon, Vol XI., 7 Dec , 1887
Burton-Peters · Peters, H.   23 Sept., 1822 (1643).
Burton-Phillipson see Turner.
           : Wright, C   8 Sept. 1792 (682)
Bury   Atcheler, S. J., of New Barnet, Herts, architect and
           surveyor   Times, d p , 14 Nov , 1881
  see Briggs-Bury
  · Collins, W H , formerly of Linwood, Blankney, Lincoln,
    gentleman, afterwards of Leeds. York, and of
    Richmond, York, maltster and brewer, now of
    Cheltenham, Gloucester   Times, d p , 9 May,
    1865
  : Collins, B B   20 Dec., 1799 (1305).
  see Howard-Bury.
   ,, Incledon
  · Tuckey, Chas , Captain. Times. 22 April, 1896
Bury-Barry : Bury, J. R B   25 Jan , 1889 (D G 65)
Busby see Aldridge-Busby
Buscomb see Hill
Busfield see Ferrand
Bush see Bushe
Bushby see Bacon
       ,, Dusgate
Bushe : Bush, E.   12 Aug., 1891 (4437)
Bussell see Pettiward
Buszard   Williams, Mabel C , of 29, Porchester Terrace, spinster
    Times, d.p , 25 Dec., 1895
Butcher see Bowcher
       ,, Pemberton

Butcher *see* Rodbard
Butcher-Lea : Butcher, G. 17 March, 1834 (540).
Butler *see* Arcedeckne-Butler.
    „ Clifford-Butler.
    Dight, J B. 9 June, 1792 (384).
    see Danvers.
    . Fowler, R. 11 Feb , 1824 (315)
    Hopson, G. B. 29 July, 1851 (1945)
    : Kilkelly, J. P. 3 June, 1878 (D.G. 549)
Butler-Bowdon : Bowdon, J 11 Jan., 1841 (112).
Butler-Clarke : Butler, C. H. 31 Oct., 1820 (2150)
Butler-Clarke-Southwell-Wandesford : Butler-Clarke, C. H. (commonly called Hon). 1 June, 1830 (1160).
Butler-Cole . Butler, T. 18 Nov., 1816 (2299)
Butler-Creagh : Butler, W. B. 12 Aug., 1889 (D.G. 873).
Butler Davies *see* Davies
Butler-Kearney : Butler, C. J. 28 April, 1876 (D.G. 253)
Butler-Shawe : Shawe, W. B., of 47, Oxford Terrace, Hyde Park, Middlesex, Col. Bengal Army Times, d.p., 18 Nov., 1881.
Butler-Smythe : Smyth, A. C. B, of 1, Hillside, Crouch Hill, Middlesex, surgeon. d.p., 27 July, 1881 (Times, 24 Aug , 1881)
Butler-Stoney : Stoney, W. C , of Portland Park, Tipperary, Ireland, etc. Times, d p., 6 May, 1893.
Butt *see* Everett.
    „ Hayward-Butt.
Butter *see* Faskally.
    „ Lance
    „ Warre.
Butterfield *see* Bancroft.
Butterworth-De Botwor : Butterworth, C H., late of Trinity College. Oxford, now of Lincoln's Inn, Middlesex, esquire Times, 15 Dec , 1871
Button *see* Freman.
    ., Newton.
Button Browning : Button, J. G , of 316, Regent Street, London, gent. Times, 13 Dec., 1879
Buttrey *see* Lister.
Buxton : Jacob, Sir R. J B. 8 July, 1825 (1268).
Buxton-Jacob : Buxton, Sir R. J. 25 March. 1825 (770)
Byfield-Higden : Byfield, G. 6 Sept., 1816 (1725)
Bykur : Baker, W , of Bournemouth, Hants, gent. Times, d.p , 27 April, 1880
Byng : Binswanger, M. and G. Times, d.p., 13 June, 1896
    see Cranmer-Byng.
Byrde : Bird. H. C., of Goytrey House, Monmouth, esq. d.p . 28 Nov., 1863

Byres Crane, P M., of Mersey Bank, Didsbury, Lancs., and of Tonley, Aberdeens., merchant. Times, d.p , 22 Mar , 1890.
Byres-Leake : Leake, J., of Weyside Lodge, Weybridge, Surrey, esq Times, d.p , 3 Jan., 1890.
Byrne, A Leicester : Byrne, A. Xavier, of Pietermaritzburg, Natal. Times, d.p., 22 Nov., 1895.
Byrom *see* Jones Byrom.
  . Fox, E. 29 Jan., 1871 (169).
Byron : Lazarus or Deraay, P., of 44, New North Road, Midx., theatrical costumier. Times, 7 Nov , 1873.
  see Noel

C

Cabbell *see* Bond-Cabbell.
Cabrier *see* Leekey
  „ Leekey-Cabrier
Caccia Birch : Caccia, W. C. B., of Ewehwon, Hawkes Bay, N Zealand, and of Junr Con. Club, Piccadilly, London, sheep farmer. Times. d p., 9 Nov., 1893
Cadby *see* Faulkner.
Cadogan *see* Greene-Cadogan
  „ Hodgson-Cadogan
Caerdoel : Kerdoel, E. C. B de M., of 6, Denmark Terrace, Hammersmith, to resume ancient orthography of surname.
Caffin *see* Crawford-Caffin.
Cain Kavanagh Cain, P., of Paris, prof. of languages Times, 16 July, 1874
Caird *see* Henryson-Caird
Cairncross : Newbigging, R 10 June, 1822 (978)
Cairns Ceains, S W., of Oxton, Chester, and of London, esq. Times, d.p., 17 March, 1881
Calcas *see* André.
Calcott *see* Evans.
  „ Berkeley-Calcott
Calcraft : Lucas, G 19 Aug , 1786 (376).
  : Lucas, J. 12 May, 1792 (293)
Caldbeck *see* Roper-Caldbeck
Caldecot : Reid, T 19 Dec , 1797 (1202)
Caldwell *see* Marsh-Caldwell.
  W. Smith : Smith, W. Caldwell, M.D., late Surg.-Maj. 27th Punjaub Infy. Times, d.p., 1 Dec., 1875

Caley : Davis, J W. 24 May, 1806 (663).
Calisher *see* Campbell
Calland *see* Forbes-Bentley
Callander : Smith, J 5 Dec., 1798 (1166).
Calliphronas *see* Locke
Calmady Everitt, C H. 9 Feb., 1788 (61).
Calthorpe *see* Gough
       Gough, Sir H 10 March, 1788 (218)
Calthorpe-Mallaby : Calthorpe-Deeley, Wm 1894
       see Mallaby
Calthrop *see* Collingwood
       ., Hollway-Calthrop
Calverly-Rudston · Rudston-Read 11 Nov., 1886 (5983).
Calverley Blayds, J 12 April, 1852 (1058)
    see Blayds
Calvert *see* Anstey-Calvert
    ,, Booth
    : Greenwood, H. C., of Park Lodge, Halifax, Yorks. bookkeeper. Times, d p, 22 Sept., 1880
    : Jackson, T 30 April, 1817 (1156).
    see Verney
Cambridge *see* Pickard-Cambridge
Cameron *see* Macmartin-Cameron
    ,, Sorel-Cameron.
Cameron-Hampden : Cameron, Geo. H. Whll., 30 July, 1866 (4349) (D G 1198)
Camm *see* Thornhill
Cammeyer *see* Doorman
Campbell *see* Blake-Campbell
     ,, Bouverie-Campbell
     ,, Bouverie-Campbell-Wyndham.
     ,, Burnley-Campbell
     Calisher, L. L. Times, d p, 26 May, 1873
    see Carter-Campbell
     ., Cockburn-Campbell.
     ,, Deans-Campbell.
     ,, Douglas-Campbell-Douglas
     Hamilton, C E 17 March, 1819 (587)
    see Hartley
     ,, Hunter Campbell
     Jekyll, S C. 25 June, 1838 (1445).
    see Lamont-Campbell
     , McIver-Campbell
     ,, Mackinnon-Campbell
     ,, Montgomery-Campbell.
     ., Pearce-Campbell
     ,, Pleydell-Bouverie-Campbell-Wyndham

Campbell *see* Purves-Hume-Campbell
    Powell, H. 4 Sept, 1800 (25)
    Smith, A., of Lisbon, Portugal, retired Major Times, d p., 7 Dec., 1877
    : Smith, A C., of Lisbon, Portugal, retired Major. Times, d.p , 14 Jan , 1878
    Watt, Rev. J A , late V of St. Luke's Church, South Lyncombe, nr Bath, Somerset, now residing at Folkestone, Kent, o s of late A , of Castlenau Villas, nr Barnes, Surrey. Times, d.p, 5 Oct , 1871
Campbell-Bannerman, of Hunton Court Campbell, Henry, M P Lyon Vol IX , 25 Oct , 1872
Campbell Bradford Bradford, A , of Millwall, Poplar, bank clerk Times, 18 May, 1875.
Campbell-Graham : Campbell, T. 23 Aug., 1815 (1945).
Campbell-Johnston Johnston, A R., of Heatherley, nr. Wokingham, Berks. Times. d p., 8 April, 1870
Campbell-Johnstone Johnstone, J , of 6, Arundel Terrace, Brighton, Sussex, esq. d p , 22 June, 1886
    : Johnstone, J C., of 6, Arundel Terrace, Brighton, Sussex, esq. Times, d.p, 25 June, 1886
Campbell-Miller-Morison, of Hetlnad Mrs Jean Buchanan with consent of her husband, Hugh Miller. Lyon Vol XI , 19 April, 1883
Campbell-M'Laren . Rohrweger, Mary F., of 3a, Poet's Corner, Westminster. Times, d.p , 6 Feb , 1895
Campbell-Orde Orde, Sir J W P 16 Jan , 1880 (287)
    of Morpeth, North Uist, and Kilmory · Orde, Sir John William Powlett, Bart Lyon, Vol. X 23 March, 1881
Campbell-Reed R. Roed, R Camillo of Middleton Street, Sculcoates, Kingston-upon-Hull, master mariner Times, d p , 10 Nov , 1890
Campbell-Wyndham . Campbell, J and C F 3 April, 1844 (1197).
Campion *see* Coates
    „ Coventry-Campion
Camplin *see* Bernard.
Camsell : Onion, J S., of Fort Simpson, Canada, trader Times, d p., 17 May, 1877
Canale *see* Thorold
Candler Helsham, W., of Kilkenny Dublin, 11 Sept , 1838.
    see Sempill.
Candler-Brown Candler, E. 10 May, 1803 (543)

Candler-Brown   Candler, W   6 July, 1857 (2551).
Cann see Skoulding Cann.
Canning see De Burgh-Canning, H.
   „   Gordon-Canning.
Canning-Doherty   Doherty, J., registrar for district of Warwickshire, at Birmingham   Times, d p., 24 Oct., 1887.
Cannon · Forgan, D., of Les Vaux Saliris, France gent.   Times, d.p., 28 Oct., 1884.
Cantrell see Whitaker-Cantrell.
Cantrell-Hubbersty   Hubbersty, A. C   3 Feb., 1894 (913).
Capel see Capell
Capel-Carnegy-Arbuthnott   Capel, A R, of 9, Bramham Gardens, S. Kensington, etc., gent   Times, d.p., 3 Jan., 1894
Capell : Capel, A A (Earl of Essex)   15 July, 1880 (4089)
Capes   Crawley, C, of The Cottage, Lebanon Gardens, Wandsworth   Times 13 Nov., 1888.
Capron see Hollist
Caradock   Cradock J F (Baron Howden)   2 Jan., 1832 (51)
Caravoglia see Carden
Carden   Caravoglia, J, of Regent's Square, London, formerly of Colville Square, Bayswater, London   Times, d.p., 23 May, 1890
Careleton : Mitchell, J.   10 Dec., 1793 (1099).
Carew see Hallowell-Carew
   Pole, R.   12th Geo. III, 1772.
   Smith, S, of Pembridge Villas, Bayswater phys and surg   Times, d p., 6 April, 1888.
   Warrington, G H   23 Sept 1811 (1914).
Carew-Gibson   Gibson, G   12 July, 1852 (1948).
Carey see Tupper-Carey
   , Wood
Carey Bouch   Bouch Frederick, of Stock Exchange, London. Times, 28 Oct., 1899.
Carill-Worsley see Tindall Carill Worsley.
Carleton   Groome, R C   18 May 1813 (1072).
   see Leir-Carleton
   Mycock, Ann, of Crewe, Chester   Times, 18 Jan., 1899.
   : Stainsby Conant Paynton Pigott, of Heckfield Heath, Hants, esq., consent of Baron Dorchester   d p., 13 June, 1864.
Carley Geo. Leyburn : Carley, G J, formerly of Reading, Berks, now of Brighton, Sussex, gent   Times, d.p., 7 Nov., 1879
Carlile-Kent   Kent, S S H, spinster, temp, residing in Florence, Italy.   Times, 21 Feb., 1880.
Carlton   Metcalfe, J   25 June, 1791 (368)

Carlyle Bell : Bell. T , of Queen's Road, Kingston Hill, Surrey,
    Major-Gen. Times, d.p , 11 April, 1892
Carlyon : Simmons   23 May, 1882 (2739)
    see Spry.
Carlyon-Britton . Britton, P. W. P.   29 April, 1897.
Carmichael   Carmichael-Smyth, Sir J R.   5 Feb , 1841 (567)
        Carmichael-Smyth, C M.   22 Aug , 1842 (2278).
      · Carmichael-Smythe, D. E P., of 6, Royal Crescent.
        Notting Hill, Middlesex, Officer R N   Times, 9
        March, 1882.
    see Gibson-Carmichael
    : M'Ostrick, Jno. C.   (St James's 1 May), 22 May,
        1868, (D.G. 573 and 581)
    : Smyth, J. D. C   16 June, 1853 (1740).
    : Smyth, L. M.   16 June, 1853 (1740)
Carmichael-Ferrall : Carmichael, Catherine C (widow).   9 July,
    21 July, 1852 (D.G. 617 and 625).
Carnegy see de Balinhard
Carnegy-Arbuthnott see Capel-Carnegy-Arbuthnott
Carpenter see Boyd-Carpenter.
    ,, Cheese-Carpenter
    : Talbot, W C   1 June, 1868 (3430).
    : Talbot, Honble W. Cecil   Whll , 1 June, 1868
        (D G 693).
Carpenter-Garnier : Carpenter, John   W., 1 July, 1864 (D G.
    747)
Carnac Rivett, J   14 May, 1801 (533)
Carne see Nicholl-Carne
    Nickoll, R   16 Dec., 1842 (3725)
    see Stradling-Carne.
Carrara see De Carrara-Rivers.
Carr . Hay, Hon. W.   28 March, 1795 (273)
    : Holwell, W   20 Nov . 1798 (1101)
    see Chace-Carr
    ,, Standish
Carr-Ellison : Carr, R   2 Feb., 1871 (486)
Carr-Forster : Foster, W R C . formerly of Worthing and
    Brighton, now at 22, Sillwood Road. Brighton, gent
    Times, d.p , 11 March, 1876.
Carr-Gomm : Carr, F. C. and E B.   9 March, 1878 (2010)
Carr-Lloyd : Carr, G K.   22 March. 1855 (1220).
Carr-Maudsley Maudsley, H of University College Hospital,
    Gower Street, Middlesex, M.D. (London), M R C.P.
    (London), and M R.C.S. (England). Times. d p . 20 May,
    1887, and 24, May, 1887
Carre see Riddell-Carre.
Carre-Riddell : Riddell, R.   21 June, 1826 (1649)

Carrington-Smith : Smith, W. Times, d.p., 31 March, 1896
Carroll *see* Farrell
 ,, Leahy
Carroll-Irwin · Carroll, E. C. 17 June, 1892 (D G. 705).
Carruthers *see* Mitchell-Carruthers
Carruthers-Wade Wade, John Peter. H E.I.C S   Lyon, Vol.
    V, 18 May, 1854.
Carson *see* Porter.
Carter *see* Bonham-Carter
  ,, Baird-Carter
   · Churchill, B 29 Aug., 1789 (569).
   see Coldrick-Carter.
   : Coldrick, A., of Hillfield Parade, nr. the City but in the
          County of Gloucester, gent d p, 8' Feb., 1869.
   . Coldrick, H. C., of Hillfield Parade, nr. the City but in
          the County of Gloucester gent. d p, 3 Feb,
          1869 (Glos Chron.).
   see Hole
   : Langham, J 23 Nov., 1813 (2432).
   see Morris
   ., Pollard.
      Shepherd, W. E. Times. d p., 31 May, 1873
Carter-Campbell, of Possil : Carter, Col Thomas Tupper
          Lyon Reg., Vol XIII, 18 Jan., 1894
        · Carter, T. of Dorchester Road, Weymouth,
          Col R. E. and Emily, his wife   Times,
          d p., 11 March, 1893
Carter-Wood . Wood, J., of Victoria Street, Westminster, and 49,
    St George's Road, Pimlico, Middlesex, esq   Times, 4
    Sept., 1865
Carteret-Silvester : Carteret, P. 31 Jan. 1822 (194)
Cartmell *see* Austen-Cartmell
Cartwright · Cobb, R 25 Oct., 1865 (5087)
       : Hogg, J. 23 Aug., 1817 (1895)
       see Anson-Cartwright
Cartwright-Enery   Cartwright, S. D. D. C on his marriage with
    Constance Isabelle Enery. 21 June, 24 June, 1864 (D G.
    1010 and 1021).
Carus-Wilson : Carus, W. W   5 March, 1793 (181)
Carver *see* Middleton
Cary *see* Goldney-Cary
Cary-Malins : Cary, E. R., of 57, Lowndes Square. Middlesex,
    spinster. Times, d p, 20 March, 1882.
Casabianca *see* Hope.
Casberd-Boteler · Boteler, J. B 22 Jan., 1867 (471)
         : Boteler, Wm J. Whll., 22 Jan., 1867 (D G.
          151)

Case *see* Morewood
„ Walker
    H. A — Walker, H. A C., Beckford Hall, Tewkesbury, Glos   Times, 12 Oct., 1898
Case Walker : Case, H. A., of Barton House, Canterbury, esq., Capt 12th R Lancers   Times, d p, 10 Feb., 1883
Caslon-Smith — Smith, S. H., A. H., and H. A., all of 22 and 23, Chiswell Street, London   Times, d p., 21 Nov., 1896
Cason *see* Winter
Castell *see* Nicholson Castell
    Stead, Fred John, of Boscombe, Bournemouth   Times, 19 July, 1899
Castle *see* Gee
Castledine *see* Tucker-Castledine
Catchmayd *see* Gwinnett
Cathrow-Disney — Cathrow, J   23 June, 1820 (1300)
Cator *see* Lennard
Catt *see* Willett
Cattermole-Davison — Cattermole, A. B., Haddesley House, Selby, Yorks   Times, d p., 17 Dec., 1894
Cattley, W. E. — Ewing, W. H. A., of 5, Crown Office Row, London.   Times, d.p., 6 May, 1892
Catton Watson : Watson, A. G., of 39, Lowndes Square, London   Times, d.p., 23 Dec., 1891
Caudle *see* Bateman
Caulfield-de Pons : Caulfield, E. H., born at Gibralter, 11 April, 1843, resided in Paris upwards of 14 years ; Secretary to his Excellency the Condé de Fernandina (Grandee of Spain), private and business address 10, Avenue de Messine, Paris.
Causens *see* Smith
Cautley *see* Pasley-Dirom
    Pasley-Dirom, H., to resume original family name   Times, d p., 29 Oct and 5 Nov., 1888
Cavan Irving : Irving, J. A. J., of 94, Eaton Place, Middlesex, esq   Times, 10 July, 1873
    Irving, J. C., of 94, Eaton Place, Middlesex, esq now at Nice, France.   Times, 15 Jan., 1875
    Irving, H., of 94, Eaton Place, Middlesex, esq   Times, 22 Jan., 1876
Cave Cumberbatch, C. C   eldest s of Lawrence Trent Cumberbatch, M.D., of 25, Cadogan Place Middlesex   Times, d.p., 6 May, 1879, 10 May, 1879.
    Otway, S   12 March, 1818 (543)
    see Verney-Cave
Cave-Orme — Robinson, G. A   19 Jan., 1889 (668)

Caven *see* Gambles.
Cavendish *see* Bradshaw.
Cavenagh-Mainwaring : Cavenagh, W. 25 Feb , 1892 (1274).
Cavis-Brown : Brown, J., of Chichester, Clerk in Holy Orders, one of the Priest Vicars of Chichester Cathedral Times, d.p., 25 March, 1884, 16 April, 1884.
Cawley *see* Floyer.
Cawthorn *see* Cawthorne
Cawthorne : Cawthorn, Jas., Jane, and E., of Hove, Sussex. Times, 29 Dec., 1894.
    Churley, G. J. 26 Dec., 1891 (255).
    Fenton, J. 15 May, 1781 (12187-8)
Cearns *see* Cairns.
Cecil *see* Gascoyne-Cecil
Cedd *see* Saint Cedd
Cerjat *see* De Cerjat
Chace-Carr : Carr, E., of Great Tower Street, London. Times, 3 Sept., 1898
Chad *see* Scott-Chad
Chaddock-Lowndes : Chaddock, T., of Old House Green, Odd Rode, Chester, esq , formerly of Congleton, Cheshire, and St. Leonards-on-Sea, Sussex, gent Times, d.p , 12 Feb., 1883.
Chadwick *see* Cooper-Chadwick.
    : Gillan, W. 1 Aug , 1834 (1429).
    Jas. Tattersall Tattersall, J Chadwick, now at 29 Spring Gardens, Buxton, gent. Times, 23 Aug., 1888
Chaffyn *see* Troyte-Chaffyn-Grove.
Chalker-Pearse Chalker, S. W. P. 8 April, 1874 (2098).
Chalmers-Hunt : Hunt, J. 19 Jan., 1889 (453).
Chaloner : Walmesley, R.G. 14 Jan., 1888 (495).
Challoner *see* Bisse-Challoner.
Chamberlain *see* Dyneley
  ,, Hughes-Chamberlain
    Jno. : Whitehorn, M. B., of Newbury, Berks, sheep and cattle dealer. Times, d p., 15 June, 1889
Chamberlaine : Pooke, W. H., and H. 5 Feb , 1872 (594).
Chamberlayne *see* Ingles Chamberlayne.
    : Wilkinson and Ackerley, otherwise Acherley, J. 1st and 2nd Will. IV., 1831.
Chamberlin-Hopkins : Chamberlin, J. 14 July, 1810 (1023).
Chambers *see* Hammond-Chambers
  ,, Hammond-Chambers-Borgnis
  ,. Hodgetts.
    : Rogerman J. 31 March, 1795 (285).
Chambres . Chambres-Jones, E. 26 June, 1812 (1258)

Chamier : Des Champs, J. 21 Oct., 1780 (12128)
Champain *see* Bateman-Champain.
Champante *see* Joggett-Champante
Champernowne : Harington, A. 7 May, 1774 (11454)
Champion . Champion-Baumgartner. H J, of 7, St Swithin's Lane, E.C., civil and mining engineer. Times, 16 Nov., 1888.
Champneys · Burt, H. W. 13 Oct., 1778 (11917)
   see Mostyn-Champneys
Champneys-Smith · Smith, E. J, of 101, Stacey Road, Cardiff, gent. Times, d p, 4 May, 1887
Chandless *see* Long.
Chandler · Gascoyne, G 15 June, 1793 (491)
Chandos-Pole Pole. S 3 Feb., 1807 (141)
Chandos-Pole-Gell Chandos-Pole, H. W., 2 April, 1863 (D G 430).
Channey *see* Snell-Channey.
Chanter *see* Roylands-Chanter
Chaplin . Smith G. H., of Crossbrook Street, Cheshunt, Hertford. Times, 30 June, 1865
Chaplin Robertson *see* Robertson Chaplin.
Chapman Chapman-Yapp, S A 7 Dec., 1842 (3867)
   Agnes Chapman, Nanny, of Green Well, Dent, near Sedbergh, York, spinster. Times, d p, 9 Oct., 1878.
   see Green.
   Ramsay, S, widow of J. Chapman, on her divorce from Dr Ramsay, of London. Times, 24 June, 1876.
   see Yapp.
Chapman-Yapp Yapp, S. A 2 April. 1839 (724).
Chappell *see* Brunning Maddison
Charles *see* Rundle Charles
Charleton *see* Anne
   ,, Maxwell.
Charlett : Newport, J. W 6th Geo. IV., 1825.
Charlton · Lechmere, N. 22 Jan., 1785 (37)
   see Meyrick
Charteris *see* Tracy.
Chase *see* Wathen.
Chassereau Weber. E, born at Hayti, nat. Br. subject, residing at Grosvenor Hotel, London. Times, d p., 12 June, 1882
Chaston . Gedny, jun., J 14 March, 1837 (683).
Chater-Fawsitt . Chater. H G., of Notting Hill, London Times, d.p., 23 and 27 Aug., 1895.
Chatfeild Clarke · Clarke, E., of 132, Westbourne Terrace, London, etc., gentleman Times, d p, 2 Nov., 1896.

Chatfeild-Clarke : Clarke, Stanley and Leslie of 132, Westbourne Terrace, London, etc. Times, d p , 5 Nov , 1868
Chatto see Potts-Chatto.
Chauncey see Snell-Chauncey.
Chauntrell : Faithfull, F D , esquire, of H M. Uncovenanted Civil Service, Bombay, India, formerly practising as a solicitor in London and afterwards at Bombay d p , 3 Aug , 1865
Chaworth Musters, J (junr) 3 Oct , 1806 (160).
    see Musters
    : Taylor, G 12 Dec , 1780 (12143).
Chaworth-Musters Musters, J P. 6 Oct , 1888 (5605)
Cheek see Foote
Cheere see Madryll-Cheere.
Cheese-Carpenter : Cheese E. 9 June, 1815 (1161)
Cheese-Lewis : Cheese, L T., of Roxton, Beds , schoolmaster, Times, 7 June, 1887
Cheiake · Chick, W., of Woodville, Hereford, architect and surveyor Times, d p , 2 Oct , 1879
Chevenix : Smith, G 10 Oct , 1836 (1785)
Cherry-Garrard : Cherry, A 30 Sept , 1892 (5679).
Cheshire Widdowson, J. 10 Dec , 1817 (2652)
Chesmer : Boomer, H C., of Toronto, Canada. Times, d p , 24 Dec , 1896
Chester see St Leger
Cheston see Sherman.
Chetham-Strode Chetham, Sir F. 23 June, 1845 (1863)
    Chetham, R 24 Oct , 1827 (2219)
    Chetham, T 16 Dec , 1808 (4)
Chetwode see Newdigate-Ludford-Chetwode
Chetwood-Aiken : Aiken, C. E. 4 Jan , 1886 (D.G 13)
Chetwynd see Stapylton
    ,, Talbot-Chetwynd
    Talbot, J C (Earl Talbot) 19 April, 1786 (165)
Cheval-Tooke Tooke, C 10 Feb , 1859 (612)
Cheviot Brown, Lilian, of Thorpe, East Molesey, Surrey spinster d p , 11 Jan , 1897
Chichester : Burnard, J C of Stoke House, Somerset, esquire Times, 9 Aug , 1865
    . Burnard (otherwise Chichester) A C 30 July, 1898 (5919)
Chichester-Constable Chichester, W G R 19 Jan 1895 (548)
Chichester-Nagle · Chichester, J. 15 Aug , 1839 (1605)
Chichester-O'Neill Chichester, Rev W. St J , 16 Mar , W , 29 Mar., 1855 (D G 546 and 562)
Chick see Cheiake
    ,, Lucas.

Child *see* Dampier-Child.
  „ Field-Child
  „ Hook-Child
Childe *see* Baldwyn-Childe
  · Childe Pemberton, C B., of Millichope Park, Salop, esq ,
    Lieut R H G. Times, d.p , 18 Nov., 1884
Childe-Freeman Childe, Rev E L , of Bolton Abbey, Yorks
    Times, d p , 13 June, 1882
Childe-Pemberton Childe. C O   2 July, 1849 (2201).
Chinnery *see* Haldane-Chinnery
Chinnery-Haldane Haldane-Chinnery, J. R. A 19 Sept , 1878
    (D G 802) Lyon, XI., 9 Oct , 1887
Chisenhale · Johnson, J. C 1 July, 1833 (1277)
Chisenhale-Marsh Marsh, T. C. 27 Oct., 1846 (3798)
Chisholm *see* Gooden-Chisholm
  „ Scott-Chisholme
Chisholm-Batten Batten, E and J 1 April, 1859 (1414)
    Mrs Jemima Chisholm Lyon, VI , 9 Feb , 1860
Cholmeley *see* Fairfax-Cholmley
  Strickland, Sir G 17 March, 1865 (1882)
  Cholmley Strickland, W R , of 14, Church Villas, Church Road,
    Willesden Times, d p , 10 April, 1886
  · Fane, H H 31st Geo III , 1791
    Grimes, R 8 Feb , 1858 (846)
Cholmondeley *see* Owen
Cholwick *see* Lear-Cholwick
Chowne Tilson, C. 10 Jan 1812 (69)
    Tilson, J H 24 Feb , 1836 (403)
Christian *see* Curwin
  „ Hare
Christie Christy, W 11 Feb., 1890 (956).
  : Plenderleath, W 24 June, 1835 (1284)
Christie-Burton Christie, N W, 16 Nov., 1784 (D G 4529)
Christopher *see* Cradock-Christopher
    Dundas, R A 25 Jan , 1836 (147)
    see Seton-Christopher
Christopher-Nisbet-Hamilton, of Bloxholm, Dirleton, &c
    Christopher, Hon Lady Mary Lyon, Vol. V , 3 Dec , 1855
Christy *see* Christie
Christy-Miller Christy, S 19 March, 1862 (1618)
Chrystie-Miller, of Craigentinny Christy, Saml Lyon Vol
    VI., 4 March, 1862
Chucker-Butty *see* Goodeve
Chudleigh *see* Stuart-Chudleigh
Church Beck, W 9 April, 1789 (226).
    see Handy-Church

Church *see* King-Church.
    ,, Pearce-Church
       Phillips, S. C   5 May, 1869 (2744)
       Phillips, S. C   5 May, 1869 (D.G 490)
Churchill : Bones, C. E., of 41, Gresham Street, London, warehouseman. Times, d p., 17 April, 1866
      Bones, E., of 15, George Street, Manchester, warehouseman Times. d.p., 18 April, 1886
    see Carter
       Davis, J. A. V., of Stretton, East Dulwich Grove Surrey Times, d p., 11 Nov., 1895
    see Jodrill
Churchward : Dimond, J   22 Feb., 1817 (576).
Churley *see* Cawthorne.
Churston, Lord *see* Bullei-Yaide-Buller
Chute *see* Wiggett-Chute.
Challice *see* Scott Challice
Clanchy *see* Johnson.
Clapcott *see* Dean
Clapp *see* Cunningham.
Clare *see* Newton-Clare.
Claremont *see* Lyne Stephens
Clarges *see* Hare-Clarges
Clark : Daws, J., of 57, Gt Northern Road. Derby railway clerk. Times, 16 Dec., 1889.
   see Dawson.
   ,, Dyer.
    Hamilton, J   20 Dec., 1777 (11832).
   see Hannam Clark.
   ,, Lee Clark.
    Onions, J. C.   17 Feb., 1877 (994).
   see Perceval-Clark
   ,, Sanders-Clark
   ,, Stott
   ,, Towers-Clark
Clark-Kennedy   Clark, Lieut.-Col. Alex. Kennedy. Lyon Vol. IV., 30 April, 1839
Clark-Smith : Smith, T. C., of Ulverston Lancs., B.A. Times, d p., 24 Oct., 1888
Clarke *see* Browne-Clarke (cancelled 13 Apr., 1802—374)
    . Butler-Clarke-Southwell-Wandesford
    . Butler-Clarke
    .. Chatfeild Clarke.
    ,, Clucas
    ,, Cooper
    ,, Fairlie-Clarke.
    Graham, J   31 Jan., 1786 (41).

Clarke see Graham-Clarke
　,, Jervoise-Clarke
　　Littlewood, H D , of 26, Essex Street, Strand, solicitor (enrolled in H M High Court of Justice). Times, 25 Sept , 1894
　　Mudd, C　5 Nov , 1850 (2912).
　　O'Donnell, of Summer Hill, co Armagh. Ir. R. L , 3 March, 1806.
　　Plomer, J　15th Geo III , 1775
　　Price, J H　13 Jan , 1787 (17)
　　Smith, W. A , officer, mercantile marine service, s s Nevasa. Times, d.p , 17 June, 1891
　　Smith, A. E , of Drigg Vicarage, Cumberland, formerly of Cheltenham, spinster　Times, d.p , 11 Mar , 1891
　see Wells-Clarke
　,, Whitfeld.
　,, Wiseman Clarke.
Clarke Baylis　Clarke, J W., of Moreton-in-the-Marsh, Gloucester, gent.　Times, d p , 11 Oct , 1890
Clarke Deeley see Mallaby.
Clarke-Earle　Clarke, G , of Hendon, Middlesex, esquire Times, 10 Aug , 1865.
Clarke-Frost　Frost, W C , of Falkland, Nightingale Lane, Surrey, gent　Times, d p , 14 Aug , 1894.
Clarke-Jervoise　Clarke, S　9 Nov , 1808 (1519).
Clarke-Lens　Clarke, B L., of 19, Bertram Road, Manningham, Bradford. Yorks　Times, d p., 1 Jan , 1884, 4 Jan , 1884
Clarke-Thornhill　Clarke　15 Jan , 1856 (155)
Clarke-Wellwood, of Comrie Castle Clarke, Andrew　Lyon Vol IV , 10 June, 1847
Clarke-Wellwood　Clarke, A　20 May, 1847 (1830)
Clapcott see Dean.
Clavell　Richards, J.　27 Aug , 1817 (1918)
Clavering see Napier-Clavering
　,, Savage
Clay Ker Seymer　Clay, H E　5 Jan , 1865 (48)
Clayfield-Ireland　Clayfield, J I　11 May, 1827 (1060)
Clayhills-Henderson, of Invergowrie Clayhills, Geo David, Captn R N　Lyon Vol XIV , 27 Nov , 1896.
Claypon see Lane-Claypon.
　　Lane, W. W. C , of Spalding, Lincoln　Times, 5 Nov., 1875
Clayton : Brack, D.　15 Nov , 1813 (2383).
　see Browne-Clayton
　,, Every-Clayton
　,, Every-Halsted
　,, Lowndes.

Clayton-East   Clayton, E G   9 April, 1829 (688)
                Gilbert-East, Sir G A, of Hall Place, Maidenhead, Berks, Bart. Times, d p, 12 Jan, 1870.
                see Gilbert-East.
Cleaver see Banks
        ,,   Peach
Clegg-Hill · Hill, R. C.   7 April, 1874 (2098).
Cleghorn see Tancred.
Cleland see Henderson-Cleland
            Lander, W H, of 88, Harley Street, Middlesex, esq Times, d p, 3 March, 1892
            Lander, W. H.   27 Dec, 1895 (2162)
Cleland-Henderson : Cleland, John Wm, Lt-Col. Lyon Vol. XI (R L. 21 Nov, 1865 and 13 Oct, 1886), 26 Apr. 1882
            · Cleland, J. W.   21 Nov, 1868 (6402) (D G 1326).
Clement see Ashburner-Clement
Clements see Lucas-Clements
Clements-Finnerty   Clements, H   Times, d p, 29 Nov., 1887
Clench see Stanley
Clennell · Fenwick, T   15 Sept, 1882 (4340)
        · Fenwick, T   2 April, 1796 (310)
Clephane see Maclean
Clerk see Collins
Clerk Eldin · Clerk, F North, of Tettenhall Wood, Staffs., esq., Times, d p, 1 Jan., 1873
Clerke : Jennings, P   26 Oct., 1774 (11504)
Cleugh : Darry, P   7 Aug, 1813 (1634)
Cleveland see Vane
        · Willett, A S   13 April, 1847 (1374).
Clibborn see Booth-Clibborn
Cliff McCulloch : Cliff, Janet and E A, on succeeding to the estates of Kirkclaugh   Times, 27 Nov, 1896
            · W E, Lyon   1 July, 1899
Cliffe see Bradbury
Clifford · Clifford Eskell, M, surgeon and M D., of 111, Great Russell Street, Bloomsbury Square. Times, d p, 23 Oct, 1877
        see Constable.
        ,, Phelps
        . Winchcombe, N.   14 Nov., 1801 (1358).
Clifford-Butler · Butler, Jas. F. and Marion, his wife   W, 13 Nov., 1860 (D G 1375)
Clifford Constable · Hartley, R, formerly widow of Sir T A. Clifford Constable, now wife of F J. Hartley, of Teddington, esq   Times, d p, 24 Aug, 1876

Clifford Constable : Trelawny, R., of Dunbar House, Teddington, Middlesex. Times, d p , 1 Jan , 1873
Clifford-Eskell : Eskell, A., of 8, Grosvenor Street, W, surg.-dentist. Times, 20 Jan., 1873
: Eskell, M., of 8, Grosvenor Street, Middlesex, M R.C S Times, 1 May 1873
Clifford-Jones : Jones, T., late of Hampton Lee, Sutton, now temp at 42, Penn Road, Wolverhampton, Staffs Times, d.p., 28 Sept., 1891
Clifton, H. A. : Abraham, H J. W., of 29, Loraine Road, Holloway, London. Times, d p., 7 June, 1895
   see Abney-Hastings
   ,, Dicconson
   Juckes, Sir G 8 Dec , 1837 (3242)
   see Juckes.
   Markham, H. R. 6 Aug., 1869 (4568) (D G. 993)
Clifton-Dicconson : Clifton, C 12 March, 1890 (1804)
   Clifton, W. C. 8 April, 1881 (1792)
Clifton-Mogg : Mogg, Rev. W. C., of Great Bedwyn, Wilts Times, d p , 20 May, 24 May, 1879
Clinton see Fynes-Clinton
   Lord see Hepburn-Stuart-Forbes
   see Pelham-Clinton-Hope.
Clitherow see Stracey Clitherow
Clive see Herbert
   ,, Windsor-Clive
Cloak see Sampson.
Clopton : Ingram, E. 9 June, 1801 (636)
   Ingram, J 18 June, 1818 (1265)
   Skrymsher, C B 22 Dec , 1792 (950)
Close-Brooks : Close, J. B. 14 Feb , 1889 (1027)
   d p , 4 Jan , 1889
   : Close, J B , of Pendleton, Lancs., banker Times,
Clough : Ellis, T P W 26 June, 1879 (6749)
   see Taylor.
Cloutt see Russell
Clovell : Richards, W. 21 March, 1797 (263)
Clucas : Clarke, G P., of The Lodge, Repton, Derby M A Times, d p , 8 June, 1875
   : Clugas, T 30 March, 1854 (1058)
Cludde : Pemberton, W 25th Geo III , 1785
Clugas see Clucas
Clulow : Rigg, H , of 5, Albion Place, Camberwell New Road, Surrey, gentleman. Times, 9 July, 1868
Clutterbuck : Parsons, A R., of 13, Conyers Road, Streatham, Surrey, spinster Times, 24 April, 1889
Clutton Brock : Clutton, T 10 July, 1810 (1005).

Coaks, J B   Bugg, J , of Bank Chambers, Norwich, and Thorpe Hamlet, Norwich, solicitor   Times, 1 Feb, 1866
Coape-Arnold   Coape, H F J., of Mirables, I of W. Times, d p., 16 July, 1867.
    see Arnold
Coape-Smith · Smith, H , of 93, Cornwall Gardens, S Kensington, Col. (H M Bengal Staff Corps), &c   Times, d p , 11 Aug., 1885
Coates, *als* Boardman *see* Bowman
    · Campion, J.   20 July, 1790 (449).
    see Thompson
    „ Webb-Coates
Coathupe *see* Day
Coats *see* Glen-Coats
Cobb *see* Cartwright
    „ Jewer
Cobden-Sanderson   Sanderson, T J., of 3, Paper Buildings, Temple, London, barrister   Times, d p , 27 Oct., 1882
Cobham   Cobham-Martyr, A   20 Aug., 1813 (351).
Coburn, Henry James : Isaacs, Henry Moses, late of Spring Villa, Clifton, Bristol, now of 7, Milner Square, Middlesex, gentleman   Times, 30 April, 1868
Cochram *see* Cochrane
Cochrane   Cochrane, M L , of 101. High St., Barry, Glamorgan, boot and shoe dealer   Times, d p , 6 Nov., 1891
    Cochrane, E J , of Gorlitz, Silesia, now at Holloway, Middlesex, student of elec engineering   Times, d p , 20 Nov , 1890
    Cochrane, W J late of Reading, Berks, but now of 101, High Street, Barry, Glamorgan, spinster   Times, d p., 6 Nov 1891
    Cochrane C E , of Moscow   M R C.V S , Eng. Times, d p , 20 Nov., 1890.
Cochrane-Wisheart-Baillie, of Lamington Cochrane Alex Dundas, Ross. Lyon Vol IV , 27 Dec , 1837
Cock *see* Haselfoot
    „ Lamb
    „ Rand
    „ Vawdrey.
Cockayne *see* Frith.
     , Medlycott.
Cockayne-Cust   Cust, H F   2 Jan , 1862 (3).
Cockburn : Wilson, J. P , of The Mount, Totnes, Devon, esq   Times, d p , 6 Dec., 1876
Cockburn-Campbell · Cockburn, Sir A T   2 Aug , 1825 (1374)
Cockburn-Hood, of Stoneridge   Hood, Jno   Lyon, Vol VII., 6 April, 1866

Cockburn-Mercer : Messer, Mary S., of Victoria, Australia, widow of late W. C. Messer. Times, 18 April, 1891
Cockburn-Ross : Cockburn, J. 29 Jan., 1791 (55).
Cockburn-Stothert : of Blacket . Cockburn, Thomas   Lyon, Vol. II., 26 July, 1814
Cockerell *see* Rushout
Cockerton *see* Higgin-Birket
Cockey *see* Morrish.
Cocking-Gladstone : Cocking, A. E., late of Somerleyton Road, Brixton, Surrey, at present residing at 15, Rue de Dunkerque, Paris   Times, 20 June, 27 June 1883.
Cocks *see* Pemberton
  „ Somers-Cocks
Cockshutt *see* Twisleton
Codd *see* Walls
Codrington *see* Bethell.
  . Millar, J. C. 8 May, 1792 (286)
Codwise *see* Bertie
Cody *see* Ormond
Coffin : Bennett, R 7th Geo III., 1767.
  see Blount.
  „ Lyddingsen
  „ Pine-Coffin
Coffin-Greenly : Coffin, Sir I. 6 April 1811 (621)
Coggins *see* Harper
Coghill : Cramer, Sir J. C 7 June, 1817 (1340)
  : Maine, J 6 March, 1779 (11958)
Coghlan *see* Colan.
  „ Hay-Coghlan
Coham-Fleming : Fleming, J. B 4 June, 1883 (3038)
Cohen *see* Agar-Hutton
  : Isidor, Albert Anders, of Wood, Middlesex   Times, 1 Sep., 1899.
  see Arthur.
  David Daniel De Lara : Cohen, David Danl., of 48, Woburn Place, Middlesex, gent   Times, d.p., 7 June, 1882.
  Michael George : Cohen, Michael, of 600, Commercial Road, E., iron merchant   Times, d.p., 14 June, 1890
  see Druce
  „ Field
  „ Freeman-Cohen
  „ Montagu
  „ Rothbury
Cohn *see* Cooke
Cokayne : Adams, G. E. 15 Aug., 1873 (3993)

Cckayne-Frith Frith, C. and C C , both of 5. Victoria Park,
    Dover, Kent. Times, d p , 4 Jan , 1881
Cokburne *see* Ker-Cokburne.
Coke Cooke, A., of 339, Oxford Street, Middlesex. umbrella
    manufacturer, to resume original family name of
    Coke Times, 7 May, 1884.
  Cooke, A. H , Lieut. Times, 11 and 19 Sept . 1895.
  Cooke, A. H , of W. Hampstead. Middlesex, gent
    Times, 9 Feb , 1888
  Cooke, A. H., to resume original family name Times,
    d.p., 10 July, 1896.
Colan Coghlan, T., M.D., M R C S. (Eng). now surgeon of
    H.M. 'Malabar.' Times, 19 April, 1867.
  Coghlan, H A , M.R C S. (Eng), staff-assistant-surg.
    H.M Army, at present stationed at Castle Hill
    Fort, Dover, Kent Times, 29 June, 1867.
Colborne *see* Ridley-Colborne.
Colborne-Veel : Colborne, J V. 16 Aug., 1853 (2252)
Colchester *see* Wemyss Colchester.
Colchester Wemyss . Wemyss Colchester, M W , of The Wilder-
    ness, Glos , esq Times, d.p., 30 Nov , 1882
Colclough *see* Biddulph-Colclough
Coldham-Fussell : Fussell, J. C Times d p , 17 Nov , 1892
Coldrick *see* Carter
Coldrick-Carter Coldrick, A., of Hillfield Parade, nr. Gloucester,
    gent. Times, d.p, 8 Feb., 1869.
  Coldrick, H C , of Hillfield Parade, nr Glouces-
    ter, gent Times, d p., 3 Feb., 1869
Coldwell *see* Thicknesse
Coldwell Horsfall : Coldwell, H H., of The Firs, Moseley,
    Worces., gent Times, d p , 8 Nov., 1877
Cole *see* Butler-Cole
  ,, Cowden-Cole
    Dicker, J. 1 March, 1833 (449).
  : Dicker, W C 18 Feb . 1833 (374)
  see Fortescue-Cole.
    Hammon.
    Loggin, W 42nd Geo III , 1802.
  see Marshall
    Van Thysen, T 6 April, 1805 (522)
  see Wells-Cole.
Colegrave Manby, W 16 Feb 1819 (380)
  : Manby, J W J M Whll . 6 July 1868 (D G 822)
  Manby, J. W J. M. L 6 July 1868 (3937).
  see Manby-Colegrave
Coleman *see* Proctor.
Coleman-Napier : Coleman, G V 25 Jan., 1860 (378)

Coles-Cowper : Cowper-Coles, C. B. 4 Feb , 1888 (893).
Coles *see* Pinckard.
Collard *see* Beverly.
: Bonn, E., of Abbotsfield, Weveliscombe, Somerset, and of Ravensworth, Hants, spinster   Times. d p , 14 Jan , 1887
Colleton *see* Garth-Colleton
Collette-Thomas Thomas. J. of Trewince, Cornwall   Times, 6 June, 1900
Colley Davies Davies, T. 25 Aug. 1865 (4283).
Colley *see* Davies-Colley
  „ Pomeroy-Colley
: Pomeroy, G. F., of Rathorngan, co Kildare   Dublin. 20 Jan , 1830
Collie-Macneill Colhe, G W and D G., of London   Times, 23 Aug , 1888
Collier-Wright Wright J R C of Great Malvern   Times 18 April, 1900
Collingwood : Calthrop, R G and A. 3 April, 1868 (2252).
   see Lempriere-Collingwood
   „ Newnham-Collingwood
. Stanhope, E P 10 Dec , 1816 (2442)
Collins *see* Browne.
  „ Bury.
   Clerk, S. V. 25 April, 1801 (445)
  see Maunsell Collins
: Metcalf, L C   31 July, 1875 (3866)
  see Sell-Collins.
   „ Edward-Collins
   „ Fenton
   „ Lovibond-Collins
   Moses, Rev. M., of 24, Woodstock Road, Poplar. Middlesex   Times. d p , 21 Oct., 1890
  see Rigby-Collins.
   „ Tenison
Collins-Trelawney . Collins, C T   26 Nov , 1838 (2778)
  or Collis *see* Ward.
Collins Harvey Harvey, W K . of 16 Auriol Road, W Kensington, Times. 21 Aug , 1879
Collins-Splatt Collins, H   14 Aug 1833 (1540).
Collis-Sandes : Collis. F S. 17 July, 1879 (D G. 558).
Collis . Supple, Ed 18 July, 2 Aug , 1859 (D G 1387).
  see Ward
Collyer-Bristow Collyer A. 16 March, 1860 (1172)
    Collyer, W. W , 15 Jan , 1859 (D G. 66)
Colman Summers, S. 21 Nov., 1786 (557).
Colmer *see* Lester

Colmore *see* Cregoe-Colmore.
Colpoys *see* Griffith-Colpoys
Colquitt *see* Goodwin
Colt : Williams, W C., one of H M inspectors of schools, of Hagley Hall, Staffs, and Christ Church, Oxford, esq. Times, d p., 17 Feb., 1892
Colthurst *see* Bowen Colthurst.
    : Bulcock, J C 14 Sept., 1790 (569).
Colthurst-Brabazon · Colthurst, N. and Elizabeth, his wife D. Castle, 17 Feb., 1845 (D.G. 122 & 129).
    : Colthurst, N., of Danesford, co Kerry. Dublin, 11 Jan , 1845
Colthurst-Vesey : Colthurst, Chas. V. 21 Nov., 6 Dec., 1860 (D G. 1465 and 1473).
Coltman *see* Pocklington-Coltman.
Colton *see* Broomhead-Colton-Fox
    : Coward, C. A , of 31, Henley Street, Paddington, Sydney, N.S. Wales. Times, 1 June, 1893
Colton-Fox Broomhead, J. S 12 April, 1894 (2241)
    : Fox, G. 11 Jan., 1833 (123).
Colvile : Webberburn, A. 22 June, 1814 (1371)
Colyear-Dawkins : Dawkins, J 24 Dec. 1835 (3 and 24).
Colyer-Fergusson : Fergusson. T. C., of The Monte, nr. Sevenoaks, and Wombwell Hall, Gravesend, of Christ Church, Oxford, and 34, Curzon Street, Mayfair, esq. Times. d p., 14 Jan., 1890
Combe : Maddison, R T 18 Dec., 1849 (3856).
Comberback *see* Swetenham
Combridge, J. T M Martin, J T , of 26 Western Road. Hove. Sussex, butcher. 25 June, 1879 ·
Commyns-Mannock : Commyns, W V 19 Jan., 1793 (50).
Compton Bugg, W 4 July, 1831 (1363)
    see Douglas-Compton.
Comyn Macfarlane *see* Macfarlane-Grieve.
Conant *see* Pigott-Stainsby-Conant.
    „ Carleton
Condell *see* Vallange
Conder · Hitchcock, S C., of New Wandsworth, Surrey Times, 30 Oct. 1877.
Conoly : Pakenham, E M of Castledown, co. Kildare Dublin, 27 Aug., 1821
Conquest *see* Oliver Conquest.
Conrahy · Morriss, E J., of Manor House, Plaistow, Essex Times, 21 Jan., 1878
Coningesby : Williams, Lady F H 2nd Geo III , 1762.
Connell *see* Lyons
Conn *see* Phillips-Conn

Constable see Brown-Constable.
,, Chichester-Constable.
Clifford, Sir T H 28 April, 1821 (963)
see Clifford-Constable
,, Goulton-Constable.
,, Nicoll-Constable
Sheldon, E 30 July, 1791 (433)
Sheldon, F 4 May, 1803 (698)
see Stanley.
,, Strickland-Constable
Constable-Maxwell-Stuart, of Traquair Constable-Maxwell, Henry. Lyon Vol X, 17 Oct, 1876
Conway see Ingram-Seymour-Conway
Potter, J C 8 Sept, 1825 (1752)
see Shipley-Conway
Conway-Gordon Conway, W 12 Aug 1839 (1584)
Conway, William R L, Lyon Vol IV
Conybeare see Bere.
Conyers Lang, H F 18 March, 1873 (1822).
Conyngham Burton Rt Hon F P (Baron Conyngham) 3 May, 1781 (12187)
see Denison
Cook see Altham
J Travis : Cook, J., of 1, Adelaide Terrace, Kingston-upon-Hull, solicitor Times. d.p., 23 Sept, 1886
see Lascelles-Astley
,, Rhodes.
,, Sheppard
,, Widdrington
Cooke Bull, F W. of Porthcawl, Glamorgan, gent Times, d.p. 13 Feb, 1889
Cohn, J J, of The Hotel Metropole, Brighton, Sussex, gent Times, d p, 26 Oct, 1891
see Coke
: Denny, T H, of Bergh Apton, Norfolk, gent Times, d.p., 17 and 19 Dec, 1890
Gane, J H 8 June, 1820 (1379)
Mathews, T A — March, 1850 (929)
see Molloy
, Pigott
: Trench, T 10 May, 25 Sept, 1850 (D G 740 and 749)
see Twemlow Cooke
, Van Mildert
,, Widdrington.
Cooke-Holland : Cooke, F G, of Boston Lincoln Times, 29 Oct, 1886
Cooke-Hurle Cooke, J W, 12 Nov, 1855 (D G 1573)

Cooke-Hurle : Cooke, J 12 Nov., 1855 (4184)
Cooke-Nicholson : Nicholson, T., of Elswick Dene, George Rd., Newcastle-on-Tyne Times, 17 Sept., 1867
Cooke-Trench Cooke, T. F St James,, 18 June, D C., 1 July, 1858 (D.G 1310 and 1317)
Cooke-Yarborough : Cooke G. 5 July, 1802 (719)
Cookes see Denham-Cookes
Cookson Crackanthorpe . Cookson, M. H., of 29, Rutland Gate. and of Lincoln's Inn, M'sex Times, d p., 24 Jan., 1888.
Cookson see Crackenthorpe
    ,, Dod
      Evans-Gordon H A. G 10 Aug. 1859 (3572)
    see Evans-Gordon
    ,, Fife-Cookson
    , Hume-Cookson
    ,, Reynard-Cookson
Cookson-Sawrey : Cookson, J 21 Nov., 1881 (5904)
    see Sawrey-Cookson.
Cookworthy Fox, W 29 July, 1780 (12104)
Coombe see Pilkington
Coombes see Johnstone-Coombes
Cooper see Aglionby.
    : Clarke, G. W 3 June, 1857 (1975)
    A Dyson Cooper, A, of St John's Coll , Oxon, and Edinson Villa, Thornton Heath, solicitor. Times, d p., 15 Nov., 1883.
    see Cowper
    ,, Erskine
    , Fisher
    ,, Hay-Cooper
    . Heap, W D. C 6 June, 1818 (1018)
    see O'Hara
    ,, Purnell
    , Paston-Cooper
    ,, Rede
    ,, Sanders
    ,, Tourle
    Tuthill, J C, of Merrin Square, Dublin Dublin, 26 April, 1844.
    : Tuthill, J. C D C., 3 June, 1844 (D.G 349 and 366) by Warrant
Cooper-Brown : Brown, W, of Hainford Hall, Norfolk, esq Times. d p., 13 Dec., 1884
Cooper-Chadwick Cooper, R and Catherine Chadwick, on their marriage St J., 15 Jan., D C, 6 Feb, 1855 (D G 222 and 263)
Cooper-Dean Cooper, J E 2 June, 1888 (3310)

Cooper-Essex Cooper (or Cowper), Jas. S Whll., 3 Aug., 1868 (D.G. 917).
Cooper-Gardiner Cooper, J G 11 March, 1823 (394)
Cooper-Key Key, Dame E., of Laggan House, Maidenhead, Berks, widow Times, d p., 7 May, 1888
    Key, A. M C., of the Royal Mil Academy, Woolwich, Kent, Lieut R. A Times, d p., 1 June, 1888
Cooper-Oakley : Oakley, A J., B A Cantab, of Oaklands, W Enfield, Middlesex Times. d p., 12 Jan., 1884
Cooper-Pattin Cooper, W. H., stud of med. at St Thomas's Hospital, and undergrad. Cambs., residing at 103, Lambeth Palace Road Times, 14 Jan., 1887
Cooper-Simpson-Cross Cross W 20 April, 1807 (555)
Coopy see Brent.
Coore see Blagrove
    „ Gale
Cope : Doolan, Rev C. of Loughgall, co Armagh Dublin, 30 May, 1844
    Doolan, R. W C D.C, 14 June, 1844 (D.G 389 and 397) by Warrant
    Garland, Anna (widow) 17 Feb., 1847 (702)
    Pinniger, J. A M 10 Aug., 1867 (4548)
    Pinniger, J A M and Georgina C., his wife Whll, 10 Aug., 1867 (D G 1053)
Cope Proctor : Cope, C W., of Clifton, Bristol, agricul chymist Times, d p., 28 June, 1876.
Copeland see Malkin
Copeman see Barker.
    Haggard, G W B., of Hemsby Hall, Norfolk, and Trinity Hall, Cambridge Times, d p., 24 June, 1895
Copestake see Bingham-Copestake
    „ Goodall-Copestake
Copland-Crawford : Crawford, R F., formerly of Harrow, now of Sudbery Lodge, Middlesex Times, d.p., 25 Sept., 1872
Copland-Griffiths : Griffiths, A E., of 25, Talbot Square, Hyde Park, &c. Times, 11 Oct., 1894
Copley see Bewicke-Copley
    . Moyle, J 7th Geo III., 1767.
    see Watson-Copley
    . Wolley, E 19 May, 1810 (712).
Coppinger see Burgh.
Coppin : Pittman, J 21 April, 1781 (12180)
Corban-Lucas : Lucas, A J 20 Aug., 1877 (D.G 583)
Corbet Davenant, Corbet 28 Jan 1783 (12409)
    Maurice, A 11 Jan., 1821 (154).

Corbet : Maurice, E   15 Feb., 1783 (12414).
 : Pigott, G. W.   29 May, 1800 (3189)
 : Pigott, J. D.   28 March, 1865 (1731)
 see Singleton
  Soden, J. and H. C   5 July, 1865 (3485)
Corbett *see* Astley-Corbett
 : Flint, R   22 Nov., 1774 (11512).
 see Holland-Corbett.
 : Jacobs, D. H., of Hyde Chester, congregl. minister.
  Times, 22 May 1889
  Plymley, J   20 Nov., 1804 (1422)
Corbett-Thompson : Corbett W   21 July, 1810 (1183)
Corbett-Winder : Corbett, U   Whitehall, 2 June, 1869 (D G. 612)
  Corbett, U. and M. A. J   2 June 1869 (3254)
Corbould-Warren   Corbould, W.   19 July, 1853 (2137).
Cordner-James   James, J. H., of Barberton, S. Africa, now at Manchester Hotel, Aldersgate Street, London. mining engineer   Times, d.p. 16 Dec., 1889
Cormack *see* Lawson.
Cornelius-Wheeler   Wheeler, J., of Nightingale Road, Southsea Portsea, Southampton. dentist   d.p, 14 Dec. 1865
Cornell *see* Viall, K.
Cornes : Corns, F., of Macclesfield, Chester, about to proceed to Yokohama, Japan   Times, d.p., 19 Feb., 22 Feb., 1864
Cornewall   Amyand, Sir G   20 July, 1771 (11162)
  see Walker
Cornfoot · Richardson, H   28 Oct., 1836 (1900)
Cornish *see* Mowbray.
 · Pitchford, S   11th Geo. III., 1771
  see Warre Cornish
Cornish-Bowden, F. J., of Avonwick, Devon, and Black Heath, Kent. esq   Times, d.p., 17 Feb., 1873
Cornish Brown : Cornish, C. B   14 Oct., 1863 (4),7)
Cornock *see* Hawkes-Cornock
Corns *see* Cornes
Cornwall *see* Lewis-Crosby.
Cornwallis *see* Mann.
  Wykeham-Martin, F   25 Oct., 1859 (5858)
Corrance · White, F   16 May, 1837 (1252)
Corry   Lowry, G., of Athenis, co Tyrone   Ulster's Office, 1769
Corsbie · Brown, J C., of Beyton, Suffolk, gent.   Times, 9 Aug., 1881
Cortis *see* Stamford
Cory : Eade, H. C.   25 May, 1864 (2868)

Cory Johnson, W., of Eton College, Buckingham, and of Halsdon, nr. Dolton, Devon, esquire, Fellow of King's Coll. Camb. Times, d p., 17 Oct., 1872.
Cory-Wright Wright, C F., of Hornsey Lane, Middlesex, also of Commercial Road, Lambeth, &c. Times, d p , 29 Nov , 1888.
Cosby, Mrs. Eliza Goring, Lady Eliza, wife of Col R G Cosby, of Queen's co., Ireland. Times, 28 Aug , 1893.
Cosens, W. Cosens, W. Reyner (Rev), D D , Vicar of Dudley, Worces. Times, 11 Dec , 1890.
Cosens-Weir, of Bogangreen Cosens, Robt. Lyon Vol. VII , 25 April, 1865.
Cosham see Hastings
Cosway see Bucknell
 ,, Halliday
 ,, Sowdon
Cotes-Preedy Preedy, Digby Hen Worthington, of Emmanuel Col. Cambs. Times, 20 Oct., 1899.
Cotgreave Johnson. J 20 June 1795 (632)
Cotham see Walmesley-Cotham
Cottam see Gregory
 ,, Milner.
Cottin see Murray.
Cotton Green, E. 14 Jan , 1820 (180)
 see Sheppard-Cotton
Cotton-Jodrell : Cotton. E. T D 10 July, 1890 (4327)
Cotton-Sheppard Sheppard, T 11 April, 1806 (448)
Cottrell-Dormer see Upton-Cottrell-Dormer
Couch see Quiller-Couch
Coull see Dixon-Coull
 ,, Forster-Coull
Counsell-Roberts Roberts, G. E , barrister-at-law, 5, King's Bench Walk, and 207, Albany Street, London, N W. Times. 5 Jan , 1898.
Coulson see Ward-Coulson
Coulter . Gardiner, J C and R P , both 1a, Portland Place, Middlesex, gent. Times, d p , 6 May, 1889
Coupland see Berne
 ,, Bergne-Coupland
 ,, Mitchell
Courcelles see De Courcelles.
Courtail · Bradley, C 8 March, 1806 (294)
 · Bradley, C 8 March 1806 (294)
Courtenay Courtenay-Anstruther, J W L., of St Albans Place, St James's, S W., etc . Capt Colonial Mil Times, d p., 1 Dec., 1884
 Throckmorton, C 22 March, 1819 (588)

Courtenay - Throckmorton, G 4 Feb., 1792 (78)
Courthope - Pousett, F. S. 18 Feb. 1862 (958).
Courtier-Dutton - Courtier. L 21 July, 1824 (1375)
Courtin see Allcard
Courtney - Mayhew, H 20 Dec., 1865 (6805)
    see Curtis
    „ Mayhew
Courtney-Mayhew - Courtney, T 23 Nov., 1821 (2344)
Coutts see Burdett-Coutts-Bartlett
    „ Burdett-Coutts
    „ Burdett-Coutts-Bartlett-Coutts
    „ Money-Coutts
Couves-Neville - Couves, F. A., formerly of Bow Middlesex Times, 29 March, 1871
Coutts Trotter, Jane : Lady Coutts Trotter, of Eaton Place, London Times, 4 March, 1899
Cowne see Tuder-Nelthorpe
Coventry-Campion - Coventry, J W 29 Dec., 1835 (2592)
Coventry - Darby-Coventry 27 April, 1798 (368)
Cowan see Baikie
Coward see Colton
    „ Mansel
Cowburn, A. see Smith-Masters
Cowden-Cole - Penney, I J. of Enfield, Middlesex assistant schoolmaster Times, 17 Aug., 1865
Cowdrey-Stanley - Stanley E, of 19, St Peter's Square, Hammersmith, Lond Times 16 Oct., 1873
Cowe see Cowen
Cowell-Stepney - Cowell, J S 29 Dec., 1857 (52) (1858)
Cowen - Cowe, H. of 22, Parade, Berwick-on-Tweed Times, 19 Sept., 1894
Cowley-Fowler - Fowler Rev J B A, formerly of Gunness, otherwise Gunhouse, Lincoln, but now residing at Steep Hill House, Lincoln d.p 16 Sept., 1878
Cowper see Coles-Cowper
    - Cooper, F of Queen's Coll, Oxford now of Lisle Court, Wootton, I W., esq Times, d p, 19 Jan., 1899
Cowper-Essex - Cowper, J S 3 Aug., 1868 (4382)
    - Cowper, J. S., late of Sandside, nr Ulverstone, esq Times, 25 July, 1868
    - Cowper, T C 15 Feb., 1879 (867)
Cowper-Smith - Smith, I. M., of Maida Hill, widow; also F. E, A. M de L and H F, her sons, all of same place Times, d p, 30 April, 1875
Cowper-Temple - Cowper W F 17 Nov 1869 (7226) (D G

Cox *see* Bingham-Cox
 „   Bompass, J. C.   31 Jan., 1820 (492)
 „   Buller-Hippesley-Cox.
    William Penn   Cox, E., of The Market Place, Leicester newspaper proprietor, etc.   Times, d.p., 3 Mar., 1881
    see Hody.
 „, Snead Cox
Cox-Edwards   Edwards (Rev.) J. C., of Emmanuel Coll., Cambridge, and Huntiscombe Place, Plymouth, chaplain R N   Times, 24 Feb., 1882
Cox-Hippisley : Cox, W. A., of High Cross Street, Leicester, and B., of same place   Times. d p., 27 Sept., 1877.
Cox-Murchison : Cox, K. M. M.   10 Nov., 1888 (6282)
Cox-Wentworth : Cox, J., of Upper Clapton, and Woburn Place, Russell Square, Middlesex, esq.   Times, 6 June, 1865.
Coxell *see* Gorey.
Coxwell *see* Grinfield-Coxwell
Coxwell-Rogers : Coxwell, R. R.   26 Jan., 1850 (279)
              Coxwell, W. R.   26 Oct., 1854 (3314).
Coyney : Hill, W.   27 March, 1790 (181).
Cozens *see* Brooke.
 „   Grimwood
 „   Napier
Crabb *see* Boucher
 „   Boulton
Crackanthorp : Cookson, C. C.   17 July, 1792 (553)
Crackanthorpe *see* Cookson Crackanthorpe
       Cookson, M. H.   28 July. 1888 (4365)
Cracroft *see* Amcotts.
       Cracroft Amcotts, E. W., of Hackthorn Hall, Lincoln, esq.   Times, d.p., 5 Feb., 1885
Cracroft-Amcotts : Cracroft, W. W., 24 July, 1857 (D.G. 714).
Cradock : Adderley, E. J.   19 May, 1886 (3032) (see 2798).
    see Caradock.
       Christopher, to continue name   W. 24 Aug., 1852 (D.G. 687)
       : Grove, E. H.   8 May, 1849 (1648).
Cradock-Hartopp : Hartopp Sir W. E.   25 May, 1849 (1716)
Cragg *see* Barker.
Cragg-Smith : Cragg, J.   27 May, 1822 (891)
Craggs   Eliot, E. L.   2 May, 1789 (334).
       : Scraggs, J.   Times, 3 Feb., 1876
Craig *see* Gibson-Craig
Craig-Laurie, of Redcastle and Myra Castle   Craig, Rowland Lyon Vol. V., 4 Sep., 1857.
       of Redcastle and Myra Castle : Craig, John.   Lyon Vol. XV., 8 Oct., 1897

Craigie-Halkett Halket-Craigie, J 16 April, 1856 (1508)
Cramer *see* Coghill.
  „   Roberts
Crane *see* Blathwayt
  „   Byres
  „   Taylor-Crane
Cranmer Dixon, E. M. 24 May, 1805 (683)
  · Mounsey, J P. 19 July, 1814 (1562)
  · Webb, A 18 May, 1813 (1016)
Cranmer-Byng Byng 1 Feb., 1882 (604).
Cranstoun *see* Trotter-Cranstoun.
Crapper *see* Foster
Craster *see* Wood-Craster
Crate Hue, E H , of Pelham Crescent, S Kensington. Times, d p , 20 Oct., 1894.
Crathorne *see* Tasburgh.
Craven : Goodwin, G C. 12 Dec , 1860 (5041)
  see Higgs-Craven
Crawford *see* Copland-Crawford.
  „   Douglas-Crawford.
  „   Hume
  „   Ramsay
  „   Sharman-Crawford
  „   Singleton
Crawford-Caffin Caffin, C., of H M Coastguard, King's Lynn, Commdr. R N Times, d p , 25 Apl., 1889
Crawford-Pollok, of Pollok Crawford, Sir Hew, Bt Lyon Vol. V , 5 June, 1852
Crawfurth *see* Smith-Crawfurth
Crawley *see* Capes
Crawhall-Wilson Crawhall, T. W. and T. F W , both of Alston, Cumberland, esq Times, d p , 22 Nov , 1880
Crawshay *see* Hiscocks-Crawshay
Creagh *see* MacMahon-Creagh.
  „   Butler-Creagh
Creasy *see* Cressy.
Cree : McMahon, J 10 June, 1815 (1105)
  : Stone, G J, of Owermoigne, Dorset, esq Times, d p , 7 Oct , 1880
Cregoe-Colmore : Cregoe, F 27 July, 1835 (1442)
Cremer Woodrow, jun , C. 26 Nov , 1785 (537).
Cremlyn . Jones, J W , Mid Temple Lane, W.C Times, 18 Dec , 1900
Crespin, C. W. Legassicke : Crespin, C W., of Gt Modbury, and Torquay, esq Times, 11 Nov , 1882
  see Legassicke-Crespin
Cressett *see* Pelham-Cressett

Cressingham : Crossingham, J   20 Dec., 1836 (2601).
Cresswell *see* Baker-Cresswell
   ,,   Baker
   : Easterby, F. 4 May, 1807 (598).
Cressy : Creasy, W. E., of Carshalton, Surrey, surgeon, and J G
   Creasey, of Southborough Kent Times 9 Feb., 1870
Creswell *see* Ward
Creswell-Ward   Creswell, R W, of Neasham Hill, Durham
   Times, d p, 15 March, 1889
Crewe Harpur, Sir H 11 April, 1808 (549)
Crewe-Milnes   Milnes. R O A 8 June, 1894 (4021)
Crewe-Read   Crewe, J O. 25 March, 1836 (584).
Cribb *see* Hatfield
Crichton *see* Morriss
   : Solomon, L A., of 34, Bedford Place, Russell Square,
       silversmith Times, d.p., 25 Oct., 1886
   see Stuart-Crichton
Crichton-Maitland *see* Makgill-Crichton-Maitland
Crichton-Stuart : Stuart, P J H 26 May 1817 (1253)
Crickitt *see* Scott-Crickitt
Crieves *see* Macpherson
Crighton-Ginsburg : Ginsburg Rev J B, of Magador, Morocco,
   and Sarah O his wife Times, d p 21 April, 1886
Cripps-Day Day, F. H 3 July, 1886 (3329)
Cripps-Dean *see* Dean
Critchley-Martin : Critchley, J. of 3, Portland Place Middlesex,
   gentleman Times. d.p, 5 Dec., 1871
Crocker *see* Eastcott Crocker
Crockford *see* Blake
Croft *see* Huddlestone
   Morgan, H 10 Nov, 1823 (2032)
   Morgan, J T. 23 Oct, 1822 (1979)
   Prichard, J R 1 July, 1824 (1374)
   Sampson, J H 13 June, 1823 (1090)
   Woodcock, J 29 Dec, 1792 (974)
Crofts W H Blackett Crofts, W H, of Welford Road,
   Leicester, temp. at Cambridge, med stud
   Times. d p, 21 May, 1875
   see Humble-Crofts
Cromey-Buck : Knight, H R, of Weymouth, Dorset Times,
   d p, 13 Jan., 1885.
Crommelin : Delacherois, S Dublin, 26 Nov. 1838
Crompton-Brown : Brown, F C J, of Kingswear, Cromer,
   Norfolk, gent Times, d p, 1 March, 1894
Crompton-Roberts Roberts, C W 9 Aug, 1861 (3316)
Crompton-Stansfield : Crompton, W H. 14 May 1872 (2439)
   : Crompton, W R. 26 June, 1832 (1519).

Cromwell *see* Frankland
Cronmire *see* Beauclerk
Crook *see* Noble
Crooke-Lawless : Crooke, W. R., Surgeon-Capt. in H. M. Army Med. Staff (Coldstream Guards) Times, 4 Aug., 1894
Crookshanks-Bailie Crookshanks. S. 2 May, 1780 (12079)
Cropley Crow, J. S., now at 50, Coomer Road, Fulham, phrenologist Times, d.p., 16 Feb., 1886.
Cropper *see* Thornburgh-Cropper
Crosbie : Brown, J. C. B., of Beyton, Suffolk, gent Times, 22 July, 1881
    Talbot, Rev. J. Dublin. 14 Feb., 1816
    see Talbot
    ,, Talbot-Crosbie
Crosbie-Hill · Hill, W. S. J., of Sutton, Surrey, esq. Times, d.p. 20 June, 1889
Crosby Lord, J. J., Dublin Dublin, 9 May, 1820
    see Lewis-Crosby
Crosdale Fatt, A., of the Stock Exchange. London Times d.p., 12 March. 14 March, 1883
Cross : Dos-Remedios, J. C., of 53, Wetherell Road, Hackney Common, Middlesex, D.D Times, d p., 1 Sept. 5 Sept., 1881
    see Cooper-Simpson-Cross
    ,, Innes-Cross
    ,. Legh
    ,, Shepherd-Cross
Cross-Starkey : Cross, J. 23 Sept., 1811 (1930)
    ,, Norman Crosse.
Crosse · Godsalve, J. 25 July, 1780 (12103)
    see Hamilton
    Ikin, T. B. 19 Nov., 1828 (2141)
    see Legh.
    ,, Norman-Crosse
Crossingham *see* Cressingham
Crossley *see* Dampier-Crossley
    : Kerschner, E. A. J. 24 March, 1880 (2308)
Croucher *see* Perocchy
Crow *see* Cropley
    ,, Marlowe
    ,, Paver-Crow
Crowder *see* Robert-Crowder
Crowther *see* Alwyn
    : Goodall, W. 4 Sept., 1828 (1669)
    see Wigglesworth
Crowther-Beynon : Crowther, R. W. B. 21 Nov., 1874 (6036)
    : Crowther, S. B. 18 July, 1879 (4804)

Crowther-Smith : Smith, Stanley Francis, of Shirley Southants.
    Times, 21 Sept, 1899.
Croxall see Tongue-Croxall.
Croxford see Spiers
Croxton see Ferrers.
Cruger see Peach
Crumpe see Bland.
        Moriarty, S. 23 July, 1881 (D.G. 698)
        see Moriarty
Cruse see Feake
Crutchley : Duffield, G. H. 28 Jan, 1806 (128).
Cruwys see Sharland-Cruwys.
Cuchet see Fleming.
Cuddon-Fletcher : Cuddon, B. J., of Somerton Hall, Norfolk,
    esq. Times, 9 April, 1869.
Cuddon see Reid-Cuddon.
Cueto see Ellerker
Cuff see Adams
Culley : Darling, G. 24 Feb, 1851 (704)
    see Leather-Culley.
Culling-Hanbury : Hanbury, R. junr, of Brick Lane, Spitalfields,
    and 10, Upper Grosvenor Street, Middlesex, esq, M.P.
    Times, 24 June, 1865.
Culme-Seymour · Seymour, Sir J. H. 9 May, 1842 (1268)
Cullum see Milner-Gibson-Cullum
Culpeper see Bishop-Culpeper.
Culverwell see Leeson.
Cumberbatch see Cave.
Cumberland-Jones : Jones, R. D., of St John's Coll, Cambridge
    Times, d p, 2 Feb, 1885
Cumberland, Stuart C F. : Garner, C. F., of South Crescent,
    Bedford Square, Middlesex Times. d p, 30 Nov., 1880.
Cumberlege see Ware.
Cuming see Leslie-Cuming
Cumins see Richards-Cumins
Cumming see Hovell-Thurlow-Cumming-Bruce
        „ Smith-Cumming.
        „ Valiant-Cumming
        „ Wynne
Cumming-Bruce, of Roseisle and Dunphail Cumming. Chas
    Lennox Lyon Vol IX, 2 Nov., 1874.
Cumming-Ince · Ince, E. J. Times. 28 Aug, 10 Sept, 1883
Cunliffe see Ingham-Cunliffe
        see Pickersgill Cunliffe.
        : Owen, H 23 April, 1774 (11450)
        see Rodger-Cunliffe
Cunliffe-Lister see Kay.
Cunliffe-Offley · Cunliffe, F. 26 Jan, 1830 (169).

Cunningham : Cunningham-Clapp, W. H., of 2, Wilmington Sq., Middlesex, gent. Times, d.p., 15 Feb., 1866.
    Clapp, W. H. C., of 2, Wilmington Square, Middlesex, gent. d.p., 1866
    see Fairlie-Cuningham
    ,, Miller-Cunningham
Cunninghame *see* Gun-Cunninghame.
    ,, Smith-Cunninghame
Cunyngham *see* Dick-Cunyngham
Cupit *see* Allsebrook
Curran *see* Tyrrell
Currer : Richardson, J. 18 May, 1771 (11146)
    see Roundell.
    Roundell, D. R. 27 June, 1806 (815)
Curryer, W. : Smith, W. C., Birmingham. Times, 12 Oct., 1900
Curson : Roper, H. 26 Feb., 1788 (93).
Curtis : Courtney, J. 9 July, 1814 (1390).
    see La Mert-Curtis
Curwin : Christian, J. 6 March, 1790 (137).
Curzon : Deeley, F. A., of 4, Clare Street, Dublin. Times, d.p., 30 Oct., 1896
    see Roper-Curzon.
    ,, Smyth.
Curzon-Howe : Curzon, Rt. Hon. R. W. P. (Earl Howe, Vis. and Baron Curzon). 30 July, 1821 (1580).
Cusack : Smith, W. Dublin, 12 March, 1800
Cust *see* Cockayne-Cust
    ,. Egerton-Cust
    .. Egerton.
    ,. Porcelli-Cust
Cutbush *see* West
Cutcliffe *see* Drake-Cutcliffe
Cuthbert-Kearney : Cuthbert, T., of Garretstown, co. Cork. Dublin, 31 May, 1832

D

D'Acosta de St. Laurent : D'Acosta, L. J. de R., of Darmstadt, Hesse, Germany, now in London. Major, late Capt. Times, d.p., 21 Jan., 1873

D'Acosta de St Laurent   D'Acosta, F J., student at Darmstadt,
        Germany   Times, d p., 21 Jan., 1873.
Da Costo-Lindo   Lindo, M.   14 July, 1812 (1365)
Dacre-Assey : Dacre, C. W   16 June, 1836 (1158)
d'Ade see Hamlin-Nott
Dades   Overton   Overton, M, of Swindon, Glos. (widow).
        Times, d p., 3 May, 1894
Da Esqeirra   Sequerra, S.   Times, 6 Oct 1866
D'Aeth see Hughes D'Aeth
Dalberg-Acton · Acton, Sir F. R E.   11 Jan, 1834 (102)
Dalby   Blunt, R.   1 March, 1853 (642)
Dale : Stennett, J D.   16 Feb., 1876 (1788)
        Albert Alfred Michell   Goodchild, Albert, of 74, Baker
                Street, Portman Square   Times, 16 May, 1872.
Dale-Roberts : Roberts, A R., of Leamington, Warwick, physician
        and sugeon   Times, d p., 30 Sept., 1895
Dalglish-Bellasis   Bellasis, W. D.   16 May, 1896 (3514)
Dalison   Hammond, M D D.   10 March, 1819 (716).
Dallas-Yorke   Dallas, T Y.   3 July, 1855 (2789)
Dalrymple see Dalrymple-Horn-Elphinstone.
        „ Hamilton-Dalrymple
        „ Hay.
Dalrymple-Horn-Elphinstone · Dalrymple-Horn, Sir Robert Bt
        Lyon Vol. III, 31 March, 1828
Dalton-Fitzgerald : Fitzgerald, Sir G R.   4 April, 1867 (2184).
                Fitzgerald, Sir J. G   31 May, 1861 (2352)
Dalton : Grant, R. F.   12 Sept., 1826 (2213)
        N C   Lillycropp, N, of 17, Devonshire Road, Balham,
                Surrey   Times, d p., 17 Sept, 1879
        see Norcliffe.
        „ Portman-Dalton.
        Edw. . Vanderpant, Edw M. D., of Kennington, Surrey,
                and 70, Finsbury Pavement, EC, broker. Times,
                27 March, 1895.
        : Wade   1879 (5274)
Dalway . Webb, N.   Dublin, 27 June, 1795.
Daly : Blake, J A (a minor aged 2).   Dublin, 5 April, 1837
Daman : Dammann, J. F. K., formerly of Edgbaston, but now of
                Broadhurst Gardens, Hampstead, Middlesex,
                gent.   Times, d p., 11 Aug, 1892
        : Dammann, H E, of 22, Harborne Road, Edgbaston,
                Warwick, gent   Times, d p, 11 Aug., 1892.
        . Dammann, M., of 22, Harborne Road, Edgbaston,
                Warwick, widow   Times, d.p, 11 Aug, 1892
        : Dammann, K A, of 22, Harborne Road, Edgbaston,
                Warwick, gent   Times, d p, 11 Aug, 1892.

Dambrill-Davies : Davies, W. R. of Sandbach, Chester, and of Manchester, M.R.C.S. Times, 5 Oct., 1881
Damer see Dawson-Damer
Dammann see Daman
Dampier see Smith-Dampier.
Dampier-Child : Child, R., of Upper Clatford Rectory, Hants, esq Times, d.p., 25 Nov., 1871
Dampier Crossley Dampier, A. C. 5 Nov. 1864 (5605)
Danby Affleck, G 10 Nov., 1879 (6493)
    Mankiewicz, S., at present residing at 2, Albemarle St., Middlesex; partner in the firm of Messrs Gisborne & Co., trading at Calcutta as merchants Times, 10 Oct., 1865
Danby Palmer Palmer, W., of Southtown Suffolk, gent Times, 13 May, 1887
Dance see Holland
Dandov Lopez, H., of Oran, Algeria, landowner Times, d.p., 3 Sept, 1886
    Lopez, V. E., of Algeria merchant. Times, d.p., 30 Jan., 1883
Dangerfield Bubb, G. of The Mount, Lightcliffe Road, Brighouse, York Times, 2 March, 1898
D'Anglebermes see Bertrand
Daniel Hardie, Emily C., of 27, Queensberry Place, S Kensington, spinster Times, d.p., 12 Dec., 1891
    see Tyssen-Daniel-Amhurst
    „ Tyssen-Amhurst
    „ Tyssen Daniel Amhurst
Daniel-Tyssen Daniel, W. G. 14 March, 1814 (650).
    see Tyssen-Amhurst
Daniell see Johnson-Daniell.
Daniell-Bainbridge Daniell, R. P. 2 July 1878 (3969).
Daniels see Harrison.
Danks : Lee, F. T. of Quinton, Halesowen, Worcestershire Times, d.p., 14 Jan., 1893
Dansey Browning Browning, G., of 16, Royal Terr., Weymouth, Dorset, gent Times, d.p., 6 May, 1892
Danson Hayward, T. 17 Nov., 1798 (1083)
    see Martinez-Danson
Danvers : Butler, Hon. A. R. 13 Sept., 1796 (881)
    Davies, E., of 36, Shenstone Street, Edge Hill, Liverpool, plumber Times, d.p., 3 Dec, 1879
Danvers Wilson Wilson, J., of Reighton, Yorks, gent. Times, 25 Nov, 1879
Darby see Miller
    „ St Quintin.

Darby-Coventry : Darby, T. 27 April, 1798 (368)
    see Coventry.
Darby-Griffith : Darby, M. C. 31 Oct., 1801 (1304)
D'Arcy see Mervyn-D'Arcy-Irvine
D'Arcy-Irvine : D'Arcy, W., of Castle Irvine, Fermanagh, and of Dover, Kent, esq. Times. d.p., 28 Jan., 1881
Dare see Grafton-Dare
  „ Hall-Dare
  „ Sheehan-Dare
Darell : Blount 6 March, 1882 (1131)
    see Trelawney
Darell-Brown : Brown, Rev. L. E., of Welland Vicarge, Worcester. Times, d.p., 22 July, 1873
Darell-Rokewode : Darell, R. 9 May, 1872 (2361)
D'Arenberg Abeltshauser, L. J., of 4, Cambridge Gardens Notting Hill. Times, 21 March, 1871
Dark see Bayley
Darley see Warren-Darley
       : Wilks, H. 9 Jan., 1808 (38)
       : Wilkes, H. 30 Sept., 1809 (1557)
Darling see Bagshaw
  „ Culley
Darling-Barker : Darling, J. 31 May, 1860 (2400)
Darlington see Kent.
Darnbacher see Darner
Darner : Darnbacher, Otto Simon, of Highfield Place, Bradford. Times, 17 Oct., 1899
Darning : Nuttall, R. 22 June, 1804 (796).
Darnley Harryson, R. 23 Sept., 1797 (907)
       : Poppy, T. and D. R. Times, 18 Aug., 1868
       : Poppy, D. R., M.A., Ph.D., of the University of Bostock, Mecklenburg, of Lincoln's Inn, London, barrister-at-law, and of the University of London. Times, 18 Aug., 1868
Darry see Cleugh.
Darwin : Rhodes, F. 21 Feb., 1850 (496)
Dashwood see Peyton
D'Aubyn see Hirsch D'Aubyn
D'Audeberts see Burdon
Dauntesey : Buck, J. 13 Oct., 1863 (5021)
         : Hull, R. 18 July, 1878 (4317)
D'avenant see Corbet
Davenport see Bromley-Davenport
  „ Hinckes
  : Humphreys, Sir S. P. 7 May, 1838 (1047)
  see Talbot

Davenport-Bromley : Davenport, W 14 Sept , 1822 (1500)
    Bromley-Davenport.
Davenport-Handley Davenport, J W H   25 March, 1881 (1435).
Davenport Hill Hill, R. and F M , of 9, Regent's Park Road, Middlesex Times, 19 March. 1877
Davidson *see* Strachan-Davidson
Davidson-Houston : Davidson, Rev B C , M A , Vicar of St John, Sandymount, Dublin Times, d.p , 22 Oct., 1879
Davie *see* Ferguson-Davie
Davie-Basset : Davie, J 25 Feb , 1803 (251).
Davies *see* Alwyn
    Banks, J 5 April, 1858 (1742).
    see Birt-Davies
    ,, Browne-Davies
    ,, Colley Davies.
    ,, Dambrill-Davies
    ,, Danvers
    E R John Wyatt Davies, E R , of 23, Finsbury Square, Middlesex Times, 4 Aug., 1883
    see Fielding-Davies
    ,, Fox-Davies
    ,, Hamblet
    ,, Hardwicke
    ,, Houghton-Davies
    ,, Hughes
    J Butler : Davies, J , of Gravels Bank, Worthen, Salop, gent Times, 10 Dec 1877
    see Kevill-Davies
    ,, Knight.
    ,, Macgregor-Davies
    Powel. J 2 Feb , 1796 (127)
    see Prescott-Davies
    ,, Price-Davies
    ,, Rees
    ,, Touchet
    : Wood, J 9th Geo III , 1769
Davies-Berrington Davies, J. 11 June, 1798 (573)
Davies-Browne Browne, E. D., of Court y Gollen, Brecon, and St John's Wood, Middlesex. Times, d.p., 2 Jan., 1891
Davies-Colley : Davies, T. Whll., 25 Aug., 1865 (D.G. 1085)
        : Davies, T. C., of 8, Marsden Street, Manchester, solicitor Times, 30 Nov., 1865
Davies-Evans . Davies, H 20 Feb., 1844 (579)
Davies-Glasspoole : Davies, Rev. R , now residing at Great Malvern Worcester. Times. d p , 9 April. 1870

Davies-Gould · Davies. F., of 164. Tulse Hill, Surrey. gent
	Times, d p., 24 April and 5 May, 1873
Davies-Jenkins . Davies, J., of Pen-y-green, Montgomerys., Capt.
	R A Times, 22 April, 1896.
Davies-Lloyd   Davies, A L   2 Feb., 1848 (370)
Davies Parnall   Davies, W., of Bishopgate Street, Lond. assistant
	clothier. Times, d p., 26 Feb., 1875
D Avigdor-Goldsmid   D'Avigdor. O E   16 May, 1896 (3065)
Davis see Birt Davis
	,, Caley.
	,, Churchill
	Charles Solomon · Davis, Solmon, of High St., Borough
		Times, d.p., 1 July, 1890.
	Herbert Lewis Davis. David, of 18. Greek Street Soho
		Times, 17 July, 1883.
	, see Millett-Davis
		Hart-Davis
	,, Tresham.
Davis-Goff   Davis, S., of Horetown, co. Wexford.   D. Castle. 23
	April, 1845 (D G. 262, 269 and 285)
Davis-Protheroe   Protheroe, jun. E   28 Jan., 1845 (248)
Davis-Rogers   Davis, A. of 140. Edgware Road, and 6, Lowndes
	Terrace, Knightsbridge, Middlesex Times. d p., 14 Dec.,
	1878, and 31 Jan., 1879
Davis-Winstone   Davis. W. E., Bromsgrove. Worc   Times 15
	Oct., 1898
Davison see Bland
	Bourman, S. M., A E. C., S. F. and M. L. Times
		12 Aug., 1882
	see Cattermole-Davison
	: Eden, M J. 31 Oct., 1812 (2167)
	see Tyzack.
	, Wood-Davison.
Davy · Barlee, L E 12 March, 1852 (769).
Dawber-Enderly . Dawber, Thomas Sidney of Boston, Lincoln-
	shire. Times, 29 March, 1898.
Dawes   Willock. C. W.   Whll, 21 April, 1870 (D G 725)
	· Willock, C W 21 April, 1870 (2541)
Dawkins see Colyear-Dawkins.
Dawkins-Pennant   Dawkins G H   2 April. 1808 (452)
		Dawkins, G H 2 April, 1808 (452)
Dawnay see Langley.
Daws see Clark.
Dawson, Oswald · Dawson, Ernest Oswald, of Caledonian Road,
	Leeds, gent. Times, 25 April, 1893
	see D'Ossone.

Dawson : Heywood, Gladys, R. I, of Caledonian Road, Leeds.
 Times, 25 April, 1893
　　see Kennett-Dawson
　　,, Lee-Dawson
　　· Mitchell, H and A, both of 14, St. James' Road,
　　　Liverpool Times, d.p, 4 Jan, 1876
　　Perfect, W. M. 20 Jan., 1879 (797)
　　W C. P Pullbrook, W C, of Ventnor Villa, Saxon
　　　Rd, Selhurst, Surrey Times, d p, 13 Jan, 1881.
　　see Squirl-Dawson
　　,, Tetlow
　　,, Westropp-Dawson
Dawson, A Clark · Clark, A, of Shu-e-crow House, Keswick,
　　spinster Times, d p, 19 Jan, 1876
Dawson-Damer Dawson, G L 14 March, 1829 (574)
Dawson Duffield · Duffield, R. D D 29 Sept., 1865 (4787)
Dawson Kilburn see Kilburn.
Dawson-Lambton Dawson, J 6 Sept, 1814 (1872)
Dawson-Margrave Dawson, W 3 Aug., 1826 (2087)
Dawson-Scott · Dawson, R N, of Fareham, Southampton, esq.,
　　Major R E Times, d p, 6 Sept, 1872.
Dawson-Smith Smith, Rev C. C, of West End, New Brampton,
　　Derbyshire 12 Oct, 1886
Dawson-Thomas Dawson, J B 6 July, 1868 (4453)
　　　　　　Dawson, J B Whll, 6 July, 1868 (D G 927)
Day see Branton-Day.
　　Coathupe, C. D, on dissolution of her marriage with Capt
　　　H. B Coathupe Times, 23 Sept, 1875
　　see Cripps-Day
　　,, Fitzgerald-Day
　　,, Daye
　　,, Galley-Day-Jackson
　　,, Gilbert-Day
　　,, Kendall
　　,, Lewis
　　,, Morton-Day
　　,, Pentelow
　　,, Sprake-Day
Day Hermitage · Day, E, Vicar of Abbey Cwmhir, Radnor
　　Times, 7 June, 1893
Day-Jackson · Day, F 31 July, 1797 (733)
　　　　　　Day, J 31 July, 1797 (733)
Daye · Day, R P, of 37, St. Paul's Road, Canonbury, Middlesex,
　　and of War Office, gent Times, d p, 23 April, 1872.
Dayrolles Thomasset, F. L 23 July, 1825 (1316)
Dayrolles-Blakeney see Eveleigh-De Moleyns
Dazley-Smith Dazley, H S 12 Nov, 1845 (5454)
Deadman see Dedman

Deakin *see* Newton-Deakin
De Almeda, E. : Emanuel, H., of 11, Hyde Park Gardens,, Midx.,
    gent Times, d p., 9 March, 1875
De Almeida Portugal *see* Edye.
Dealtry *see* Procter.
De Ameland : Murray, A. 15 Oct., 1806 (1364)
Dean Brietzke, R. B 5 May, 1801 (481).
    Clapcott, W C 6 July, 1855 (2699)
    see Cooper-Dean
        Cripps-Dean, J., compositor, of 17, Wilmot St., Brunswick
            Square, Middlesex Times, 9 Feb., 1872.
        Goodyear, L. H., of Scawsby Hall, Halifax, Yorks, gent
            Times, d.p., 10 April, 1874.
Deane *see* Digby
Deanesly Deane, Sly S., of Wincanton, Somerset, wine
    merchant Times, 17 December, 1881
Deans-Brown : Brown, J., of The Cottage, Weyhill, Hants,
    brewers' manager Times, d p., 29 April, 1892.
Deans-Campbell, of Culraith Deans John Lyon, Vol III., 27
    Feb., 1835.
Deans-Whitley-Dundas Deans, J 20 April, 1808 (584).
Dearden *see* Griffith-Dearden.
Dearling *see* Penfold
Deas-Thomson, of Norton Thomson, John Lyon, Vol II., 20
    Dec., 1810
Death *see* Morton-Day
    ,, Syrett.
De Balinhard *see* Bahnhard
De Bathe Bath, J. M. 26 March, 1793 (242).
De Beauchamp De Beauchamp, Strickland G., of Warwick
        Lodge, Hatcham, Surrey, gent Times, d p.,
        4 Oct 1869
    see Beard De Beauchamp
De Beauvoir *see* Benyon De Beauvoir.
    Browne, J. E. 14 Oct., 1826 (2465)
De Beer Baruchson, Arnold de Beer, of 29, Elm Park Gardens,
    Middlesex, esq., barrister-at-law d.p., 30 Nov., 1882.
De Bermere Smart, H. J. de B., Major in H M Worces Reg.
    Times, d.p., 21 Dec., 1886
De Berry : Berry, Lieut.-Col and Brevet-Col G. F., of Birken-
    head Times, d p., 22 Dec., 1878, 19 Feb., 1879
De Blutstein *see* Paget.
De Botwor *see* Butterworth-De Botwor.
De Burgh Burgh, F 21 Dec., 1790 (761).
        Burgh, Rt Hon U Lord Baron Downes, Thos., Rev.
            W., John, and Rev Wm Office of Arms, Dublin
            Castle, 6 March, 1848 (D G 355 and 367).

De Burgh : Bourke, J. F.   15 June, 1811 (1086)
: Lill, J. G   11 Feb., 1800 (128)
De Burgh-Canning : de Burgh, H.   9 July, 1862 (3534).
De Burgh-Lawson   Lawson, H., of Gatherley Castle. Yorks, esq.
    Times, 23 Jan., 1877
De Buriatte *see* Isaac de Buriatte
De Capell-Brooke : Supple, R. B.   28 Nov., 1797 (1125).
De Cardonnel : Dinevor, Baroness C.   9 June, 1787 (274)
    see Rice.
    . Rice, Hon. G. T.   4 May, 1793 (356).
De Carrara-Rivers   Carrara, A., of Gibraltar.   Times, Oct., 31, 1898
De Carteret *see* Mallet de Carteret.
De Carteret-Bisson, Fredk. Shirley Dumaresq   de Carteret-Bisson, Frederick Shirley, of 52, Sutherland Gardens, St Peter's Park, W., Middlesex, a Captain in the First Reg. of Royal Jersey Light Infantry   Fredk. Shirley de Carteret-Bisson jun.   Times, 19 Aug., 1881
Decie *see* Prescott-Decie.
De Cerjat : Cerjat, H. S., Rector of Horsley, Surrey, and C. T. W. G. Cerjat, Commdr R.N., of Ripley House, Surrey   Times, 20 Aug., 1867.
De Courcelles : Courcelle, or Courcelles, J. H., of 10. Fellowes Place, Devonport, formerly of Worcester Coll., Oxon. and Crowan, Cornwall   Times, d.p., 19 Jan., 1877.
De Courcy-Benwell   Benwell, Rev. H. F., of Shepherd's Bush, Middlesex   Times, d.p., 11 Jan., 1888.
De Courcy Helbert : de Courcy Helbert Helbert, F., Capt. Naval and Mil. Club, Piccadilly.   Times, d.p., 26 Feb., 1894
De Courcy Perry   Perry, G. R., of the Brit. Consulate, Antwerp. Belgium, H. Brit. Maj. Consul-Gen for Belgium   Times, d.p., 9 Dec., 1890
De David Teixeira *see* Teixeira
Dedman : Deadman, J. J., R. Deadman and N. Deadman, all of 18, Polygon, Clapham, Surrey   Times, 5 March, 1864
Deeley *see* Calthorpe-Mallaby
     „   Curzon.
     „   Mallaby.
Deere : Thomas, R.   8th Geo III., 1768
Deering : Gandy, J. P.   19 June, 1827 (1428)
De Faubert Maunder : Maunder, J. F., of West Kensington. London.   Times, d.p., 4 Dec., 1896
De Freville   Greene, E. H.   15 July, 1885 (3474)
    see Greene de Freville.
     „   Greene.
Degacher : Hitchcock W. H., of Horsham, esq., H. J., Major 24th Infry., W., Capt. same Reg., and W. F., at Amelia Court House, Va., U.S.A.   Times, d.p., 18 Feb., 1874

De Gallimare : De Schmitt, J A and E M, daughters of Baron Alex de Schmitt, of the Old Guard, Legion of Honour, etc. Times, 20 April, 1874
De Garston Garstin, N. of St Helier, Jersey, D D d p , 1 July, 1864
De Grailly De Grailly Evans, G. of 17, Salisbury Street, Strand. Times, 24 Dec , 1875
De Grave Jones, J W , of Letherhead, Surrey, and of H M Customs, London, to assume name of his maternal ancestors. Times. d.p., 17 Jan , 1888.
De Grenier-Fonblanque · Fonblanque, J 14 May, 1828 (949)
Dehane-Small · Small, F W D , Brompton Sq Times, 2 Feb 1900
De Havilland Haviland, R J. L , of Cambridge Square, Hyde Park, London, and of Winstone, Glos., esq., M.A Cantab. Times, d p , 4 July, 1884
De Heriz : Smith, J. C (originally De Heriz, but family assumed name of Smith for many generations) Office of Arms, 3 Oct , 1850 (D G 765 and 773).
   see Smith de Heriz
De Hochepied : Porter, G. 6 May, 1819 (842)
De Hochepied-Larpent : Larpent, G G.
          Larpent, J J 14 June, 1819 (1045)
De Hoghton Hoghton, Sir H 6 Aug , 1862 (3995 and 4039)
De Horsey · Kilderbee, S H. 20 April, 1832 (916)
De Hyde Wytt : White, W H Hyde, Br. Subj., La Tourelle, Alfortville, Seine, France Times, 8 June, 1891
Deighton *see* Braysher
De Kierzkowski-Steuart de Kierzkowski, C. F. 10 April, 1878 (2692)
De Knevett *see* Knevett
De Krauchy Russell, J. G , of Villa Neri, Monaco, gent Times, d p , 12 Jan. 1895
De la Beche Beach, J H. 23 Oct , 1790 (634)
        Beach. T. 23 Oct , 1790 (634)
De la Bere *see* Baghot de la Bere
De la Bère : Driver, C. R., Capt. and Staff Officer of Pensioners,
        · Driver, H. T., of War Office. d p , 16 Sept., 1864
De Labilliere Labilliere, F. P , of Harrow-on-the-Hill, to resume ancestral name Times, 5 April, 1888
De Lacy . Lacy, Rev T., Archd. of Meath Betham's List
Delacherois *see* Crommelin.
De la Cour *see* Smith de la Cour
     ,, Bizouard de la Courtine de Montille
De la Fontaine *see* Mottet
Delahay Tallmadge. W H 3 Nov , 1898 (380) 1899

De la Hey Hayes, Rev G , late of Icklesham, Sussex, but now of Tewkesbury, Glos., M A., to resume family surname   Times, d.p , 31 Dec , 1883
    see Oldridge de la Hey
Delamaine *see* Delmaine.
De Lancy Smith, W. G., of Park Farm, nr Dorking, Surrey. organist. Times, 19 Dec., 1868
Delando-Osborne Delando, O 13 April, 1833 (75c)
Delap *see* Dunlop
De la Pole Pole, Sir J. W 13 Oct , 1789 (649)
    see Reeve de la Pole
De Lasaux *see* Ayerst
Delaune *see* Faunce-Delaune
De Legh : Rickard, H., of Plympton St Mary, Devon, retired Staff Surg R N. Times, d.p , 18 Oct , 1876
De Liefde-Temple : De Liefde, J , of 41, Camden Rd., Middlesex M.D., M R.C.S Times, d.p , 25 April, 1872
Delisser *see* Lymburner
Delmaine, A Dowling, Alfred Richard Bayly, at present staying at 38, Cannon Place, Brighton (signed Delamaine) Times. 2 Aug., 1872.
Delmar *see* Tompson-Delmar
Delmar Williamson : Williamson, F of 87, Ladbroke Road, Notting Hill, gent Times, d p , 14 April, 1894.
Delmé-Rafcliffe : Delmé, E. H. 14 Aug , 1802 (841)
Deloraine-Roquette-Palmer-Palmer : Palmer, A. T , of 5, Westbourne Terr., Middlesex, esq Times, d p , 23 Oct . 1884
Del Strother Strother, E , of Stuttgart, Germany. formerly of Yorks, Eng Times, 21 Dec , 1880
Delves Broughton, Sir T. 7th Geo III., 1767
De Mattos Lumbazo, A 13 Nov., 1790 (682)
De Moleyns Mullins, T T. A., Lord Baron Ventry (for him and the descendants of his grandfather the 1st Baron Ventry) Dublin, 16 Feb . 1841
De Moleyns-Eveleigh *see* Dayrolles-Blakeney
De Montille *see* Bizouard de la Courtine de Montille
De Montmorency Morres, H F 5 Aug., 1815 (1830)
    Morres, R H 5 Aug , 1815 (1830)
    Morres, Sir W. R. 5 Aug., 1815 (1830)
    Mountmorres, Lord Visct and Bart , Rt. Hon Sir F. H. 5 Aug , 1815 (1830)
    Pratt, Harvey Dublin, 31 Aug. 1831
De Morlaincourt *see* Hales
Dempster *see* Hawkins Dempster
    „ Soper-Dempster
De Moro Phillips, M Times, 21 Oct , 1895
De Moulin *see* Brown

Denham-Cookes : Cookes, G 12 June, 1891 (3299)
Denis-Tottenham : Denis, W. Dublin, 20 Aug., 1835.
Denison : Beckett, E. 29 July, 1816 (1725)
    see Beckett.
        Conyngham, A D (Lord) 4 Sept , 1849 (2809)
        Wilkinson, J. 16 April, 1785 (213)
De Nittis see Hallam de Nittis
Denman see Aitchison Denman
Denne : Hollingbery, D 16 Oct , 1822 (1745).
Denness see Berrie.
Denny see Cooke.
Denroche Smith : Smith, T., of the Bengal Civ. Service Times. 6 Dec., 1887.
Dent see Bernard Dent
  „ Dent-Dowson.
    Hedley, W. D 12 Sept., 1831 (1900)
  see Hinrich-Dent.
  J. Bernard O'Brien, J., of 189, Blackfriars Road, London. late 97th Reg. Times, 24 Dec., 1887
  . Rippon, R. E. 14 Oct , 1850 (2775).
  Tricket, J. 11 Sept , 1834 (1696).
Dent-Dowson : Dent, John Henry, Newlands, Wolsingham, Dur Times, 12 Dec , 1898
Dent-Price : Price, R. H 5 March, 1885 (2214).
Denton see Ladbroke
    „ Parker
De Poix see Tyrel de Poix
De Pons see Caulfield-de-Pons
De Portugal see Edye
Deraay see Byron
De Rodes : Gossip, W. H. 4 April, 1844 (1198).
De Ros see Fitzgerald-de Ros.
De Rustafjaell : Fawcus-Smith, R., of 127, Queen's Gate, London. Times. 9 Oct . 1894
Dervicke-Jones : Jones, A. D. Chiswick, Midx. Times, 12 June. 1900
De Salis see Fane.
Despard : Wright, W, of Kellaghy Castle, co Tipperary Dublin, 4 June, 1838
De St. Laurent see D'Acosta de St Laurent
Des Champs see Chamier.
De Schmitt see De Gallimare.
De Sidenham : Sydenham, G 14 Sept., 1841 (2298)
Desmond see Egan-Desmond
De Stafford : O'Brien, H de Stafford, of Blatherwycke Park co. Northampton Times, d.p., 8 Nov . 1896.
D'Este : Eastes, G J., late of Keppel Street, Russell Square, now of Bradford. Times, 17 Nov, 1865.

D'Esté East East, H. H E., of Bourton House, Moreton-in-the-Marsh, Glos. Times, 2 Nov., 1895
D'Esterre *see* Madden-D'Esterre
De St Romaine : Romaine, E. Times, d.p., 12 May, 1891
De Tavora Fernandez : Fernandez, A. L., of Army and Navy Club, Pall Mall, and of Wakefield, esq Times, d.p, 17 Jan., 1889.
De Trafford : Trafford, Sir T. J. 8 Oct., 1841 (2471).
    Trafford, W. W., of Chaddesley Corbett, Worces., esq., ret. Major. Times, d.p, 20 Dec., 1882
De Uphaugh : Turbutt, R. D. 5 May, 1888 (2828)
De Vere, Aubrey Weare, R P., of Barmyside and Paille Castle, co Ayr, esq Times, 19 March, 1877.
  · Hunt, Sir A. de Vere, Bart. Dublin, 3 Feb , 1832
  O'Fflahertie, A. H. B Times, d.p., 2 March, 1864
Deverell : Pedley, R. 25 June, 1793 (532).
De Vesian *see* Ellis de Vesian.
Deville-O'Keeffe : Deville, N. G. 30 May, 1797 (484)
Dew *see* Aulton
 ,, Smith-Dew.
Dew-Smith . Dew, A G WII , 21 July, 1870 (D.G. 1013).
D'Ewes *see* Granville
Dewes *see* Granville
De Wesselow *see* Simpkinson De Wesselow
De Wilton, Gerald : Wilkins, J., M D., Surg. Major 29th Madras Native Iny, of Waterloo Street, Brighton. Times. d p . 18 Sept , 1876
De Windt Jennyns, J C. 26 Feb , 1851 (602)
De Winton : Wilkins, C. 6 July, 1839 (1363).
De Witt Witt, E. E., of 1, King's Bench Walk, Temple. and of Cambridgeshire. Times, d p , 5 March, 1888
De Wynter Baker, C. J , late of Southampton and of Cheltenham, Glos., esq Times, d.p , 14 Dec., 1874
De Yarburgh *see* Bateson-de Yarburgh
D'Eye *see* Rust.
D'Eyncourt *see* Tennyson-D'Eyncourt
Dicas *see* Leacroft.
Dicconson Clifton, E. 11 Feb., 1861 (792)
   see Clifton-Dicconson
    Eccleston, C. 8 May, 1810 (675)
    Eccleston, Mary 19 March, 1834 (570).
   see Gerard-Dicconson
   ,, Scarisbrick
Dick Hume, Q. D 23 Nov , 1892 (7002).
  Hume. W. W. F. 17 June, 1864 (2317).
Dick-Cunyngham : Dick, Sir R K 8 & 9 Vict. c 23 (R) Index to pub and priv Statutes, p. 503.

Dick-Melbourne   Dick, Charles Sydney, of Rockhampton, Queensland, solicitor, at present residing in London, Middlesex. Times, d p., 8 March, 1870.
Dickant : Dickhant, Marie M D. O., of West Brighton, Sussex, spinster. Times, d.p., 26 Jan, 1893
Dicken *see* Temple.
Dickens-Scarse   Dickins, C   24 March, 1792 (189).
Dicker *see* Cole
Dickerdine *see* Fellowe
Dickey Faulkner : Dickey, A, late of Abingdon Berks, now of 9, Fenchurch Street, London, solicitor. Times, d.p., 5 Oct, 1877.
Dickhant *see* Dickant.
Dickin *see* Lloyd-Dickin
Dickinson *see* Ehret Dickinson.
          „   Robert-Crowder
          „   Walrond.
Dickinson Stanley-Dodgson   Dickinson. S. D., of Whitehaven, Cumberland, land agent. Times, 16 July, 1886.
Dickson   Dickson-Thorold, F. (born Dickson), to resume original name. Times, d.p., 15 Dec., 1893
          see Thorold.
Dickson-Poynder   Dickson, E   21 March, 1881 (1791)
                  Poynder, Sir J. P   12 Jan, 1888 (551).
Dickson-Thorold   Thorold, F T. (born "Dickson") Times, d.p., 1 July, 1892.
Digby   Boycott, E. G. D., late Capt. 14th Hussars, now of 90. Piccadilly, Middlesex Times, 31 Dec, 1891
        Deane, J   Dublin, 24 July 1809
        see Wingfield-Digby.
Digby-Wingfield   Wingfield. G. D. 2 July, 1856 (2377)
Dight *see* Butler.
Dignum Mitchell : Dignum, F B, of 43, Arundel Gdns. Notting Hill, Middlesex Times, d p., 17 Aug., 1876.
Dilke *see* Fetherston.
     „   Fetherston-Dilke
Dillon *see* FitzGibbon
      „   Tennent.
Dillon-Trant   Trant, H   5 March, 1816 (505).
Dillon-Trenchard   Dillon, H L. S   10 Nov, 1846 (3949)
                  . Dillon, W T   15 June, 1841 (1536)
Dillwyn-Venables-Llewelyn   Dillwyn-Llewelyn, C I.   27 June, 1893 (3842)
Dimond *see* Churchward
Dineley   Goodere, Sir J D   29 June, 1776 (11678)
Dinevor *see* de Cardonnel.
Dinkelspiel *see* Dunk.

Dinsdale *see* Moses-Dinsdale
    ,, Trotter-Dinsdale.
Diprose *see* Birchill
Dirom *see* Pasley-Dirom
Disney *see* Cathrow-Disney
    ,, Ffytche.
Dixon · Brown, D. 25 July, 1825 (1316)
    see Cranmer
    ,, Jameson-Dixon
Dixon Beavan : Dixon, A. B., of Glascwm, Radnor, esq Times, d.p., 5 Jan , 1880.
Dixon-Coull · Dixon, R. 31 July, 1875 (3866).
Dixon-Brown : Brown, Rev D., of Northank Hall, N'berland Times, 13 June, 1882
Dixon Johnson Johnson, C. F , of Oakwood Croft, York, esq Times, d.p , 28 Dec , 1893
    : Johnson, C. G., of Oakwood Croft, York, and Aykley Heads, Durham, esq Times, d p , 21 Dec , 1893
    : Johnson, Chas W., of Oakwood Croft, York, esq Times, d.p., 28 Dec , 1893.
Dixon-Nuttall Dixon, F 13 June, 1860 (2263)
Dixon-Stewart, J. Fletcher · Dixon, J (Rev), of Sutton, Cambridge. Times, d.p , 8 Dec , 1879
Dixwell *see* Oxenden-Dixwell
Dobie-Wilson : Dobie, W 5 Sept , 1822 (1539)
Dobinson *see* Logan
Dod · Cookson, J Y 8 Dec., 1834 (2229)
    see Wolley-Dod.
Dodd-Thomas : Thomas, F , of Chester, med stud Times, 27 Sept., 1886
Dodds-Philipson Philipson, R H 28 Aug., 1883 (4358)
Dodgson *see* Dickinson Stanley-Dodgson
Dodington *see* Marriott-Doddington
Dodsworth : Smith, Sir Chas. 6 March, 1846 (863)
    : Smith, Sir E 20 June, 1821 (1350).
Doel *see* Webb
Doherty *see* Canning Doherty
Doherty-Holwell Doherty, M , Lieut 2nd Batt Worc Reg Times, 24 Sept , 1881
Doherty-Waterhouse Doherty, D. W 9 July, 1872 (3104)
Dolben *see* Mackworth-Dolben
Dolland : Huggins, G. 22 June, 1852 (1753)
Domvile · Barrington, Rev. B , vicar of St Anne's Dublin. Ulster's Office, 1769
    · Pocklington, C. Dublin, 11 Oct , 1814
Donald *see* Harvey.

Donaldson Matthews, C. G. 24 Sep , 1879 (D.G. 773).
Donaldson-Hudson Donaldson, C. 10 Feb , 1862 (720).
Donaldson-Selby Donaldson, J S 3 May, 1839 (951).
Donkin *see* Palmer Donkin
Donnithorpe *see* Harris
Donston Huthwaite, Geo W., 14 Sept , 1784 (D G 4502)
Doolan *see* Cope
Doorman Cammeyer, C. 15 May, 1813 (919).
Doo-Rawlings Doo, H , of Nassau Street and Charles Street, Middlesex Hospital, Middlesex, manufacturer of mineral waters Times. d p , 28 Sept , 1863.
Dopping-Hepenstal Dopping. R A 24 June, 5 July, 1859 (D G 1241 and 1261)
Dorling . Helms, G , of Walton-le-Soken. Essex, spinster Times. d p., 3 March. 1874.
Dormer *see* Upton-Cottrell-Dormer
Dorrien-Magens Dorrien, M 30 Sept , 1794 (985).
Dorrien *see* Smith-Dorrien-Smith
 ,, Smith-Dorrien
Dosell-Smith Smith, Agnes of Paddington Times, 22 Nov . 1898.
D'Ossone Dawson, C., of Brixton, formerly of Little Britton, Yorks, gent Times, d p , 15 Jan., 1877
Dos-Remedios *see* Cross
Dougall *see* Heriot-Maitland-Dougall
Dougal *see* Roney-Dougal
Doughty . Tichborne, E 7 June, 1826 (1403).
Doughty-Tichborne Tichborne, Sir J. F 26 April, 1853 (1264).
Douglas *see* Akers Douglas
 Barnes, W M A , of Hurstpierpoint. Sussex Times, d p., 6 Dec , 1877
 see Edmeston
 . Gilbert-Douglas
 . Home Douglas
 ,. Houstan-Douglas
 (of Baads) *see* Houston-Douglas
 see Houstoun-Douglas.
 ., Irvine.
 ,. Keith-Douglas
 Mackenzie, Sir K 31 Oct., 1831 (2279)
 see Monteath-Douglas.
 ., Scott-Douglas.
 ,, Stoddart-Douglas
 Snodgrass, J. D., Capt R.A Times. d p , 28 July. 1883
Douglas - Campbell - Douglas. of Douglas Support Douglas-Campbell, Sholto. Lyon Vol VIII , 20 Jan . 1871

Douglas-Compton · Compton, C. (com. called Earl Compton) 3 Feb., 1831 (244)
Douglas-Crawford : Crawford, Douglas D , of Arundel Avenue, Liverpool Times, 3 July, 1899
Douglas-Gresley Douglas, R. A 17 Dec , 1829 (461)
Douglas-Hamilton : Hamilton, O., Major-General, of Blackham, Sussex Times, 23 Nov., 1875.
: Hamilton, H. A., of Manor House, Barkham, Sussex Times, 26 Oct., 1875
· Hamilton, F. R V , eldest son of F. Douglas-Hamilton, H M. Minister at Quito. Times, 5 July, 1876
: Hamilton, F , H.M. Minister at Quito, Ecuador Times, 20 March, 1876.
Douglas-Pennant Douglas, E. G. 14 Jan., 1841 (138).
Douglas-Scott-Montagu Montagu-Douglas-Scott, H J. (Baron Montagu) 26 May, 1886 (3679).
Douglas Starey Starey, E , of Eastbourne Times, d p , 22 April, 1896
Douglas-Willan · Douglas, J. K 21 Jan , 1829 (130).
Douglass Blacker, St John T. 21 June, 1880 (D G 641).
Douse *see* Le Marchant
Doust, W. H. L Dust, W. H. L , of 23, Mervan Road, Brixton. Times, 21 Oct , 1897.
Dove : Jones, T. D 25 June, 1841 (1754)
Dove-Haly Haly-Dove, J A , of 50, Tregunter Road, S. Kensington, esq., Major 5th Rifles. Times d p., 27 Oct., 1885
Dowell-Akerman Dowell, E. A , late of Clifton, co Gloucester. Times, 29 Sept , 1870
Dower *see* Gandar-Dower
Dowling *see* Delmaine (signed Delamaine).
Downes *see* Panter-Downes
: Berrill, T. J Times, d p , 8 May, 1896
Downes-Shaw Shaw, A D (Rev.), of Littleton, Middlesex Times, d p , 28 July, 1892
Downing Downing, G (son of T Hamersley) 9 June, 1812 (1092) *see* Fullerton.
Downing-Macdonald : Downing, Elizabeth Times, 21 July, 1876
Downing Wallace Downing, T S , of Curtain Road, Shoreditch, and Dalston, Middlesex Times, 11 Aug , 1876.
Downs *see* Bottom Downs.
, Nibblett.
Dowson *see* Dent Dowson.
Doyle : North.
Drake *see* Brockman.
„ Fuller-Elliott-Drake.
„ Hillas-Drake.
„ Tyrwhitt-Drake.

Drake-Cutcliffe   Drake, C H   18 May, 1867 (2996).
Drakeford-Lewis : Drakeford, Rev L A, of St. John the Baptist Vicarage, Leeds Times, d.p., 12 June, 1890.
Drax *see* Egginton-Ernlé-Erle-Drax.
   „   Erle-Drax
   „   Sawbridge-Erle-Drax
Drayton *see* Grimké
Dredge : Harkett, E 12 May, 1894 (4395).
Drew Bickerstaffe, F B. D., of St. Chad's College. Denston, Staffs , gent Times, 13 April, 1878
Drewe-Mercer   Drewe, A   5 July 1889 (3951) (see 5197).
Drewett · Brown, T D   4 Sept , 1867 (5110)
 . Brown, T. D   Whll., 4 Sept., 1867 (D.G. 1189).
Driffield : Waddington, W   24 May, 1860 (2040)
Drinkwater *see* Handforde-Drinkwater
Drinkwater-Lawe : Drinkwater, J. 24 Feb., 1879 (1791).
Driver *see* de la Bère.
   „ White
Driver-Holloway, H   Driver, H. Diggs, of 78, New Oxford Street, London, esq Times, d p , 6 March, 1884.
Drought *see* Samwell
Druce, J. Wyatt   Cohen, J , of Harrow Road, Middlesex Times, d.p., 29 March, 1884
Drudge *see* Miller.
Drummond *see* Beresford-Drummond
              of Cromlix and Innerpeffray. Drummond Hay, Hon. Robert. Lyon Vol V., 27 Jan., 1853.
              see Heathcote-Drummond
                „ Heathcote-Drummond-Willoughby.
              . Pinkerton, F. 23 April, 1791 (240).
              see Walker-Drummond
                „ Williams-Drummond
Drummond-Buller-Elphinstone : Drummond-Elphinstone, J. 24 Feb., 1824 (330).
Drummond-Stewart, of Grandtully   Stewart, Sir Wm   Lyon Vol IV , 15 Oct , 1839
Drury . Bottomley, J D , of Oak Villa, Charlton, Kent, Lieut Royal Marines Light Infantry d p , 15 Jan , 1866
   see Lowe
Drury-Lowe   Lowe, W D N. 16 Aug , 1884 (4587)
Dryden · Scholey, E   28 Jan., 1819 (266).
       · Turner, J. 31 Dec., 1791 (717).
Drynan *see* Grey.
Duncan *see* Haldane-Duncan-Mercer-Henderson
Ducie *see* Moreton
         : Moreton, Lord T. 11th Geo III., 1771.
Duck *see* Duke.
         Richard Gelson *see* Grahame, Richard

Ducke *see* Duke.
Ducker *see* Littler
Duckett Jackson, Sir G. 14 Feb., 1797 (145).
Duckett-Steuart · Duckett, C. E H. 19 April, 1894 (D.G. 441)
Duckworth-King : King, Sir G St. V. 13 Feb., 1888 (1154).
Dudgeon *see* Hartley.
Dudley *see* Aspinall-Dudley
 „ Jelly-Dudley.
 Parr, A. D., of Brasenose Coll., Oxon, and of Cossington, Leicester. Times, d p., 5 March, 1880.
 see Roberts-Dudley.
 „ Waddell-Dudley.
Dudley-Jauns : Dudley, S F. 31 Dec, 1874 (D.G 17).
Dudley Pegus *see* Pegus Dudley.
Dudley-Scott : Scott, J., of Hildenborough, Kent Times, 23 Aug., 1898
Dudman *see* Shirreff
Duesbury *see* Thornton-Duesbury
Duff *see* Leslie.
 „ Petre.
 „ Wharton-Duff.
Duff-Assheton-Smith : Duff, G W. 19 Oct., 1859 (3921).
 Duff, R G (on behalf of G. W., a minor).
 W , 19 Oct , 1859 (D G 1709)
Duff-Gillespie . Gillespie, S., Vetnary. Capt. in H.M Forces at Mhow, Central India Times, 15 March, 1893
Duff-Gordon Gordon, W. 9 Oct , 1813 (2032).
Duffield *see* Crutchley.
 „ Dawson Duffield
 „ Elwes
Duffield-Harding : Harding, A. A , late of Harwood Sq , Middlesex, now of Basingstoke Times, d p , 4 Feb 1888
Dugdale : Geast, R. 16 March, 1799 (239)
 see Geast-Dugdale.
Dugué *see* Lacouture-Dugué
Duguid *see* Leslie-Duguid
Duguid-McCombie, of Cammachmore Duguid. Peter Lyon, Vol. XII , 31 July, 1890
Duke : Ducke, J. H. (Rev.), of Glencraig Vicarage, co Down Times, 4 Dec , 1875
 Duck, F., late of Newbury, Berks, now of 27. Sidney Place, London, clerk Times, 20 July, 1871.
 Thompson, W. A., L R C S , at St Stephen's Green, Dublin Times, 15 Sept , 1868
Dumpleton *see* Barton
Dun-Waters, of Craigton Waters. Jas Cameron Lyon Vol XII , 7 Dec . 1888

Dunbar *see* Abbott-Dunbar, J. S.
    : Orr, G. D. Dublin, 18 March, 1833
    see Dunbar-Whittaker
    ,, Walker Dunbar.
Dunbar-Brander, of Pitgaveny : Brander or Dunbar, Dame Mary, relict of Sir Archd. Dunbar, of Northfield. Lyon Vol. V., 15 Nov., 1854.
Dunbar-Brunton : Brunton, J., of Ladhope, Roxburghshire, N.B., esq., M B., C. M. Times, 30 Oct., 1893
Dunbar-Buller : Buller, C. W. 2 Dec., 1891 (6841).
Dunbar-Dunbar. Dunbar, E Warrant of Lords of Council and Session, 24 Nov., 1848.
Dunbar-Whitaker : Dunbar, D. J., Liverpool. Times, 10 April, 1900.
Duncan *see* Anstruther-Duncan.
    ,, Beveridge-Duncan
    ,, Bluett-Duncan
    ,, Haldane-Duncan-Mercer-Henderson.
    : Smith, H M. D, of 139, Buckingham Palace Road, Middlesex, M D Times, 19 Aug., 1869.
Duncan Morison, of Naughton Duncan, Adam Alexr Lyon Vol. V., 8 Sept. 1853.
    see Morison-Duncan.
Duncombe : Moffat, A. 3 Nov., 1835 (2190)
    see Pauncefort-Duncombe.
    ,, Peirse-Duncombe.
Duncombe-Jewell : Jewell, R., of 2, Staple Inn, Holborn. Times, d p, 4 Nov., 1895.
Duncombe-Shafto : Duncombe, R. E. 9 Oct., 1802 (1073).
Dundas *see* Christopher.
    ,, Deans-Whitley-Dundas.
Dunk : Dinkelspiel, S., of 7, Prescott Street, New Brighton, Cheshire Times, d p, 14 April, 1887
    : Dunkelspiel, M., of 2, Lime Street Square, London, wine merchant Times, d.p., 1 Jan., 1886.
Dunkelspiel *see* Dunk.
Dunlap Paramore, Rev J D., of Chewton House, Earley, Berks. Times, d p, 15 March, 1884.
Dunlop *see* Buchanan-Dunlop.
    Delap, W. D St J., 24 Jan., D. Castle, 4 Feb., 1861 (D G 157 and 169).
    George H. M Dunlop, H M., of Leith Walk, Edinburgh, physician Times, 26 June, 1884
Dunn *see* Bower
    Marian Dunn, Sarah, wife of Rev. J. C. Dunn, of Nethersole, Bath, Somerset. Times, d p, 11 March, 1891
    see Marsh-Dunn.

Dun : Robson, H. G., of 3, East Parade, Whitby, N'berland,
        art. solicitors' clerk. Times, d.p., 28 Feb. and 3
        March, 1885.
Dunn-Gardner : Townshend, C. M. B. 20 April, 1847 (1446).
        : Townshend, J. 10 Aug., 1843 (2703).
        : Dunn, W. 1 May, 1804 (590).
Dunne *see* Amphlett.
Dunnington-Jefferson : Dunnington, J. 29 Jan., 1812 (226).
        : Dunnington, J. 21 May, 1841 (1282).
Dunton Orr, G. D., of Belfast Dublin, 18 March, 1833
    W. T. W. : Watts, W. T., of The Pines, Putney Hill,
        Middlesex. Times, d p., 18 April, 1896
Dunworth-Nugent . Dunworth, M and R., of Edgware Road,
    Middlesex. Times, d p., 9 Sept., 1881.
Duppa : Hancorn, R. 5th Geo. III., 1765.
        : Hancorn, B. D. 31st Geo. III., 1791.
        : Lloyd, T. D. 1 Nov., 1837 (3080).
Durand : Goose, H. E., of North Bailey, Durh. Times, 22 March,
    1899
Durell : Evans, T. 20 July, 1771 (11162).
        : Stables, D. 31 May, 1823 (898)
        see Stables.
Du Riche Preller : Scheibner, C., Ph D., Assoc. Mem Inst C.E..
    18, Margaret St., Cavendish Sq. Times, d p., 9 Nov., 1892.
Durieu *see* Durrieu
Durieux *see* Tyrel de Poix.
Durning-Lawrence : Lawrence, Edwin, M.P., and Edith Jane, his
    wife 2 Feb., 1898 (871).
Durrant : Bugg, W. C Times, d.p., 20 March, 1896
Durrieu · Durieu, L. A, of 71, Mornington Road, N.W. Times,
    10 April, 1865
Du Santoy-Anstis . Du Santoy, B., of the Royal Nav Reserve.
    Times, d.p., 5 July, 1882.
Dusgate : Bushby, R. D. 17 June, 1875 (3243).
Dust *see* Doust
Dutton *see* Courtier-Dutton.
    ,, Napier-Dutton.
    ,, Pickop-Dutton.
Duxbury *see* Whitlow.
Dyer : Clark, N. 2 Nov., 1833 (2075).
    see Maitland Dyer
    ,, Thiselton-Dyer.
Dyke *see* Poore
Dyke Acland *see* Troyte.
Dykes *see* Ballantine-Dykes.
    ,, Ballantine.
Dyman *see* Grey.

Dymoke *see* Wells Dymoke.
Dyne *see* Bradley.
   „ Bradley-Dyne
Dyneley : Chamberlain, M. 16 July, 1861 (3000).
Dyot : Bucknall, T. S. 17 Nov., 1792 (853).
Dyott : Burnaby, R. 18 May, 1891 (2725)
Dyson *see* Cooper.
Dyson-Holland : Dyson, T. 28 June, 1817 (1543).

E

Eade *see* Cory.
Eadon : Mitton, H. 1 Jan., 1836 (79).
Eady *see* Grant.
Eady-Borlase Eady, Mary E., of Combe Royal, Kingsbridge, Devon, widow. Times, d p , 19 Feb., 1889.
Eames, Fredk Abraham Knight : Eames, F , of 127, Richmond Road, Hackney, Middlesex, 13 Oct., 1886.
   see Waight-Eames.
Eardley · Eardley Smith, Sir C. W., 17 May, 1847 (D.G 691).
   : Gideon, S 17 July, 1789 (493)
   : Smith, Sir C. E. 17 May, 1847 (1793).
Eardley-Twisleton-Fiennes : Twisleton-Fiennes, Rt. Hon. G. W. 16 March, 1825 (459).
Eardley-Wilmot : Wilmot, J. 20 Jan., 1812 (170, 198)
Earl *see* Rudgard.
Earle *see* Biscoe.
   „ Clarke-Earle.
   „ Willis.
Earnshaw-Wall : Earnshaw, S W. (Rev.), of Ellough Rectory, Beccles. Times, d p , 11 Aug., 1885.
East *see* Clayton-East.
   „ D'Esté East.
   „ Gilbert-East
   : Maclaverty, H. H. E. & G. C M. D. 28 July, 1879 (5452)
Eastbrooke *see* Rowels.
Eastcott Crocker : Crocker, W., of The Mount, Wellington, Somerset, gent. Times, d.p , 7 May, 1894
Easterby *see* Cresswell
Eastes *see* D'Este.

Easton *see* Greengrass-Easton.
Eastwick-Field, C. : Field, C. A. E. A., of Midhurst, Sussex, surgeon Times, 4 June, 1890
Eastwood *see* Badger-Eastwood.
Eaton *see* Applebee-Eaton.
 ,, Browne
 ,, Haywood
 ,, Loftie-Eaton.
 : Lott, E. 28 Nov., 1807 (1632).
 : Monins, R. W., 1 April, 1769 (D.G. 1997)
 · Potter, G. 8 Aug., 1789 (529).
 : Selby, R. 17 Feb., 1781 (12162)
Eaton-Iddins Eaton, W. F., late of Bisley, now of Sutton House, Maida Vale, Middlesex, gent. Times, d p, 15 Dec., 1880.
Eaton-Matthews · Matthews, H., of Borough High Street, Southwark, London Times, 12 July, 1898.
Ebb-Smith : Smith, J. 4 Aug., 1890 (4602).
Eccles, Joseph Snape : Eccles, J., of Runcorn, Chester, manufr's assistant. Times, d p, 11 Nov., 1875.
Eccleston *see* Dicconson.
 see Scarisbrick.
 . Sheils, G. Dublin, 5 March, 1818.
Echlin Smith : Smith, Geo. of Newtown House, Leixlip, Ireland Times, 7 Jan., 1891
Eckford Morris, C. R., of 55, Clephane Road, Canonbury, London, baker, &c. Times, d.p., 5 Feb., 1890.
Ecroyd *see* Farrer.
Eddowes : Ellis, W. 31 March, 1800 (313).
Eden *see* Davison
 ,, Henley.
 ,, Johnson-Eden
 : Methold, J. 26 Sept., 1844 (3355).
 : Shafto, T. D. 20 May, 1885 (3291)
Edgar *see* Samuel Edgar.
Edgcumbe *see* Pearce Edgcumbe
Edge *see* Harris Edge
 : Hurt, J. T. 16 Oct., 1848 (3732) (see 3767).
 see Webb-Edge.
Edgell *see* Verney-Cave.
 ,, Wyatt.
Edgerley · Freebody, P. G., formerly of Brompton Crescent, Middlesex, now temp. residing at 2, Royal Cres., Ramsgate, Kent, esq Times, d p, 12 Aug., 1893
 · Freebody, Fanny J., formerly of Guildford, Surrey, now temp. at 2, Royal Crescent, Ramsgate, Kent, spinster. Times, d.p., 12 Aug., 1893.
Edgeworth : Kitchiner, G. M. 27 April, 1863 (2402).

Edgeworth-Johnstone · Johnston, W., Capt. in H M. Royal Irish
 Reg Times, d.p , 7 Feb , 1895
Edmeston Douglas, F A , S Africa. Times, 9 May, 1900
Edney Thomas, J J., of the Inland Rev., Somerset House
 Times, 27 Sept , 1877.
Edon-Brown : Brown, H. E , 5, Villa Dupont, Rue Pergolèse,
 Paris Times, 3 Jan , 1898
Edridge : Lucas, J 2 Nov., 1821 (2176)
Edward-Collins Collins, C M 20 March, 1850 (907)
Edwardes *see* Hope-Edwardes
Edwards *see* Baghot de la Bere.
  · Bedford, W. 3 Nov., 1792 (821).
  see Christian-Edwards.
  „ Cox-Edwards.
  R G. : Goldstein, R , of 95, High Holborn, London
   Times, d p , 7 Feb , 1894.
  : Hodges, T., or Edwards Hodges, T , of Fermoy,
   Ireland, Capt. R I. Rifles   Times, d p , 18 Oct ,
   1893.
  see Hodges
  „ Jervis-Edwards
  „ Marsh-Edwards
  „ Noel
  : Raynsford, G N   28 Feb., 1809 (292)
  · Richards, T. W   1 Dec , 1823 (787).
  see Smith-Edwards
Edwards-Brettell-Vaughan : Edwards, W. 21 May, 1850 (1480)
    see Shipley Hewett
Edwards-Gwynne · Edwards, H. L. 21 Jan , 1806 (128)
Edwards-Heathcote · Edwards, J H. 5 March, 1870 (1632)
 (D G 302)
Edwards-Moss · Moss T. and A C   4 April, 1851 (919, 955)
Edwards-Taylor : Edwards, R. Whll., 7 Jan , 1868 (D G 62)
  : Edwards, R   7 Jan , 1868 (155)
  · Edwards, R., of Moreton, Lancaster, Vicar of
   Mytton, West Riding, York. Times, 17
   Sept., 1867
Edwards-Vaughan Edwards, J. 29 July, 1829 (1438).
Edwards-Wood . Edwards, W and Luana, his wife. W., 24 Oct.,
 1851 (D.G 870)
Edwin Wyndham, C 18th Geo III., 1778
Edye : Edye de Portugal, L., of Penlee, Stoke, Devonport, Devon.
 Times, 13 Dec , 1866.
 : de Almeida Portugal, E   Times, 23 Aug., 1870.
Edyvean-Walker : Walker, H. E , of Rugby, Warwick. Times,
 d p , 1 Nov , 1890

Egan-Desmond : Egan, Rev. H. M., M.A., only s. of late W. M., of Stillorgan, Dublin, now residing at Beneavin, Dublin. Times, d.p., 1 Nov., 1869.

Egerton : Home-Cust, J. W. S. B. (Vis Alford) 6 Sept., 1853 (2449).
    see Grey-Egerton
    : Grosvenor, Rt. Hon. T (Earl of Wilton). 27 Nov., 1821 (2344).
    : Hayter, F. T. 13 Nov., 1792 (847).
    · Home-Cust, J. H. (Vis. Alford) 15 March, 1849 (932).
    : Leveson-Gower, Rt Hon F. (co called Rt. Hon. Lord). 24 Aug., 1833 (1589).
    : Lockall, J. 30 Aug., 1788 (413).
    see Marjoribanks Egerton.
    · Tatton, H. 9 May, 1780 (12081).
    see Tatton.

Egerton-Bone : Bone, G., of 52, Prince George Street, Portsea, Hants, gent. Times, 7 Aug., 1878.

Egerton-Cust : Egerton, J. W. S. B. (Earl Brownlow). 6 July, 1863 (3509).

Egerton-Green Green, C. E. 14 Nov., 1887 (6133)

Egerton-Warburton · Egerton, R. 10 Aug., 1813 (1635)

Egginton-Ernlé : Egginton, J L 6 May, 1887 (5046)

Egginton-Ernlé-Erle-Drax : Egginton-Ernle, J. L. 27 Sept., 1887. (5377).

Egremont : Silley, J., of Damerham South, Wilts, farmer. Times, d p., 4 March, 1867.

Ehret Dickinson : Dickinson, J., of Hemel Hempstead, Herts, esq. Times, d.p., 22 Dec., 1885

Ekins · Kerry, J. 40th Geo III., 1800.

Eldin *see* Clerk Eldin

Eliot *see* Craggs.

Eliott *see* Fuller-Eliott-Drake.

Ellard *see* Burnsall.

Elleker *see* Mainwaring-Elleker-Onslow.

Ellerker : Cueto, J. E. 6 Sept., 1816 (1725).
    : Smith, T. 1 May, 1826 (1029).

Ellerton *see* Lodge-Ellerton

Elliot : Badcock, J., of Warkworth House, Devons , and 128, Fore Stret, Exeter, provision merchant. Times, d.p., 30 May, 1883
    see Greig-Rutherford-Elliot.
    ,. Tracey-Elliot.

Elliot-Bates · Elliot, J. E. 14 March, 1879 (2307)

Elliot Risdon : Risdon, W. N., of Smallack, Egg Buckland, Devon, and of Hornsey Lane, Middlesex, M D. Times, d.p., 25 Aug., 1890.

Elliott . [late Stanford], W., S , J S , to continue the name. 10 Dec., 1796 (1194).
   see Fogg-Elliott
   . Glass, G H 15 Aug., 1811 (1636).
   see Greig-Rutherford-Elliott
   . Johnson, J. A , now a stud. of Wesleyan Theolg Instn , Richmond, Surrey, late of Benares, India Times, 16 Jan., 1882
    Ovens, O E 12 May, 1792 (293)
   . Stanford, W. 11 Dec., 1792 (922)
Elliott Drake *see* Fuller-Elliott-Drake
Elliott Townsend : Elliott, T S., of 219, New Kent Road, Surrey Times, 30 March, 1876
Ellis Buckley, C , of Heywood, Lancaster Times, 21 Feb., 1899
   see Clough.
   ,, Eddowes.
  : Ezra, E (formerly of Calcutta). Times, 28 Aug., 1896.
   see Gregson Ellis.
   ,, Heaton.
   ,, Heaton-Ellis.
   ,, Israel-Ellis
   ,, Joel-Ellis.
   ,, Lloyd
   ,, Saville
   Sharpe, A J 24 Nov., 1825 (2165)
   see Scott-Ellis.
   ,, Towell Ellis
  : Vezian, E 11 Feb., 1792 (90).
   Welbore, Rt. Hon. H (Visct. and Baron Clifden) 4 Feb , 1804 (199).
Ellis de Vesian Ellis (to resume former name) E J , E. E , R. E , J. S. Times, d.p , 19 Oct., 1889.
Ellis Fermor : Ellis, C A , of Ashmansworth, Southampton, esq Times, d p , 14 April, 1876
Ellis-Jervoise · Ellis, F and M. 28 Feb , 1848 (924)
Ellis-Viner Ellis, J 6 July, 1811 (1297).
Ellison *see* Carr-Ellison
Ellison-Macartney *see* Porter.
         Ellison, J Wm St. J., 4 Apr , Dublin Castle, 11 April, 1859 (D G 546 and 558).
Elphinstone *see* Dalrymple-Horn-Elphinstone
    ,, Drummond-Buller-Elphinstone
    ,, Osborne-Elphinstone
Ephinstone-Holloway : Holloway, W C. 26 Feb , 1823 (353)
Elphinstone-Stone : Stone W E 10 May, 1879 (3379).
      : Stone, W., of 7, Brunswick Terrace, Exeter retired Capt. R N Times, d p , 8 April, 1879

Elphinstone-Stone : Stone, W. E , of 7, Brunswick Terrace, Exmouth, Devon, esq., a retired Captain R.N. d.p., 2 April, 1879.
Elrington *see* Bisset.
Elsley *see* Baker.
Elsegood *see* Lloyd-Elsegood.
Eltham *see* Bass-Eltham
Elton *see* Marwood-Elton.
Elwes : Duffield, H 20 July, 1846 (2676)
Elwin *see* Woodyeare.
Elwood : Jones, A. S., G. A , and G. M , children of Dr. O Jones, all of 33, Manor Rd., Folkestone. Times, 3 Oct., 1885.
    see Bowen.
Emanuel *see* De Almeda.
Embleton-Fox : Embleton, T. F. 14 May, 1862 (2732)
        : Embleton, W. 6 Feb., 1877 (688).
Embury *see* Tollett.
Emerson *see* Amcotts.
Emery *see* Wetherell.
Emmerson-Harding : Harding, E. Times, 6 Sept., 1866.
Emmerton *see* Wescomb-Emmerton
Emmerton-Wescomb : Wescomb-Emmerton, J. 25 May, 1824 (908) (s. 949).
Emmitt : Baines, W. 21 Nov., 1826 (2866) (see 2926)
Emmott *see* Green-Emmott-Rawdon.
    „ Oswald-Emmott
Empson Lister, R. C., of Ousefleet Grange and Goole Hall, West Riding, Yorks, esq. Times, 13 May, 1871
        Stephenson, T. 29 Jan , 1812 (226).
Empson Rhodes : Empson, Alice, of The Elms, Market Rasen, Lincolns., spinster. Times, d.p., 11 May, 1883.
Emsall *see* Greaves-Emsall.
Enderby *see* Dawber-Enderby.
Enery *see* Cartwright-Enery.
Engelhart *see* Erskine.
England : Tiley, G., of Hatcham Lodge, New Cross, Deptford, Surrey, gent. Times, d p., 24 Oct., 1893.
Englefield *see* Silvertop.
Entwistle : Markland, J. 19 June, 1787 (289).
Enys · Hunt, L. A. 27 Dec , 1813 (188)
Erichson-Parrott : Parrott, J., of 44, Camberwell Road, Surrey, chymist. Times, 19 Sept , 1871
Erle *see* Egginton-Ernlé-Erle-Drax.
    „ Sawbridge-Erle-Drax.
Erle-Drax : Sawbridge, J. S. W. 16 March, 1829 (502).

Ernest Seligsen, G P , of The Albany, Piccadilly, and 57, Moor-
gate Street, London, merchant Times, d p , 2
March, 1894
Ernlé *see* Egginton-Ernlé.
„ Egginton-Ernlé-Erle-Drax.
Errington *see* Gladwin-Errington
: Stanley, Sir J. M , of Puddington, Cheshire, and Great
Glemham, Wickham Market, Suffolk, Bart.
Times, d.p , 2 March, 7 March, 1876
Stanley, Sir J. M , Bart 27 Aug., 1877 (4627)
Stanley-Massey-Stanley, Sir T 27 June, 1820 (1338)
see Turbutt
Ward, G 1 Dec , 1789 (749)
Eroll : Willis, G. H R , of Queen's Gate, Kensington, retired
Commdr R N Times, d p , 21 Aug , 1884.
Erskine : Cooper, W E , of Ivy Lodge, Ramsgate, Kent, late H M
Civil Service Times, d p , 29 May, 1877
: Engelhart, D 26 Sept , 1820 (1825)
of Linlathen Paterson, Jas. Erskine. Lyon Vol VIII ,
20 May, 1870.
see St Clair
„ West-Erskine
Zwilchenbart, M M A. 15 Sept , 1884 (4133).
Escott *see* Sweet-Escott
Eskell *ees* Clifford
„ Clifford-Eskell
Eskell-Paget · Eskell, E E., of 445, Strand, and 58, Ludgate Hill,
London, dental surgeon Times, d.p , 19 Dec., 1885.
Esmead *see* Moore-Michell-Esmead
Esmée : Gooderich, Elinor Mary, of Regent St , London Times,
15 Aug , 1899
Essex, Earl of, *see* Capell.
see Cowper-Essex
„ Evans-Essex
„ Quaintrell
Essington Ward, W W. 4 Jan., 1828 (50).
Estcourt *see* Bucknall
: Bucknall, T.G. 3 June, 1823 (1175)
see Sotheron
„ Sotheron-Estcourt
Ethelston *see* Peel
Etheredge : Murrell, T R. 29 March, 1864 (2219)
Eustace Malpas, F. J. W. E , Lieut. R.N. Times, d.p , 22 Aug.,
1873.
Robertson. (1875). In Index only no particulars.

Evans see Bennett Goldney.
,, Bevan
,, Bradney Marsh.
: Calcott, G. 15 Oct., 1834 (1911).
see Davies-Evans.
,, De Grailly Evans.
,, Durell.
John Bethell Sackville : Evans. J. Times, d.p., 7 Sept., 1889.
see FitzHenry.
, Gwynne
Jones, J., of Bronygog, Montgomery. esq Times, 26 March, 1877
see Lombe
,, Pugh.
, Westyr-Evans
Wills, Hannah E. Times, d.p., 3 March, 1877.
see Wilson
Evans-Blackwall · Evans, J B , of Blackwall, Kirk Ireton, Derby Times, d p., 18 Feb., 1871.
Evans-Essex : Evans, Mary A 19 Sept , 1851 (2645)
Evans-Gordon : Evans, C S S. 6 Feb , 1846 (410)
· Evans, Mrs Frances Emma Valentina Lyon. Vol. IV , 13 Feb., 1846.
: Cookson, H. A. G. 23 March, 1865 (1731).
Evans-Gwynne : Evans, G F. J. G. 13 June, 1882 (3292).
Evans-Lloyd : Evans, E., of Plas Newton and Plasyndre, esq Times, d.p., 4 Jan., 1876.
Evans Vaughan : Evans, J., of Upper Brooke Street, Oswestry, Salop, gent. Times, d p., 15 Dec., 1891.
Eveleigh-De Moleyns ; Dayrolles-Blakeney (Lord Ventry). 14 Dec., 1874 (D G. 813).
Evelyn . Hume, A 22 July, 1797 (699).
: Shuckburgh, Sir G. A. W 34th Geo. III , 1794
Everard see Welby-Everard.
Everard-Hutton : Hutton, T , of Middleton Hall, Lynn, Norfolk, esq Times, 1 March, 1865.
Everett : Butt, J. 15 Feb , 1811 (381)
Everitt see Calmady.
: Stiffe, F. W. E 15 Aug., 1860 (D.G. 970).
Wm. : Webb, W John Wesley, Rector of Allhallows, Goldsmith Street, Exeter. Times, d p., 30 Oct., 1880
Everley-Taylor : Taylor, W C, of Scarboro', Yorks, surgeon, L R.C.P. Times, d p., 5 Sept., 1879.
Eversfield : Markwick, W. 28 May, 1807 (731).

Eversleigh, H. A E. · Wilkins, H. J , of Moor Park, Fulham Road, Middlesex, and of Wellington, New Zealand, gent. Times, 2 Jan., 4 Jan , 1879.
Evers-Swindell : Evers, C. and E M , also E. J. and A J   24 June, 1851
Every-Clayton . Every, E.   21 Aug , 1835 (1645)
Every-Halsted   Every-Clayton, C. E   17 July, 1886 (3619)
  : Every-Clayton, E.   17 July, 1886 (3619).
Evors-Smith · Smith, J , of 21 St James' Square, Notting Hill, Middlesex, gent.   Times, 12 April, 1866.
Ewbank see Kay
Ewbanke . Wilson, M R , of Borrenthwaite-upon-Stainsmore. Westmoreland   Times, 2 May, 1867
Ewens-Gorney · Ewens, G., of U S A   Times, 16 Sep , 1899.
Ewing see Cattley.
Ewins see Barwell-Ewins
Eyre see Archer-Houblon
  Houblon, C. A.   27 Sept , 1831 (2082)
  · Purvis, W   30 June, 1795 (678)
  see Richardson-Eyre.
Eyre-Matcham : Matcham, W. E., of Whiteparish, Wilts, esq   Times, d.p , 13 April, 1889.
Eyres   Kettlewell, H W.   7 Sept., 1878 (5219)
  : Kettlewell, C. T , of Piccadilly, London   Times, 15 April, 1898
Eyton see Stubbs
Ezra see Ellis.

F

Faber · Smith, A , of 11 and 12. Clement's Lane, and Lloyd's, London, and of E. Dulwich, Surrey, marine insur broker and underwriter. Times, d p , 5 Jan , 1886
  : Smith, G H., of 11 and 12, Clement's Lane. and Lloyd's. London, and of Beckenham, Kent. marine insur broker and underwriter. Times, d p, 5 Jan., 1886
  Smith, W , of 11 and 12, Clement's Lane, London, and of E Dulwich, Surrey, mercantile clerk   Times, Times, d p , 5 Jan , 1886
Fairfax   Martin, D   10 Aug. 1782 (12320)
  · Martin, D.   37th Geo III , 1797
  see Ramsay-Fairfax.

Fairfax-Cholmeley : Cholmeley, T. C. 10 July, 1886 (3679)
Fairles Humphreys : Fairles, N W. Times, 24 Jan , 1877
Fairlie *see* Brown-Fairlie.
Fairlie-Clarke Clarke, Allan Johnston, of Southborough, Kent
 Times, 29 Aug , 1899
Fairlie-Cuningham, of Robeland : Cuningham-Fairlie, Sir Chas
 Arthur Lyon Vol. XI., 14 March, 1882.
Fairs *see* Hare.
Faithfull *see* Chauntrell
Falcon *see* Harrison
Falcon-Steward : Falcon   3 June, 1882 (2739)
Falconar *see* Stewart
Falder *see* Roddam.
Fall *see* Nicholson-Fall.
Fancourt *see* Michell-Fancourt.
Fane *see* Cholmley.
 „ Ponsonby-Fane.
Fane-de Salis : de Salis, Count J   11 Dec , 1835 (2476)
Fanning *see* Burton-Fanning.
Farewell : Hallet, S   33rd Geo II , 1760.
Faria Van Réable, A J L., of Cornwall Road, Notting Hill
 Times, d.p., 17 Aug , 1875.
Farley *see* Turner Farley
Farmar-Bringhurst : Farmar, E D , of Dorset Lodge, Bourne-
 mouth, Army surgeon. Times, d p , 3 Nov , 1884
Farmer *see* Haywood-Farmer.
Farmer-Atkinson Atkinson, H J , esq , M.P., and E., his wife,
 both of Ore, Hastings, Sussex   Times, d p , 11 Aug , 1891.
Farmer-Jones Farmer, J.   29 April, 1869 (2683)
     · Farmer, Jas.   Whitehall, April, 29, 1869 (D G.
     461)
Farquhar. H. D   Huggins, H. J., of Sheen Park, Richmond,
 Surrey, widow   Times, d p , 4 Oct , 1894.
Farquharson Ross, J. 19 Aug , 1805 (1145)
  see Macdonald-Macdonald.
  of Whitehouse : Young-Leshe, George. Lyon Vol.
  XIV , 4 June, 1896
Farrant : Binsteed, G 16 June, 1795 (619).
   . Binsteed, T. 16 June, 1795 (619)
Farrel *see* Skeffington
Farrell Carroll, C St J., 21 Feb , D C , 3 March, 1855 (D G
 409 and 427)
Farrer : Ecroyd, W   29 July, 1896 (4571)
 see Fawkes
Farrer-Baynes . Baynes, T , of Blackburn, Lancs., cotton
 manufacr   Times, d p , 20 Sept., 1879
Farside : Watson, G J   22 June, 1826 (1686)

Farside · Hutton, W 15 Nov., 1877 (6674)
Farthing-Beauchamp   Farthing, R   10 April, 1820 (762)
Faskally : Butter, G. B., F R C S   Times, d p., 26 Sept., 1876.
Fatt *see* Crosdale
    ,,   Pierssené .
Faudel-Phillips · Phillips, S H   23 Dec., 1895 (3)
Faulkner *see* Allen-Faulkner
        . Cadby, F. G., of 1, Margaret Road, Harborne, Staffs,
            polisher   Times, d p., 7 Aug., 1894.
        see Dickey Faulkner.
        Todd, Tho., nephew of Geo. F., *c.* 1775.   Betham
Faunce Delaune   Faunce, C D   12 Aug. 1864 (4451).
Faussett *see* Godfrey-Faussett
Fawcett *see* Pulteney.
        Sedgwick, W.   8 Aug., 1867 (4548).
        Sedgwick, Wm   Whll., 8 Aug., 1867 (D G 1053).
Fawcus-Smith *see* de Rustafjaell
Fawkes · Farrer, F   29 Aug., 1786 (398).
        Hawksworth, W   2 Sept., 1786 (407)
        · Hawksworth, W. R   1 Dec., 1792 (891).
Fawsitt *see* Chater-Fawsitt
    ,,   Ferguson Fawsitt
        · Hornby, J   1 March 1805 (276).
        Wetherell, R   31 May, 1831 (1140).
Fawssett   Ward, Rev R F, of Elmley House, Surbiton, Surrey.
    Times, d p., 2 June, 1883
Fazakerley . Gillibrand, M.   — ——, 1829 (2221).
        Gillibrand, T.   11 June, 1814 (1205).
        · Radcliffe, T   20 June, 1767 (10738)
Fazakerley-Westby   Westby J. T., and Fazakerley, M H   15
    April, 1863 (2071).
Feake   Cruse, J   3 Nov., 1800 (1258)
Fearnley-Whittingstall   Fearnley. E   29 March, 1825 (605)
Fearon *see* Brown
Featherston *see* Langton-Featherston.
Featherstonehaugh *see* Bullock Featherstonehaugh
Fector *see* Laurie, of Maxwelton.
Feely *see* Lovell
Feilding *see* Powys
Fellowe   Dickerdine, G R   14th Geo III., 1774
Fellowes *see* Benyon
        · Wallop, Hon N   9 Aug. 1794 (805).
Fellows *see* Woodbridge
Felvus *see* Young.
Fenton *see* Cawthorne
        Collins, C. G. F. C   14 May, 1889 (2688).

Fenton Fenton-Jones, W. H., of 29, Brook Street, Grosvenor Square, phys. Times, d.p, 13 March, 1888.
Fenton-Jones Jones, J., J.P., of 12, Northumberland Houses, Hackney, London. Times, d p., 4 Jan., 1893.
Fenton-Livingstone, of Westquarter Livingstone-Fenton, Thos. Livingstone. Lyon, Vol. V., 26 July, 1854
Fenton-Wingate Wingate, W. E., Torquay. Times, 31 July, 1900.
Fenwick *see* Clennell.
    J. Fenwick : Fenwick, J (jun.), of Spencer House, Wimbledon Common, Surrey, esq., and of 57, Gracechurch Street, London. d p, 6 July, 1887.
    : Jeffrey, J. 21 Aug., 1860 (3186).
    : Jeffrey, W. 17 June, 1830 (1419).
    : Lambert, T. 30 July, 1801 (930).
    : Reid, E. M. 3 June, 1851 (1451)
    : Tatham, N. 2 Feb , 1796 (176).
Fenwick-Bisset, of Lessendrum . Fenwick, Mordaunt. Lyon, Vol. VIII , 23 Feb., 1870.
Fenwick-Stuart : Fenwick, M. 25 Nov., 1816 (2351).
Ferguson : Berry, W. 12 Jan., 1782 (12260)
    : Beyfus, L., of Mare Street, Hackney, Middlesex. Times, d p., 16 Oct., 1876
    : Magennis, of Burt House, co. Donegal. Dublin, 21 Dec , 1842.
    see Oliphant-Ferguson
    Anthony : Orsinigo, Antonino, of Canning Town, Mid , engineer. Times, d p., 4 July, 1883.
    see Tepper.
Ferguson-Davie : Ferguson, H. R and F. 13 Feb., 1846 (603).
Ferguson Fawsitt Ferguson, J. B. 19 Dec., 1866 (7113)
Ferguson-Walker : Walker, J., of 11, King's Bench Walk, Temple, E C. Times, 22 Nov., 1894
Fergusson *see* Colyer-Fergusson
Fergusson-Buchanan, of Auchentorlie : Fergusson, George James. Lyon Vol. XII , 1 May, 1890.
Fergusson-Pollok : Fergusson, William. Lyon Vol. XI., 21 June, 1886.
Fermor *see* Ellis Fermor
Fermor-Hesketh . Hesketh, Sir Thos. Geo., and Lady Anna Maria Arabella, his wife, and Thos. Geo. Hesketh, his second son. Whll . 8 Nov., 1867 (D.G. 1401).
Fernandez *see* De Tavora Fernandez
Ferrall *see* Carmichael-Ferrall.
    „ O'Ferrall.
Ferrand : Busfield, S. 2 Aug., 1837 (2217).
    : Busfeild, W. 18 March, 1890 (1709).
    : Waddington, T. 3 June, 1788 (265).

Ferrars : Townshend, G 9 May, 1786 (197)
Ferrers Croxton, H. F 16 Jan., 1885 (676)
Fetherston : Dilke, J. 17 May, 1833 (950)
             : Dilke, T. 16 Dec., 1783 (12501)
Fetherston-Dilke Fetherston, W. G., of Maxstoke Castle, Warwicks., esq Times, d p., 14 Sept., 1877
             : Fetherston, C 7 April, 1858 (2298)
              Fetherston, W G., of Fakenham, Norfolk, congregational minister. Times, d p., 17 Oct., 1878
Fetherston-Whitney : Fetherston, J. H 4 Nov., 1880 (D G 934).
             : Fetherston, E. W. 5 July, 14 July, 1859 (D G 1289 and 1298).
Featherstone see Harding.
Fetherstonhaugh see Smalwood-Fetherstonhaugh
             ,, Turnour-Fetherstonhaugh.
Fetherstonhaugh-Whitney · Fethertonhaugh, H. E. W. R.L., St. James's, 23 Aug., D. Castle, 6 Sept., 1881 (D G 841).
              Fetherstonhaugh, H E. W 6 Sept., 1881 (D G 841)
Fetherstonhaugh-Frampton : Fetherstonhaugh, R P., of Moreton House, Dorset, esq., and his wife, L M., and his children. Times, d p., 13 March, 1888
Fettiplace Georges, R 13 Jan., 1806 (80).
Fewtrell-Wylde : Wylde, C E 9 July, 1852 (2097)
Ffooks see Woodforde
Ffytche : Disney, L. 30 Sept., 1775 (11600).
Ficklin · Brown, C B. 28 Nov., 1888 (329)
        · Brown, P B. 28 Nov., 1888 (329).
Field, D Cohen, David Field, of Burgundy Villa, Pagoda Avenue, Richmond. Times, 10 Feb., 1898
          see Eastwick-Field
          ,, Parker.
Field-Child Field, J. C. 23 May, 1822 (916)
Fielden see Warnock Fielden
        ,, Smith-Fielding
Fielding-Davis : Fielding, A., of Amington, Tamworth, Warwick, terra-cotta moulder Times, 18 March, 1890
Fielding-Ould : Ould, R., of Aigburth, Lancaster Times, 3 Oct., 1898.
Fiennes see Eardley-Twisleton-Fiennes.
        ,, Twisleton-Fiennes
        ,, Twisleton-Wykham-Fiennes.
        ,, Wykeham-Fiennes

Fife-Cookson : Fife, J C, of Whitehill, Durham, a Capt in H.M.
65th Regiment. Times, d p, 9 Nov, 1878,
4 Jan, 1879.
: Fife, J C 2 Dec., 1878 (7076)
Figg see Ainsworth
Figgins see Leighton.
Filgate . Macartney, T. P. H St J., 4 June, D.C., 26 June, 1862
(D.G 760 and 778)
Filkin : Sugden W, formerly of Bruton, now of 97, Kingsdown
Parade, Bristol, Somerset Times, 10 Oct, 1871
Finch . Ingle, W. F. 6 June, 1778 (11880)
. Steward, P. F. 5 June, 1861 (2538).
see Wykes-Finch
,, Wynne-Finch
Finch-Hatton-Besly Finch-Hatton, W D   28 Nov., 1893 (7183).
Finchett-Maddock . Moss, Hy., of Chester and Carnarvon,
solicitor   Times, d p., 16 Jan, 1893.
: Finchett, J 12 Feb., 1824 (370).
Finlayson see Harding-Finlayson
Finnerty see Clements-Finnerty.
,, Hussey
: Stack, E F Times, d p, 7 May, 16 May, 1884.
Finney : Tate, S 30 Aug, 1788 (413)
Finn-Kelcey Finn, F. 25 March, 1881 (1792).
Fiott see Lee
Firth see Bottomley-Firth.
Turner, G F, of Wakefield, Yorks, machinist Times,
d p, 20 Feb., 1874.
Firth-Heatly . Firth, J 1 March, 17 March, 1848 (D G 366 and
377)
Fisher see Appelbee Fisher
,, Boghurst-Fisher.
,, Brocklebank
· Cooper, H 31 July, 1797 (733)
see Horman-Fisher
Jones, F. C, formerly of 29, High Street, Newport,
Monmouth, then of Buenos Ayres, S. America,
now of Bristol, stock and exchange broker.
Times, d p., 11 Jan, 14 Jan, 1879.
see Philipps
,, Ponsonby
,, Rowe
,, Viviane
Fisher-Rowe : Fisher. E. R 5 Feb., 1881 (607)
Fishre see Jeddere-Fishre.
Fiske see Wilkes.
Fiske-Harrison : Harrison, F. G. 20 April, 1840 (1016)

116   *An Index to Changes of Name.*   [FIT

Fitzalan-Howard : Howard, B. T. (Lord), Howard, E. G. (Lord) and Howard, H. G., (Earl of Arundel and Surrey). 26 April 1842. (1170)
    see Talbot
FitzClarence *see* Hunloke
FitzGerald *see* Dalton-FitzGerald.
   ,, Foster-Vesey-FitzGerald
   : Galaher, E. F., of 27, Winchester Street, Pimlico, Times, 17 May, 1864
   J Edward : Guntrip, J (Rev), of 14, Dents Road, Wandsworth Common, Surrey. Times, 16 Dec, 1890.
   : Healy, Lieut. J. G., of Royal Milford, Surrey. Times, d.p., 16 Oct., 1896.
   : Healy, J. G. 26 Dec., 1896 (125).
   : Magrath, J F Dublin, 29 May, 1810
   : Molloy, J. Fitzgerald, of Barrow-in-Furness, Lancs., retired Staff-Comdr R N Times, d.p., 5 Dec, 1874.
   · Noding, M. R., of Richmond, Surrey, gent Times, d.p., 26 July, 1892.
   see Nugent
   : Purcell, J 3 Oct., 1818 (1768)
   Chas. Wm Tuckfield, Chas., of 9, Giltspur Street, London, watch manufacturer. Times, 29 Sept, 1868.
   see Vesey-FitzGerald.
   ., Wilson-Fitzgerald
FitzGerald-Day : Fitzgerald, J. R. and E., both of Spring Hill, co. Kerry. Dublin, 26 July, 1841.
Fitzgerald-De Ros . Fitzgerald, Rt. Hon. H (com called Lord). 6 Oct. 1806 (1336)
Fitz-Gibbon Dillon, G N and Lady 24 Nov., 1873 (5508) (D.G. 861).
FitzHenry Evans, W Dublin, 11 June, 1812.
FitzHerbert . Rothwell, Thomas. St J, 19 Sept., D.C., 1 Oct., 1863 (D.G. 1093 and 1105)
Fitzherbert-Brockholes Fitzherbert. W 21 June, 1783 (12450). Fitzherbert, W J. 25 Aug., 1875 (4325)
Fitzwilliam *see* Wentworth-Fitzwilliam
FitzWygram : Wygram, Sir R. Bart. Dublin, 22 Oct., 1832.
Flamank *see* Phillipps-Flamank.
Flanders *see* Howard-Flanders
Fleck-Basil : Fleck, H. C. J., of Brompton Road, Middlesex, baker Times, d.p., 28 Oct., 1882
Fleetwood *see* Hesketh.

Fleetwood-Buckle : to use for the future, notwithstanding the entry in St Philip's Parish Church, Birmingham, being in the name of William Henry Fleetwood Buckle, and the entry in the Register at Somerset House being in the name of Thomas Fleetwood Buckle. Times, 31 Jan., 1867.
Fleming *see* Coham-Fleming.
 : Cuchet, J. L. 12 Oct., 1805 (1271).
 : Raincock, J 19th Geo. III., 1779.
 : Willis, J. 7th Geo. III., 1767.
 : Willis, J. F. B. 53 Geo. III , 3. c 78.
 : Worsley, S. D. 27 Sep., 1805 (1217).
Fletcher *see* Boughey
 ,, Bradshaw.
 ,, Cuddon-Fletcher.
 ,, Hewitt-Fletcher.
 ,, Hunter.
 : Jack, J. C 12 Oct., 1855 (3798).
 : Jack, C., of 21, Clarges Street, Piccadilly, and of the Inner Temple, esq., barrister; and Jack, J. F., formerly of Wilts., now of 8, Carlton Chambers. Regent Street, Middlesex, esq Times, d.p., 18 Dec., 1882.
 see Powell
 : Ramsden, J. F. 29 Sept., 1843 (3179).
 see Stanley.
 ,, Watkins.
 ,, Wynne.
Fletcher-Bennett : Bennett, Ann B., of Carisbrooke Villa, Tulse Hill, widow. d.p., 30 Nov., 1878.
Fletcher Helleley · Fletcher, J. H., of Brierley, Yorks, esq., Times, d.p, 1 Dec., 1874
Fletcher-Twemlow . Royds, G. F. 8 June, 1894 (3381).
Fletcher-Welch : Fletcher, S. J. W 19 Sept., 1815 (1946).
Flint *see* Corbett
Flood *see* Hanford
 ,, Lloyd-Flood.
 : Solly, F Dublin, 14 Oct., 1818.
Flower *see* Walker.
 : Walker, Rt. Hon. H. (Vis. Ashbrook) 21 July, 1847 (2691).
Floyer *see* Burnes-Floyer.
 : Cawley, W. H. 14 Dec., 1793 (110).
Flutter-Steevens · French, F. 14 Jan., 1807 (90).
Flynn *see* Pilkington.
Foard *see* Huskisson
Fogg : Barlow, J. 9 April, 1811 (655).
Fogg-Elliott : Fogg, J. 11 June, 1828 (1141).

Foley *see* Hodgetts.
Foljambe : Moore, F F 16th Geo III , 1776
Fonblanque *see* de Grenier-Fonblanque
Foord-Bowes   Foord, T F   2 Jan , 1813 (2)
        Trollope, B 30 Oct., 1861 (4403 and 4455)
Foord-Kelcey   Foord, G , F., W , E , J   22 May, 1872 (2475 and 2712)
Foote   Cheek. S , of 31 and 32, Beech Street, Barbican, London, hosier and shirt maker Times, d p , 2 April, 5 April, 1881.
    see Williams-Foote
Foote-Macdonald Foot, Gregory Grant, one of H M Corps of Gentlemen at Arms. Lyon Vol V , 16 Oct., 1850
Forbes : Forbes-Robertson, Jas and Geo   Times, d p , 23 June, 1896
    : Gordon, B   18 Aug , 1823 (1431)
    see Gordon
    „ Hepburn-Stuart-Forbes
    „ Hepburn-Stuart-Forbes-Trefusis
    „ Holmes-Forbes
    „ Smith-Forbes
Forbes-Bentley : Calland, J F. 24 April, 1854 (1294)
    : Forbes, T 25 Jan., 1822 (153).
Forbes-Leith, of Fyvie : Leith, Alexr John. Lyon Vol. XII., 26 Aug., 1889.
Forbes-Leslie, of Rothie and Badenscoth Forbes, Jonathan Lyon Vol. VI., 20 May, 1862.
Forbes-Morgan · Forbes, Jane C., wife of Rt. Hon. G A H. Forbes 3 March. 21 March, 1859 (D G 441 and 454)
Forbes-Muller : Muller, C. F., of the Grammar School, Cranbrook, Kent Times, d p , 15 Sept , 1896.
Forbes-Stuart Forbes, W 31 July, 1821 (1617)
Forbes Winslow Winslow, L S., of 23, Cavendish Square, and Sussex House, Hammersmith. M B and D.C.L , M R C P. Times, d.p , 2 April, 1874
Ford, Albert Ernest Alsor Clair Ford, A. E , of 19, Upper Glos Place, Middlesex, mus. composer. Times, d p , 8 Aug., 1889.
    see Hilton-Ford.
    „ Jones-Ford
    „ Napier Ford
Fordyce-Buchan, of Kelloe Fordyce, Geo. Wm. Lyon Vol. V., 15 Feb , 1856.
Foreman : New, J. F , of 60, Chippenham Road, London, and of Manilla, merchant. Times, d p , 12 May, 1885.
Forester French, R F. 1 April, 1797 (298)
    see Townsend-Forester.

Forester *see* Weld-Forester.
Forgan *see* Cannon.
Forrest *see* Forsyth-Forrest.
Forrester *see* Birkley-Forrester
Forsdyke : Reid, F. W., of Camden Town, Middlesex. Times, 7 Feb., 1876.
Forster *see* Arnold-Forster.
    ,, Bacon.
    ,, Baird
    ,, Blake Forster
    ,, Carr-Forster.
    : Foster, G C., son of R. C Foster, bap " Forster," late of Worthing, Sussex, gent Times, 19 May, 1885.
    see Haire-Forster
    Storey, W 2 April, 1808 (452).
Forster-Brown . Brown, S. and G H., of 3, Gordon Road, Ealing. Times, 24 Feb., 1894
Forster-Coull : Forster, W D. 15 Sept., 1887 (5320)
Forster-Walker Walker, I, of 7, Stanhope Terrace, Bayswater, Middlesex, spinster. Times, d p, 28 May, 1867.
Forsyth-Brown, of Whitsome Newton : Forsyth, Robt Brown. Lyon Vol. V., 10 March, 1856.
Forsyth-Forrest : Forsyth, T. 20 Nov., 1855 (4588)
Forsyth-Grant : Grant, J, Cheltenham, Glos. Times, 19 Sept., 1898
Fortescue Inglett, R. 8 Feb., 1776 (11742).
Fortescue-Brickdale Brickdale, J F 12 Feb., 1861 (603)
Fortescue-Cole Cole, J. H. W., of Newport Road, Cardiff Times, d p., 20 June, 1884.
Fortescue-Knottesford Fortescue, F. 20 April, 1793 (310)
Forward . Howard, Hon W. 14 Nov., 1780 (12135).
Forward-Howard Forward, W (Earl of Wicklow). Dublin, 22 Dec., 1815.
Foss : Smith, C. H. Times, d p, 20 Nov., 1885
Foster *see* Betton-Foster.
    ,, Blake
    ,, Blake-Forster
    ,, Carr-Forster
    : Crapper, J, of Bradford, Yorks, coal merchant Times, d.p., 20 April, 1882.
    see Forster.
    ,, Francis.
    ,, Graham-Foster-Pigott
    ,, Hyatt-Foster
    ,, Hylton Foster.
    ,, Pigott.
    ,, Skeffington
Foster-Melliar : Foster, A. 13 Nov., 1840 (2521).

Foster-Stackhouse : Stackhouse, H , of 41, Newborough Street, Scarborough Times. 28 April, 1870
Foster-Vesey-FitzGerald : Foster, Honble Letitia L (widow) 7 May, 17 May, 1860 (D G 613 and 625)
Fothergill : Grainger, J   1 Dec , 1778 (11931)
        see Price-Fothergill
        „ Tarleton-Fothergill.
        „ Watson Fothergill.
Foulis *see* Sidney-Foulis.
Foulston *see* Hunt-Foulston.
Fountaine : Price, B 5th Geo. III , 1765
Fountaine *see* Addison-Fountaine.
Fountayne *see* Wilson-Fountayne
Fountayne-Wilson *see* Montagu
Fowden Weatherhilt, R F   25 Nov , 1819 (2174)
Fowell-Watts Watts, P. H , of West Hackney, Middlesex, solicitor. Times. d p , 9 Aug., 1877
Fowle : Middleton, Sir W. 6 Jan., 1823 (26)
Fowler-Berdmore Fowler, C B   16 Aug , 1841 (2103)
Fowler *see* Butler
        „ Cowley-Fowler.
        „ Moir-Fowler.
        „ Piggin Fowler.
        · Robinson, M. 19 Aug 1828 (1576).
Fowler-Smith *see* Smith-Dampier.
Fownes *see* Somerville.
Fox *see* Broomhead-Colton-Fox
  „ Byrom.
  „ Colton-Fox.
  „ Cookworthy.
  „ Embleton-Fox.
    Fuchs, J. C F E. Times, d p , 8 Jan , 1896
    · Littlefield, Bessie, of Belgrave Mansions, Grosvenor Gardens, spinster Times, d p., 12 Oct., 1895
    see Stuart-Fox.
  „ Suckling.
Fox-Adams Adams H , of Knightsbridge, London Times, 4 Feb., 1899
Fox-Davies : Davies, A C   d.p., 28 Feb., 1890.
        · Davies, T. E R L , 26 Sept , 1894 (not gazetted).
Fox-Kirk, Stanley · Fox, Harold, O. S., of Gainsborough, Lincoln, gent Times, d p, 29 March, 1894.
Fox-Pitt-Rivers Fox, A H L   25 May, 1880 (3326)
Fox-Pitt : Fox, A. H L. (children). 1880.
Fox-Powys . Powys, J. W. H   7 Nov., 1890 (6213)
Foxcroft Jones, E. T. D., of Hinton Charterhouse, Somerset, and Halsteads, York, esq Times, d.p , 12 Aug., 1868.

Foxlow *see* Murray.
Fradelle *see* Smith.
Frampton : Badcock, H F , of Lydiard Millicent, Wilts, gent.
   Times, d.p., 3 Nov., 1883.
  : Badcock, H. F., of Lydiard Millicent, Wilts, gent.
   d.p, 15 Oct , 1883.
  see Fetherstonhaugh-Frampton
France *see* Hayhurst
  : Hayhurst, W. J. A 18 March, 1876 (2155)
  see Hayhurst-France
  : Hayhurst, T. 6 Oct , 1795 (1033).
  see Wilson-France.
France-Hayhurst · France, T   13 Oct., 1870 (4553)
    · France, Thos. Whitehall, 13 Oct , 1870
    (D.G. 1343).
Francis · Foster, G , of 19, Woodpecker Road, New Cross, Kent,
   Times, d.p , 5 April, 1873.
  : Morgan, F. 4 Aug., 1846 (2843).
  see Temple-Allen.
Francklyn *see* Webbe.
Franco *see* Lopes.
Frankland : Cromwell, H. 28 Jan., 1806 (147).
  see Gill
  ,, Payne-Frankland
Frankland-Russell · Frankland, Sir J. 9 Feb., 1837 (327 & 350).
Frankland-Russell-Astley · Astley, R. A , of 7, Cavendish Square,
  Middlesex, r. of Lieut.-Col. Francis L'Estrange. Times,
  d.p , 17 Feb., 1872.
Franklin-Adams : Adams, J., of Lloyd's, London, underwriter.
  Times, d p , 1 May, 1879
Franklin-Hindle : Franklin, J , of Well Bank, Haslingdon, Lancs ,
  gent. Times, d.p., 19 May, 1884
Franklin-Littlegroom-Nicholas . Franklin, J   16 Aug , 1806
  (1093)
Franklin Franklinski, J. A , of 4, Prince's Square, Bayswater.
  Times, 25 Jan., 1867.
Franklinski *see* Franklin.
Frary *see* Serjeant.
Fraser *see* Allan-Fraser
  ,, Mackenzie-Fraser.
  ,, Newby-Fraser.
  ,, White Fraser.
Fraser-Mackintosh : Fraser, C   18 Sept., 1857 (3251)
Fraunceis *see* Gwyn.
Frazer *see* Gordon-Frazer.
Freakes *see* Parson.

Frecheville, R R F. · Fretwell, R R., late of Manor Hill, nr. Halifax, Nova Scotia, now of Percy Lodge, East Sheen, Surrey, gent   Times, d p , 26 July, 1866.
Freebody *see* Edgerley.
Freeman *see* Childe-Freeman
    : Mackereth, J. 15 Sept , 1787 (418)
    see Thomas.
    ,, Williams-Freeman
Freeman-Cohen   Cohen, H F., Portman Square   Times, 31 March, 1899
Freeman-Mitford   Mitford, A B. 30 June, 1886 (3188).
    Mitford Rt Hon J (Baron Redesdalle) 28 Jan., 1809 (131).
Freeman-Thomas : Thomas, F , of Ratton, Sussex, esq. Times, d p., 20 Aug. and 18 Nov., 1892
Freer-Meade : Meade, or Meadows, T., of Alvecote Priory, Tamworth, Staffs. Times, d p , 29 Dec , 1894.
Freind *see* Robinson.
Freke · John, H   7 Aug., 1835 (1567).
    see Hussey-Freke
Freman : Button, J. 14 May, 1831 (974).
French *see* Flutter-Steevens.
    ,, Forester
    ,, Le Poer.
    ,, Leslie
    ,, St George
    ,, Stuart-French
French-Brewster   French, R. A. 13 Aug , 1 Sept , 1874 (D G 521)
Fretwell, R. R. *see* Frecheville, R R. F.
Frey *see* Bellamy.
Freyburg *see* Proschwitzky-Freyburg.
Friend Thompson   Thompson, G , of Bury St Edmunds, and Hart Plain, gent   Times, 3 May, 1877.
Frith   Cockayne   16th Geo. III , 1776.
    see Cokayne-Frith.
Frith-Hudson · Frith, C., of 8, Sunderland Terrace, Bayswater, Middlesex, gent   d p , 3 Oct , 1878
Frost *see* Clarke-Frost.
    ,, Marcham-Mears
    ,, Player-Frowd.
Frostick Aldridge · Frostick, H W. T , of Rotherhithe, Surrey, cheesemonger.   Times, 19 May, 1881
Frowd *see* Player-Frowd.
Frye : Newton, W M.   17 March, 1801 (429)
Fryer *see* Page Fryer.
Fuchs *see* Fox

Fuller *see* Kenyon-Fuller.
Fullarton of Kilmichael Bowden, M. James Lyon Vol. VII, 17 Feb, 1866.
Fuller-Acland-Hood : Hood, A B. P. 7 Sept 1849 (2747)
Fuller-Elliott-Drake : Fuller, Sir F G A. 3 Oct, 1870 (4414)
    . Fuller, T T 31 March, 1813 (679).
Fuller-Maitland . Maitland. E 20 Nov, 1807 (1579).
Fuller-Meyrick Fuller, A E 27 May, 1825 (954)
Fuller-Palmer-Acland : Palmer-Acland, Sir P. P. 12 Aug, 1834 (1545)
Fullerton : Downing, G A 6 Dec, 1794 (1189).
    . Downing, D F. 6 Dec, 1794 (1189)
Fullwood *see* Abbott Fullwood
Furse Johnson, C W. 13 Feb, 1855 (609)
Fussell : Gendre, M M. Countess de, of 68, Westbourne Terrace, Middlesex. Times, 10 Nov, 1871
    see Coldham-Fussell.
Fust *see* Jenner-Fust.
    : Langley, Flora. 18 July, 1827 (1562).
Fynes-Clinton : Fynes, C. 26 April, 1821 (978).

G

Gabbett-Mulhallen . Gabbett, M 17 May, 1895 (D.G 537).
Gabbit : Spiers, J. 29 April, 1795 (410)
    . Spiers, T. 29 April, 1795 (410).
Gage *see* Baillie-Gage
    „ Rookwood.
    „ Rokewode-Gage
Gage-Brown : Brown, E E., of 88, Sloane Street, Chelsea, spinster. Times, d.p, 13 April, 1881
    . Brown, W P., of 88, Sloane Street, Chelsea, gent Times. d p . 3 April, 1882
    Brown, C. H, of 88, Sloane Street, Chelsea, undergrad Edin. University Times, d p, 13 April, 1881.
Gage-Rokewode . Gage, J 20 Nov., 1838 (2592).
Galaher *see* Fitz-Gerald
Gale *see* Braddyll.
    : Coore, H M. G, of Scruton Hall, Bedale, Yorks, esq Times. d p, 8 Aug, 1890
    : Morant, E. 2 Jan, 1796 (7)
Gale-Braddyll *see* Richmund-Gale-Braddyll.
Gallaher *see* Wilson.

Gallenga Hardwin : Gallenga, G. H., Capt. Dublin Fusiliers. Times, d p , 1 May, 1890.
Galley *see* Jackson.
Galley-Day-Jackson : Galley, J. 8 Dec., 1837 (3242)
Gallway *see* Payne
Gally *see* Knight.
Galmoye, T Lawrence : Alley-Jones, T , of Coleherne Road, S. Kensington, and 40, Chancery Lane, solicitor. Times, d.p., 20 Nov , 1875.
Galpine *see* Sampson.
Galway *see* Arundell.
Galwey : Payne, Sir W., Bart. 54 Geo. III , c. 4 (Index to pub. and priv. Statutes, p. 504).
Gambles Caven, J , of East Croft, Cumberland, gent Times, d p., 18 July, 1876.
Games *see* Hughes Games.
Gammie-Maitland Gammie, G , of Shotover House, Oxford, and of Stockbridge, Hants, esq. Times, 21 April, 1865.
Gammon *see* Gariman.
  „ Gretton.
Gammon-Grenville : Gammon, Rev. R. P., L.L.B., of 8, Queen's Square, Glasgow; G. P Gammon, of Hollowel Barton, East Down, North Devon ; W B Gammon, of 18, Wood Street, London, s. of Rev. William, of Norton-Fitzwarren, Somerset Times, 22 April, 1869
Gandar-Dower Gandar, J W., of Regent's Park, Middlesex, esq. Times, d p, 26 July, 1890.
Gandolfi *see* Hornyold.
Gandy Brandreth, F. 20 Jan., 1859 (293)
  see Deering.
  : Rogers, R. N. 20 Jan., 1859 (293).
Gane *see* Cooke.
Gapp-Arlington · Gapp, C., of Ryder's Wells, Lewes, Sussex. Times, 16 July, 1864.
Gapper *see* Southby
Garbett *see* Hughes-Garbett.
Garbett-Walsham · Garbett. J. 12 May, 1800 (461).
  see Walsham
Gard, W. Garrard Snowdon · Gard, W. S., of Hampstead and Basinghall Street, London, L L.B , solicitor. Times, 20 Dec., 1873.
  see Gostwyck.
Gardiner *see* Cooper-Gardiner.
    „ Coulter.
    „ Richmond.
    „ Smythe.
    „ Smythe-Gardiner.

Gardner see Agg-Gardner.
„ Dunn-Gardner.
„ Gardner-McTaggart.
„ Kynnersley
: Panting, L.   2 May, 1801 (465).
: Panting, R.   30 Aug., 1844 (3012)
see Richardson-Gardner.
Gardner-McTaggart   Gardner, G. H. S., of Reading, Berks. Times, 7 Oct., 1898.
Gardner-Medwin   Gardner, F. M.   2 March, 1868 (1865).
Gardner-Waterman   Gardner, W. and W.   3 April, 1867 (2184).
Gardner, Waterman and William   Whll, 3 April, 1867 (D.G. 495)
Waterman, J. C., of Street End, Willesborough, Kent, widow   Times, 13 April, 1867
Gardner-Woolloton   Gardner, A. W., of Stamford Hill, Midx., gent.   Times, d.p., 11 May, 1877
Garfit see Bellwood.
Gariman   Gammon, H., of 15, Somerset Terrace, Stoke Newington, Middlesex, and of 11, Fenchurch Buildings, London, ship broker   Times, 1 July, 1865.
Garland see Cope.
„ Lester
Garlick : Barber, J   10th Geo. IV., 1829.
see Rothwell
Garner see Cumberland
Garner-Richards : Garner, D. R.   9 Nov., 1860 (4408)
Garnett   Orme.   6 March, 1882 (1131)
Garnett-Botfield   Garnett, W. B.   30 Oct., 1863 (5193).
Garnier see Carpenter-Garnier.
Garrard see Cherry-Garrard.
Garrard Snowdon Gard see Gard.
Garrett-Pegge : Pegg, Jn. Wm. Garrett, of Chesham Bois, Bucks. Times, 18 Aug., 1899
Garrick see Trevor-Garrick
Garstang see Hodgson
Garth-Colleton   Garth, C.   13 April, 1805 (522)
Garstin see de Garston.
Garth   Lowndes, R.   20 March, 1837 (876).
Gartside, Fredk : Neville, Geo. Fredk., of 41, Fitzroy Square, Middlesex, actor   Times, d.p., 14 May, 1888
Gascoigne · Gaskin, J. H., of Croydon Road, S. Penge Park, Surrey and Home Office, Whitehall, gent.   Times, d.p., 25 Nov., 1881.
see Oliver-Gascoigne
„ Trench-Gascoigne.

Gascoyne *see* Chandler
Gascoyne-Cecil : Cecil, J. B. W. 27 March, 1821 (728).
Gaskell : Hookey, H., of 26, Westbourne Park, Bayswater, Midx., esq. Times, d p., 19 June, 1877.
   see Penn-Gaskell.
Gaskin *see* Gascoigne
Gastrell *see* Harris-Gastrell
   ,, Houghton-Gastrell
Gates-Warren : Warren, G. G , of Jamaica, W. Indies, assistnt surveyor Roy Engineers. Times, d p , 19 Jan., 1892.
Gathorne-Hardy : Hardy, G (Visc. Cranbrook). 11 May, 1878 (3044) (D.G 486)
Gatty *see* Barfoot-Saunt.
   ,, Scott-Gatty.
Gaudet *see* Bunning.
Gausset Lanagan : Gausset, F E., of 9, Brownlow St , Holborn. Times, 13 May, 1875
Gawan Jones : Jones, J. E., Holland Park, W. Times, 13 Dec., 1900
Gawen *see* Roberts-Gawen
Gawler *see* Ker Bellenden.
Gay : Rivers, Sir P. 28 July, 1767 (10749).
Gay Roberts : Roberts, E C , of Turlake, Devon, and of Nuneaton, Warwick, esq. Times, d p., 10 April, 1880.
Gaylard *see* Ratcliff-Gaylard.
Geale-Brady : Geale, B., of Mount Geale, co Kilkenny, and of Dublin. Dublin, 6 Feb , 1841.
Geale-Wybrants : Geale, W 29 March, 1877 (D.G 235)
Geary *see* Ruiz-Geary.
Geary-Salte : Geary, W. 5 May, 1798 (368).
Geast *see* Dugdale
Geast-Dugdale : Geast, H 10 April, 1822 (785)
Gedney *see* Holgate-Gedney.
Gedny *see* Chaston.
Gee : Castle, T 8 May, 1863 (2525,
   Parson, A. B 15 Jan., 1885 (233).
Geisenhainer *see* Watson.
Gelderd : Airey, M. A 12 Feb. 1878 (1730).
   : Somervel, F and A. 29 Feb., 1878 (1788)
Gelderd-Somervell : Gelderd. 29 March, 1882 (1696).
Gell *see* Chandos-Pole-Gell.
   ,, Hamilton Gell
   ,, Thornhill Gell
Gendre, Countess de *see* Fussell.
Gennys : Henn, E 24 April, 1802 (406)
Gent *see* Tharp-Gent
Geoghegan *see* O'Neill.

George *see* Bryan.
      ,, St. George.
      ,, Thorne-George.
Georges *see* Fettiplace
      William : Goergs, Wilhelm, of 31, Hampton Place, Brighton, Sussex, prof. of languages and music. Times, 7 March, 1871
Gerard-Dicconson : Gerard, R J. 18 Jan., 1896 (503).
Germaine *see* Sackville.
German Reed : Reed, A. G., of Maude Grove, Fulham Road, Middlesex. Times, 14 Jan., 1888
Gervis *see* Tapps-Gervis.
      ,, Tapps-Gervis-Meyrick
Gery *see* Wade-Gery.
Gibb *see* Hughes-Gibb
    : Scott, H. W. 9 Jan., 1819 (153).
Gibb-Samson *see* Alexander
Gibbard *see* Stileman-Gibbard.
Gibbon *see* Samuel-Gibbon
Gibbons *see* Blythe.
Gibbs *see* Brandreth.
Gibbs-Heagren : Heagren, E. 13 April, 1819 (756)
Giblett *see* Montagu
Gibson : Carew-Gibson.
      see Mackenzie-Gibson
      ,, Milner-Gibson.
      ,, Milner-Gibson-Cullum.
      ,, Sugars Gibson
Gibson-Carmichael, of Skirling : Gibson, Sir Thomas, Bt. Lyon Vol III., 28 Nov., 1823.
Gibson-Craig, of Riccarton : Gibson, James. Lyon Vol. III., 17 June, 1823.
Gibson-Leadbitter : Gibson, T. 4 Dec., 1874 (203)
Gibson-Maitland *see* Ramsay-Gibson-Maitland.
Gibson-Watt : Gibson, J. W. 29 Dec., 1856 (147)
Giddy *see* Gilbert.
Gideon *see* Eardley
Giebelhausen *see* Greene.
Gieve : Neale, J. W., of 111, High Street, Portsmouth. Times, d p, 25 Sept., 1877.
Gifford *see* Bennet.
Gigg *see* Jones
Gigger *see* Mace-Gigger.
Gilbert : Giddy, D. 10 Dec., 1816 (2)
      · Price, J. 10 May, 1822 (916)
      : Price, T. 10 May, 1822 (916)

Gilbert-Day : Day, Rev. J., of Pitsford, Northampton Times, d.p., 28 May, 1874
Gilbert-Douglas Gilbert, A. 24 Nov., 1807 (1580).
Gilbert-East : Clayton-East, G. E. 11 April, 1839 (800)
    see Clayton-East.
Gilbert-Smith · Smith, E., of 8, Easy Row, Birmingham, Warwick, surgeon Times, 11 Sept., 1874.
Gilbertson-Pritchard Gilbertson, W. E., of Cemarth, Montgomerys. Times, d.p., 23 March, 1881
Gilchrist *see* Bothwick-Gilchrist
Giles-Puller Puller, C. W. 27 Nov., 1857 (4217).
    Puller, C. G., of Youngsbury, Herts, and of Gt. Stoatley, Surrey, esq Times, d.p., 9 June, 1885.
Gill Frankland, M. D. 15 June, 1867 (3475).
    Frankland, Mary D. Whll., 15 June, 1867 (D G 811)
    see Gyll
    · Kerr, Agnes Stewart (widow) Whll., 15 June, 1867 (D G. 811).
    see Pretor
    „ Varenne.
Gill-Anderton Gill, A. W. 9 April, 1892 (2318)
Gill Houghton Gill F. G., H.M. Army Times, 4 April, 1900.
Gill-Russell · Gill, J. R. W., at Charing Cross Hotel, Middlesex, gent. Times, d.p., 2 June, 1887.
Gillan *see* Chadwick
Gillespie *see* Duff-Gillespie
Gillespie-Stainton : Gillespie, R. W., of Biggarshiells, Lanark, and Bitterswell House, Leicester, esq Times, d.p., 6 May, 1873. Lyon Vol. IX. 4 June, 1873
Gillibrand *see* Fazakerley
    Hawarden, T. 18 May, 1779 (11979).
Gillies-Smith Smith, Adam Gillies Lyon Vol. XIV., 20 Mar., 1896
Gilling *see* Smith
    Lax, T. 11 Dec., 1843 (4350).
Gilling-Lax Gilling, Geo. R. Whll., 20 May, 1868 (D G. 585)
Gillyatt Marris, E. G. 12 Oct., 1807 (1400).
Gilmour *see* Gordon-Gilmour.
    „ Little-Gilmour.
Gilpin Purcell, P. V. 12 Feb., 1884 (D G. 219)
Gilpin-Brown : Gilpin, G. 3 March, 1854 (787).
Gilson *see* Shield
Gilstrap *see* MacRae-Gilstrap
Ginger *see* Glyn.
Ginsburg *see* Crighton-Ginsburg
Gist · Sellick, J. 23 Feb., 1815 (391).
Gladell-Vernon : Gladell, J. W., 8 May, 1784 (D G. 4447).

Gladston : Gladstone, A E C, of 23, Rue de Rocroy, Paris, commission agent Times, d p , 21 Feb , 1890.
Gladstone *see* Cocking-Gladstone.
„ Gladston.
· Gladstones, John R.L., 10 Feb., 1835.
Gladwin *see* Goodwin-Gladwin
Gladwin-Errington Errington, J L., of Midgham Vicarage, Reading, Berks Times, 15 March, 1898
Glass *see* Elliott
Glass-Turner : Glass, H 8 Sept , 1804 (1101).
Glasse *see* Shaw.
Glasspoole *see* Davies-Glasspoole
Glaze Hall, R. L, of Waterloo Road, Wolverhampton, Staffs. Times. d p , 27 Nov , 1896
Gledstanes : Hornidge, M V. 11 July, 24 July, 1871 (D.G 545 and 549)
Glen-Coats, of Ferguslie Park · Coats, Sir Thomas, Bart Lyon Vol. XIII , 20 May, 1895
Glyn : Ginger, W , of 47, Denbigh Street, Pimlico, gent. Times, d p , 1 Jan., 1867.
: Wills, J., widow of late Ed Wills, and subsequently Mrs. Dallas, of 6, Hanover Square, London. Times, 11 July, 1874.
Glynn *see* Oglander.
: Greensmith, T., of 82, Mason's Hill, Bromley, Kent, butler Times, d p , 30 Aug , 1889.
Glynton : Brownjohn, C M., esq , and A , his wife, both of 8, Lansdown Place East, Bath Times, d p , 18 May, 1888
Goatley *see* Gotley.
Goddard *see* Reeve.
Goddard-Mason Sirr, Penelope M Times, 7 Aug , 1862.
Godden-Smith Godden, A S , of 18 Oriel Street, Bootle, Lancs , ship-broker. Times, d.p., 28 Sept , 1888.
Godfrey . Jull, T 39th Geo III , 1799
. Jull, J 6 June, 1810 (821).
Mackenzie. 11th Geo. III , 1771.
see Thurlow
Godfrey-Faussett · Faussett, G T., of Heppington, Kent , G Faussett, of Cheltenham, co Gloucester , H. C. Faussett, of S Littleton, co Worcester ; Lieut W. Faussett, in H M 's Army ; R. Faussett, student of Ch Church, Oxford , T G. Faussett, barrister-at-law, of Lincoln's Inn and precincts of Canterbury Cathedral , J T Faussett, of 49, Pall Mall, Westminster, student of Ch. Church, Oxford; S. Faussett, spinster, of Cheltenham , S Faussett, spinster, of Great Marlow, Bucks. Times, 24 June, 1870.
Godfrey-Faussett-Osborne : Godfrey Faussett, Rev. H G , of Hartlip Place, Kent Times, 11 Dec , 1871

Godin *see* Bigot
Godsalve *see* Crosse
Godwin-Austen : Austen, R A C.   24 Oct., 1854 (3219).
Goergs, Wilhelm *see* Georges, William
Goff *see* Davis-Goff
  „ Mallard
Goggs *see* Pemberton.
Goldie-Scott, of Craigmuie : Scott, Thos. Lyon Vol VIII., 30 Nov., 1868.
Goldie-Taubman : Goldie, A J. 2 Aug., 1824 (1452).
Golding : Graves, G G. 44th Geo. III., 1804.
Golding-Bird Bird, Rev R J, of 26, John Street, Bedford Row, London. Times, d p., 8 Jan., 1890.
Golding-Palmer Golding, H   13 Oct., 1880 (5431)
Goldney *see* Bennett Goldney
Goldney-Cary Cary, G, of Burleigh House, Willesden, and of Old Square, Lincoln's Inn, barrister. Times, d p, 30 Nov., 1881
Goldsmid *see* D'Avigdor-Goldsmid.
  „ Hoffnung-Goldsmid
  „ Meredith
     Moses, E. 6 Aug., 1804 (1040).
Goldsmid-Montefiore · Montefiore, C J. 22 Feb., 1883 (998)
Goldstein *see* Edwards
Goldstrom *see* Grosvenor
Goldwyer-Lewis : Lewis, A G, formerly Archdeacon of Bombay, India, now of Bushmead Avenue, Bedford. Times, d.p, 21 Nov., 1891.
Gomm *see* Carr-Gomm
Gooch *see* Hill
Goodall *see* Crowther
Goodall-Copestake · Goodall, T   2 Feb., 1827 (598)
Goodchild, Albert *see* Dale, Albert Alfred Michell
Goode *see* Wyatt
Gooden-Chisholm : Gooden, J. Chisholm, of 33, Tavistock Square, Middlesex, esq Lyon Vol XI., 3 May, 1887. Times, 17 June, 1887
Goodere *see* Dineley
Gooderich *see* Esmée
Goodeve, Arthur Chucker-Butty, Arthur Tims Goodeve. of Walmer, Kent   Times, 24 Aug., 1899
Goodlake *see* Surman
Goodliffe Vereker-Bindon, H, of 10. Manor Mansions, Belsize Park Gardens, London. cadet   Times, d p., 3 Sept., 1889
Goodman *see* Berliner-Goodman
  „ Goodwin.
Goodricke *see* Holyoake.

Goodwin : Goodman, B , late of Manchester, Lancaster, now
    of 24, Burlington Road, Bayswater, Middlesex.
    Times, 19 July, 1867.
  : Bones, J. 19 Nov., 1793 (1031)
  : Colquitt, G. C. 10 Feb , 1842 (356).
  see Craven
  : Maxwell. H 13 Feb , 1815 (338).
Goodwin Brown : Goodwin, H., of Deptford Times, 22 Dec ,
  1863.
Goodwin-Gladwin : Goodwin, R H. 28 April, 1881 (2554).
Goodyear *see* Dean.
Goose *see* Durand
  „ Sewell.
Goppy *see* Warre
Gordan *see* Evans-Gordon
Gordon *see* Bentley
  „ Conway-Gordon
  „ Duff-Gordon
  „ Evans-Gordon.
  „ Forbes
  Forbes, B 26 Aug , 1836 (1654)
  Forbes, B. 30 Nov , 1816 (2478)
  Sir Hugh, Bt Gordon, Hugh, s of late Hugh Wm., of
    The Knoll, Elgin, nearest of kin to late Sir
    F. Gordon, Bt , of Lesmoir. Times, 28 Sept , 1870
  see Hay-Gordon
  „ Jordan.
  : Jordan, L J., of Harley Street, Cavendish Square.
    Times, d p , 24 ct , 1879
  . Lloyd, Clara A Times, 10 Feb , 1900
  see McHaffie-Gordon
  : Matchett, W. 29 Nov , 1837 (3189).
  see Smith-Gordon
  • Straube, F G Times, d p , 15 May, 1896.
Gordon Baillie : Whyte, A., of 4, Bryanston Street, Portman Sq ,
  W Times, d.p., 31 March, 1885
Gordon-Canning : Gordon, P. R. and H 16 March, 1849 (1205)
Gordon Craig : Gordon Wardell, E. H , of 22, Barkston Gardens,
  S Kensington, actor. Times, d p , 24 Feb , 1893
Gordon-Frazer : Frazer, C E., of 4, John Street, Hampstead,
  Middlesex Times d p . 20 April, 1887.
Gordon-Gilmour, of Craigmillar Robert Gordon Wolrige-Gordon.
  Lyon Vol. VII., 7 July, 1865
Gordon-Kerr : Jones, H G , of 39, Euston Grove, Oxton,
  Cheshire, gent Times, d p , 28 Sept., 1883.
  • Jones, T. C., of 6, Preesons Row, Liverpool,
    merchant Times, d p , 28 Sept., 1883

Gordon-Lennox   Lennox, C , Duke of   9 Aug., 1836 (1441)
Gordon-Moore : Gordon, Hon C. and Emily, his wife.   27 April, 22 May, 1850 (D.G 473 and 481)
Gordon-Oswald, of Scotstown   Gordon, Jas.   Lyon Vol VII, 7 July, 1865
Gordon Pugh : Pugh, W T , Forest-gate, Essex   Times, 3 Feb , 1899
Gordon-Short : Short, C H , Lieut 104th Bengal Fusiliers, of London   Times, 11 March, 1873
Gordon-Stuart   Gordon, D   9 March, 1835 (439)
Gordon-Wolrige : Perkins-Wolrige, H , of 15, Pembridge Square, London   Times, 8 July, 1864
    see Wolrige-Gordon
Gordon-Woodhouse · Woodhouse, J. G., of 6, Upper Brooke St , Grosvenor Square, &c.   Times, d p , 12 Dec., 1895
Gore *see* Hickman
   „ Hume-Gore.
   Knox, J. D C , 23 April, 1813.
   see Langton
   „ Ormsby-Gore.
   „ Saunders-Knox-Gore
   „ Vernon-Gore.
Gore-Booth   Gore, Sir R.   30 Aug , 1804 (1161).
Gore-Langton *see* Temple-Gore-Langton.
Gorey   Coxell, R H , 8, Fore Street, Devonport, refreshment-house keeper.   Times, d p , 16 May, 1893
Gorges *see* Meredyth
Goring *see* Cosby
Goring-Bankes : Bankes, H. A , of 34, Moorgate Street, London.   Times, d p , 7 Feb., 1893
Gorman-Monkhouse   Gorman, E S   9 June, 1810 (821)
Gorney *see* Ewens-Gorney.
Gorst *see* Lowndes
Gortzacoff *see* Zacharoff Gortzacoff.
Gorwyn *see* Arden-Gorwyn
    „ Lambert
Gosling *see* Hamlyn
Gosnall *see* Walford-Gosnall
Gosselin *see* Lefebvre
Gossip *see* De Rodes
   „ Hatfield
   „ Wilmer.
Gostling-Murray   Murray, C E   18 May, 1875 (2773)
Gostwyck   Gard, W G   29 Jan., 1897 (1166).
Gothard *see* Baker-Gothard.
Gotley, G Henniker   Goatley, G (Rev) of Tysoe, Warwicks   Times, d.p.; 22 Dec., 1887.

Gotobed see Loft.
,, Vipan.
Gott : Greening, H. T. 9th Geo III., 1769.
Gottheimer see Grant.
Gough : Astley, jun., R. 2 Nov., 1816 (2378)
   see Calthorpe.
   : Gough-Calthorpe, F. (Hon.) 12 June, 1845 (1764)
   : Jones, J. H., of 90, Aspen Grove, Liverpool. Times, 1 March, 1887
   see Seare.
Could see Baring-Gould.
   ,, Davies-Gould
   . Jackson, H. L. 20 April, 1871 (2268).
   see Morgan.
   , Yelverton
Goulton-Constable : Marriott, Jas. P. and Lucy H., his wife. Whll., 18 Dec., 1865 (D.G. 22).
   : Marriott, J. P. 18 Dec., 1865 (26)
Govett-Romaine · Govett, W. 24 May, 1827 (1273)
Gow : Gow Smith, W., of Assam, E. Indies, now of Gt. Tower Street, London, tea planter. Times, d.p., 8 Sept., 1879.
Gow-Stewart, of Little Colonsay . Gow, James. Lyon Vol. VI, 3 Oct., 1864.
   : Gow, A., of Newcastle-upon-Tyne, lead manufacr. Times, 13 May, 1886.
Gow-Steuart-Gow . Gow-Steuart, M. J. 13 July, 1895 (4159).
Gowan see Mauleverer
Gower see Egerton.
Grace see Hamilton-Grace.
   ,, Hensman.
Grace-Hensman : Grace, C. J., of Clarendon Road, Notting Hill, London. Times, 9 May, 1899.
Græme see Hamond-Græme.
   ,, Jones-Græme
Græme Watt : Watt, R., of 37, Ashley Avenue, Belfast Times, 23 March, 1895
Grafton-Dare : Grafton, J. M. 13 Dec., 1805 (1611).
Grafton see Tomkyns-Grafton.
Grafton Wignall : Wignall, F., of 38, Calthorpe Road, Edgbaston, Warwicks., gent. Times, d.p., 20 July, 1882.
Graham see Campbell-Graham.
   . Clarke, Revd. E. G. W., 10 June, 1862 (D.G. 707).
   see Clarke.
   ,, Graham-Barns-Graham.
   : Graham-Clarke, E. 10 June, 1862 (2991)
   see Lacon-Graham.
   ,, Martone-Graham

Graham *see* Maxwell-Graham.
   „ Munn-Graham
   „ Savage-Graham
   : Vernon. H. C E.   13 Sept , 1800 (1030)
   see Vernon.
   „ Webberburn.
   „ Webster.
   : White, T. G.   4 April, 1845 (1050)
Graham-Barns-Graham, of Craigalhan : Graham, Allan   Lyon, Vol. XI., 7 May, 1884.
Graham-Clarke *see* Graham.
Graham-Foster-Pigott · Graham, G. E.   12 March, 1827 (631).
Graham-Hodgson *see* Hodgson
Graham-Maxwell, of Monksworth : Maxwell-Graham, James, Lyon Vol. VI , 7 Aug , 1858.
Graham-Montgomery, of Stanhope : Montgomery.   Lyon Vol. IV., 3 Sept , 1844.
Graham-Toler : Toler, Hon. H. J.   Dublin, 26 Nov., 1825.
Graham-Wigan · Wigan, J. A.   8 Dec., 1896 (7487)
Grahame, Richard : Duck, Richard Gelson, of Newmarket Chambers, Strutt Street, Manchester, Lancaster, and of Chelford House, Chelford, Chester, stock and share broker.. Times, d p , 14 May, 1872
Grainger *see* Fothergill.
   : Liddell, H , of Middleton Hall, nr. Belford, N'berland. Times, 4 May, 1893.
   see Liddell-Grainger
   „ Parry
Grant *see* Dalton
   : Eady, C. G., of Bylock Hall, Ponder's End, Middlesex, gent.   Times, d.p., 19 March, 1868
   see Forsyth-Grant
   . Gottheimer, A., late of Bedford Villas, Croydon, Surrey, now of 80, Lombard Street, London, and of Stafford House, Carlton Road, Maida Vale, Middlesex, esq   Times, d p., 11 July, 1863.
W. Robertson : Grant, W., of Buenos Ayres, and of Cromdale, N.B   Times, 18 Sept., 1877.
   see Keir-Grant.
   „ McPherson-Grant.
   „ Mounsey.
   „ Mounsey Grant.
   „ Napier Grant.
   : Peterkin, G. G., of Invererne, co Moray, formerly Lieut. 45th Reg., now in Western Virginia, U.S A. Times, 26 March, 1879.

Grant see Philipps.
,, Powell
: Sim, P., of 5, Mabledon Place, Kings' Cross, printer's timekeeper. Times, d p., 16 July, 1881
see Thomlinson-Grant
,, Willoughby Gordon
Grant-Browne-Sheridan : Sheridan, R. B. 8 Feb, 1836 (286)
Grant-Ives : Grant. W. D. 18 Aug., 1888 (5021)
Grant-Thorold : Grant, A. W. T. 8 Nov., 1864 (5265).
Grantham-Hill : Hill, S. G., of Denham Court, Hants. Times, d.p., 26 April, 1893
Grantley : Walter, H. J., formerly of Oxford, but now of Missouri, U.S.A., attorney-at-law. Times, d p., 14 June, 1889.
Granville : Dewes, C. 4 April, 1827 (942)
· D'Ewes, J. 22 Nov., 1785 (533)
Granville-Smith : Smith, R. W., of 75, Victoria Street, Westminster, gent. Times, d p., 30 Dec., 1886.
Grattan, Ernest : Smith, John, of H M Commissariat Staff, Woolwich. Times, d p., 1 June, 1880
Grattan-Bellew : Bellew, T. A. 19 March, 28 March, 1859 (D G. 467 and 515)
Grattan-Guinness : Guinness, Rev W S St. J., 28 Feb., D.C., 10 March, 1856 (D G. 337)
Gratwicke see Archdall-Gratwicke.
,, Kinleside-Gratwicke
Graver-Brown · Graver, J T. 13 May, 1815 (894)
Graves see Golding
,, Sawle
,, Steele-Graves, Sir. J M
Graves-Knyfton : Graves, R. B. 24 Nov., 1894 (7451)
Graves-Russell : Russell, J. 27 May, 1822 (956)
Graves-Sawle : Sawle, J S. 30 Nov., 1827 (2506).
Gray : Hall, G. (formerly Gray), of 37, Carlyle Square, Chelsea esq. Times, d p., 13 Aug., 1889.
see Hall
Hunter, W. 29 Jan., 1851 (335).
see Ross
(Baroness Eveleen) : Smith Lyon Vol. XIV., 8 June, 1897.
of Gray, Kinfauns, etc. Stuart, Edmund Archibald Lyon Vol. X., 30 Jan., 1879
see Wallace
Gray-Archdall : Gray, H A., of Derryargan, co. Fermanagh Dublin, 27 Jan., 1840.
Gray-Jones : Jones, T., of Newport, Monmouth, collector of H.M. Customs, formerly of Preston, Lancaster. Times, 7 June, **1872.**

Gray-Murray · Buist, Milton Gray, Gloucester Crescent, Regent's Park, London. Times, 12 July, 1898.
Grayrigge : Rigge, G , of Jesus Coll , Camb., Sub-Lieut Lancs Mil. Times, d p , 28 Oct., 1875.
Greame *see* Lloyd-Greame
    „ Yarburgh
Greathed : Harris, E. 22 March, 1806 (375).
Greatheed *see* Bertie-Greatheed
Greatheed-Percy : Percy, Hon. C 10 April, 1826 (878).
Greaves Bradshaw, J 2 June, 1824 (950).
    see Brown-Greaves
    „ Ley.
    „ Myers
Greaves-Bagshaw Greaves, W. H 29 May, 1879 (2730).
Greaves-Banning Banning, C B. 6 Nov., 1865 (5403).
Greaves Emsall Greaves, J. E. 26 April, 1817 (1002).
Green *see* Ashman
    „ Beddow.
    : Chapman, E. 29 June, 1776 (11678).
    see Cotton
    „ Egerton-Green
    T Harold Mortimer : Green, T., Lieut., now at Plymouth, Devon Times, d.p., 1 March, 1890.
    see Horwood
    : Kent, J 26 Jan., 1793 (70).
    see Kent-Green.
    . Kent, R. 27 July, 1829 (1464).
    see Lowthorpe-Green
    „ Leedham-Green
    „ Penrose Green.
    „ Richardson
    Verral, A. 13 July, 1835 (1351)
    see Wilkinson-Green
    · Wilson, J 12 June, 1827 (1273).
Green-Armytage : Green, J. 26 June, 1807 (895).
Green-Emmott-Rawdon : Green, E A, of 29, Promenade, Cheltenham, Gloucester, and of Rawdon, York, Maj -Gen on H M retired list. Times d p., 7 March, 1872
Green-Thompson : Green, A W, 13 July. 1855 (D G 1068).
Green Ward Green, C. S , of Maida Vale, Paddington Times, d.p , 23 Oct., 1880
Greene *see* Armelle
    „ de Freville
    : Giebelhausen, J. 20 March, 1820 (624).
    : Quarrill, T A , of 18, Greville Place, St. John's Wood, Middlesex d p , 13 May, 1865

Greene - Quarrill, C J., of 18, Greville Place, St John's Wood, Middlesex, lamp and lustre manufacturer. d p., 13 May, 1865.
  · Thomas, H. 55th Geo III, 1815
Greene-Cadogan : Greene, J. F. C., of Alum Bay, I.W., esq Times, d.p , 5 Dec. 1879
Greene-de Freville : Greene, E. H 4 June, 1850 (1569)
  : Green, Rev F. P., of Pusey Rectory, Faringdon. Berks. d p., 19 May, 1894.
Greengrass-Easton : Greengrass, Edwin, of Westminster, London Times, 4 July, 1899.
Greenhill-Russell Greenhill, R. 27 May, 1815 (996).
Greenhough : Bellas, G. 3 Jan., 1795 (1).
Greenhow-Relph : Greenhow, G. R. 29 Nov., 1844 (5086).
Greening *see* Gott.
Greenland : Hooker, G T 25 Aug., 1820 (1629).
Greenley Allen, C. W 10 March, 1865 (1448).
Greenly *see* Coffin-Greenly.
Greensmith *see* Glynn.
Greenwollers *see* Kent.
Greenwood *see* Brown.
  „ Calvert.
  „ Holden.
  „ Stanyforth.
Greenwood-Penny . Greenwood, R. P 13 April, 1841 (977).
Gregge · Hopwood, E 13th Geo III., 1773.
Gregor . Booker, G. W F. 14 Nov., 1825 (2189).
Gregory · Cottam, W. G., of Swinshawe, Lancs., tanner and currier. Times, d.p., 9 Sept , 1876
  see Mogg.
  „ Pearson-Gregory.
  : Sherwin, J. S 11 Sept , 1860 (3401).
  see Welby-Gregory
Gregory-Welby *see* Welby-Gregory.
Gregson : Knight, H 28 July. 1842 (2077)
Gregson Ellis : Ellis, R. G., of Ruthin, Denbigh, J.P. Times. d p., 25 Nov., 1887.
  : Ellis, C J., of 1, Paper Buildings, Middlesex, and of 41, Penywern Road, Middlesex, barrister-at-law. Times, 1 March, 1889.
Greig *see* Rutherford-Greig.
Greig-Rutherford-Elliot · Bogie, J., of Newington, nr. Edinburgh, formerly of Victoria Street, Edinburgh, esq , F S S. Lond. Times, 4 Aug., 1885.
Greive *see* Browne-Greive.
Grenville *see* Gammon-Grenville.
  „ Morgan-Grenville.
  „ Neville-Grenville.

Grenville-Nugent-Temple . Grenville, Rt Hon. G (E. Temple, Vis. Cobham) 4 Dec , 1779 (12036).
Grepe . Gripe, J , of Burrington Park, Pennycross, Devon, gent . formerly of Melbourne, Victoria, merchant Times. 24 April, 1871
 Gripe, W. S , of Compton Gifford, Devon, gent., formerly of Melbourne, Victoria, merchant. Times, 24 April, 1871
Gresham *see* Aikman-Gresham.
Gresley *see* Douglas-Gresley.
Greswolde *see* Meysey-Wigley-Greswolde.
 : Wigley 4 Feb., 1833 (274)
 see Williams-Greswolde
Greswolde-Williams Williams, W. G W., 1 Sept, 1860 (D G 1040).
 . Williams, F. W G. 7 March, 1893 (2120).
 . Williams, H J., of The Mount, Torquay, Devon Times, 11 Oct., 1895.
 · Williams, W. G 1 Sept., 1860 (3333).
Gretton . Gammon, J H , of 26, Maida Vale, Middlesex, manag direcr Lond Internatnal Exhib Soc Times, 12 May, 1881.
Greulich *see* Grey.
Greville . Murray-Greville, R. F. 24 Aug , 1824 (1478).
 . Greville-Nugent-Algernon, W F (Baron Greville) 7 April, 1883 (2024)
 : Greville-Nugent, G. F. 6 June, 1883 (2982)
Greville-Nugent · Greville, F. S., and his wife, Lady Rosa 8 Aug. and 16 Aug , 1866 (D G 1245 and 1266).
Grevis-James . Grevis, D. 18 Dec , 1817 (2590)
Grews *see* Loraine-Grews
Grey *see* Bacon-Grey
 · Drynan, G S , of Malcolm Peth, St. Leonard's-on-Sea Sussex Times, d.p , 3 Nov , 1870.
 : Greulich, C., of Newent, Gloucester, Lieut H M. Royal Naval Reserve Times, 11 March, 1868
 see Robinson
 ,, Scurfield
 ,, Smith.
Grey-Egerton : Egerton, Sir P. 30 June, 1822 (1246)
 . Grey, Sir J 17 Oct., 1814 (103)
Greyham : Benjamin, S., of Russell Square, formerly of Cape of Good Hope, merchant Times, d p., 13 March, 1876
 · Benjamin, H. I , of Russell Square, formerly of Cape of Good Hope, merchant Times, d p , 13 Mar., 1876

Grice-Hutchinson Hutchinson, G W, of Avening, Glos, Capt. (Army), and L E M., his wife. Times, d p, 9 March, 1885.
Grieve : Brown, W S. 25 Aug., 1884 (3913)
    see Macfarlane-Grieve
    ,, Mackenzie-Grieve, J. A and F J.
Griffies-Williams Griffies, G 2 April, 1875 (161)
Griffin Neville, R A (Lord Aldworth) 38th Geo. III , 1798.
    . Parker, M 6 June, 1797 (511)
    see Parnell
    ,, Stonestreet
    . Tyler, G. G. 16 Feb., 1877 (2133)
Griffith *see* Booth
    ,, Darley-Griffith
    Griffith Jones, G C., of 17, Henrietta Street, Covent Garden, journalist. Times, d p , 5 June, 1894
    see Jermyn
    ,, Murhall-Griffith.
    ,, Poyer
    ,, Waldie-Griffith
    : Watkins, L. A 30 Nov, 1841 (3137).
Griffith-Apsley . Reeve, Griffith ap, lately commonly known as ap Griffith, of 4, St. Peter's Place, Brighton Times, d p , 5 Dec., 1868
Griffith Boscawen Griffith, B T., of Trevalyn Hall, Denbigh, esq. Times, d p., 19 May, 1875
Griffith-Colpoys : Griffith, E. 15 June, 1821 (1439)
Griffith-Dearden : Dearden, J , of Manor House, Rochdale, Lancaster, barrister-at-law d p , 24 Nov , 1865.
Griffith-Williams · Williams, A M , Sol , & F L , assumed about 1883
Griffith-Winne Wynne, F 26 June, 1804 (839)
Griffith-Wynne *see* Wynne-Finch
Griffiths *see* Benson Griffiths
    ,, Copland-Griffiths
    Albert Edwin : Griffiths, Rich Albert Edwin, of Maida Vale, Middlesex, stock jobber. Times, d p., 23 May, 1888
    see Hazelby.
    : Morgan, Hannah, of 48, Aughton Road, Birkdale, Lancs , spinster. Times, d p., 4 Dec., 1889
    see Parry
    ,, Thackray
Griffiths-Aubrey Griffiths, M 17 April, 1813 (773)
Griffiths-Averill : Griffiths, J. 8 Aug., 1891 (4437)
Grimes *see* Avery
    ,, Cholmley
Grimké-Drayton : Grimké, T. D. 18 Feb., 1891 (1202).

Grimshaw *see* Atkinson-Grimshaw
Grimston *see* Bucknall.
    : Wilmot, J. 21 July, 1860 (2779)
Grimwood : Cozens, J. G 15 May, 1851 (1296).
Grindall *see* Sturt-Grindall
Grinfield-Coxwell · Coxwell, J. E , of 7, Marlborough Place, Brighton, at present residing at 7, Woburn Place, Middlesex, Times, 16 April, 1886.
Gripe *see* Grepe
Grodsenski *see* Morris.
Grogan-Morgan : Grogan, H. K , of Johnstown Castle, co Wexford Dublin, 29 Oct., 1828
    . Grogan, G G., of Johnstown Castle, co Wexford. Dublin, 29 Oct , 1828.
Grombridge or Groombridge · Lipscombe, J , of 217, Hampstead Road, London, and of Mount Sion, Tunbridge Wells, Kent Times d p , 20 Dec , 1866
Groom *see* Napier.
Groome *see* Carleton
Groome Anderson · Groome, A , of Salt-Hill, Bucks, market gardener, formerly of N.W. Canada Times, d p , 21 Dec , 1889.
Grosett *see* Steuart-Grosett-Muirhead
Grosse *see* Twells
Grosvenor *see* Egerton
    : Goldstrom, F S , of 126, Southampton Row, London, gent Times, d p , 16 April, 1890
    Sowdon, Rev F., Rector of Dunkerton, Somerset Times, d.p , 21 Jan , 1874
    Richard Williams, Edward, of 17, Sweeting Street, Liverpool, gent Times, d.p , 14 Nov., 1879
Grote-Joyce · Joyce, Rev C. Times, 17 March, 1900
Grove *see* Brooke.
    ,, Cradock
    ,, Hillersdon
    · Price. S G. 21 Dec , 1870 (5916) (D G. 1699)
    see Troyte-Chafyn-Grove
Groves *see* Harris
Grubb *see* Bell
Grubb Belgrave : Grubb, T., of 22, Oakley Crescent, Chelsea, Middlesex, com clerk Times, d p , 30 June, 1875
Gruggen *see* Seymour
Grundy *see* Swinfen
Gubbins . Legh, J R , Bruree, Limerick, Ireland, gent Times, d.p , 27 July, 1891
Guinness *see* Grattan-Guinness
Gulley *see* Slade-Gulley.

Gulston : Brigg, F 7 June, 1798 (497)
    see Stepney-Gulston
Gulston-Stepney . Gulston, Eliza 1 May, 1855 (1730).
Gun-Cunninghame Gun, G. 19 May, 1826 (1328)
        . Gun, G., of Riversdale, co Kerry Dublin,
            3 March, 1827
Gunning-Sutton . Gunning, O. G S. 26 March, 1850 (960).
Guntrip see Fitzgerald
Gurden see Price
Gurbs, Eliza Elise, Baroness de Gurbs, of Montpeller Street,
        Brighton Times, 6 May, 1899
Gurdon-Rebow Gurdon, J 5 Sept , 1835 (1698)
Gurney see John-Gurney
Gurney-Salter Salter, Jane and Emma, 40, Ladbrooke Road,
        W. Times, 15 Jan., 1894.
        see Salter
Gurney-Randall Randall, T , Haverstock Hill, Middlesex
    Times, 26 Sept., 1898.
Guthrie, of Mount, co. Ayr : Browne, Honble Dominick
        Augustus Frederick Lyon Vol VI . 2 May, 1860
    see Lingard-Guthrie.
Guy see Parsons Guy.
Gwatkin see Ashton-Gwatkin.
Gwillym see Atherton
Gwilt see Newport Gwilt
Gwinnett . Hayton, W C 13 Nov., 1840 (2679)
    · Catchmayd, G. 9 Feb., 1793 (465)
    · Catchmayd, W 17 Aug., 1782 (12322).
Gwyn : Fraunceis, J 5 Aug , 1780 (12106)
    : Powell, N. 27 Feb., 1841 (600).
    · Thompson, R 2 March, 1840 (520).
Gwynn-Mason Gwynn, F. M., of Smethwick. Staffs Times, 10
    Aug., 1898.
Gwynne see Edwards-Gwynne
    . Evans. G F J. G. 13 June, 1882 (2849)
    see Evans-Gwynne
        Howell. H. G., of Llanelwedd Hall, Radnor, esq
            Times, d p , 28 April, 2 May, 1879
    see Jones-Gwynne
Gwynne-Holford Holford, J P 13 May, 1831 (974)
Gwynne-Vaughan · Jones, H 4 May, 1855 (1831)
Gwyther see Leslie
    ,, Philipps.
Gyll see Hamilton-Gyll-Brooke.
    to con. same name—formerly Gill . B. H , G W.. J , Sir R .
        F. C (widow), H F C, and B C J (minors)
        W , 14 Dec , 1844 (D.G 948)

H

Habberfield-Short : Short, R. H., of 91, Queen Victoria Street, London, and of Streatham, Surrey, merchant. Times, d.p., 31 Dec., 1891.
Hamilton : Brown, p. 2044, Lond. Gaz., 1865 [*erroneous reference*]
Hacker *see* Heathcote-Hacker
,, Marshall-Hacker.
Haddington, Earl of *see* Baillie-Hamilton.
Haden *see* Barrs-Haden
,, Hamilton.
Podmore-Jones, W. H., M.D., of 66, Harley Street, Cavendish Square, London. Times, 24 March, 1871
Haden-Best : Best, G. A. H. 31 May, 1879 (4281).
Hadgley *see* Burrell.
Hadsley : Raymond, J. 5th Geo. III., 1765.
Hadwen *see* Ward.
Haffenden *see* Wilson-Haffenden.
Hagan *see* Mahon-Hagan.
Haggard *see* Copeman.
Hagger *see* Page.
Haggitt *see* Wegg-Prosser.
Haigh *see* Shaw.
Haire-Forster : Haire, A. N. 26 June, 1875 (D.G. 421).
Haldane-Chinnery : Haldane, J. R. A. 29 July, 1864 (4124)
Lyon, X., 12 June, 1876
Haldane-Chinnery *see* Chinnery-Haldane.
Haldane-Duncan-Mercer-Henderson : Haldane-Duncan, H. A. D. 3 June, 1882, (2739)
see Mercer-Henderson.
Haldane-Oswald, of Auchencruive and Cavers : Oswald, Alexr. Lyon, Vol VI., 3 April, 1861
Hale *see* Hildyard.
,, Hilton
,, Rigby.
Hales : de Morlaincourt, E. 15 May, 1829 (913)
see Roling
Hales-Tooke : Hales, J. T. 30 Aug., 1842 (2355)
Hales, B. 24 Nov., 1876 (6683)
Haley *see* Berry

Halford : Vaughan, Sir H. 55th Geo. III., 1815
: Hyam, Simon, of 69, 71, 73, and 75, Cannon Street, London, and 47, Gloucester Square, Hyde Park, Middlesex, merchant Times, d p, 8 Feb., 1872.
: Hyam, E E, of 18, Leinster Square, Middlesex, and of 56, Cannon Street, London, merchant. Times, d.p. 22 Oct, 1872
Montagu · Hyam, Moses, of 69, 71, 73, and 75, Cannon Street, London, and 116, Westbourne Terrace, Hyde Park, Middlesex, merchant Times, d p, 8 Feb., 1872
: Hyam, B, of 56, Cannon Street, and 3, Cleveland Gardens, Cleveland Square, Hyde Park, Midx., esq Times, 27 June, 1872.
Hyam, F. B, of 56, Cannon Street, and 26, Cleveland Gardens, Cleveland Square, Hyde Park, Midx., esq Times, 24 July, 1872
Hyam, A, of 31, Glo'ster Gardens, Hyde Park, Midx, gent Times. d p., 10 July, 1875
Hyam, F M, of 62. Inverness Terrace, Hyde Park, Middlesex, gent Times, d p, 10 July, 1875.
Robt. Hyam. R A. L, of Westbourne Terrace, Hyde Park, Midx., gent. Times, d p, 25 March, 1875.
: Hyam, E, of Wansee, nr Berlin Times, d p, 6 Nov, 1894
Hyam, M, of Maida Vale, London Times, d p, 6 Nov, 1894.
Halford-Adcock · Adcock. Rev. H. H, of 23, Earl's Court Sq, Middlesex Times. d.p., 24 May, 1881
Halkett : Smith, R H Times. d.p., 29 June. 1882
Halkett-Craigie *see* Craigie-Halkett.
Hall Adcock. T 5 July, 1836 (1226)
    see Brettell
    Bullock, W. H 26 July, 1872 (3439)
    see Glaze.
    Gray, G 12 Feb, 1884 (790)
    see Gray
    Hall, W., to con the name 13 Jan, 1798 (33)
    see Halls
    ,, Knight.
    ,, Laurington Hall
    ,, Lines
    : O'Toole, L K 28 April, 1834 (814).
    see Shute
    ,, Wharton
Hall-Dare Hall, R W 25 April, 1823 (730)

Hall-Houghton Houghton, F, of 10, York Place, Clifton, spinster. Times, d.p., 15 Jan, 1876.
Hall-Say : Hall, R. 17 May, 1855 (2016).
Hall-Standish Hall, F 29 Dec, 1814 (63)
Hall Stephenson : Hall, J T. S., of Somerton Court, Somerset, retired Major. Times, d p, 15 June, 1877
Hall-Watt · Hall, E R. B., of Bishop Burton, Yorks., esq Times, d p, 25 Nov, 1886.
Hallam de Nittis Hallam, C, of Saint Germain-en-Laye (Seine-et-Oise), France Times, 17 Nov., 1868
Hallet see Farewell
 ,, Hughes-Hallett
    A Miller Miller, A, of 53, Bedford Gardens, Kensington, antimony refiner. Times, d p, 28 April, 1877.
Halliday · Cosway, W H 9 May, 1872 (2305)
  see Tollemache
Hallidie see Smith Hallidie
Hallwell see Phillips
Hallwell-Phillipps Phillipps, J O. and Katherine E, of Hollingbury Copse, Brighton, Sussex, and Tregunter Road, South Kensington, Middlesex, by R L, 29 Feb, 1872. Discontinued the surname of Hallwell and assumed Phillipps only. Times, d.p, 28 May, 1879.
  : Phillipps, J O., of Brighton, and S. Kensington, esq, and K E, spinster, his daughter Times, d p, 31 May, 1879.
Hallowell-Carew · Hallowell, Sir B 28 June, 1828 (1273)
Hallows · Inman, H F, of Walthamstow, Esssex, lic victualler. Times, d p, 27 March, 1889
Halls . Hall, C. E, of 74, St George Street East, Middlesex, manufacr. Times, 28 Oct., 1875
Halse see Otton-Halse
Halsey see Moore-Halsey
  Whateley J T 45th Geo III., 1805
Halsey Bircham . Halsey, B E, of 104, Drayton Gardens, S Kensington Times, d p, 23 Nov, 1894
Halsted see Every-Halsted
   · Holgate, A 2 Feb, 1846 (493)
    Holgate, E 2 Feb. 1846 (493)
   see Poole
Haly-Dove see Dove-Haly
Hamblet Davies (junr), J H. of West Bromwich. Staffs., brick manufacr. Times, d p, 24 Nov. 1891.
Hambleton see Hamilton
Hambly see Burbridge-Hambly

Hamill-Stewart : Stewart, J. T.   24 Oct., 8 Nov., 1865 (D.G. 1361 and 1377).
Hamilton   Adams, A H , of 31, Marylebone Road, Middlesex, gent Times, d.p., 15 March, 1875
    see Baillie-Hamilton
    ,, Barrett-Hamilton
    (Calcutta) Brown, Claud   Lyon Vol. VII., 29 Mar., 1865.
    see Brown.
    Birnie, J.   6 July, 1773 (11367)
    ,, Buchanan-Hamilton.
    ,, Campbell
    ., Christopher-Nisbet-Hamilton
    ,, Clark
    : Crosse, J   15 March, 1859 (1139)
    see Douglas-Hamilton
    · Haden, M   10 July, 1802 (719)
    : Hambleton, G W, of 1, Trafalgar Square, Christ Coll., Cambridge, etc., gent., to resume ancestral name.   Times, 18 March, 1879
    Hitchcock, F C and E M, his wife, both of Breakspears Road, Brockley, and of Bedford Street, Strand, ecclesiastical surveyor   Times, d p., 21 Sept., 1889
    · Johnson, C   31 Dec , 1833 (56)
    Kelso, A H   23 March, 1811 (528)
    · Lesassier, A   15 April, 1815 (697)
    : Levy, J L., of 100, Westbourne Terrace, Bayswater, physician.   Times, d p , 31 Jan , 1873
    see Nisbet-Hamilton-Ogilvy
    ,, Ormsby-Hamilton
    Stevens, T. N   9 March, 1835 (439)
    see Shaw-Hamilton
    ,, Stevenson-Hamilton
    ,, Stirling-Hamilton
    Taylor, F G. and H R., both of Guernsey   Times, 30 Jan , 1899
Hamilton-Dalrymple, of North Berwick · Dalrymple, Sir Walter, Bart.   Lyon Vol XII , 18 Jan , 1889.
Hamilton Gell : Hamilton, Rev F A W., Vicar of Holy Trinity, Stanton-in-Peak, Derbys   Times. d p , 12 Sept , 1877
Hamilton-Gordon *see* Hamilton
Hamilton-Grace : Grace, S.   21 Feb , 1880 (1905).
Hamilton Gyll Brooke   Gyll   Lyon, Vol. IV., 15 Oct , 1844.
Hamilton-Hoare · Hoare, H N   15 Sept , 1882 (4381)
Hamilton-Russell : Hamilton, G F and E M, his wife   W., 27 Feb , 1850 (D G 263).

K

Hamilton-Starke, of Troqueer Holm : Starke, Jas. Gibson Lyon
   Vol. XI , 21 Nov., 1885.
Hamilton-Tyndall-Bruce, of Grangehill and Falkland : Hamilton,
   Walter. Lyon Vol. IX , 22 Jan., 1873.
Hamlin-Nott : d'Ade, J R., late of Trinidad, West Indies, now of
   11, Russell Road, Kensington   Times, 7 Feb., 1898.
Hamlyn : Gosling, F. 27 April, 1889 (2560).
   : Gosling, F., of Manton House, Oakham, Rutland, esq.
      Times, d.p , 15 May, 1889.
   : Hammet, J. 33rd Geo II , 1760.
   see Sillifant-Hamlyn.
    „ Williams
Hammet see Hamlyn.
Hammon : Cole, J. W. H., of the Victoria Tavern, Essex, mercan-
   tile clerk. Times, d.p., 30 Oct , 1873.
Hammond see Dalison
          „ Lucy.
Hammond-Chambers : Hammond, R. S. B. 30 July, 1859 (2971).
Hammond-Chambers-Borgnis : Hammond-Chambers, J A 17
   Dec., 1891 (3).
Hammond-Sampson : Hammond, J G. 16 July, 1811 (1323).
Hammond-Spencer : Hammond, H. 13 Aug., 1873 (1894).
Hamond-Græme : Hamond, Sir A. S. 3 April, 1873 (1873).
Hampden see Cameron-Hampden
       „ Hobart-Hampden.
Hampden-Jones : Jones, B., of Emmanuel Coll , Cambridge, gent.
   Times, d.p., 4 July, 1881
Hampton-Lewis : Hampton, J H. 1 June, 1830 (1127)
Hanbury see Bateman-Hanbury.
        „ Bateman-Hanbury-Kincaid-Lennox
        „ Culling-Hanbury.
        : Hanbury Leigh, J. C., E C., F. C. 22 Jan., 1864
           (315)
        : Leigh, Emma E. H., on behalf of her son, John C. H ,
           and her daughters, Emma C. H and Frances
           E. H (all minors). W., 22 Jan , 1864 (D G. 90).
        see Leigh.
         „ Tracy.
Hanbury Leigh see Hanbury.
Hanbury-Sparrow : Sparrow, A H B 4 April, 1899 (3254)
Hanbury-Tracy : Leigh, T. C (com called Hon.). 30 March,
   1839 (724).
Hance-Pigot : Hance, A , of Chieveley, nr Newbury, Berks, late
   of Commdr -in-Chief's Office. Times, 10 Nov., 1871.
Hancock see Burford-Hancock.
        : Hillier, S., of 24, Newton Road, Westbourne Grove,
           Middlesex Times, 30 June 1864.

Hancock *see* Liebenrood.
Hancorn *see* Duppa.
Handasyde *see* Sharp-Handasyde.
Handforde-Drinkwater : Drinkwater, J., late of Duckinfield, Cheshire, now of Richmond Villa, Redhill, Surrey, gent. Times, 23 Sept., 1871.
Handley *see* Davenport-Handley
Hand-Newton : Hand, N. D. 18 April, 1806 (511).
Handy-Church : Handy, Maj. 15 Oct , 1832 (2371).
Hanford · Hanford-Flood, J. C. 6 March, 1893 (1540)
Hanford-Flood Lloyd-Flood, W. 4 June, 1861 (2575)
Hanham *see* Swinburne-Hanham
Hankey *see* Alers-Hankey.
Hankin, Hy A. Trulock : Hankin, H. A., of 116, Church Road, Canonbury. Times, d.p., 28 Sept., 1876.
    see Turvin
Hanmer *see* Hervey.
Hannam-Clark : Clark, F., of Queen Street, Glos., solicitor. Times, d p., 31 Jan , 1889.
Hanning *see* Lee.
Hanning-Lee Lee, E. H., of Bighton, Hants, Lieut. 2nd Life Guards. Times, d.p., 13 June, 1876.
Hansard : Yockney, V. H. 8 July, 1898 (4274).
Hanson : Kershaw, W. B. 20 June, 1844 (2133).
    see Lucas
Hanson-Inglish : Hanson, B. 3 May, 1800 (423).
        Hanson, B 26 Dec., 1834 (2)
Hanson Torriano · Hanson, L L., of Ryde, I.W., widow. Times, d.p., 29 April. 1875.
Hanway : Balack, H. 15 July, 1775 (11578).
Harcourt, Francis Vernon Harcourt, Francis Geo. Randolph, of Buxted Park, Carlton Gdns , and St. Clare, I W , Col. Times, 1 Jan , 1874.
    Harcourt-Ainslie. G. S. 15 Feb , 1823 (251).
    : Masters, C. H 20 March, 1810 (407).
    : Vernon, Rt. Hon. E. V 15 Jan., 1831 (123)
Hardcastle *see* Burghardt-Hardcastle.
    „ Smith Hardcastle.
Hardie *see* Daniel.
Harding *see* Duffield-Harding.
    „ Emmerson-Harding
    · Harding-Featherstone, R. 26 May, 1853 (1665).
    see Hardinge.
    E. W *see* Jefferson-Conkling, P.
    see Newman
    „ Nott.

Harding-Finlayson : Harding, M. H M., Port of Spain, Trinidad.
Times, d p., 2 Jan, 1892
Hardinge   Harding, E, of Old Springs, Staffs, esq, to restore
the ancient spelling of family name. Times, 4
Nov., 1886
Harding, H, of Hammersmith and the War Office,
Pall Mall, Middlesex Times, 11 Nov., 1874
Hardtman *see* Berkeley.
Hardwicke   Davies, H L. and P. L. 29 May, 1880 (3327)
Hardwin *see* Gallenga Hardwin
Hardy *see* Cozens-Hardy.
" Gathorne-Hardy
" Harris
Nathan, P., of Kensington and Old Broad St, London,
merchant. Times, d p, 26 April, 1877
Nathan, L, of Bradford, Manchester, and Old Broad St,
London, merchant. Times, d.p, 26 April, 1877
Nathan, J., of Hamburg, Germany, and carrying on
business in London, Manchester, and Bradford,
merchant Times, 13 June, 1877
Hare : Beevor, A   18 Oct, 1821 (2072)
Christian, E   5 Dec., 1798 (1166)
: Fairs, J J., of Hornton St., Kensington, and of St. James's
Theatre, Westminster, comedian   Times, d p,
27 Nov., 1883
Henley, J   24 Nov., 1778 (11950)
: Leigh, T   31st Geo III., 1791.
Hare-Clarges   Hare, R G   18 June. 1844 (2093)
Harford *see* Battersby-Harford.
" Battersby
" Lyne
Harford Battersby *see* Battersby Harford
Hargood-Ashe   Snooke, W C A, of Portsmouth,. Southampton,
esq   Times, d p, 6 Nov., 1877
Hargrave *see* Pawson-Hargrave
Harington *see* Champernowne
Harkett *see* Dredge
Harland *see* Appleton.
" Hoar-Harland
: Hoar, W   17 April, 1827 (942)
Hoar, W. C   29 Sept, 1824 (1717)
Harle   Atkinson, T   11 Sept, 1807 (1243)
Harley : Bickersteth, J E (Lady Langdale)   14 March, 1853
(884)
see Rodney-Harley.
: Teleki, A. J. J. (Count)   2 Nov., 1859 (4077)

Harling . Todd, J., of Burnley, Lancaster, machinist.   Times, d.p , 24 May, 1867.
Harman *see* King-Harman
Harmar *see* Rivington-Harmar.
Harmon   Phillips, P., of 69, Lady Margaret Road, Kentish Town. Times, 27 May, 1895
Harmer, Minnie Jemima Fanny Harmer, of Streatham, Surrey. Times, 23 April, 1898
Harmood Banner   Banner, J. S., of 12, Canning St., Liverpool, accountant   Times. 22 Aug , 1876
Harnage   Blackman, Sir G.   11 Oct., 1821 (2035)
Harnett *see* Meredith-Harnett
Harper   Coggins, Emily M , of Astwick Manor House, Hatfield   Times, d.p., 9 Nov., 1875.
  see Hosken-Harper
Harper-Smith   Smith, S H , late of Norham-on-Tweed, but now of Gordon House, Cambs   Times, d p , 1 June, 1889.
Harpur *see* Crewe.
Harries *see* Lloyd
  ,,   Lloyd Harries
Harrington-Stuart, of Torrance   Harrington, Robt Edwd. Stuart   Lyon Vol. X , 20 Nov., 1879.
Harris : Badcock, J. H., of Gosport, Hants   9 May, 1865
    : Badcock, C. H., of Gosport, Hants.   Times, 9 May, 1865
    see Brunel-Norman.
    · Donnithorne, J   6 April, 1799 (313).
    see Greathed.
    : Groves, G T., of Manor Farm, Southfleet, Kent, farmer.   Times, 25 Dec., 1889.
    : Groves, H. W., of Manor Farm, Southfleet, Kent, farmer   Times, 25 Dec., 1889.
    : Hardy, T , of Tuticorin, India   Times, 18 Jan., 1864.
    Peter Benjamin   Harris, B , of 55, Gracechurch Street, and White Lion, Gracechurch Street, London   Times, d p , 28 Feb , 1874
    see Norris.
    ,,   Penson Harris
    Peppercorn, Charles, late of Highfield Road, Derby, now of Bardon Villa, Charnwood Street, Derby.   Times, 9 Feb., 1898.
    see Roope
    ,,   Temple.
    : Tothill, S. J and M I , his wife, of Sunnyside, Kingkerswell, Devon   Times, d p , 4 July, 1890.
    see Whitmore-Jones
Harris-Arundel   Harris, W. A.   11 July, 1822 (1194)

Harris-Burland : Harris, J. B. 13 July, 1835 (1351).
Harris-Edge : Edge, J., of Shifnal, Salop, manufacr. Times, d.p., 28 May, 1887.
Harris-Gastrell . Harris, J P., of Stanley Hall, Wakefield, York, at present residing at Berlin, Prussia. Times, d.p., 20 Nov., 1868
Harris-Liston : Harris, L., of 1, Tressillian Road, Kent, gent. Times, 22 Sept., 1882
Harris-Matthews · Harris, T. M. 27 June, 1871 (3005).
Harris-Williams Harris, O 3 April, 1824 (538)
Harrison, Hy : Aaronson, A., of Shepherd's Bush, London. Times, d p, 19 Sept. 1894.
    Daniels, C A., of " The Three Compasses," Dalston Lane, N.E Times, d.p., 2 Nov, 1896.
    Daniels, H. L., of " The Three Compasses," Dalston Lane, N.E. d.p., 29 April, 1896.
: Falcon, J. 23 Aug., 1844 (2933).
see Fiske-Harrison
Richd. Charlton : Harrison, R., of Shepherd's Bush, Middlesex, L.R.C.P., M.R C S., etc Times, d p., 9 July, 1879
    Lamdin, A., of Silchester, Southampton, yeoman. d.p., 10 Aug., 1864.
see Mackinlay.
,, North
,, Rogers-Harrison
,, Slater-Harrison.
Steere, R. 8 May, 1819 (802)
see Ward.
,, Wayne
Harrison-Andrew Harrison, T. 26 March. 1796 (289).
Harrison-Batley · Harrison, C 10 May, 1822 (916).
Harrison-Broadley Harrison, H B. 1 July, 1896 (3911)
    Harrison, W H 16 March, 1865 (1558)
Harrison-Osborne · Long, W. 30 Nov., 1877 (7071)
Harrison-Powles Harrison, P 7 Dec. 1808 (5)
Harrison-Rowson Harrison, J T 8 Nov. 1875 (5517)
Harrison-Watson : Watson, G A., of 70, Elm Park Gardens, Kensington, esq Times, d.p., 28 March, 1885.
Harrop *see* Hulton-Harrop.
. Hulton, Elizabeth M (widow), on behalf of her son, Wm. E. M. (a minor). 8 Dec., 1866 (D G. 1839)
Harryson *see* Darnley
Hart *see* Arnold.
· Blondeau. W N 3rd Geo III., 1765.
see McHarg

Hart : Solomon, E., late of Henrietta Street, Covent Garden, now
of Brighton Times, d p., 7 Oct , 1879.
   see Thorold
    ,, Tulk
    : Tulk, E. H. 19 Nov, 1832 (2601).
    : Tulk, M H 19 Nov, 1832 (2601).
Hart-Davis Davis, S. O. H , of 7, Hereford Gardens, Middlesex,
gent Times, d.p., 13 Dec., 1880
Hart-Smith : Smith, C. M., spinster ; C. L H , solicitor ; E P ,
spinster ; A. M , spinster ; T E , gent.; P. L ,
gent , G M C, gent , H M, gent ; all of St
Peter's Rectory, Bedford. Times, d.p , 9 May,
1888.
    : Smith, F C , of St. Peter's Rectory, Bedford, M B ,
and G L., of W Kensington, spinster Times,
d p , 27 April, 1888
Harter *see* Hatfield
Hartland-Perkins : Hartland, G 16 Oct., 1843 (3363).
Hartley : Campbell, L L 7 Dec , 1841 (3163).
   see Clifford Constable
    : Dudgeon, G 1 Oct , 1841 (2422)
   see Holliday Hartley.
Hartley-Smith · Smith. H., of Cornhill, London, and Wimbledon,
Surrey, stockbroker Times, d p . 23 March, 1881
Hartnell *see* Beavis
    ,, Braine-Hartnell
Hartopp Bunney, E 18th Geo III., 1778.
   see Burns-Hartopp.
    ,, Cradock-Hartopp.
    ,, Wigley.
Hartstonge *see* Weld-Hartstonge
Harvey : Aberdeen, J 10 Jan., 1792 (13)
   see Barcley-Harvey
    . Bateson, R 20 Sept , 1788 (449)
   see Collins Harvey
    Donald, R ,10 Jan , 1792 (13).
    Lee, J 3 Feb , 1821 (368)
   see Lugg-Harvey.
    ,, Norton.
    Rae, J 10 Jan , 1792 (13).
   see Savill-Onley.
Harvey-Bonnell : Bonnell, J 21 July, 1860 (2721).
          Harvey, M. A 8 April, 1841 (944)
Harvey-Hawke . Hawke, Hon E 31 Aug., 1798 (809)
Harvey-Jellie Jellie, Rev W H , of 4, St Stephen's Road,
Canterbury, Presby. minister Times, 25 Sept , 1884.
Harvey-Kelly Kelly, H , Lieut Col Times, d p., 22 Feb , 1890

Harvey-Piper : Piper, E. W., of Camberwell, Surrey, reporter. Times, d p, 19 April, 1882
Harward : Blake, C 24 April, 1816 (850).
Harwood *see* Blackwell.
    : Penny, H. H. 11 March, 1853 (785).
Harwood-Nash : Harwood, F. G. 11 Jan, 1895 (774).
Hase *see* Lombe.
Haselfoot *see* Paske-Haselfoot, T.
    : Cock, F. K. H., of 18, Sunderland Terrace, Paddington, Middlesex, and of the Inner Temple, London, barrister-at-law. Times, 30 Dec, 1865.
Haslam Steinthal, A. J, of Cheetwood, Manchester, student. Times, 7 Sept., 1881.
    Steinthal, G. J., of Cheetwood, Manchester, med. stud Times, 28 Sept., 1880.
Hassard *see* Short
    Short, E. H., Marian, Gertrude, of Wimbledon Times, 2 Jan., 1899
Hassell *see* Ogden.
Hastings *see* Abney-Hastings.
    Barnett. E. 7 May, 1812 (934).
    Cosham, W T. (also called W. T Cosham Hastings), of Franklands, Burgess Hill, Sussex, late Lieut. R.S. Fus. Times, d p., 11 April, 1885.
    : Rawdon, Lord F. 16 Feb., 1790 (98).
    see Woodman-Hastings.
Hatchett *see* Owen.
Hatfield : Gossip, R. and C 22 Oct., 1844 (3602).
    : Harter, J 26 April, 1816 (874)
    Hatfield-Cribb, J., of 5, West Street, Poole, Dorset Times, 14 Oct., 1871.
    : Marshall, W. 26 Dec., 1833 (2394)
Hathornthwaite : Bradshaw, W 19 Dec., 1868 (6825).
    : Bradshaw, Wm. Whll., 19 Dec., 1868 (D.G. 1446).
Hatsell-Powys : Powys, L. 11 March, 1853 (811).
Hatton *see* Finch-Hatton-Besley.
Hatton, Stormont-Finch : Hatton, The Hon Henry Stormont Finch. Times, 4 April, 1887.
Haughton : Arnold, G. 13 Jan, 1798 (33).
    . Arnold, H. 13 Jan., 1798 (33).
Havard, L Laud : Havard-Jones, L, of Alpheton Rectory, Long Melford, Suffolk, gent. Times, d.p, 12 Dec., 1884.
Havelock-Allan : Havelock. Sir H M 17 March, 1880 (2190).
Haverfield *see* Balguy.
Haviland *see* de Havilland
Haviland-Burke : Haviland, T. W. A. 22 April, 1818 (736).

Haward : Jeaffreson, H.   29 Nov., 1785 (545)
Hawarden *see* Gillibrand.
Hawe   Awe, or Aughe, G J. of Mason Street, Liverpool, printer
 Times, d p., 18 Aug., 1873
Hawke *see* Harvey-Hawke
Hawkes-Cornock : Hawkes, J. 9 April, 1883 (D G 407).
Hawkes-Strugnell : Strugnell, W., of H M S Aurora, Staff-
 Commdr. R.N. Times, d p., 22 June, 1893.
Hawkesford *see* Bone Hawkesford.
Hawkesworth *see* Fawkes
Hawkey *see* Whitford-Hawkey.
Hawkins *see* Black-Hawkins.
Hawkins-Dempster, of Dunnichen : Hawkins, George. Lyon Vol
 V, 9 Feb, 1855.
Hawksworth *see* Fawkes
Haworth-Booth   Haworth, B. B   6 July, 1869 (3821).
  Haworth, B. B   6 July, 1869 (D.G. 809)
Haworth *see* Leslie.
Haworth-Leslie . Haworth, M. E   20 March, 1886 (1467).
Hay *see* Baird-Hay
 „ Carr.
 · Dalrymple, J. 20 April, 1798 (321)
 see Drummond Hay
 . Leith, A   5 Dec., 1789 (757)
 see Paterson-Balfour-Hay.
Hay Burgess   Boggers, J H. of 33. Kenilworth Rd., Newcastle-
 on-Tyne, clerk. Times, 31 Dec, 1895.
Hay-Coghlan : Coghlan, W M, late of H M Bombay Civ.
 Service, now at Boulogne, France Times, d p., 20 April,
 1888.
Hay-Cooper   Cooper, H, of Durrington House, Wimbledon,
 Surrey, esq Times, d p., 17 Jan, 1883.
Hay-Gordon, of Avochie : Hay, Adam. Lyon Vol V, 26 Jan,
 1858.
Hay Morgan : Morgan, Geo, of 17, West Bank, Stamford Hill,
 London, Baptist minister Times, d p, 7 Sept., 1895
Hay-Williams   Williams, Sir J 16 May, 1842 (1333)
Haycock *see* Hine-Haycock
Haydock   Haydock-Boardman, J   5 March, 1813 (503)
Hayes *see* De la Hey
 „ Oldridge de la Hey
Hayes-Stracy . Hayes, R., warehouseman, of Manchester, residing
 at Clifton Villa, Fallowfield, Lancaster, s of late William
 Miller, of Liverpool Times, 12 Sept, 1871.
Haygarth *see* Parry
Hayhurst *see* France

Hayhurst : France, H. H., of Ystymcolwyn, Montgomery, esq. Times, d p., 30 Jan., 1871.
    see France-Hayhurst.
Hayhurst-France : Hayhurst, G. H. H. 30 April, 1887 (2581).
Hayne *see* Seale-Hayne.
Haynes : Jones, J. H. 12 May, 1843 (1556).
    see Topham-Haynes
Haynes-Thomas : Thomas, E. J., of Chester, physician. Times, 27 Sept., 1886.
Hayter *see* Egerton.
Hayton *see* Gwinnett
Hayward : Arno, A. C M. 6 Aug., 1811 (1571)
    see Danson.
Hayward Butt : Butt, F. W., of 21, Lansdowne Terrace, Cheltenham, gent. Times, d.p., 24 May, 1894.
Hayward-Southby : Perfect, T. 1 Nov., 1822 (1869).
Hayward-Wilkins : Wilkins, W. 6 April, 1835 (669).
Haywood Eaton, C. 3 May, 1875 (2394).
    : Truefitt, L. H., now of 3, Roxburghe Terrace, Shoeburyness, Essex, B.M. and Mast. of Surgery (Aberdeen), surg. in H.M. Army. Times, d.p., 11 July, 1891.
Haywood-Farmer : Haywood, C. 5 Aug., 1871 (3594)
Hazelby : Griffiths, A., of 70, David Street, Park Road, Liverpool, hosier's assnt. Times, d.p., 9 June, 1888.
Head *see* James.
   „ Jones.
    : Roper, A. G. 29 May, 1770 (11047)
Headley *see* Balls-Headley.
Heagren *see* Gibbs-Heagren.
Healy *see* Fitzgerald.
Healey : Holgate, H. 23 Aug., 1824 (1397)
Heap *see* Cooper.
Heaps-Moore Heaps, T. M., of 9, Florence Street, Islington, bookseller, 2nd s. of Thomas, of Liscard Park, Liscard, Cornwall, gent. Times, d.p., 3 Nov., 1871.
Heath : Blood, R. 22 April, 1801 (445).
    · Jones, Grace, of Holly Mount, Hagley Road, Edgbaston, spinster. Times, d p., 3 Sept., 1894.
Heathcoate-Amory : Amory, J. H. 28 Feb., 1874 (1453).
Heathcote *see* Boothby Heathcote.
   „ Edwards-Heathcote.
    : Shepley, A H. 20 June, 1821 (1351).
    see Sinclair.
   „ Unwin-Heathcote.
Heathcote-Drummond · Heathcote (Lady Aveland). 16 Nov., 1870 (5215).

Heathcote-Drummond : Heathcote, C. E (Dowager Lady Aveland) widow. Whitehall, 16 Nov., 1870 (D.G 1571).
Heathcote-Drummond-Willoughby . Heathcote-Drummond (Lady Willoughby D'eresby). 4 May, 1872.
Heathcote-Hacker : Heathcote, J 25 June. 1840 (1571)
: Heathcote, R 12 May, 1871 (2414).
Heathcote, R 16 Dec., 1819 ,(2282)
Heathcote Martin Martin, S. J., of Catterall, Worcester, esq. Times, d.p., 14 May, 1875.
Heatly see Firth-Heatly.
„ Tod-Heatly
Heaton Ellis, C. A H. 11 July, 1805 (903).
Heaton-Armstrong : Armstrong, J., of Mount Heaton, King s County, son of Hon. W H. Armstrong D Telegraph, 27 Oct 1884.
Heaton-Ellis Heaton, C A H. 9 Aug., 1838 (1839)
Heaviside see William-Spicer.
Heaviside-Whitmarsh . Whitmarsh, W M , of Albemarle House, Hounslow, M D Times, d p , 3 Nov , 1887.
Heber-Percy · Percy, A. C 4 Feb , 1847 (413)
Hecker see Teush Hecker.
Hedley see Dent.
Hedley Armstrong Armstrong. W , junr , of Southwood, Caterham, Surrey. Times, 20 Aug., 1875.
Heitland-Browne · Browne, A . of Amberley House, Crouch Hill, Middlesex, gent. Times, d p , 24 Jan , 1888.
Helbert . Israel, H. 30 Aug 1833 (1608)
see de Courcy Helbert
Hele see Selby-Hele
Hellberg see Booth-Hellberg.
Helleley see Fletcher
Hellier Shaw, T. 18 July, 1786 (321)
Helme see Mashiter
Helms see Dorling
Helsham see Candler.
: Jones. 29 Dec , 1891 (66) (D G 1892)
Helsham-Brown Helsham, E 18 July, 1826 (4983)
Helsham-Jones : Jones, A., of Middle Temple, London, barrister. Times, d p., 10 April, 1874
: Jones, H H and H E., both of Woodbridge, Suffolk Times, d p , 25 April, 1888.
Heming see Phipps.
Hemingway see Watson.
Hemment Bull, G., of Pontefract, York, esq. Times, d p , 15 Oct., 1867.
Hemming see Phipps.

Henderson *see* Clayhills-Henderson.
,, Haldane-Duncan-Mercer-Henderson.
,, Macdonald-Henderson.
,, Mercer-Henderson.
,, Mitchell-Henderson
,, Page-Henderson.
Henderson Cleland : Cleland-Henderson, J W   23 Feb., 1893 (1395).
Henderson-Roe : Henderson, C. H.   28 June, 1879 (4531).
Hendrick-Aylmer : Aylmer, H H.   6 Feb., 1890 (D G 173).
Heneage : Walker, J.   8 March, 1777 (11750)
    see Walker.
Henley : Eden, Rt Hon. R. H. (Baron Henley)   4 April, 1831 (646).
    see Hare.
Henn *see* Gennys.
Hennah *see* Oglander-Hennah.
Henniker *see* Major.
    ,, Gotley.
Henniker-Major : Henniker, Rt. Hon J M.   27 May, 1822 (956).
Henniker-Wilson : Henniker, J.   18 May, 1839 (1034).
Henochsberg *see* Nathan Henochsberg
Henry, I. : Isaacs, Henry, of 17, Gt Russell Street, Bloomsbury, W C   Times, 7 March 1874
    see Jones Henry
    ,, Yelverton
Henry-Benjamin : Benjamin, D. H., late of Cape Town, South Africa, now of 58, Great Cumberland Place, Hyde Park, Middlesex, and 27, Throgmorton Street, London   Times, d.p., 14 March, 17 March, 1883
Henryson-Caird, of Cassencary : Caird, James Alexr.   Lyon Vol. XIV, 14 March, 1897.
Henshall : Alcock, M J, of 29, White Rock Street, Liverpool, spinster   Times, 7 Jan., 1874
    : Alcock, E., of 29, White Rock Street, Liverpool, book-keeper.   Times, 7 Jan., 1874.
    Alcock, H, of 29, White Rock Street, Liverpool, cashier.   Times, 7 Jan., 1874.
Henshaw : Smith, F. B   14 March, 1843 (860).
Hensley Owen : Owen, J., junr., of 55, Northfield Road, Stamford Hill Middlesex   Times, d p., 26 April, 1890
Hensman *see* Grace-Hensman
Henville *see* Burgess-Henville.
Henzell *see* Pidcock-Henzell.
Hepburn-Stuart-Forbes-Trefusis : Trefusis, Chas W. R (Baron Clinton), and Harriet W., his wife.   Will, 4 Sept., 1867 (D G 1205).

Hepburn-Stuart-Forbes : Trefusis (Lord Clinton) 4 Sept., 1867 (5161).
Hepenstal *see* Dopping-Hepenstal
Hepworth *see* Molesworth-Hepworth.
    ,, Williams-Hepworth.
Herbert   Beilby, S 16 Jan., 1798 (42)
    Clive, E 9 March, 1807 (379).
    Hogsflesh, J. E., of Kintbury, Berks, gent. Times, d.p., 18 Sept., 1877.
    Jones, William, of Clytha House, Monmouth. esq Times. d.p., 18 Feb., 1862.
    Jones, J. A. E. 2 Oct., 1848 (3585)
    Jones, J. A. E., A. J., E. P., G. H., M. L. W., 2 Oct., 1848 (D G 1063).
    see Kenney-Herbert.
    ,, Morton-Herbert
    Sparks, H. H., late of Clapham, Surrey, now of Felpham, Sussex. gent. Times, d.p., 14 Jan., 1893
Herbert-Spottiswoode : Herbert, J. R. C., of Spottiswoode. Lyon, 21 June, 1900
Heriz-Smith Smith, J. C. T., of Bideford, Devon Times, 21 Feb., 1899
Hercy . Smallwood, T. H. 10 Dec., 1821 (2486).
Heriot-Maitland-Dougall Heriot-Maitland, W 5 Jan., 1852 (69)
Hermann *see* Ashby.
Hermine *see* Roeper
Hermitage *see* Day-Hermitage
Hermon-Hodge : Hodge, R. T., of Wyfold Court, nr Henley-on-Thames, esq Times, d.p., 16 Feb., 1885
Herne *see* Burchell-Herne.
    ,, Buckworth-Herne-Soame
Heron : Hiron, H, of Sydney, N S. Wales, formerly of Bath, Somerset, gent. Times, d.p., 2 Sept., 1874.
Herrick *see* Perry-Herrick
Herring *see* Barnwell
Herriot, of Ramornie : Makgill-Maitland, James Lyon Vol II, 4 Feb., 1814
Herschel Hirschl, L. K., of Bordighera, Italy, M.D. Times, d.p., 5 Jan., 1889.
Hersch Hersch, I. H., heretofore known as Herschkowitz, formerly of 3, Grittleton Road. Paddington, Caius College. Camb., and Manchester, now of 184, Burrage Road. Plumstead Times, 5 and 15 Jan., 1898
Herschkowitz *see* Hersch
Hertz *see* Hurst
Hervey *see* Bathurst
    Hanmer, T 26 Feb., 1774 (11434)
    see Timms-Hervey-Eleyes

Hervey-Bathurst : Hervey, F. A. 31 Oct., 1818
Hesketh *see* Bamford
        „ Bamford-Hesketh.
        „ Bibby-Hesketh.
        „ Fermor-Hesketh.
        „ Juxon.
Hesketh-Fleetwood : Hesketh, P. 14 March, 1831 (517)
Heslop *see* Stitt-Heslop.
Hesse *see* Legrew-Hesse.
Hetherington : Warwick, J 28 July, 1824 (1358).
Hethersett . Barker, Maj.-Gen. J. 9 Sept, 1803 (1179).
Hewett *see* Prescott-Hewett.
        „ Shipley Hewett.
Hewitt *see* Hitchins Hewitt.
        „ Hughes.
        „ Ludlow.
        „ Smallwood
Hewitt-Fletcher . Fletcher, S., of the Br. Cen. Africa Administration, Zomba, Africa. Times, d.p., 24 Oct., 1895.
Hewlings *see* McAllister Hewlings
Heysham *see* Mounsey Heysham
Heywood *see* Dawson.
Heywood-Lonsdale : Lonsdale, A. P. 15 Nov., 1877 (6893).
Heyworth-Savage : Heyworth, C. F. 16 Feb., 1895 (1248).
Hibbert-Ware : Hibbert, S., M D., late of Edinburgh, but now of York. Dublin, 8 March, 1837.
Hibbert *see* Holland-Hibbert.
Hibbit *see* Wight.
Hickman *see* Bacon-Hickman.
     : Gore, F. W. 4 Dec., 1878 (D.G. 1065).
Hicks : E., enabling him to bear Surname and Arms of Hicks 6 & 7 Will. IV., c. 42. (Index to pub. and priv Statutes, p. 503). See below, Simpson.
    see Braxton Hicks.
      „ Beach.
      „ Ross
    : Simpson, junr., E 21 Aug., 1835 (1605).
Hicks-Austin : Austin, E. C. W., of the Inner Temple, barrister-at-law. Times, d.p., 15 Jan., 1892
Hicks-Beach *see* Beach
Hicks Palmer *see* Palmer.
Higden *see* Byfield-Higden.
Higford Burr, H. 20 June, 1860 (2400).
     . Parsons, J 6 Sept., 1825 (1650).
Higgin *see* Winfield.
Higgin-Birket : Birket. 16 Jan., 1897 (463)

Higgin-Birket . Cockerton, D. (children). 13 Aug., 1880 (5383).
: Cockerton, W H B. 16 Feb., 1895 (1249)
Higginbotham *see* Higginbotham-Wybrants
,, Price
Higgins *see* Brabazon
,, Jodrell
,, Platt-Higgins
Higginson . Allman, R., of 76, Portland Street, Manchester.
Times, d p. 25 Jan., 1881.
: Barneby, E 8 Jan., 1825 (84).
see Royle Higginson
Higginson-Whyte-Melville Higginson, Rev H P., of The
Bartons, Tetbury, Glos., and of Twickenham, Middlesex
Times, d.p., 23 Nov., 1886.
Higgs-Craven : Higgs, S. C., of Ceylon, agent of the Oriental
Bank Corporation in Point de Galle, now residing at West-
leigh, co. Devon Times, d p., 31 Oct., 1870
Higgs-Walker . Higgs, J. W., of Netherton, Dudley, Worces.,
nail manufacr Times, d p., 8 Feb., 1887.
Higham · Hyam, L M., of St John's Wood, Middlesex. Times.
27 Oct., 1898.
Highton-Reade Highton, A., formerly of Bedford Square, also
Upper Berkeley Street, Portman Square, now of 28, York
Street, Portman Square, gent., and A C., his wife. Times,
d.p., 29 March, 1884.
Hignett . Litherland, J. 6 Aug., 1819 (1452)
Litherland, J 1 Nov., 1800 (1258)
Litherland, W. 6 March, 1820 (523)
Hildyard : Hale, J R W 19 June, 1855 (2403)
: Thoroton, T B 23 May, 1815 (1076)
Hiley : Moses, H. S., of Lyndhurst, Talbot Place, Cardiff,
architect. Times, d.p., 10 May, 1894
Hill *see* Brooks Hill.
: Brunyce, J S 6 May, 1859 (1940).
: Buscomb, J H., of Park Villa, Trelights, Cornwall, gent.,
formerly of Bombay, India, stevedore. Times,
d p., 4 Sept., 1893
see Clegg-Hill
,, Coyney.
,, Crosbie-Hill
,, Davenport-Hill
. Gooch, C. H 9 May, 1831 (950)
see Grantham-Hill.
: Johnson, R. 20 May, 1783 (12441)
see Kesteven-Hill.
: Lowe, A C 10 Oct., 1865 (4941).

Hill *see* Medlycott.
„ Noel-Hill.
„ Paterson.
(Lord Sandys) *see* Sandys.
see Sale-Hill. -
: Smith, W. A., of 4, Rupert Lane, Liverpool, accountant. Times, d.p., 27 Oct., 1877.
Hill-Hutton : Hill, J. H. 26 Feb., 1861 (792).
Hill-Littler : Hill, R 31 July, 1893 (4355)
Hill Lowe : Lowe, A H O P., of Salop and of Devonshire, esq. Commdr. R.N Times, d.p., 3 Feb., 1886.
Hill-Trevor : Hill, A. E. 26 Sept., 1862 (4633).
Hill-Wilson : Wilson, A E., of 280, Goldhawk Road, Shepherd's Bush, Middlesex, M R.C.S and L.R.C.P. (Lond.). Times, d.p., 14 March, 1891.
Hill-Wontner : Hill, Gerald Arthur, of Egham, Surrey. Times, 9 May, 1899
Hillas : Webb, G W and Esther H , his wife D. Castle, 5 Sep., 1846 (D.G. 865).
Hillas-Drake · Hillas, E K. 21 Dec., 1882 (6650).
Hillersdon : Grove, J. 14 July, 1807 (974).
Hillier *see* Hancock
Stump, J. H , of Clapham Com., Surrey, in H M Office of Works Times, d p , 19 Nov., 1885.
Hillman *see* Howis Hillman.
Hills · Astle, P. 9 Jan. 1790 (13).
see Rand.
Hills-Johnes : Hills, Sir J 6 Sept.. 1883 (4400)
Hilton . Hale, W. 11 April, 1885 (1669).
see Johnson
: Smith, J., of 104, Old Kent Road, Surrey Times, d.p., 17 April, 1871.
Hilton-Ford : Hilton, J. 24 Aug., 1835 (1844).
Hilton-Simpson : Hilton, W. 28 Dec., 1888 (70)
Hinckes Davenport, H. T. 12 Nov., 1890 (6105.
: Davenport, H T 3 March, 1896 (1680)
Hind *see* Archer-Hind.
„ Hodgson-Hind.
Hinde *see* Lloyd.
Hinde-Lloyd : Hinde, M C., d. of late Capt. Jacob William. now residing at Spa. Belgium. Times, 24 June, 1869
Hindermann-Maulère *see* Hindermann (also as Maulère), C., of 56, York Street, Midlesex, spinster. Times, 8 July, 1882.
Hindle *see* Franklin-Hindle
Hine-Haycock : Haycock, W. H., of 4, College Hill. London, and of Belmont, Sidmouth, Devon. Times, d p., 31 Dec., 1878, 3 Jan., 1879.

Hingeston-Randolph Hingeston. C., M.A., Clerk in Holy Orders, of Exeter Coll. Oxford; R., of Ringmore, Devon. Times. 21 Dec., 1868.
Hinrich-Dent : Hinrich..H D 18 June 1879 (4338)
Hipkiss see Pedley
Hipper see Brownsmith
Hippesley Cox see Buller-Hippesley-Cox
Hippisley see Cox-Hippisley.
Hippisley-Tuckfield : Hippisley, R. 24 Nov., 1807 (1600).
Hipwell see Wood.
Hird see Wickham
Hiron see Heron
Hirons Brewerton, J. H. 6 Nov., 1826 (2625).
Hirsch D'Aubyn : Hirsch, C H., of Wurtemburg, S. Germany. Times, 23 Jan., 1877.
Hirschl see Herschel.
Hirst Shirt. H J. 19 Aug., 1820 (2296)
Hirst-Bracken · Hirst. T., of Halifax, York. Times. d.p., 15 Feb., 1871
Hiscocks-Crawshay : Hiscocks, C. M., of 3, Park Place. Greenwich. and of Wandsworth, Surrey.
Hitchcock see Conder
     ,,   Degacher.
     ,   Hamilton
Hitchcock Burgess : Hitchcock, W., of 20, Piccadilly. Middlesex. wine merchant Times. d.p., 29 April, 1880.
Hitchcock-Spencer Hitchcock C S., of Brighton, Sussex, spinster ; Wm., of Hampstead, Middlesex, M. L, wife of Wm ; and M G. C, his daughter Times, 23 Mar., 1885.
Hitchin-Kemp · Hitchin, F. W. 13 June, 1868 (3430)
Hitchins, E J. : Pace, E J, of 29, Kildare Terrace, Bayswater, widow Times, d p., 8 May, 1894.
Hitchins Hewitt : Hitchins J H., of Havant. Southampton, gent. Times, d.p., 6 June, 1879
Hoadly-Ashe : Ashe. R. 6 Feb., 1797 (133).
Hoar see Bertie
  ,,   Harland.
Hoare see Hamilton Hoare
Hoar-Harland : Hoar, C. 2 Nov., 1802 (1141)
Hoare Ward Hoare, J. of The Ferns, and of Royal Parade, Chislehurst, Kent Times. d.p., 12 Feb., 1885.
Hobart-Hampden · Hobart (Earl of Bucks), A. E. 5 Aug., 1878 (4646)
Hobbs see Webber.
Hobday-Horsley · Hobday, H H. 21 Feb., 1832 (416)
Hobgen · Percival , C. H. of Manor House, Aldingbourne, Sussex, spinster Times, d p., 26 Feb., 1880.

Hoblyn *see* Peter-Hoblyn.
Hockenhull *see* Molyneux
Hodge *see* Blake.
　　„ Hermon-Hodge
　　　　Jackson, A Whall., 18 April, 1869 (D G 406).
　　. Jackson, A   18 April, 1869 (2429)
Hodges *see* Edwards.
　　: Edwards, F D 17 June, 1862. (3101).
　　: Hodson, J. F. 23 Feb 1844 (621)
　　. Parry, W   25 April, 1788 (205)
　　see Richardson-Eyre.
Hodgetts . Chambers, W. T. H. 4 March, 1867 (1531).
　　　　Chambers, W T H   Whll., 4 March. 1867 (D G 307)
Hodgetts-Foley Foley, J. H   14 April 1821 (839).
Hodgkins *see* Hodgkyns
Hodgkinson *see* Montagu.
　　　　„ Patten
Hodgkinson-Morewood Hodgkinson, W   5 June, 1802 (570)
Hodgkyns : Hodgkins. J., late of S Africa, but now at Hotel
　　Metropole, London. Times, d p, 1 March, 1889
Hodgson. Ge Graham : Hodgson, George Goodfellow, of
　　Chertsey, Surrey. Times, 2 Aug., 1899
　　W. : Bond, W H B., of Poulton-le-Fylde, Lancaster,
　　　　gent Times, d p., 1 Jan., 6 Jan., 1879
　　. Garstang, T and M   2 Aug., 1872 (3529).
　　see Pemberton
Hodgson-Cadogan : Hodgson, W   14 Oct., 1833 (1842).
Hodgson-Hind Hodgson, J   11 Aug., 1836 (1441).
Hodgson-Minns · Hodgson, John. Times, d p, 14 Aug., 1896.
Hodgson-Nicoll · Hodgson, C   6 Sept., 1883 (4491)
Hodson : Pickering, J. E   16 Oct., 1849 (3077)
　　　Pickering, T H   19 Feb., 1840 (361)
　　see Hodges
Hody · Cox, W T., of Dorset, esq.; W. T. H., of Hants, esq;
　　R A H., of Devon, esq., and A M H, of Dorset,
　　spinster. Times, d.p., 23 Feb., 1886
Hoel-Walsh Welch, Capt. R. G, R N Times 3 July, 1867.
Hoffnung-Goldsmid . Hoffnung, S F. 13 Feb., 1896 (1744)
Hogg *see* Cartwright
　　　　„ McGarel Hogg
Hogge-Allen : Hoggs, F   13 July. 1857 (2444) (D G 690).
Hoghton *see* Bold-Hoghton.
　　　　,. de Hoghton
Hogsflesh *see* Herbert
Holden : Greenwood, E   28 July, 1840 (1804)
　　see Lowe
　　„ Rendall.

Holden *see* Rose.
   · Shuttleworth, C. 12 April, 1791 (222)
   Shuttleworth, J 8th Geo. III., 1768
Holdich-Hungerford . Holdich, H. H 11 Feb., 1824 (316)
Holdsworth *see* Owen-Holdsworth
Hole : Carter, junr., C. 27 Sept., 1852 (2617).
Holford *see* Gwynne-Holford.
Holgate-Gedney : Holgate, P. 4 Feb., 1847 (413).
Holgate *see* Halsted.
   „ Healey.
Holland, Rose Montague Montague, Elizabeth Rose Times, 26 Jan., 1899
  see Bateman-Robson
  ., Cooke-Holland
  Dance, N 4 July, 1800 (774)
  see Dyson-Holland
Holland-Corbett : Holland, F. 25 June, 1872 (3015)
   Holland, C 2 May, 1839 (951).
Holland Hibbert Holland, A H 17 May 1876 (3110).
Holland-King King. W., of 9, Old Square, Lincoln's Inn, Middlesex, barrister-at-law Times. d.p, 3 July, 6 July, 1883
Holland-Robinson Robinson, Florence Ellen of Notting Hill, London Times, 25 Aug., 1898
Holland-Schwann Schwann, F.. of Wimbledon, Surrey Times, 24 June, 1898
Holland Wynne Wynne, Rev. T. E. H., of The Rectory, Llanvaches Monmouth Times d.p., 12 July, 1894.
Hollest *see* Williams
Hollick *see* Van Hollick.
Holliday Hartley Simonds, E A., of Skirbeck, Boston, Lincoln Times 28 Feb., 1880
Hollingbery *see* Denne.
Hollinshead *see* Blundell-Hollinshead.
   . Blundell-Hollinshead-Blundell
   Brock, L 23 Sept., 1803 (1274).
   Brock, W 10 Sept., 1802 (953)
Hollist · Capron, A 2 Sept., 1883 (1627)
Holloway *see* Driver Holloway.
  ., Elphinstone-Holloway.
  : Martelli. H F K 5 July, 1828 (1326).
  see Martin-Holloway.
  ., Turner
Hollway-Calthrop Hollway, H. C 10 June, 1878 (4423).
Holman Peacock, S 11 May, 1807 (636).
Holme *see* Bankes
  „ Simmer-Holme.

Holme : Torre. H J 31 Jan , 1834 (185).
: Torre, N. 15 Nov., 1811 (2374)
Holmes *see* a'Court-Holmes
„ , Boulderson
Holmes A'Court : A'Court Holmes. W L. 9 Aug., 1860 (3087)
Holmes-Forbes : Holmes, A., M A , barrister Times, d p , 23 May, 1879.
Holmes-Tarn : Tarn, H , of 94, Lancaster Gate, Hyde Park. Middlesex. Times, d p ,12 March, 1895
Holroyd *see* Smyth
Holt : Holt-Robinson, J 24 Nov 1818 (2171)
: Mills. W. 19 April, 1841 (1056)
see Preston-Holt.
Holt-Lomax : Lomax. R , of Alveston Leys. Stratford-on-Avon, Warwick, esq Times, 8 Feb . 1870.
Holt-Needham : Holt. O. N 26 April, 1893 (2616).
Holte *see* Orford-Holte.
Holtzapffel : Budd, G W 19 March, 1898 (2287)
Holwell *see* Carr
„ , Doherty-Holwell
Holyoake-Goodricke : Holyoake. F. L 12 Dec., 1833 (2330).
Homan-Mulock : Mollov, T. M , of Bellair, King's County. Dublin, 14 Feb , 1843
Home *see* Logan-Home.
Home-Cust *see* Egerton
Home-Daniel, Douglas *see* Lyon. Daniel Home
Home-Douglas, of Douglas Home, Chas Alexr. (commonly called Lord Dunglass) Lyon, Vol X , 14 March. 1878
Home-Ramey Home, Rt. Hon Earl of. 31 March, 1814 (810).
Homersham *see* Osborn
Homfray *see* Addenbrooke.
Honey-Atkinson · Honey, P., late of the Exchequer Office, Stone Buildings, Lincoln's Inn. Times, 6 Feb , 1864
Hood *see* Cockburn-Hood.
„ Fuller-Acland-Hood.
„ Jacomb-Hood.
„ Tibbits
Hook-Child Hook, A. T. 7 Aug , 1872 (3885)
Hooker *see* Greenland
„ Ottley
Hookey *see* Gaskell
Hoole-Lowsley-Williams Hoole. G. W L. 31 July, 1890 (4602)
Hooper *see* Purnell
Hooper-Rastrick Rastrick. R. J. of Elm Grove. Southsea, gent. Times, 2 Nov.. 1887
Hooper-Wathngton Hooper. J 25 Sept , 1852 (2574)

Hope, W. Casabianca, W. H L Times, d.p., 9 Feb 1891
    see Beresford-Hope
    . Hopps, G. F. W., of Sandbach, co. Chester. Times, 28 Sept., 1870.
    . Hopps, H. E , of 40, Fitzroy Square, London Times, 22 March, 1869.
    see Pelham-Clinton-Hope
    „ Williams
    „ Williams-Hope.
Hope-Edwardes : Hope, T. H. 7 Nov., 1854 (3519)
Hope-Scott, of Abbotsford : Mrs Charlotte Harriet Jane Lockart-Hope and her husband Hope, Jas Robert Lyon Vol V., 15 March, 1853
Hope-Wallace Hope, J. (com called Hon.) 9 April, 1844 (1198)
Hopewell *see* Samborne.
Hopkin *see* Lane-Hopkin
    . Ward W H., of the Oriental Hotel, Montpelier Road, Brighton Times, 10 Oct., 1889
Hopkins : Bond, jun., B 12 Dec., 1772 (11308)
    see Chamberlin-Hopkins
    „ Hopkyns.
      Northey, R 10 May, 1799 (434).
    see Seaborne
Hopkinson-Sedge Sage, W., of 17, Mincing Lane, London, gent. Times, d p., 23 Dec., 1878, 24 Jan, 1879.
Hopkyns Hopkins, T. D (Rev), of Southsea, Hants, and of Montagu Square, London Times, 21 Feb , 1879.
Hopper *see* Shipperdson
Hopps *see* Hope.
Hopson *see* Butler
    . Ongley, W 8 March, 1824 (395).
Hopton Hunt, John Dutton, of Folkestone, Kent Times, 11 May, 1899.
    : Mynors-Baskerville, Sybil M. 19 March, 1898 (2437)
    Parsons, W 21 March, 1817 (1002)
Hopwood *see* Gregge.
Horman-Fisher : Fisher, R. S. 10 July, 1832 (1583)
Horn *see* Dalrymple-Horn-Elphinstone
Hornby *see* Fawsitt
Horne · Warren, Thos. W., 24 April, 1784 (D.G 4441)
Hornidge *see* Gledstanes
Hornyold Gandolfi, J V. 28 Feb , 1859 (953)
Horsey *see* Terry Horsey
Horsfall *see* Coldwell Horsfall.
    „ Jarratt.

Horsley see Hobday.
: Miniken, H., Vicar of Northleach, Gloucester, M.A. d.p., 30 June, 1865.
Hort see Reading.
Horton see Anson-Horton.
· Kolle, J. H   17 Nov., 1869 (D.G. 1344)
Kolle, J. H.   17 Nov., 1869 (6183)
see Wilmot Horton
„ Wilmot.
Horton-Wilmot : Wilmot, R. J   8 May, 1823 (755).
Horwood : Green, C.   13 Sept 1849 (2910)
Hosken-Harper · Hosken, J   19 Oct., 1816 (1996)
Hoskyns see Wren-Hoskyns
Hotchkiss see Littler
Hotham : Knott, W   25 Feb., 1799 (191)
Houblon see Archer-Houblon.
„ Eyre
Houblon-Archer : Houblon, J   6 Jan., 1801 (28).
Houblon-Newton : Houblon, S   29 June, 1819 (1199).
Houghton see Gill-Houghton.
„ Hall-Houghton
. Rafferty W.   25 June, 1808 (872)
Houghton-Davies · Davies, Thomas John, of Pwllheli, Carmarthen. Times, 1 Dec., 1899
House see Newell
Houston see Blakiston-Houston
„ Davidson-Houston
„ Houston-Boswell
Houstoun-Boswall · Houstoun. Sir G. A. F., on his marriage to E. Boswall.   15 Feb., 1847 (702).
Houstoun-Boswall-Preston · Houston-Boswall, T. A.   15 Sept., 1886 (4625)
· Houston-Boswall, R., of Blackadder, Berwick. esq   Times, d.p., 15 April, 1874
Houstoun-Douglas   Houstoun. A.   2 Nov., 1833 (2049).
Houston-Douglas, of Baads : Houston, Eliz.   5 Aug., 1852 (2154)
Houssonleer see Trist
Hovell-Thurlow-Cumming-Bruce, of Kinnaird and Roseigh and Dunphail : Hovell-Thurlow (Lord Thurlow).   6 Aug., 1874 (4018).
Howard   Alvarenga, D.   1 March, 1785 (109)
Bagot, R   29 April, 1783 (12435)
see Fitzalan-Howard
„ Forward.

Howard, Alfred . Joseph. Abraham, of 2, Aldermanbury, London warehouseman   Times, d p. 28 March, 1871
    Bertram   Joseph, Benjamin, of 108, Guilford Street, Russell Square, stock jobber   Times, d p , 13 Oct., 1883
    see Molyneux
    „ Norfolk-Howard
    Upton, Hon. F. G   6 Aug . 1807 (1085)
Howard Brealey *see* Brealey
Howard-Brooke : Brooke. R   3 Jan , 1835 (43).
Howard-Bury : Howard, K   23 Dec., 1881 (D G 1441)
Howard-Flanders : Howard, W F., of Tyle Hall, Latchingdon Essex. esq   Times, d.p., 3 Oct., 1874
Howard-McLean   McLean, J   5 May. 1859 (1940)
Howard-Stafford   Stafford, B B de B   Times, 2 Aug . 1865.
Howard-Vyse : Vyse, R W H   14 Sept., 1812 (1862).
Howarth *see* Wood.
Howe *see* Curzon-Howe
    „ Mansel-Howe
Howel *see* Hughes
Howell *see* Gwynne.
    : Wright, A   27 June, 1807 (895)
Howey   Taylor, Violet H , widow, of 33, Albion Street, Hyde Park, London   Times, d p , 15 Feb., 1893
    see Taylor.
Howie-M'Ewan   Howie, J T.   Times, d p., 16 Oct , 1872.
Howis Hillman : Hillman, E . of Schoolhill, Lewes, Sussex, solicitor   Times, d p., 26 Sept , 1874
Howitt-Ludlow : Ludlow, T A   14 Sept . 1857 (3173)
Howman *see* Little.
Howson : Taylor, J., of Hanley, Staffs, potter's manager   Times, d p., 26 Nov . 1879
Howson Potter *see* Neville.
Hoy   Barlow, J   26 Jan . 1829 (156)
Hoyle : Ashworth, John, of Holme House, Warley, Halifax, worsted spinner   Times, d p., 26 Dec., 1869
    J . : Hoyle, J Craven, of Moorlands, Bacup, Lancs., cotton spinner, J.P   Times, d p , 18 June, 1892.
    see Wheelwright
Hubbard *see* Sherlock-Hubbard
Hubbersty *see* Cantrell-Hubbersty
Huck *see* Saunders
Huddleston *see* Lawlor-Huddleston.
Huddlestone · Croft. G   29 May, 1819 (952)
Huddy, Saml. : Huddy. Saml F. Ouseley   Times, 28 Feb., 1893
Hudleston   Simpson, J   18 April, 1867 (2433)
Hudson *see* Bateman.

Hudson *see* Donaldson-Hudson
  „ Frith-Hudson.
  „ Moses, Geo. Times. d p., 18 April. 1893
  see Palmer
    Thexton, J F, of Ashton House, Beetham, spinster.
      Times, d p , 27 Feb , 1875
Hudson-Kinahan Kinahan, Sir E H. 8 Nov, 1887 (D G 1341)
Hue *see* Crate
Hugessen *see* Knatchbull-Hugessen.
Huggeson : Spratt, W. H. 6 Oct., 1801 (1217)
Huggett Potter, S 12 Jan , 1847 (154)
    Towle, S D 21 April, 1851 (1080)
Huggins *see* Dolland.
  „ Farquhar.
Hughes *see* Ball-Hughes
  „ Buller
    Davies, T. H F., of Abercery, Cardigan. esq Times,
      d.p., 11 Oct., 1873
    Hewitt, W H. 25 May, 1825 (1019)
    Howel, T. 27 July, 1816 (1480).
    G C. *see* Hughes le Fleming
    James, F 20 March, 1810 (407)
    see Otway
    „ Parry.
    Pringle, G H. 3 March. 1835 (392)
    see Thomas
    „ Young-Hughes.
Hughes Agutter : Hughes, M E and A F, of London. Times,
    3 Oct., 1874.
Hughes-Bonsell Hughes. J. G F 7 Feb , 1879 (668)
Hughes-Chamberlain Hughes, R. E 9 April, 1892 (2481)
    Hughes, T. C. 7 Dec, 1793 (1081)
Hughes-D'Aeth Hughes, G W 4 June. 1808 (773)
Hughes Games Jones, Rev J D C L , of Lincoln Coll , Oxon.
    Prinl of King William's Coll . I Man. Times, d p , 17
    March. 1880
Hughes-Garbett Garbett, P L , of Island House, Laugharne,
    Carmarthen, esq Times, d p , 12 Feb , 1886
Hughes-Gibb Gibb, F , of Greenford Lodge. nr. Southall. Midx
    Times, 14 June, 1882
Hughes-Hallett Hughes, C 21 May, 1823 (859)
Hughes le Fleming Hughes, G. C 19 April, 1862 (2101).
Hull *see* Brown
  „ Dauntesey.
Hulton *see* Harrop
  „ Hill-Hulton
  „ Hulton

Hulton *see* Preston.
Hulton-Harrop : Hulton, W. E. M 8 Dec. 1866 (7056)
Humble-Crofts Humble, W. J 29 May, 1879 (4027)
Hume Crawford, M 27 Sept., 1815 (2081)
    see Dick.
    ,, Evelyn.
    : Kennedy, J H 13 Aug., 1877 (2736)
    L : Levy, L M , of 14, Somerset Street, Portman Square,
        gent Times, d.p., 2 May, 1892.
    see Macartney.
    : Macleod, A. 28 Nov., 1801 (1411)
    see Purves-Hume-Campbell.
    ,. Sharp Hume
Hume-Cookson Hume, J C 20 Sept., 1889 (5920)
Hume-Gore : Hume, E C (Lady) 23 Oct., 1895 (5921).
Hume-Long . Long, C A , of Dolforgan House, Exmouth, Devon,
    widow Times d.p., 23 May, 1891
Hume-Rothery Rothery, Rev. W. H late of Hexham Northumberland, and now of 3, Richmond Terrace, Middleton, nr
    Manchester, Lancaster. d.p., 1 Jan., 1866
Hume Spry · Spry, G F , of 2nd Life Guards at Knightsbridge
    Barracks, Middlesex Times d.p. 8 Dec., 1875
Humfrey *see* Blake-Humfrey
Humfrey-Mason Blake-Humfrey, R H 8 March 1879 (2138)
Humfrey-Mason *see* Mason
Humphreys *see* Davenport
    ,, Fairles Humphreys
    ,, Porter-Humphreys
Humphrys-Alexander · Humphrys, A 24 March, 1824 (524).
Humphreys-Owen Humphreys, A C 11 Nov., 1876 (6097)
Hungerford *see* Holdich-Hungerford.
    Walker, H M 17 March, 1789 (130)
Hunloke *see* Eccleston
    . FitzClarence, F C G and Adelaide A W. his wife
        W., 19 Dec., 1863 (D.G. 1498 and 1509)
    see Scarisbrick
Hunt *see* Andrews.
    , Beaumont
    ,, Brooke-Hunt
    : Brown, C 4 Oct., 1794 (999)
    see Chalmers
    , De Vere
    ,, Enys
    ,, Hopton.
    ,, Husey-Hunt
    ,, Medley
    ,, Mickelfield

Hunt, Ella : Tomlinson, M. E , of Leicester, spinster   Times,
    d p , 6 Oct , 1875.
    see Whitaker.
    ,, Wilson
Hunt-Boyse : Hunt H. S., of Bannon House, Wexford, Ireland,
    Commdr R N. Times, 14 June, 1864
Hunt-Foulston Hunt. J. F. 23 April, 1875 (2283)
Hunt-Leaman Hunt, T L   1 Jan , 1844 (34).
Hunt-Powell Hunt, M A   24 Sept , 1806 (1270)
Hunt-Prinn Prinn, W H   25 Nov., 1803 (1743)
Hunter Aschkenasi, C., of 29, Greenwood Road, Dalston,
    Middlesex, B A.   Times, d.p , 19 Nov . 1889
    Fletcher, H   15 Dec., 1792 (933)
    see Gray
    ,, Muskett-Hunter
Hunter Campbell Hunter, C. H , widow of W M. Hunter, esq
    Times, 16 April, 1875.
Hunter-Arundell : Hunter, W. F. 26 Feb., 1825 (354)
Hunter-Marshall, of Callander Marshall. Wm   Lyon Register
    Vol IX , 1 Oct , 1872
Hunter-Weston, of Hunterston · Hunter, C R.   8 May, 1880
    (3106).
    : Hunter or Weston, Mrs. Jane.
    Lyon Register Vol. X., 21 June, 1880.
Huntingtower, Lord see Talmash
Hunton see Raper-Hunton
Hurker see Anderson
Hurle see Cooke-Hurle
Hurst . Hertz, J. P., of 12, Furnival's Inn, London, gent   Times.
    d.p , 26 Sept , 1879
Hurst-Whitworth Hurst, R S   14 June, 1822 (1018)
Hurt see Edge
    ,, Sitwell
    ., Wolley.
    ,, Woolley-Hurt.
Husenbeth : Rogerson, J. 13 Jan 1821 (193)
Husey-Hunt : Senior, L. G   15 June, 1833 (1203)
Huskison or Huskisson see Tilghman-Huskinson
Huskisson Foard, E. J, of Sillwood Road, Brighton, spinster
    Times, d p , 28 July, 1874.
    see Milbanke Huskisson.
Hussey Freke Hussey, A. D. 1 Sept , 1863 (4285).
Hussey Finnerty, E   12 April, 5 May, 1847 (D G 646 & 658)
    · Moubray, R H. — April, 1832 (917)
    Rowe, J 11 Oct , 1788 (485)
    : Stronge, —   Betham's List.
Hustler Peirse, Thos. W , 8 May, 1784 (D G. 4447).

Hutchinson *see* Grice-Hutchinson.
  „ Parker-Hutchinson
  : Robson, A. 8 Aug., 1891 (4378).
  · Robson, J. H. 13 March, 1867 (1726)
    Robson, J. H. Whll , 13 March, 1867 (D G. 381).
    Synge, Rev Sir S , Bart. Dublin, 3 April, 1813
    see Staveley
    „ Sutton
Hutchinson-Lloyd-Vaughan Hutchinson, S. D. of Mount Heaton, King's Co , and Mary, dau. and sole heir of John Lloyd, late of Birr, King's Co. (immediately after their intended marriage). Dublin, 26 July, 1843.
Hutchinson-Russell . Hutchinson, R. 22 June, 1847 (2269)
Huthwaite *see* Donston
Hutton *see* Everard-Hutton
  „ Farside.
  „ Hill-Hutton.
Hutton-Squire : Hutton, R. 31 July, 1869 (D G. 950).
              Hutton R. 31 July 1869 (4313)
Hyam *see* Halford.
  „ Higham
  Moses *see* Halford. Montagu.
Hyatt-Foster . Foster C. W. 31 May, 1824 (949)
Hyde Beck, S. 18 Dec., 1888 (D G. 1321)
Hyett · Adams W. H. 1 June, 1813 (1122).
  see Warner
Hylton-Foster : Foster H , of Tolworth Hall, Surrey, esq , and his infant children Times, d p , 29 Jan., 1892
Hyman *see* Sewell
Hyslop Maxwell Hyslop, M. 9 Aug. 1867 (4476)

I

Ibbetson *see* Selwin
Ick *see* Brodrick
Iddins *see* Eaton-Iddins
Idris *see* Williams Idris.
Ikin *see* Crosse.
Iliewicz *see* Illington
Ilive *see* Wyndham.
Illington · Iliewicz, J. T. Times, d p , 19 Dec., 1891
        Iliewicz E. M., of Margate, surgeon. Times. d p , 26 March, 1895.
Impey-Lovibond . Impey, A. 21 Oct , 1872 (5105).

Imrie : Pollard, Amy E. R., of Holmstead, Mossley Hill, nr. Liverpool. Times, d.p, 20 Oct , 1891.
Ince *see* Cumming-Ince.
„ Whittington-Ince.
Incledon-Bury : Incledon, R.   14 Aug., 1802 (841).
Incledon-Webber *see* Webber-Incledon.
Ingham *see* Cunliffe.
Ingle *see* Finch.
   , Wright-Ingle.
Ingilby *see* Amcotts-Ingilby.
   : Wright, J. 20th Geo. III., 1780
Ingilby-Amcotts : Ingilby, E 3 Oct., 1800 (1130).
Ingles Chamberlayne : Ingles, H., of Maugersbury, Glos., esq. Times. d.p., 2 Nov., 1874.
Inglett *see* Fortescue.
Inglis-Jones : Jones, W I., of Derry Ormond, co Cardigan. Times, 29 Dec , 1898
Inglish *see* Hanson-Inglish.
Ingram *see* Clopton
   „ Meynell-Ingram.
   „ Winnington-Ingram.
Ingram-Seymour-Conway : Seymour-Conway, Hon F. 18 Dec., 1807.
Inman *see* Hallows
Innes *see* Mitchell-Innes
   „ Rose-Innes.
   „ Norcliffe
Innes-Cross : Innes, A. C 23 July, 1888 (D G. 766)
Innes-Vine : Mitchell-Innes, A. V., of Puckaster, Niton, I.W., and of Chelsea. Middlesex, esq Times, 18 Feb., 1890.
Ion *see* Ringrose-Ion
Ireland : Allison, G. I , of Skeeby, Yorks, farmer Times, 10 Sept , 1879
   see Clayfield-Ireland.
Irish *see* Thomas
Ironmonger : Sola, A 27 June, 1837 (1658)
Ironmonger-Sola : Ironmonger, J A Times, d.p., 11 April, 1870
Ironside *see* Bax-Ironside
   „ Briscoe-Ironside
Ironside-Jackson : Jackson, M , of 3, St Alban's Terr , Hammersmith, spinster Times, d.p., 29 Oct , 1877.
Irton : Ryder, J I 2 March, 1885 (1311).
   : Turner, R. L 25 Jan , 1884 (487).
Irvine *see* D'Arcy Irvine.
   : Douglas, W 13 May, 1845 (1439)
   : Leslie, W. 17 Feb , 1778 (11849).

Irvine *see* Mervyn-D'Arcy-Irvine
Irving *see* Cavan Irving.
,, Winter-Irving
Irwell & Co. : Israel & Co., Julius   Times, 1 Jan., 1872.
    Israel, J., of Highfield House, Headingly, Leeds. Yorkshire, wool merchant, and of Alfred Street, Leeds, and Station Street, Huddersfield   Times, d.p., 1 Jan., 1872.
  : Israel, H., of Huddersfield, York, wool merchant in Alfred Street, Leeds, and Station Street, Huddersfield. Times, d.p, 1 Jan., 1872
  : Israel, J., of Wheatfield Lodge, Headingly, Leeds, York, wool merchant in Alfred Street, Leeds, and Station Street, Huddersfield.   Times, d.p., 1 Jan., 1872.
Irwin *see* Carroll-Irwin
  : Nolan, Jas. D   St. James's, 6 Feb., Whll., 18 Feb 1867 (D.G. 221)
Isaac *see* Bunbury-Isaac
,, Woolley-Hurt.
Isaac-Biggs : Isaac. T   W, 29 June 1784 (D G. 4469).
Isaac de Buriatte : Isaac. F. A. W., of Queen Street, Brompton, and E., of Euston Square, Middlesex   Times, d p, 17 July, 1876.
Isaac Nicolson : Isaac, W., of 98, Leadenhall Street. London, merchant, formerly of Melrose, N.B   Times, 28 Nov., 1873
Isaacs. Henry Moses *see* Coburn, Henry James
  see Henry.
Isherwood *see* Ramsbottom
Isidor *see* Cohen
Israel-Ellis : Israel, I H   14 March, 1829 (574)
Israel *see* Helbert.
,, Irwell.
& Co., Julius *see* Irwell & Co., Julius
Ivers *see* Thecothick
Ives *see* Grant-Ives.

J

Jack *see* Fletcher

Jackson *see* Bennett.
　　,, Calvert.
　　,, Day-Jackson.
　　,, Duckett
　　,, Galley-Day-Jackson
　　: Galley, R 21 Aug., 1821 (1724).
　　see Gould.
　　,, Hodge.
　　,, Ironside-Jackson.
　　: Jacob, D. 13 Nov., 1816 (2378)
　　: Jacob, J. 26 Aug., 1814 (1732).
　　: Jacobs, F S, of 12, Pembroke Road, Kensington.
　　　　　Times, 17 Feb., 1885
　　see Massey-Jackson.
　　: Orange, S. 9 Sept., 1793 (768).
　　: Pavier, T. 30 Nov., 1871 (5475).
　　see Pavior.
　　,, Sadleir-Jackson.
　　,, Saint Cedd.
　　,, Scott-Jackson.
　　: Shackerley, P. 17 Dec, 1806 (1627).
　　see Whitfield-Jackson.
Jackson-Shapland : Jackson, S 3 Nov, 1892 (6475).
　　　　　: Jackson, Susan, of Cradley, Great Malvern.
　　　　　　　Hereford, spinster. Times, d.p., 25 Feb.,
　　　　　　　1892.
Jackson-Smith : Smith, Rev. T. J., of Patcham, Sussex. B.A,
　　Vicar of Patcham Times, d.p, 29 Dec, 1888.
Jacob *see* Buxton-Jacob
　　　　,, Buxton
　　　　,, Jackson
　　　　,, Jackson.
　　　: Jacobs, W., of 41, Norland Square, Notting Hill, and of
　　　　　　Law Dept., Inland Revenue, Somerset House,
　　　　　　attorney-at-law and solicitor. Times, d p., 30
　　　　　　July, 1872
　　　: Jacobs, William, of the Isle of Wight. Times, 23 April,
　　　　　　1898.
Jacobs *see* Corbett
　　　　,, Jackson
　　　　,, Jacob
　　　　,, Jay.
Jacobs-Smith : Jacobs, G E., of The Cottage, Brockhurst.
　　Warwick. gent, late of Holborn, Middlesex Times, d p.,
　　13 March, 1890
Jacomb-Hood : Jacomb, R. 13 May, 1834 (858).
Jacson *see* Widdrington.

Jaggers *see* Jordan-Jaggers.
Jago Baynes, J., of Trejago, Hammersmith, and an assistant in the British Museum. d p., 27 Dec., 1878.
Jago-Arundel : Jago, F V. 28 Feb, 1815 (509).
Jago-Trelawny : Jago, J 19 April, 1886 (1898).
Jalfon Allen, H. J, of Chatham, Kent, gent. Times, d.p., 15 Feb , 1871.
: Allen, O. W. J., of Chatham, Kent, gent. Times, d.p., 15 Feb., 1871
John James : Allen, John, of Chatham, Kent, gent Times, d p., 9 Sept., 1872.
James *see* Brookesbank-James
„ Cordner-James.
„ Grevis-James.
Head, W. 10th Geo III , 1770.
: Head, W. 18th Geo. III., 1778
see Hughes
„ Peck.
James-Trevor James, T C. G., of The Bank House. Builth Wells, Brecon, esq Times. d p. 25 June, 1868.
Jameson-Dixon : Jameson. Amelia M., of Holton Park. and of Caistor. Lincoln Times. d.p , 8 Aug , 1893
Jamieson *see* Young-Jamieson
Jamison *see* Schiesser-Jamison
Janns *see* Dudley-Janns.
Janvrin : Valpy dit Janvrin, D. 30 Nov., 1826 (2946).
: Valpy dit Janvrin, F. 30 Nov , 1826 (2946)
Valpy dit Janvrin. J. 30 Nov , 1826 (2946).
Valpy dit Janvrin, P. 30 Nov., 1826 (2946)
Jaques-Jones Jaques. J 27 Sept., 1841 (2421)
Jarratt : Horsfall, G. J. Oct., 1846 (3548).
Jarvis. William *see* Jarvis. William Elliott
Wm Elliott Jarvis, Wm., master mariner, of The Parade. Is of St. Mary. Scilly, Cornwall. Times 7 Dec., 1869
see Young.
Jarvis-Makepeace : Jarvis, A E., of Streatham Hill, Surrey, gent Times, d.p., 19 Aug., 1885
Jausz *see* Jenner.
Jay : Jacobes, A W. and D. F. Times, d.p., 12 June, 1896.
· Joseph, A. H , of Bath Place, Kensington. Midx, merchant Times d p , 2 Dec 1881
see Rawlins
Jeaffreson *see* Haward
: Pigott, W. 21 Jan , 1839 (119)
see Robinson
Jebb : Bowker, R. 12 Jan., 1788 (13).

Jeddere-Fishre : Jeddere, J 9 Oct , 1813 (2032).
Jefferson see Dunnington-Jefferson.
  ,, Sergison.
Jefferson-Conkling, Paul Harding, E W , 29, Duke Street, Manchester Square, Middlesex, esq d p., 13 Dec., 1878
Jeffery see Burnell-Jeffery.
  ,, Orchard.
  ,, Spilsbury
Jeffrey see Fenwick.
Jeffreys see Allen-Jeffreys.
Jeffreys-Powell Jeffreys, David Whll , 3 May, 1867 (D.G. 612)
  : Jeffreys, D 3 May, 1867 (2639)
Jeffrey see Fenwick
Jekyll see Campbell.
Jelf-Pettit : Jelf, L W., late Lieut. 15th Reg , now of Lichfield gent , also Helen, his wife Times, d p , 6 July, 1886
Jelf-Reveley : Jelf, E P., esq., and F. J, his wife, both of Brynygwin, Dolgelly, Merioneth Times, d p., 18 July, 1891
Jelf-Sharp Jelf, H 7 April, 1831 (666)
Jelhe see Harvey-Jelhe
Jelly-Dudley Jelly, J B and E A 29 Aug 1868 (4991)
  Jelly, J B Whll , 29 Aug , 1868 (D G 1030).
Jenkin, Mary Patten Jenkin, Maria Patten, of St Leonards-on-Sea Times, 2 Feb., 1899
  C see Vernon
Jenkins see Blandy-Jenkins
  ,, Davies-Jenkins
  ,, Steynor.
  ,, Turberville-Llewellin
  ,, Vaughan-Jenkins
  ,, Walford.
  ,, Wolseley-Jenkins
Jenkins-Vaughan Vaughan, F. 20 Nov , 1871 (6747).
Jenkyn Osborn, Jas 8 Nov , 1799 (1138).
Jenner Jausz, F , of 5, Bromley Road, Lee Kent, banker's clerk Times. d p , 26 Jan , 1883
  see Worge
Jenner-Fust Jenner, Rt. Hon Sir H 14 Jan , 1842 (117).
Jenner-Tyrell : Tyrell. C T 5 May, 1828 (1074).
Jennings : Bramley 17 Dec., 1798 (1203)
  see Clerke
  . Jennion, J 25 July. 1795 (767)
  see Smith.
  Ed Smith · Smith, E. St. Clare, of 16. Duke Street, Midx , carver and gilder Times, 12 Jan 1876
Jennion see Jennings.

Jennyns *see* de Windt.
Jennyings *see* Starkey.
Jenyns *see* Blomefield.
Jephson-Rowley · Jephson, J. 2 July, 1844 (2270).
Jephson-Norris : Jephson, C. D. O., of Mallow, co. Cork. Dublin, 18 July, 1838.
Jermy · Preston, I. 6 Sept., 1838 (1946 and 1965)
Jermyn · Griffiths, S, late of Naples, Italy, now of Dublin, spinster. Dublin, 22 April, 1843.
Jerningham *see* Stafford-Jerningham.
Jerome *see* Smith-Jerome
Jerrard *see* Spencer.
Jervis *see* Parker-Jervis
    Pearson, W. H and M. 22 May, 1865 (2806).
    Markham, O 3 June, 1823 (965).
    Ricketts, Rt Hon. E. J. (Vis St. Vincent). 7 May, 1823 (818).
    · Ricketts, W. H. 10 June, 1801 (645)
Jervis-Edwards : Edwards, T., of Trematon Hall, by Saltash Cornwall, esq., late a Cornet in Her Majesty's Fourth or Royal Irish Dragoon Guards. d p, 18 July, 1864.
Jervis-White : White, J. J. 19 Nov., 1793 (1031).
Jervoise *see* Clarke-Jervoise
    ,, Ellis-Jervoise.
    : Purefoy, G. H. J. 31 Jan., 1793 (97).
    see Purefoy-Jervoise.
Jervoise-Clarke : Clarke, C. J. 17th
Jessop Bomford, R., of Mount Jessop, co Longford. Dublin, 18 May, 1825.
Jeune *see* Symons-Jeune.
Jewell *see* Duncombe-Jewell.
Jewer · Cobb, J. H. 28 Aug, 1798 (809).
    : Cobb, T. 28 Aug., 1798 (809).
Jex-Blake : Blake, W. 25 Aug., 1837 (2245).
Jobson *see* Warburton.
Jobson-Smith : Smith, M. E. and L. K., both of Lilburn Dore, Derby. Times, d.p, 11 Dec, 1888
Jodrell · Bower, J. 4 Feb, 1775 (11532).
    see Cotton-Jodrell.
    Higgins, A V. 26 Jan., 1883 (594)
    see Phillips Jodrell.
Jodrill Churchill, H. H. 31 March, 1883 (1844)
Joel-Ellis : Joel, J., of Brompton Hall, Kensington, Middlesex. Consul for Montevideo. Times, d p., 19 Aug., 1863.
Joggett-Champante Joggett J. 19 Aug., 1820 (1629).
John *see* Freke.
John-Gurney · Gurney, J. 17 July, 1818 (1440).

Johnes *see* Hills-Johnes.
Johns' *see* Beldam-Johns.
Johnson *see* Appleby.
„ Britten.
„ Bulkeley-Johnson
„ Chisenhale.
· Clanchy, C. M. and R. 26 March, 1851 (1046)
see Cory.
„ Cotgreave.
„ Dixon Johnson
„ Elliott.
„ Furse.
„ Hamilton.
„ Hill.
: Hilton, J. W. D. 7 Sept., 1872 (4042).
see Johnstone.
„ Kember
„ Kemeys-Tynte
Edward William : Johnson, William, of 10, St Mary's Street, Lambeth, Surrey. Times, 1 Jan., 1868.
William *see* Johnson, Edward William.
: Lillingston, G. W. 28 April, 1859 (1765)
see Lillingston.
„ Lindsay-Johnson
„ Luttman-Johnson
„ Lynn.
„ Mackenzie-Steuart.
„ Prior-Johnson.
Wm Prior · Richardson, James. 16 Sept., 1839 (1775).
see Pugh-Johnson.
„ Savell.
: Steer, R. P. 26 March, 1832 (828).
see Torrens-Johnson
„ Sharpe.
„ Walshe.
Johnson-Brooke : Johnson, J. B. 23 May, 1848 (2010).
Johnson-Daniell · Johnson, A. 10 Feb., 1842 (402).
Johnson-Eden : Eden, R. 18 Feb, 1811 (316)
Johnson-Jones : Jones, J., of 11, Exchange Alley, Chapel Street, Liverpool, and Sunnyside, Seaforth, both in Lancaster, stock and share broker. Times, d p., 16 Dec., 22 Dec., 1879
Johnson-Kember : Johnson, A. K., of High Street, Notting Hill, London. Times, 8 Feb., 1900.
Johnson Townley : Johnson, A. P. T., of Hoxne, Suffolk, gent. Times, d.p., 3 Nov., 1888.

Johnston *see* Campbell-Johnston.
      ,, Edgeworth-Johnstone.
Johnston Vaughan : Johnston, W. J., of St. Nicholas House, Glos., gent. Times, d.p , 28 May, 1888.
Johnstone *see* Campbell-Johnstone
      ,, Johnstoun-Coombes
     : Bempdé, R. J. 9 June, 1795 (386).
      Johnson, J. H. W. of 8, Suffolk Place, Pall Mall, Middlesex, F R.C.S Times, d.p., 21 April, 1870.
      Johnson, H., of North Dulwich, London. Times, 5 July, 1898
     : Montgomery, Rev A D.G , 14 July, 1813.
     see Schonswar-Johnstone.
     ,, Vanden-Bempde.
Johnstone-Scott : Johnstone, H. R. 17 April, 1860 (1555)
Johnstoun-Coombes : Johnstone, W Times, 31 Jan., 1896
Joiner *see* Visconti Powlett.
Jolliff : Milner, W. 23 Feb , 1807 (260)
Jones *see* Adair.
    ,, Alley-Jones.
    ,, Arderne.
    ,, Atcherley
    ,, Barker
    ,, Bence-Pembroke.
    ,, Birch-Jones.
    ,, Bowen.
    ,, Brock-Jones
    ,, Brooke-Jones.
    ,, Browne.
    : Burdett, Sir F. 5 April. 1800 (321).
    · Burnell, N. 16 April, 1807 (495)
    see Burnes-Floyer.
    ,, Chambres
    ,, Clifford-Jones.
    ,, Cumberland-Jones
    ,, De Grave.
    ,, Dervicke-Jones
    ,, Dove.
    ,, Elwood.
    ,, Evans.
    ,, Farmer-Jones
    ,, Fenton.
    ,, Fenton-Jones.
    ,, Fisher.
    ,, Foxcroft
    ,, Gawan-Jones.

Jones : Gigg, R. H , of 12, John Street, Pentonville, gent. Times, d.p , 25 March, 1879
    see Gordon-Kerr.
    ,, Gough.
    ,, Gray-Jones
    ,, Griffith
    ,, Gwynne-Vaughan.
    ,, Haden.
    ,, Hampden-Jones
    ,, Havard.
    ,, Haynes.
    ,, Heath.
    ,, Helsham.
    ,, Helsham-Jones.
    ,, Herbert.
    ,, Hughes Games.
    ,, Inglis-Jones.
    ,, Jaques-Jones.
    ,, Johnson-Jones.
T. Ridge : Jones, T., of 19, Chapel Street, Belgrave Sq., Middlesex, M D. Times, d.p , 12 Feb., 1876.
Wm. Phillip · Jones, Wm , of Glyncorrwg, Glamorgan Times, 6 Aug., 1898.
    see Kendrick
    ,, Kinghorn-Jones.
: Langham, W. 28 May, 1768 (10836).
    see Lawford Jones.
: Leach, W. H   12 June, 1849 (1988) (see 2225)
    see Lloyd-Jones.
    ,, Madoc.
    ,, Meredith Jones.
    ,, Meyrick-Jones.
    ,, Milner-Jones.
    ,, Mitton
    ,, Montford
    ,, Morgan.
    ,, Newell-Jones
    ,, Norbury
    ,, Ovington-Jones.
    ,, Paske-Jones.
    ,, Protheroe.
    ,, Pryce-Jones
    ,, Purnell.
    ,, Reynell-Upham.
    ,, Rowlands
    ,, Rowland.

Jones *see* Ryde-Jones.
,, Simpson-Jones.
,, Skelton.
,, Skelton.
,, Smith
,, Spencer
J. S. *see* Spencer, J.
see Stanley
,, Stanley-Jones
,, Stephens.
,, St. Paul
,, Taylor Jones
,, Thaddeus
,, Thomas-Jones
,, Trevaldwyn
,, Tudor.
: Tyrwhitt, T 6 March, 1790 (137).
see Tyrwhitt.
,, Vaughan
,, Vaughan-Jones
,, Veel
,, Vere.
,, Vincent
,, Walker-Jones
,, Wallis-Jones.
,, Whitmore-Jones
,, Willding-Jones.
,, Williams-Jones-Parry.
,, Wilym-Jones
Jones-Bateman : Jones, J 8 May, 1834 (834)
Jones-Brydges : Jones, Sir H. 4 May, 1826 (1160).
Jones-Byrom : Jones, W. H. and Byrom, S. H. 24 Sept, 1863 (4645).
Jones-Ford : Jones, C. C 16 June, 1875 (3561)
Jones-Græme Jones, V. 15 April, 1822 (639)
Jones Henry H : Jones, H. (Rev.), Rector of Llanberis, Carnarvon Times, d p, 23 Sept, 1876
Jones-Gwynne : Jones, A T 21 Jan, 1806 (127)
Jones Langston : Jones, Rev C., of Sevington Rectory, Kent. Times, d p, 26 Sept, 1879
Jones-Long Jones, D 22 March, 1814 (701)
Jones-Lloyd . Jones, J. R, of 120, Goswell Road, Middlesex, manufacr Times, d.p, 3 March, 1876
Jones-Marsham : Marsham, H. S 24 Nov., 1857 (4128)
Jones Mortimer : Jones, H. M., of Plasnewydd, Denbigh, esq, J.P., Lieut.-Col. Times, d.p, 30 Dec., 1874.

Jones-Parry : Jones, T. P. 14 Feb., 1807 (193).
    see Lloyd.
    „ Yale.
    „ Yate.
Jones-Perrivel : Jones, C., of 7a, Manchester Square, Marylebone d.p., 9 March, 1864.
Jones-Saltoun Jones, M., of Fronfraith, Montgomery, esq. Times, 7 Jan., 1868.
Jones-Vere : Jones, V. of Centra, Upper Norwood, Surrey, esq. Times, d.p., 29 Dec., 1880
Jones-Wilkinson Jones, T. 15 Feb, 1811 (381)
Jones-Williams Jones, T. J 15 Aug., 1871 (3726)
Jones-Willoughby : Jones, W. W., of Stoney Croft, Liverpool, Lancashire, esq. Times, d.p., 28 Sept., 2 Oct., 1883
Jordan *see* Gordon
    Gordon, L. J., of the Brunswick Hotel, Jermyn Street, Middlesex. Times, d.p., 26 June, 25 July, 1883
    Price, G. B. J. 15 Jan., 1835 (102)
Jordan-Jaggers . Jordan, T. J., of 5, Smith's Terrace, Chelsea Times, 13 April, 1869.
Jortin *see* Lee-Jortin
Joseph, Abraham *see* Howard, Alfred.
    see Jay
    M. : Maurice, J., formerly of 3, Langham Place, Midx., now of 61, Finchley New Road, gent Times, 29 Oct., 1874.
    see Lewin
    „ Morice
    „ Uttermare
Joseph Thal : Josephthal, Ernest, of Piccadilly, London 1c June, 1899
Joseph-Watkin Joseph, T. M. 13 Aug., 1894 (5141).
Joubert de la Ferté *see* Joubert.
Joubert : Joubert de la Ferté, C. H., of Newton Lodge, Hungerford, Berks, and of St. Mary's Hospital, Paddington, Middlesex, M.R.C.S., England Times, d.p., 12 April, 1869.
Jowett *see* Atkinson-Jowett
Joyce *see* Grote-Joyce
Joyner-Ellis : Joyner, W. 5 Feb., 1817 (263).
Joynt-Annesley . Joynt, R., of Bernagher, King's Co. D.C., 15 April, 1844 (D.G. 237 and 245) by Warrant
Jubb *see* Bedford
Juckes Clifton, J 11th and 21 Sept., 1790 (561 and 581)
    see Clifton.
Judd-Spark : Spark, L. M. and G. E. (spins.). Times, d.p., 28 Aug., 1896.

Juer *see* Pryce Juer
Jull *see* Godfrey
Juxon : Hesketh, Sir R   2 June, 1792 (363)

K

Kaeser *see* Keser
Karr *see* Ramsay-Karr.
: Seton, J.   18 June, 1799 (640)
see Seton-Karr.
Kavanagh *see* Cain Kavanagh
Kay *see* Arundale
Cunliffe-Lister   20 June, 1844 (2132).
Ewbank, W.   7 June, 1798 (584)
see Maden.
Kay-Shuttleworth : Kay, J. P.   18 Feb., 1842 (495).
Kaye *see* Lister-Kaye
Kay *see* Arundale.
Keane : Meara, J., of Dublin, Capt. R N. Dublin, 31 July, 1824.
Kearney *see* Aylward-Kearney.
  „ Butler Kearney.
  „ Cuthbert-Kenney.
Kearsey : Thomas, F.   23 July, 1841 (1927).
Keck *see* Legh.
  „ Powys-Keck
  „ Tracey.
Keene *see* Perry-Keene
  „ Ruck-Keene.
Keiffenheim-Trubridge : L. W. A , of Newcastle-on-Tyne, M.D.
Times, d.p , 14 Jan , 1892
Keily *see* Usher.
Keighley : Timothy, M. J , of Limewood, Lewisham, Kent, widow.
Times, d p., 25 Jan., 1887.
Keighly-Peach   Keighly, E. S.   19 Oct , 1838 (2252).
Keir-Grant . Keir, Sir W G   13 March, 1822 (443)
Keir-Mackintosh, of Dalmegavie . Keir, Campbell.   Lyon, Vol
XI., 21 June, 1882.
Keir, C. M., late of Portman Square, now of
Wimpole Street, London, gent   Times, d.p.,
20 April, 1882
Keith-Fraser : Fraser, H. C., Life Guards' Bararcks, London.
Times, 24 Oct., 1898.
Keith *see* Pusey-Keith.

Keith-Douglas, S Marischal : Douglas, S., of 18, Welbeck Street, Cavendish Square, and of the Oriental Club, London, esq Times, d p., 17 Aug., 1885.
Kelcey *see* Finn-Kelcey.
  „ Foord-Kelcey
Kelham : Kelham-Langdale, R 2 May, 1812 (804).
Kellett *see* Long.
Kellie : Kelly, K H. A., of Hyde Park, London. Times, 30 Nov., 1900
Kelly *see* Harvey-Kelly
  „ Kellie.
Kelly Kenny : Kelly, T., of Staff College, Farnboro', and Treanmand, co Clare, Capt 2nd Foot. Times, d p, 17 Nov., 1874
Kelly-White : Kelly, J B., of 3, Coleman Street, London, medical student at London Hospital. Times, 16 Oct., 1868
Kelsall *see* Peckham-Phipps
Kelsey *see* Atkins.
Kelso *see* Hamilton
Kember *see* Johnson-Kember
Kemble : Knebel, S. F., junr., of 2, Staning Lane, Gresham Street, London, accountant. Times, 4 Feb., 1888.
Kemeys *see* Allard-Kemeys.
Kemeys-Tynte Johnson, J. W., 29 Oct., 1785 (D G. 4677).
Kemmis-Betty : Betty, C. H., widow of Rev William, of Castle Cor, and Old Castle, co Meath, Ireland ; William Thomas Betty ; Joshua Frederick Betty. Times, 3 Dec., 1867
Kemp *see* Brookes-Kemp.
  „ Hitchin-Kemp
Kemp-Miller : Kemp, M. A., of Warminster, Wilts. Times, 23 Dec., 1867.
Kemp-Welch Kemp, M 16 May, 1795 (450).
Kempe : Russell, W. 33rd Geo. II., 1760.
Kendall Day, W. H H., of Philbeach Gardens, Middlesex, phys and surg. Times, d p, 8 March, 1888.
  : Masser, J., of Harrogate, Leeds, York, banker in Albion Street. Times, d p., 11 April, 1872
  see Mitchelson
Kendall-Lumb Kendall, P. 12 July, 1870 (3384) (D G. 975).
Kendrick, A J. : Jones, A., of Lower Bebington, nr. Birkenhead, and 64, Victoria Street, Liverpool, accountant and estate agent Times, d p., 30 Dec., 1893
Kennedy *see* Clark-Kennedy.
  „ Hume
  „ Shaw-Kennedy.
  „ Skipton.

Kennedy-Baillie : Kennedy, J., D.D., Rector of Ardtrea, in the
    Archdioc of Armagh. Dublin, 2 March, 1836
Kennedy-Lawrie : Kennedy, W   15 July, 1802 (782)
Kennedy-Purvis   Purvis, Mary J , of 29, Clifton Gardens, Maida
    Vale, Middlesex, widow; Arthur Purvis, of Darsham
    House, Suffolk, Capt. 2nd Batt Royal Sussex Regiment,
    Charles Purvis, Commander R N , Alex Purvis, of 29,
    Clifton Gardens, Madia Vale, solicitor, Frank Purvis, of
    29, Clifton Gardens, Maida Vale, gent., and Mary
    Eleanor Purvis, of 29, Clifton Gardens, Maida Vale,
    spinster. Times, d.p , 29 June, 3 July, 1883.
Kennedy-Skipton . Skipton, C S   15 April, 1893 (D.G. 449)
Kennett see Barrington
    ,, Barrington-Kennett.
Kennett-Dawson : Kennett, B.   6 Feb , 1807 (176).
Kenney see Kingsmill.
    ,, Cuthbert-Kenney.
Kenney Herbert   Herbert, Rev A. R., Rector of Bourton-on-
            Dunsmore, Warwick, and M L. and E. M ,
            his children   Times, d.p , 27 July, 1875.
        : Kenney, A. R , Capt Madras Cav , and A E.,
            his wife. Times, d p., 8 Dec., 1875
Kenney-Herbert : Kenney, J., of Lockarrig, co Cork. Dublin,
    29 June, 1842.
Kenny see Kelly-Kenny.
Kenrick see Kyffin
Kensington Salaman : Salaman, Chas.   Times, 1 Nov., 1867
Kent see Blake-Kent
    ,, Carlile-Kent
    : Darlington, B.   19 Nov., 1793 (1031).
    see Green
    : Greenwollers, A   15 July, 1780 (12100).
    see Ramsey-Kent.
Kent-Green   Green, Rev. Ed. K., of The Rectory, Claughton,
    Lancs. Times, d p , 28 July, 1890
Kenyon : Bedford, B.   8 April, 1824 (643).
Kenyon-Fuller : Fuller, H. A. K., of Pomeroy, nr Honiton,
    Devon, esq , and who lately held a Commission in H M.
    83rd Infantry. Times, d.p , 9 Feb., 1866,
Kenyon-Slaney   Kenyon, W. and F C   23 July, 1862 (3777).
Kenyon-Stow : Stow, M K., late of Moor Allerton Hall, York,
    now of Stoke Bishop, Gloucester. Times, 22 Aug., 1871.
Keown see Boyd.
Keppel see Roos-Keppel
Ker see Clay-Ker-Seymer.
Ker Bellenden : Gawler, J. B.   5 Nov., 1804 (1378).

Kerchever-Arnold : Arnold, Bessy May, of Whitethorns, Acton, Middlesex, and Meadow Brow, Grasmere, Westmorland Times, 5 and 12 Feb , 1898
Ker-Cokburne   Ker, H.   3 May, 1833 (860).
Ker Seymer *see* Clay Ker Seymer.
Kerdoel *see* Caerdoel
Kerr *see* Gill
  „ Gordon-Kerr
  „ Nelson
  „ Scott-Kerr
  „ Taylor.
    Triggs, L. K., now at 42, Stanford Road, Brighton, Sussex Times, d p , 16 July, 1891.
  see Williams-Kerr
Kerr-Pearse : Pearse, B. K. W.   3 Dec., 1889 (7279).
    of Ascot, co Bucks   Kerr, Revd. Beauchamp Kerr Warren   Lyon Register Vol. XII , 12 Sept., 1891
Kerrick-Walker : Kerrick, H. W.   13 Jan., 1877 (317).
Kerrison *see* Palmer Kerrison.
Kerry *see* Ekins
Kerschner *see* Crossley.
Kershaw *see* Hanson
Kershaw-Lumb : Kershaw, R.   28 Jan., 1836 (170)
Kerslake : Blyth. Rev. E. K. R., of Burnham Deepdale, Norfolk Times, d p , 16 March, 1870
Keser : Kaeser, J. S., formerly of Switzerland, now of 60, Queen Anne Street, Cavendish Square, London, M D. (Bâle), F R C S. (Eng)   Times, d.p , 8 Aug , 1884.
Kesteven-Hill : Hill, T., of 14, Bedford Row, Middlesex, architect and surveyor   Times, 5 Feb., 1870.
Kettle-Young : Kettle, A   1 Jan , 1835 (2)
Kettlewell *see* Eyres
Kevill-Davies : Kevill, W. T.   11 Nov., 1844 (3875)
    : Davies, A   12 July, 1838 (1613).
Key *see* Cooper-Key.
Keys-Wells : Keys, Rev. W., late of Scarborough, now of Clifton Rectory, nr Penrith, Cumberland, M A.   Times, d.p , 22 June, 1871
Khonstamm *see* Konstam.
Kilborn *see* Burrowes
Kilburn, J. Dawson · Kilburn, J., of Isleworth, Middlesex, Indep minister   Times, d.p , 3 Nov , 1876.
Kilderbee *see* de Horsey
Kilkelly *see* Butler

KIR]   *An Index to Changes of Name.*   187

Killam : Matthews, T. K   7 Feb , 1880 (730)
    see Newsome-Killam
Killikelly *see* Lynch-Killikelly
Kinahan *see* Hudson-Kinahan.
Kincaid *see* Bateman-Hanbury, C S
    „ Bateman-Hanbury-Kincaid-Lennox.
Kincaid-Lennox : Kincaid, John Lennox. Lyon Register Vol. III , 12 June, 1833.
Kincaid-Lennox, of Woodhead and Kincaid : Smythe, Viscountess Strangford   18 June, 1859 (2472).
    Smythe, Margaret C. (widow).   W , 18 June, 1859 (D.G. 1224).
King *see* Duckworth-King.
    „ Holland-King.
    „ Martin.
    „ Meade-King
    „ Milbanke
    „ Reeve-King
    : Sampson, Rev. R K., of Pevensey, Sussex.   d.p , 25 April, 1865
    Simpkinson, J.   10 April, 1837 (955).
    : Simpkinson, J. K.   22 Nov., 1842 (3566)
    see Wolfenden.
King-Church : King, H. J.   13 Feb , 1849 (471)
King-Harman : King, H L   26 July, 1838 (1690).
King-Noel : King, W. (Earl of Lovelace).   29 Sept., 1860.
King-Sampson : King, R.   31 May, 1814 (1233)
King Tenison : King, H. E. N. (Earl of Kingston).   20 March, 1883 (D G. 297).
Kingesmill Brice, R   6th Geo. III., 1766.
Kinghorn-Jones : Jones, J A., of 247, Selhurst Road, S Norwood, stationer.   Times, d.p., 9 Feb., 1892.
Kingsford *see* Burton.
Kingsmill · Brice, E.   22 Dec., 1787 (585)
    Kenney, T. N and Isabel A. B., his wife.   18 Jan , 25 Jan., 1866 (D.G. 142 and 168).
    : Stephens, J.   28 Jan., 1806 (147).
    see Woodham-Kingsmill
Kinleside-Gratwicke   Kinleside, W. G   4 Jan , 1822 (18)
Kinnear *see* Balfour-Kinnear
Kinsey *see* Rowbotham.
Kirby *see* Morgan-Kirby.
    „ Nassau.
Kirby-Smith · Smith, H , of Rose Cottage, Brisley, Norfolk, gent. Times, d.p , 15 Dec., 1896.
Kirk : Bull, G. E. K.   11 July, 1881 (D.G. 652).

Kirk : Bull, P. A. K. B.   11 July, 1881 (D.G. 652).
  see Fox-Kirk
Kirkby see Bagnall-Wild
Kirklinton   Saul, G. G. K., of Kirklinton Hall, Cumberland,
    esq   Times, d.p., 25 Jan., 1877
Kitchiner see Edgeworth
Kiville see Newcombe
Knapp O'Brien : Knapp, T., formerly of Brighton, London,
    Weston-super-Mare, and now of Florence, Italy, esq
    Times, d.p., 20 Oct., 1876
Knapton see Abel-Knapton
    Brine, A. J.   30 July, 1860 (2933).
Knatchbull-Hugessen : Knatchbull, E. H., R. B., R. A., H.T.,
    W. W., M. C., and L. S.   13 Aug., 1849 (2533)
Knebel see Kemble
Knevett de Knevett   Knevett, J. S., of 2, Belle Vue, Hounslow,
    Middlesex, esq   Times, d.p., 2 Sept., 1882
Knight : Austen, E.   10 Nov., 1812 (2347).
    see Bruce.
    „ Cromey Buck.
    Davies, J.   5 May, 1772 (11245)
    see Eames
    : Gally, H.   29 Jan., 1805 (130)
    see Gregson
    : Hall, J.   16 July, 1849 (2327)
    see Leake-Knight
    „ Lysaght-Knight.
    „ Nuttall
    „ Rouse-Boughton-Knight.
Knight-Bruce   Knight, J. L.   4 Sept., 1837 (2344)
Knill-Abel : Abel, W. H., of 110, Great Portland Street, Midx.,
    gent   Times, d.p., 17 July, 1875
Knollys   Welldale, F.   19 April, 1794 (343)
    see Weldale-Knollys
Knott see Hotham.
    Newbery, T.   5 Sept., 1780 (12115).
Knottesford see Fortescue-Knottesford
Knowles-Tillotson   Tillotson, T., of Whatton House, Leicester,
    esq.   Times, d.p., 9 Jan., 1873
Knox see Saunders-Knox-Gore
Knox-Browne   Browne, H.   13 April, 1874 (D.G. 233).
Knyfton see Graves-Knyfton
Kolle see Horton.
Konstam   Khonstamm, Teresina, of 142, Ebury Street, London,
    widow   Times, d.p., 26 Feb., 1892
Kruszinski see Newman
Kyffin : Kenrick, E.   28 April, 1842 (1172).
    : Kenrick, H.   1 March, 1839 (460)

Kyffin · Lenthall, W. K. and Elizabeth, his wife. Whll., 3 March, 1870 (D G 339).
Kynaston . Owen, W. C. E 2 Jan., 1867 (51)
: Owen, W. C. E. 2 Jan., 1868 (D.G. 31).
see Powell.
· Snow, Rev. H., Princ. of Cheltenham College. Times, 11 Jan and 3 Feb., 1875.
Kynnersley : Gardner, T. K. 19 Sept., 1887 (5488).
see Sneyd-Kynnersley.
Kyrke-Smith : Smith, H., of Liverpool. Times, 29 July, 1900.
Kyrle *see* Money-Kyrle.

L

Labilliere *see* de Labilliere.
Lacon · Atkinson, W. L 12 June, 1826 (1446).
Lacon-Graham : Lacon, Ida C., of Duntrune, Forfarshire. Times, d.p, 27 Sept., 1894.
Laconture-Dugue : Laconture, L. P , late of Marseilles, but now of Bordeaux, France Times, d p., 5 June, 1889
Lacy *see* de Lacy.
· Newnham, W. 30 Oct , 1790 (646).
C. E : Long, Chas Edw Lacy, of Barnet, Middlesex Times, 24 Jan , 1899.
Ladbroke : Denton, O. 6 June, 1818 (1018)
see Weller-Ladbroke.
Lade *see* Milles-Lade.
Lagra : Langenbach, L., of Tottenham, Middlesex, gent. Times, d.p., 8 June, 1869.
Laing *see* Meason.
  „ Oldham.
  „ Shields.
  „ Wolryche-Whitmore
Laird-MacGregor : Laird, W, of Liverpool, co. Lancaster. Times, d p., 17 June, 1870.
: Laird, J. L., now at Everleigh, Wilts, Dep. Conservator of Forests, Bombay. Times, d.p , 3 July, 1883.
: Laird, W S , at present residing at Craigcrostan Archacon (Gironde, Fr), esq. Times, d p , 15 June and 15 Dec., 1892.
: Laird, W. S., of Craigcrostan in the Gironde, France. Times, d p , 15 Feb and 15 April, 1893

Lake *see* Watson
La Mark *see* Lamarque
Lamarque : La Mark, W A , gent , Sarah La Mark , F. W. La Mark , F. V La Mark , M. L La Mark, spinster , S. A M. La Mark, spinster ; H E La Mark, all of Kingston-on-Thames, Surrey ; and G. J. L La Mark, of Faversham, Kent. Times, d p , 10 March, 1868.
Lamb *see* Armstrong-Lamb.
    Andouin, G D.G., 10 Nov., 1801.
    Burges, Sir C M 2 Nov., 1824 (1801).
    Burges, J B. 25 Oct , 1821 (2113)
    Cock, T H 13 March, 1798 (217)
Lambden *see* Yalden.
Lambe Arathoon, H J. G., Lieut. Lt. Inf Times, d.p., 13 May, 1885
    see Armstrong-Lambe.
    Torbett, G V. L. 14 Aug., 1850 (2247)
Lambert *see* Bence Lambert
    : Binns, F W , of Farsley. nr. Leeds, York, surgeon's assistant Times, 20 June, 1866.
    see Fenwick
    : Gorwyn, G., of Trayhill, Devon, gent. Times, 1 Jan., 1875
    see Ruttledge,
    · Smith, J. W. L., of Bayswater, Middlesex, financial agent. Times, d.p., 10 Dec , 1873
Lambton *see* Dawson-Lambton
Lamdin *see* Harrison
La'Mert, Lewis *see* Lewis, Louis
La Mert-Curtis : La Mert, J., of 15, Albemarle Street, Piccadilly, Middlesex, M R.C.S , M.D Times, 14 Feb., 1873
    . La Mert, J , of 15, Albemarle Street, Piccadilly, Middlesex, M.D., of Rostock, Germany. Times, d p , 19 March, 1866.
Lamplugh Brougham, P. 11 March, 1783 (12421)
Lamont-Campbell, of Possil Lamont, Celestine Lyon Register Vol. XII., 14 July, 1892.
Lamplugh-Rapier : Rapier, J. L. 10 March, 1825 (459).
Lampson Locker, F 25 June. 1885 (3178).
L'Amy *see* Ramsay-L'Amy
Lanagan *see* Gaussett Lanagan
Lancaster-Lucas Lancaster, S L. 3 July, 1849 (2127)
    : Lancaster S L W , 3 July, 1849 (D G 650)
Lance · Butler, A F , of Brookside, Bournemouth, Hants. Times, d.p , 6 June, 1881
Landale *see* Phillip

Lander *see* Cleland.
Lane *see* Claypon
   ,, Lane-Scott
   ,, Lucas-Lane.
   ,, Lutwyche.
Lane-Claypon : Lane, W. W. 28 Feb., 1877 (2026).
Lane-Hopkin : Hopkin, J., formerly of St James' Rectory, Wednesbury, Staffs, now of Carrington Wootton Gardens, Bournemouth Times, 19 Jan., 1898.
Lane-Scott : Lane, W. F., of Manchester. Times, 22 June, 1900.
Lanfear *see* Stanfield.
    : Viereck, C. S., formerly of Germany, but now of Letcombe Regis, Berks. Times, d.p., 12 July, 1881.
Lang *see* Conyers.
   ,, Tomlinson.
Langdale *see* Kelham.
   : Stourton, Hon. C. 3 Jan., 1815 (23).
Langdale-Moreton : Pheasant, Wm., Walton-on-the-Hill, Lancs. Times, 3 April, 1899.
Langdon *see* Lazarus-Langdon.
    : Lazarus, M. J., of Sunbury, Rusholme, Manchester, chem manufacr. Times, d p., 2 Oct., 1890.
    : Lazarus, E. H., of Sunny Oaks, Fallowfield, Manchester, merchant. Times, d.p., 2 Oct., 1890.
Langenbach *see* Lagra.
Langford *see* Pooll.
   ,, Sainsbury.
Langford-Brooke : Brooke, H. L. B., of Mere Hall, Cheshire, esq., Capt 17th Foot Reg. Times, d p., 11 May, 1874.
Langford Pearse : Pearse, Emily J., of Lindesay, Ryde, I.W., widow. Times, d p., 22 July, 1892.
Langham *see* Carter.
   ,, Jones.
Langhorn *see* Lansdell Langhorn
Langley Dawnay, Hon. M 18 May, 1824 (851)
   see Fust.
Langley-Smith : Smith, W T., of Croydon, Surrey, gent. Times, d.p., 5 Nov., 1886.
Langmead *see* Taswell-Langmead.
Langridge Brown · Brown, E. A., of Lee, Kent, spinster Times, d p., 20 Aug., 1881.
Langston *see* Jones Langston.
Langton *see* Allibone Langton
   : Gore, W. 9 Aug., 1783 (12465)
   see Massingberd

Langton *see* Temple-Gore-Langton.
Langton-Featherston : Featherston, Rev. R. N , Vicar of Ravensthorpe, Northampton. Times, d p , 24 Oct , 1885.
Lanigan *see* O'Keefe.
Lansdell Langhorn : Lansdell, A., of 10, Stonefield Street, Islington, clerk in Civ Service Times, d.p., 1 Jan , 1887
Lara *see* Lopez
Larkins-Walker : Walker, W. L., of Hove, Sussex, Lieut -Col. Times, d p., 4 Feb., 1889.
Larmour : Lazarus, D. A., of 61, Bentick Street, Calcutta, E Indies, accountant. d p., 5 Feb , 1881.
 : Lazarus, C F., of 61, Bentick Street, Calcutta, E Indies, cabinet-maker. d p., 5 Feb , 1881.
 : Lazarus, F. D A., of Calcutta, E Indies, accountnt. Times, d p , 9 March, 1881.
Larpent *see* De Hochepied-Larpent
Lascelles : Moore, W 5 Aug , 1777 (11793).
 see Toby-Lascelles.
Lascelles-Astley : Cook, Fredk., of Funchal, Portugal Times, 7 Dec., 1889.
Latchmore *see* Lechmere
Lateward : Schrieber, J 25th Geo. III , 1785
Latham *see* Ashby.
 ,, Smith-Latham.
Latour *see* Young
La Trobe-Bateman Bateman, J. F 28 May, 1883 (D G 681)
Laud Du Boys : Laud Wood, H S., of Ludgate Hill, London. Times, 28 Feb , 1899.
Laurence Lazarus, A L , late of 83, Pembroke Rd., of Dublin, Ireland, but now of Chancery Lane and of S. Kensington Hotel, Queen's Gate Terrace, London, Middlesex B A. (Trin. Coll , Dublin), and solicitor of Supreme Court of Judicature in England Times, d p , 4 Nov , 1878.
Laurie Bayley, Sir J R. L E 26 Feb , 1887 (1161)
 see Brown-Laurie
 ,, Craig-Laurie.
 of Maxwelton : Fector, J. M. W., 12 Feb , 1848 (D G 233)
 Laurie- Brown, Annie B , St. Mary's Vicarage, Warwick, spinster Times, d.p , 1 March, 1893
 see Northale-Laurie
Laurie-Brown Brown, A B , formerly of Leamington, Warwick, now in Naples, Italy, spinster. Times, d.p., 2 Feb , 1889.
Laurington Hall : Hall, C., of 5, Lowndes Terrace, Middlesex. draper's assistnt. Times, d.p., 12 July, 1890
Lavallin Puxley : Puxley Lavallin, J., of 36, Bury Street, St James, London, esq Times, d.p, 6 Jan., 1885.

Lavers-Smith : Smith, C. of Oakfield, Walton-on-Thames, Surrey, formerly of Highbury New Park, Middlesex Times, d.p., 20 Jan., 1883.
La Vettée de la Dubeterre Morris : Morris, J. J. Times, d.p., 27 Nov., 1885.
Law *see* Lawrence-Law
Law *see* Peel-Law
Law-Schofield : Law, G. W. 1 Jan., 1855 (4)
Lawe *see* Drinkwater-Lawe
Lawford Jones : Jones, H., of Alexandria House, Brigstocke Road, Bristol, accountant. Times, d.p., 3 Dec., 1885.
Lawless *see* Crooke-Lawless.
Lawley *see* Thompson
Lawlor-Huddleston : Lawlor, D. A S. 20 June, 1891 (3378)
Lawrell *see* Bebb.
Lawrence *see* Barnes Lawrence.
    ,, Durning-Lawrence.
    : Morris, W. 25 Aug., 1815 (1945)
    see Lawrence-Pitt.
    : Lazarus, C. L, of 23, St. George's Road, Kilburn, Middlesex. Times, 12 July, 1864
    Levy, W., of 53, Sutherland Gardens, Maida Vale, Middlesex, gent. Times, d.p., 29 Oct, 1878
Lawrence-Law : Lawrence, C G., King's Cliffe, Northampton Times, 3 Dec., 1898
Lawrence-Morris *see* Lawrence
Lawrence-Townsend : Lawrence, R 5 May, 1803 (526)
Lawrie *see* Kennedy-Lawrie.
Lawson : Cormack, A. D. 10 Sept., 1801 (1135).
    see De Burgh-Lawson
    ,, Levy-Lawson
    ,, Maire
    ,, Nixon-Lawson
    Wright, W 12 May, 1834 (857).
    Wybergh, W. 2 Oct., 1812 (1987).
Lawson-Bell : Lawson, E., late of Scarborough, York, now of 29, Great-Western Street, Moss Side, Manchester, Lancaster Times, 24 April, 1882.
Lawson-Smith : Lawson, E. M. 3 Jan., 1881 (179).
Lax *see* Gilling-Lax
    ,, Gilling.
Layland-Barratt : Barratt, F 1 May, 1895 (2630)
Lazarus *see* Byron.
    ,, Langdon
    ,, Larmour.
    ,, Lawrence
    ,, Venis-Lazarus.

Lazarus-Barlow   Lazarus, W. S., of 55, Penn Road Villas, Islington, and of Downing Coll., Cambs., med stud. Times, 27 July, 1886
Lazarus-Langdon · Lazarus, A M, of Victoria Park, Rusholme, Manchester, and of 2, St. James' Square, Manchester, barrister-at-law. Times, d p, 26 Sept., 1890
Lea *see* Butcher-Lea.
Leach *see* Jones.
   „   Lloyd.
Leacroft : Dicas, T.   6 May, 1823 (755)
Leadbitter *see* Gibson-Leadbitter.
Leadbitter-Smith   Leadbitter, J.   7 April, 1843 (1236)
Leahy : Carroll, T.   13 Feb, 1882 (D G 287)
Leake-Knight . Leake, G B   13 May, 1815 (894)
Leake *see* Byres-Leake
Leaman *see* Hunt-Leaman
Leaper-Spell   Spell, W.   3 Aug, 1802 (805)
Leaper *see* Newton.
Lear . Vaughan, A. A., of Abergavenny. Times, 7 Sept, 1865
Lear-Cholwick : Lear, W T   23 Oct, 1835 (2050)
Leasland-White : White, W J, of Forest Row, nr East Grinstead, Sussex. Times, d p, 6 April, 1895.
Leather-Culley   Leather, A. H., of Fowbery Tower, Belford, Northumberland. Times, d.p, 10 Nov., 1894
   Leather, A H   20 Aug, 1896 (4817)
Leathes *see* Stanger-Leathes
Leavins *see* Waters Leavins
Le Breton-Simmons   Simmons, G F H, Lieut R E. Times, d p, 7 Sept, 1887
Lechmere *see* Charlton
   Latchmore, E , of 14, Stratford Place, Oxford Street Middlesex, lic dent surg, R C S. Eng. Times, d.p, 1 March. 1889
Lecky *see* Browne-Lecky
Lecky-Browne · Browne C W L.   29 May, 1874 (D G 333)
le Dixon-Sutton : le Dixon, T. A, of Brandon Parva. Norfolk, farmer   Times, d p, 11 Sept, 1895.
Lee : Ayton, R   24 April, 1773 (11346)
   see Ayton.
   „ Bosvile
   „ Danks
   : Fiott, J   4 Oct., 1816 (2123).
   · Hanning, J L   21 March, 1825 (517)
   see Hanning-Lee.
   „ Harvey.
   : Levy, E L, of St. John's Wood, Middlesex, gent   Times, d p, 15 Oct, 1888.

Lee *see* Norman-Lee
　　,, Thornton.
　　,, Vaughan
　　.. Vaughan-Lee
Lee-Acton : Acton, N. L. 19th Geo III , 1779
Lee-Bellasyse   Bellasyse, E 10 March, 1870 (1736) (D G 339)
Lee Clark   Lee, J C.   Times, d p. 28 July 1896
Lee-Dawson Dawson. R   15 April 1836 (682)
Lee-Jortin   Lee, W 18 June 1844 (2132)
Lee-Mainwaring · Lee, C. B 2 Nov. 1859 (4077).
Lee-Norman   Norman, L. A.   23 March. 1876 (D G 181 and 189)
　　　　　: Lee, T D G , 21 Oct , 1817
Lee-Warner : Bagge, W. W. 21 May, 1814 (1488)
　　　　　: Woodward, D H   45th Geo III.. 1805
Lee-Wood   Wood, T . of Southport. Lancs , gent   Times. d p , 7 April. 1893
Leedham-Green   Green. C A., of Didsbury Coll , nr. Manchester, Lancs., M R.C S. (Eng) and L R C P (London)   Times. d p. 29 Nov , 1892
Leekey . Cabrier. G L   28 July, 1803, L.G. 1804 (365).
Leekey-Cabrier   Leekey, G.   23 Feb.. 1802 (199)
Leeming *see* Brettargh-Leeming
　　　　,, Marshall
Lees *see* Luxmoore
　　,, Worsley
Lees-Milne   Lees. J H   31 May. 1890 (3241).
Leesmith : Smith, J L , of Slingsby, York, now at Dunedin   Times, d p., 23 Aug , 1879
Leeson   Culverwell. F M., of 56. Wimpole Street, Cavendish Square, Middlesex   Times. d p. 7 Sept., 1877
　　see Marshall.
Lefebvre   Gosselin, B M H.   19 Feb., 1885 (759)
Lefevre   Shaw, C   8 Aug , 1789 (529).
Le Fleming *see* Hughes-le Fleming
Le French *see* Bannerman.
Lefroy *see* Maxwell-Lefroy.
Legassicke-Crespin : Crespin. C W.. of the Manors of Great Modbury and Modbury, and of The Chase, Torquay, Devon, esq 9 Nov., 1882
Legg *see* Rowan-Legg.
Legh : Cross, T   24 July, 1823 (1222).
　　· Crosse, R   15 Aug., 1806 (1121)
　　see Gubbins.
　　: Keck, G A   31 July, 1792 (596)
　　: Renny, A. M. R and C. M. F , both of Adlington Hall, Chester. Times, d p., 24 Oct , 1896

Legh Rowlls, E. 6 Oct, 1781 (12230).
Legrew-Hesse Legrew, O. 12 July, 1794 (696)
Le Hunt *see* Bainbrigge-Le Hunt
Leibrandt Nash, J T., of 23, Blomfield Road, Shepherd's Bush, Middlesex, gent., late officer 66th Foot Times, d.p, 9 Sept., 1873
Leicester *see* Bryne
,, Warren.
Leicester-Warren : Leighton (calling himself Leicester-Warren), C 9 Feb , 1899 (1040).
Leigh *see* Austen-Leigh
· Hanbury, C 30 May, 1797 (483).
see Hare.
,, Hanbury
,, Hanbury-Leigh.
John Nash Leigh, J. E R N , of Guildhall Chambers, Cardiff, solicitor Times, 14 March, 1885
H. Levy : Levy, H., of 42, Westbourne Park Road, Midx., antiquarian Times, d.p., 10 Aug , 1882
see Mallory.
,, Pemberton-Leigh
Smith, J 10 April, 1802 (358).
. Tracy, H. (Viscount) 23 Feb , 1793 (-49).
· Tracy, T. C. (Viscount) 19 Sept., 1789 (605).
see Trafford
,, Walker-Leigh
,, Ward-Boughton-Leigh
Yates, R (a minor) 10 Oct , 1850 (2681)
Leighton Figgins, Rev J L . of The Rectory, Blackley, nr. Manchester. Times, d.p , 20 March, 1873
see Leicester-Warren
H · Leipziger, H S, of The Ferry, Shepperton, Middlesex Times, d.p., 6 Dec., 1892.
Leighton-Warren : Leighton. Dame E. L.. of Knutsford. Times, 28 May, 1900
Leipziger *see* Leighton.
Leir *see* Wilkins-Leir
Leir-Carleton : Leir, R. L , of Greywell Hill, Hants, Maj.-Gen. Times, 26 May, 1888
Leith *see* Forbes-Leith.
,, Hay.
Leman Orgill, T 22 Jan , 1808 (5 and 144).
Le Marchant *see* Thomas.
Le Marchant Douse Douse, T , of 4, Richmond Terr., Clapham Road, Surrey, B.A., clerk to Senate of Lond. University Times, d.p., 10 Dec.. 1880.
Lemon *see* Taylor

Lempriere-Collingwood : Lempriere, Anne   25 July, 1831 (1532)
Leney : Levy, J A, of 81, Broadhurst Gardens, S Hampstead, London, gent   Times, d p, 5 May, 1892
Leng-Smith . Smith, C., of 12, Milk Street, London, and 17, Crescent Road, Brockley, Kent, accountant   Times, d p, 22 April, 1890
Lenigan see Ryan-Lenigan
Lennard see Barrett-Lennard
     : Cator, J. F   26 Nov, 1861 (5067)
Lennox see Bateman-Hanbury, C. S.
    ,, Bateman-Hanbury-Kincaid-Lennox
    ,, Gordon-Lennox.
    ,, Kincaid-Lennox
Lens see Clarke-Lens
Lenthall see Kiffin.
Leonard see Bolden
Leonard-Willey : Leonard, D   19 May, 1870 (2825) (D G 803)
Lenwood : Peppercorn, Rev W, B A, LL B, of Sheffield, Yorks, Ind minister   Times, 14 Nov., 1874
Le Poer : Trench, R. (Earl of Clancarty)   D G., 27 Oct., 1807
Lernoult : Vaux, A. L.   9 June, 1795 (586)
Le Roy-Lewis : Le Roy, H., of Westbury House, nr. Petersfield, Southampton. Times, d p, 20 Jan., 1886.
Lesassier see Hamilton.
Leschallas see Pige Leschallas
Lesingham : Biggs, F. J., of Notting Hill and Leadenhall Street, London, merchant. Times, d p, 1 Feb, 1888
Leslie . Beers, F. C   8 March, 18 March. 1850 (D G 319 and 330)
    Duff, Mary   19 April, 1802 (418)
    see Forbes-Leslie
    ,, Farquharson
    · French, R. C. L.   6 July, 1885 (D G 665)
    : Gwyther, G.   4 June, 1817 (1339)
    : Haworth, M H.   17 Jan, 1865 (214)
    see Haworth-Leslie
    ,, Irvine
    James   Levy, Jonah, of 22, Bedford Square, Middlesex
    see Levvy Leslie
    ,, Levvy Sandbach.
          Times, 7 May, 1869
    · Levy, C., of 116, Wilmslow Road, Rusholme, Lancs, manufacr, formerly of Manchester, clothier   Times, d.p., 24 May, 1881
    see Levy-Leslie
    ,, Slingsby.
    ,. Roberts.
    ,, Waldegrave-Leslie.

Leslie-Cuming : Leshe, J 14 Aug., 1818 (1456).
Leslie-Duguid, of Balquhan : Leslie, of Balquhan, Chas Stephen. Lyon Register Vol. XII., 25 Oct., 1889.
Leslie-Miller : Miller, L J. H , of the I of Java and of Hurst House, Hurst, Bucks, merchant. Times. d p , 17 Nov., 1893.
Lesly Sole. R , of Edinburgh Scotland, med. stud. Times, d.p.. 8 Oct , 1880.
Lester . Colmer, W., of Connaught Street. Hyde Park, and 27, Red Lion Square, Middlesex Times, d p., 2 June, 1880
: Garland, B. L 17 May, 1805 (649)
: Garland, L. B. 23 Dec, 1853 (3748).
: Garland, L 8 Dec., 1854 (4054)
: Letztergroschen, Julius, of Keppel Street, Middlesex Times, 9 March, 1899
Le Strange *see* Styleman-Le Strange.
Styleman Le Strange, C., Lieut R N. Times, d p. 5 May, 1874
Styleman Le Strange, H., of Hunstanton, Norfolk, esq Times, d p , 5 May, 1874.
Styleman Le Strange, G , of Hunstanton, Norfolk, esq. Times. d p, 17 Aug., 1875.
Letztergroschen *see* Lester.
Leverton-Spry : Leverton, E. J , of St Keverne, Cornwall, surgeon. Times, d.p.. 31 March. 1888
Leveson-Gower *see* Egerton.
,, Sutherland.
Levett *see* Mirehouse.
,, Scrivener.
Levett-Prinsep : Levett 7 July, 1835 (1332)
Levi, G Montefiore : Levi, G , of Brussels, civil engineer, Times, d.p., 3 Feb, 1876
see Rickman
,, Waley.
Levi-Newton : Levi, A 23 Feb.. 1824 (442).
Levingston *see* Smith Levingston
Levvy Leslie : Levvy, F. J.. of Edgbaston. Warwicks.. merchant Times, 11 Aug, 1879.
Levvy Sandbach . Levy. G.. of 21. St Aubyn's, Hove. Brighton Times, 24 Nov., 1879
Levy *see* Annesley
,, Hamilton.
,, Hume.
Jonah *see* Leslie, James.
see Lawrence.
,, Lee

Levy *see* Leigh
„ Leney
„ Leslie.
„ Lewis.
„ Lumley
„ Meyrick
Levy-Lawson : Levy, E. 11 Dec., 1875 (6467)
Levy-Leslie . Levy, H., of Douro House, Edgbaston, Warwicks., gent Times, d p., 13 Sept., 1881.
: Levy, H., of Douro House, 36, Wellington Road, Edgbaston, Birmingham, Warwick, gent., until recently one of the partners in the late firm of J Emanuel Davis & Co, of Birmingham. d.p., 29 Aug., 1881
Levy-Newton : Levy, M. 12 Aug., 1800 (921).
Levy Tebbitt : Levy, A. P., of 3, Highbury New Park, and 66, Commercial Street. Spitalfields Times, d p., 10 March, 1888.
Lewes *see* Lloyd.
Lewin, Joseph Joseph, Lewin, Hatton Garden, London. Times, 13 Oct., 1898
Lewis : Bones, J., of Clarendon House, Maida Vale, Middlesex, esq., J. C. A. Bones, M.A., barrister-at-law, Capt. Kent Artillery Militia, Governor of H.M. Pentonville Prison, esq., and Rev H. C. Bones, B.A., R. of Binsted, Sussex. Times, d.p., 13 Aug., 1869
see Cheese Lewis.
: Day, Geo. W. 13 Oct., 26 Oct., 1865 (D.G. 1321 and 1310)
see Drakeford-Lewis
., Goldwyer-Lewis.
„ Hampton-Lewis.
„ Le Roy-Lewis
: Levy, J., of Southampton Buildings and Clement's Inn, Middlesex, auctioneer and estate agent Times. d p., 7 July, 1877.
Thos. Young · Lewis, T., of 3, Napier Street, Cardigan, bank clerk Times, 16 Sept., 1891
see Lloyd
: Lutto, J., of Houndsditch and Finsbury Circus. Times, d.p., 6 May, 1879.
Louis : La'Mert, Lewis, of 37, Bedford Square, Bloomsbury, Middlesex, M R.C S., England. Times. d.p., 16 Jan., 1868.
see Owen

Lewis see Philpps.
,,   Pitt-Lewis
        Solomons, S., Limehouse, London, tailor and outfitter.
            Times. d p . 29 April, 1893
        see Villiers
Lewis-Barned   Lewis, L. J   24 July, 1888 (3553)
Lewis-Bird : Lewis, W. C.   3 March, 1809 (308)
Lewis-Crosby   Cornwall, R C   17 Aug., 1885 (D G 835).
                Cornwall, E. H.   28 April, 1891 (D G. 977).
Lewis-Lloyd   Lewis, T.   20 Dec , 1824 (2144)
Lewis-Minet   Mason, G   27 April, 1832 (963)
                Mason, J   4 May, 1832 (1017)
Lewys-Lloyd : Lloyd, E.. Abergynolwyn, Merioneth. Times, 19 Dec., 1898
Ley   Greaves, R C   16 Sept , 1820 (1783).
Leyland   Bullin, C   8 May, 1845 (1438)
        : Naylor, C J., of Leighton Hall and Brynllwyarch,
            Montgomery, esq   Times, d p , 30 April, 1891
        Bullin, R   19 June, 1827 (1396).
Leyborne-Popham   Leyborne, E W   22 Dec   1805 (80)
Leyburn see Carley.
Lichigary see Bertie
Liddell see Grainger.
Liddell-Grainger : Liddell, H.   29 May, 1893 (3182)
Liebenrood : Hancock, J.   13 Jan , 1865 (214)
                Ziegenbein, J E   24 Jan., 1795 (71)
Liebmann   Benjamin, H., of Oak Villas. Bradford, Yorks, trade
            assistnt   Times, d p , 1 April, 1875
Lightfoot   Schofield, S   1 Oct , 1820 (1942)
Light see Lyte.
Lill see De Burgh
Lillingston see Johnson
        . Johnson, W G. L., of Ulverscroft, Leicestershire.
            Capt Royal Irish Rifles   Times, d p , 29 Dec ,
            1894
            Spooner, A   16 Aug , 1797 (807)
Lillycropp see Dalton.
Lindeman see Bird Lindeman
Lindley   Sleigh, A   20 Aug . 1782 (12323)
            Sleigh, J   28 Nov , 1772 (11304)
        : Wilkinson, J   28 Dec , 1782 (12400)
Lindow see Burns-Lindow
        : Rawlinson, H. L   19 May, 1792 (317).
Lindo see Da Costo-Lindo.
Lindo-Abarbanel : Abarbanel, D L   2 Jan , 1802 (1)
Lindon see Brawne-Lindon
Lindsay see Alexander-Lindsay.

Lindsay *see* Bethune.
   ,, Lloyd-Lindsay
   : Sloper, C. A. L. Times d.p., 7 May, 1896.
Lindsay-Johnson : Johnson, C. M., of 4, Albert Road, Brighton, Sussex, esq. Times, d.p., 28 July, 1890
Lindsay-Renton : Renton, G. H., of Walworth and Clapham Road, Surrey, timber merchant Times, d.p., 13 June, 1882.
Lines : Hall, A. W. 2 Dec., 1882 (6320).
Lingard-Guthrie : Lingard, Rev. Roger Rowton. Lyon Register Vol. VIII., 17 Feb., 1871.
Lingard-Monk : Lingard, R. B. M. 11 Oct., 1875 (4904)
Lings Scott : Lings, James Scott, of Stockport, Lancs., and of Levenhulme, Lancs., esq., J.P. Times, d.p., 28 Nov., 1892
Linnington *see* Martyn-Linnington.
Lintorn-Simmons : Simmons, Eleanor Julia, Walton-by-Clevedon, Somerset. Times, 21 Sept., 1898.
Lintott Aylmer : Lintott, A., of 3, Chichester Place, Brighton, Sussex, gent. Times, d.p., 23 Dec., 1880.
Liot *see* Ludlow
Lipscombe *see* Grombridge or Groombridge
Lisburne, Earl *see* Vaughan
Lisgar (Baron) : Young, Sir John, Bart. Whitehall, 8 Oct., 1870 (D.G. 1307).
Lisle : Moises, H. and J. 13 Aug., 1860 (3088)
   : Orde, W. B. 27 July, 1882 (3515)
   : Taylor, E. H. 5 Oct., 1822 (1619)
Lister : Buttrey, J. A., formerly of Leeds, now of Bedford, gent. Times, d.p., 8 Sept., 1874
   see Cunliffe-Lister
   ,, Empson
   ,, Harris-Liston
   ,, Kay
   ,, Marsden.
   : Simpson, J. B., of Dunsa Bank, Kirby, Ravensworth, York, esq. d.p., 27 March, 1865.
   : Stovin, G. 4 Nov, 1783 (12489).
Lister-Kaye : Kaye, J. 22 June, 1806 (160)
Litherland *see* Hignett
Lithgow, R. A. Douglas : Lithgow, R. A., physician, surgeon, &c., of Broomfield House, Hendon, Surrey. Times 8 Dec., 1874
Little : Acres S. W. 30 Aug., 1834 (1605)
   : Howman, Rev. G. E., Rector of Barnesley, Glos., residing at Newbold Pacey Hall, Warwicks. Times, d.p., 8 Jan., 1874

Little   Howman, G. A. K.   14 June, 1879 (4028)
  see Lyttel
  „ Parker.
     Woodcock, J   6 March, 1834 (405)
Littlefield see Fox
Little-Gilmour, of Liberton : Gilmour, Walter Jas.   Lyon Register Vol II., 9 Jan., 1811
Littlegroom see Franklin-Littlegroom-Nicholas
Littlehales see Baker
Littler · Ducker, M.   29 Dec., 1883 (1)
  see Hill-Littler
     Hotchkiss, T   7th Geo III., 1767
Littleton   Walhouse, E. J.   18 July, 1812 (1365)
Littlewood see Clarke.
Livesey   Bell, R   13 April, 1803 (499).
Livingstone-Macdonald, of Flodigarry House : Livingston, Randal Jno Macdonald   Lyon Register Vol. XIII., 9 March, 1894.
Livingstone see Fenton-Livingstone.
        Thompson, J G   12 May, 1863 (2525)
Llewellin see Purcell-Llewellin
        „ Turberville-Llewellin
Llewelyn see Dillwyn-Venables-Llewelyn
Lloyd see Alderson.
   „ Carr-Lloyd
   „ Davies-Lloyd.
   ., Duppa.
   : Ellis, J.   17 Dec., 1811 (2412)
   see Evans-Lloyd
   · Hinde, J. Y W.   Whll., 12 Dec., 1868 (D G 1421)
   see Hinde-Lloyd.
     Jones-Parry, T E J   19 April. 1871 (2122).
   see Jones-Lloyd
     Leach, F. E   13 March, 1849 (932).
     Lewes, D. E.   24th Geo III , 1783
   see Lewis-Lloyd
   ., Lewys-Lloyd
     Lewis, T   33rd Geo II., 1760
   . Lloyd-Harries, E P., late Dep.-Commiss of Nowgong, Assam, at present a Major on H.M Half-pay List   Times, 14 July, 1871
   see Philipps
   : Price, L. L., of Glanwilly, Llanllawddog, Carmarthen, esq   Times, d p , 14 Oct., 1871
   see Topp
   „ Treherne

Lloyd *see* Whitelocke-Lloyd
„ Yarburgh
Lloyd-Anstruther : Anstruther, J. H. 17 April, 1837 (1002)
Lloyd-Dickin : Dickin, J., Major in H.M. Glos. Reg Foot, Times, d p., 13 Feb., 1888.
Lloyd-Elsegood : Lloyd, J, of 6, Oriental Place, Brighton, Sussex, gent Times, 26 July, 1865.
Lloyd-Flood *see* Hanford-Flood.
        Lloyd, W, of Farmley, co. Kilkenny Dublin, 31 Jan, 1839
Lloyd-Greame Lloyd, Y G Whll, 12 July, 1867 (D.G 925)
Lloyd Harries : Lloyd, T, of Clifton, Bristol, gent Times, d.p., 17 Aug., 1875.
Lloyd-Jones : Jones, W., of Budleigh Salterton, Devons, land agent. Times, d.p, 24 March, 1885
Lloyd-Lindsay Lindsay, R. J. 17 Nov, 1858 (4907).
Lloyd-Mostyn Lloyd, E. M. 7 May, 1831 (924)
Lloyd-Owen : Owen. D C L., of 51, Newhall St. and Clermont, Edgbaston, Birmingham, surg Times, d p, 28 July, 1888
Lloyd-Powell Lloyd, E 16 July, 1838 (1613)
Lloyd-Shirreff Lloyd. M 1 July, 1863 (3399)
Lloyd-Wheate : Lloyd, F S 10 July, 1807 (974).
Lloyd-Vaughan *see* Hutchinson-Lloyd-Vaughan.
Lloyd-Verney Verney, G. H. 11 Feb., 1888 (1499)
Loader *see* Webb
Lock . Luck, J. L., of Adelaide Road, Surbiton. Surrey, Lieut. Royal Welsh Fusiliers, now stationed at Pembroke Dock. Pembroke d.p., 20 July, 1883
  see Rideal-Lock.
  „ Roe-Lock
Lockall *see* Egerton.
Locke, C L Calliphronas Calliphronas, C L, M A, of Clifton. Glos Times, 10 Jan., 1881
  see Luck.
  . Luck, F, of Hartlip, Kent, and West Brighton, Sussex, esq, J.P., Lieut R E Kent Yeo. Cav. Times. d.p, 19 Nov., 1875
Lock-Beveridge : Beveridge, J E. of Darland House, Luton, Chatham, Kent, esq Times. d.p. 23 Jan., 1869
Lock-Roe Roe, R., of The Manor House. Lynmouth, Devon, esq Times, 4 July, 1871
Locke-Anstruther : Locke, J W., of the Junr Nav and Mil Club, Piccadilly, and of Virginia, U.S., gent, late Capt. Times, 15 Sept, 1882
Locker *see* Lampson.
Lockhart-Ross Ross, A H 17 July, 1863 (3669).
Lockhart *see* Wastie.

Lockhart-McKonchie : Lockhart, A 23 Aug., 1794 (853).
Lockhart-Scott, of Abbotsford : Lockhart, Walter Scott. Lyon,
    Vol. IV , 28 July, 1848.
Lockwood see Wood.
    . Wood, A. R. M., of Audley Square, Middlesex, and
        Bishop's Hall, Essex, Lieut. and Capt. Cold-
        stream Foot Gds Times, d p , 3 June, 1876
    Wood, W. R. P , of Stonedon Lodge, nr Brentwood,
        Dep.-Lieut. for Essex, and late Capt. 4th Light
        Infantry. Times, d p., 6 Jan., 1887.
Lockwood-Maydwell : Lockwood, W. 7 Oct., 1797 (955).
Loder . Stephens, C. L 20 May, 1844 (1764)
    Stephens, C. L. W., 20 May, 1844 (D G 336)
    . Stephens, C. 23 Oct., 1807 (1409)
Loder-Symonds : Symonds 8 Feb., 1882 (874).
Lodge see Wilcocks.
Lodge-Ellerton : Lodge. J. 15 June, 1838 (1362).
Lofft-Moseley : Lofft, H. C. 8 April, 1864 (2054).
Loft : Gotobed, Mary Ann, of Finchley Park, Middlesex, spinster
        (adopted name Loft in 1878) Times, d p., 24
        June, 1892.
    see Wallis.
Loftie-Eaton : Loftie, J. S. 24 Nov., 1807 (1600).
Logan : Dobinson, L., of Lockington Rectory, Beverley, York-
        shire; F. Dobinson, of Lincoln's Inn, esq., late
        of East Grinstead, Sussex, and now residing at
        Ardverikie, Kingussie. N B.; and J. Dobinson
        and E Dobinson, both lately of Manilla Crescent,
        Weston-super-Mare, Somersetshire, spinsters, now
        residing at Malvern—all four parties were
        formerly at Egham Lodge, Egham, Surrey.
        Times, d.p , 11 June, 1866.
    . O'Neill, J., of St. Ann's Chambers, Ludgate Hill,
        London, commer. clerk. Times, d.p., 31 Oct.,
        1892
Logan-Home : Logan, G., of Broomhouse 31 Dec., 1840 (25)
Logie-Pirie · Pirie, F. L., of Tottingworth Park, Heathfield,
    Sussex. Times, d p., 21 Nov., 1895.
Loggin see Cole.
Logue-Pascoe : Logue, W. R., of Woodcroft Tidenham, Glos.,
    gardener Times, d.p., 14 April, 1882.
Lomax see Trappes-Lomax.
    ,,   Holt-Lomax.
    : Lomax-Smith, M., M.R.C.S., about to reside at 25,
        Newport Road, Cardiff Times, 4 Nov., 1896
    see Trappes-Lomax

Lomax-Smith : Smith, M., of Cheltenham, Glos, and of S.
    Belgravia, Middlesex, physician. Times. d p, 11 Dec.
    1888.
Lombe : Beevor, E. 10 Aug, 1847 (3073 see 2954)
    : Beevor, E. 57th Geo III., 1817.
    · Evans. H. 14 Nov., 1862 (5455).
    : Evans, E. 27 Oct., 1860 (4024).
    . Hase, J. 2nd Geo III., 1762
Londonderry *see* Stewart.
Long : Chandless, C. 29 Dec. 1843 (4578).
    : Harrison-Osborne
    see Hume-Long
    „ Jones-Long.
    „ Lacy.
    : Longbottom, A. R., of 1, Raine's Mansions, St. George's-
        in-the-East, London. Times, d p., 13 Apl., 1896.
    : Kellett. R 30 June, 1797 (612).
    see Mainstone
    ., North.
    · North, D 2 May, 1789 (334).
    see Pole-Tylney-Long-Wellesley.
    „ Sugden.
Long-Tylney · Long, Sir J 9 June, 1775 (11568)
Longbottom *see* Long.
Longden *see* Sherwin.
    „ Sherwin and Gregory.
Longmore *see* Skinner.
Longworth : Baller, T. J. 11 Jan., 1889 (389).
    : Baller, R C., F., H R., all of Cheltenham, Glos.
        Times, 7 Feb., 1899.
Lonsdale *see* Heywood-Lonsdale.
    Lowenthal. N. N. L, of Lonsdale House, Brighton;
        A L. Lowenthal, H L. Lowenthal, and D. L.
        Lowenthal. Times, 3 June, 1863
Lopes · Franco, Sir R 7 May, 1831 (924)
    see Massey-Lopes.
Lopez *see* Baldomero Hyacinth de Bertodano
    : Lara, J. 12 July, 1794 (696)
    see Dandoy.
Loraine-Grews : Loraine. R A. 13 Aug. 1849 (2532)
Loraine *see* Smith.
Lord *see* Crosby.
Losh *see* Arlosh
    : Brown, J., of Gas Coy.'s Buildings, Newcastle-on-Tyne,
        solicitor. Times, d p, 14 Nov., 1889
Lotery : Loteryman. J., of Whitechapel Road, London. Times,
    24 June, 1899

Loteryman *see* Lotery
Lott *see* Eaton.
    „ Rogers-Harrison.
Loveden : Pryse, P. 18 July, 1849 (2327)
    see Pryse.
Lowenthal *see* Lovell.
Lowry *see* Corry.
Lovedon : Townsend, E 10 Oct , 1772 (11290)
Lovegrove *see* Saunt
Loveland · Oldershaw. J. P 28 March, 1861 (1423).
        . Oldershaw, J. P. and Harriet H., his wife W., 28 March, 1861 (D G 414).
Lovell Badcock, L B. 10 April, 1840 (946).
    . Feely, W. L , clerk in Savings bank, G.P O., London Times, d p., 7 Aug., 1886.
    see Palmer-Lovell.
    „ Pugh-Lovell.
    · Teek, J. L. 28 July, 1803 (938).
    . Lowenthal, A E., of Hamburg, Germany Times, 15 April, 1898
Lovell-Marshall . Marshall. Mary K., of The Priory, Bridgwater, and of Windsor, Berks, spinster Times, d p , 8 Sept and 15 Sept., 1893.
Lovibond-Collins : Lovibond, A 25 Oct., 1783 (12486)
        . Lovibond, J. 24 Sept., 1785 (437)
Lovibond *see* Impey-Lovibond
Lowdham *see* Allsopp-Lowdham
Lowe : Drury, W. 10 July, 1790 (421)
    see Hill.
    „ Drury-Lowe
    ., Hill Lowe.
    Holden, W. D 27 Jan , 1849 (282).
    see Mosley
    ., Mosley-Lowe
    „ Strode.
    · Taylor, T P , of Beech Holme, Bocking, Essex, M.R C.S. (Eng.) and L.S A Times, d p , 16 June, 1893.
Lowenstein, George S M : Lowenstein, S. M Times, d.p , 2 June, 1874.
Lowenthal *see* Lonsdale.
Lowis *see* Merrikin.
Lowndes *see* Chaddock Lowndes
        . Clayton, G. A 5 Vict c 4 (Index to pub and priv. Statutes, p 503)
    see Garth.
    · Gorst, E. C 18 July, 1853 (2004).
    : Gorst, T M. 18 Jan., 1841 (164)

Lowndes see Selby-Lowndes
Lowndes-Salmon : Salmon, Wm. Arth Hughes, of Woodbridge, Suffolk   Times, 13 Nov., 1899
Lowndes-Stone-Norton : Norton, R. T. L. and C. C.   6 March, 1868 (2803).
      : Norton, R T L.   Whll., 6 May, 1868 (D G 547)
Lowsley see Hoole-Lowsley-Williams
Lowten : Robinson, T. L   6 Aug., 1830 (1714)
   : Wainwright, T.   6 June, 1814 (1323).
Lowther-Small : Lowther, J. S., of Guisbrough, North Riding, York, gent   Times, 22 Aug., 1867
Lowthorpe-Green : Green, J W., of Owmby Rectory, nr Market Rasen, Lincoln, and of the Middle Temple, London, student-at-law   d.p., 4 Dec., 1865.
Loyd-Lindsay : Lindsay, R J., on his marriage with Harriet S. Loyd.   W., 17 Nov., 1858 (D.G. 1985).
Luard-Selby : Luard, L M and R   Times, 13 July, 1867
    : Luard, Marianne, of the Mote Estate Ightham, Kent   Times, 13 July, 1867
    : Luard, R., of the Mote Estate, Igtham, Kent Capt and Brevet-Major on the retired list of the Royal Regiment of Artillery   Times, 13 July 1867
Luard see Wright
Lubé see Rockliff-Lubé
Lucadou see West
Lucas see Braithwaite
 ,, Calcraft.
 : Chick J R G, of Buckland, Portsea, Hants, gent   Times, d p., 25 March, 1880
 see Corban-Lucas
 ,, Edridge.
 : Hanson, J   23 Jan., 1798 (64)
 see Lancaster-Lucas
 ,, Major-Lucas
 : Reynolds, W St J., 19 June, 1784 (D G 4465)
 : Woodwright, T L., Lieut. 36th Infantry, at Barracks, Cork   Times, d p., 4 Aug., 1880
Lucas-Clements : Lucas, T E., of Rakenny, co Cavan   Dublin, 2 July, 1823
Lucas-Lane : Lane, H.   4 March, 1856 (958).
Lucas-Rennie : Rennie, G   7 May, 1832 (1113).
Lucas-Shadwell : Shadwell, W   4 June, 1811 (1045)
    : Stent, W D W., 7 Dec., 1844 (D G 931)
Luck see Lock
 ,, Locke.

Luck Locke, C A., late Lieut. R.M Light Infantry, now in Punjaub, India Times, d.p., 22 May, 1890.
    Locke, W. H., formerly of Kent, England, but now of Bombay Military Police, at Jalgaon, Bombay, India Times, d.p 29 May, 1891.
Luckman-Bennett Bennett, Alice H., of 23, Brunswick Road, Brighton, spinster. Times, d p., 15 Dec., 1896.
Lucock-Bragg Lucock T. 23 May, 1805 (683)
Lucy : Hammond, J. 17 Feb , 1787 (77)
Ludby, Max : Pyne, W B., of Ye Hutte, Cookham Deane Times, d.p , 17 Aug., 1894.
Ludford *see* Newdigate
    ,, Newdigate-Ludford-Chetwode.
Ludford-Astley : Astley, J N. F., of The Manor House, Ansley, Warwicks. esq Times. d p., 30 Dec., 1878. and 2 Jan , 1879
    · Astley, Rev. B. B. G , of Cadeby Rectory, Leicester Times, d.p , 4 Jan and 7 Jan., 1879.
Ludlow *see* Howitt-Ludlow.
    : Liot, E 27 Aug., 1889 (5049).
    · Smith, L. C. Times, d.p., 30 Dec., 1890
Ludlow-Bruges : Ludlow, W. H 30 March, 1835 (600)
Ludlow-Hewitt : Ludlow, T A W. 14 Sept., 1857 (D G. 890)
Lugg-Harvey : Lugg, J., costumier, late of Wigmore Street, Cavendish Square, now of Pentonville Road. Pentonville Times, 17 June, 1872
Lukin *see* Windham.
Lumb *see* Kendall-Lumb.
    ,, Kershaw-Lumb
Lumbazo *see* de Mattos.
Lumley · Levy, J. 1 Dec., 1823 (2071)
    see Savile-Lumley
    ,, Saville
Lumley-Savile Lumley, J 28 Sept. 1807 (1317)
    : Savile. J S. (Baron Savile, of Rufford, Notts) 11 Feb , 1898 (1116)
Lunn *see* Rockliffe
Lushington-Tulloch : Armstrong, W. C. 12 Sept., 1884 (4133)
Lushington *see* Tilson-Marsh-Lushington-Tilson
    ,, Wildman-Lushington.
Lush-Wilson : Lush, H W. and R F 4 Aug., 1879 (5876)
Luther-Watson : Watson, L. A., widow, and R L., spinster, both of 36, Harley Street, W. Times, d.p., 12 July, 1875
Lutley *see* Barneby-Lutley.
Luttman-Johnson Michell, H W. R. 16 Nov., 1831 (2457).
Lutto *see* Lewis.

Luttrell *see* Olmius.
Lutwyche : Lane, W. 3 Aug., 1776 (11688).
Luxmoore *see* Brooke
        Lees, A. D., S. D. D., L L D   12 Oct., 1899 (6531).
        : Nainby, W. C.   29 Jan., 1885 (676).
        Nainby, W. C.   25 July, 1885 (3474).
        : Luxmoore-Brooke, C. F. C.   9 May, 1894 (3049).
Lyall-Wilson : Wilson, Amelia Pearce, of St Ermins Mansions, Westminster. Times, 6 Nov., 1899.
Lybbe *see* Powys-Lybbe.
Lyddingsen : Coffin, Mrs Sophia Lydia, of Sewardstone, Essex. Times, 25 May, 1899.
Lyde : Ames, L.   6 Feb., 1806 (192).
    see Ames-Lyde.
    : Poole, L.   21 July, 1792 (562).
Lygon *see* Pindar.
Lymburner . Delisser, A.   27 Feb., 1836 (403).
Lynch-Killikelly : Killikelly, P. de.   23 Dec., 1780 (12146).
Lynch-Power Lynch, E. D.G., 1 June, 1814.
Lynch-Staunton Lynch, G. S.   2 Dec., 1859 (3607 and 4591).
    . Lynch, G. S.   4 Oct., 1859.
Lyne : Harford, H.   20 Dec., 1826 (236).
    : Harford, R.   9 March, 1820 (493).
Lyne-Stephens : Claremont, H. A., of Roehampton, Surrey. Times, d.p., 7 Nov., 1894.
    : Lyne, C.   20 Dec., 1826 (3002).
Lynes *see* Temple Lynes
Lynn : Johnson, G. F.   26 March, 1796 (329).
Lyon *see* Blakeney-Lyon-Stewart
    Daniel Home : Home, Daniel Dunglas.   Times, d.p., 3 Dec., 1866.
Lyon-Winder : Lyon, E. W.   17 June, 1859 (2472)
    : Lyon, J. W.   28 June, 1820 (1339).
Lyons · Connell, C.   D.G., 29 March, 1814.
Lysaght-Knight : Knight, F. B., of 134, Barras-Bridge, Newcastle-on-Tyne, esq.   Times, d.p., 26 June, 1891.
Lyster : West, J.   D.G., 2 Dec., 1805.
Lyte : Light, A., Major-Gen. R.A., of U. Service Club, Pall Mall. Times, d.p., 19 April, 1895 ,
Lyttel . Little W. C., 2, Sidney Street, Sidney Square, London, E. Times, 5 Dec., 1867.
    : Little, E. Z., Cit of London, residing at Caermarthen. Times, 5 Dec., 1867
Lyttleton-Annesley : Annesley, A. L.   29 Sept., 1884 (5780).
Lytton *see* Bulwer-Lytton

M

Maas : Mauss, T., of 4, Lancaster Road, Westbourne Park, W Times, 12 Dec., 1867.
Mabbett, W. Scott : Mabbett, W., of Essex House, Dursley, Glos., gent. Times, d.p., 23 Nov., 1886.
Macalester *see* Somerville-Macalerton.
McAllister Hewlings : McAllister, W. F., of Prince's Street, Leicester, med stud. Times, d.p, 14 Sept., 1889.
Macallum-Buchanan : Macallum, W. B., of Edinburgh, esq. Times, 9 Jan., 1864.
MacAndrew, Sir J. *see* MacGregor.
Macarthur-Onslow : Onslow, E 12 March, 1892 (1701).
Macartney, Ellison- *see* Porter.
   see Ellison-Macartney.
   „ Filgate.
   : Hume, G. D.G., 8 Oct., 1814.
Macaulay *see* Pickles-Macaulay.
Macaulay-Anderson : Macaulay, F. A. 4 Jan., 1886 (D.G. 13).
Macbean *see* Bell.
Macbeth-Raeburn : Macbeth, H. R., of 43, Bloomsbury Square, artist. Times, d.p., 2 June, 1883.
McBurnie : Skinner, Fanny M., of Dresden, Saxony, spinster. d.p., 25 Feb., 1879.
McCausland *see* Bacon.
McCulloch *see* Cliff McCulloch.
MacCulloch *see* Mansell-MacCulloch.
McCutchon see M'Gill.
McCombie *see* Duguid.
Macdonald *see* Bosville.
    „ Bosville-Macdonald.
    „ Foote-Macdonald.
    „ Downing-Macdonald.
    „ Livingston-MacDonald.
    „ Macdonald-Stewart
    „ Robertson Macdonald.
    „ Wood Macdonald
Macdonald-Henderson : Henderson, J. Times,s 6 Sept., 1865.
Macdonald-Macdonald, of St. Martins : Farquharson, William. Lyon, Vol. V, 30 June, 1849.
Macdonald-Stewart : MacDonald, Ranald. Lyon Vol II., 15 April, 1813.
M'Donnell : Kerr, H S. (Earl of Antrim). 27 June, 1836 (1226)
MacDonnell *see* Armstrong-MacDonnell.
McEvoy *see* Netterville
M'Ewan *see* Howie-M'Ewan.

Mace-Gigger : Mace, J. 11 Jan., 1803 (177)
McCreagh *see* Thornhill
McCumming *see* Beaumont.
McDonnell : Kerr, M. W., 30 Oct., 1855 (D G. 1503).
: Kerr, M. (Earl of Antrim). 30 Oct., 1855 (3994).
: Phelps, E. 27 June, 1817 (1621).
Macfarlane-Grieve, of Edenhall, Impington, etc. : Comyn-Macfarlane, William Alexr. Lyon Vol. XIV., 12 June, 1896.
Macfie *see* Shaw.
Macgaie *see* Tait.
MacGeough Bond Shelton : MacGeough Bond, R., of the Argory Moy, Armagh, esq., late Capt. 12th Royal Lancers. Times, 7 May, 1873.
McGarel Hogg : Hogg, Sir J. M. 8 Feb., 1877 (1967).
M'Gill : M'Cutchon, P. 20 March, 1821 (728).
MacGregor *see* Laird-MacGregor.
: MacAndrew, Sir J. 24 July, 1863 (3837).
Macgregor : Macgregor-Skinner, Capt. Francis Henry. Lyon Vol. IX., 8 March, 1872.
: Macgregor-Skinner, Capt. Francis Nugent, R.A., Lyon Vol. XI., 13 July, 1883.
: Macgregor-Skinner, Philip Leighton, Major R.A. Lyon Vol XI, 15 April, 1887.
: Macgregor-Skinner, Capt Cortland George. Lyon Vol. IX., 8 March, 1872.
: Macgregor-Skinner, Cortlandt Alexr., Major R.E. Lyon Vol. X., 3 Oct., 1881.
Macgregor-Davies : Davies, F., of Brampford Speke, Devon. Times, 9 Nov., 1900.
McHaffie Gordon : McHaffie, G. W. G., esq. Times, d.p., 24 May, 1886.
McHaffie-Gordon, of Corsmalzie : McHaffie, Geo. Wm Gordon. Lyon Vol. XI., 20 July, 1886.
McHarg : Hart, W., Quarter-Master of H M. 44th Reg., at present stationed at Belgaum, East Indies Times, d.p., 18 March, 1865.
Macie *see* Smithson
M'Innes *see* Nicholson.
MacIver *see* Randall-MacIver. Times, 11 Aug., 1900.
McIver-Campbell, of Asknish : Paterson, James Duff. Lyon Vol. X., 11 Oct., 1881.
of Asknish · Campbell, Paterson Duncan. Lyon Vol. V., 7 June, 1853
: Vivian, Lt.-Col. Aylmer. Lyon Vol. XI., 25 Jan., 1884.
McKerrell-Brown : Brown, Jas. A. Lyon Vol. XI., 10 Nov., 1887

M'Knight see Webb
McKonchie see Lockhart-McKonchie.
Mackay see Aberigh-Mackay.
  : Prevost, J 2 Sept., 1775 (11592 see 11593).
Mackenzie-Ashton : Mackenzie, A 2 July, 1879 (4338).
Mackenzie see Burton-Mackenzie.
  „ Douglas
  „ Godfrey
  „ Montague-Stuart-Wortley-Mackenzie.
  „ Nutt-Mackenzie.
  „ Shaw-Mackenzie.
Mackenzie-Fraser : Mackenzie, A 22 July, 1803 (1003)
Mackenzie-Gibson Gibson, Rev. John Lyon Vol. XIII., 4 Dec., 1894.
Mackenzie-Grieve : Grieve, Jno. Andrew, Major R.A. Lyon Vol. XII., 9 March, 1891.
  Grieve, Frederick John, Commr. R N. Lyon Vol XII , 1 March, 1891
Mackenzie-Richards : Richards, P. F., of 21, Gt. George Street, London, civil engineer Times, d.p., 24 June, 1893.
Mackenzie-Steuart : Johnson, Rev. E. C', M.A., Oxon, one of Assistant Clergy of St. Paul's, Knightsbridge. Times, d.p., 23 Nov., 1896
Mackerdy see Scott-Mackerdy.
Mackereth see Freeman
McKerrell-Brown · Brown, Lt.-Col. Wm , R.A Lyon Vol. XIV., 15 July, 1896.
Mackinlay : Harrison, J. J., of Coatham, Redcar, York, engineer's student Times, d p , 23 Jan , 1891.
  : Harrison, W H , of Redcar, York, temp residing 29, Lauriston Gardens, Edinburgh, med. student. Times, d.p , 23 Jan., 1891
Macklin see Wilson.
Mackinnon see Bundock Mackinnon
Mackinnon-Campbell : Mackinnon, J. 27 March, 1806 (422).
Mackintosh see Fraser-Mackintosh.
  „ Keir-Mackintosh.
    McLean, B 21 Feb., 1797 (170).
  . Smith, Regina C. M., of 44, Upper Bedford Place, Russell Square, London. Times, d p , 15 Oct., 1892.
Mackintosh Mackintosh Mackintosh, Shaw A., of 36, James Street, Buckingham Gate, Middlesex. Times, d p., 21 March, 1893
Macknish-Porter Porter, W M 9 Oct., 1816 (2225).
  see Macnish-Porter.
Mackrell see Smith
Mackreth see Williams-Mackreth.

Mackworth-Dolben : Mackworth, W. H. I. 20 July, 1835 (1400).
M'Laren *see* Campbell-M'Laren.
McLaughlin *see* Berens.
McLaughlin *see* Berens.
Maclaverty *see* East.
Maclean : Clephane, W. D 6 Nov , 1790 (659).
McLean *see* Howard-McLean.
    ,, Mackintosh.
McLean *see* Howard-McLean.
McLean Buckley : Buckley, G. A , Lieut., of Woodstock Road, Oxford. Times, d.p., 27 Jan., 1888.
MacLeod *see* Annesley.
    ,, Hume.
MacLeroth *see* Mountjoy.
M'Clintock-Bunbury : M'Clintock, W. 21 July, 1846 (2919).
M'Loughlin *see* Barnewall.
McMahon *see* Cree.
MacMahon-Creagh MacMahon, H. M. M. 1 Oct., 1885 (D.G. 957)
Macmartin-Cameron : Cameron, of Argyllshire, N B., esq. Times, d.p., 13 May, 1892.
McMaster-Allen *see* Allen.
McMillan, A Douglas : McMillan, A., of 100, Sutherland Gardens, Maida Vale, Congrel. minister Times, 28 Sept., 1881.
MacNaghten *see* Workman.
MacNair : McNair, J., Capt. H.M. Bengal Staff Corps. Times, 16 Jan., 1874.
McNair *see* Macnair.
Macnamara *see* Nugent-Macnamara.
MacNeal : MacPherson, C. 1 Sept , 1798 (907).
Macneill *see* Collie-Macneill.
Macnish-Porter Macnish, W. 21 Aug., 1804 (1021).
    see Macknish-Porter.
M'Nicol *see* Nairne
McCombie *see* Duguid-McCombie.
Maconochie-Wellwood, of Garvock and Meadowbank : Maconochie, Alex Lyon Vol V., 2 Oct., 1854.
M'Ostrich *see* Carmichael
Macpherson : Crieves, Rev. W. A. G., of Lynsted, Kent Times, d p. 20 May, 1876
MacPherson *see* MacNeal.
Macpherson-Grant, of Inverishie : Macpherson, George Lyon, Vol. II., 5 June, 1806.
McPherson-Grant : McPherson, Margaret G. 14 June, 1854 (1868).
MacRae-Gilstrap : MacRae, J. 9 Jan., 1897 (257).

McTaggart-Stewart, of Southwick, Blair, Derry and Ardwell :
   Stewart, Sir Mark John. Lyon Vol. XIV., 5 Nov., 1895.
McTurk *see* Alexander.
McVane : Augier, L..N. J. J. T., of the Hon. Soc. of the Inner
   Temple. Times, 25 Sept., 1890.
Madan-Mayers : Mayers, F. H., now at Harrogate, Yorks, esq.
   Times, 16 June, 1882.
      : Mayers, F. H., now of 14, Cornfield Road,
        Eastbourne, esq. Times, d.p., 14 Feb.,
        1883.
Madden-D'Esterre : Madden, E. C., of 46, Albion Road, Stoke
   Newington, N. Times, d.p., 18 Oct., 1887.
Madden-Medlycott : Madden, C. W. C., of West Horrington,
   Wells, Somerset. Times, 30 Nov., 1865.
Maddison *see* Brunning Maddison.
   „ Combe.
      : Rawling, G. 1 Feb., 1812 (198).
Maddock *see* Ashby.
   „ Finchett-Maddock.
Maden : Kay, J. H., of Rockliffe House, Bacup, Lancs., cotton
   spinner. Times, d.p., 13 June, 1885.
Madoc : Jones, F. V. M., of Oswestry. Times, 12 Dec., 1900.
Madryll-Cheere : Madryll, C. 12 Feb., 1808 (519).
Magennis *see* Ferguson.
      : Vaughan, G. Dublin, 13 Nov., 1840.
Magens *see* D'orrien-Magens.
McGeough-Bond : McGeough, W. D.G., 5 Nov., 1824.
Magill-Aston : Magill, Amy, Elmdene, Sandown, I.W., spinster.
   Times, d.p., 22 Aug., 1892.
Magra *see* Mario-Matra.
Magrath *see* FitzGerald.
Mahon *see* Pakenham-Mahon.
Mahon-Hagan : Mahon, C. P. 23 Aug., 1888 (D.G 865).
Maillard *see* Stubber.
Maine *see* Coghill.
Mainstone : Long, S. W., late of 2, Park Villas, Park Lane, nr.
   Bath, now lodging at 2, Laura Place, Bath, gent. Times,
   d.p. 20 Dec., 1866.
Mainwaring *see* Cavenagh-Mainwaring.
   „ Lee-Mainwaring.
   „ Massey-Mainwaring.
   „ Milman-Mainwaring.
      : Wetenhall, T. 9 May, 1797 (455).
Mainwaring-Elleker-Onslow : Onslow, G. J. H. 19 Aug., 1861
   (3573).
      : Onslow, E. M. (com. called Hon.)
        31 Jan., 1843 (335).

Maire : Lawson, H. 19 May, 1772 (11249).
Maitland see Fuller-Maitland.
 „ Gammie-Maitland.
 „ Heriot-Maitland-Dougall.
 „ Makgill-Crichton-Maitland.
 „ Ramsay-Gibson-Maitland.
Maitland Dyer : Dyer, H. L. M., of Camden House, Folkestone, Kent, spinster. Times, d.p., 1 March, 1886.
Maitland-Makgill-Crichton see Makgill-Crichton-Maitland.
Major : Henniker, J. 16 Aug., 1792 (630).
 see Henniker-Major.
 : Mauger, J. M., of St. Helier, Jersey, gent· Times, d.p., 30 Jan., 1866.
Major-Lucas : Major, E. M. 16 Jan., 1860 (224).
Majoribanks see Robertson.
Makdougall-Brisbane : Brisbane, Sir T. 21 Aug., 1826 (2064).
Makepeace see Scott-Makdougall.
 „ Williams.
Makgill-Crichton-Maitland : Maitland-Makgill-Crichton, D., Major and Lieut.-Col. and Col. (Gren. Gds.). Times, 14 June, 1884.
Makgill-Maitland see Herriot.
Makin see Thompson.
Malet : Mallet, R. P., M.A., Oxon, W. E. Mallet and C. E. Mallet de Carteret. Times, d.p., 4 Feb., 1864.
Malins see Cary Malins.
Malkin, S. W. · Copeland, S. M. Times, d.p., 31 July, 1896.
Mallaby see Calthorpe-Mallaby.
 : Clarke, Deeley, of St. Aubyns, Jersey. Times, d.p., 5 March, 1894.
Mallard : Goff, P. 12 April, 1794 (313).
Mallet see Malet.
 „ Mallet de Carteret.
Mallet de Carteret : Mallet, E. C. 5 April, 1859 (1484).
Mallett see Veale.
Mallory : Leigh, G. 18 Dec., 1832 (2835).
Malpas see Eustace.
 : Folie, J. Betham, 1 Feb., 1783.
Mammatt see Wynter.
Manby see Colegrave.
Manby-Colegrave : Colegrave, J. W. J. M. L., of Cann Hall, Essex, and of Little Ellingham, Ellingham, Norfolk, and 66, Eccles Street, Dublin. Times, d.p., 16 Jan., 1871.
Manbey : Tidy, W. 28 March, 1821 (728).
Mandeville see Power.
Mankiewicz see Danby.
Manley see Pillin.

Mann : Bolton, G. 6 May, 1852 (1291).
: Cornwallis, C J. 16 Sept., 1823 (1630).
: Cornwallis, F. S. W. 10 June, 1884 (2683).
: Cornwallis, J 9 April, 1814 (858).
: Cornwallis, J. J.
Manners *see* Talmash.
„ Tollemache.
Mannheimer *see* Manning.
Manning : Mannheimer, W. G., of Berlin, Germany, bank manager. Times, d.p., 12 March, 1889.
J. : Watts, J. M., of Kislingbury, Northamptons., esq. Times, d p, 8 May, 1877.
Manningham-Buller : Buller, E 4 Jan., 1866 (210).
Mannock *see* Commyns-Mannock
: Power, P. 23 Sept., 1830 (2021).
Mansel : Coward, R S., formerly of Otterburn, afterwards of Rothbury, both in Northumberland, now of Rugby, Warwick, gent. Times, d p, 7 July, 1862.
: Philipps, C. 18 May, 1866 (3015).
Mansel-Howe : Joseph, S. W. I., of Godstone, Surrey, M D. Times, d.p., 6 Oct., 1890.
Mansel-Pleydell : Mansel, J. C., of Whatcombe, Dorset, esq. Times, d.p., 4 July, 1871.
Mansell : Shewen, E. W. R 24 Feb., 1802 (199).
: Villiers, Hon. W. A. H. 4 June, 1802 (570).
Mansell-MacCulloch : MacCulloch, William, of The Touillets, Guernsey, and 6, Lower Bedford Place, Russell Square, London Times, 3 March, 1870.
Mansergh-St George : Mansergh, M. 13 Sept., 1774 (11494).
: Mansergh, R. St. G. 13 Sept, 1774 (11491).
Mansfield *see* Bridgman-Mansfield.
Manville : Moseley, B E., of 5, Grosvenor Street, Bond Street, Middlesex, surg. dentist, M R.C.S Times, d.p, 2 July, 1875.
Manwaring : Manwaring-Parker, R 21 Jan., 1809 (74).
March *see* Weeley.
March-Phillipps : March, T. 23 Aug., 1796 (803).
Marcham-Mears : Frost, Mary A., formerly of Marcham, now of Seymour House, Acton, Middlesex. 8 March, 1879.
Marchant *see* Wallace Marchant.
Marcus *see* Binden Marcus.
Margrave *see* Dawson-Margrave
Mario-Matra : Magra, J. 24 Feb., 1776 (11642).
Marjoribanks Egerton : Egerton, Rev. J., of Odd Rode Rectory, Cheshire, M.A. Times, 8 March, 1888.

Markeloff *see* Simonds
Marker : Smith, G T.   22 May, 1855 (1965)
Markham *see* Clifton
  ,,   Jervis.
  ,,   Salisbury.
Markland *see* Entwistle.
Marks *see* Seawell
Markwick *see* Eversfield.
Marlow : Vaughan, B.   12 June, 1784 (12550).
Marlowe : Crow, M. S.   26 March, 1776 (11651).
Marrett Edwardes or Edwardes : Edwards, S. J., of El Nido, St.
    Tropez (Var), Fr Republic. Times, d p., 22 Sept., 1896.
Marriott-Dodington : Marriott, T.   12 July, 1853 (1947).
Marriott, J. P. *see* Goulton-Constable
    see Siddons.
    ,,   Smith-Marriott.
    : Wakefield, G. P.   6 Dec., 1799 (1255).
    : Walker, H. M.   8 Feb , 1879 (737)
Marris *see* Gillyatt.
Marrow *see* Armfield-Marrow.
Marsden : Lister, A   27 Feb., 1827 (503)
    James : Marsden, Tobias Child Lovell, of Sheffield,
      Yorks, paper-maker. Times, 22 Feb., 1889.
    see Montagu-Marsden.
    ,,   Moses-Marsden.
Marsden Smedley : Marsden, J. T., of Riber Castle and Lea
    Mills, Derby. Times, 18 Sept., 1874.
Marsden-Smith : Smith, B., of 10, Well Walk, Hampstead, N.W.
    Times, 1 Jan , 1892
Marsh *see* Bradney Marsh.
    ,,   Chisenhale-Marsh.
    John Moses : Moses, Jacob, of 6, Bedford Square,
      Middlesex, gent. Times, d p , 8 Sept , 1868
    see Tilson-Marsh-Lushington-Tilson.
Marsh-Caldwell : Marsh, A.   18 May, 1860 (2494).
Marsh-Dunn : Dunn, R. M., of Carlton Lodge, Teignmouth.
    Times, d p , 20 April, 1876.
Marsh-Edwards : Edwards, Rev. H. M., of Tunbridge Wells,
    Kent   Times, 17 May, 1893.
Marshall *see* Burt-Marshall
    : Cole, J.   12 June, 1828 (1141).
    see Hunter-Marshall
    ,,   Hatfield.
    : Leeming, R.   24 Dec., 1802 (1358).
    : Leeming, R.   25 Feb., 1848 (767) (see 834, 26 Feb ,
      1847).

Marshall · Leeming, W. 26 Feb , 1847, 25 Feb , 1848 (834) (see
    767).
    : Leeson, R. J. 10 Feb., 1 March, 1852 (D.G. 241 and
        250)
    : Leeson, R. 20 Feb., 10 March, 1849 (D.G. 341)
    see Lovell-Marshall.
    ,, Orloff.
Marshall-Hacker : Marshall, E 31 May, 1827 (1195)
    : Marshall, N. 30 Nov., 1819 (2230)
Marshall-West : West, J. W. H., of West Kensington, and of 25,
    Alfred Place West, S. Kensington, Capt 4th Batt. Somerset
    Lt Infantry. Times, d.p , 22 Dec., 1893.
Marsham see Jones-Marsham
    ,, Savill-Onley.
Marsham-Townshend : Marsham, R. (com. called The Hon.) 27
    March, 1893 (2078).
Marston see Vann.
Martelli see Holloway.
Martin see Atkins
    ,, Bainbridge.
    : Bell, A. E, on his marriage to Mary L Martin 15
        Sept., 8 Oct., 1847 (D.G. 1074 and 1098).
    see Combridge.
    ,, Cornwallis
    ,, Critchley-Martin.
    ,, Fairfax.
    ,, Heathcote Martin
    : King, I. H. C. E. 19 April, 1862 (2227).
    : Phelps, E 11 Aug., 1787 (373).
    see Wood-Martin.
    ,, Wykeham-Martin.
Martin-Holloway, G : Martin, G. F., of Sunninghill, Berks, esq.
    Times, d p., 6 March, 1884.
Martin Pooley : Martin, W., of Lewisham, Kent, gent. Times,
    d p., 10 July, 1883.
Martin-Rebow : Rebow, I. M. 17th Geo III., 1777.
Martindale-Vale : Vale, H. E., of Coddington Court, Hereford,
    Major (retired). Times, d p , 23 May, 1895.
Martinez see Armstrong-Martinez
Martinez-D'anson : Martinez, R. J 15 Dec., 1894 (7529)
Martone-Graham, of Cultoquhey and Redgorton : Martone,
    James. Lyon, Vol VI., 15 July, 1861
Martyn-Linnington Martyn, R. L 27 Sept., 1889 (5245).
Martyr see Cobham.
Marwood · Metcalfe, W. 5th Geo III., 1765
    . Metcalfe, E. 49th Geo III., 1809.
Marwood-Elton . Elton, A 8 Jan., 1885 (358)

Marwood-Elton : Elton, G.   23 June, 1830 (1345)
Maryon-Wilson : Wilson, Sir S., of Charlton House, Kent, and Searles, Sussex, Bt   Times., d.p, 24 June, 1876.
Mashiter : Helme, R.   13 April, 1876 (2669).
   : Helme, T.   23 May, 1884 (2645).
Mason   Bear, T. A., of 6, Coburg Place, Kensington Gardens, esq.   Times, 24 May, 1888.
   see Blomefield.
   „ Browne-Mason.
   „ Goddard-Mason.
   „ Gwynn-Mason.
   „ Humfrey-Mason.
   : Humfrey Mason, R. H., of Necton, Norfolk, esq   Times, d.p, 12 July, 1880.
   see Lewis-Minet
   „ Pomeroy.
   „ Shiers Mason.
   „ Wormald.
Masser *see* Kendall.
Massereene *see* Skeffington.
Massey *see* Oliver-Massey.
   „ Errington.
   : Watkiss, W.   30 Jan., 1807 (176).
Massey-Lopes · Lopes, M   15 Oct, 1805 (1285).
Massey-Jackson : Massey, M.   11 March, 1802 (279)
Massey-Mainwaring : Massey, W. F. B. & I. A.   8 May, 1874 (2993).
Massey-Spencer : Waters, A., of 29, High Street, Coventry, wine and spirit merchant   Times, d.p, 17 Aug., 1888.
Massey-Stanley *see* Errington.
Massey Westropp, J. · Westropp, J., of Longlands, Lancs., Capt. R. Lancs Militia.   Times, d.p, 20 Sept., 1875
Massicks *see* Barlow-Massicks
Massingberd : Langton, E. C. L., of The Red House, Bournemouth, and of Gunley Hall, Lincoln, widow   Times, d p, 19 March, 1887.
   : Langton, E. C. L.   20 May, 1887 (6869).
   · Langton, P   2 Feb., 1803 (138).
Massingberd-Mundy : Mundy, C. J. H.   8 May, 1863 (2461)
Massy *see* Beresford-Massy.
   : Bolton, J. M.   D G., 14 Sep., 1842.
Massy-Beresford : Beresford-Massey, J M.   5 Feb, 19 Feb, 1872 (D G. 125)
Massy-Richardson . Massy, Augusta, L. R. (widow).   28 Jan., 11 Feb., 1865 (D.G. 153)
Master Whitaker : Master, M. C., of The Holme, Lancs., wife of the Rev A. Master Whitaker.   Times, 17 Sept., 1889.

Master Whitaker : Master, Rev. A., of The Holme, Lancs.
Times, 17 Sept , 1889.
: Master, A. 4 Dec., 1889 (7202).
Masterman : Barlow, H. 18 April, 1823 (627).
: Patton, J. 11 March, 1788 (117)
Masterman-Sykes . Masterman, M. 27 Sept., 1796 (1117) (see 1234).
Masters see Harcourt
" Smith-Masters.
Matcham see Eyre-Matcham.
Matchett see Gordon.
Mathew see Bertie-Mathew.
" Buckley-Mathew.
" Sclater-Mathew.
Mathews see Ashburner.
" Attwood-Mathews.
" Cooke
Mathews-Attwood . Mathews, B. St. John, of Pentrilas, Hereford d p, 22 Aug., 1881.
Matthews see Donaldson.
" Eaton-Matthews.
" Harris-Matthews.
" Killam
" Povoleri.
Matra see Mario-Matra
Maturin-Baird : Maturin, D. B. 11 March, 1875 (D G 189).
Maude see Moorson-Mitchinson-Maude.
: Rycroft, J. 9 April, 1851 (1012)
see Roxby.
Maudsley see Carr-Maudesley.
Mauger see Major.
Maule see Blossett-Maule.
Maulère see Hindermann-Maulère.
Mauleverer : Gowan, W. 13 May, 1834 (898).
Maunder see De Faubert Maunder.
Maunsell see Tibbits.
Maunsell Collins : Collins, W., M D , surg. to Scots Fusiliers Gds. Times, 5 July, 1873
Maurice see Bonnor-Maurice.
" Corbet.
" Joseph.
Mauss see Maas.
Maxwell see Brown.
: Charleton, R. 16 Feb., 1790 (99).
see Constable-Maxwell-Stuart.
" Goodwin.
of Glengaber : Hyslop Maxwell. Lyon Vol. VII., 24 June, 1867.

Maxwell *see* Hyslop Maxwell.
,, Perceval-Maxwell.
: Waring, D. M. 9 April, 1803.
see Wedderburn-Maxwell.
Maxwell-Brown : Maxwell, E. W., 14 Oct., 1786 (D.G 4828).
Maxwell-Graham : Graham, James Lyon Vol. IV., 8 April, 1837.
see Graham-Maxwell.
Maxwell-Lefroy : Lefroy, C. J, of Itchel, Southampton, esq., late Capt. 14th Hussars, and E. C., his wife. Times, d.p., 2 March, 1875.
: Lefroy, C. J M. 27 Feb., 1875 (D G. 179).
May *see* May-Bourne.
,, Bourne-May.
May-Bourne : May, J. W. S. 22 June, 1892 (3719).
Maydwell *see* Lockwood-Maydwell.
Maydwell : Smith, H. L. 8 April, 1841 (944).
Mayelston, James Mayel : Mayelston, J, of Elloughton, Yorks., gent. Times, 8 Jan., 1883.
Mayer · Solomon, H. M., late of Deal, Kent, now of Snow Hill, Holborn, china and glass merchant. Times, d.p., 8 Oct., 1881.
Mayer-Ashby : Mayer, G. J., of 47, Enmore Park, S. Norwood, pyrotechnist. Times, d p., 11 April, 1892.
Mayers *see* Madan-Mayers.
Mayes *see* Blomefield.
Mayhew : Courtney, H. 7 Jan., 1828 (145).
see Courtney-Mayhew.
,, Courteney.
Maynard-Page : Page, T. E., of Ambleside, Westmorland. Times, 26 Sept., 1900.
Mayo *see* Newman-Mayo.
Mayor *see* Brown.
Maze *see* Blackburne-Maze.
Meackham *see* Berkin-Meackham.
Mead : Phillips, J. M, of 2, King's Bench Walk, Temple, and of Beckenham, Kent, solicitor. Times, d p., 17 Dec., 1887.
Mead-Waldo : Mead, E. W. 8 June, 1830 (1127).
Meade *see* Freer-Meade.
Meade-King : Meade, R. 19 Nov., 1830 (2422).
Meade Oliver · Meade, O. B., of Middlezoy, Somerset, farmer. Times, d.p., 14 Feb, 1893.
Meadows *see* Braham.
(or Meade) *see* Freer-Meade.
see Theobald.
Mealy *see* O'Mealy.
Meara *see* Keane.
Meare : Stephens, M. 16 Nov., 1801 (1411)

Mears *see* Marcham-Mears.
Meason, of Lindertis : Laing, Gilbert. Lyon Vol. II , 14 Dec, 1804.
Meatyard *see* Meteyard.
Medland Soper, J M., of Belgrave Road, Torquay, Devon, butcher. Times, d p., 27 Jan., 1888
Medley : Hunt, H. C., of Thames Cottage, Datchet, Bucks, boat proprietor Times, 30 Aug , 1886
Medhurst *see* Wheler
Medlycott : Cockayne, Hon. B. 42 Geo. III., 1802.
    : Hill, A. B. 3rd Geo III., 1763
    see Madden-Medlycott
Medows · Norie, W. H 22 Aug., 1864 (4160).
    : Norie, Wm. H. W., 22 Aug , 1864 (D G 966)
    see Pierrepont.
Medwin *see* Gardner-Medwin.
Mehrhagen *see* Rhiner-Waring.
Meeke : Meyer, A. J 22 Oct., 1839 (2017).
    see Taylor.
Meggison *see* Pearson.
    ,, Rochester
Melbourne *see* Dick-Melbourne.
Melhuish *see* Smart-Melhuish
Melliar *see* Foster-Melliar.
Mellifont-Townsend : Townsend, R 14 Dec , 24 Dec., 1869 (D G 1530)
Melville *see* Balfour-Melville.
    ,, Higginson-Whyte-Melville.
    ,, Milbanke.
    ,, Pomfret Melville.
Menzies *see* Murray-Menzies.
Mercer *see* Drewe-Mercer
    ,, Cockburn-Messer.
    ,, Haldane-Duncan-Mercer-Henderson
    ,, Tod-Mercer.
Mercer-Henderson : Mercer, D 14 Jan., 1853 (201).
    : Haldane-Duncan-Mercer-Henderson, E. J 19 Aug , 1882 (3917)
Meredith · Goldsmid, Moses J., of 32, Elgin Road, Middlesex, gent. Times, d.p., 24 Jan., 1880.
    see Warter-Meredith.
Meredith-Harnett : Harnett, E , of 35, Piccadilly, London, Major-Gen. Times, d.p , 29 April, 1890
Meredith Jones Jones, R., of Rockland, Chester, bank manager Times, d p , 16 June, 1875
Meredyth : Gorges, R. 15 April, 1775 (11552).
Mernkin : Lowis, G. M 15 Sept , 1865 (4541).

Mervyn-D'Arcy-Irvine : Irvine, Hy W , 10, St. J , 27 April, 1861 (D.G 586).
Meryweather *see* Turner.
Messer *see* Cockburn-Mercer.
Messiter-Terry Messiter, G. T. M 30 June, 1894 (3939).
: Messiter, G. T. M., Vicar of Payhembury, Devon R.L. Times, 7 Aug., 1894
Metcalfe *see* Barton.
„ Carlton.
„ Collins.
„ Marwood.
„ More.
Methold *see* Eden.
Meteyard : Meatyard, Mary A. and Martha, of St. Leonards-on-Sea, spinsters. Times, 18 April, 1894.
Meyer *see* Meeke
„ Meyrick.
„ Thompson.
Meynell-Ingram . Meynell, H C. 25 Oct., 1841 (2626).
Meyrick : Charlton, T. 31 March, 1858 (1793).
see Fuller-Meyrick
· Levy, C A , of Cherry Orchard, Staines, gent. Times, d p., 13 and 16 June, 1894.
· Meyer, J., of Lindo House, South Road, Nottingham, merchant Times, d p., 13 March, 1893
see Tapps-Gervis-Meyrick
„ Williams-Meyrick.
Meyrick-Jones . Jones, Rev G M., of Clapton Court, Crewkerne, Somerset, also his wife and children Times, d p , 28 Sept , 1893
Meysey-Thompson : Thompson, H. S , of Kirby Hall, Yorks., esq. Times, 23 Feb , 1874
Meysey-Wigley Wigley, E 15 June, 1811 (1173).
Meysey-Wigley-Greswolde · Meysey-Wigley, E 20 Aug., 1829 (1710)
Michaelson *see* Yeates.
Michael : Smith, Amelia, L , of Bath. Times, d p , 4 Nov., 1884.
: Westbrooke, J 6 July, 1793 (564)
Michell *see* Luttman-Johnson.
„ Moore-Michell-Esmead.
Michell-Fancourt : Michell, St J. F., of Harborne Park, Staffs. ·Times, 4 May, 1900.
Mickelfield : Hunt, R 18 Nov , 1786 (551).
: Hunt, W. 22 Feb , 1803 (197).
Middlecott White, Montague : White, Montague, of Clarence House, East Cowes, I.W , and Malvern College. Times, d.p , 9 April, 1896.
Middlemore-Whithard : Whittard, Rev. T. M. d.p., 13 June, 1879

Middleton *see* Athorpe.
    „ Broke-Middleton.
    : Carver, M. M. 11 April, 1795 (319).
    see Fowle.
    · Monck, Sir A. E., of Belsay Castle, N'berland, Bt., and H. N., late Rifle Brigade, of Montreal, Canada, esq Times, d p., 17 Feb., 1876.
    see Monck.
Middleton-Biddulph : Biddulph, R. 29 Dec., 1807 (1531).
Middleton-Wybrants : Middleton, Isabella H. L. 11 Jan., 1876 (D.G. 17).
Midgley *see* Munro.
Milbanke : King, R. G. N. 14 Nov., 1860 (4783).
    . Melville, W. 12 June, 1792 (396).
    see Noel.
Milbanke Huskisson : Milbanke, Sir J. R. 5 March, 1866 (1647).
Milborne-Swinnerton-Pilkington : Swinnerton, Sir W. M. M. 17 and 18 Vict. c. l. e. 52.
    : Pilkingtond. Dame M. 6-7 Will. IV., c. 52.
    : Swinnerton, Sir L. W., 15 Feb., 1856 (D.G. 250).
Milbourne *see* Thistlethwayte-Pelham.
Mildmay : St. John, Sir H. 14 Dec., 1790 (745).
Miles-Wynne · Miles, R. 1 May, 1813 (833).
Miller : Aarons, J. A., late of St Mark's College, Chelsea, Middlesex, now of Wiltshire Place, Brixton Times, 17 March, 1865.
    : Abrahams, E. J., of 68, Fore St., London, etc. Times, 13 Nov., 1895.
    W. : Abrahams, H. W. Times, d.p., 31 Jan., 1896.
    : Bowen, C. Dublin, 1 Feb., 1812.
    see Campbell-Miller-Morison.
    „ Christy-Miller.
    „ Chrystie-Miller.
    : Darby, B. 10 Jan., 1800 (26).
    : Drudge, H., of Henley Cottage, Carrisbrook Road, Newport, I. of W. Times, 18 June, 1869.
    see Hallett.
    „ Kemp-Miller.
    „ Leslie-Miller.
    R. Tamplin : Miller, R., of Travancore, S. India, temp residing at 53, Bedford Gardens, Kensington. Middlesex, tea-planter Times, 13 Nov., 1893.
    : Muller, Hy. J., of 16, Rue de la Monnaie, Paris, dentist, Br. subject. Times, 25 June, 1895.
    see Percival.
    „ Riggs-Miller.

Miller-Cunningham, of Leithen . Cunningham, George. Lyon, Vol. XI., 24 Oct., 1887
Miller Millner : Miller, J., A., G., and P., all of Gibson Square, Islington. Times, d p., 14 Aug., 1873
Milles-Lade : Milles, H. A., of Lees Court, Faversham, Kent. Times, 12 Feb., 1900.
Millett-Davis : Davis, G. M. W., 6 Aug., 1856 (D.G. 864).
Millner *see* Miller Millner.
Mills (junr.) . Wrigglesworth, C., of The Grange, 23, Highbury New Park, N., gent. Times, d p., 5 Sept., 1894
Milman-Mainwaring : children of E. C. W. M. Milman. 8 May, 1874 (2993).
Milne *see* Lees-Milne
: Smith, S. M. 4 Dec., 1877 (52)
see Stott-Milne.
Milner *see* Browne.
: Cottam, C. 17 May, 1788 (229).
see Jolliff.
Milner-Gibson-Cullum : Milner-Gibson, G. G. 9 Dec., 1878 (7135).
Milner-Gibson : Gibson, T. 7 Feb., 1839 (239)
Milner-Jones Jones, E. W., of Lincoln's Inn, barrister. Times, d.p., 23 Oct., 1883.
Milner Walker Walker, J, of St Mary's Cottage, Charnwood Forest. Leic., gent Times, d p., 2 April, 1886.
Milner-White . White, H., of Westwood Park, Southampton, barrister Times, 11 Oct., 1894.
Milnes *see* Crewe-Milnes.
: Rich, J 13 Jan., 1803 (114)
: Rich, R. 12 Oct., 1805 (1271)
see Rich.
„ Smith-Milnes.
„ Walthall.
Milward : Parkinson, R. 30 Sept., 1844 (3423).
Parkinson, L., of The Old Hall, E. Bridgford, Notts. esq Times, d p., 14 May, 1888
. Sayer, H. C. 4 April, 1836 (644).
see Sayer-Milward.
Mill *see* Barker-Mill.
„ Brown-Mill.
Millar *see* Codrington.
Milles : Watson, G. J. 27 Dec., 1820 (8).
Millett-Davis : Davis, G. M. 6 Aug., 1856 (2746).
Mills *see* Holt.
Mills-Baker : Baker, Gertrude M. and Florence M. Times, 3 Nov., 1900.
Minet *see* Lewis-Minet.

Minett *see* Sorel-Cameron.
Miniken *see* Horsley.
Minns *see* Hodgson-Minns
Minton-Senhouse : Minton, Rev. S., of Fair Head, Putney, Surrey, M.A. Times, d.p., 18 Oct., 1884
Minton, R. M., of Stoke-on-Trent, Staffs, gent. Times, d.p., 22 Nov., 1884.
: Minton, E., of Fair Head, Putney, spinster; H., of Stoke-on-Trent, Staffs, china manfr., and H. M., of Cheltenham Glos., B.A. (Rev.). Times, d.p, 4 Nov., 1884
Mirehouse . Levett, R. W. B. 17 March, 1865 (1559 and 1614)
Mitchell *see* Careleton
: Coupland, E. and A. 4 Jan., 1879 (469)
see Dawson.
„ Dignum Mitchell.
„ Mitchell-Withers.
„ Parry-Mitchell.
: Van Gheluwe, A., of 49, Harley Street, London, colonial merchant Times, d p, 27 May, 1891
Mitchell-Barnard · Mitchell, Thomas B, of Southbury Road. Enfield, florist, etc. Times, d.p., 18 April, 1885.
Mitchell-Carruthers : Mitchell, Wm. Lyon, Vol X., 30 June, 1876.
Mitchell-Henderson . Michell, H., Gloucester Road, London. Times, 21 Dec., 1899.
Mitchell-Innes *see* Innes-Vine
. Mitchell, W. 3 April, 1840 (945).
Mitchell, William. Lyon, Vol. IV., 30 March, 1840.
Mitchell-Withers · Mitchell, J. B. 27 Feb, 1862 (1248)
Mitchelson Kendall, J. 27 Oct., 1860 (3962)
Mitchinson *see* Moorsom-Mitchinson-Maude.
Mitford *see* Aynsley.
., Freeman-Mitford.
„ Osbaldeston.
„ Osbaldeston-Mitford
Mitton *see* Eadon.
G. J. Jones, G., of Donnington, Salop, esq. Times, d p., 27 June, 1881.
Moffatt *see* Duncombe.
„ Story
Mogg *see* Clifton-Mogg.
: Mogg-Gregory, H. H., of New Bridge Hill, nr. Bath. Times, d.p, 12 March, 1895.
see Rees-Mogg.

Moir Fowler : Moir, H A. L., wife of Dr J W. Moir, of Challon House, St. Andrews, Fifeshire, N B. Times, 9 Nov , 1895.
Moises *see* Lisle.
Moke-Norrie : Moke, G. E. 9 June, 1893 (3639).
Molecey *see* Twigge-Molecey.
Molesworth-Hepworth : Molesworth, E. N., of Littleboro', Lancs., esq Times, d.p., 23 Jan., 1880.
Molesworth-St. Aubyn · Molesworth, H. 18 March, 1844 (954).
. Molesworth, J. 15 Nov., 1839 (2413)
Molineux *see* Montgomerie.
Mollov · Cooke, C 1st Geo. III , 1761.
   see Fitzgerald.
   ,. Homan-Mulock.
Molyneux : Howard, E. 16 March, 1825 (459).
   · Howard, H. T. — July, 1812 (1505)
   : Hockenhull, W. H. 24 May, 1806 (649)
Molyneux-Seel : Unsworth, T 12 Jan., 1815 (147)
Monck *see* Middleton.
   Middleton, Sir C. M. L. 25 Feb , 1799 (191)
Monckton-Arundell : Arundell, Rt. Hon. W. G. M. (Vis. Galway and Baron Killard). 10 April, 1826 (910).
Moncrieff *see* Scott-Wellwood.
Money-Coutts : Money, C. M and F. B T. 20 Sept , 1880 (5069).
Money-Kyrle : Money, J. 26 April, 1809 (603)
. Money, W. 11 Aug., 1843 (2703)
Money-Shewan . Shewan, G., at Arrah, Bengal, Surgeon-Maj Ind Med. Service. Times, 22 Dec , 1892
   : Shewan, Geo , of Agra, Bengal, Surgeon-Major 5th Bengal Native Infantry. Times, d p., 19 Jan., 1895.
Mongan *see* Warburton.
Monier-Williams : Williams, M. F., of 1 and 2, Bucklersbury. London, gent.; C. F., of Royal Crts Jus . Strand, gent ; O T., of Buckingham Street, Strand, gent. ; and S F , of Buckingham Street, Strand. architect. Times, d p , 1 Jan., 1880.
Monins *see* Eaton.
Monk *see* Lingard-Monk
Monkhouse *see* Gorman-Monkhouse
Monkhouse-Tillstone : Monkhouse, R. 16 Jan., 1830 (264).
Montagu · Cohen, Anna R and Violet R , of 4c. Hyde Park Mansions, London Times, 19 Aug 1893.,
   see Douglas-Scott-Montagu.
   : Fountayne-Wilson, A 27 Feb., 1826 (783).
   : Giblett. J 30 Aug , 1804 (1069).

Montagu Robinson, M 4 June, 1776 (11671)
    Ed Augustus : Thompson, E M., of 329, Vauxhall Bridge Road, S.W. Times, 23 June, 1877.
    : Wilkinson, M. 24 Jan., 1797 (61).
    see Wroughton.
    Thomson, D. I 4 Feb., 1841 (309)
    : Hodgkinson, F. B. 26 Sept., 1867 (5340).
Montagu-Marsden : Montagu, M., of 26, Brondesbury Villas, Kilburn, Middlesex Times, d.p., 14 Jan., 1867.
Montagu-Pollock : Pollock, Sir F. and Dame. 11 Aug., 1873 (3770)
Montagu-Stuart-Wortley-Mackenzie : Stuart-Wortley, Mackenzie (Earl of Wharncliffe), and Stuart-Wortley, F. D. 18 Oct., 1880 (5431)
Montague *see* Holland.
Monteath-Douglas : Monteath, T. 18 Dec., 1850 (3477).
Montefiore *see* Goldsmid-Montefiore.
    : Sebag, J. 29 Aug, 1885 (4178).
Montefiore Brice : Montefiore, A. J. Times, d.p., 19 June, 1896.
Montefiore-Levi *see* Levi.
Montford : Jones, Rev. E M, Rector of Llamerewig, Montgomery. Times, d.p., 2 Sept, 1879
    : Mountford, E., of Brockton. Lydbury North, Salop, and J. W Mountford, of Oswestry, Salop. Times, 14 Dec, 1870.
Montgomerie : Molineux, G 9 Sept, 1780 (12116)
Montgomery *see* Graham-Montgomery.
    „ Johnstone.
    „ Powell-Montgomery.
    : Heatley, C. D.G., 29 July, 1820.
    Henry Greville · Montgomery, H, of 20, New St., Westminster. Times, 1 Aug., 1883
Montgomery-Campbell . Campbell, A. 4 June, 1785 (265)
Montgomery-Smith : Smith. E. C, of 8, Seymore Terrace, Anerley. Times, d p, 20 Sept, 1894
Montgomrey : Allenby, S. H 25 Oct., 1893 (6144).
Moon-Parker Moon, G E. B, of Beyrout, Syria, dep manager of Beyrout Waterworks Co. (Ltd.). Times, d.p., 3 May, 1883.
Mooney *see* Thornburgh.
Moore-Radford : Radford. A., of Hyde Park, London. 22 May, 1900.
Moore *see* Bramley-Moore
    „ Foljambe.
    „ Gordon-Moore.
    „ Heaps-Moore
    „ Lascelles.

Moore . Papineau, O W., of College Street, London Times,
8 May, 1900.
    see Parkin-Moore
    ,, Smyth.
    ,, Stevens.
    Streatfeild, A E C. 19 June, 1885 (3372)
    . Strutt, H F , of Leigh, Essex, gent. Times, d p , 22 Nov., 1893
    see Thomas-Moore
    ,, Tonkin.
    ,, Tunstall-Moore
    Wood, C G , of Gloucester Street, Belgrave Road, and Fleet Street, Middlesex Times, d p , 26 May, 1876.
Moore-Brabazon : Moore, W J. 4 July, 1845 (1985)
    : Moore, Jno. A. H. Whll , 13 March, 1868 (D G 335)
Moore-Halsey : Moore, J F. 6 Feb , 1821 (329).
Moore-Michell-Esmead : Moore, G F. 14 Feb , 1845 (601)
Moore-Stevens · Moore, J. 17 July, 1832 (1704)
Moore-Tyrrel : Smith, W. M. T., of Gordon Avenue, Southampton, retired farmer Times, d.p., 6 Oct , 1891
Moorsom-Mitchinson-Maude Moorsom, C R 13 June, 1892 (4958)
Moorson-Roberts : Roberts, O W., of Swiss Cottage, Debenham, Suffolk, esq Times, d p , 11 May, 1886
Morant *see* Gale.
Mordant : Moses, A I , stockbroker, of Birmingham. Times, d p, 12 Jan , 1877.
Mordaunt Stead Stead, J. Times, 3 April, 1886
More . Metcalfe, T 1 July, 1797 (612)
    Wills, R 19 Feb , 1780 (12058).
    : Wills, T 19 Feb., 1780 (12058).
Moreton *see* Ducie.
    : Ducie, Lord F. 26th Geo III , 1786
    see Langdale-Moreton
Morewood : Case, H. 9 Feb , 1793 (107)
    see Hodgkinson-Morewood
    ,, Palmer-Morewood
Morgan *see* Croft.
    ,, Forbes-Morgan
    ,, Francis
    : Gould, C 20 Nov , 1792 (866)
    : Gould, Sir C. 20 Nov , 1792 (866)
    see Griffiths
    ,, Grogan-Morgan

Morgan *see* Hay Morgan.
　　　　: Jones, W. M., of Woodland Park, Monmouth, and 34, Gt St. Helen's, London. Times, 5 Sept., 1892.
　　　see Mulcahy-Morgan
　　　　,, Stratford.
　　　　: Thomas, L., V. of St. Hilary, Cowbridge, Glamorgan. Times, d.p., 16 Feb., 1866
Morgan-Bletsoe : Morgan, J. 30 Jan., 1813 (203).
Morgan-Bulmer : Bulmer, F. 25 April, 1817 (1088).
Morgan-Grenville : Morgan, L. F. H. C. 6 Dec., 1890 (7051)
Morgan-Kirby : Morgan, Rev. D., Rector of Stradishall, Suffolk. Times, 10 March, 1877.
Morgan-Payler : Morgan, F. 18 Aug., 1854 (2566).
Morgan-Richardson, C. E. Davies : Richardson, C. E., of Cardigan, gent. Times, d.p., 13 Jan., 1880.
Morgan-Spencer, Ernest : Morgan, Arthur Ernest, of Avechurch Lane, London. Times, 2 Nov., 1900.
Morgan-Stratford : Morgan, H. 27 Oct., 1887 (5937)
Moriarty *see* Crumpe.
Morice, Morris Hubert Jay : Joseph Morris, of Hatchett's Hotel, Piccadilly, Middlesex, gentleman. Times, d.p., 23 Dec., 1864.
Morin *see* Tirel.
Morison *see* Brown Morison.
　　　　　　　,, Campbell-Miller-Morison.
　　　　　　　,, Duncan Morison
　　　　　　　,, Walker Morison
Morison-Duncan of Naughton Duncan-Morison, Catherine Henrietta Adamina. Lyon, Vol. IX., 4 Feb., 1876.
　　　　　　　Duncan-Morison, Catherine Eunice Mackenzie. Lyon, Vol IX., 4 Feb., 1876
Morisset Window *see* Window Morisset.
Morland : Bernard, S. 15 Feb., 1811 (336).
Morley *see* Baxter
　　　　: Moseley, A., of 16, Sunderland Terrace, Westbourne Park, Middlesex, surgeon-dentist. Times, d.p, 21 Jan., 1870.
　　　see Stark.
　　　　,, White.
Morres *see* de Montmorency.
Morris : Carter, E. A., of 42, Calthorpe Road, Edgbaston, Warwick. Times, d.p., 6 April, 1892.
　　　see Eckford.
　　　　: Grodsenski, B., of 1, Russell Street, London, W.C. Times, 10 May, 1893
　　　see La Vettée de la Dubeterre.

Morris *see* Morice.
,, Lawrence
Squire, E., of Birchwood, Sydenham Hill, Upper Norwood, Surrey, esq. Times 4 July, 1865
Morris Pugh · Morris, W., of Astley Lodge, Salop Times, 18 Feb., 1876.
Morris-Wall : Morris, Sir Benjamin 23 Jan., 1875 (D.G. 58).
Morrish Cockey, W 7 Feb. 1807 (176)
Morriss *see* Conrahy
: Crichton, E. J., of Manor House, Plaistow, Essex Times, 17 June, 1879
Morse-Boycott : Morse. J H 23 July, 1844 (2549)
Morshead *see* Anderson-Morshead
Mortimer *see* Siddall
,, Bird Mortimer
,, Green.
,, Jones Mortimer.
Mortlock : Rawlins, S. E., late the wife of D A D Rawlins, of Market Harborough, Leicestershire, attorney-at-law Times, 30 June, 1865
Morton-Day . Death, R., of 15, Bartholomew Villas, Kentish Town, N.W Times, 25 April, 1866.
Morton-Herbert · Morton, M 18 April, 1820 (810)
Morton-Paggett · Morton, T C. P 26 July, 1817 (1646)
Moseley *see* Lofft-Moseley
,, Manville
,, Morley.
,, Walsh
Moseley-Williams : Moseley, J. 28 June, 1851 (1735)
Moses *see* Bargate
,, Beddington
,, Collins
,, Goldsmid
,, Hiley.
,, Hudson.
Jacob *see* Marsh, John Moses
see Meredith.
,, Mordant
,, Moss.
,, Mostyn
,, Murray
,, Sims.
,, Sinclair
Moses-Dinsdale : Moses, R 11 March, 1814 (650)
Moses-Marsden · Moses. I, of 23, Kensington Palace Gardens, Middlesex. Times, d.p, 4 Jan., 1865
Moses-Walter : Moses, F. E of 18. Isledon Road, Holloway, London. gent Times, d p , 2 Jan , 1891.

Mosley Mosley Lowe, M., late of Southgate. Middlesex. now of
    Combe Down, Somerset, spinster. Times, 10 April, 1879
Mosley Lowe Mosley, Maria, late of Loughboro, now of South-
    gate, Middlesex, spinster. Times, 24 Nov., 1873.
Moss *see* Edwards-Moss.
    „ Finchett-Maddock.
    Moses, A., of Kilburn, Middlesex, clothier. Times, d p,
        28 April, 1888.
    Moses, I., of 95, Charing Cross Road, Middlesex, clothier.
        Times, d.p., 12 May, 1891
    see Scott
    „ Slazenger.
Moss-Breakell-Moss : Breakell, A. E., of The Manor House,
    Longton, Lancs., gent. Times, d.p, 21 Feb., 1885.
Mostyn *see* Lloyd-Mostyn.
    Moses, A. A., late of Cheltenham, silversmith, now of
        Maida Vale, Middlesex, gent. Times, d p., 10
        Jan, 1881.
Mostyn-Champneys : Champneys, Sir T. S. 16 May, 1831 (975)
Mottet de la Fontaine : Mottet. E. H., late of Hassan and
    Shimoga, India, now at Dieppe, France, retired Col.
    Times, d p., 21 June, 1880
Moubray *see* Hussey.
Moulton *see* Barrett
Mounsey *see* Cranmer.
    . Mounsey-Grant, Mary T., widow, of The Hill,
        Cumberland Times, d.p., 29 Oct., 1896
Mounsey Grant · Mounsey, C J and M T., of Inverness, N B,
    and of The Hill, Cumberland. Times, d.p, 25 July, 1882.
Mounsey-Heysham : Mounsey, G. W. 31 May, 1871 (3414).
Mounteney *see* Power-Mounteney
Mountford *see* Montford.
    : Mycock, Josiah, of 12, Giles Gate, Durham,
        superindt. wesleyan minister of the Durham
        Circuit. Times, 28 March, 1872.
    see Newte.
Mountjoy McLeroth, T., formerly of Killenyther, Down, Ireland,
    now of Newport, I. of W., Southampton, esq, J.P. for
    Down Times. 1 Feb., 1866.
Mountmorres *see* De Montmorency
Mowbray Cornish, J R. (on his marriage to E J. Mowbray)
        26 July, 1847 (3033)
    : Wiggin, B. H. 12 Nov., 1855 (4232)
Moyle *see* Copley
Moyse-Belward . Moyse, H B. 19 July, 1813 (1411).
Moyser : Whyte, R. 26 May, 1815 (1076)
Mudd *see* Clarke.

Mugeridge, J. : Bridger, J. M., of Binney Farm, All Hallows. nr.
Rochester. Kent, farmer Times, d p., 28 July, 1892
Muir see Strange-Muir.
Muirhead see Steuart-Grossett-Muirhead
Mulcahy Morgan : Mulcachy, Susan, W. Times, 18 March, 1879.
Mulhallen see Gabbett-Mulhallen.
    „ Wallace-Mulhallen.
Mullins see de Moleyns.
Muller see Binden Marcus.
    „ Forbes-Muller.
    „ Miller.
Mulock see Homan-Mulock.
Mumford . Abercrombie, C. 1 March, 1788 (97).
Mundy see Massingberd-Mundy
    : Patch, Rev. J. T., M.A., Oxon, formerly of Heavitree, Devon, now Vicar of Cornwood, Devon. Times, d.p., 24 Nov., 1888
Munn see Brydges
Munn-Graham : Munn, A., of 35, Duke Street, St. James's, London, hosier. Times, d p., 20 June, 1893
Munro : Midgley, C. M. 29 April, 1859 (1866)
    : Munro-Scott, T. 23 May, 1816 (1046).
    see Walker-Munro.
    „ Watson Munro.
Murdoch see Pasley-Dirom.
Murchison see Cox-Murchinson
Mure : Rae, J. 5 May, 1807 (636).
    see Strange-Mure.
Murhall-Griffith : Griffith, T. 7 July, 1813 (1381).
Murphy see Burgoyne.
    „ Ventris.
Murray see Ade-Murray.
    „ Allan.
    „ Aynsley
    „ Bankes.
    ., Browne-Clarke
    · Cottin, A. 27 Dec., 1835 (25).
    see De Ameland.
    : Foxlow, W. 7 May, 1782 (12293).
    see Gostling-Murray
    „ Greville.
    : Moses, C., of Kylemore Eton Avenue, Hampstead, diamond merchant. Times, d p., 3 July, 1893.
    see Pulteney.
    : Robertson, J. M. 21 July, 1798 (669).
    see Scott-Murray.

Murray see Stewart-Murray.
Murray of Broughton : Murray, A D.G., 18 March, 1812.
Murray-Anderdon : Murray, H. E., of Chislehurst, Kent, esq.
  Times, d.p, 26 Feb., 1873.
Murray-Browne : Browne, C. C., Rector of Uley, Glos. Times,
  d.p., 22 July, 1885.
Murray-Menzies of Pitlochie . Murray, Gilbert Innes, Lt. 42nd
  R H Lyon, Vol. V., 25 Jan., 1853.
Murray-Oliphant-Murray : Murray, Alexr. Oliphant (Baron
  Elibank). Lyon, Vol IV., 22 Sept. 1843.
Murray-Shirreff see Shirreff.
Murray-Stewart : Murray, H G S. 7 Nov., 1855 (4184),
  (D.G. 1573).
Murrell see Etheredge.
Murton-Neale : Murton, A C., of Buckhurst Hill, Essex, and
  Barge Yard Chambers, Bucklersbury, London, solicitor.
  Times, d.p., 3 April, 1869.
Musgrave-Sagar see Sagar-Musgrave.
Musgrave see Sagar Musgrave.
    : Norman. 6 March, 1882 (1131).
    see Tattersall-Musgrave
    ,, Wykeham-Musgrave
Muskett-Hunter Hunter, R., of East Moulsey, Surrey. Times,
  30 April, 1867.
Musters : Chaworth, J. 14 Aug., 1823 (1365).
  see Chaworth-Musters.
Muter see Straton
Mycock see Mountford.
  ,,   Gibson.
Myers-Beswick : Myers, W B. 10 Dec., 1895 (7367)
Myers : Greaves, J. M., of Horsforth, Guiseley, Yorks, butcher.
    Times, d p , 10 Dec., 1875
  see Waskett-Myers.
Mynors-Baskerville : Mynors, T B 3 July, 1817 (1572).
    see Hopton.
Mynors · Rickards, P. 15 Sept., 1787 (418).
Mytton see Thornycroft.

N

Nagle see Chichester.
Nainby see Luxmoore
Nairn · Aveling, W. — July, 1834 (1392)
Nairne : M'Nicol, J. 6 March, 1834 (405).

Nanson *see* Walker-Nanson.
Naper-Dutton . Dutton, W. 17th Geo. III., 1777
Napier *see* Coleman-Napier
    . Groom, C O., of Southwell Cottage, Kingsdown, Bristol. Times, 1 March, 1865
    . Mutter, A. D. (and nine others). 20 July, 1900, Lyon Register
    see Williamson-Napier.
Napier-Clavering : Napier, J. W. 8 Feb, 1894 (985).
    of Axwell Park : Napier, Rev John Warren. [R.L., 8 Feb., 1894.] Lyon, Vol XIII, 1 June, 1895.
Napier Ford : Ford, A., of Regent's Park and of Cavendish Sq., London, surgeon. Times, d.p , 25 Aug 1885
Napier Grant : Grant, C. D., of 54, Penywern Road, S Kensington, Middlesex. Times, 26 Sept, 1888
Nash *see* Harwood-Nash.
  ,, Beigh.
  ,, Leibrandt.
  : Palmer, jun., J. 6 March, 1809 (292)
  see Roston-Nash
  ,, Skillicorne.
  . Williams, F. 4 Nov., 1834 (1949).
Nash-Woodhouse *see* Beldams-Johns.
Nash-Woodham Nash, W. 1 May, 1825 (787).
Nassau : Kirby D'Arcy, N., of 13, Guildford Terrace, Dover, Kent. d.p , 29 April and 3 May, 1884.
Naters *see* Sharp-Naters.
Nathan *see* Hardy.
  ,, Norbury.
Nathan Henochsberg Nathan, D , of 20, Islington, Liverpool, manager to Messrs. Henochsberg & Ellis, clothiers Times, d.p., 2 Feb., 1888.
Naylor *see* Leyland.
Neale *see* Bailey-Neale.
  ,, Barry.
  · Burrard, H 8 April, 1795 (339)
  see Gieve.
  ,, Murton-Neale.
  Van Sittart, E. 14 Nov., 1805 (1485).
Neale-Watson : Neale, S. D.G., 8 March, 1837.
Need *see* Welfitt.
Needham *see* Holt-Needham
    ,, Kilmorey, Earl of.
    ,, Redfern.
Neison *see* Nevill.
Nelson : Kerr, G. 13 Sept , 1806 (1235)
    : Walter, R 26 Nov., 1791 (649).

Nelson-Ward : Ward, H N , Rector of Radstock, Somerset Times, 19 April, 1881
Nelthorpe-Newman *see* Nott.
Nelthorpe : Sutton, R. N. 13 Oct , 1884 (4494)
    see Tuder-Nelthorpe
Neruda *see* Norman-Neruda.
Nesbitt : Ravizzotti, R. B. Times, d.p., 21 Oct , 1882.
Ness *see* Burdett.
Netterville : McEvoy, J J , and The Hon Mary his wife. D. Castle, 14 July, 1865 (D G 893 and 905)
Neumann Norman Neumann, L. 1. Times, d p , 10 Sep , 1886.
Neville or Neville-Aldworth : Aldworth, R. N. W , 4 Sept., 1762 (D.G 1252).
Nevile *see* Noel.
Nevill, E Neville : Neison, E , of the Observatory, Natal, esq Times, 2 Jan., 1888
Neville : Benjamin, E. D., of Westbourne Terrace, Hyde Park, gent. Times, d p , 28 Nov , 1879.
    see Couves-Neville
    ,, Gartside
    ,, Griffin.
    Howson Potter, Rev. F , of Charlton Kings, Gloucester Times, d p., 27 Sept , 1880, and 12 Feb., 1881
    White, J. S 25 July, 1885 (3651).
Neville-Bagot Bagot, J. L 17 Feb., 1878 (D G. 199).
Neville-Grenville : Neville, Hon G 7 July, 1825 (1295)
Neville-Rolfe · Neville, S C. E 8 April, 1837 (955)
Nevins, Hy W. Probyn Nevins, H W , of Cheltenham, Glos Times, d.p , 19 March, 1880.
New *see* Alderman.
  ,, Birch
  ,, Foreman
Newbery *see* Knott
Newberry *see* Power
    ,, Wilson
Newbigging *see* Cairncross
Newbury *see* Smith
Newby-Fraser Newby, W. (to continue use of surname Fraser). W., 20 June, 1851 (D G. 510)
Newby-Fraser Newby, W 20 June, 1851 (1603)
Newcastle, Duke of *see* Pelham
Newcombe, Jas Kivelle · Newcombe, J , M D., L R C P., M.R.C S. Times, 14 Sept , 1886.
Newcomb *see* Todd-Newcomb
Newcomen : Gleadowe, Sir W., Bt. Betham, 16 Nov., 1781.
Newdegate. Parker, J. 25 Jan., 1807 (176)
    see Newdigate-Newdegate

Newdigate-Ludford-Chetwode : Chetwode, J 21 Aug , 1826 (2064)
Newdigate-Ludford Ludford, J 12 July, 1808 (977).
Newdigate-Newdegate Newdigate, E 18 Aug., 1888 (4735)
Newdigate Parker, F 29 May, 1773 (11356)
Newell . House, W. 19th Geo. III., 1779
Newell-Atkins : Newell, J 3 May, 19 May, 1848 (D G 537 and 545).
Newell-Birch : Birch, J W 31 May, 1847 (2008).
Newell-Jones Jones. A E., of Hillersdon House, Barnes. Surrey, spinster. Times. d p , 22 June, 1881.
Newey *see* Soley.
Newland-Pedley Pedley, F. N., of 32, Devonshire Place, Middlesex, dental surgeon. Times, d p , 9 Jan , 1889
Newman Harding, R N 23rd Geo. III., 1783
· Kruszinski, M , of 9, Wood Street, Spitalsfield, tailor Times, 7 March, 1873
see Nelthorpe-Newman
Prohowsky, S., formerly of St George's Street, E , clothier, now of Woodsome Villas, Forest Hill Times, 16 Aug , 1871
Toll, C 9 Sept , 1775 (11594)
· Toll, R. N 24 April. 1802 (406).
Newman-Mayo Newman, T M 30 July, 1828 (1470)
Newman-Wilson, J. R. · Wilson, N J R., of Brisbane, Queensland, now at St George's Club, Hanover Square. solicitor and notary pub Times, d p , 26 June, 1888.
Newnham *see* Lacy.
Newnham-Collingwood : Newnham, G L 11 June, 1819 (1064).
Newport *see* Charlett.
  ,, Wakeman-Newport
Newport Gwilt Newport, G., of Lewisham. Kent, timber merchant, etc Times, d p 18 Sept., 1897
Newsome-Killam : Newsome, H 29 June 1871 (3225)
Newson-Smith . Smith, H , E C L., H. H., F E, and C C , all of 8, Gordon Street. Gordon Square. London Times, d.p., 4 Sept , 1890
Newte : Mountford. T 16 Aug , 1806 (1093)
Newton : Button. W. 18 Feb , 1797 (157)
  see Bagenal.
  ,, Frye.
  ,, Houblon-Newton
  ., Hand-Newton
  : Leaper, J. 6 Oct., 1789 (637)
  see Levi-Newton
  ,, Levy-Newton
  ,, Watson

Newton-Clare · Newton, E A. 14 Aug., 1879 (5452)
Newton-Robinson : Robinson, C. E , of Regent's Park, Middlesex.
    esq   Times, d p , 6 June. 1889
Nibblett : Downs, Laura, of Carlton Vale, London, spinster.
    Times, d p., 28 March, 1893
Nibloch-Stuart of Edenaneane   Nibloch, Revd Jas Lyon, Vol.
    XI , 22 Nov , 1882
Niccol *see* Searancke.
Nicholas *see* Franklin-Littlegroom-Nicholas
Nicholl *see* Carne.
Nicholl-Carne *see* Stradling-Carne
Nicholls . Whitaker, C K   18 July, 1834 (1355)
Nicholson-Fall : Nicholson, W. 13 Feb., 1812 (381).
Nichols *see* Broadhurst.
Nichols-Stewart of Dalpowrie House . Nichols, Franc   Lyon,
    Vol. VIII., 8 Oct , 1869
Nicholson *see* Cooke-Nicholson.
            : Custis, Jas. St. J., 28 Feb , D C. 9 March, 1861
                (D.G 317 and 333).
            : M'Innes, A. 5 Dec., 1821 (2422)
            : Phillips, W. N. 5 Nov., 1827 (2274).
            see Shaw.
Nicoll *see* Hodgson-Nicoll
Nicoll-Constable   Nicoll, J   28 Oct , 1845 (3228).
Nicolls *see* Trafford.
Nicolson *see* Isaac Nicolson
Nicholson Castell Nicholson, F. B , of 759. Old Kent Road,
    formerly of Liverpool, civ and elec engineer   Times,
    d.p., 22 March, 1886
Nightingale : Shore, W. E   21 Feb., 1815 (338)
            see Shore Nightingale
            W. Shore : Smith, W Shore, of Embley Park,
                Hants. etc., gent   Times, d p . 22 Feb , 1893
Nisbet *see* Christopher-Nisbet-Hamilton
Nisbet-Hamilton-Ogilvy   Ogilvy. Hy Thos   Lyon Vol. XII , 4
    Oct , 1888
Nixon *see* Wilson
Nixon-Lawson : Nixon, R L , of Burgh-by-Sands. Cumberland.
    land agent   Times. d p , 30 May, 1891
Nixon-Wensley   St J 2 Nov., 1784 (D G 4523)
Noble   Crook, C J   30 April 1825 (812).
    see Walker
Nouaille *see* Rudge-Nouaille.
Noding *see* FitzGerald
Noel : Byron, Baron, Rt. Hon. G. G   2 March, 1822 (385).
    : Edwards. G N   8 May, 1798 (387)

Noel *see* King-Noel.
,, Milbanke, Sir R. 29 May, 1815 (1018).
,, Nevile, C. 11 June, 1798 (512).
Noel-Hill : Hill, Hon. W. 24 March, 1824 (500).
Nolan *see* Irwin.
Nolan-Whelan : Nolan, J. 31 Aug., 1886 (D.G. 741).
Nooth *see* Vavasour.
,, Wright-Nooth.
Noott *see* Van der Noot.
Norbury : Jones, T. 9 Nov., 1840 (2480).
,, Nathan, H. F., staff surgeon H.M.S. Impregnable, Devonport, of Devons. Times, d.p., 30 Sept., 1874.
Norcop *see* Radford-Norcop.
Norcliffe : Robinson, R. 9 May, 1862 (2430).
,, Dalton, T. N. 7 Aug., 1807 (1059).
,, Innes, Sir J. 31 May, 1769 (10944).
Norfolk-Howard : Bug, J., of Wakefield, York (late of Epsom, Surrey), landlord of Swan Tavern. Times, d.p., 23 June, 1862.
Norie *see* Medows.
Norman *see* Blake.
,, Brunel-Norman.
,, Lee-Norman.
,, Musgrave.
,, Neumann Norman.
Norman-Crosse : Norman, G. S., of Middlesborough, Yorks. Times, 9 Aug., 1900.
Norman-Lee : Lee, F. B. N., of St John's Coll., Cambridge, residing at 82, Church Street, Islington, Middlesex. Times, 21 May, 1881.
Norman-Neruda, Waldemar : Norman, F. W. W., of 19, Holland Park, London. Times, d.p., 6 June, 1895.
Norrie *see* Moke-Norrie.
Norris : Harris, R. J. J. 1 Aug., 1808 (1052).
,, *see* Jephson-Norris.
North *see* Beesley.
,, Bomford-North.
,, Burton, N. 18 April, 1866 (2568) (D.G. 711).
,, Doyle, J. S. 20 Aug., 1838 (1860).
,, Harrison, W. 11 July, 1789 (477).
,, *see* Long.
,, Long, D. 2 May, 1789 (334).
,, *see* Ouvry-North.
North Wates *see* Wates

Northale-Laurie · Laurie, P   17 Oct, 1850 (2775) (*see* 2831)
Northey *see* Hopkins
Northland · Robinson, G, of Leamington, Warwicks, Capt R N
	Times, d p., 1 Feb, 1886.
Norton   Bradbury, J   21 March, 1797 (263).
	. Harvey W F. N. 30 June. 1807 (915)
	see Lowndes-Stone-Norton
	,, Wilson-Norton
Norton-Taylor · Taylor, A. N, of Southsea, Hants, surgeon
	Times, 7 Jan, 1880
Nott · Harding, R   27 June, 1856 (2342).
	. Nelthorpe-Newman, F. L. 2 April, 1825 (655).
	see Pyke-Nott
	,, Hamlyn-Nott.
Nowell   Robinson, M   1 Nov., 1843 (3816).
Nowell-Usticke : Beauchant, S. U.   28 Feb, 1852 (672) (D G. 253).
Nowlan · Jones, T., D.G., 28 Aug., 1900 (1261)
Nugent *see* Dunworth-Nugent.
	FitzGerald, P D.G., 31 Sep. 1831.
	see Greville-Nugent-Algernon.
	,, Greville-Nugent
	. Grenville-Nugent-Temple
	Reilly, Sir H, Bart. D.G., 11 Sept., 1812
	Savage A. D.G, 10 Sept., 1812
	Smith, H J, of Brighton, Sussex, spinster, and W T.,
		Wimbledon, Surrey, esq Times, 12 Feb, 1875
Nugent-Macnamara   Macnamara.   1 Dec, 1816 (2478)
Nunn-Rivers : Nunn, A R., of St Andrew's Clergy House, Gt
	Grimsby, Lincoln gent Times, 29 April, 1891.
Nutcombe : Quick, N   32nd Geo. III., 1792
Nuttall *see* Darning.
	,, Dixon-Nuttall
	. Knight, Lucy A., of Farnworth. nr. Bolton, Lancs.
		spinster Times, d p, 25 June, 1891
	: Knight, C. H., of Farnworth, nr Bolton, Lancs, cotton
		spinner Times, d p, 25 June, 1891
Nutt-Mackenzie   Nutt, C H   28 June, 1888 (5107)

O

Oakeley *see* Oakley
Oakley *see* Cooper-Oakley

OLD] *An Index to Changes of Name.* 241

Oakley : Oakeley, R. B , of Leadenhall Street, E.C., and Gravesend. Times, 27 Nov., 1874.
O'Brien *see* Bainbridge.
„ Bernard Dent.
„ Dent.
„ De Stafford.
„ Knapp O'Brien.
O'Brien-Stafford : O'Brien, S. A. 11 June, 1847 (2788).
O'Callaghan-Westropp : O'Callaghan, G. 19 June, 1885 (D.G. 610).
O'Donel *see* Thomas-O'Donel
O'Donnell see Clarke.
O'Ferrall Ferrall, J. E., of Longsdon House, Oundle, Northants. Times, 1 Nov., 1889.
see Ambrose.
O'Fflahertie *see* De Vere.
Offley *see* Cunliffe-Offley.
Ogden, F. H. B. : Brown, F. H., of N. Shields. Times, d.p., 31 Jan., 1893.
: Hassell, P. 3 April, 1866 (2206).
Ogilvie : Brown, G. A., of Fonnereau Road, Ipswich, Suffolk, engineer. Times, d p., 3 June, 1893.
: Perry, R V. 17 March, 1801 (429).
Ogilvy *see* Nisbet-Hamilton-Ogilvy.
: Ogilwy, A. C., of St. Mark's School, Windsor, and T. of Eton College. Times, 22 Dec., 1887.
Ogilwy *see* Ogilvy
Oglander, Jno. Hy. Glynn : Glynn, H. O. G., barrister, 12 Onslow Crescent, Kensington Times, d.p., 6 April, 1889.
Oglander-Hennah : Hennah, W. H., of E. Cowes, I.W., Lieut. D. Guards. Times, d.p., 19 May, 1882.
Ogle Wallis, W. O. 23 Sept., 1786 (451).
: Williamson, J. O. 24 April, 1787 (193)
O'Hara : Cooper, C. W. 7 Nov., 21 Nov., 1860 (D.G 1345 and 1373).
Ohren Ovington : Ohren, J., C. S., and A., all of Oaklands, Surrey. Times, d.p., 23 June, 1891.
O'Keefe :, Lanigan, S. M. 22 July, 1895 (D.G. 841).
O'Keeffe *see* Deville-O'Keeffe.
Oldershaw *see* Loveland.
Oldham : Laing, J. 16 June, 1830 (1245).
Oldnall : Oldnall-Russell, H. C 9 March, 1897 (1668).
: Oldnall-Russell, R. W 9 March, 1897 (1668)
Oldnall-Russell *see* Russell-Oldnall
Oldnall-Wolley : Oldnall, E. 24 July, 1843 (2512).
Oldridge de la Hey : Hayes, E., Vicar of St. Martin's Marple, Chester, has resumed the original family name of de la Hey. 13 Feb., 1879.

Q

Oliphant *see* Murray-Oliphant-Murray.
: Wilson, Janet M., of 8 and 9, Clarence Crescent, New Windsor, Berks, spinster   Times, d p., 18 April, 1895.
Oliphant-Ferguson : Oliphant, G. H H   29 Sept., 1860 (3753).
Oliver *see* Meade Oliver
 ,, Smith-Oliver
Oliver-Bellasis : Oliver, R J. E   11 Feb., 1879.
Oliver Conquest · Oliver, G. A., of Tufnell Park, Middlesex, theatrical proprtr   Times, d p., 27 April, 1883.
Oliver-Gascoigne. Oliver, R   7 April, 1810 (506)
Oliver-Massey · Oliver, R M   14 May, 1844 (1641)
Oliver-Orton   Oliver, R., of Bank House, Tattenhall, Chester. Times, 11 Jan., 1866
O'Mealy : Mealy, W., of Gt. Malvern, Worces., gent.   Times, 27 April, 1880
Olmius : Luttrell, Hon J   3 April, 1787 (161).
Olney *see* Allen-Olney.
O'Neill *see* Chichester-O'Neill.
 · Geoghegan, J.   13 Feb., 1808 (217).
 see Logan.
Ongley *see* Hopson.
Onion *see* Camsell
Onions *see* Clark
 ,, Wenyon.
Onley *see* Savill-Onley.
Onley-Prattenton   Onley, Rev. G D., of Bransford, Worcester. d.p., 15 May, 1865
 · Onley, E. J., formerly of Bransford, Worcester, but now of Rainbow Hill, Worces., gent. Times, 24 Sept., 1889.
Onslow *see* Mainwaring-Elleker-Onslow
 A E Mainwaring Elleker : Onslow, A. E., of 2, Elliot Terrace, Plymouth, Lieut.-Col., late Scots Gds. Times, d p., 14 Dec., 1882.
 see Macarthur-Onslow.
 ,, Williams-Onslow.
Openshaw   Sargeant, F. O., of Sheffield, Yorks, Capt. and Paymaster 19th Foot Reg.   Times, d p., 8 Feb., 1876.
Orange *see* Jackson.
Orby-Wombwell   Wombwell, C.   20 May, 1836 (1029)
Orchard : Jeffery, J W.   13 June, 1807 (819)
Ord *see* Blackett-Ord.
 ,, Wright.
Ord-Willis   Ord, J   6 Sept., 1814 (1872).
Orde *see* Campbell-Orde.
 ,, Lisle.

Orde *see* Powlett.
Orford-Holte : Orford, R. 10 June, 1825 (1019)
Orgill *see* Leman.
Orloff : Marshall, M. A. B., of 37, Guildford Street, London, late of 15, Clifton Road, Brockley, Kent, spinster. Times, d.p., 19 Nov., 1886
Orme *see* Cave-Orme.
,, Garnett.
Orme-Webb : Webb, R. O., of Ponsbourne Park, Herts, esq., retired Commdr. R.N., J.P. Times, 2 March, 1882.
Ormsby-Gore · Gore, W. 10 Jan., 1815 (63).
Ormsby-Hamilton : Ormsby, A. H. 26 Nov., 1892 (7100).
Ormsby-Rebow : Ormsby, Mary M. 7 July, 1835 (1332).
Orton *see* Previté Orton.
,, Oliver-Orton.
O'Rorke Rorke, E., of Dinard, France, banker. Times, d.p., 1 Aug., 1892.
: Rorke, A., of St. Servan, France, banker. Times, d.p., 1 Aug., 1892.
Ormond Cody, A., of 19, Holland Street, Kensington. Times, d.p., 7 July, 1879.
Orpen Palmer : Palmer, Rev. A. H. H., B.D., of St Peter's Vicarage, Cheltenham, Glos., and Killowen, Ireland. Times, d.p., 30 July, 1892.
Orr *see* Dunbar.
,, Dunton.
Orsinigo *see* Ferguson.
Osbaldeston : Brookes, H. 30 July, 1770 (11063).
see Brooke.
: Mitford, B. 6 Feb., 1836 (255).
: Wickins, G. 30 July, 1770 (11063).
Osbaldeston-Mitford : Mitford, E. L., of the Hunmanby and Mitford estates. Times, 16 Dec., 1895.
: Mitford, P., tenant for life in possession of the Hunmanby estates, co. York, and of the Mitford estates, co. Northumberland. Times, 18 Aug., 1870.
Osbaldestone *see* Brooke.
Osborn : Homersham, O., temp. residing at 14, Park Street, Grosvenor Square, Middlesex, esq. Times, d.p., 28 Sept., 1876.
see Jenkyn.
,, Homersham.
Osborne . Bernal, jun., R. (on his marriage to C. J. Osborne). 19 Aug., 1844 (2933).
see Delando-Osborne.
,, Godfrey-Faussett-Osborne.

Osborne *see* Harrison-Osborne.
Osborne-Elphinstone of Banheath and Stonehaven Mareschal :
    Villiers or Elphinstone, Lady Wm. Godolphin. Lyon,
    Vol. VIII, 8 June, 1870.
Osbourne *see* Smyth-Osbourne.
O'Shea *see* Roche.
Osmaston : Wright, J., of Osmaston Manor, Derby, esq. Times,
        d p, 11 Sept, 1876
    : Wright, J., J.P., D L., of Osmaston. d.p., Notts
        Guardian, 22 Sept, 1876
Osmond : Webber, C O. 8 Aug., 1807 (1045)
Ossington *see* Scott.
Oswald *see* Gordon-Oswald.
    „ Haldane-Oswald.
Oswald-Brown : Brown, Major Chas. Robt. Lyon, Vol. XIV.,
    14 Nov., 1895
Oswald-Emmott Oswald, A. 23 Aug., 1821 (2095) (*see* 2071).
O'Toole *see* Hall.
Otter-Barry · Otter, R. M. B. 19 May, 1873 (2586).
Ottiwell *see* Bennet.
Otton-Halse : Halse, G A. Times, d.p., 14 July, 1884.
Ottley : Hooker, J B 4 Sept., 1820 (1704).
Otway *see* Cave
    : Hughes, W. J. M. 14 Jan., 1873 (321).
Ould *see* Fielding-Ould.
Ourry *see* Treby.
Ouvry-North : Ouvry, J N. 16 March, 1838 (658).
Ovens *see* Elliott
Overton *see* Dades Overton.
Ovington *see* Ohren Ovington.
Ovington-Jones Jones, D. V., of 28, Bridge Avenue, Hammer-
    smith, gent Times, 28 Oct., 1884.
Owen-Barlow Owen, Sir W 5 Aug., 1844 (2984).
Owen *see* Barlow.
    : Cholmondeley, T 23 June, 1863 (3294).
    see Cunliffe
    : Hatchett, H. 24 Aug., 1804 (1040).
    see Hensley Owen
    „ Humphreys-Owen.
    „ Kynaston.
    : Lewis, T. 7 May, 1798 (387)
    see Lloyd-Owen.
    : Pemberton, E. W S. 24 Dec., 1814 (22).
    · Smythe, N O. 27 Feb., 1790 (121).
    see Swaffield
    „ Wynne-Owen.

Owen-Holdsworth : Owen, H L., of Crowhurst, Battle, Sussex, gent Times, d.p, 12 Oct., 1892.
Owen-Swaffield . Swaffield, C. J. O , of Wyke Regis, Dorset, esq., late Lieut.-Col. Times, d p, 27 Nov., 1879
Owst-Atkinson : Atkinson, E. G , E E. Atkinson and E. A. Atkinson, of Kingston-upon-Hull Times, d p., 28 Feb., 1866.
Oxenden-Dixwell · Oxenden, P. D. N 28 June, 1890 (4602).
Oxley : Braithwaite, jun., C. 18 March, 1775 (11544).

P

Pace *see* Hitchins
Pack *see* Reynell-Pack.
Packe *see* Reading.
Packe-Reading Packe, C. W. 7 Nov., 1821 (2206).
Packer : Woolsey, Ellen J, of New Buckenham, Norfolk. Times, d.p., 5 July, 1892
Page : Hagger, W. 24 Aug , 1836 (1550).
    see Maynard-Page.
    ,, Selfe.
    : Seymour, R. P. 21 May, 1862 (2780).
    : Turner, Sir G. 18 Nov., 1775 (11614).
Page-Bailey · Bailey, J. P 15 Dec , 1816 (229)
Page-Fryer : Fryer, H. E., r. of Rev. Charles Gulliver, of Eltham, Kent, d. of late Sir Gregory Osborne Page Turner, of Battlesden Park, Bedford, Bart. Times, d p., 15 Aug , 1871
    Fryer, H. E. 29 April, 1875 (2394)
Page-Henderson Page, R. H. 29 Jan , 1867 (634)
Paget, Alfred : De Blutstein, Alphonse, esq , of Ladbroke Grove Road, Notting Hill, Middlesex. Times, d.p., 17 Nov., 1876.
    see Eskell-Paget
    : Paget (Lord), Hon. Hy , Baron of Beaudesert. L. Gazette, 8 March, 1770 (D.G. 2141).
Paget-Tomlinson : Paget, W. S. 7 Feb , 1890 (956)
Paige-Browne : Paige, J B, of Great Englebourne, Harberton, Devon. Times, d p , 19 Sept., 1870.
Paggett *see* Morton-Paggett.
Paine, Charles Abrahams, Solomon, of 39, White Horse St , Stepney, wholesale glass and china dealer. Times, d p., 25 Feb., 1885.

Pakenham-Mahon : Pakenham, H. S. 26 March, 15 April, 1847 (D G. 578 and 595).
    see Conoby
Pakington · Russell, J. S. 14 March, 1831 (496).
Palgrave . Turner, D. 30 Sept., 1823 (1615)
Palliser : Thomas, G 31 March, 1796 (323).
    : Walters, Sir H P. 13 Dec , 1798
Palmer : Budworth, J. 21 March, 1812 (520).
    : Danby Palmer.
    see Deloraine-Roquette-Palmer-Palmer.
    „ Golding-Palmer.
    : Hudson, Sir C. T. 11 Dec., 1813 (2516).
    see Nash.
    „ Orpen Palmer
    „ Roquette-Palmer-Palmer
    : Younghusband, J P 22 Oct., 1850 (2775).
Palmer-Acland *see* Fuller-Palmer-Acland.
Palmer Donkin · Palmer, Carl Times, d p , 25 June, 1896.
Palmer, Jas Hicks : Palmer, J., of 43, St Paul's Churchyard, London, mantle manufr Times, d.p., 4 June, 1887.
Palmer Kerrison : Palmer, G. W. D., of Kirstead and Ranworth, Norfolk, esq. Times, 27 April, 1887.
Palmer-Lovell : Palmer, C G., of 53, Lowndes Square, Middlesex, spinster Times, d p., 13 June, 1890.
    : Palmer, H. M., of 53, Lowndes Square, Middlesex, spinster Times, d p., 13 June, 1890
    . Palmer, Clarissa M, of 53, Lowndes Square, Middlesex, widow Times, d p, 13 June, 1890.
Palmer-Morewood : Palmer, W. 1 Aug , 1825 (1357).
Palmer-Samborne : Palmer, S. S 24 March, 1840 (795).
Palmer-Willey : Palmer, D. W. 26 March, 1839 (672)
    : Palmer, R. 21 May, 1833 (1047).
Panter-Downes · Panter, E. D. 21 Aug., 1855 (3361)
Panting *see* Gardner
Pantry Price · Price, J., of 3, Batsford Road, St John's, Kent. Times, d p , 8 June, 1894.
Papineau *see* Moore.
Paramore *see* Dunlap.
Parham : Barfoot, G. P. 28, March, 1845 (1017)
Park-Yates · Park, E. W. 8 Dec., 1857 (4402)
Parker *see* Biddulph-Parker
    : Denton, H. P , of Styrrup, Nottingham, farmer. d.p., 24 Aug., 1865
    : Field, J 19, June, 1790 (373)
    see Griffin
    : Little, H. C. 26 Nov., 1878 (L.G. 1, 1879).
    see Manwaring.

Parker see Moon-Parker.
    „ Newdegate.
    „ Newdigate.
    . Thorpe, W. 6 Aug., 1831 (1660).
    see Townley-Parker.
    „ Warren.
Parker-Hutchinson : Parker, S. G. J. 28 April, 1891 (D.G. 977 and 990)
Parker-Jervis : Jervis, E. S. 23 April, 1861 (1900).
Parkin see Beer.
    „ Sherwin.
Parkin-Moore : Parkin, W., of Whitehall, Cumberland, esq. Times, d.p., 24 Jan., 1889.
Parkinson see Milward.
    : Wilson, J. P. 14 Feb., 1842 (495).
Parnall see Davies Parnall.
Parnell : Griffin, T. P. 12 Nov., 1877 (6674).
Parr see Dudley.
Parrott see Erichson-Parrott.
    „ Wood.
Parry : Grainger, E. W., and to R. E. Grainger, and to W. J. Grainger, and to C. J. Grainger, and to Eliza R. Grainger, and to Adele Grainger, and to Rose Parry his wife. St. James's, 4 Nov., and D. Castle, 24 Nov., 1864 (D.G. 1305 and 1345).
    : Griffithes, R. 30 March, 1838 (836).
    : Haygarth, H. E., of Wimbledon, Surrey, esq. Times, d.p., 22 June, 1881.
    see Hodges.
    : Hughes, E. 30 Oct., 1848 (3875).
    see Jones-Parry.
    : Pritchard, J. 15 Sept., 1787 (418).
    see Richmond-Parry.
    „ Webley.
    „ Williams-Jones-Parry.
    „ Yate.
Parry-Mitchell : Mitchell, H. D. 14 Aug., 1880 (4902).
Parson : Freakes, J. 23 Oct., 1802 (1113).
    · Freakes, J. 5 Nov., 1808 (1491).
    see Gee.
Parson-Smith : Smith, H. H., of Westbourne Park Crescent, London. Times, 11 April, 1900.
Parsons see Clutterbuck.
    „ Higford.
    „ Hopton.

Parsons Guy · Parsons, R., of Waterstock, Oxford, farmer. Times, d p, 27 Nov., 1880.
Parsons-Peters : Parsons, W. 7 Oct., 1858 (4463).
Partridge *see* Penyston.
Pascoe *see* Logue-Pascoe.
Paske-Haselfoot : Paske, T. 24 Sept., 1863 (4645).
Paske-Jones : Paske, G. 27 Sept., 1841 (2421).
Pasley : Sabine, Sir T. S. 3 March, 1809 (292).
Pasley-Dirom *see* Cautley.
           : Cautley, H. (on his marriage with E. L. Pasley-Dirom). Times, d.p., 13 Oct., 1887.
           Dirom, T. A., of Lerce and Mount Annan. 27 April, 1864 (2399).
           : Murdoch, Mrs. Madeline E. and Patrick Alexr. Lyon, Vol. XIII, 13 April, 1894.
Passawer Percival : Percival, E., of 53, Conduit St,, Middlesex, LL.D. Times, d.p., 23 May, 1887.
Passey : Pawsey, F. 3 Aug., 1842 (2128).
Passingham *see* Anwyl-Passingham.
Paston-Bedingfeld : Bedingfield, Sir H. R. 26 March, 1830 (758).
Paston-Bisshopp-Bedingfeld : Paston-Bedingfeld, M. A. 6 April, 1841 (943).
           : Paston-Bedingfield, R. S. 23 Sept., 1887 (7063) (*see* 7247).
Paston-Cooper : Cooper, Sir A. P. 19 Nov, 1884 (5436).
Patch *see* Mundy.
Paterson *see* Erskine
           : Hill, Rebeckah J., of 16, Ebury Street, London. Times, 31 May, 1895.
           see McIver-Campbell.
Paterson-Balfour-Hay, of Leys and Carpow : Paterson, Edmund de Haya. Lyon, Vol IX, 31 Jan., 1872.
Paterson-Wallace : Paterson, Robt. Alexr. Lyon, Vol. III, 8 April, 1824.
Pateshall *see* Burnam-Pateshall.
           · Thomas, E. and A. E. 9 March, 1855 (2789).
Patrick *see* Ralston-Patrick.
   ,, Wilson-Patrick.
Patten · Hodgkinson, H J. 16 July, 1884 (3484)
Pattenson *see* Tylden-Pattenson
Patterson · Turner, M. L., of Southwick, Sussex. Times, 11 Dec., 1899.
Pattin *see* Cooper-Pattin.
Patton *see* Bethune.
   ,, Masterman.

Patton-Bethune : Patton, A. L., of Army and Navy Club, Pall
    Mall, late Capt. and Hon Major. Times, d p., 21 Nov.,
    1889.
Paul *see* St Paul
    : Tippetts, J. P. 20 Feb, 1787 (548).
Paulet *see* Borroughs.
Pauncefote : Bromley, Sir G. 6 April, 1803 (434).
    : Smith, R. 14 Dec., 1808 (1690).
Pauncefort-Duncombe : Pauncefort, P. D. 29 July, 1805 (985)
Parry see Lloyd.
Paver-Crow : Paver, R., of Ornham's Hall, nr. Boroughbridge,
    York, esq. Times, d.p., 30 March, 1872.
Pavier *see* Jackson.
    „ Russell-Pavier.
Pavior : Jackson, J. 10 July, 1860 (2655).
Pawsey *see* Passey.
Pawson-Hargrave : Pawson, G. 19 March, 1817 (787).
Payler *see* Morgan-Payler.
Payne : Gallway, S. 9th Geo. III., 1769
    see Galwey.
    : Row, J. 18 Oct., 1796 (985).
      Pène, E. L. N, of 121, Regent Street, Middlesex, hosier
        and glover Times, d.p., 5 April, 1869.
    : Piper, R. 2 Aug., 1803 (1003).
    : Richardson, W. J. 18 May, 1891 (3785).
Payne-Frankland : Payne-Gallwey, E. A. 2 Oct., 1882 (4655).
Payne-Townsend : Townsend, H., and Mary S. his wife W., 18
    Nov., 1863 (D G. 1342).
Peach : Cleaver, J. J., and Ellin S. his wife   30 June, 1845
    (1939).
    : Cruger, S. P. 10 May, 1788 (219)
    see Keighly-Peach.
    „ Stanway.
Peacock *see* Holman.
    „ Willson.
Peacock-Yate : Peacock, W. M 6 Dec., 1848 (4508).
    : Peacock, W. M W., 6 Dec., 1848 (D G. 1266).
Peacocke *see* Sandford.
Pearce-Campbell : Campbell, W. N. 15 Nov., 1841 (2856).
Pearce-Church · Pearce, J. C. 16 Oct., 1845 (3118).
Pearce Edgcumbe : Pearce, E R., of 5, Paper Bldgs., Temple,
    E.C., and of 18, Halsey Street, Chelsea, barrister. Times,
    d.p., 16 June, 1884
Pearce-Serocold : Pearce, E. S. 30 July, 1842 (2243)
Pears-Archbold · Pears, J. A. 1 Feb., 1870 (753).
Pearse *see* Chalker-Pearse.

Pearse *see* Kerr-Pearse.
    ,, Langford Pearse.
Pearse-Thompson : Pearse, C B. 3 April, 1875 (2030).
Pearson *see* Baker.
    ,, Jervis.
     Meggison, R. 23 Feb., 1782 (12272).
    see Pennant.
    : Pinchbeck, W. A., of 11, Alexander Road, Middlesex, architect Times, 5 Sept., 1890.
Pearson-Gregory : Pearson, T. S. 29 Sept., 1892 (6402).
Peart *see* Scrope.
Pease *see* Aldam
    ,, Watkin
Peck : James, J. A. J., of Cretingham, Suffolk, farmer, only child of late Rev. Thomas, of Debenham, Suffolk. Times, 17 Dec., 1868.
Peckham-Phipps : Kelsall, S. 3 Oct., 1837 (2535).
Peckham : Phipps, T 30 April, 1793 (332).
    · Smith, J. P. 3 Jan., 1820 (106).
Peckwell *see* Blossett.
Pedlar *see* Shield.
Pedley *see* Deverell.
    : Hipkiss, T. W., of Oak Bank Hse., Willaston, Cheshire, yeoman. Times, d.p., 24 Dec., 1877.
    see Newland-Pedley
Peel : Ethelston, E. 29 March, 1851 (919)
Peers *see* Symonds.
Pegg *see* Pegge.
    ,, Garrett-Pegge.
Pegge : Pegg, J. T., of Scarboro', Yorks, gent. Times, d.p., 6 April, 1888.
    : Pigg, C., of Vernon House, Briton Ferry, Glamorgan, surgeon. Times, 21 June, 1865.
Pegge-Burnell : Steade, B. B. 11 March, 1836 (475).
Pegus Dudley : Dudley Pegus, F. H., of Sydney, N.S. Wales, now in London. Times, 2 Oct., 1876.
Peirse *see* Hustler.
    ,, Beresford-Peirse.
Peirse-Duncombe : Duncombe, G. T. 12 July, 1887 (4002).
Peirson *see* Bradshaw-Peirson.
Pelham : Henry, Duke of Newcastle, to take name of. St. J., 3 Dec., 1768 (D G 1946).
    see Thistlethwayte-Pelham
    ,, Thursby-Pelham.
Pelham-Clinton-Hope : Pelham-Clinton, H F. H. 7 April, 1887 (2252).
Pelham-Cressett : Pelham, H. 28 Aug., 1792 (661).

Pemberton : Butcher, E. R. 9 June, 1842 (1587).
   see Childe-Pemberton.
   ,, Childe.
   ,, Cludde.
   : Cocks, E. 10 June, 1802 (613).
     Cocks, S. 10 June, 1802 (613).
   : Goggs, R. G., of Blackheath, Kent. Times, d.p., 15 May, 1895.
   : Hodgson, H. W. 13 Oct., 1855 (4035).
   see Owen.
Pemberton-Barnes : Pemberton, W. 29 Nov., 1850 (3361)
Pemberton-Leigh : Pemberton, T. 10 March, 1843 (816)
Pembroke *see* Bence-Pembroke.
Pendarves : Wood, E. W. W. (a minor—on behalf of) W., 6 Feb., 1860 (D G. 213).
Pendarvis *see* Wynne-Pendarvis.
Pène *see* Payne.
Penfold *see* Wyatt.
   : Dearling, T., of Lingfield, Surrey. Times, 17 Dec., 1887.
Peniston-Bird : Bird, E. J., of Holly Lodge, Brook Green, Hammersmith, esq. Times, d.p., 12 Aug., 1886.
Penkivil *see* Tompsett.
Penn-Gaskell : Gaskell, P. 31 May, 1824 (949).
Pennant *see* Dawkins-Pennant.
   ,, Douglas-Pennant.
   : Pearson, P. P. 27 Oct., 1860 (3962).
Penney *see* Cowden-Cole
Pennington : Sparrow, T. S. 29 Nov., 1838 (2778).
   : Sparrow, J. J. H. S., of Willesboro', Kent (Rev.), M.A. Times, d p., 17 March, 1886.
   see Tetlow.
Penny *see* Greenwood-Penny.
  ,, Harwood.
Pennyman : Worsley, J. W. 28 April, 1853 (1226)
Penoyre *see* Baker-Stallard-Penoyre.
   ,, Brodbelt-Stallard-Penoyre.
   ,, Raymond-Stallard-Penoyre.
   ,, Stallard-Penoyre.
Penrose Green : Penrose, W., of Roundhay, Leeds. Times, 10 July, 1886.
Penson Harris : Penson, G. A., of Ascott-under-Wychwood, Oxford, yeoman. Times, d.p., 12 March, 1888.
Pentelow : Day, J. T., of Raunds, Northampton, miller. Times, d.p., 13 Dec., 1895.
Penyston : Partridge, E. T. 2 May, 1894 (2850).
   : Partridge, J. F. 29 Aug., 1873 (4095).

Peploe : Webb, D. P. 17 May, 1845 (1540)
    : Webb, J. B. 16 July, 1866 (4038).
Peppercorn *see* Lenwood
  ,, Harris.
Pepperell *see* Royal.
Perceval-Clark : Clark, P., of 9, Queen Anne's Gardens, Chiswick, esq., Capt. 9th Lancers. Times, d p, 16 June, 1885.
Perceval-Maxwell : Perceval, R. 2 Aug., 1839 (1624).
Percival *see* Hobgen.
    : Miller, C. 18 Aug., 1792 (635).
  see Passawer Percival
Perocchy : Croucher, E., of 23, Cranbourn Street, Middlesex, spinster. Times, d.p., 21 June, 1875.
Perry *see* De Courcy Perry.
Pepperrell : Sparhawk, A. P. 28 Feb., 1775 (11539).
Pereira . Tibbs, Rev. H. W., of Waterville Terrace, North Shields, co. Northumberland, V. of Bobbington. Times, d.p., 4 June, 1870.
Percy *see* Greatheed-Percy.
  ,, Heber-Percy.
Perfect *see* Dawson.
  ,, Hayward-Southby
Perkins *see* Hartland-Perkins
  ,, Vivian
  ,, Wolrige-Gordon.
Perkins-Wolrige *see* Gordon-Wolrige.
Perrins, Mary Anne Perrins . Barton, Mary Anne, of 13, St. George's Terrace, Hyde Park, Middlesex, widow. Times, d.p., 15 Feb , 1865
Perrivel *see* Jones-Perrivel.
Perry-Herrick . Herrick, W. 9 May, 1853 (1972).
Perry-Keene : Perry, W. T. K. 28 May, 1839 (1072).
Perry *see* Ogilvie
  ,, de Courcy Perry.
Perry Ayscough : Perry, Rev. G. B., Vicar of Brabourne, and Rector of Monks Horton, Kent. Times, d.p , 21 Dec., 1881.
Perry-Watlington : Perry, J. W. 10 April, 1849 (1205).
Peter *see* Thomas-Peter
Peter-Hoblyn : Peter, D 13 Sept., 1836 (1636)
    Peter, J. H 18 July, 1865 (3675).
Peterkin *see* Grant
Peters *see* Burton-Peters
  ,, Parsons-Peters.
  ,, Turton

Petre : Duff. 14 March, 1882 (1212)
: Varlo, J. 30 June, 1802 (719).
Pettit *see* Jelf-Pettit.
Pettiward : Bussell, R. J. 22 Jan., 1856 (237).
Peyton : Dashwood, H. 12th Geo. III., 1772.
Pfander *see* Swinborne.
Pheasant *see* Langdale-Moreton.
Phelps : Clifford, W. 18 Nov., 1891 (6647).
    see Martin
     ,, McDonnell.
Philip *see* Wilson-Philip.
Philipps *see* Allen-Philipps.
    : Fisher, C. E. G. and M. P. 29 July, 1876 (4374).
    : Grant, R. B. P. 10 Feb., 1824 (252).
    : Gwyther, J. H. A. 7 Feb., 1857 (537).
    : Lewis, J. and W. W., 31 Jan., 1845 (D.G. 114)
    : Lewis, J. 31 Jan., 1845 (395).
    : Lewis, W. 31 Jan., 1845 (395).
    : Lloyd, J. P. 1 June, 1824 (949).
    see Mansel.
     ,, Scourfield.
     ,, Walters-Philipps.
Philips *see* Scott.
Philipson *see* Dodds-Philipson.
Philipson-Stow : Stow, F. S. P. 28 Feb., 1891 (1266).
Phillimore : Stiff, W. P. 22 April, 1873 (2126).
Phillip, T. L. : Landale, T., of California, U.S.A. Times, d.p.,
    12 July, 1892.
Phillipps *see* Halliwell-Phillipps
      ,, March-Phillipps.
      : Plume, W. G., of 20, Fleming Street, Kingsland
          Road, Middlesex. Times, 3 Aug., 1871.
Phillipps-Flamank : Phillipps, W. 17 Feb., 1848 (816).
Phillips see Bannerman-Phillips.
    : Barnet, Sarah, of 46, Portman Square, Middlesex.
        Times, d.p., 4 March, 1875.
    see Church.
     ,, de Moro.
     ,, Faudel-Phillips
    · Halliwell, J. O. and H. E. M. 29 Feb., 1872 (1404).
    see Harmon
     ,, Mead.
     ,, Nicholson.
    Edw. : Phillips, M. E. C., of St. Mary Axe, wharfinger,
        and Lewisham. Times, 21 Aug., 1874.
    Alfred : Salaman, Abraham, of 57, Gower Street,
        Bedford Square, Middlesex, gent. Times, d.p.,
        18 Aug., 1862.

Phillips : Solomon, P. A., of Bedford Place, Russell Square, art student Times, d.p., 14 Nov , 1888.
   see Spencer-Phillips.
   : Winsloe, T. 17 Nov , 1798 (1083).
Phillips-Conn : Phillips, H. 18 July, 1894 (D G 837).
Phillips Jodrell : Phillips, T. J. 29 June, 1868 (3737).
Phillips-Treby . Phillips, P. W. 31 Jan , 1877 (1967).
Phillips-Wolley : Phillips, E. C. O. L. 7 July, 1876 (3890).
Phillipson *see* Burton-Phillipson.
   : Burton, R. 6th Geo. III., 1766.
   see Turner.
Phillpot *see* Philpott.
Philpott : Phillpot, E., of Bungay, Suffolk, merchant. Times, 2 Jan , 1893
Phipps - Heming, T. 2 Dec., 1851 (3453).
   : Heming, J. 11 June, 1850 (1700).
   . Hemming, J. 10 April, 1827 (962).
   see Peckham.
    ,, Peckham-Phipps.
    ,, Waller.
Phipson-Wybrants : Phipson, T. L. 29 March, 1877 (D.G. 235)
Physick *see* Vernon.
Pickard *see* Trenchard
Pickard-Cambridge : Pickard, G 19 May, 1848 (1941).
Pickering *see* Hodson.
Pickersgill-Cunliffe : Pickersgill, J. C. 6 March, 1867 (1596).
Pickford *see* Radcliffe.
Pickles *see* Tattersall.
   ,, Wilsden.
Pickles-Macaulay : Pickles, Joe, publisher's assistant, of 32, Cloudesley Street, Islington, London. Times, 18 July, 1866.
Pickop-Dutton : Pickop, F., of Trefnant, Denbigh, and of Blackburn, Lancs Times, d.p., 29 Nov., 1893.
Pickwick *see* Sainsbury
Picton : Beete, J P. 25 Oct., 1883 (5146).
   see Turberville.
   : Williams, J 2 June, 1840 (1342)
Pidcock-Henzell : Pidcock, H. H F. ,of Pinehurst, Farnborough, Hants, esq., late Capt. 19th Reg. Times, d p., 14 Dec , 1883
Piddington · Smith, J. G., of Sloane Street, Middlesex. Times, 28 April, 1900.
Pierce-Seaman : Pierce, B. C. 15 June, 1835 (1150).
Pierce *see* Seaman.
Piercy *see* Brown.

Pierssené : Fatt, H., late of Fenchurch Street, London, commsn
   agent, also of Lee, Kent. Times. d.p., 1 Nov., 1888
Pierrepont . Medows, C 20 Sept., 1788 (449).
Pige Leschallas : Pige, H., of Page Green, Tottenham, Midx,
   esq. Times, d.p., 9 March, 1874
Pigg *see* Brown.
   ,, Pegge.
   ,, Theobald.
Piggin Fowler · Piggin, J. H., of Langley Hall, Langley, Worces.,
   scholar of Trinity Coll, Oxford. Times, 19 May, 1884
Piggott *see* Royston-Piggott
Piggott-Royston . Piggott, G. W. 25 April, 1860 (1596)
Pigot *see* Hance-Pigot
Pigott · Cooke, S. F. 31 July, 1824 (1358).
   see Corbet.
   ,, Conant.
   : Foster, W. 6 July, 1805 (903)
   see Graham-Foster-Pigott
   ,, Jeaffreson
   ,, Smyth-Pigott.
Pigott-Stainsby-Conant · Pigott, Francis, of Heckfield Heath,
   Hants, and of Government House, I of Man, esq., Lieut.-
   Gov. of that Island; and Francis Paynton Pigott his son
   Times, 30 Dec., 1862
Pike-Scrivener · Pike, J. P. 9 April, 1839 (762).
Pilgrim : Ross, Mary A. E., spinster, of Bournemouth. Times,
   d p., 13 March, 1895.
Pilkington · Coombe, E. A. and M. E.; also Flynn, M. J. P. S.
               and E., all of Summerseat House, Southport,
               Lancs. Times, 29 March, 1882
         see Milborne-Swinnerton-Pilkington.
           ,, Windle-Pilkington.
Pill *see* Thomas.
Pillin · Manley, E. M., of 23, Clermont Terrace, Preston, nr.
   Brighton, Sussex, spinster. Times, d p, 26 Sept., 1891.
Pilling-Taylor : Pilling, M. 9 Nov., 1876 (6683).
Pim, Ed. H Bedford : Pim, Ed H., Lieut. in H.M. R.A.
   Times, d.p., 24 July, 1890
Pinchbeck *see* Pearson.
Pimbury *see* Wilkinson-Pimbury.
Pinckard : Coles, G. H. 29 May, 1893 (3570)
Pindar Lygon, Hon. J. R. 22 Oct., 1813 (2117).
       · Woodbridge, J. 6 Feb., 1790 (73).
Pine-Coffin : Pine, J. 20 March, 1797 (328).
Pinfold-Tate : Pinfold, Louisa 17 July, 1849 (2265)
Pinhorne *see* Stanley Pinhorne.
Pinkerton *see* Drummond

Pinniger *see* Cope.
Piozzi-Salusbury : Piozzi, J. S.   4 Dec., 1813 (2492)
Pipe *see* Wolferstan.
Piper *see* Harvey-Piper.
  „   Payne.
Pippard *see* Blundell.
Pirie *see* Logie-Pirie.
Pistor *see* Worthington.
Pitchford *see* Cornish.
Pitt : Ready, Rev. E. M., of Westerham, Kent. Times, d.p , 1 Dec., 1874.
   see Lawrence
Pitt-Lewis : Lewis, G.   17 June, 1876 (3615).
Pitt-Rivers *see* Fox-Pitt-Rivers
         : Beckford, Rt. Hon. W. H.   26 Nov., 1828 (2249).
Pittman *see* Coppin.
Pizzey *see* Boyman.
Plaistow-Trapaud : Plaistow, F.   18 June, 1803 (740).
Platt-Higgins : Higgins, E.   13 Dec , 1889 (7279).
         : Higgins, F.   13 Dec , 1889 (7279).
         : Higgins, W.   13 Dec., 1889 (7279).
Player-Frowd   Player, J., s. of the late Rev. E. Player, of Salisbury, nephew of the late Rev. E. Frowd, R. of Upper Clatford, Hants.   Times, 29 Feb., 1868.
Plenderleath *see* Christie.
Pleydell *see* Mansel-Pleydell.
Pleydell-Bouverie-Campbell : Pleydell-Bouverie, P. A., of Dunoon, Argyll, Scotland, and of Yately, Southampton, esq. Times, 6 Jan., 1869
Pleydell-Bouverie-Campbell-Wyndham : Pleydell-Bouverie-Campbell, P. A., of The Beeches, Winchester, esq.   Times, 29 May, 1890.
Plomer *see* Clarke.
Plumbe-Tempest : Plumbe, J.   1 June, 1824 (891).
Plume *see* Phillipps
Plumer-Ward : Ward, R.   16 July, 1828 (1456).
Plymley *see* Corbett.
Pobgee *see* Bennett
Pocklington *see* Domville
Pocklington-Coltman : Pocklington, R. and M. L.   8 May, 1876 (3040).
Pocklington-Senhouse : Pocklington, J.   27 Sept., 1842 (2634).
Podmore-Jones *see* Haden.
Poë *see* Bennett-Poë.
Poer, de la : Power, Frances, widow.   St. J., 14 May, D.C., 29 May, 1863 (D.G. 633 and 649)
Pole *see* Carew.

POR] *An Index to Changes of Name* 257

Pole *see* Chandos-Pole-Gell.
   „ Chandos-Pole.
   „ De la Pole.
   : Van Notten, C. 17 March, 1787 (129).
   see Van Notten-Pole.
Pole-Tylney-Long-Wellesley : Wellesley-Pole, W. 18 Jan., 1812 (129).
Pollard : Carter, J. 4th Geo. III., 1764.
   see Imrie.
Pollard-Urquhart . Pollard, W. 11 June, 24 June, 1847 (D.G. 791 and 802).
Polhill-Turner : Polhill, F. C. 21 Feb., 1853 (481).
Pollen *see* Boileau-Pollen.
Pollock *see* Montague-Pollock.
Pollok *see* Crawfurd-Pollok.
   „ Fergusson-Pollok.
Pomeroy : Mason, H. W. 19 Sept, 1789 (605).
   : Wakefield, R. 29 Aug., 1841 (2203).
   see Colley.
Pomeroy-Colley : Colley, Sir Geo P. 13 May, 1880 (D.G. 469).
Pomfret : Burra, W. P. 2 Oct., 1882 (4507).
Pomfret Melville : Pomfret, W., of Spedhurst, Kent, gent. Times, 14 Dec, 1886
Ponsonby . Brannagan, J, late of Dublin, now of London. Middlesex, gent. Times, d.p., 12 July, 1862.
   see Barker.
   : Fisher, J. 24 April, 1816 (769).
   see Talbot-Ponsonby.
Ponsonby-Fane : Ponsonby, S C. B. 5 Feb., 1875 (547).
Pont *see* Springett.
Pooke *see* Chamberlaine
Poole : Halsted, D. 13 July, 1782 (12312)
   see Lyde.
   „ Theobald
   · Tribe, B. F. 5th Geo. III., 1765.
Pooley *see* Martin Pooley.
Pooll : Langford, R. P. 12 June, 1871.
Poore : Dyke, E. 5 Dec, 1803 (1743).
Popham *see* Leyborne-Popham.
   „ White-Popham.
Popkin *see* Bassett.
Poppy *see* Darnley.
Porcelli-Cust : Porcelli, A. R. C 26 Dec, 1893 (82)
Porch Reeves, T P. 8 Dec., 1830 (2606)
Porcher *see* Powney.
   „ Powney-Porcher.
Porter : Archdall, J P. 29 May, 1876 (D.G. 337).
   see Boyd.

R

Porter   Carson, J.   6 Feb., 1808 (175)
   see De Hochepied.
   : Ellison-Macartney, T. S.   24 Sept., 1875 (D.G 589).
   see Macknish-Porter
   „   Macnish-Porter.
   · Tayler, H.   11 April, 1877 (2618)
   · Walsh, P P   19 Dec., 1783 (12502).
   see Ward-Porter.
Porter-Burrall . Burrall, G A. P.   16 Aug., 1886 (D.G 693).
Porter-Humphreys   Humphreys, J   22 Oct., 1819 (1871).
Porter Whiteside   Porter, J., formerly of Blackpool, now of Exeter, traveller.   Times, 18 April, 1876.
Portman-Dalton : Portman, S B   10 Dec., 1887 (7064).
Portugal *see* Edye.
Postlethwaite *see* Thom-Postlethwaite.
Potter *see* Conway.
   „   Eaton.
   „   Huggett.
   „   Neville
Potter Veltmann · Veltmann, L. H., of Wavertree, nr. Liverpool, gent   Times, 26 Dec., 1879, and 2 Jan., 1880.
Potts *see* Wardell-Potts.
Potts Bromley : Potts, F. E., of Powis Street, Woolwich, Kent Times, d p, 22 Sept., 1873.
Potts-Chatto : Potts, W. J.   27 July, 1864 (3828).
Poulett *see* Buncombe-Poulett-Scrope
   „   Thomson-Buncombe-Poulett.
Poulter : Sayer, E.   2 May, 1778 (11870)
Poussett *see* Courthope.
Povoleri, Arnaldo Girolamo . Matthews, Arnold Jerome, of Broadhurst Gardens, S. Hampstead, gent   Times, d p, 10 Oct., 1890.
Powel *see* Davies
   : Price, H Penry P., of Castle Madoc, Brecon, esq.   Times, 22 Sept., 1875
   : Price, H Powell, of Castle Madoc, Brecon, esq   Times, 22 Sept., 1875.
   · Roberts, A. A.   29th Geo III., 1789.
Powell *see* Campbell.
   : Fletcher, C.   10 May, 1806 (570)
   : Grant, P.   26 Aug., 1814 (1732)
   see Gwyn
   „   Hunt-Powell.
   „   Jeffreys-Powell
   : Kynaston, J.   11 Feb., 1797 (133).

Powell *see* Lloyd-Powell.
    Roberts, J. P. : estab. the assumption of name and arms.
        54th Geo. III., 1814
    : Roberts, J. P. 12 July, 1813 (1381).
    : Richards, W. 2nd Geo. III., 1762.
    see Sweetman-Powell.
    : Skyrme, W. H. P., junr., of Ross, Hereford, and Corpus
        Christi Coll., Cambridge, gent. Times, d.p., 28
        Sept., 1893.
Powell-Montgomery : Powell, H. B., of Wilverley Park, Lynd-
    hurst, Southampton, esq Times, d.p., 28 April, 1871.
Powell-Rodney : Rodney, W. 15 Feb., 1841 (400).
Powell-Williams : Williams, Rowland, of Beckenham, Kent.
    Times, 12 April, 1900.
Power *see* Mannock.
    : Mandeville, F. D.G., 12 Jan., 1814.
    : Newberry, T. 5 Sept., 1778 (11906).
    see Poer, de la.
Power-Mounteney : Power, C. W., of Katoomba, Chislehurst,
    Kent, clerk in Holy Orders Times, 26 Sept., 1894
Powles *see* Harrison-Powles.
Powlett (Duke of Cleveland) *see* Vane.
    : Orde, J. M. 12 Jan., 1795 (29).
    : Orde, Rt. Hon. T. 12 Jan., 1795 (29).
    : Vane, Hon. W. J. F. 20 April, 1813 (773).
    : Vane, (Duke of Cleveland). 18 Nov., 1864 (5797).
    see Visconti Powlett.
    ,,   William Powlett.
Powlett-Wrighte : Benyon. 18 Aug., 1814 (1855).
    see Benyon-de Beauvoir.
Pownall *see* Beaty-Pownall.
Powney-Porcher : Powney, C. du P. P. 22 June, 1894 (3735).
Powney : Powney-Porcher, C. du P. P. 15 Nov., 1894 (7045).
    Thompson, E. P. 15 March, 1876 (2154).
Powys : Feilding, H. W. 26 July, 1832 (1810).
    see Fox-Powys
    ,,   Hatsell-Powys.
Powys-Keck : Powys, H. L. 12 Feb., 1861 (651).
Powys-Lybbe : Powys, W. R. L., of Wallingford, Berks, formerly
    of Boulogne, France, now at Tunbridge Wells,
    Kent, esq Times, d.p., 24 July, 1882
    : Powys, P. L. 18 Feb., 1863 (1298)
Poyer : Griffith, junr., J. P. 27 May, 1834 (966).
Poynder *see* Dickson-Poynder
Praed *see* Tyringham.
Prance, J. C. : Pranz, J. C. H. J. Times, 23 March, 1894.

Pranz *see* Prance.
Pratt *see* de Montmorency.
,, Tynte.
Prattenton *see* Onley-Prattenton.
Preedy *see* Cotes-Preedy.
Preller *see* Dukiche-Preller.
Prescott-Davies : Davies, N., of 12, Chalcot Gardens, Haverstock Hill, Middlesex, artist   Times, d p., 14 Nov., 1891.
Prescott-Decie : Decie, R. and A   1866.
Prescott-Hewett : Hewett, Agnes S., of Chestnut Lodge, Horsham, Sussex, spinster. Times, d p., 6 Aug., 1891.
Prescott-Roberts : Roberts, H P., of 11 Haven Green, Ealing, W. Times, 29 Dec., 1891.
: Roberts, H., of 11, Haven Green, Ealing, W. Times, 1 Jan., 1892.
Prescott-Westcarr : Prescott, C. W.   10 Apr., 1882 (2075).
Preston *see* Agar.
,, Houston-Boswall-Preston.
: Houston-Boswell, W. 7 April, 1883 (1961).
: Hulton, T. 22 May, 1805 (683).
see Jermy.
,, Richard-Preston.
Preston-Holt · Preston, W. 10 Nov., 1840 (2481).
Preston-Thomas : Thomas, H. P., of Broomfield, Weybridge, and of Whitehall. Times, 28 Sept., 1888.
Pretor · Gill, S   7 April, 1813 (699).
Pretyman *see* Tomline.
Previté-Orton : Previté, Rev. W., of St. John's Coll., Camb., M.A., of Little Wratting, Suffolk. 18 Oct., 1870
Prevost *see* Mackay
Price Blackwood, J. 2 Aug., 28 Aug., 1847 (D.G. 962 & 970).
see Clarke.
,, Dent-Price
,, Gilbert.
,, Fountain.
,, Grove.
: Gurden, B. 29 April, 1808 (601).
. Higginbotham, J. 6 March, 1781 (12167).
see Jordan
,, Lloyd.
,, Pantry-Price
,, Powel
T. Spiers : Price, T., of 89, Holland Road, Brixton, Surrey. Times, 14 April, 1876.
see Rugge-Price.
: Watkin, R. T. 26 Aug., 1777 (1777).
Price-Davies : Price, L. R. (children). 7 Jan., 1880 (1905).

Price-Fothergill : Price, Dame I. 3 Aug., 1895 (4551).
Prichard *see* Croft.
Prigg *see* Trigg.
Pringle *see* Hughes.
Prinn *see* Hunt-Prinn.
      : Prowse, G. B. 20 Oct , 1825 (2046)
      : Russell, J E. 22 Feb , 1841 (473)
Prinsep *see* Leyett-Prinsep.
Prior *see* Alexander-Prior.
    ,, Wandesforde.
    ,, William-Prior-Johnson.
Prior-Johnson Richardson, W. 14 April, 1781 (12178).
Prior-Wandesforde : Prior, R. H. 16 June, 1894 (D.G 713).
Pritchard *see* Burdett.
    ,, Gilbertson-Pritchard.
    ,, Parry
    ,, Sergison.
Probyn *see* Nevins.
Probyn-Williams . Williams, R J, A C., and H. E , all of 9, Woburn Square, London. Times, d p., 31 Oct., 1893.
Procter *see* Atkinson.
      : Dealtry, C. 22 March, 1847 (1144)
Proctor : Coleman, E B. 28 Oct., 1878 (5937).
    see Cope Proctor.
    ,, Waller
Proctor-Beauchamp : Beauchamp-Proctor, T. W. B 9 July, 1852 (1974).
Prohowsky *see* Newman.
Proschwitzky-Freyburg Proschwitzky, F., of West Brighton, Sussex, artist. Times, d p , 25 March, 1891.
Prosser *see* Wegg-Prosser.
Protheroe *see* Davis-Protheroe.
      : Jones, E. 22 Nov , 1813 (2384).
      : Schow, W. G. B. 1 June, 1819 (1177).
Protheroe Smith : Smith, H. B , Lieut. Times, d.p., 22 March, 1893.
Prowse *see* Prinn.
Prowting-Roberts : Roberts, W., of 14, Powis Square, Kensington Park, W , and The Depot, Winchester, Lieut. 2nd Batt Hants. Times, d.p., 9 July, 1886.
Pryce : Bruce. J B 4 Sept., 1837 (2344).
Pryce-Jones : Jones, P., of Dolcrw, Montgomerys , Kt Times, d.p., 16 July, 1887
Pryce Juer : Pryce, R , of Park Road, Battersea, gent. Times, d p , 14 June, 1881.
Pryer *see* Speed-Pryer
Pryse : Loveden, C. 28 July, 1863 (3995).

Pryse : Loveden, P. W., 29 July, 1863 (D G. 914).
: Loveden, P 26 March, 1798 (246)
see Loveden.
John Pugh Vaughan : Pryse, John Pugh, of Bwlchbychan Cardigan, esq. Times, d.p., 26 Jan., 1866
see Rice-Vaughan-Pryse.
,, Vaughan-Pryse-Rice.
Pryse-Rice *see* Vaughan-Pryse-Rice
Puddicombe : Austen, S. W. 24 Sept., 1827 (2097).
Pudsey *see* Aston-Pudsey.
: Aston, J. 4 March, 1847 (956)
: Aston, T. P. 4 May, 1807 (636)
Pugh *see* Bockett-Pugh.
: Evans, L. P. 26 May, 1868 (3168)
see Gordon-Pugh.
,, Morris Pugh.
Pugh-Johnson : Johnson, M. A., and daughters. 22 Feb., 1879 (1791)
Pugh-Lovell : Lovell, M. J. 17 June, 1882 (2694).
Pullbrook *see* Dawson.
Puller *see* Giles-Puller.
Pullman-Baker : Pullman, G. A., of 4, The Terrace, Albion Road, Stoke Newington, Middlesex, gent. Times, 19 Feb., 1869
Pulteney : Fawcett, J 9 Aug., 1813 (1558).
: Murray, Sir J. 22 July, 1794 (759)
Punch *see* Wadeson
Purcell *see* Fitzgerald
,, Gilpin.
Purcell-Llewellin : Purcell, R. L., M.A., of Exeter College, Oxford. Times, d.p., 27 June, 1871.
Purefoy *see* Bagwell-Purefoy.
,, Jervoise.
Purefoy-Jervoise : Purefoy, G. 17 July, 1792 (553 and 562).
Purkis : Webb, C., of Brighton, Sussex, servant Times, 28 July, 1863
Purnell : Cooper, P. B. 2 March, 1805 (276).
: Hooper, R. J. 21 Aug., 1826 (2064)
: Jones, T. 14th Geo. III., 1774
Pursall *see* Seymour.
Purves-Hume-Campbell of Marchmach : Purves, Sir William Lyon, Vol. II., 10 May, 1812
Purvis *see* Atkinson.
: Barker, C. D. 7 April, 1792 (220).
: Barker, T. P. 7 April, 1789 (210).
see Eyre
,, Kennedy-Purvis.

Pusey-Keith : Pusey, W. A., of Croydon, Surrey, Prof. of Music Times, d p, 28 April, 1886
Puxley Lavallin *see* Lavallin Puxley.
Pybus *see* Rigg
Pybus-Sellon   Sellon, J. S., of 78, Hatton Garden, Middlesex, and The Hall, Sydenham, Kent, esq.   d p, 21 and 26 March, 1883
Pyddoke : Whateley, E   10 Feb , 1847 (565).
Pye : Alington, H.   7 July, 1828 (1829).
　　 : Woolcock, J. P   21 July, 1846 (2675)
Pye-Benet · Pye, W. B   21 Aug , 1802 (899)
Pyemont · Smith, J.   28 Jan , 1853 (263)
　　 : Smith, Samuel, D D , of University College, Durham, V of Whitwick, Leicester   Times, 30 Dec , 1868
Pyke-Nott   Pyke, M.   1 Sept., 1863 (4285)
Pym *see* Reading.
Pyne *see* Ludby.
Pytches *see* Revett.

Q

Quaintrell : Essex, H Q., of 2, Albion Terrace, Somerset Road, Tottenham, builder   Times, d p., 16 May, 1885
Quarrill *see* Greene.
Quiller-Couch : Couch, M , of 21, St Margaret's Road, Oxford, widow   Times, d p., 25 Dec., 1888
Quick *see* Nutcombe
Quilter : Rumball, J.   18th Geo. III , 1778
Quin *see* Wyndham-Quin.
　　 : Taylor, Lord G.   D.G., 10 Feb., 1812

R

Radcliffe *see* Fazakerley
　　 : Pickford, J   14 Jan , 1796 (65)
Radcliffe-Smith   Smith, R. W., of Normanton Avenue, Sefton Park, Liverpool   Times, 20 March, 1900.

Radford : Bottom, H. R., formerly of Derby, accountant clerk, now of the Midland Grand Hotel, Middlesex, cashier. d p., 15 Feb., 1879
: Brown, G. W., of 145, Tottenham Court Road, and formerly of Maidenhead, Berks, clerk. Times, d.p., 5 Feb., 1884.
  see Moor-Radford.
  ,, Tempest Radford.
Radford-Norcop : Radford, A. W. 8 April, 1862 (1970).
Rae see Bruce Rae.
  ,, Harvey.
  ,, Mure.
Rae-Arnot : Rae, Hy., of Auchermuchty, Scotland, LL.D. Times, 9 May, 1895.
Rae-Wilson : Rae, W. 16 Aug., 1806 (1235).
  of Kelvinbank : Wilson, W. Lyon, Vol II., 6 March, 1807.
Raeburn see Macbeth-Raeburn.
Rafferty see Houghton.
Raiemond : Webb, G., of 60, Dalberg Road, Brixton, Surrey. Times, d.p., 25 June, 1888.
Raincock see Fleming.
Raines : Raines-Baines, R. R., merchant, and H. R. Baines, of Kingston-upon-Hull, gent., H. R. Baines, jun., A. R. Baines, R. R. Baines, C. R. Baines, and I. R. Baines. Times, 17 July, 1869.
Rainford : Tibbitts, F. A., of 41, Lansdowne Crescent, Notting Hill, London, gent. Times, d.p., 15 Jan., 1892.
Ralston-Patrick of Roughwood : Patrick, William. Lyon, Vol. VI., 12 June, 1861.
Ramey see Home-Ramey.
Ramsay : Burnett, A. 4 March, 1806 (282).
  of Balmain : Burnett, Alexr. Lyon, Vol. II., 31 March, 1805.
  see Chapman.
  : Crawford, G., of Newport, Mon. Times, d.p., 27 Nov., 1895.
Ramsay-Fairfax of Maxton : Fairfax, Sir Wm. George Herbert Taylor, Bt. Lyon, Vol X., 2 March, 1877.
Ramsay-Gibson-Maitland of Cliftonhall and Barnton : Gibson-Maitland, Sir Alex. Chas., Bt. Lyon, Vol. VII., 6 July, 1866.
Ramsay-Karr : Ramsay, D. 30 Dec., 1794 (1209).
Ramsey-Kent : Kent, P. R., of Claremont Lodge, Brixton, Surrey, esq. Times, d.p., 1 Sept., 1887.
Ramsay-L'Amy of Dunkenny : Ramsay L'Amy, John. Lyon, Vol. VI., 19 March, 1864.

Ramsbottom-Isherwood Ramsbottom, J R, of Maidstone, Kent, esq, Capt. 97th Foot Times, d p., 14 Jan, 1871.
· Ramsbottom, A F, a lieut. 23rd Foot Times, d p., 14 Jan., 1871.
Ramsden *see* Fletcher
Rand : Cock, E. 17 Dec, 1812 (2523).
: Hills, E. 6 Aug, 1791 (449 and 457).
Randall *see* Bruxner-Randall
,, Gurney-Randall
Randolph *see* Hingeston-Randolph.
Randolph-Symmons Symmons, F R, of Colchester, Essex, solicitor. Times, d p., 2 July, 1891.
Raper-Hunton : Raper, J 16 April, 1812 (757).
Rapier *see* Lamplugh-Rapier
Rastrick *see* Hooper-Rastrick
Ratcliff-Gaylard Gaylard, J R, of The Ferns, New Shildon, Durham, phys and surg. Times, d p., 20 Dec., 1889.
Ratcliffe *see* Delmé-Ratcliffe
Ravizzotti *see* Nesbitt
Rawdon *see* Green-Emmott-Rawdon.
,, Hastings.
Rawlence : Teasdale, M 23 March, 1793 (232).
Rawling *see* Maddison.
Rawlings *see* Doo-Rawlings
Rawlins Jay, Annie, of Fairview House, Upton-cum-Chalvey, Bucks Times, d p, 18 July, 1893
see Mortlock.
,, Wilberforce.
Rawlinson *see* Lindow
Raworth Boyd, J. T., of Leicester, sewing cotton manufacturer Times, d p., 3 Dec., 1879.
Rawson : Adams, Sir W 9 March, 1825 (459).
see Trafford-Rawson.
Rawson-Ackroyd Rawson, J W 5 Nov, 1875 (5452)
Ray Wheeler, H. R. 4 June, 1864 (2977).
Raymond *see* Barker.
: Breach, T. 12 Nov., 1808 (1519)
see Hadsley.
,, Symons.
: Syndercombe, G 11 Sep., 1804 (1122).
Raymond-Stallard-Penoyre Raymond, Rev. W. F , of The Moor, Herefords., and of Cheltenham, Glos. Times, d p, 11 June, 1886.
Rayne : Allen, W. T 21 July, 1807 (974).
Rayner *see* Burton.

Raynsford *see* Edwards.
,, Sheldon.
Razzano-Romano · Romano, G., of Westbourne Park, Middlesex, prof. of mus and singing. Times, 27 Aug, 1888
Read *see* Calverly-Rudston.
,, Crewe-Read.
,, Revell
,, Rudston-Read
Reade *see* Highton-Reade.
,, Rutherford-Reade.
: Wakefield, J. 20 July, 1868 (4117)
Reading Hort, K J 10 Sept, 1807 (1279)
· Packe, K J 3rd Geo IV., 1822
see Packe-Reading
. Pym, C. 6 April, 1870 (2540)
Ready *see* Pitt.
Reaston-Rodes : Reaston, C H. 20 April, 1825 (897)
Rebow *see* Gurdon.
,, Martin-Rebow.
,, Ormsby-Rebow.
,, Slater-Rebow.
Rede : Cooper, R. R. 17 Sept., 1822 (1579)
Redfern · Needham, M., of Bank House, Crich, Derby, spinster. Times, d.p., 11 Dec, 1882.
Redfern Russell · Redfern, F., of Northwood, I.W., trade merchant Times, d.p, 18 Sept., 1883
· Redfern, J. and S W, both of Berkeley Sq, Middlesex, and of Forest Hill, Kent, trade merchants. Times, d p, 11 June, 1883
Redman-Thompson . Redman, H. 10 Jan., 1801 (39).
Reed *see* German Reed
,, Campbell-Reed
,, Verelst
Rees : Davies, E W., of South Norwood, Surrey, formerly of Croydon, mechan. engineer. Times, d.p, 13 March, 1879.
see Ruutz-Rees.
Rees-Mogg . Rees, J 14 Nov., 1806 (354).
Rees-Williams : Williams, J J., of 58, Sutherland Avenue, Maida Hill, esq Times, d.p., 8 March, 1888
Reeve *see* Brooke.
: Goddard, C. 26 Jan., 1830 (217)
Griffith ap *see* Griffith-Apsley.
Reeve-de la Pole · De la Pole, J G. 4 Dec, 1838 (2820).
Reeve-King . Reeve, N H 29 July, 1896 (5140)
Reeve-Tucker : Tucker, W R., of Bronala Lodge, Ramsgate, Kent, gent. Times, d.p., 6 Oct., 1883.

Reeves *see* Porch
Reid *see* Baillie.
   „ Caldecot
   „ Fenwick.
   „ Forsdyke
Reid-Cuddon : Reid, J. E. 22 Nov., 1893 (6985)
Reid-Seton of Oxmantownhall : Reid, Ellen Elizbeth Lyon, Vol. VII., 9 Oct., 1866
Reilly *see* Nugent
Relph *see* Greenhow-Relph.
Rendall · Holden, F. S. and R. F. 9 May, 1877 (3214).
Render *see* Wakefield-Render.
Renn Stansfield : Renn, H. W., of 67, High Street, Peckham, Surrey, stationer, &c Times, d.p., 21 Jan., 1873.
Rennie *see* Lucas-Rennie.
Renny *see* Legh.
Renny-Tailyour of Borrowfield : Renny, T. 16 Nov., 1849 (3472).
Renton *see* Lindsey-Renton.
Repington *see* A'Court-Repington.
           „ Ashe-a'Court
Repinder *see* Bradshaw-Peirson.
Restell *see* Taylor-Restell.
Reveley *see* Jelf-Reveley.
Revell · Read, H 10 March, 1809 (308)
Revett : Pytches, J 4 April, 1820 (1379)
Rewse *see* Smith-Rewse
Reynard Cookson : Reynard, G. H. and A. S. 30 Nov., 1864 (6545).
Reynardson *see* Birch-Reynardson
Reynell-Pack : Pack, A. J. 13 Jan., 1857 (173)
Reynell-Upham : Jones, W
Reyner *see* Brooksbank.
       „ Cosens.
Reynolds *see* Lucas
        „ Reynolds Reynolds
        · Young, R. D.G., 19 July, 1808.
Reynolds Reynolds : Reynolds, J. J., of High Park, Devons., esq. Times, d.p., 23 Nov., 1877.
Rhiner-Waring : Wehrhangen, D. H., of 32, London Wall, London, and of 72, South Hill Park, Hampstead, underclothing manufacr. Times, d.p., 24 June, 1892
Rhodes : Cook, A. R. 26 Dec., 1814 (22).
   see Darwin
   „ Empson Rhodes
Ricarde-Seaver : Ricarde, F. I. 28 April, 1881 (2495)

Rice : De Cardonnel, Rt. H. G. T. (Baron Dynevor). 4 Feb.,
    (1816) (336).
    see De Cardonnel.
    ,, Vaughan-Pryse-Rice.
    ,, Watkins
Rice-Trevor : Rice, Hon. G R. 2 Nov, 1824 (1801).
Rice-Vaughan-Pryse *see* Vaughan-Pryse-Rice.
    : Vaughan-Pryse, J. C. P. 26 July, 1887
        (4134).
Rice-Wiggin : Wiggin, E. H. R., formerly of Gloster, now of
    Chancery Lane, Lond., barrister. Times, 22 Feb., 1873.
Rich : Bostock, C. 11 June, 1791 (337).
    : Milnes, J 17 Aug., 1802 (898).
    : Milnes, R. 13 Jan., 1803 (114).
    see Milnes.
    Williams, R 21 Jan., 1786 (21).
Richard *see* Bonaparte.
    ,, Yeldham-Richard.
Richard-Preston : Preston, C. 1 July, 1813 (1313).
Richards *see* Bennet.
    ,, Clavell.
    ,, Edwards
    ,, Garner-Richards.
    ,, Mackenzie-Richards.
    ,, Powell.
    : Wilmsdoff, J. L. G. E. R. D. G., 8 May, 1802
    see Yeates.
Richards-Cumins : Richards, J. C., nav. lieut., R.N. Times, 7
    June, 1871.
Richardson *see* Cornfoot
    ,, Currer.
    : Green, F R, of Upton St Leonards, Glos, gent
        Times, d p., 21 Jan., 1885.
    see Johnson.
    ,, Massy-Richardson.
    ,, Morgan-Richardson.
    ,, Payne
    ,, Prior-Johnson.
    ,, Saunders.
    ,, Stuart-Richardson.
    ,, Whelpdale
    ,, William-Prior-Johnson
Richardson-Allsup : Richardson, W., of Aston-upon-Ribble,
    Lancs, and of Ribble Mills, secretary. Times, 18 Jan,
    1881.
Richardson-Bunbury : Richardson, J. M. 20 April, 1822 (734).

Richardson-Eyre : Hodges, J. (Rev.), of St. John's Wood, Middlesex. Times, d.p., 7 May, 1888.
Richardson-Gardner : Richardson, R. and M. 6 May, 1865 (2496)
Richmond : Gardiner, J., and Jane his wife. 19 July, 1845 (2224)
Richmond-Parry : Parry, E. S., of Thornclyffe, Wandsworth Times, d p., 4 Feb., 1887.
Richmund-Gale-Braddyll : Gale-Braddyll, T. 18 Oct, 1819 (1852).
Rickard *see* De Legh
Rickards *see* Mynors.
Ricketts *see* Aubrey.
   ,, Jervis
   ,, Tempest.
: Wilkinson, G. L. 21 March, 1865 (1614).
see Wilkinson.
Rickman : Levi, S. P. 2 Dec., 1823 (108).
Riddell *see* Buchanan.
   ,, Carre-Riddell.
Riddell-Carre : Riddell, Captn. Robert. Lyon, Vol. III., 31 Jan., 1828
Rideal-Lock : Lock, G., of 17, Worcester Terrace, Oxford, gent, and E. H. his wife. Times, 5 Sept, 1879.
Ridge Jones *see* Jones.
Ridler Rowe : Ridler, W. R. R., of Stogursey, Somerset, gent. Times, 17 Feb, 1876.
Ridley-Colborne : Ridley, N. W. 21 June, 1803 (740).
Ridsdale *see* Stoveld.
Rigby-Collins : Rigby, C. 29 Aug., 1810 (1326).
Rigby : Hale, F. 1 July, 1788 (313).
Rigbye : Baldwin, J. 2 Aug., 1787 (361).
   : Baldwin, R. 4 June, 1796 (538).
Rigg *see* Chulow.
: Pybus, W. H., of Patrick Brompton, Yorks, gent Times, d.p., 21 June, 1876.
Rigge *see* Grayrigge.
Riggs-Miller : Ryan, T. J. 15 April, 1889 (D.G. 417).
Riley-Smith : Riley, F., of Tadcaster, York, brewer. Times, d.p., 3 Feb., 1887.
   : Riley, H. H., of Toulston Lodge, nr. Tadcaster, York, brewer Times, d p., 3 Feb., 1887.
Rimington-Wilson : Rimington, S. 24 July, 1840 (1759).
Ringrose : Voase, R. T. R., of Anlaby House, E. Riding, Yorks., esq. Times, 14 Feb., 1885.
see Voase.

Ringrose-Ion . Ion, J. W., of Bury St. Edmunds, Suffolk, esq
    Times, 14 Oct , 1882.
Ringrose-Voase : Ringrose, W. R., of Chilworth Tower, Hants,
    esq. Times, d.p., 27 April, 1885.
Rippon *see* Dent.
    : Urwin, C. S.   4 Jan , 1884 (532).
Risdon *see* Elliot Risdon.
Rissowe *see* Sharpe.
Ritchie *see* Barclay
Rivers *see* Fox-Pitt-Rivers.
    ,, de Carrara-Rivers.
    ,, Gay.
    ,, Nunn-Rivers
    ,, Pitt-Rivers.
Riversdale *see* Alcock-Stawell-Riversdale.
Rivett *see* Carnac.
Rivington-Harmar : Rivington, H. J.   5 Sept., 1892 (5153).
Rix Spelman : Rix, C. C., of St. Giles St., Norwich, auctioneer.
    Times, 7 Feb., 1874.
Rix-Wells   Rix, G , of Park House, Wallingford, Berks. Times,
    d.p., 15 Sept., 1887.
Robartes *see* Agar-Robartes.
Roberts *see* Armour.
    ,, Austen.
    : Atkin, J R.   23 Dec., 1882 (85).
    see Counsell-Roberts.
    : Cramer, J.   9 Oct., 1801 (1227)
    see Dale-Roberts.
    ,, Gay Roberts
    ,, Moorsom-Roberts.
    ,, Powel
    ,, Powell.
    ,, Prescott-Roberts.
    ,, Prowting-Roberts.
    Hugh Leslie   Roberts Hugh Lloyd, of Plymouth Grove,
        Manchester, M.B., M.C.   Times, d.p , 28
        March, 1889.
    see Stoakes.
    ,, Crompton-Roberts.
Roberts-Dudley : Roberts, F. J. and A.   18 Jan., 1870 (477).
Roberts-Gawen : Roberts, C. G. W., 1 Feb., 1851 (D G. 97)
    : Borough, C. G.   13 May, 1875 (2682).
Robert-Crowder : Dickinson, W. I.   4 April, 1842 (1017)
Robertson *see* Askew-Robertson
    ,, Eustace.
    ,, Forbes-Robertson.
    ,, Grant.

Robertson : Majoribanks, D. 26 Sept., 1834 (1736, see 1751).
    see Murray.
    : Robinson, H. C., of Bishopsgate Street, London, merchant. Times, d.p., 18 Feb., 1873.
    see Souter-Robertson.
    ,, Winton-Robertson.
Robertson-Barclay : Robertson, J. 19 Oct., 1799 (1067).
Robertson Chaplin : Chaplin Robertson, G., of Murlingden, Forfar, N.B., esq. Times, d.p., 23 June, 1880.
    Chaplin Robertson, T., of Murlingden, Forfar, N.B., Capt. Times, d p, 23 June, 1880.
Robertson Grant *see* Grant.
Robertson Macdonald : Robertson, D., of 41, Lansdowne Road, Bayswater, retired Rear-Admiral. Times. d p., 25 Oct., 1876.
Robertson-Ross : Robertson, P. 10 Dec, 1864.
Robertson-Shersby, jun : Robertson, R. H. S. 7 April, 1883 (2024).
    : Robertson, T. H. S. 7 April, 1883 (2024).
Robertson-Souter *see* Souter-Robertson.
Robertson-Walker : Robertson, J, of Gilgarran, Cumberland, etc., esq Times, d p, 21 June, 1893.
    : Robertson, J 3 Sept., 1824 (1478).
Robertson-Williamson of Balgray : Williamson, David. Lyon, Vol. II., 7 Sept., 1814.
Robinson *see* Adams-Robinson.
    : C. W., to con. name (late Jeaffreson, formerly Pigott). 28 Aug., 1857 (2923).
    see Brown.
    ,, Burton.
    ,, Cave-Orme.
    ,, Fowler.
    : Freind, J. 30 Nov, 1793 (1061).
    : Grey, W. R. 22 Sept, 1838 (2092)
    see Holland-Robinson.
    ,, Holt
    ,, Lowten.
    ,, Montagu.
    ,, Newton-Robinson.
    ,, Norcliffe.
    ,, Northland.
    ,, Nowell.
    ,, Robertson.
    F Cayley : Robinson, F., of Colville Sq., Bayswater, and Wool Exchange, London, merchant Times, d p., 30 Sept., 1881.

Robinson *see* Vyvyan-Robinson.
    „ Vyvyan.
    : Watson, R. R. 25 Sept., 1798 (907).
Robson *see* Bateman-Robson.
    „ Bell.
    „ Brooke.
    „ Dunn.
    „ Hutchinson.
Robson-Burrows : Burrows, D. H. W., of Long Stratton, Norfolk, undergrad., Cambs. Times, d.p., 18 Dec., 1888.
Roby *see* Burgin.
Roby-Burgin : Roby, W. 7 March, 1851 (704).
Roche : O'Shea, C. 28 Sept., 1830 (2049).
    : O'Shea, M. 28 Sept., 1830 (2049).
Rochester : Meggison, T. 9 Nov., 1848 (4021).
Rochfort-Boyd : Boyd, Geo. Augustus. 16 Nov., 25 Nov., 1867 (D.G. 1445 and 1478).
    see Boyd-Rochfort.
Rockliffe : Lunn, W. C. 13 June, 1870 (3001).
Rockliff-Lubé : Rockliff, Wm. St. J., 31 July, D.C., 14 Aug., 1862 (D.G. 947 and 961).
Rockliffe *see* Wayne.
Rodbard : Bean, M. 7 & 8 Vict. c. 43.
    : Butcher, J. 33rd Geo. III, 1793.
    : Butcher, W. 51st Geo. III., 1811.
    : Whitley, E. 7 & 8 Vict. c. 43.
Roddam : Falder, R. J. 2 March, 1865 (1448).
    : Stanhope, W. S. 20 March, 1818 (696).
Rodes *see* Reaston-Rodes.
Rodger-Cunliffe : Rodger, W. W. 19 Nov., 1887 (6225).
Rodney *see* Powell-Rodney.
Rodney-Harley : Rodney, T. J. 4 Nov., 1806 (294).
Roe *see* Henderson-Roe.
    „ Lock-Roe.
    „ Turner-Roe.
Roe-Lock · Roe T. 18 Jan., 1834 (122).
Roebuck : Taylor, J. T., of Stocksbridge, near Sheffield, York, mechanic. d.p., 7 Jan., 1884.
Roed *see* Campbell Reed.
Roeper : Hermine, T., of 2, Trinity Street, Cambs., spinster. Times, d.p., 8 April, 1884.
Rogers *see* Coxwell-Rogers.
    „ Davis-Rogers.
    „ Gandy.
    „ St. Clair-Rogers.

Rogers-Harrison, Daniel Charles : Lott, Valentine. 5 May, 1821 (978).
Rogers-Tillstone . Rogers, B. T. 23 Nov., 1868 (6705)
Rogerman *see* Chambers.
Rogerson *see* Husenbeth
Rohrweger *see* Campbell-M'Laren
Rokewode *see* Darell-Rokewode
    ,, Gage-Rokewode.
Rokewode-Gage : Gage, Sir E. 6 March, 1867 (1725)
    Gage, Sir T 10 Aug., 1843 (2703)
Rolfe *see* Boggis-Rolfe
  ,, Neville-Rolfe
Rolfes *see* Anichini-Rolfes
Roling Hales, W G N, now of Florence, Italy, artist, Br subject, formerly of Gt. Yarmouth. Eng Times, d p, 16 Nov., 1882
Roll *see* Winfield-Roll
Rolle . Trefusis, M G K. 7 Nov. 1851 (2894)
    Walter, D. 21 July, 1781 (12208)
Romaine *see* de St. Romaine
  ,, Govett-Romaine
Romano *see* Razzano-Romano
Ronald Taylor . Taylor, N of Turnberry and St Faiths, formerly of Belmont, N.B., Commissary in H.M. Control Depnt Times, 12 June, 1875
Roney-Dougal · Roney, R. 12 June, 1871 (2847)
Rooke Worrall, H 8 Aug, 1840 (1904).
Rookwood Gage, R 12 April, 1799 (358)
Roope Harris, R 15 Oct., 1771 (11187)
Roos-Keppel . Roos, G O, of Montford House, Sunbury-on-Thames, Lieut Times, d p., 6 Oct., 1890
Roper *see* Curzon
  ,, Head
  ,, Trevor-Roper.
Roper-Caldbeck · Roper, W C, of Moyle Park, Glendalkin, Dublin, esq. Times, d p, 8 May, 1880
Roper-Curzon : Curzon, H. F. 22 June, 1813 (1313)
Roquette *see* Deloraine-Roquette-Palmer-Palmer
Roquette-Palmer-Palmer . Palmer, J, of the Oxford and Cambridge University Club, Pall Mall, Middlesex, and of Clifton, Bristol, M A. d p., 12 Nov., 1878
Rorke *see* O'Rorke
Rose Holden, W L 25th Geo III, 1785
  see Smith-Rose.
Rose-Innes of Netherton . Rose, Thos Gilzean Lyon, Vol XIV., 25 Feb., 1897.
Rose-Swindell . Rose, J 5 July. 1819 (1177)

Rosedale Rosenthall, A. L., of 158, Queen Victoria Street, London, and of Forest Hill, Kent. paper merchant. Times, d p , 18 Dec., 1892
Rosenthall *see* Rosedale
Ross *see* Cockburn-Ross
  ,, Farquharson
  : Gray, A 11 April, 1786 (157).
  : Hicks, J. C , Capt. H M. 2nd Dragoons, now stationed at Cahir, Tipperary, Ireland. Times, d p , 17 July, 1869
  see Lockhart-Ross.
  ,, Pilgrim
  ,, Robertson-Ross
Roston-Nash Roston, A. S 15 April, 1831 (740).
Rothbury : Cohen, E. S. and R , of 302, Amhurst Road. Stoke Newington, and W., of Denman Road, Peckham Times, d p , 14 Dec , 1896
Rothery *see* Hume-Rothery
Rothwell *see* FitzHerbert
  : Garlick, J., of Colchester, Essex Times, 12 June. 1900.
Roundell · Currer, D. R 21 Oct., 1851 (2778)
  see Currer
Round-Turner : Round, H L. 8 Nov , 1871 (4713).
Rouse-Boughton-Knight · Rouse-Boughton, A. J 28 Jan , 1857 (472)
Routh : Tebb, S. A , of Edmonton, spinster. Times, d p , 28 April, 1882
Rousselet-Whitefoord : Rousselet, J 29 April, 1797 (435)
Row *see* Payne
  ,, Thomas-Row
Rowan-Legg : Rowan, Wm 21 June, 4 July, 1864 (D G 813 and 833)
  : Rowan, E. L 26 May, 12 June, 1874 (D G 357)
Rowbotham Kinsey, J 27 March, 1852 (954)
Rowden Shittler, J R. 16 Dec , 1884 (5919)
Rowe · Fisher, E. R., of 8, Wilton Crescent, Middlesex, and of Thorncombe, Surrey, esq Times, d p , 14 Feb , 1880
  see Fisher-Rowe
  ,, Hussey
  ,, Ridler Rowe.
  Snook, T., of Dickenson Road, Rusholme, Manchester. oil merchant and general agent Times, d p , 15 Nov., 1892
Rowels Eastbrooke, C. H. 21 Aug., 1806 (1109)

Rowland, J. Daniel : Jones, J. R., of 23, Rood Lane, London.
Times. d p., 18 Dec., 1879
see Wiltshire
Rowlands : Jones, J. R., late of Machynlleth, Montgomery, now
of Shrewsbury, Salop, clerk in National Prov. Bank of
Eng. Times, d p., 26 March, 1863
Rowley *see* Jephson-Rowley
: Taylor, C. D. G., 11 April, 1796.
Rowlls *see* Legh
Rowson *see* Harrison-Rowson
Roxby : Maude, H. R. 3 Feb., 1837 (327)
Royall : Pepperell, W. 30 June 1787 (305)
Royds *see* Beswicke-Royds
,, Fletcher-Twemlow.
Roylands-Chanter Roylands Smith, I. J., formerly of Ventnor
and Torquay, now of Morley's Hotel, London, esq.
Times, d p., 5 Feb., 1876
Royle-Higginson : Royle, T. and E. 1 June. 1867 (3228)
Royston *see* Piggott-Royston
Royston-Piggott Piggott, G. W., and Anne Hitchin (widow), on
their marriage. W., 25 April, 1860 (D.G 558)
Ruck-Keene : Keene, C. E. 19 July, 1841 (1894)
Ruddell : Ruddell-Todd, J. A. 9 Feb., 1872 (645)
Ruddell-Todd : Ruddell 12 Jan., 1814 (188)
Rudgard Earl, E. W. R. 11 June, 1841 (1510)
Rudge-Nouaille : Rudge, Walter Wm. Nouaille, of West View,
Shirley, Hants, esq., Dep Lieut for Lincoln Times.
d p., 21 Jan., 1886
Rudston-Read *see* Calverly-Rudston.
: Rudston, T. C. 19 May, 1801 (549)
Rugge-Price : Price, Sir A. J., Bart. 7 March, 1874 (1644)
Ruiz-Geary Ruiz, T., of Malaga, Spain Times, d p., 14 Jan
1892
Ruutz-Rees : Rees, L. O. R., of Calcutta. E. Ind., merchant,
temp. residing at 3, Suffolk Place, Pall Mall. Middlesex
Times, d p., 5 Nov., 1862
Rumball *see* Quilter
Rump *see* Ward.
Rushout : Cockerell, Sir C. R. 6 June, 1849 (1913)
Rundle-Charles Charles, E. R., of Combe Edge, Hampstead,
widow. Times. 30 Dec., 1887
Russell Branfill. B 16 March 1829 (527)
Cloutt, W. 3 June, 1823 (1175)
see De Krauchy.
, Frankland-Russell.
., Frankland-Russell-Astley
,, Gill-Russell

Russell *see* Graves-Russell.
  „ Greenhill-Russell.
  „ Hamilton-Russell.
  „ Hutchinson-Russell
  „ Kempe
  „ Oldnall
  „ Pakington.
  „ Prinn.
  „ Redfern Russell.
  „ Ward
  „ Watts-Russell.
Russell-Oldnall : Oldnall-Russell, H. C., of Sion House, Chaddesley Corbett, Worcs., Lieut R A. Times, d.p., 9 Feb., 1892
  Oldnall-Russell, J. E., of Sion House, Chaddesley Corbett. Worces., Sub-Lieut. R N. Times, d.p., 2 April, 1888
Russell-Pavier . Russell, W. A. 24 July, 1874 (3859)
Rust-D'Eye . Rust, E. W., 24 July, 1852 (D.G. 635)
Rutherfoord-Reade : Rutherfoord, P. A., of Ballymena, co. Antrim, lieut., now quartered at Dinapore, India. Times, 28 Sept., 1889.
Rutherford *see* Ainslie.
  „ Atkinson.
Rutherford-Elliot *see* Greig-Rutherford-Elliot
Rutherford-Greig : Greig, John. Lyon, Vol IV., 18 Nov., 1846
Rutherforth *see* Abdy
Rutherfurd-Ainslie · Rutherfurd, J., W. 11 July, 1786 (D.G. 4787)
Ruthven . Trotter, Edwd. Southwell, resumed the surname of Ruthven, R. L. Lyon, Vol. II., 18 July, 1805
  Trotter, Captn. John, Ayrshire Militia, resumed the surname of Ruthven. Lyon, Vol II., 3 Nov., 1809
  · Trotter, W. C. B. 21 April, and 28 April, 1865 (D.G. 525 and 541)
  · Trotter, E. S. 24 Jan., 1801 (98)
Ruttledge . Lambert, Rev. F. 7 April, 1818
  : Watson, D. D.G., 1 Jan., 1834.
Ryan *see* Riggs-Miller
  „ Tenison.
Ryan-Lenigan Ryan, J. V. 9 Dec., 1878 (D.G. 1074)
Ryan-Tenison Ryan, E. T., of 8, Keith Terrace, Shepherd's Bush, Middlesex, M D. (St. Andrews, Scot.), L R.C.P., M.R.C.S (Eng.), assist. surgeon, R.N. Times, d.p., 22 Aug., 1862

Ryan-Tenison : Tenison, E. H , of Kilronan, Bexhill-on-Sea, surgeon. Times, 16 Oct., 1888
Rycroft *see* Maude.
Ryder *see* Bromwich-Ryder.
    ,, Irton.
    ,, Wood-Ryder.
Ryde-Jones : Jones, T., of Queen Street, Chester, bank manager Times, d p., 26 Oct., 1893.
Rye *see* Brograve.
Ryland *see* Smith-Ryland.

S

Sabben-Clare : Sabben, J. W., of John Street, Bedford Row, London. Times, 18 Dec., 1900.
Sabin Smith : Smith, A., late of Clifton, Bristol, now of Harbury, Warwicks., gent. Times, d.p., 25 June, 1881.
Sabine *see* Pasley.
Sackvill *see* Stopford-Sackville
Sackville : Germaine, Lord G. 10th Geo. III., 1770.
    : Sackville-West, R. W. (Lord Buckhurst). 24 April, 1871 (2122).
    see Stopford.
    ,, Evans.
Sackville-West : West, Rt. Hon G. J. (Earl de la Warr). 6 Nov., 1843 (3604).
Sadleir-Jackson : Sadleir, N. H and C. R. A., of 10 York Street, St. James's, Middlesex. Times, d.p, 10 Jan., 1894
Sagar *see* Wilkinson.
Sagar Musgrave : Sagar, J. M. 17 April, 1863 (2071)
Sage *see* Hopkinson-Sedge.
Sainsbury : Langford, S. 21 Feb., 1800 (169).
    . Pickwick, C. H. S., of Bradford-on-Avon, Wilts. esq. Times, d p., 8 March, 1872
St Aubyn *see* Molesworth
    ,, Molesworth-St. Aubyn.
Saint Cedd : Jackson, W., formerly of Spital Square, Middlesex. but temporarily in Paris. Times, d.p , 29 June. 1876.
St. Clair *see* Bower-St. Clair.
    : Erskine, Sir J. 11 July, 1789 (477).
    : Smith, T. S. St. C., of Hoole Lodge, Chester, Capt 49th Foot. Times, d.p., 27 Dec., 1875, and 1 Jan., 1876.

St. Clair-Rogers : Rogers, E., of Drumpellier House, Gloster Times, d.p., 9 March, 1880.
St George see Mansergh St. George
— French, A. D.G., 30 April, 1811.
— George, H. I., of Pendleton, Lancs., schoolmaster Times. 1 Feb., 1879.
— : Mansergh, Richard, son of James M. and Mary St. George. Betham.
St Gerrans : Smith, H P., of The Limes, Yateley, Hants, gent. Times, d p., 4 Nov., 1890.
St John : Bunny, E J 21 March 1877 (2263)
 — see Mildmay
St. Leger : Chester, J. 1 April, 1863 (1937).
St. Maur-Wynch : Wynch, H S., Col., of 24. Rectory Grove. Clapham, Surrey. Times d p, 18 May, 1889
St Paul Jones, D R., formerly of H M. 53rd Foot and late of Walcott Lodge, Lutterworth, Leicester now of Everdon Hall, Northampton, Maj. and Dep-Lieut. for Leicester Times, d p., 12 June, 1862.
— Paul, J. 8th Geo. III, 1768.
St Quintin : Darby, W. T. 31 Oct., 1795 (1140).
Salaman, Abraham see Phillips, Alfred.
 — see Kensington Salaman
 — Chas Kensington : Salaman, C., of 36, Baker Street, Portman Square, W. Times, 1 Nov., 1867
Sale-Hill : Hill, R., Major-Gen., C B Times, d p., 26 April, 1889
Salisbury : Markham, A. 24 Sept., 1785 (437)
Salmon see Lowndes-Salmon
Salte see Geary-Salte
Salter, Wm. Hy Gurney : Salter, W H., of 26, Abingdon Street, Middlesex. Times, 28 Nov., 1873.
 — see Gurney Salter.
Saltoun see Jones-Saltoun.
Salusbury see Burroughs
 ,, Piozzi-Salusbury
 — : Trelawney, W. L. 30 Oct. 1802 (1129)
Salusbury-Trelawney : Salusbury, W. L 19 Dec 1807 (1734)
Salvidge see Tutton
Samborne : Hopewell, M. 6 Jan 1778 (11838).
 — see Palmer-Samborne
Samo-Waller : Samo, J. W. 24 March, 1823 (483)
Sampson see Croft
 — Galpine, A. 25 Aug., 1803 (1483)
 — see Hammond-Sampson
 ,, King
 ,, King-Sampson.

Sampson : Sampson-Cloak, B 22 Dec., 1840 (3046)
    see Tilden-Sampson
Samson *see* Gibb Samson.
Samuel Edgar : Samuel, E., of Thornleigh, Salford, Lancaster Times, 2 Dec., 1896
    see Saville
Samuels, Joseph Naphtali *see* Saville, Herbert
Samuel-Gibbon : Samuel, J 10 Nov., 1863 (5303)
Samwell Drought, T F 6 & 7 Vict c. 30 (Index to pub. and priv. Statutes, p. 503).
    : Watson, W. L. 1st and 2nd Will. IV, 1831.
    : Watson, T. S. 30th Geo III., 1790
Sandbach *see* Levvy-Sandbach
Sandeman Solomon, E A, late of Hong Kong, now of 12, Leadenhall Street, London, gent Times, d.p., 15 Sept., 1893
    see Vernon
Sanders-Bradfield : Sanders, J. B 14 Nov., 1814 (2263)
Sanders-Clark : Clark, H. of 4, Stafford Place, Buckingham Gate. Times, d.p. 16 Aug, 1895
Sanders : Cooper, Hy S. W, 30 Jan., 1860 (D G 141)
Sanderson : Burdon, R 4 April, 1815 (631).
    see Cobden-Sanderson.
    ,, Smirthwaite
    : Winter, S 2 Oct., 20 Oct., 1873 (D G. 718).
Sandes *see* Collis-Sandes
Sandford : Peacocke, G M W. 25 Jan., 1866 (773).
    see Wills-Sandford-Wills.
    ,, Wills-Sandford
    ,, Winston.
Sandys *see* Bayntum-Sandys.
    Hill (Lord Sandys). 15 Feb., 1861 (792).
    see Speer
Sargeant *see* Openshaw.
Sargent *see* Arnold
Sauerwein *see* Thomas
Saul *see* Kirklinton.
    ,, Wingate-Saul.
Saunders · Arundell, F W A. 16 July, 1873 (3451)
    Badcock, A., Stratton, Cornwall. Times, 29 March, 1900
    : Huck, R 18 March, 1777 (11753)
    . Richardson R. W 11 Oct., 1837 (2615)
    see Webb.
Saunders-Knox-Gore : Saunders, W. B 23 April, 1891 (D G 965).
Saunt *see* Barfoot-Saunt

Saunt Lovegrove, T. W., of 14, Gloucester Row, Weymouth
also the children of the above ı c , M H ,
B. V., T. E., W. F., and L S. Times, d p., 31
Jan., 1894.
Savage : Clavering, R * 21 Oct, 1797 (997).
    see Heyworth-Savage
    „ Nugent
    ., Tyers
Savage-Graham · Graham, C. R. 12 July, 1878 (D.G. 627).
Savell, A. . Johnson, A. Geo., of 7, Gt Marylebone St., London,
artist in stained glass Times, d p., 27 April, 1887.
Savile : Atkinson, C. 8 Aug., 1798 (741).
    : Lumley, F. 4th and 5th Will. IV., 1834.
    see Lumley-Savile.
    : Lumley, Hon. R. 24th Geo III , 1783
    see Stewart-Savile.
    : Savile-Lumley, Rt. Hon. Sir J. 28 May, 1887 (3148).
Savile-Lumley : Savile, A. W 15 Nov., 1881 (5904)
Savill-Onley : Harvey, C. 14 Dec., 1822 (2044)
    Marsham, C. A O 21 May, 1891 (2926).
Saville Lumley, H. 30 Jan, 1857 (386)
    Herbert · Samuels, Joseph Naphtali, of Chalcott Villa,
Alexandra Road, St. John's Wood, Middlesex
gent Times. d.p , 9 Oct., 1871.
    Frank · Samuel, J F., of 17, Keppel Street, Russell Sq
Times, d.p., 13 July, 1883.
    see Smith Saville.
Sawbridge-Erle-Drax : Sawbridge, W. E. 7 Oct., 1887 (5545)
Sawbridge see Erle-Drax.
Sawle : Graves, J. S. 7 April. 1815 (749).
    see Graves-Sawle.
Sawrey see Cookson-Sawrey
Sawrey-Cookson : Cookson-Sawrey, J., of Neasham Hall,
Durham, and Broughton Tower, Lancs Times, 27 Feb.
1882.
Say see Hall-Say.
Sayer-Milward Sayer, E H. 11 Aug., 1856 (2839)
    : Sayer, W. C. 21 March, 1874 (1922).
Sayer see Milward.
    „ Poulter.
Scarbrow-White : White, C. S 7 July, 1837 (1882)
Scarisbrick : Dicconson, C. (heretofore Eccleston). 30 Aug.,
1833 (1607)
    . Eccleston, T. 8 May, 1810 (674).
    : Hunloke, Dame Anne (widow). W., 17 Oct., 1860
(D.G. 1178)

Schank Wight, J M S G 10 June, 1843 (1979)
Schapira-Windeck Schapira, J. late of Vienna, now at Royal Hotel, Blackfriars, London, nat. Br subject, gent Times, 10 Nov., 1883
Scheibner *see* Du Riche Preller
Schenck *see* Woodhead
Schiesser-Jamison, A Schiesser, A., of Milan, Italy. Times, d p., 30 Sept , 1874.
Schilizzi-Vafiadacchi Schilizzi, J, L and M. 1 June, 1875 (3047)
Schlesinger *see* Selwyn.
  ,,   Sinclair.
Schlesinger Selwyn . Schlesinger, Sophia, of 13, Augusta Strasse, Wiesbaden, widow. Times, 31 Jan., 1894
  Schlesinger W M., of Havana, Cuba, elec engineer Times, d p., 23 June, 1894
Schmidt-Temple . Schmidt, A , formerly of Sunset, Cornwall, but now of Munich, Bavaria, gent Times, d p., 15 Aug., 1885.
Schofield *see* Law-Schofield.
  ,, Lightfoot
Scholes *see* Whittam.
Scholey *see* Dryden
Schonswar-Johnstone : Johnstone, J., of Leamington, Warwick. wife of C Johnstone, esq Times, d.p., 9 Feb., 1878.
Schow *see* Protheroe
Schrieber *see* Lateward.
Schultz-Weir : Shultz, H., of Durban, Natal Times, 27 Aug., 1900.
Schwan *see* Swab.
Schwann *see* Holland-Schwann.
Sclater-Booth : Sclater, G 13 Nov., 1857 (3919).
Sclater-Mathew Sclater, T. L. 27 March, 1802 (304)
Scobbe *see* Scobell.
Scobell Scobbe, R W, of 14, Billiter Street, London, and 2, Park Place, Grosvenor Road, S.W , auctioneer, land and estate agent Times, 23 April, 1864
Scott *see* Altham
  ,, Bentinck-Scott.
  ,, Dawson-Scott
  ,, Douglas-Scott-Montagu
  ,, Gibb
  ,, Goldie-Scott.
  ,, Hope Scott.
  ,, Johnstone-Scott.

Scott *see* Lane-Scott.
,, Lings-Scott.
,, Lockhart-Scott.
,, Mabbett.
Moss, M. 4 Dec., 1838 (2912)
see Munro
Ossington, Charlotte D. (Vis. Ossington). 26 June, 1882 (3099)
Philips, E. 1 June, 1816 (1046).
Skues, R. 12 March, 1827 (631).
Stuart, L. S. 26 March, 1892 (2318)
see Waring
,, Williams.
,, Young-Scott.
Scott, Isaac Temple: Isaacs, I., of West Hampstead, London Times, 1 May, 1900.
Scott-Bentinck *see* Bentinck-Scott.
Scott-Chad: Scott, J. S. 27 Nov., 1855 (4535)
Scott Challice: Challice, J., of 14, Coverdale Road, Shepherd's Bush, medical student. Times, d.p. 12 April, 1894
Scott-Chisholme of Stirches · Chisholm, John, Lyon, Vol. V. 15 March, 1853.
Scott-Crickitt: Crickitt, P. S. H., of 4, Pump Court, Temple, and Merton Coll., Oxford, and of Inner Temple, London, B.A. Times, d.p., 31 Oct., 1890
Scott-Douglas: Douglas, Sir J. J. 10 July, 1822 (1353).
Scott-Ellis: Ellis, L. J. (Baroness Howard de Walden) 26 Nov., 1889 (6755)
Scott-Gatty: Gatty, A. S. York Herald, 23 Nov., 1892
Scott-Jackson: Scott, T. 20 Sept., 1768 (10869)
Scott-Kerr of Chatto. Kerr, Wm., resumes the surname of Scott which he had dropped. Lyon, Vol. IV., 26 Dec., 1837.
Scott-Mackerdy of Birkwood. Scott, Wm. Augustus. Lyon, Vol. XIII., 15 Feb., 1894
Scott-Makdougall: Scott, J. E., of Makerstoun, co. Roxburgh. Times, 12 Jan., 1900.
Scott-Murray: Murray, C. R. S. 27 Oct., 1847 (3828).
Scott-Stonehewer: Scott, S. 22 March, 1811 (555).
. Scott, W. 30 June, 1825 (1246)
Scott-Wellwood of Garvoch: Scott-Moncrieff, Robert. Lyon, Vol. IV., 25 May, 1847
Scott Williams *see* Williams.
Scourfield · Philipps, J. H. 30 Sept., 1862 (4723).
Scraggs *see* Craggs
Scrase *see* Dickens-Scrase

Scrivener Levett, E. B. B., of Suffolk and Oxford, esq, late Lieut. R.N. Times, d.p., 6 April, 1889
    see Pike-Scrivener.
Scroope *see* Scrope.
Scrope *see* Buncombe-Poulett-Scrope
    : Peart, J. 2 June, 1792 (363).
    Scroope, S. T. 7 Oct., 1852 (2724).
Scourfield : Philipps, Jho H. W, 30 Sept, 1862 (D G. 1123)
Scudamore-Stanhope : Stanhope, Sir E. F. 25 Jan., 1827 (185).
Scurfield Grey, J. 27 Dec., 1831 (2771).
Seaborne : Hopkins, C. E., of Kimberley, Tulse Hill, Surrey, gent Times, d p., 24 Aug, 1887.
Seale-Hayne : Seale, C. H. 28 Oct., 1831 (2222).
Sealy *see* Vidal
Seaman : Pierce, S. 9 Feb., 1825 (329).
    see Pierce-Seaman.
Searancke : Niccoll, F. C. 13 Feb., 1781 (12161).
Searancke Archer *see* Archer
Seare Gough, C. J. 24 Dec., 1800 (1438).
Searle *see* Van Dam.
    „ Whitmore-Searle.
Searles-Wood : Appleton, H. D, of 157, Wool Exchange, London, and of Benfleet Hall, Sutton, Surrey, F R I B A, &c. Times, d p., 5 July, 1890
Seaton, Catherine Thomas, Charity, of 4, Montagu Terrace, Richmond, Surrey, spinster Times, d.p, 4 July, 1891.
Seaver *see* Ricarde-Seaver.
Seawell : Marks, T. S. S., of Guildford, Surrey, gent Times, d p, 12 Jan, 1877.
Sebag *see* Montefiore
Sedawee, Halesh *see* Sedway, Herbert James
Seddon, John Strettell · Seddon, Strettell, of 29, Stockport Road, Manchester, gent. Times, 22 March, 1866.
Sedge *see* Hopkinson-Sedge.
Sedgwick *see* Fawcett.
Sedley Vernon, Hon. H. V. 27 March, 1779 (11964).
Sedley-Tillstone · Sedley, E. S. 23 Jan, 1843 (246).
Sedway, Herbert J. : Sedawee, Halesh, of Beyrout Times, 21 Feb., 1871.
Seel *see* Molyneux-Seal.
Selby : Browne, J. 23rd Geo. III., 1783.
    see Donaldson-Selby.
    „ Eaton.
    „ Luard-Selby
    „ Swinfen.
Selby-Bigge : Bigge, L. A., of St. Margts Road, Oxford, esq, M.A. Times, d.p., 20 Sept., 1887.

Selby-Hele : Selby, R H   17 May, 1791 (287)
Selby-Lowndes : Lowndes, W   19 June, 1813 (1166)
Selfe : Page, H. J. S.   1 Feb, 1832 (260)
Seligsen *see* Ernest.
Sell-Collins : Sell, T.   27 March, 1871 (1631)
Sellick *see* Gist.
Sellon *see* Pybus-Sellon
    :-Smith, W. R. B.   2 Jan., 1847 (47).
Selous   Slous, J. G, son of T D. Slous, of 7, Morden Terrace, Lewisham Road, Greenwich. Times, 1 Aug, 1865.
Selwin   Ibbetson, C.   18 Feb., 1817 (576).
    Ibbetson, J. T.   3 Sept., 1825 (1600).
Selwyn : Schlesinger, C. H., of 12th Bengal Cav. (lieut). Times, d.p., 8 Nov., 1893.
    see Schlesinger Selwyn.
    : Solomon, A. H., of 14, Piccadilly, Middlesex   Times, d.p., 9 Dec, 11 Dec., 1879.
Semon   Simon, A. C., late of Kingston-on-Thames, Surrey, but now of Hampton-Wick, Middlesex, and of Claremont. Jersey, M R.C.S., L.R C.P   Times, d.p , 3 Aug., 1889.
Sempill   Candler, E   25 Aug., 1853 (2362)
Senhouse   Bell, R., of the Fitz, Cockermouth, physician. Times, d.p., 8 May, 1875.
    see Minton-Senhouse.
    „ Pocklington-Senhouse.
Senior *see* Husey-Hunt.
Sentleger . Aldworth, S   12 March, 1767 (10727).
    : Aldworth, S., and Mary his wife. St. J., 12 May, 1767 (D.G. 1747).
Serjeant : Frary, T.   27 Feb, 1810 (317).
Sequerra *see* Da Esqeirra.
Sergison : Jefferson, F. W., 27 Nov., 1784 (D G 4535)
    : Pritchard, W. S.   28 April, 1812 (782).
    : Skutt, T.   23 Dec., 1803 (1797)
Serocold *see* Pearce-Serocold.
Seton : Anderson, A.   10 Feb , 1812 (275).
    see Karr
    „ Reid-Seton
Seton-Christopher : Christopher, A. C., of Elm Lodge, Childwall, Lancs., esq., Capt. in H.M. Land Forces.   Times, d.p., 25 Sept, 1893.
Seton-Karr : Seton, A.   16 May, 1815 (924)
Seton-Smith : Smith, B. S, formerly of Ware, Herts, at present residing at San Remo, Italy, esq. Times, d p , 11 Feb., 1885.
Sewell   Goose, A. J, of Picardy Road, Belvedere, Kent, clerk (G.P.O.).   Times, d.p., 11 July, 1892

Sewell Hyman, L 23 July, 1859 (2933)
Seymer *see* Clay-Ker-Seymer
Seymour *see* Culme-Seymour
        Gruggen, W W M., of 82, Gloster Crescent, Hyde Park, Middlesex. Lieut R A Times, d.p., 28 June, 1873
        : Gruggen, M. H M., of H M S Antelope, at Malta. Sub-Lieut. R.N. Times, d p, 15 April, 1876
        see Page
        Pursall, F., of Seymour Villa. Portland Road, Edgbaston, being surname of late husband. Chas. Seymour Times, d.p. 7 Oct, 1886
Seymour-Conway *see* Ingram-Seymour-Conway.
Shackerley *see* Jackson
Shadwell *see* Lucas-Shadwell
Shafto *see* Duncombe-Shafto
    „ Eden
Shakerley : Buckworth, C W. J. 29th Geo. III., 1789
Shakespear · Bowles, C. 15 Nov 1858 (5073)
Shand *see* Smith-Shand
Shapland *see* Jackson-Shapland.
Sharland-Cruwys : Sharland, G. 9 Nov, 1831 (2355)
Sharman-Crawford : Sharman, W. D.G., 14 March, 1827
Sharp : Bowlt, A 12 Aug., 1817 (1750).
    see Jelf-Sharp
    „ Troughton
Sharp-Handasyde : Sharp, W. 27 Feb, 1808 (285)
Sharp Hume : Sharp, M A., of Essex. and also of Madrid esq, Major 5th Essex Vol Rifles Times, 7 April 1877
Sharp-Naters : Sharp, J. G 5 Sept., 1892 (5384)
Sharpe *see* Banks
    „ Bethune.
    „ Brabazon
    „ Ellis
    : Johnson, R 14 April. 1798 (306)
    : Rissowe, C T 27 Dec., 1800 (1453)
Shattock Betty, S G., of 1, Park Street. Regent's Park, Middlesex Times, d.p., 19 Oct., 1877
Shaw *see* Alexander.
    , Alexander-Shaw
    Alexander, W. J D. Castle. 10 June, 1846 (D G. 593 and 606).
    see Bull-Shaw
    „ Downes-Shaw
    Glasse. G H 25 June. 1802 (719)

Shaw   Glasse, M. L. 25 June, 1802 (719)
  . Haigh, W   d p , 19 Nov , 1883
   see Hellier.
   ,, Lefevre
  : Macfie, J. 6 Oct , 1807 (1353)
   see Mackintosh
  : Nicholson, J R   11 Jan., 1837 (92)
   see Vernon
   ,, Wedgner
Shaw-Brooke : Shaw. 13 Dec , 1796 (1208).
Shaw-Hamilton : Shaw, R. I. 10 April, 1889 (D.G. 403).
Shaw-Kennedy : Shaw, J   15 March, 1834 (480).
Shaw-Mackenzie of Newhall, Cromarty Shaw, John Andrew Lyon Vol, V., 5 Sept. 1857.
Shaw-Yates   Shaw, R. B , of Moorgate, Rotherham, York Times, d p , 23 May, 1870
Shawe *see* Butler-Shawe
Shawe-Storey . Shawe, L. P   12 May, 1873 (2586)
Shawe-Taylor : Shawe, F. M . and Albinia his wife   25 March, 1844 (1037)
Shayer *see* Veysie
Sheehan-Dare : Sheehan, J R , of Hatfield, Herts, schoolmaster and organist. Times, 3 March, 1882
Sheepshanks *see* York.
Sheepshanks-Burgess : Sheepshanks, W. 4 Sept , 1837 (2344)
Sheilds *see* Wentworth-Sheilds
Sheldon *see* Constable.
       Raynsford, A   14 Feb , 1828 (438)
       Vincent. Mercy   14 Feb , 1828 (438)
Shelley *see* Sidney
Shelton *see* MacGeough Bond Shelton
Shepheard *see* Walwyn-Shepheard.
Shepheard-Walwyn : Shepheard, Rev. C. C. W , of Highlands, Guildford, Surrey Times, d p , 3 June, 1881
        Shepheard, A. W , of the Grange, Windermere. esq. Times, d p , 5 Aug , 1881
Shepherd *see* Carter.
Shepherd-Cross Cross, H. 13 May, 1884 (2610)
Shepley *see* Heathcote.
        Winterbottom, R. S , now of Harefield. Torkington. Chester, esq. Times. d p., 20 March, 1891
Sheppard Cook. H. 25 Feb., 1864 (1254)
       see Cotton-Sheppard.
Sheppard-Cotton : Sheppard, W. T   13 Sept , 1799 (925)
Sherburne : Tench, J. S   28 March, 1853 (924)
Sheridan *see* Grant-Browne-Sheridan.

Sherlock-Hubbard : Hubbard, I. S., of Wellington, Salop.
   Times, d p , 19 April, 1886.
Sherman : Cheston, J. 15 July, 1780 (12100).
Shersby see Robertson-Shersby
Sherwin see Gregory
   · Longden, J. S. 22 Aug., 1825 (1530).
   : Parkin, A. 10 Aug , 1820 (1590).
Shewan see Money-Shewan.
Shewen see Mansell.
Shield : Gilson, W W., 2 April, 1851 (D.G. 326)
   . Pedlar, G. H O. (on his marriage to Ann Shield). 28 Jan., 1845 (359).
   see Spencer.
Shields see Eccleston.
Shields, Cuthbert : Laing, Robt., of Corpus Christi Coll., Oxon, now at Hotel Metropole, London. Times, 30 Sept., 1886.
Shiers Mason : Mason, R. S, of Gargrave, York, and of Queen's Coll , Oxford, gent Times, 4 June, 1886
Shimmen-Vivian : Shimmen, J, temporarily residing at Parker's Hotel, Surrey Street, Strand, Middlesex, gent. Times, d.p., 16 July, 5 Sept., 1881.
Shipley-Conway : Shipley, C 1 Aug., 1825 (1357)
Shipley-Hewett, Brettell-Vaughan-Edwards Hewett, Edwards, of Clunbury, Salop, gent. Times, d.p., 5 March, 1895
Shipperdson : Hopper, E H 25 March, 1856 (1160).
Shirley Smith, W. E. of Doncaster, York, attorney and solicitor Times, d.p., 23 Nov., 1863
   · Tremearne, C. E , of London, late of Calcutta, Bengal Times, 6 June, 1874.
Shirreff Dudman, J. H. S., of Pitney House, nr. Langport, Somersets. esq Times, 23 Jan., 1885.
   see Lloyd-Shirreff
   Murray-Shirreff, Jane M., wife of T. W Murray-Shirreff, of 83, Sutherland Avenue, Middlesex. Times, d.p., 28 March, 1888
Shirt see Barton.
   „ Hirst.
   „ Staveley-Shirt
Shittler see Rowden.
Shore see Nightingale
Shore Nightingale : Shore Smith, S. and M. T., both of Embley Park, Hants, and L. H S., of Jermyn Street, London. Times, d.p , 20 April, 1893.
Shorrock · Ashton, E S 6 Jan , 1854 (83).
Short see Gordon-Short.
   „ Habberfield-Short
   Hassard, H 25 Jan , 1794 (76).

Short · Hassard, J. G.   30 June, 1807 (882)
       · Hassard, R. S.   7 Aug., 1807 (1045)
       Robt. John : Short, R. J. English, of Hill-Martin Road, Holloway, mem. of Stock Exchange   Times, d.p., 22 Dec., 1875.
Shotter Trimmer, J. 2 Dec., 1795 (1345)
Shuckburgh *see* Blencowe-Shuckburgh.
       ,, Evelyn.
       Wood, R H. 9 May, 1876 (2982)
Shum-Storey : Shum, E. A. 3 Dec., 1870 (5701)
       Shum, G   8 Feb., 1823 (235)
Shute . Hall, E. J., of Queen's Road, Teddington, Middlesex, spinster Times, d.p., 26 Sept., 1884
Shuttleworth *see* Holden.
       ,, Kay-Shuttleworth
Sibthorpe *see* Waldo-Sibthorpe.
Siddall : Mortimer, T. 18 April, 1843 (1281)
Siddons : Marriott, E., of 9, Wellington Street, Middlesex, widow, to resume name formerly borne. Times, d.p., 6 Dec., 1873
Sidebottom *see* Venner.
Sidney-Foulis Sidney, P. and M   6 June, 1850 (1666)
Sidney Adams, H., of 223, Piccadilly, artist   Times, d.p., 24 May, 1875.
       Shelley, J   12 March, 1793 (202)
       Shelley, P   10 April, 1799 (383)
Siemens, Wm : Siemens, Sir Chas W., Kt., F.R.S., D.C.L., etc., of Sherwood, Kent, and of 3. Palace Houses, Bayswater Times, 12 June, 1883
Sikes Baines, F   14 Dec., 1857 (4552)
Silley *see* Egremont.
Sillifant-Hamlyn : Fanny G Sillifant-Hamlyn (widow), of No 17. The Beacon, Exmouth. Mrn. Post, 8 Nov., 1897
Silvertop : Englefield, H   4 April, 1849 (1161).
       see Witham
Silvester *see* Carteret-Silvester.
Sim *see* Grant.
Simmer-Holme Simmer, G   16 Aug., 1796 (781)
Simmons Carlyon, G F   16 Feb., 1858 (772)
       see Carlyon
       ,, Le Breton-Simmons.
       ,, Lintorn Simmons.
       . Smith.
Simmons-Atkinson · Simmons, J   5 Dec., 1821 (2422)
Simon *see* Semon.
Simonds *see* Holliday Hartley

Simonds Markeloff, Marie, of 81, Richmond Road, Barnsbury, Islington, spinster, formerly of St Petersburg. Times, d p., 3 March, 1886
Simpkinson *see* King
Simpkinson de Wesselow Simpkinson, F. G., of 67, Victoria Street, Westminster, esq Times, d.p., 18 Nov. 1869
Simpson Bridgman, J. 25th Geo III, 1785.
    see Bridgeman.
    „ Cooper-Simpson-Cross
    „ Hicks.
    „ Hilton-Simpson
    „ Hudleston
    „ Lister.
Simpson-Baikie . Simpson, E., of 21, York Terrace, Regent's Park, London, and Baden Times, 3 March, 1876
    : Simpson, F., late Lieut. 4th Lt. Dragoons, of Army and Navy, and Oriental Clubs. London Times, 7 March, 1876
Simpson-Jones : Jones, J. G., of High Street, Pwllheli, Carnarvon Times, 10 May, 1900.
Sims . Moses, D. W., of 60, Russell Square, Bloomsbury, late of Kimberley, S Africa surg. dentist Times, d p, 15 Nov, 1887.
Simson *see* Bruce-Simson
Sinclair *see* Alexander-Sinclair
    . Heathcote, F. G. 13 March, 1890 (1709)
    of Fairmead, Cambridge : Heathcote, Fredk Granville. Lyon, Vol. XII., 24 Jan., 1891
    : Moses, C. A, of Oakwood, Brampton, Cumberland, gent. Times, d p., 14 Nov., 1876
    Schlesinger, L, of 3, Pembridge Place, Bayswater, gent., late of Sydney, N S Wales. Times, d p, 16 Oct., 1886
Sing *see* Synge
Singleton : Corbet, F. D.G . 9 Nov., 1820.
    Crawford, T D G . 26 Jan., 1843.
Sirr *see* Goddard-Mason.
Sisson-Wayet : Sisson, W. L. 31 Dec., 1831 (106)
Sitwell : Hurt, F. 8 March, 1777 (11750).
    or Wilmot-Sitwell : Wilmot, R. S. St J., 19 Dec., 1769 (D.G. 2112).
    Wilmot, E. S. 1 Dec., 1772 (11305)
Sivwright *see* Bedell-Sivwright.
Skeffington Farrel, W. C. 13 June, 1772 (11256)
    : Foster, Right Hon. T. H. D.G., 8 Jan., 1817

Skeffington Massereene (Visct.) Foster, Thos. Henry D Castle.
9 Jan., 1844 (D G. 16 and 24)
Skelton : Jones, A 24 Nov, 1772 (11303)
see Wood
Skillicorne : Nash, R. S 6 May, 1803 (526)
Skidmore Westwood · Skidmore, W W, of Stourbridge,
Worcester Times, d p., 2 Aug., 1886
Skinner . Longmore, S J 26 Oct , 1825 (1975)
see McBurnie
,, Macgregor-Skinner.
,, Steuart
,, Stewart
Skipton : Kennedy, G. C 13 Feb , 1802 (199)
see Kennedy-Skipton.
Skoulding-Cann : Skoulding, F. J. 29 Nov., 1866 (6885)
Skryne *see* Powell.
Skrymsher *see* Clopton.
Skues *see* Scott.
Skutt *see* Sergison.
Slacke-Barnes : Barnes. W. S 14 Nov., 1878 (6275)
Slade-Gulley Gulley, S T 9 March, 1854 (939)
Slaney *see* Kenyon-Slaney.
Slater · Wilson, H. B. D.G., 5 May, 1835.
Slater-Harrison : Slater, J. H 21 Nov , 1834 (2163).
Slater-Rebow : Slater, F. 12 April, 1796 (342).
Slazenger · Moss, R. S., of 56, Cannon Street, London. merchant
Times, 15 April, 1886.
Sleep *see* Southlan
Sleigh *see* Lindley.
Slingsby : Barraclough, Lucy, of Fairholme, Broxbourne, Herts.
Times, d.p, 15 March, 1894
Leslie, T. and E L C. 9 April 1869 (2234)
Sloane *see* Bidgood
Sloane-Stanley Sloane, H. 28 Dec.. 1821 (2504)
Sloper *see* Lindsay
Sloughter *see* Stanwix.
Slous *see* Selous.
Sly. Deane *see* Deanesly
Slyman *see* Betenson.
Small *see* Lowther-Small
Smallwood *see* Hercy
: Hewitt, T 27 May, 1794 (488)
Smalwood-Fetherstonhaugh : Smalwood, C 1 Sept., 1797 (859)
Smart *see* de Berniere

Smart-Melhuish : Smart, D. C., of 434. Oxford Street, London,
    esq. Times, d.p., 13 Feb., 1888.
Smedley *see* Marsden Smedley.
Smijth *see* Bowyer-Smijth.
Smijth-Windham *see* Windham
          : Smijth, J. 22 May, 1823 (875)
          see Windham.
Smirthwaite : Sanderson, J. 16 Feb , 1871 (587).
Smith *see* Ackers.
    „ Alder-Smith
    „ Allen-Smith.
    „ Anderton.
    : Asheton, T. 14th Geo III., 1774.
    see Atwell-Smith.
    „ Austen.
    „ Ayscough.
    „ Barclay-Smith.
    „ Barker.
    „ Bassett-Smith
    „ Bell.
    „ Bickford Smith.
    „ Blakelock.
    : Bolster, Martha E. S , of Bayley Street, Bedford Square,
        London, spinster. Times, d.p., 11 July, 1893.
    see Booth-Smith
    „ Braikenridge
    „ Bright-Smith
    „ Brodrick-Smith-Brodrick
    „ Bromley.
    „ Brooke-Smith.
    „ Broughton
    „ Burges
    „ Burnell.
    „ Caldwell.
    „ Callander.
    „ Campbell.
    „ Carew.
    , Carrington-Smith.
    „ Caslon-Smith.
    : Causens, H., of 1, Denmark Place, Chapel Road, Lower
        Norwood Times. d.p , 10 March, 1869
    see Champneys-Smith.
    „ Chaplin
    „ Chenevix
    „ Clark-Smith
    „ Clarke

Smith see Coape-Smith
,, Cowper-Smith.
,, Cragg-Smith
,, Crowther-Smith.
,, Cusack.
,, Dawson-Smith.
,, Dazley-Smith.
E H. Dean : Smith, E H , of Paramatta, N S. Wales.
    Times, 4 Sept., 1886.
see De Heriz.
,, De Lancy.
,, Denroche Smitn.
,, De Rutafjaell.
,, Dew-Smith.
,, Dodsworth.
,, Duff-Asheton-Smith.
,, Duncan.
,, Eardley.
,, Eardley-Smith.
,, Ebb-Smith.
,, Echlin Smith
,, Elleker.
,, Evors-Smith.
,, Faber.
,, Foss.
Fradelle, C. B., née Farren, widow of W. J. Fradelle.
    Times, 24 Oct., 1881.
see Gilbert-Smith.
,, Gillies-Smith.
M. Gilling, M. Anne, of Linkfield Court, Bournemouth.
    Hants., spinster Times, d.p., 19 Dec., 1892.
see Godden-Smith.
,, Gow Smith.
,, Granville-Smith.
,, Grattan
,, Gray, Baroness Eveleen
: Grey, J. W. 2 Sept., 1883 (1643)
see Halkett.
,, Harper-Smith.
,, Hart-Smith
,, Hartley-Smith
. Henshaw
,, Heriz-Smith
,, Hill
,, Hilton

Smith see Jackson-Smith
,, Jacobs-Smith.
,, Jennings
: Jennings, J. 5th Geo. III., 1765
see Jobson-Smith.
Jones, W. 27 March, 1798 (257)
see Kirby-Smith.
,, Kyrke-Smith.
,, Lambert
,, Langley-Smith.
,, Lavers-Smith
,, Lawson-Smith
,, Leadbitter-Smith
,, Leesmith
,, Leigh.
,, Leng-Smith.
,, Lomax.
,, Lomax-Smith
,, Loraine, C.
,, Ludlow.
,, Mackintosh.
Mackrell, C. R. 18 Dec., 1843 (4442)
see Marker.
,, Marsden-Smith.
Wm Marsden : Smith, Wm., of 1, Copthall Chambers, Copthall Court, London, gent Times, 28 Sept., 1868
see Maydwell.
,, Michael
,, Milne.
,, Montgomery-Smith.
,, Moore-Tyrrel.
,, Newson-Smith
,, Nightingale.
,, Nugent.
,, Parson-Smith.
,, Pauncefote
,, Peckham
,, Piddington.
,, Protheroe Smith
,, Pyemont.
,, Radcliffe-Smith.
,, Riley-Smith.
,, Roylands-Chanter.
.. Sabin Smith.
,, St Clair

Smith *see* St Gerrans
  „ Sellon.
  „ Seton-Smith.
  „ Shirley.
  Simmons, A 19 Nov., 1774 (11510)
  E. T. Aydon : Smith E T., of Bermondsey, Surrey, med.
      stud of Lond. Hosp. Times, 18 Oct , 1882.
  E Stanley : Smith, E , of Blackheath. Kent. Times, 6
      Aug., 1875
  see Smyth.
  „ Stallard.
  Emily Ethel : Stamp, Emily Sarah, of Eastbourne, Sussex,
      spinster. Times, d.p., 21 Nov , 1891
  see Stemman
  „ Stephens.
  „ Stephenson.
  „ Stevens
  „ Sundius
  „ Swainson.
  „ Taylor-Smith.
  „ Telford-Smith.
  Thackwell, E J, of Norman's Land, Dymock
      Gloucester, barrister-at-law Times. 13 Feb,
      1866.
  see Todd
  „ Vernon.
  „ Wanless-O'Gowan.
  „ Webber
  Webber. J 24 April, 1804 (590)
  see Weir-Smith.
  „ Wilkins-Smith.
  „ Wontner-Smith.
  „ Woodrouffe--Smith
  „ Wyatt-Smith.
  „ Wyke-Smith.
Smith-Bannerman · Smith, J M 18 July, 1855 (2789)
Smith-Barry Smith, R. S. 20 Dec., 1821
Smith-Bingham : Smith. O. 8 March, 1893 (2078).
Smith-Bosanquet Smith, H. J 8 Sept., 1866 (5102)
Smith-Chatterton . Smith, W P 17 March, 26 March. 1874
    (D.G. 201).
Smith-Crawfurth : Smith, T. 28 July, 1824 (1358).
Smith-Cumming : Smith, M. G., of London, and Morayshire,
    N.B. Lieut. R.N. Times, 15 April, 1889.
Smith-Cunninghame : Smith, J 1 Aug. 1834 (1447)
Smith de la Cour Smith. E. now at 1, Belle Vue, Bradford,
    York, H M. Consul at Delagoa Bay, Africa Times, d.p,
    11 Jan., 1890

Smith-Dampier : Fowler-Smith, Jane M., of Thetford, Norfolk, widow. Times, d p, 12 July, 1893.
Smith-de Heriz : Smith, Rev F., of Aston Botterell, Salop, J.P. Times, 13 June, 1865.
Smith-Dew : Dew, A. G 21 July, 1870 (3521).
Smith-Dorrien-Smith : Smith-Dorrien, T. A. 2 Oct, 1874 (4790)
Smith-Dorrien : Smith, R. A. and M A 4 April, 1845 (1049).
　　　　　: Smith, R. A., and Mary Ann his wife. W., 4 April, 1845 (D G. 230)
Smith-Edwards : Smith, J. 6 Jan., 1825 (394).
Smith-Fielding : Smith, G W., late of the 11th Hussars, of Denbeigh, Haslemere, Surrey, and of Shaldon Lodge, Alton, Hants Times, 26 Sept., 1866.
Smith-Forbes : Smith, C. J. F. 2 June, 1863 (2970)
Smith-Gordon : Smith, Sir L. E 4 Feb., 1868 (772).
Smith Hallidie · Smith, A. H, of 36, Gloucester St, Middlesex, surgeon. Times. d p. 18 July, 1891.
　　　　　: Smith, A R., of Gloucester St. and Lincoln's Inn, Middlesex, barrister-at-law. Times, d.p., 18 July, 1891
Smith Hardcastle : Smith, H., of the Temple Hotel, Booksellers' Row, Strand, hotel proprietor. Times, d.p, 16 Nov., 1887.
Smith-Jerome : Smith, W. J., of Monteith Lodge, Sydenham, Kent Times, d p, 2 Oct, 1894.
Smith-Latham Smith, J., of Buckland, Surrey, gent Times, d.p, 12 Feb., 1872.
Smith Levingston : Smith, R. J. S., of Rotterdam, Holland, ship-broker. Times, d.p., 25 April, 1890.
Smith-Marriott · Smith W. M. 15 Feb., 1811 (712)
Smith-Masters : Cowburn, A. 10 April, 1862 (1901).
Smith-Milnes : Smith, T. M 26 Aug., 1830 (1830).
　　　　　: Smith, W. B. 8 Oct., 1873 (49).
Smith-Oliver : Smith, I. T., of Portland Villas, Varna Road. Birmingham, co Warwick Times, 3 Oct., 1870
Smith-Rewse : Smith, G. F. 9 April, 1889 (2376)
　　　　　: Smith, H S. 9 April, 1889 (2376)
Smith-Rose : Smith, W., of Bayswater, London. Times, 18 Dec., 1900.
Smith-Ryland Smith, W. C. H. A 17 May, 1889 (2812)
Smith Saville : Smith, R W., of Swaithe House, Worsborough, Yorks, architect and civ engineer. Times, 18 Sept., 1886
Smith-Shand of Templeland : Smith, Jas Wm. Fraser. M D. Lyon, Vol X., 31 Oct., 1876
Smith, Shore *see* Shore Nightingale.

Smith-Trevor   Smith, C. M., of Magdalen College, Oxford, and
    Apsley Guise, Bedford, esq   Times. d.p. 1 Oct., 6 Oct.,
    1887
Smith-Turberville   Smith, H. T   Times d p 28 Nov. 1884
Smith-Tyler : Smith, E T., Lieut. 2nd Brigade, Southern
    Division, Royal Artillery. Times. d.p., 29 Aug.,
    6 Sept., 1883.
    Smith, W S., of 4, Ormond Terrace, Richmond,
    Surrey, gent Times, d p., 18 June, 1884
Smith-Wilmot   Smith, Harry, formerly of Radford, Nottingham,
    now temp. residing at Almond's Hotel, Clifford Street,
    Bond Street. Times, d.p., 23 April, 1866
Smith-Windsor   Smith, James, cotton manufacturer of Spring-
    field, Bacup, Lancaster   Times, 17 July, 1866
Smithson · Macie, J   16 Feb., 1801 (202)
    Taylor, J. 20 July, 1782 (12314).
Smollett *see* Telfer-Smollett
Smyly *see* Beresford
Smyth *see* Butler-Smythe
    . Blood M.   D.G., 15 Dec., 1808.
    see Carmichael.
    . Curzon, Honble L., & Alicia Maria his wife 16 Nov.,
    26 Nov., 1866 (D G 1652 and 1679)
    . Holroyd, J. H. G.   30 Aug., 1892 (D G. 1029)
    Moore, Hon C. W St J. 29 July, D.C., 7 Aug., 1858
    (D G. 1533).
    Smith J H., of 2, The Terrace, Upper Norwood,
    Surrey; for 35 years in Rio Janeiro doing
    business in name of Smith Times, 24 Feb.,
    1874
    : Smith, M G., of Bathampton House, Bath, spinster.
    Times, d p., 20 March 1877
    : Smith, Rev. C. J. M., of Duncan Terrace, Islington,
    R C Priest Times, d p., 20 March, 1877
    Smith, J A. M, of Bathampton House, Bath, widow.
    Times, d p., 20 March, 1877
    see Temple
    ,, Thompson-Smyth
    . Upton, J. H. G. 21 Aug., 1852 (2303)
    Upton, F 3 July, 1849 (2127)
    see Vallois-Smyth
    ,, Wilson.
    ,, Watson-Smyth
Smyth-Osbourne : Osbourne, J. S., of Heath House, Stapleton,
    Gloucester, esq., grand-nephew and heir-at-law of the late
    John Smyth, formerly of Holbeck, Leeds, and of Bowcliffe
    House, Bramham, both in county of York d p., 3 Dec.,
    1878

Smyth-Pigott : Smith, J H   4 June, 1824 (908)
Smythe see Burke-Smythe
   ,, Carmichael-Smythe
      Gardiner, Sir J W   20 Feb., 1787 (85)
   see Kincaid-Lennox.
   ,, Owen
      Viscountess Strangford see Kincaid-Lennox of Woodhead and Kincaid
Smythe-Gardiner : Whalley, Sir J. 22 Dec., 1797 (1221)
Smythies see Blatch
Snape Eccles see Eccles
Snead Cox : Cox, J G, of 63, Montagu Square, London, esq. Times, d.p., 23 March, 1892.
Snell-Chauncey : Snell, W. 16 Dec., 1780 (12144)
             : Snell, C. 29 April, 1783 (12435).
Snell see Bisset-Snell
Snelling, Robert C B : Snelling, C B, watchmaker and silversmith, of Silver Street, London Times, 22 Jan., 1876
Sneyd-Kynnersley : Sneyd, T 9 May, 1815 (872)
Snodgrass see Douglas
Snook see Rowe
   ,, Weddell.
Snooke see Hargood-Ashe.
   ,, Woods
Snooke Woods Snooke, L. F, of Chichester, Sussex, spinster Times, d p, 11 Dec., 1877
Snow see Kynaston.
   ,, Strahan.
Snowdon see Gard
Soame see Buckworth-Herne-Soame
Soden see Corbet
Sola see Ironmonger
   ,, Ironmonger-Sola
Sole see Lesly
Soley : Newey, W., of 6, Fitchett's Court Noble Street, and of Milton, Gravesend, Kent, manufer's manager Times, d p, 28 May, 1883
Solly see Flood
Solomon see Crichton
         ,, Hart
         ,, Mayer
         ,, Phillips
         ,, Sandeman
         ,, Selwyn
Solomons see Lewis
Soltau-Symons : Soltau G W 1 May, 1845 (1324).

Somers : Sussmann, A. W. and W. T. W., of Bradford, Yorks. Times, d.p., 2 Oct., 1896.
Somers-Cocks · Cocks, Rt. Hon. J. S. 27 April, 1841 (1112)
Somervel *see* Gelderd.
Somervell *see* Gelderd-Somervell.
Somerville · Fownes, J. S. 15 Jan., 1831 (146)
Somerville-MacAlester of Loup : MacAlester, Chas. Lyon, Vol. IV., 29 July, 1847
Sonnenthal *see* Stanley
Soper *see* Medland.
Soper-Dempster : Soper, W. 28 July, 1803 (924).
Sorel-Cameron · Minett, H. W., of Lower Westonhouse, nr Ross, Hereford Times, 11 Oct., 1870
Sotheron : Bucknall-Estcourt, T. H. S. 17 July, 1839 (1436).
Sotheron-Estcourt : Bucknall-Estcourt, G. T. J. 10 March, 1876 (2013).
               Sotheron, T. H. S. 4 Sept., 1855 (3323)
Souter-Robertson . Robertson-Souter, D. 16 July, 1860 (2721)
South *see* Archer-Burton.
Southan : Brown, A. H., of Lansdown Crescent, Worcester Times, 9 Oct., 1867
Southby : Gapper, A. 30 April, 1835 (858)
    see Hayward-Southby.
Southgate *see* Yates-Southgate.
Southlan : Sleep, J. S., of Sydney, New South Wales. Times, d.p., 6 Nov., 1878, 24 Jan., 1879
Southwell *see* Butler-Clarke-Southwell-Wandesford
    . Trafford, J. 31st Geo. III, 1791.
    see Trafford.
    ,, Trafford-Southwell
Sowdon . Cosway, W. 26 June, 1855 (2884)
    see Grosvenor
Sparhawk *see* Pepperrell
Spark *see* Judd-Spark.
Sparke *see* Astley-Sparke
Sparks *see* Buist.
    ,. Buist-Sparks
    ,, Herbert
Sparrow *see* Bence.
    ,, Beridge
    . Brown, W. A. 18 May, 1881 (2859).
    see Hanbury-Sparrow.
    ,, Pennington
Sparvel-Bayly : Sparvel, J. A., of Knockhold Lodge, Swanscombe, Kent. Times, 21 March, 1865
Speed-Pryer Speed, H. P., of 2, Bembridge Villas, E. Cowes, I.W. Times, 13 July, 1893

Speer : Sandys, H. 26 Dec., 1871 (1)
Speers : Allwright, W., of Manchester, now residing at São Paulo, Brazil. Times, 7 Sept., 1872.
Spelman *see* Rix-Spelman
Spell *see* Leaper-Spell
Spence, Edmund Lionel Warren *see* Spence, James Edwin
    J. E. : Spence, E. L. W., of 6, Almorah Crescent, Jersey, infant son of James Atkinson West Spence, F.R.C.S.E., L.R.C.P.E., Surgeon-Major in H.M. Indian Army.
Spencer *see* Hammond-Spencer.
    ,, Hitchcock-Spencer.
    : Jerrard, A. E., of Bath, Somerset, spinster. Times, d.p., 30 Nov., 1874.
    : Jones, J. S., of Baltimore, U.S. America. Times, d.p., 25 March, 16 June, 1879
    see Massey-Spencer
    ,, Morgan-Spencer.
    Shield, H. 29 Aug., 1842 (2355)
    : Stanhope, W. 10 Feb., 1776 (11638)
Spencer-Bell : Bell, J. 29 Jan., 1866 (585)
Spencer-Phillips : Spencer, J. R. 20 Oct., 1809 (1672)
Spenlove : Waite, J. F. S. 12 May, 1863
Spicer *see* William-Spicer.
Spieker *see* Brander
Spiers : Croxford, T. 20 June, 1833 (1203).
    see Gabbit.
Spiers Price *see* Price.
Spilsbury : Jeffery, R. S., of Clapham Common, Surrey, esq. Times, d.p., 3 May, 1892.
Splatt *see* Collins-Splatt
Spooner *see* Lillingston.
Sprake-Day : Sprake, Eliz. L. Times, d.p., 7 March, 1896
Spratt *see* Huggeson
Springett : Pont, A., M.B., and S. E. his wife, formerly of Yalding, Kent, now of Hawkhurst, Kent. Times, d.p., 12 June, 1876.
Sprott *see* Yate-Sprott
Spry : Carlyon, T. H. 30 Dec., 1893 (174).
    see Hume Spry.
    ,, Leverton-Spry.
Squire *see* Hutton-Squire.
    ,, Morris.
Squirl-Dawson : Squirl, W., of The Lodge, Higham, Suffolk, Major (retired). Times, d.p., 15 Nov., 1888.
Stables *see* Durell
    . Durell, J. P. L. D. 13 July, 1895 (4300).

Stacey Harrie Stacey, H. Michael Wm., of Redhill and Merstham Surrey, auctioneer and valuer. Times, d p., 27 Oct., 1886
Stack *see* Finnerty
Stackhouse *see* Foster-Stackhouse
    „ Wynne-Pendarvis.
Stafford : Abbs, J. 12 June, 1805 (918)
    see Howard-Stafford
    „ O'Brien-Stafford.
Stafford-Jerningham Jerningham, Rt. Hon G W 6 Nov., 1826 (2659).
Stafford-King-Harman : Stafford, E C. D.G. 13 Feb., 1900 (209).
Stainsby Conant *see* Carleton
Stainsby *see* Pigott-Stainsby-Conant
Stainsfield *see* West-Stainsfield
Stainton *see* Gillispie-Stainton
St. Albyn : Gravenor, L. 19 Aug, 1806 (1093)
Stallard *see* Brodbelt-Stallard-Penoyre
    · Smith, J., R. L. J., and J. G. L. J 20 Aug, 1878 (4872)
Stallard-Penoyre *see* Baker-Stallard-Penoyre
    · Brown, T. J., of The Moor, Hereford, esq. Times, d.p., 12 May, 1874
    Stallard, T. 12 July, 1783 (12456)
    see Raymond-Stallard-Penoyre.
Stanford Cortis, E.C., O.C, and W H 15 June, 1858 (2963)
Stamp *see* Smith.
Stancombe-Wills . Stancombe, Janet S. C. and Yda E M., of 25, Hyde Park Gardens, spinsters. Times, 8 June, 1893
Standing Tetlow Standing, W., of Skirdon, Yorks., yeoman Times, 7 Nov., 1884.
Standish : Carr, W. S. 6 May, 1841 (1165).
    see Hall-Standish.
    : Stephenson, R. 6 June. 1834 (1046).
    see Strickland-Standish.
Stane Bramston, J 21 April, 1801 (421).
Stanfield : Lanfear, J. 30 May, 1809 (765)
Stanford *see* Benett-Stanford
    „ Elliott
    Vere Benett Stanford, Vere Fane Benett, of Tisbury, Wilts., and of Ennismore Gardens, Middlesex, J.P Times, d.p., 23 Nov., 1891.
Stanger-Leathes : Stanger, T 27 Dec., 1806 (1679)
Stanhope *see* Collingwood.
    „ Roddam
    „ Scudamore-Stanhope
    „ Stott-Stanhope

Stanhope *see* Spencer.
Stanier, F. : Broade, F. S. P., of Salop and Staffs., esq Times, d.p., 4 Aug., 1876.
Stanier-Broade : Stanier, F. 7 Jan., 1857 (147).
Stanier-Philip-Broade : Stanier, Fres W, 7 Jan., 1857 (D G 63).
Stanley : Bontein, E. S. 6 April, 1835 (750)
  : Bontein, J. T. 6 April, 1835 (750)
  see Bontein-Stanley.
  H. Clench . Clench, H., of The Lodge, Coborn Road, Bow, gent. Times, d.p, 22 March, 1873
  Constable, C. H. 3 Aug., 1793 (653).
  see Cowdrey-Stanley.
  „ Errington.
  : Fletcher, R J., of Poland Street, Oxford Street, Midx., prof. of music. Times, 3 May, 1875
  . Jones, M (widow), M. S. (spinster), and W. F. (son of M. Jones), all of Lavender Hill, Surrey. Times, d.p., 7 March, 1889.
  : Sonnenthal, S., of Manchester, but now at Wiesbaden, Germany, gent Times, d.p., 1 Jan., 1886.
  see Sloane-Stanley.
  „ Smith.
  : Wentworth, S. 19 July, 1856 (2554).
Stanley-Adams : Adams, W. S., formerly of Hong Kong, now of Oakthorpe, Edmonton, Middlesex. M.D Times, d.p., 31 Oct, 1888
Stanley-Dodgson *see* Dickinson Stanley-Dodgson.
Stanley-Jones : Jones, H. S, of 5, Fenchurch Buildings, London, and "Benenden," Tulse Hill, Surrey. Times, d.p., 18 Sept, 19 Sept, 1883
Stanley-Massey-Stanley *see* Errington.
Stanley Pinhorne . Pinhorne, W E., widow of Rev G. S. Pinhorne, of St. John's, Beckermont, Cumberland. Times, 26 May, 1873.
Stanley Smith *see* Smith
Stansfield. D Wolryche : Stansfield, D, late of Ilkley York, now of Leamington, Warwicks, gent Times, 8 Nov., 1886.
  see Crompton-Stansfield
  „ Renn Stansfield
Stanway . Peach, A H., of 44, Nutford Place, Bryanstone Square, London, W. student. 19 Dec, 1878
Stanwix : Sloughter, T. 16 Oct., 1790 (622).
Stanyforth : Greenwood, E. W. 7*Dec., 1887 (7064).
Staples-Browne . Staples, R T. 14 Jan. 1843 (159)

Stapleton : Stapleton, Tho., to confirm the use of the name. 25 May, 1773 (11355).
Stapleton-Bretherton . Stapleton, M. 7 Sept., 1868 (4919).
Stapylton : Bree, M 13 July, 1811 (1297).
— : Chetwynd, The Hon G. A. 2 Aug., 1783 (12463)
Starey see Douglas Starey
Stark. Aug. Mozley : Stark A. Times. 10 Feb. 1885.
Starke see Hamilton-Starke.
Starkey see Cross-Starkey.
—, Barber-Starkey
—: Jennings, W 23 Sept., 1811 (1930)
Staunton : Ashpinshaw, J. 20 June, 1807 (839).
— see Lynch-Staunton, G. S.
Staunton-Wing Wing, G., of Gt. Berkhamsted, Herts., esq. Times, d.p, 2 April, 1889.
Staveley : Hutchinson, T. K. 14 Jan., 1815 (87)
Staveley-Shirt : Staveley, J 3 June, 1852 (2184)
Stawell see Alcock-Stawell
Stawell-Riversdale, Alcock see Alcock-Stawell
Stead see Mordaunt Stead
—, Castell
Steade see Pegge-Burnell
Steele see Topham-Steele
Steele-Graves · Steele. Sir J. M., Bart.. and E A. 30 July. 1862 (3828)
Steer see Johnson
Steer-Watkins : Steer, P W., formerly of Lahore, E. Indies, now of 411, Mare Street, Hackney. Middlesex, gent. Times, d.p., 2 Aug., 1871
Steere see Harrison
— : Witts. L. S 19 Jan., 1796 (79).
Sternchuss see Strong.
Stevens see Flutter-Stevens
Steigenberger . Berger, J. C., formerly of Lower Clapton, Midx, but now of Sandgate, Kent, gent. Times, d.p., 26 July 1883
Steinheim : Steinheimer, B., a native of Bavaria, but now of Lothbury, London, and Bayswater, Middlesex, gent. Times. d.p., 21 Jan., 1891
Steinheimer see Steinheim
Steinman Smith. G. S. 25 Oct., 1832 (2371)
Steinthal see Haslam
Stent see Lucas-Shadwell
Stennett see Dale
Stephens . Jones, E.. of Pencuwe, co Cardigan, late of 27, Arlington Square. Islington, now of 44, Regina Road. Times 29 Dec., 1868

Stephens *see* Kingsmill.
,, Loder.
,, Lyne-Stephens.
,, Meare.
: Smith. C. R., of Castle Vale, Radnor. Times. d.p. 21 March, 1893.
: Townsend, M F. 27 Jan 1827 (210)
see Trelawney.
: Wilkinson, P 25 Aug , 1820 (1825)
: Willis. H 16 June, 1801 (659)
Stephens-Townsend : Stephens, H J. T 1554 (40)
: Stephens, M. F. 8 Aug., 1845 (2385)
Stephenson *see* Empson.
,, Hall Stephenson
: Smith, H., of St. James's Square, Manchester, barrister-at-law. Times, d.p., 23 May, 1892
see Standish.
,, Thomas-Row.
Stepney *see* Cowell-Stepney.
,, Gulston-Stepney.
Stepney-Gulston : Gulston, A. S., of Derwydd, nr. Llandilo. Carmarthen, J.P., Capt R C.A. Mil Times, d.p , 20 May, 1886.
Steuart *see* de Kierskowski-Steuart
,, Duckett-Steuart
,, Gow-Steuart-Gow.
,, Mackenzie-Steuart
: Skinner, J., presently residing in London Times. 10 June, 1876.
Steuart-Grosett-Muirhead of Bredisholme : Steuart, R D 10 Aug., 1863 (3995)
Stevens *see* Hamilton
,, Moore-Stevens
: Moore, T. 19 June, 1817 (1389).
: Smith, R. P., of Risley, and formerly of Sawley, both in the county of Derby, gent Times. 12 Sept. 16 Sept., 1885
see Vaughan-Stevens
Stevenson : Bellairs, J. 15 Oct. 1844 (3519).
see Wharton.
Stevenson-Hamilton of Braidwood : Stevenson, Captn. James Lyon, Vol. VII., 6 Nov., 1867.
Steward *see* Falcon-Steward
,, Finch.
Stewart *see* Alston-Stewart
,, Balfour-Stewart
,, Blakeney-Lyon-Stewart.

Stewart *see* Dixon-Stewart.
,, Drummond-Stewart
of Binny : Falconar, Geo Mercer   Lyon, Vol. X , 9 Feb , 1880.
see Gow-Stewart
,, Hamill-Stewart.
: Vane-Tempest, Chas (Marq of Londonderry). 3 Aug., 1885 (3600).
see MacDonald-Stewart
,, McTaggart-Stewart.
,, Murray-Stewart.
,, Nichols-Stewart.
of Ballachin : Skinner, John   Lyon, Vol. X., 14 June, 1876
see Stuart.
,, Vane.
,, Wilson-Stewart
Stewart-Balfour · Stewart, Lieut.-Col. Wm   Lyon, Vol. IV, 16 March. 1837
Stewart-Murray *see* Murray-Stewart.
of Broughton : Stewart, H. G.   21 May, 1846 (1938)
Stewart-Savile : Savile, F. A , M.A , Rector of Torwood, Torquay, J.P. Times, 26 June. 1874.
Stewart-Wilson : Wilson. C , of N W Bengal, India. Times, d p , 11 March, 1887.
Steynor : Jenkins, Jas., of Birkdale, Edgbaston, Warwick. gent Times, d p., 23 Feb , 1894
Stidston-Broadbent · Stidston, C , of Chapel Street, Southport, and Birkdale Lancs , draper   Times, d p , 21 April, 1888
Stiff *see* Phillimore
Stiffe *see* Everitt
Stileman Gibbard · Stileman, L G , of Sharnbrook House Beds , esq. Times, d p , 5 Sept , 1877
Stirling-Hamilton : Hamilton, Sir W , of Woodgaters, Horsham, Sussex. Bart , Lieut.-Gen. Times d p , 7 Dec , 1889.
Stitt-Heslop Stitt. J , of Liverpool, Lancaster, esq retired merchant Times. d.p , 23 May, 1868
Stoakes Roberts. E   29 July, 1858 (3667).
Stoddart-Douglas Stoddart, J. D   19 Oct., 1833 (1929).
Stone *see* Cree
,, Batstone-Stone.
,, Elphinstone-Stone.
, Lowndes-Stone-Norton
,, Warry-Stone.
Stoffold *see* Austen

Stonehewer *see* Scott-Stonehewer
Stoneman, Jas Alford : Stoneman, J., of The Castle, Tynemouth, assnt. commissary in Ord. Dep. of Army. Times, 22 May, 1879
Stonestreet : Griffin, G. 25 Feb., 1794 (169).
Stoney *see* Bowes
,, Butler-Stoney.
Stooke-Vaughan : Stooke, Rev. F. S., of The Vicarage, Weddington Heath, Hereford. Times, d p., 6 Nov., 1875.
Stopford *see* Tucker.
Stopford-Blair : Stopford, W H. 15 May, 1842 (1333)
Stopford-Sackville : Stopford, Caroline H. Whll., 26 March, 1870 (D G. 427)
: Stopford, W. B. 26 March, 1870 (2057)
Storey *see* Forster.
: Moffatt, J. and R. S. W., 10 Sept., 1860 (D G 1062)
see Shawe-Storey.
,, Shum-Storey.
Stormont *see* Hatton.
Stothert *see* Cockburn-Stothert.
Stott : Clark, N. S. 1 Sept., 1884 (3953)
Wilson, W. J. S. 17 Jan., 1828 (262).
Stott-Milne : Stott, J. 31 Jan., 1844 (406)
: Stott, J. 17 May, 1854 (1573).
Stott-Stanhope : Stott, G. 4 March. 1856 (1004).
Stott-Stanhope : Stott, Geo. W., 4 March, 1856 (D G. 330)
Stoughton *see* Trent-Stoughton
Stourton *see* Langdale.
,, Vavasour.
Stoveld : Ridsdale 8 Dec., 1881 (46).
Stovin *see* Lister.
Stow *see* Kenyon-Stow.
,, Philipson-Stow.
Stow-Baldrey : Stow, J. 12 April, 1794 (313)
Stoyle, W. Blin : Stoyle, W., of Crediton, Devon, and St Catherine's Coll, Cambs., gent. Times, d p., 11 March, 1891.
Strachan-Davidson : Strachan, G. A., of Dornton, Wilts Times, 12 July, 1900
Stracey-Clitherow : Stracy, E. J. 20 July, 1865 (3676).
Stracy *see* Hayes-Stracy
Stradling-Carne : Nicholl-Carne, J. W., and M. S. his wife, of Bridgend, Glamorgan. Times, d p., 4 Sept., 1877.
Strahan : Snow, W. 24 Sept., 1831 (1998)
Strange-Mure : Strange, W. T. H. Whll., 24 Dec., 1867 (D G 3).
Strange-Mure : Strange, W T H. 24 Dec., 1867 (7110)

Strangford *see* Kincaid-Lennox.
Strangways *see* Swainston-Strangways
Stratford : Morgan, H. S 11 April, 1842 (1017)
    see Morgan-Stratford.
    ,, Wingfield-Stratford.
Strathmore, Earl and Countess of : Bowes-Lyon, from Lyon, 7 Geo. III, 1766.
Straton : Muter, J 10 Sept., 1816 (1873)
Straube *see* Gordon
Streatfield *see* Moore
Street *see* Wright
Streeter *see* Bisshopp.
Strey *see* Brougham
  ,, Broughton-Strey.
Strickland *see* Cholmeley.
  ,, Cholmley.
  ,, De Beauchamp.
Strickland-Constable : Strickland, H 26 March, 1863 (1873)
Strickland-Standish : Strickland, T. 11 May, 1807 (656).
Stringer : Belcher, W. 16 May, 1817 (1208).
Strode *see* Chetham-Strode
    Lowe, G. S. S 27 Feb., 1897 (1470)
Strong : Sternschuss, P. H., of Cagedale, Clehonger, Hereford. Incumbent of Newton d.p., 6 May, 1865
Strother *see* Del Strother.
Stronge *see* Hussey.
Strugnell *see* Hawkes-Strugnell.
Strutt *see* Moore
Stuart : Belches, E. 7 Oct., 1797 (955).
   : Belches, Sir J 7 Oct., 1797 (955).
    see Constable-Maxwell-Stuart.
    ,, Crichton-Stuart
    ,, Cumberland.
    ,, Fenwick-Stuart.
    ,, Forbes-Stuart.
    ,, Gordon-Stuart
    ,, Gray.
    ,, Harrington-Stuart
    ,, Hepburn-Stuart-Forbes-Trefusis
    ,, Hepburn-Stuart-Forbes
    ,, Nibloch-Stuart
    ,, Scott.
    ,, Toby-Stuart.
    ,, Villiers-Stuart
   Stewart, J., of Bishopwearmouth, formerly of Portsmouth, Presby minister. Times, 16 Dec., 1875.
Stuart-Chudleigh : Stuart, H de C 17 May, 1895 (D.G. 537)

Stuart-Crichton : Stuart, J. 26 Aug., 1805 (1091).
Stuart-Fox : Fox, Jas., of 55, Marquess Road, Canonbury, London, to cont. name of Stuart-Fox used prior to and ever since 1886. Times, 21 April, 1896.
Stuart-French : Stuart, T. G. 3 Nov., 1894 (D.G. 1264).
Stuart-Richardson : Stuart, Visct. Hy. James, and Augusta L his wife. St. James's, 11 May, 23 May, 1867 (D.G 673 and 693).
Stuart-Wortley *see* Montague-Stuart-Wortley-Mackenzie.
Stubber : Maillard, Nicholas D. P. St. J., 15 May, D.C., 30 May, 1863 (D.G. 633 and 649).
Stubbs . Eyton, H., junr., of 7, Church Street, Manchester, merchant. Times, d.p , 15 Jan., 1876.
Stubbes : Taylor, J. S. 6 April, 1861 (1532).
Stubington : Yeulett, I. F., of Westfield, Horndean, Hants., spinster. Times, d.p., 7 March, 1893.
Stuckey : Wood, V. 14 March, 1861 (1372).
Stuckey-Bartlett : Bartlett, B. J. 15 May, 1810 (693).
Stucley : Buck, G. S. 27 July, 1858 (3632).
Stump *see* Hillier.
Sturges-Bourne : Sturges, W. 6 Dec., 1803 (1743)
Sturt-Grindall · Grindall, H. E P S. 20 Aug., 1830 (1807).
Styleman *see* Le Strange.
Styleman-Le Strange : Styleman, H. Le S 18 July, 1839 (1436)
Styleman Le Strange *see* Le Strange.
Suckling : Fox, A. I. 28 Dec., 1820 (35).
Suffield : Brown, P. S., of Victoria Street, Westminster. Times, 3 Dec., 1900.
Sugars Gibson : Gibson, J., of H.M.S. Rover, assisnt. engineer Times, d p., 21 May, 1886.
Sugden *see* Filkin.
  · Long, W. J. 9 Sept., 1834 (1641).
Sulman *see* Wagener.
Summers *see* Colman
Sumner *see* Brockhurst
  : Wiggin, Catherine, of Queen Anne's Mansions, Westminster, Middlesex, spinster. d.p., 25 Nov., 1878.
Sunderland-Taylor : Sunderland, C., of Long Sutton, Lincoln, farmer. Times, 27 March, 1871.
Sundius : Smith, Rev C. S., of Driffield, York. Times, d.p., 12 Feb., 1890
Supple *see* Collis.
  ,, De Capell-Brooke
Surman : Goodlake, J. S. 1st & 2nd Will IV, 1831
Surridge *see* Andrews
Surtees-Allnatt : Allnatt, E. A., of The Firs, Frant, Sussex, wife of R. H. Allnatt, esq Times, 11 March, 1880

Susskin *see* Van Werner.
Sussmann *see* Somers.
Sutcliffe-Witham   Sutcliffe, J. 6 March, 1839 (522).
Sutherland-Leveson-Gower : G G, Duke of Sutherland, to continue to use the name of Sutherland before Leveson-Gower   12 May, 1841 (1223)
Sutherland-Walker : Sutherland, E. C   13 Dec, 1856 (2485)
Sutton *see* Gunning-Sutton
   . Hutchinson, G W. 14 Dec., 1822 (2044).
   see le Dixon-Sutton.
  ,, Nelthorpe.
Swab, Edw Wilson . Schwab, Siegfried Moritz. Times, 14 Oct., 1874
Swaffield   Owen, R H. 26 Oct, 1840 (2353)
   see Owen-Swaffield.
Swainson   Smith, C. S., of The Parsonage, Grange-over-Sands, Lancs., gent. Times, d p, 16 April and 23 April, 1887
Swainston-Strangways   Swainston, E   2 Jan., 1804 (14)
Swann Teasdale, W   15 Nov, 1831 (2457)
Sweet-Escott . Sweet, T. 29 Sept, 1810 (1538)
Sweetman-Powell . Sweetman, J. M. 4 March, 1874 (D. Castle only), (D.G. 154).
Swettenham *see* Willis.
Swete : Tripe, J. 21st Geo. III., 1781.
Swetenham · Comberback, R. 6 July, 1790 (413)
Swettenham *see* Warren-Swettenham.
Swinborne, L. P . Pfander, Thos. L., of London, and of Essex, merchant. Times, 8 July, 1884
   : Pfander, F W, E. E., and L H., all of Gt. Coggleshall, Essex   Times, 8 July, 1884
Swinburne-Hanham : Swinburne, J C, of Manston House, Dorset. esq   Times, d.p, 7 Feb., 1883
Swindell *see* Evers-Swindell.
  ,, Rose-Swindell
Swinfen · Grundy. 8th Geo. III., 1768
   : Grundy, T. 11th Geo III., 1771
     Selby, Alice J., of St. Margaret's House, Bethnal Green, E , spinster   Times, 7 Oct., 1895.
Swinnerton *see* Milborne-Swinnerton
  ,, Milborne-Swinnerton-Pilkington
Sydenham *see* De Sidenham
Syers Barnett, A W S. Times, 11 Sept., 1900
Sykes *see* Masterman-Sykes
Syme *see* Boswell.
Symes-Bullen : Symes, J. B. 25 Aug, 1868 (5038).
Symmons *see* Randolph-Symmons
Symonds *see* Breedon.
  ,, Loder-Symonds

Symonds - Peers, R. 4th Geo III., 1764
Symonds-Tayler : Symonds, J. F. 29 Jan., 1886 (560)
Symons : Raymond, T. 21 July, 1797 (699)
    see Soltau
    „   Soltau-Symons
Symons-Jeune . Jeune, J. F. 28 Oct., 1878 (5996).
Sympson *see* Walcott-Sympson
Syndercombe *see* Raymond.
Synge : Sing, M., of Aigburth, nr. Liverpool, B.A. Times, d.p., 31 Oct., 1894.
    - Sing, H. M., of Russell Square, London Times, 3 Oct., 1900
Syrett Death, C. S., of Abberton Hall, Essex, and Stevens Hospital, Dublin, med. stud. Times, 16 Sept., 1874.

T

Tabberer Brown : Tabberer, H., of Burton-on-Trent, Staffs., brewer. Times. d.p, 13 July, 1874.
Tagg-Arundel : Tagg, A., B.A., of the Madras Civil Service, District of Cuddapah, Madras Presidency, India. Times, 11 Aug., 1870.
Tagg Arundell - Tagg, W. A., of Grenville Street and Dorset Street, Middlesex, architect and surveyor Times, d.p., 6 April, 1882
Tagg *see* Arundell.
Tailyour *see* Renny-Tailyour.
    : Taylor, G. R., of Nav. and Mil. Club, Piccadilly, late Capt. "The Buffs" Reg., W. S., of Old Ormsby, Yorks., esq. and A. T., of Lamberton, co. Wicklow, esq. Times, d.p., 30 May, 1891
Tait : Macgaie, M. 20 March, 1810 (407).
Talbot *see* Carpenter.
    „   Chetwynd
    ,   Crosbie.
    Crosbie, J. 23 Sept., 30 Oct., 1851 (D.G 877 and 881)
    - Davenport. W. 16 May, 1778 (11874)
    Fitzalan-Howard, E. B. 19 July, 1876 (4254)
Talbot-Chetwynd . Talbot, Rt. Hon. J. C. W., 19 April, 1786 (D G 4752)
Talbot-Crosbie . Crosbie, W. T. 22 Nov., 1880 (D G 1029)
Talbot-Ponsonby : Talbot, Chas. Wm. 11 Oct., 20 Oct., 1865 (D.G 1501).

Tallmadge *see* Delahay.
Talmash : Manners, Sir W. (com. called Rt. Hon. Lord Huntingtower). 4 April, 1821 (838).
   see Tollemache.
Taliacarne *see* Bertie.
Tamplin Miller *see* Miller
Tancred : Cleghorn, G. 8 Sept., 1885 (4278).
Tannas, George : Ball, J. G. C. Times, 27 May, 1881.
Tanqueray-Willaume : Tanqueray, T. B. 10 March, 1848 (1087).
Tapps-Gervis-Meyrick : Tapps-Gervis, Sir G. E. M., Bart. 16 March, 1876 (2154).
Tapps-Gervis : Tapps, Sir G. I. 3 Dec., 1835 (2363).
Tarbolton : Tarbotton, W. G., of Fakenham, Norfolk, Congregational minister, A. C. Tarbotton, of 4, Holly Mount, Hampstead, and of New College, London, Middlesex, gent.; Mary S. Tarbotton, of Sunset View, Ilkley, York, spinster; Jessie M. Tarbottom, of Sunset View, Ilkley, York, spinster. Times, d.p., 17 Oct., 1878
Tarbotton *see* Tarbolton.
Tarleton-Fothergill : Tarleton, A. 21 Dec., 1887 (7248).
Tarn *see* Holmes-Tarn.
Tarrant-Turner : Tarrant, Rev. F. H. T., of 102, Burton Road, Lincoln. Times, d.p., 22 Feb., 1888.
Tasburgh : Anne, M. 8 May, 1810 (661).
   . Crathorne, G. 26th Geo. III., c. 16, 1786.
Taswell *see* Taylor-Taswell.
Taswell-Langmead : Langmead, T. P., of St. Mary's Hall, Oxford, and Lincoln's Inn, esq., barrister-at-law. Times, d.p., 7 April, 1864.
Tatchell : Bullen, J. T., 2 April, 1823 (563).
Tatchell-Bullen : Tatchell, J. T. 12 May, 1852 (1403)
Tate *see* Finney.
   ,, Pinfold-Tate.
Tatem : Upham, J. G. 1 Oct., 1807 (1317)
Tatham *see* Fenwick
Tatham-Warter : Tatham, M. E., of 10, Upper Phillimore Gardens, London, widow. Times, d.p., 25 Feb., 1885.
Tathwell : Baker, B. 22 May, 1804 (663)
Tatnall-Boone : Tatnall, T. B. 6 Sept., 1824 (1478)
Tattersall *see* Chadwick.
   : Pickles, F. W., of Bradford, Yorks. Times, d.p., 17 Oct., 1890
Tattersall-Musgrave : Tattersall, E. 9 Feb., 1869 (1453)
Tatton : Egerton, T. W. 9 June, 1806 (733).
   see Egerton.
Taubman *see* Goldie.

Tawke : Tuck, C. 31 Dec., 1816 (108).
Tayler *see* Porter.
   ,, Symonds-Tayler.
Taylor : Aynsley, H. 12 May, 1812 (978).
   see Bamford-Taylor.
   ,, Bentley-Taylor.
   ,, Bradshaw-Taylor.
   : Brind, A. C., of 46, Park Street, Dorset Square, Midx., gent. Times, 5 Feb., 1875.
   see Burrowes
   ,, Chaworth.
   : Clough, E. 15 April, 1807 (495).
   see Edwards-Taylor.
   ,, Everley-Taylor.
   ,, Hamilton
   : Howey, R. T. N. 1 Dec., 1883 (6374)
   see Howey
   ,, Howson.
   : Kerr, R. T. 15 Sept., 1883 (D G. 1224)
   : Lemon, Jane, of Hampstead, Middlesex, spinster Times, 12 April, 1893
   see Lisle
   ,, Lowe.
   : Meeke, W. B. 2 March, 1840 (520)
   see Norton-Taylor.
   ,, Pilling-Taylor.
   ,, Quinn.
   ,, Roebuck.
   ,, Ronald Taylor.
   ,, Rowley
   ,, Shawe-Taylor.
   ,, Smithson
   ,, Stubbs
   ,, Sunderland-Taylor.
   ,, Tailyour.
   ,, Watson-Taylor.
   ,, Wigsell.
   : Williams, W. 10 July, 1781 (12205).
   see Worsley-Taylor.
   : Wyeth, C. J., 354, Goldhawk Road, Hammersmith Times, 6 Jan., 1894.
Taylor-Crane : Taylor, G., of The Ivy House, Hoxton, Middlesex, victualler. Times, 11 Nov., 1875
Taylor Jones : Jones, E. W. T., and H. G. T., both of Herne House, Margate, Kent, respectively B A.'s. Times, d p., 22 Sept., 1891.

Taylor-Restell : Taylor, J. S., of S. Kensington, Middlesex, gent. Times, 2 June, 1893
Taylor-Smith : Taylor, E.   7 April, 1843 (1236).
Taylor-Taswell : Taylor, Rev. S. T., of St Mary's Hall, Oxford. Times, d.p., 5 Aug., 1869
Taylor-Whitehead : Taylor, S.   26 March, 1866 (2206).
               : Taylor, S , of Upper Phillimore Gardens, Kensington, Middlesex, esq. Times, 18 April, 1866.
Teale, Herbert Greenwood : Teale, H., of Leeds, Yorks. gent. Times, d p., 25 Aug., 1890.
Teasdale *see* Burn
      „ Rawlence.
      „ Swann.
Tebb *see* Routh.
Tebbitt *see* Levy Tebbitt.
Teek *see* Lovell.
Teixeira : De David Teixeira, A.   6 Jan., 1804 (14).
Teleki *see* Harley.
Telfer-Smollett : Telfer, C. E. D., of Bonhill, Major (retired), and barrister. Times, 27 July, 1895.
Telford-Smith : Smith, T., of Lancaster. Times, d.p , 25 Feb., 1895.
Tempest *see* Plumbe-Tempest.
       : Ricketts, R. T.   23 April, 1884 (1298).
       : Vane, Sir H.   35th Geo. III., 1795.
       see Vane-Tempest.
Tempest Radford · Radford, T., of Greenhill, Kidderminster, carpet manufacr. Times, d p., 30 Dec., 1881.
Temple *see* Couper-Temple.
      „ De Liefde-Temple.
       : Dicken, J.   27 Sept., 1796 (923).
       see Grenville-Nugent-Temple.
       · Harris, Hon A. E. D.G., 11 May, 1900 (681).
       : Harris, R. T.   R. Signet, "Office of Arms," 26 Jan., 1852 (D.G. 62).
       see Schmidt-Temple.
       : Smyth, F J. H.   1 Sept., 1835 (1697).
Temple-Allen · Francis, E. A , of Clapham, Surrey, gent. Times, d.p., 20 Oct., 1879.
Temple-Barrow : Barrow, W. J. M., of Southwell, Notts., esq. Times, d.p., 3 Aug., 1881.
Temple-Gore-Langton : Gore-Langton, W. S. (Earl Temple).   12 March, 1892 (1700)
Temple Lynes : Temple, C , of Blakeney, Norfolk, merchant. Times, d.p , 28 Aug. and 4 Sept., 1877.
Temple-West : West, J. T.   1 June, 1868 (3237).
Tench *see* Sherburne.

Tenison : Collins. C. M. 27 Dec., 1890 (165).
    see King Tenison.
    „ Ryan-Tenison
    E. T. R. : Ryan, E. T., of 8, Keith Terrace, Shepherd's Bush, Middlesex, M D (St. Andrews, Scot.), L.R.C.P (London), M.R.C.S (Eng.), late assistant surgeon R.N. Times, d p., 22 Aug., 1862.
Tennent : Dillon-Tennant, R. 5 April, 1836 (666).
    : Tovey, H. 3 Feb., 1832 (316).
    : Tovey, J. 25 Feb., 1867 (1024)
    : Vidler, H. D. 24 April, 1876 (2735).
Tennyson-D'Eyncourt : Tennyson, C. (Rt Hon). 30 July, 1835 (1464).
Tennyson *see* Turner.
Teush-Hecker: Teush, S. H. 26 Feb., 1825 (354).
Tepper : Ferguson, P. 12 June, 1779 (11986).
Terry *see* Messiter-Terry.
Terry Horsey : Terry, F. J., of 11, Billiter Square, London, auctioneer and surveyor. Times, d.p, 24 Oct., 1890.
Tetlow : Dawson, W., late of Waddington, Yorks, now of Skerdon, Yorks., yeoman. Times, d p., 8 Nov., 1890.
    see Standing Tetlow.
    : Walker, B., widow, A. Walker, spinster, and M. Pennington, spinster, all of Skirden, Bolton-by-Bowland, West Riding, York. Times, 14 May, 1865.
Thackabery *see* Thackeray.
Thackeray : Thackabery, J., of 1, Grosvenor Terrace, Buxton, Derby, preceptor. 8 April, 1876.
Thackray : Griffiths, H., of Kirton-in-Lindsey. Times, 7 June, 1900.
Thackwell *see* Smith
Thaddeus, H. Jones : Jones, H Thaddeus, of S. Kensington, artist. Times, d.p., 24 June, 1885.
Thal *see* Joseph-Thal.
Tharp-Gent : Tharp, W. M. W., 16 Aug., 1861 (D.G. 1050)
Thecothick : Ivers, J 24 June, 1775 (11572).
Theobald : Meadows, J. 16th Geo III., 1776.
    : Pigg, F., formerly of the Haymarket, Norwich, Norfolk, woollen draper and shoe manufacr, now of 7, High Street, Bromley, Kent, commercial traveller. Times, 5 Aug., 1869.
    Pigg, F., formerly of the Haymarket, Norwich, now of 7, High Street, Bromley, Kent, commercial traveller. Times, 12 Aug., 1869

Theobald Pigg, A., of Savile Park Terrace, Halifax, co. York,
	and of Old Market, Halifax, silk mercer and
	draper. Times, 14 June, 1872.
	: Poole, T 17 May, 1816 (962).
Thexton *see* Hudson.
Thicknesse : Coldwell, F. H., and Anne his wife. W., 29 March,
	1859 (D.G. 529)
Thiselton-Dyer · Thiselton, W. M. 16 April, 1840 (990).
Thislethwayte-Pelham · Milbourne, C. 27 Dec., 1811 (48).
Thom, Patrick Baeda : Thom, Peter, born at Bogfouton,
	Aberdeens. Times, 20 Oct., 1880.
Thom-Postlethwaite : Thom, A. T. and G., of Whitehaven.
	Cumberland. Times, 26 Oct., 1900.
Thomas *see* Barrett-Lennard.
„ Battie-Wrightson.
„ Berry
„ Collette-Thomas.
„ Dawson-Thomas
„ Deere.
„ Dodd-Thomas
„ Edney.
: Freeman, G. T. 11 Feb., 1792 (90).
see Freeman-Thomas.
: Freeman, I. 4 July, 1786 (298).
see Greene.
„ Haynes-Thomas.
. Hughes, Charlotte 29 Nov., 1853 (3479)
Irish, E. W. B., of 22, Queen's Road, Brownswood
	Park, London, N., mercantile clerk. Times,
	d.p., 12 March, 1884.
see Kearsey
see Morgan.
„ Palliser.
„ Pateshall.
: Pill, Eliz., of 22, Angus Street, Roath, Cardiff,
	spinster Times, d.p., 31 Aug., 1893
see Preston-Thomas.
: Sauerwein, H., of 53, Warwick Street, Westminster,
	Middlesex Times, 30 Jan., 1888.
see Seaton.
„ Treherne.
„ Vaughan
„ Watkyn-Thomas
Thomas-Jones : Thomas, A. 3 Oct., 1797 (955).
Thomas-Le-Marchant · Thomas, Le-M 10 March, 1865 (1448).
Thomas-Moore · Thomas, W. W. 11 June, 1873 (2882).

Thomas-O'Donel · Thomas, E. T., and M. A. his wife, both of Newport, co. Mayo. Times, d.p., 20 June, 1889.
Thomas-Peter . Peter, J. F. T., of Blomfield Street, Middlesex, esq. Times, d.p., 10 June, 1876.
Thomas-Row : Stephenson, E.   10 July, 1843 (2351).
Thomasset *see* Dayrolles.
Thomlinson-Grant : Thomlinson, M.   12 May, 1864 (2632).
Thomlinson-Walker : Walker, W., of Clifton Grove, and Walmgate, York, ironfounder. Times, d.p., 2 April, 1877.
Thompson : Arnall, H. T.   19 June, 1885 (3372).
    see Arnall-Thompson.
    „ Bullock
    „ Bunbury Thompson
    „ Buncombe-Poulett-Scrope
    : Coates, W.   14 April, 1836 (682).
    see Corbett-Thompson.
    „ Duke.
    „ Friend Thompson.
    „ Green-Thompson.
    „ Gwyn.
    : Lawley, P. B.   27 Sept., 1820 (1919).
    see Livingstone.
    : Makin, W. T.   8 Dec., 1806 (1599)
    : Meyer, W   28 March, 1794 (246).
    see Meysey-Thompson.
    „ Montagu.
    „ Pearse-Thompson.
    „ Powney.
    „ Redman-Thompson.
    „ Valentine Thompson.
    : Whitehouse, E., of Chesterfield, Anerley, Surrey, spinster. Times, 15 Oct., 1885.
Thompson-Smyth : Thompson, R.   6 June, 20 June, 1871 (D.G. 461).
Thompson-West · Thompson, T.   30 Aug., 1783 (12470)
Thompson-Yates : Thompson, S. A., of Thingwall Hall, nr. Liverpool, Lancaster. Times, 1 July, 1867.
Thomson *see* Deas-Thomson.
    „ Montagu.
    : Toker, R. E   28 Aug., 1851 (2206).
    see White-Thomson
Thomson-Balcarras : Thomson, W. R., of South Tottenham, cashier. Times, d.p., 31 March, 1894
Thomson-Buncombe-Poulett : Thomson, J.   27 June, 1814 (1610)
Thorbou *see* Wilson-Thorbou.

Thornburgh : Mooney. Rev. T., vicar of Heywood, nr. Westbury,
Wilts. Times, d.p., 8 Sept, 1885
Thornburgh-Cropper : Cropper, E D. 14 Nov., 1874 (5757).
Thorne, B. B Thorne Thorne, B. B, of Inverness Terrace,
Hyde Park, W Times, d p., 19 Jan, 1889
Leslie Cavendish Thorne . Thorne, L C, of 45, Inverness Terrace, Hyde Park, W. Times, d p , 15 Oct , 1889
Thorne-George *see* Wyndham.
Thornhill : Camm, C T. 13 Nov , 1802 (1178).
    see Clarke-Thornhill.
    : McCreagh. 1 March, 1882 (1064).
Thornhill Gell : Thornhill, I., of Stanton-in-Peak, Derby, of Eaton Square and Brighton, widow. Times, d p , 23 March, 1876.
Thornton *see* Astell.
    : Lee, R. N 1 Aug., 1865 (3823).
    see Todd-Thornton
    „ Welch-Thornton.
Thornton Burt *see* Burt.
Thornton-Duesbury Thornton, W D. 21 Aug , 1837 (2217)
Thornycroft : Mytton, C. 29 Oct , 1831 (2355)
Thorold Canale, S 9th Geo. III , 1769
    see Dickson.
    Dickson, F T. Times, d p , 10 Aug., 1886
    see Dickson-Thorold.
    „ Grant-Thorold
    Hart, B. 29 Feb , 1820 (412)
Thoroton *see* Hildyard
Thorpe *see* Parker
Throckmorton *see* Courtenay
Thurgood, Hannah Bunce · Bunce, C. H , at G E Ry Station, Liverpool Street, London Times, 9 Jan., 1878
Thurlow : Godfrey, W. T., of the Admiralty, Spring Gardens, Middlesex, esq Times, d p , 17 June, 1873
    see Hovell-Thurlow-Camming-Bruce
Thursby-Pelham : Thursby, H 2 Aug., 1852 (2184).
Tibbits : Hood, Rt. Hon. S. (Vis. Hood) 12 Feb., 1841 (371)
    Maunsell, J. B. 10 July, 1858 (3377).
Tibbitts *see* Rainford
Tibbs *see* Pereira
Tichborne *see* Doughty
    „ Doughty-Tichborne.
Tidy *see* Manbey.
Tighe-Bunbury Tighe, D 2 May, 13 May, 1872 (D G. 294)
Tilden-Sampson Tilden, J 22 Nov , 1797 (1114)
Tiley *see* England.

Tilghman-Huskison : Tilghman, W. H. 1856 (2808).
Tilghman-Huskisson : Tilghman, W. H. W, 7 Aug., 1856 (D G. 882)
Tillotson *see* Knowles-Tillotson.
Tillstone *see* Monkhouse-Tillstone.
    „ Rogers-Tillstone
    „ Sedley-Tillstone.
Tilney : Tinley, R. J., T., and G. A. 10 Oct., 1879 (6115)
Tilson *see* Chowne.
Tilson-Marsh-Lushington-Tilson : Tilson-Marsh, Rev Sir W., of Ely, Herts, and St. Leonards-on-Sea Times, d.p, 20 Aug., 1873.
Timms : Adams, G. W., of Preston, The Hyde, Middlesex Times, d.p., 14 June, 1886
Timms-Hervey-Elwes : Timms, J 25 May, 1793 (419)
Timothy *see* Keighley
Tincler *see* Blennerhassett
Tindal-Carill-Worsley : Tindal, N. and E. 22 Feb., 1878 (1828)
Tingling *see* Widdrington.
Tinling-Widdrington : Tinling. D 3 March, 1809 (269)
Tinley *see* Tilney
Tinson *see* Bailey
Tippet *see* Vivian.
Tippetts *see* Paul.
Tirel : Morin, J. 10 Nov., 1787 (521)
Tittle-Hamilton : Tittle, I D.G., 3 May, 1898 (545)
Toby-Lascelles : Toby, H. J, of 12, Rue Caumartin, Paris, gent Times. d.p., 6 June, 14 June, 1883
Toby-Stuart Stuart, W. J, of 4, Cobden Villas, Dagnall's Park, South Norwood, Surrey, and of 47, Brompton Road, Knightsbridge, Middlesex Times, d.p., 5 Aug., 1868.
Tod-Heatly : Tod, G. H. 16 Oct., 1848 (3732).
Tod-Mercer of Scotsbank : Tod, James Lyon, Vol XI, 17 April, 1884.
Todd *see* Ruddell-Todd
    : Smith, T. 29 Dec., 1787 (597).
    see Wilson-Todd
Todd-Newcombe Todd, J 24 Jan., 1867 (551).
Todd-Thornton Todd, J H 8 Sept and 27 Sept, 1866 (D.G 1405 and 1421)
Toker *see* Thomson.
Toler-Aylward Toler, H. J. C. 23 May, 1884 (D.G 582)
Toll *see* Newman
Toler *see* Graham-Toler.
Tollemache · Halliday, J. R. D 3 Aug., 1821 (1617)
    Manners, Hon. C 30 March, 1821 (783)
    · Manners, Hon. J 30 March, 1821 (783)

Tollemache Manners, Lady L (Rt. Hon. Countess of Dysart). 30 March, 1821 (782).
    see Tollemache-Tollemache.
    „ Talmash.
Tollemache-Tollemache : Tollemache, R. W. L, esq, Hon. M.A., J.P., Rector of South Wytham, Lincoln Times, 25 Jan., 1876.
Tollet see Wicksted.
    : Embury, G. 20 Aug., 1796 (789).
Tom see Tomn.
Tombleson : Waddingham, T 8 June, 1853 (1665)
Tombs see Boys-Tombs
Tomkins see Berkeley.
Tomkinson see Westenhall.
Tomkyns-Grafton : Tomkyns, W., of Southern House, Pittville, Cheltenham, Gloucestershire. Times, 21 Dec., 1865
Tomline : Pretyman, G. 3 Nov., 1803 (1589).
Tomlinson see Hunt.
    : Lang, J. T 18 Jan, 1854 (207).
    see Paget-Tomlinson.
Tomn : Tom, Mary A. J. S., of Rosedale, St. Clement, Cornwall, widow Times, d.p., 21 Nov., 1888.
Tompsett : Penkivil, J. S. S 12 May, 1883 (2614).
Tompson-Delmar : Tompson, F. O., now of Ruislip Park, Middlesex, gent. Times, 20 March, 1863.
Tongue-Croxall : Tongue, E R 10 Dec., 1887 (7247).
    : Tongue, R. F. 27 May, 1863 (2855).
Tonkin : Moore, W. 15 June, 1811 (1086).
Tooke see Baseley-Tooke.
    „ Cheval-Tooke.
    „ Hales-Tooke
Tooker see Whalley-Tooker.
Topham-Haynes : Topham, J R, of Wensor Castle, Deeping Common, West Deeping, Lincoln, farmer. Times, d p, 18 Jan., 1869.
Topham-Steele . Steele, E. W., of 31, Prince's Avenue, Liverpool, gent Times, d.p., 22 March, 1895
Topp see Bunton.
    : Lloyd, R. 19 May, 1778 (11875).
Torbett see Lambe.
Torre see Holme.
Torrens-Johnson · Johnson, M., G J, E., and J, all of 16, Kensington Gate, Middlesex Times, d p., 25 Sept., 1894
Torriano see Hanson Torriano.
Tothill see Harris.
Touchet-Davies · Touchet H 26 April, 1823 (706).

Tourle : Cooper, T. 28 Nov., 1801 (1411).
Tournay : Allen, H. T. 23 Feb., 1870 (1524).
    : Allen, W. T. 13 March, 1871 (1631).
Tournay-Bargrave Tournay, R. 15 July, 1800 (812).
Tovey *see* Tennent.
Towell Ellis : Towell, E. G., gent., of Norfolk. Times, d p, 10 Dec., 1875.
Tower *see* Baker.
Towers *see* Alcock-Bech (or Beck?).
Towers-Clark of Wester Moffat : Towers, Wm. Lyon Register, Vol. VII., 29 Nov., 1867.
Towerson : Bell, J., of The Cottage, Hensingham, Cumberland, civ. engineer Times, d.p., 9 July, 1880.
Towle *see* Huggett.
Townley *see* Johnson Townley.
Townley-Parker : Parker, T T. 20 Sept., 1879 (5689).
Townsend *see* Elliott Townsend.
    ,, Lawrence-Townsend.
    ,, Lovedon.
    ,, Mellifont-Townsend.
    ,, Payne-Townsend.
    ,, Stephens.
    ,, Stephens-Townsend.
    ,, Townshend.
Townsend-Forester : Forester, G. 10 Dec, 1791 (677).
Townshend *see* Brooke.
    ,, Dunn-Gardner.
    ,, Ferrars.
    ,, Marsham-Townshend.
    : Townsend, H. P., of Derry, Cork, and of Wem, Salop, esq. Times, 4 Sept., 1874.
Tozer-Aubrey : Tozer, H. P. 1 Oct., 1813 (1940).
Tracey-Elliot : Tracey, H. E. 12 May, 1892 (2904).
Tracey : Keck, Hon. H C. 14th Geo. III., 1774.
Tracy : Charteris, S. (Lady Elcho). 58th Geo. III., 1818.
    : Hanbury, C. 1 Jan., 1799 (2).
    see Hanbury-Tracy.
    ,, Leigh.
Trafford *see* De Trafford.
    : Leigh, T 10 Dec., 1791 (677).
    : Nicolls, E. T. 5 May, 1823 (730).
    : Nicolls, T. S 13 Oct., 1837 (2615).
    see Southwell.
Trafford-Rawson : Trafford, H. 25 May, 1892 (3515).
Trafford-Southwell : Trafford, Margaret E 24 April, 1849 (1424).
    Trafford. S. 10 Jan., 1810 (138).

Trant *see* Dillon-Trant.
Trapaud *see* Plaistow-Trapaud
Trappes-Lomax : Trappes, E   17 May, 1892 (3071).
　　　　　　: Trappes, Helen, of Clayton Hall, Clayton-le-Moors, Lancs., widow   Times, 30 April, 1892.
Travers : Weatherhog, P. T., of 27, Albemarle Street, Middlesex, chartrd. accnt.   Times, d p , 9 May, 1888.
Travis *see* Cook.
Treacher *see* Bowles.
Treby : Ourry, P. T.   25 June, 1785 (305).
　　see Phillips-Treby.
Treffry : Austen, J T.   14 Feb., 1838 (345).
　　　Wilcocks, E. J.   4 May, 1850 (1418).
Trefusis *see* Hepburn-Stuart-Forbes
　　　,, Rolle
Treherne · Lloyd, O. W , of Cheltenham, Glos.   Times, 28 Nov., 1890
　　　Thomas, G. T , of Mulberg, Canton of Thurgovie, Switzerland.   Times, d p , 14 Dec , 1866
　　　Thomas, G. G., of 86, Piccadilly, The New Club, St. James' Street, and 77, Gresham House, Old Broad Street, London, Middlesex, esq   d p., 1 July, 1865.
Trelawney *see* Brereton
　　　,, Clifford Constable
　　　,, Collins-Trelawney
　　　. Darell, C.   22 Oct., 1795 (1083)
　　　Darell, H St G   22 Oct , 1795 (1083)
　　　see Jago-Trelawney.
　　　,, Salusbury.
　　　,, Salusbury-Trelawney
　　　: Stephens, E   22 Oct , 1795 (1083).
　　　: Stephens, R   22 Oct , 1795 (1083)
Tremayne *see* Bouch-Tremayne.
Tremearne *see* Shirley.
Trench *see* Cooke.
　　　,, Cooke-Trench
Trench-Gascoigne · Trench, F C. and M.   15 Aug , 1851 (2148).
Trenchard *see* Ashfordby-Trenchard
　　　,, Dillon-Trenchard
　　　: Pickard, J. T   21 Nov., 1840 (3046).
Trengrove *see* Williams Trengrove.
Trent-Stoughton . Trent, H W J.   1 March. 1889 (1474)
Tresham   Davis, J C.   16 Jan.. 1813 (186)

Trevaldwyn : Jones, Rev. B W., R of Nether Whitacre,
Warwick. Times, d p., 19 Oct., 1872
Trevanion *see* Bettesworth-Trevanion.
  „ Bowling Trevanion.
Trevor : Brand, Hon. H. O. 18 Nov., 1824 (1970).
  : Brand, Thos. W., 12 April, 1851 (D.G. 352)
  see Hill-Trevor.
  „ James-Trevor.
  „ Rice-Trevor.
  „ Smith-Trevor.
Trevor-Battye *see* Battye-Trevor
  : H D 23 Sept, 1890 (5267)
Trevor-Garrick : Trever, Rev. F. S, of Fernhill Gate, Bashley,
Hants. Times, d p., 6 May, 1886.
Trevor-Roper · Roper, C. B. 17 Jan., 1809 (61)
Triandafillidi *see* Triandás.
Triandás : Triandafillidi, T. G., of Chatham Street, Liverpool,
clerk. Times, d p., 14 April, 1893
Tribe *see* Poole.
Trice *see* Wright.
Tricket *see* Dent.
Trigg · Prigg, H , esq., The Friary, Farnham, All Saints, Bury
St. Edmunds Times, March, 1892.
Triggs *see* Kerr
Trimble *see* Brackenridge.
Trimmer *see* Shotter.
Tripe *see* Swete.
  „ Veysey.
Trist : Houssonleer, J. M. 27 June, 1799 (641)
Tristram-Valentine : Valentine, J T, of 1, Sheffield Gardens,
Kensington. Times, d p., 25 Jan., 1899
Trollope *see* Foord-Bowes
Trotter : Brown, W. 3 Dec., 1868 (6528).
  see Ruthven.
  „ Coatts-Trotter.
Trotter-Dinsdale : Trotter, F. 4 Feb., 1848 (370).
Trotter-Cranstoun of Dewar · Trotter, Joseph Young, Lyon
Register, Vol. XII., 4 June,
1890.
  : Trotter, Thomas Lyon Register,
Vol. IV., 15 Dec., 1848.
Troughton : Sharp, W., of Woodhouse Tebay, W'moreland,
fireman. Times, d.p. 31 Jan, 1885.
  Sharp, J. T., of Tebay, Westmoreland, railway
guard. Times, d.p., 12 and 15 July 1880.
Trower *see* Bence Trower
Troyte *see* Acland-Troyte.

Troyte   Acland, A. H. D. W., 26 Aug., 1852 (D G. 697).
    . Acland, T. D. 26 Aug , 1852 (2332).
    : Bullock, G   31 Dec., 1852 (3942).
Troyte-Chafyn-Grove. · Troyte-Bullock, G. 5 May, 1892 (2829)
Trubridge see Keiffenheim-Trubridge
Truefitt see Haywood.
Trulock Hankin see Hankin
Trundley see Turner.
Tuck see Tawke
  ,,   Bennett.
Tucker see A'Deane
    ,,   Beauchamp
    ,,   Booth-Tucker.
    ,,   Reeve-Tucker
    · Stopford, A B., of Holloway, London. Times, 21 July, 1900.
    see White.
Tucker-Castledine : Tucker, T. 17 Dec., 1856 (4285).
Tuckey see Bury.
Tuckfield, Chas see Fitzgerald, Chas Wm
        see Hippisley-Tuckfield
Tuder-Nelthorpe   Cowne, J. 26 Aug., 1806 (1122).
Tudor : Jones, E A. T , of 5, Marine Lines, Bombay, Lieut. R. Engineers Times, d.p., 15 Oct., 1890.
    . Jones F. C. T , of 80, Mount Ararat Road, Richmond, Surrey, Lieut R.N Times, d.p., 1 Jan., 1891
    : Jones, H M. T , of 80, Mount Ararat Road, Richmond, Surrey, Commder R N. Times, d p., 14 Oct., 1890.
Tudsbery : Turner, F. W. T. 26 Dec., 1893 (3)
Tufnell-Tyrell : Tufnell, J. L 15 Jan., 1878 ((272).
Tufton, R.—continue to bear name of Tufton—son of Rt Hon H. Tufton, Earl of Thanet. 17 May, 1850 (1418) naturalized 1849, 12-13 Vict., c. 31.
Tulk · Hart, M J. 26 Nov., 1889 (7015).
    see Hart
Tulloch see Lushington-Tulloch.
Tunstall-Moore   Moore, R. T., of co. Meath. Ireland, and co Dublin, Ireland, esq., J.P. Times, d.p 21 March, 1889
Tupper-Carey : Carey, A D., of Christ Church, Oxford, B A. Times, d p., 10 Nov., 1887
Turbervill   Warlow, T. P. 5 July, 1867 (3972).
    : Warlow, J P. (Col.). late of Madras Staff Corps, now residing at Bridgend, Glamorgan. Times, 24 Dec., 1891
Turberville   Picton, R. T. 25 Aug., 1797 (859).
    see Smith-Turberville

Turberville-Llewellin . Jenkins, N. E , of Oakfield, Weston,
    Somerset, spinster. Times, 26 Nov , 1888
Turbutt *see* de Uphaugh.
    Errington, J. L 13 Nov., 1895 (7501).
Turner : Agor, W. 5th Geo. III , 1765.
    see Dryden.
    á Beckett, T 48th Geo III , 1808
    Beckett, W 2 & 3 Vict c. 48 (Index to pub. and priv
        Statutes, p 503).
    : Beckett, G. T. 32nd Geo. III., 1792
    see Bravo.
    : Burton-Phillipson, J T. 23 Sept , 1854 (2936).
    see Firth.
    ,, Glass-Turner.
    : Holloway, W T 17 Sept , 1844 (3423)
    see Irton.
    : Meryweather, M J 26 Nov., 1830 (2686)
    : Meryweather, M. W. 26 Nov , 1830 (2686).
    : Meryweather, W. S T. M. 26 Nov , 1830 (2686)
    see Page.
    ,, Palgrave
    ,, Polhill-Turner.
    ,, Round-Turner.
    ,, Tarrant-Turner
    Tennyson, C. 1 Sept , 1835 (1677).
    Jas. · Trundley, Josiah G., of 330, Old Ford Road, Bow
        Times, d p , 27 April, 1894
    see Tudsbery.
    ,, Wright.
Turner-Burnett, Amy . Turner, A Elizth., of 44, Bernard Street,
    Russell Square, spinster Times, d p , 23 June, 1885
Turner-Farley Turner, C 22 April, 1848 (1612)
    Turner, F. M. 28 May, 1867 (3163 and 2398)
    : Turner, Thos. Macnaghten. 28 May, 1867
        (D.G. 737 and 769)
Turner-Roe : Turner, T. 15 Feb , 1811 (335)
Turnor-Barnwell Barnwell, F H 17 May, 1826 (1446).
Turnur-Fetherstonhaugh · Turnour, K 27 Dec , 1895 (969)
Turton : Peters, E. 16 May, 1817 (1208).
Turvin . Hankin, J M. 11 Feb., 1839 (292)
Tuthill *see* Cooper
Tutton Salvidge, C 26th Geo III , 1786
Twaddle *see* Tweeddale
Tweddle *see* Tweeddale
Tweeddale . Twaddle, W. T , of Camberwell, then of Nunhead,
        now of Brockley, Surrey, draper Times, 4 Jan ,
        1890.

Tweeddale : Twaddle, H. J., formerly of Camberwell, then of Nunhead, now of Brockley, all in Surrey, surveyor's assistant. Times, 4 Jan 1890
: Tweddle, Rev. T., of Fring, Norfolk. Times, d p, 9 Sept., 1874
Twells : Grosse, M. E., of St. George's Vicarage, Brentford. Times, d p, 11 Feb, 1881.
· Grosse, R. L., of Ealing, Middlesex. Times, d p., 17 May, 1877.
Twemlow Cooke : Cooke, Rev. D J, of 176, Junction Road, Upper Holloway, M.A., Vicar of St Mary, Brookfield, Middlesex Times, d.p., 28 Jan., 1882
Twemlow *see* Fletcher-Twemlow.
Twigge-Molecey . Twigge, J M 20 July, 1835 (1422).
Twisleton : Cockshutt, J 30 July, 1801 (930).
Twisleton-Fiennes *see* Eardley-Twisleton-Fiennes.
: Twisleton, Rt. Hon. G. W. (Baron Saye & Sele) 26 Feb., 1825 (371).
Twisleton-Wykeham-Fiennes : Twisleton, F. (Baron Saye & Sele). W., 27 Feb., 1849 (D G 282)
Tyers Savage, T. T. 14 Nov., 1827 (2362).
Tylden-Pattenson : Tylden, R C 10 Sept., 1799 (911)
Tylden-Wright : Wright, C. C. O. 25 Aug., 1860 (3223).
Tyler *see* Griffin.
„ Smith-Tyler
Tylney *see* Long-Tylney.
„ Pole-Tylney-Long-Wellesley.
Tyndale *see* Biscoe.
„ Warre.
Tyndale-Biscoe : Biscoe, F. E. A. ; A. S. (Lieut. R.A.) . C. E. ; E. C. (Midshipman R.N.) ; J. D. T. ; G. W. T.; and A. A T., all of Holton Park, Oxford Times, d.p., 6 July, 1883
Tyndall *see* Hamilton-Tyndall-Bruce.
Tyndall-Bruce : Bruce, O. T. 19 May, 1829 (935)
Tynte *see* Kemys-Tynte.
: Pratt, J. T. D.G., 29 July, 1836.
Tyrel de Poix : Durieux. E A J E. M., of 3, Argyll Street, Kensington, Middlesex, artist. Times, d p., 27 March, 1875.
Tyrell *see* Jenner-Tyrell
„ Tufnell-Tyrell.
Tyringham : Praed, W. B. 6 Aug., 1859 (3071).
Tyrrell : Aylon, S. 7th Geo III., 1767.
. Barnard. G T. 10 Nov., 1879 (6425)
: Curran, T F. 31 Oct., 1892 (D.G. 1225).
Tyrwhitt · Jones, E. W. 13 April, 1841 (977).

Tyrwhitt *see* Jones.
,, Wilson.
Tyrwhitt-Drake : Tyrwhitt, T. 20 Dec., 1796 (1234).
Tyrwhitt-Wilson : Tyrwhitt, R. R. (commonly called the Hon.). 13 Sept. 1892 (5503).
Tyssen *see* Daniel-Tyssen.
Tyssen-Amherst : Tyssen-Amhurst, W. A. 16 Aug., 1877 (7018).
Tyssen-Amhurst : Daniel-Tyssen, W. G. T. 6 Aug., 1852 (2154)
: Tyssen-Daniel-Amhurst, W. A. 30 March, 1871 (1804)
Tyssen-Daniel-Amhurst : Tyssen-Amhurst, W. A. 10 July, 1867 (3972).
Tyzack : Davison, E. 2 Jan., 1843 (3).

U

Underwood : Buggin, Lady Cecilia L. R.L., 2 March, 1834.
Unsworth *see* Molyneux-Seel.
Unwin-Heathcote : Unwin, S. H. 27 Feb., 1813 (407).
Upham *see* Tatem.
,, Reynell-Upham.
Upton *see* Howard
,, Smyth
Upton-Cottrell-Dormer : Cottrell-Dormer, C. 30 June, 1876 (3890).
Upward *see* Weston
Uren *see* Wren.
Urquhart *see* Pollard-Urquhart.
,, Binks-Urquhart.
Urwin *see* Rippon.
Usticke *see* Nowell-Usticke.
Uthwatt : Andrewes, H., of Gloucester Cottage, Bayham Street, Middlesex, gent. Times, d.p., 25 April, 30 May, 1885.
: Andrews, H. W. 18 March, 1803 (371).
Uttermare : Joseph, A. G. and E. 25 Aug., 1874 (4167).

V

Vade-Walpole : Walpole, R. H. 4 Nov., 1844 (3759)
: Walpole, C. 6 Jan., 1887 (166).
: Walpole, H. S. 27 Oct., 1892 (6235).

Vade-Walpole : Walpole, J 6 Jan., 1887 (166).
Vafiadacchi *see* Schilizzi-Vafidacchi
Vale *see* Martindale-Vale
Valentine *see* Tristram-Valentine.
Valentine Thompson : Thompson, H., formerly of York, now at 2, Norris Street, Middlesex, esq. Times, d.p., 16 May, 1879.
Valiant-Cumming of Logie, co Moray : Valiant, Lockhart Mure. Lyon Register, Vol. VI., 11 March, 1859.
Vallange : Condell, C. V V., of Chastleton House, Chipping Norton, and of Merton Coll., Oxford. Times, d p , 9 Feb, 1891.
: Condell, U. C. V , of Chastleton House, Chipping Norton, spinster (formerly of London) Times, d p , 9 Feb, 1891
Vallois-Smyth Vallois, H E. L., of 4, Quai de Remblai, Sables d'Olonne, France Times, d.p., 19 Oct , 1895.
Valpy dit Janvrin *see* Janvrin.
Van der Noot : Noott, Revd. E. F. C., Rector of Barley, Hertford. Times, d.p , 31 Dec., 1891
Vanderpant *see* Dalton
Van Gheluwe *see* Mitchell.
Van Hollick : Hollick, F., of 9, Clapton Square, Clapton Times, d p , 9 June, 1879.
Van Braam *see* Blake
Van Dam · Searle, A. Van Dam 9 June, 1828 (1118).
Vanden-Bempde · Johnstone, R. 33rd Geo. III., 1793
Van Mildert Cooke, E V 11 Oct , 1859 (3703)
Van Notten *see* Pole.
Van Notten-Pole : Pole, C 19 July, 1853 (2059).
· Pole, Sir P. 11 June, 1853 (1701).
Van Thysen *see* Cole
Van Réable *see* Faria.
Van Sittart *see* Neale.
Van Werner, G A : Susskin, A , native of New Jersey. U S A , now travelling in Gt. Britain and Continent Times, d p., 28 Feb , 1888.
Vane, Duke of Cleveland *see* Powlett
: Powlett, W J. F., Duke of Cleveland. 4 March, 1864 (1429)
see Powlett
„ Tempest.
: Stewart, C. W (Marquis of Londonderry) R.L., 5 May, 1829.
Vane-Tempest Vane A F. C W 28 June, 1854 (2038).
: Vane, E. M. 28 June, 1854 (2038)

Vane-Tempest — Vane, Rt. Hon G H R C W (Earl Vane). 28 June, 1854 (2038)
Vann — Marston, M. A. 21 June, 1794 (578).
Varenne.: Gill, J. 25 April, 1816 (795)
Varlo see Petre.
Vassal — Webster, Sir G. 30 Oct., 1795 (1021)
Vaughan see Bowman-Vaughan.
„ Edwards-Brettell-Vaughan.
„ Edwards-Vaughan.
„ Evans Vaughan.
„ Gwynne-Vaughan.
„ Hutchinson-Lloyd-Vaughan
„ Jenkins-Vaughan
„ Johnston Vaughan.
· Jones, J. 26 Dec., 1846 (6026)
H F John : Jones, H. F., of 30, Edwardes' Square, Kensington, esq., B A., student of Civil Law. Times, d p., 13 April, 1876.
see Lear
Lee, J. E. V., of Rheola, Glamorgans., and New Coll., Oxford. Times, 5 May, 1883
: Lisburne, Rt. Hon. Earl of, r.l to subscribe surname Vaughan before all titles of honour 17 Nov., 1831 (2655).
see Marlow
„ Magennis.
„ Pryse.
„ Stooke-Vaughan
: Thomas, H V 11 Aug., 1885 (3701).
see Williams-Vaughan.
Vaughan-Arbuckle — Vaughan, B. H 8 Nov., 1843 (3665).
Vaughan-Jenkins : Vaughan, W. 27 Aug., 1814 (1856)
Vaughan-Jones : Jones, E. V., of 17, Water Lane, London, and of Hampstead, merchant Times, d.p., 6 Oct., 1879
: Jones, H. T., of Llanengan, Carnarvon, Lieut.-Col., J P. Times, d p., 12 June, 1882
Vaughan-Lee — Lee, V H., of Lanelay, Glamorgan, esq Times, d.p., 17 March, 1874.
Vaughan-Pryse see Rice-Vaughan-Pryse
Vaughan-Pryse-Rice — Rice-Vaughan-Pryse, J. C P. 10 Dec., 1887 (7182)
Vaughan-Stevens — Stevens, A., of Bedford Park Chiswick, and of 4, Trafalgar Square, esq Times, d p., 20 Aug., 1890.

Vaux *see* Lernoult.
Vavasour : Nooth, H. 26 March, 1791 (185).
    . Stourton, E. M. 11 April, 1826 (878).
Vawdrey : Cock, C., assnt. paymaster, H.M.S. Salamis. Times, 29 June, 1881.
Veale : Mallett, J. 7 July, 1781 (12204).
Veel *see* Colborne-Veel.
    : Jones, D. 5 Dec., 1848 (4507).
Veltmann *see* Potter Veltmann.
Venables . Argles, S V. 20 July, 1848 (2789).
    see Dillwyn-Venables-Llewelyn
Venables-Vernon, Hon. W. J. *see* Borlase-Warren-Venables-Vernon.
    see Warren
Venis : Venis-Lazarus, A., 2nd Lieut. 38th Reg. Times, d p., 18 Oct., 1880.
    : Venis-Lazarus, W., med. stud. of King's Coll. Hospital Times, d.p., 30 Dec., 1880.
Venner · Sidebottom, Rev., of Swithland Rectory, Loughborough, Leicester. 19 Jan., 1884.
Ventris : Murphy, A. V., of the Royal Mint, London Times, d.p., 29 Dec., 1876.
Ventry. Lord, *see* de Moleyns.
    see Eveleigh de Moleyns.
Vere *see* Broke-Vere
    Jones, V., infant son of Thomas J. Jones, of Cintra, Upper Norwood. Times, 2 July, 1863
    see Jones-Vere.
    „ Weir-Vere.
Vereker-Bindon *see* Goodliffe.
Verelst : Reed, C 1 Oct., 1851 (2834)
Verling-Brown : Brown, C. R., of Bournemouth. Times, 19 Dec., 1896.
Verner · H F., to continue to bear surname of Verner. 9 Oct., 1891 (D.G. 1613).
Verney : Anthony, C. C., temp. residing at 18, Russell Square, Brighton, Sussex Times, d.p., 2 Aug., 1892
    : Barnard, R J. (Baron Willoughby de Broke) 24 May, 1853 (1445).
    Calvert, Sir H 23 March, 1827 (726).
    see Lloyd-Verney
    : Wright, R. 16 Feb., 1811 (316).
Verney-Cave · Wyatt-Edgell ·(Lord Braye), A. T. T. 5 Feb., 1880 (683).
Vernon *see* Borlase-Warren-Venables-Vernon.
    „ Gladell-Vernon
    „ Graham.

Vernon *see* Harcourt
: Jenkin, C. 17 April, 1860 (1474)
: Physick, H. V., of Craigfoot, Weston-super-Mare, esq. Times, d.p., 17 Feb., 1877.
: Sandeman, Laura V., of 15, Eldon Road, Kensington, Middlesex (formerly L. V. Van Nyvel, spinster, and afterwards wife of David George Sandeman, late a Lieut. in H.M. 16th Lancers). Times, d.p., 21 Oct., 1878.
see Sedley.
: Shaw, J. Y. V., of Upper Norwood, Surrey, but now in Paris. Times, d.p., 21 April, 1875.
: Smith, C. J. 8 Aug., 1845 (2385).
: Smith, F. P. H. 8 Aug., 1845 (2385).
: Smith, G C. 8 Aug., 1845 (2385).
: Smith, G. R. 8 Aug., 1845 (2385).
: Smith, L V. 3 May, 1850 (1268).
: Vernon-Graham, H. C E. 11 June, 1838 (1362).
see Venables-Vernon.
„ Warren.
„ Wentworth.
Vernon-Gore : Vernon, G. K. 19 Jan., 1876 (410)
Vernon Harcourt *see* Harcourt.
Verona-Avidor : Verona, L., of Turin, Italy, now of London. Times, 1 Aug., 1867.
Verral *see* Green.
Vertue : Virtue, J., Rt. Rev., of Bishop's House, Portsmouth. Times, d.p., 30 Nov., 1895
Vesey *see* Colthurst-Vesey.
„ Foster-Vesey-FitzGerald
Vesey-Fitzgerald : FitzGerald Right Hon. W. and Rev. H. D.G., 13 Feb., 1815.
Veysey · Tripe, C., of E. Dulwich, Surrey, bank clerk Times, d.p., 10 March, 1893.
Veysie : Shayer, H., of Silvertown, Essex, engineer. Times, d.p., 10 Aug., 1889.
Vezian *see* Ellis.
Viall, King : Cornell, J. J. Q., of Brentwood and Baythorne Park, Essex, and of 4, Adam's Court, Old Broad Street, London, stock-broker, decd. Times, d-p., 16 Nov., 1893.
Vice *see* Vyse.
Vidal : Sealy, E. W. 17 Feb., 1842 (436)
Vidler *see* Tennent.
Viereck *see* Lanfear.
Villiers *see* Elphinstone.
· Lewis, V. W. 19 March, 1791 (167)

Villiers *see* Mansell.
Villiers-Stuart : Stuart, C.
    . Stuart, G.
    : Stuart, W.
    : Stuart, H   17 May, 1822 (867)
Villers-Wilkes : Wilkes, E. C., of Old Square, Birmingham, spinster. Times, d.p. 24 Sept., 1881
Vincent : Jones, J. V.   29 Aug., 1820 (1761)
Vine *see* Innes-Vine.
Vincent *see* Sheldon
Viner *see* Ellis-Viner
Vipan Gotobed, J., of New Constantia, Cape of Good Hope, also of Cambridge, England. Times, 31 Dec, 1867.
Virtue *see* Vertue.
Visconti Powlett · Joiner, J. A., master mariner. Times, 30 Dec., 1873
Viveash *see* Baskerville
Vivian, Burton : Blowers, A. T. B., of Kensington, Middlesex, artist d.p., 23 Jan, 1895.
    see McIver-Campbell.
    : Perkins, R. F. G., of 5, Alfred Place, S. Kensington, Middlesex, gent. Times, d.p., 3 Oct., 1884
    see Shimmen Vivian
    · Tippet, J. V.   23 June, 1817 (1542)
    : Tippet, J.   4 May, 1820 (934)
Viviane, St. John Ely : Fisher, J. E., of Bath, gent. Times, 11 March, 1863
Voase *see* Ringrose
    : Ringrose, T. and F. V. E.   30 Dec., 1859 (37).
    see Ringrose-Voase
Von Angern *see* Von Zedlitz
Von Roemer : Boheim, Justina, C., on the dissolution of her marriage with R. Boheim. Times, 28 July, 1892.
Von Skala, Anna Maria : Biedermann, Anna, formerly of Albert Mansions, Westminster Times 26 Nov, 1895
Von Winckler : Winckler, W. J., of Leytonstone, Essex, L.R.C.P., M.R.C.S., &c. Times, d.p., 7 Oct, 1887.
Von Zedlitz · Von Angern, M. H. R., of 25, Craven Street, Strand, gent. Times, d.p., 17 Dec., 1887.
Vyse *see* Howard-Vyse
    : Vice, C. F., Lieut 41st Bengal Nat. Infy., in E. Indies. Times, d.p., 22 Nov, 1876
Vyvyan : Vyvyan Robinson, H. N., H., C. S., and F. A. Times, 3 July, 1879
    : Warschawski, Rev. R. R. V. of 5 St. Peter's Terrace, Cambs Times, d.p., 31 July, 1888
Vyvyan-Robinson : Vyvyan, P.   19 June, 1818 (1153).

W

Waddell-Dudley : Waddell, W. D. 29 Nov., 1878 (6988).
Waddingham *see* Tombleson.
Waddington *see* Driffield.
    ,, Ferrand.
Wade : Baseley, A. 7 April, 1821 (838)
    see Carruthers-Wade.
    ,, Dalton.
    ,, Wilkinson.
Wade-Gery : Wade, H. 14 Aug., 1792 (630).
Wadeson : Punch, E. G., B.A., of St. John's Coll., Cambridge, and of Sedbergh, York, gent. Times, d.p., 4 Dec., 1884.
Wadsworth : Ayrton, M. 3 March, 1840 (556).
Wagener : Sulman, F. G. Times, d.p., 4 March, 1896.
Waghorn *see* Wilder.
Waight-Eames : Eames, J. 17th Geo. III., 1777.
Wainwright *see* Lowten.
Waite *see* Spenlove.
Wakefield *see* Marriott.
    ,, Pomeroy.
    ,, Reade.
Wakefield-Render : Wakefield, Sarah, of Barnsley. Times, 19 June, 1900.
Wakeman-Newport : Wakeman, H. A., of Hanley Court, Worcester, esq. Times, d.p, 12 Nov., 1862.
Walcott-Sympson : Walcott, J. 9 July, 1819 (1254) (see 1200).
Waldegrave-Leslie : Waldegrave, G. and H. 27 Jan., 1862 (447).
Waldie-Griffith : Griffith, G. R., of Hendersyde, Kelso. Times, 24 Aug., 1865.
Waldo-Sibthorpe : Sibthorpe, H. 22 May, 1804 (718).
Waldo *see* Mead-Waldo.
Waley : Levi, S. J. 16 Sept., 1834 (1672).
Walford *see* Ashton.
    : Jenkins, F. 28 Sept., 1799 (979).
Walford-Gosnall : Walford, J. D. 3 Feb., 1847 (621).
Walhouse *see* Littleton.
Walker *see* Ainley-Walker.
    ,, Blandy.
    Case, T. E. 28 May, 1870 (2826).
    see Case Walker.
    : Cornewall, jun., F. 21 July, 1781 (12208).
    see Edyvean-Walker.
    Flower, H. (com. called Hon.). 23 Nov., 1827 (2531).

Walker *see* Ferguson-Walker.
„ Flower.
„ Forster-Walker
„ Heneage
„ Higgs-Walker.
„ Hungerford.
„ Kerrick-Walker
„ Larkins-Walker.
„ Marriott.
„ Milner Walker
: Noble, Rev. M. H. D.G., 5 May, 1809
see Robertson-Walker.
„ Sutherland-Walker
„ Tetlow.
„ Thomlinson-Walker.
„ Waller.
„ Wood.
Walker-Aylesbury : Walker, J. H. T. 27 Nov., 1857 (4217).
Walker-Drummond *see* Williams-Drummond.
of Hawthornden : Walker. Lyon Register, Vol. III., 1 March, 1828.
Walker Dunbar : Walker, E. L., M.D., of Bristol, daughter of Alex. Walker, M.D Times, 9 Dec., 1874.
Walker-Heneage : Wyld, G. H. 20 Aug., 1818 (1580).
Walker-Jones : Walker, F. G. 18 June, 1830 (1546).
Walker-Leigh : Walker, W., of Ballyseedy, Tralee, and Regent's Park, Middlesex, late Major, Lanc Art. Mil. Times, d p, 10 May, 1873.
Walker Morison of Fawfield or Falfield · Walker, Bethune James Lyon Register, Vol. V., 30 March, 1854.
Walker-Munro Munro, E. L. 30 July, 1887 (5046).
Walker-Nanson : Walker, J. H. C., of Ealing Common, M'sex, gent. Times, d.p., 7 March, 1888.
Walshe . Johnson, Sir J. H., Bart. D.G., 9 May, 1809.
Wall *see* Bramall Wall.
„ Earnshaw-Wall.
„ Morris-Wall.
: Wallgate, R. W. 16 May, 1842 (1333)
Wallace *see* Downing Wallace.
: Gray, F. 11 Feb., 1778 (11848)
see Hope-Wallace.
„ Paterson-Wallace.
Wallace Marchant : Marchant, Jane, of Springfield Villa, Acton Times, 25 May, 1888
Wallace-Mulhallen : Wallace, M E 31 Jan., 1895 (D.G 122).
Waller : Phipps, J. W. 7 March, 1814 (513).
: Proctor, N. 15 July, 1816 (1502).

Waller *see* Samo-Waller.
    : Walker, Mrs. Stephen. Times, 30 Dec., 1881.
    : Walker, S. H. Times, 2 Dec., 1881.
Wallgate *see* Wall.
Wallinger *see* Arnold-Wallinger
    : Arnold, J. 8th Geo. III., 1768
Wallis *see* Bayly-Wallis.
  ,, Boyd-Wallis.
    Loft, A. A. 23 March, 1837 (805)
  see Ogle.
    C. J. Boyd : Wallis, C. J. Times, d.p., 6 April, 1889.
Wallis-Jones : Jones, R. J., of Lily Lodge, Vale of Health, Hampstead, M.I.E.E and A M I C E. Times, d p, 6 Sept., 1892.
Wallop *see* Fellowes.
  ,, William-Powelett.
Walls : Codd, E. 26 May, 1778 (11877).
Walmesley-Cotham Walmesley, A. A. 14 Oct., 1889 (5665)
Walmsley *see* Chaloner
Walmesley : Warmsley, J., of Ripley, Surrey, formerly of Lambeth. gent Times, d p., 15 Aug., 1867.
Walpole *see* Vade-Walpole
Walrond Dickinson. B. B. 22 April, 1845 (1220)
Walsh · Benn, J. 11 April, 1795 (319).
  see Hoel-Walsh.
  : Moseley, W. 9th Geo. III., 1769.
  see Porter
Walsham : Garbett-Washam, Sir J. J 19 May, 1837 (1275)
  see Garbett-Walsham
Walter *see* Grantley.
  ,, Marriott.
  ,, Moses Walter.
  ,, Nelson
  ,, Rolle.
Walters *see* Palliser
Walters-Philipps Walters, J. 26 Feb., 1825 (372)
Walthall : Broughton, E. W. D. 10 Nov., 1887 (304)
  · Milnes, H. W 4 June, 1853 (1587)
Walton-Wilson : Walton, J. M 19 Oct., 1880 (5383)
Walwyn *see* Shepheard-Walwyn.
Walwyn-Shepheard . Shepheard, L. H and E. C., of 100, Guildford Street, Russell Square Times, 1 Sept., 1881.
Wandesforde : Prior, Sarah (widow of Rev John Prior) 11 Sept., 1882 (D.G. 970)
  see Prior-Wandesforde
Wandesford *see* Butler-Clarke-Southwell-Wandesford

Wanless-O'Gowan : Smith, R. W., of Clonard, Dundrum, co. Dublin, Lieut. Scot. Rifles. Times, d.p., 20 April, 1895.
Warburton *see* Egerton-Warburton
        : Jobson, R. 31 Jan., 1786 (41)
        : Mongan, C 22 May, 1792 (334).
Ward Collins, E. 18 Feb., 1783 (12415)
   Collins or Collis, J. 17 April, 1827 (942).
  see Creswell-Ward.
  · Creswell, R. W. 26 Nov., 1883 (6265)
  see Errington.
  „ Essington
  „ Fawssett
  „ Green Ward
  : Hadwen, T., of Low Branthwaites, Howgill Sedburgh, West Riding, Yorks, yeoman Times, 7 April, 1869
  : Harrison, E. E., of Jesus College, Cambridge, and 2, Northgate Street, Bury St Edmunds Times, 20 Aug., 1868
  see Hoare Ward
  „ Hopkin.
  „ Nelson-Ward
  „ Plumer-Ward.
  . Rump, J., of Bellevue Park, Dublin, butler to Henry Moutray Jones, of Bellevue Park, esq. Times, 25 Dec., 1880
  : Russell, W 18 May, 1852 (1469)
  Wolfe, J., of Queen's Road, Bayswater, Midddlesex, gent Times, d.p., 17 March, 1876.
Ward-Broughton-Leigh : Ward, J 24 Sept. 1831 (1973)
Ward-Coulson : Ward, Jas St J, 26 Sept., D C, 12 Oct., 1855 (D G 1421 and 1439)
Ward-Porter · Ward, jun, P S. 18 April, 1824 (810).
Warde-Aldman : Aldam, W W. 23 April, 1878 (2772).
Wardell, or Gordon Wardell *see* Gordon Craig
  see Yates
Wardell-Potts Potts, E 5 July, 1880 (3879)
Wardell-Yerburgh : Yerburgh, O. P 26 Nov. 1888 (140)
Ware Cumberleye, E N 24 Oct, 1862 (5284)
  see Hibbert-Ware.
Waring *see* Rhiner-Waring
       · Scott, J 17 Nov., 1798 (1083)
  see Maxwell.
Warlow *see* Turbervill.
    T. P. *see* Turbervill
Warmsley *see* Walmesley
Warneford *see* Wetherell-Warneford.

Warner *see* Lee-Warner.
    Rev Richd Hyett Warner : Warner, Rev. Richard, of
        Wrydescroft Parsonage, Thorney, Ely, Cambs
    Edith Warner : Warner, E, of Chelmsford, Essex,
    Richd : Warner, Richd Hyett
        Times, 8 March, 1869.
Warnock Fielden : Warnock, J. G., of 51, Moscow Drive, Green Lane, Stoneycroft, Lancs., commercial traveller. Times, d.p., 4 April, 1885.
Warre : Butter, T W 29 July, 1813 (1534)
    : Goppy, C. B., of Townlands, Sussex, esq Times, d p, 3 May, 1873
    . Tyndale, J. 24 Sept, 1791 (529).
Warre Cornish : Cornish, F. W., of Eton, Bucks, assistnt master master at Eton Times, d p, 19 Feb, 1892
Warren *see* Borlase-Warren.
    ,, Borlase-Warren-Venables-Vernon
    ,, Corbould-Warren.
    ,, Gates-Warren
    ,, Leighton-Warren
    see Horne
    : Parker, T L 18 Feb, 1832 (415)
    see Spence.
        Venables-Vernon, Rt. Hon G. (Lord Vernon) 16 Nov, 1837 (2974)
    . Venables-Vernon, G C. 16 June, 1826 (1480)
    . Leicester, Sir G. (Lord de Tabley). R.L., 8 Feb., 1832.
    : Wright, R 21 March and 29 March, 1849 (2159).
Warren-Bulkeley : Bulkeley (Vis and Baron Bulkeley) 25 Sept, 1802 (1014)
Warren-Darley : Darley, H. B. D.G, 10 March, 1838.
Warren-Swettenham : Warren, R. 28 Oct, 1876 (5907)
Warrington *see* Carew.
Warry-Stone : Warry, W J. F, of Badbury, Wilts, and now residing at 72, Elm Park Gardens, Chelsea, Middlesex, esq. Times, d p, 11 Dec., 1886. 1 Jan., 1887.
Warschawski *see* Vyvyan
Warter *see* Tatham-Warter.
Warter-Meredith : Warter, H 15 June, 1824 (1038)
Warwick Bonnor, R 4 Feb, 1792 (78)
    see Hetherington
Waskett-Myers : Waskett, F. 10 Feb, 1818 (286)
Wassermann *see* Waterman.
Wastie Lockhart J I 2nd & 3rd Will IV, 1832
Waterhouse *see* Doherty-Waterhouse
Waterman *see* Gardner-Waterman

Waterman : Wassermann, I. F., of 59, Leazes Terrace, Newcastle-on-Tyne, spinster. Times, d p., 4 April, 1890
Waters *see* Dun-Waters.
,, Massey-Spencer.
Waters Leavins : Waters, W., of Heigham, Norwich, printer. Times, 21 April, 1885.
Wates, J. North : Wates, J., junr., of 131, Powis Street, Woolwich, accountant's clerk. Times, 28 April, 1873
Wathen *see* Baghott.
: Chase, M S., of Ashley House, Ashley Down, Bristol, spinster. Times, d.p., 30 June, 1882
: Chase, Edith, of Ashley House, Ashley Down, Bristol, spinster. Times, d p., 23 Aug., 1884
: Chase, M. A, of Ashley Down, Bristol. Times, d p., 4 Jan., 1888.
Wathen-Bartlett · Bartlett, W. W. Times, d.p., 3 Jan., 1896.
Watkin *see* Joseph-Watkin.
: Pease, E. T., of Oak Lea, Darlington, merchant. Times, d.p., 19 Jan., 1878.
see Price.
Watkins *see* Griffith.
: Rice, G W. 11 Nov., 1865 (5246).
see Steer-Watkins
Watkyn-Thomas : Thomas, W., fomerly of Cardiff, now of Cockermouth, Cumberland, civ. and min. engineer. Times, 29 March, 1884
Watkiss *see* Massey.
Watlington *see* Hooper-Watlington
,, Perry-Watlington
Watson : Aked, M J., of 15, Ovington Gardens, Middlesex, widow. Times, d p., 4 Jan., 1888.
: Baker, R 15 Aug., 1817 (1895)
L. B. : Bowen, Danl., of 30 Rue Godot de Mauroy, Paris. Times, d.p., 9 March, 1893
: Brough, R. 14 March, 1854 (904).
see Bullock.
,, Catton Watson
,, Farside.
· Geisenhainer, J. H. Times, 28 March, 1896
see Harrison-Watson
Hemingway, S W. 8 May, 1848 (1803)
. Lake, P., late of Papcastle, C'berland, now of Scarboro', Yorks. widow. Times, d.p., 9 May, 1879.
see Luther-Watson
,, Milles.

Watson *see* Neale-Watson.
  ― Newton, W. 16 Dec., 1839 (2634)
  see Robinson.
  ,, Ruttledge.
  ,, Samwell.
  M H. Conchita : Watson, Mabel H, formerly of California, U.S.A., now of Bailey's Hotel, Gloucester Road, S. Kensington, spinster, Brit. subject Times, d,p., 23 Jan., 1892.
  : Wood, J. W. 14 Nov., 1839 (2191)
  : Wood, W. 7 May, 1803 (543)
Watson-Armstrong : Watson, W. H. A. F. 1 June, 1889 (3224)
Watson-Copley : Watson, Sir C. 12 March, 1887 (1615).
Watson Fothergill : Watson, M., A. F., and E. A., all of Mapperley Road, Notts. Times, d.p., 12 Dec., 1892
    : Watson, F, of Mapperley Road, Notts., architect. Times, d p, 12 Dec., 1892.
Watson Munro · Watson, C. J., of York House, Redcar, Yorks., ironmaster. Times, d p., 29 July, 1881
Watson-Smyth Watson, G 4 Dec., 1797 (1151)
Watson-Taylor : Watson, G 19 June, 1815 (1220)
Watt *see* Campbell.
  ,, Gibson-Watt.
  ,, Graeme Watt.
  ,, Hall Watt
Walter Schroeder, A. F. W., of Cheshunt, Herts., esq., M.A., naval instrucr., H.M.S. Britannia Times d.p., 18 May, 1882.
Watts *see* Dunton.
  ,, Fowell-Watts
  ,, Manning
Watts-Russell Russell, J 28 March, 1817 (1002)
Wayet *see* Sisson-Wayet
Wayne Harrison, T. M. 18 June, 1808 (872)
  : Rockliffe. T 20 Feb., 1808 (302)
Weale *see* Beddoes
Weare *see* De Vere
Weatherhilt *see* Fowden
Weatherhog *see* Travers
Webb *see* Bowen
  ,, Cranmer
  ,, Dalway
  : Doel, F., of Castle Villa Salisbury, Wilts, gent, also his wife and children Times, d p., 29 Aug., 1893
  see Everitt
  ,, Hillas

Webb : Loader, F. 28 Feb., 1795 (188).
: M'Knight, M 28 May, 1805 (749).
see Orme Webb.
„ Peploe.
„ Purkis
„ Raiemond
: Saunders *see* McKnight 1805
C. Ford : Webb, C. Hamilton, of 7, Burnley Road, Stockwell, Surrey Times, 19 June, 1874.
Webb-Aston : Webb, Katherine, of 7, St. George's Terrace, Queen's Gate, Kensington, Middlesex, and of 16, Wynnstay Gardens, Allen Street, Kensington, spinster. Times, d p , 24 Nov., 27 Nov., 1884
Webb-Coates : Webb, M C. 17 Aug., 9 Sept., 1869 (D.G. 1069).
Webb-Edge : Edge, T. 10 May, 1803 (543)
Webbe Francklyn, A. A. 23 Jan., 1852 (184).
see Weston.
Webber *see* Osmond
„ Smith
J Hobbs Hobbs, J., late of Burton-on-Trent, Staffs , now of Marston Magna, Somerset. Times, d p , 8 July, 1886
: Smith, J. W , Col., now Commanding 18th Reg. District at Clonmel, Ireland Times, d.p., 2 Dec., 1892
Webber-Gardiner Gardiner, J 16 Dec., 1881 (143).
Webber-Incledon Incledon-Webber, L C., of Yeovil, Somerset Times, d p , 19 June, 1884.
Webberburn *see* Colvile.
. Graham, D. 26 Aug , 1829 (1607)
Weber *see* Chassereau.
Webley-Parry : Webley, W. H. 28 Oct., 1816 (2329)
Webster *see* Bullock-Webster
: Graham, J 22 July, 1816 (1545).
: Wedderburn 19 Jan , 1790 (34)
see Vassal
Webster-Wedderburn-Webster of Clapham, Surrey : Wedderburn, James. R.L., Lyon Register, Vol. II., 4 Feb., 1811.
Weddell . Snook, H , of 14, Clayton Park Square, Newcastle-on Tyne. Times, d p., 30 March, 1893.
Wedderburn *see* Webster
„ Webster-Wedderburn-Webster.
Wedderburn-Maxwell of Middlebie and Glenlair : Wedderburn, Andrew Lyon, Vol X , 10 Dec , 1879
Wedgner · Shaw, H. Times, 6 Dec., 1867.
Weeding : Badgley, A J. 16 July, 1870 (3521)
: Baggallay, T W. 8 July, 1868 (3938)

Weeley : March, J. 8 Oct., 1796 (973)
Wegg-Prosser : Haggitt, F. R. 21 July, 1849 (2597)
Wehrhagen *see* Rhiner-Waring.
Weir *see* Cosens-Weir.
 „ Schultz-Weir.
Weir-Smith : Smith, J., of Ashogle, Banffs., Scot., and of Pernambuco, Brazil, mechan. engineer. Times, 7 July, 1887.
Weir-Vere : Weir. J. 11 Jan., 1776 (11734)
Welby-Everard : Welby, E. E. E. 6 April, 1894 (2241)
Welby-Gregory : Gregory Welby. Sir W. E. 27 Dec., 1875 (1).
 : Welby, Sir J. E. 5 July, 1861 (2962)
Welbore *see* Ellis.
Welch *see* Fletcher-Welch.
 „ Hoel-Walsh
 „ Kemp-Welch.
Welch-Thornton : Welch, H. S. and A. B. 8 Feb., 1861 (603).
Weld *see* Hartstonge.
Weld-Blundell : Weld, T. 11 March, 1843 (949).
Weld-Forester : Forester. C. 24 Aug., 1811 (1636)
Weld-Hartstong : Weld, Lorenzo. 19 Dec., 1849. 7 Jan., 1850 (D. G. 37)
Weldale-Knollys : Weldale, J. 6 April, 1812 (684).
Welfitt : Need. S. W. 6 June, 1844 (2005)
Welldale *see* Knollys.
Weller-Ladbroke : Weller, J. 16 July, 1819 (1299).
Wellesley-Pole *see* Pole-Tylney-Long-Wellesley.
Wells *see* Arding
 H. B. : Beman, H. H. W., of 28, Thornton Street, South Street, Walworth, Surrey, gent. Times, d p. 26 Aug., 1862.
 see Keys-Wells.
 „ Rix-Wells.
Wells-Clarke : Wells. W. C. 1 May, 1835 (878)
Wells-Cole : Wells, G. 8 July, 1822 (1194)
Wells Dymoke : Wells. E. L. 27 Aug., 1866 (4918)
Wellwood *see* Clarke-Wellwood.
 „ Maconochie-Wellwood.
 „ Scott-Wellwood.
Welsh : Williams, J. 10 Dec., 1812 (2473)
Wemyss Colchester *see* Colchester Wemyss
 : Wemyss. M. W., of Regent's Park Road, and The Wilderness, Glos., esq. Times, d p., 29 May, 1877.
Wemyss-Whittaker : Whittaker. Rev. E. J., of The Vicarage, Falfield, Glos. Times, 26 July, 1881
Wensley *see* Nixon-Wensley

Wentworth see Stanley
: Armytage, G. W   24 March, 1789 (149).
see Cox-Wentworth.
· Vernon, F T. W   16 Oct , 1804 (1284).
. Wilson, R. G., formerly of Scarborough, Yorks.
Times, 29 March, 1871.
Wentworth Buller   Buller, E A , of Strete, Ralegh, Devon,
spinster   Times, d p., 18 Aug , 1882.
· Buller, E A , of Strete, Ralegh, Devon,
spinster   Times, d p, 18 Aug , 1883
Wentworth-Fitzwilliam, Chas. W., to con. same   W , 25 Aug.,
1856 (D G. 917).
: Fitzwilliam, Earl   25 Aug , 1856.
Wentworth-Sheilds : Sheilds, J G   13 Feb., 1877 (D.G. 103)
Wenyon : Onions, S., of Cotherstone , C Onions, of Preston ;
E. J. Onions, of Guy's Hospital, London , J Onions, of
Cape Town, Africa , W F Onions, of Kendal , and Janet
L Onions, of Cotherstone.   Times, 21 May, 26 May,
1879.
Wescomb see Emmerton-Wescomb.
Wescomb-Emmerton : Wescomb, J   2 Dec , 1823 (2143)
Westbrooke see Michael
West . Cutbush, C.   12 Oct , 1830 (2156)
Lucadou, I. L   13 May, 1816 (1046)
see Lyster.
„ Marshall-West.
„ Sackville.
„ Sackville-West.
„ Temple-West
„ Thompson-West.
West-Erskine . West, W. A E   25 April, 6 May, 1872 (D.G.
277)
West-Stainsfield   West, C , of Hoxton, p of St Leonard's,
Shoreditch, Middlesex, clerk   Times, 1 Sept , 1869
Westby see Fazakerley-Westby
Westcarr see Prescott-Westcarr
Westcott see Austin
Westenhall   Tomkinson, E.   1 Oct , 1798 (953).
Westfailing · Brereton, T   34th Geo III., 1794
Westhead see Brown-Westhead
Weston see Hunter-Weston.
: Upward, Edith Eliza, of Oak Cliff, Devon   Times,
d p , 7 April, 1893.
: Webbe, J   22 June, 1782 (12306)
Westropp see Massey Westropp
„ O Callaghan.

Westropp-Dawson : Westropp, W M 14 Oct., 25 Oct , 1859
  (D.G 1674 and 1686).
Westwood *see* Skidmore Westwood
Westyr-Evans : Evans, J. H., of 20, Church Street, Cardiff,
  residing at Springfield, Routh, solicitor Times, d p., 1
  Jan , 1881
Wetenhall *see* Mainwaring.
Wetherell : Emery, W. J., of 12, Amersham Grove, Newcross,
  Kent, gent , o s of William, late of Wellington,
  New Zealand, gent. Times, d p, 18 Oct , 1871.
   see Fawsett.
Wetherell-Warneford : Wetherell, Lady H. E. 30 Sept., 1847
  (3475).
Whalley *see* Smythe-Gardiner
Whalley-Tooker : Whalley. 12 May, 1836 (845).
Wharton : Hall, J. 20 Nov., 1807 (1554).
  : Stevenson, J. H. 6 May, 1788 (213).
Wharton-Duff : Wharton, R. 12 July, 1805 (1017).
Whateley *see* Halsey.
  „ Pyddoke.
Wheate *see* Lloyd-Wheate.
Wheatley-Balme . Wheatley, E. B. 20 March, 1857 (1135)
Wheeler *see* Cornelius-Wheeler.
  „ Ray.
Wheeley : Wilson, T. H., of 3, Cavendish Villas, Grosvenor Rd.,
  Richmond. Times, 2 Jan., 1878.
Wheelwright : Hoyle, J. 20 March, 1815 (604).
Whelan *see* Nolan-Whelan.
Wheler : Medhurst, C. 24 Nov., 1843 (4001)
Whelpdale : Richardson, J. 10 May, 1794 (415).
Whetham *see* Boddam-Whetham
Whitaker . Hunt, C 5 April, 1888 (2136).
  see Master-Whitaker.
  „ Nicholls.
  : Wikeley, T. 29 Nov , 1821 (2385)
  see Wikeley-Whitaker.
Whitaker-Bean : Whitaker, J. 23 Nov., 1857 (4128).
  J., to con. same name. W., 23 Nov., 1857
  (D.G. 1167)
Whitaker-Cantrell : Whitaker, H. E. 21 May, 1891 (2926).
Whitaker-Wilson : Whitaker, G 23 July. 1874 (3669)
  : Whitaker, J. 5 Feb , 1869 (723)
White *see* Ashton.
  „ Barrington White.
  „ Corrance.
  „ de Hyde Wytt.
  : Driver, S. W. 2 May, 1835 (902).

White *see* Graham.
   ,, Jervis.
   ,, Kelly-White
   ,, Leasland-White.
   ,, Milner-White
   ,, Neville
   ,, Scarbrow-White
: Tucker, W. W. 3 May, 1817 (1208).
C Morley White, C., of The Elms, Epsom, esq. Times, d p 3 April, 1884
: Whitehair, J. C., of Kentish Town, Middlesex, fruit and potato salesman Times, d p., 26 Oct , 1888.
see Whyte
White Fraser : White, M H , of Winterden, Lillington, Warwicks. Times, d p , 6 Jan., 1883
White-Thomson : Thomson, R T 14 July, 1875 (3665)
White-Popham White, F. 30 Dec , 1852 (3941)
White-Young : White, J. G 3 June, 1805 (749)
Whitefoord *see* Rousselet-Whitefoord
Whitehair *see* White.
Whitehead *see* Taylor-Whitehead
Whitehorn *see* Chamberlain.
Whitehouse *see* Thompson
Whitelocke-Lloyd : Lloyd, G W 12 Feb , 1880 (D G. 138)
Whiteside *see* Porter Whiteside
Whiteway-Wilkinson : Wilkinson, of Teignmouth, Devon, F R.C S Times, d.p., 21 Nov., 1890.
Whitfield : Clarke, J 21 May, 1814 (1083).
Whitfield-Jackson : Jackson, J., of 50, Torrington Square. Midx., gent Times, d p , 9 July, 1884
Whitford-Hawkey Whitford, E T T., of Treventon, St. Colomb, Major, and of Trewollack, St Wenn, both in Cornwall Times, 16 Jan., 11 Jan , 1879.
Whitley *see* Brodhurst
   ,, Deans-Whitley-Dundas
   ,, Rodbard
Emma Daisy · Whitley, Emma, of Greenroyd, Halifax. spinster. Times, d p , 28 March, 1893
Whitlow : Duxbury, R M 2 Oct., 1812 (1987)
Whitmarsh *see* Heaviside-Whitmarsh.
Whitmore *see* Wolryche-Whitmore.
Whitmore-Jones : Whitmore, J. H 8 April, 1829 (688)
: Harris, T. W., of Lincoln's Inn, London Times, 12 July, 1900.
Whitmore-Searle : Whitmore, J., of Edensbridge, Kent, gent Times, d.p., 4 June, 1880.
Whitney *see* Fetherston-Whitney

Whitney *see* Fetherstonhaugh-Whitney
Whittaker *see* Wemyss-Whittaker.
Whittaker-Dunbar *see* Dunbar-Whittaker.
Whittam : Scholes, M., of 42, Nuttall Street, Accrington, Lancs., tobacconist Times, d.p., 20 Sept., 1893
Whittard *see* Middlemore-Whithard.
Whittingstall *see* Fearnley-Whittingstall.
Whittington-Ince Ince, J C. 11 Aug., 1893 (4825)
Whitworth *see* Aylmer-Whitworth
    ,, Hurst-Whitworth
Whyte *see* Gordon Baillie
    ,, Moyser
    : White, E. T., late of Carlisle, now of Bessboro' Gardens, Middx., esq. Times, d p., 17 Sept., 1873.
Whyte-Melville *see* Higginson-Whyte-Melville
Wiber *see* Wybergh.
Wickham : Hird, H. W. 17 Feb., 1843 (554).
Wickham-Boynton : Wickham, T L. Times, 11 Dec., 1899.
Wickins *see* Osbaldeston.
Wicksted : Tollet, C. 25 March, 1814 (731).
Widdowson *see* Cheshire.
Widdrington Cook, S. 3 May, 1798 (537)
    : Cooke, S. E. 17 Feb., 1840 (326).
    : Jacson, S. F 14 Feb., 1856 (624)
    : Tingling, G. J. 3 March, 1809 (269).
    see Tinling-Widdrington.
Wigan *see* Graham-Wigan,
Wiggett-Chute : Wiggett, W. L 22 Feb., 1827 (503)
Wiggin *see* Mowbray.
    ,, Rice-Wiggin.
    ,, Sumner.
Wigglesworth : Crowther, G. 5 Sept., 1864 (4456).
Wight *see* Schank
    : Wight-Hibbit, J 3 Oct., 1818 (1768),
Wight-Boycott : Wight, C. B 1 March, 1886 (1028)
Wigley *see* Greswolde.
    : Hartopp, E. 31 March, 1781 (12174).
    see Meysey-Wigley.
    ,, Mersey-Wigley-Greswolde
Wignall *see* Grafton Wignall
    ,, Witham-Wignall.
Wigsell : Taylor, A. W 31 Jan., 1807 (141)
Wikeley *see* Whitaker.
Wikeley-Whitaker Whitaker, T S., of Everthorpe Hall, E Riding, Yorks, The Manor House, North Runcton, Norfolk, and Goldsmith's Building, Temple, barrister-at-law. Times, 24 July, 1869. Cancelled, see Times, 3 Aug., 1869.

Wilberforce : Rawlins, W., of Stogursey, Somerset late of 2nd Somerset Militia, now residing at Brighton Times, d p., 23 Nov., 1868.
Wilbraham *see* Boottle-Wilbraham.
Wilcocks Lodge, J 6 Feb., 1796 (136).
    see Treffry.
Wilcox *see* Britten
Wild *see* Bagnall-Wild.
Wilde · Wylde, A. C., of 26, Pembroke Gardens, Kensington, W Times, d.p., 10 Feb., 1894.
Wilder : Waghorn, P., of Maidstone, Kent. Times, 25 March, 1893
Wildman-Lushington : Wildman, J. L. 27 Dec., 1869 (227)
Wilkes *see* Darley.
    : Fiske, R. 23 Nov., 1857 (4003)
    see Villers-Wilkes.
Wilkie *see* Allen-Wilkie
Wilkins *see* De Wilton
    „ De Winton.
    „ Eversleigh
    „ Hayward-Wilkins.
Wilkins-Leir Wilkins, E. J. P. 28 Oct., 1881 (5494)
Wilkins-Smith Smith, W., of Hatfield, Hertfordshire Times, 19 Dec., 1900.
Wilkinson *see* Atkinson.
    „ Berdoe-Wilkinson.
    „ Chamberlayne
    „ Denison.
    „ Jones-Wilkinson
    „ Lindley.
    „ Montagu.
    Ricketts, G. Y 1 Oct., 1831 (2019)
    see Ricketts
    Sagar, H. W., of 30, Reservoir Street, Leeds, dyer. Times, d.p., 3 May, 1890.
    see Stephens
    Wade, G. W., of Pannall, Yorks., farmer. Times, d.p., 5 May, 1874
    see Whiteway-Wilkinson
    Fredk. Henry : Wilkinson, Henry Bury, of Oswaldtwistle, Lancs., manuf. chemist. Times, d.p., 16 March, 1889.
Wilkinson-Green Green, J. (junr.). 21 Jan., 1806 (94).
Wilkinson-Pimbury · Wilkinson, C. J., of 32, De Crespigny Park, Denmark Hill Times, d.p., 23 July, 1886
Wilks *see* Darley.
Willan *see* Douglas-Willan.

Willaume see Tanqueray-Willaume
Willding-Jones : Jones, W. 28 July, 1891 (3313).
Willett : Adye, J. W. 28 Feb., 1795 (188).
    : Catt, E. H. 19 June, 1863 (3239 and 3294)
    : Catt, W. 27 June, 1863 (3239 and 3294).
    : Catt, J. 15 Aug., 1863 (13).
    : Catt, E. 27 Oct., 1863 (4233 and 5193).
    see Cleveland.
Willey see Leonard-Willey.
   ,, Palmer-Willey.
William-Browne : Browne, J. 14 July. 1851 (1918).
    : Browne, P. 27 June, 14 July, 1851 (D.G. 553 and 561)
William Powlett : Wallop, B. W. P. 29 Jan., 1867 (634).
William-Prior-Johnson : Richardson, W. P. J. 28 Jan., 1845 (248).
William-Spicer : Heaviside, R. 21 April, 1853 (1226).
Williams see Abbey Williams.
   ,, Alsagar.
   ,, Bacon.
   ,, Barnes-Williams.
   ,, Basset.
   ,, Beynon-Williams
   ,, Buszard.
   ,, Colt.
   ,, Coningesby.
   ,, Greswolde-Williams
   ,, Griffies-Williams.
   ,, Griffith-Williams.
   ,, Grosvenor.
   : Hamlyn, J. 6 March, 1798 (193).
   see Hay-Williams
   : Hollest, J. L. 21 July, 1842 (2017).
   see Harris-Williams.
   ,, Hoole-Lowsley-Williams.
   . Hope, J. W. 11 March, 1811 (479).
   see Jones-Williams
   : Makepeace, S., of Tunbridge Wells, Kent, gent. Times, d.p., 29 Aug., 1877.
   see Monier-Williams.
   ,, Moseley-Williams.
   ,, Nash.
   ,, Picton.
   , Powell-Williams.
   ,, Probyn-Williams.
   ,, Rees-Williams.
   ,, Rich.

Williams R Scott Scott, R D., late of Island Bridge, co.
        Dublin, Ireland Times, 20 June, 1876
    see Taylor.
    ,, Welsh
    : Wood, J. 26 Feb , 1833 (474).
Williams-Bulkeley Williams, R B. 26 June, 1826 (1584)
Williams-Drummond Walker-Drummond, Sir J 30 Dec , 1862
        (24).
        of Hawthornden Walker-Drummond, Sir
            James, Bt Lyon Register, Vol. VI.,
            Jan., 1862.
Williams-Foote : Williams, P L., Capt. R A. Times, 26 Sept ,
        1887
Williams-Freeman : Williams, W. P. 19 Jan , 1822 (153)
Williams-Greswolde · Williams, J F. 7 Jan , 1875 (255)
Williams-Hepworth Williams, E. W G. 12 April, 1881 (1864).
Williams-Hope · Hope, W 14 July, 1826 (1752)
        Williams, J. 16 March, 1782 (12278).
Williams Idris Williams, T H., of 58, Lady Margaret Road,
        London, senr. partner in firm of Idris & Co ,
        Camden Town Times, d.p , 6 Feb , 1893
Williams-Jones-Parry Williams, S. E. M 29 July, 1892 (4492).
Williams-Kerr · Williams, W A D Castle, 15 Sept., 1846
        (D.G. 977).
Williams-Mackreth Williams, H. 16 Dec., 1819 (2282).
Williams-Meyrick Williams, J 23 May, 1877 (3448).
Williams-Onslow Williams, J. 1 March. 1777 (11748)
Williams Trengrove : Williams, E , of Honeycoombe, Cornwall,
        late Capt. 9th Lancers Times, d.p , 22 April, 1874
Williams-Vaughan · Williams, E , of Broom Hall, Oswestry,
        Salop, gent. Times, d p , 8 Dec , 1891.
Williamson : Williamson (formerly Hopper), J. W 14 Dec ,
        1829 (2327).
    see Delmar Williamson
    ,, Ogle.
    ,, Robertson-Williamson
    ,, Winn.
Williamson-Napier · Williamson, James. Arnheim, Holland.
        Lyon Register, Vol. XIII., 30 April,
        1895.
Williamson-Napier : Williamson, Jas., presently residing in
            Arnheim, Holland, being the only
            Brit. representative of Jno. Napier, of
            Kilmahew, reg about 1672. Times,
            15 May, 1895
Willis, A. : Abraham, A W., of W Hampstead, Middlesex. steel
        wire manufacturer. Times, d.p., 5 May, 1893

Willis Earle, R. 29th Geo III., 1789
    see Eroll
    ,, Fleming
    ,, Ord-Willis.
    ,, Stephens
  : Swettenham, T. 7th Geo. III., 1767
Willis-Bund : Willis, J. W B 15 Aug., 1864 (4159)
Willock see Dawes
Willoughby Gordon : Grant, Lt.-Col. John Willoughby (92nd). R.L., Lyon Register, Vol. II . 16 Jan., 1808
Willoughby *see* Heathcote-Drummond-Willoughby.
       ,, Jones-Willoughby.
Wills *see* Evans
    ,, Glyn.
    ,, More
    ,, Stancombe-Wills.
Wills-Sandford : Wills, W. R. D. Castle, 13 Sept., 1847 (D G. 1010 and 1003).
Wills-Sandford-Wills : Wills-Sandford, E. 25 Jan., 1889 (D.G 65)
Willson : Peacock, A. 1 May, 1851 (1162)
Willson-Arnold · Willson, C. 26 Jan., 1818 (190)
Wilmer : Gossip, T G 25 Oct., 1832 (2395)
     : Gossip, W 25 Oct., 1832 (2395)
Wilmot : Bedwardine, J. S. 14 May, 1785 (230).
    see Eardly-Wilmot
    ,, Grimston
    ,, Horton-Wilmot.
    ,, Sitwell.
    ,, Smith-Wilmot.
      Wilmot-Horton, Sir R E 12 Jan., 1842 (85)
Wilmot-Horton : Wilmot, Sir R. E., Bart. 22 May, 1871 (2478).
Wilmsdorff *see* Richards
Wilsden : Pickles, J S , M.A., Vicar of Wooler, N'berland, and Hon Canon of Newcastle Cathedral Ch Times, 6 April, 1889.
    : Pickles, L. W., of Trin Coll., Cambs., and Wooler Vicarage, N'berland Times, 6 April, 1889.
Wilson *see* Anthony-Wilson.
    ,, Ashburner.
    ,, Atkinson.
    ,, Bagster Wilson.
    ,, Bailey.
    ,, Bromley-Wilson
    · Bugg, J , E., M. A , F. C., all of Prospect House, Felixstowe, Suffolk, formerly of Laurel Farm, Felixstowe. Times, d.p., 12 May, 1887

Wilson see Carus-Wilson.
    „ Cockburn.
    „ Crawhall-Wilson.
    „ Dobie-Wilson.
    „ Danvers Wilson
    Evans, J. G. 21 April, 1808 (565)
    see Ewbanke
    : Gallaher, J. W., of Cockermouth, Cumberland, Inland Revenue Officer. Times, d p., 18 Feb., 1886
    see Green
    „ Henniker.
    „ Hill-Wilson.
    : Hunt, J 10 Jan., 1839 (81)
    see Lush-Wilson
    „ Lyall-Wilson.
    : Macklin, Thos. W., 8 May, 1784 (D G 4447)
    see Montagu.
    „ Maryon-Wilson.
    : Newberry. C W. 7 Jan., 1832 (73)
    see Newman-Wilson
    : Nixon, T. 16 Oct., 1773 (11396)
    see Oliphant
    „ Parkinson
    „ Rae-Wilson
    „ Rimington-Wilson
    „ Slater.
    . Smyth, G 4 Jan., 1825 (84).
    see Stewart-Wilson.
    „ Stott
    : Tyrwhitt, H T 23 Feb., 1876 (1669)
    see Tyrwhitt-Wilson
    „ Whitaker-Wilson.
    „ Walton-Wilson
    „ Wentworth.
    „ Wheeley
    Geo. Bailey Wilson, G, of Thorny Hills, Kendal, W'moreland Times. 21 June, 1881.
    John Patrick Wilson, Patrick, perpetual Curate of Moxley, Stafford Times, 13 May, 1867
    „ Whitaker-Wilson
    „ Wright-Wilson.
Wilson-Atkinson : Wilson, G. C, and Jane A his wife W, 23 Nov., 1860 (D G. 1474).
Wilson-Fitzgerald Wilson, W H 20 July, 1872 (3299)
Wilson-Fountayne Wilson, R 20 July, 1803 (1003)
Wilson-France Wilson, T. 25 June, 1817 (1543)
Wilson-Haffenden : Wilson, J. 23 Dec, 1871 (1).

Wilson-Norton : Wilson, C., of 12, Crescent Place, Mornington Crescent, Middlesex, gent. Times, 10 July, 1867.
: Wilson, C., of 60, Oseney Crescent, Kentish Town, Middlesex Times, 20 Feb , 1871.
Wilson-Patrick *see* Wilson, John Patrick
Wilson-Philip : Wilson, A P. 15 Feb , 1811 (406).
Wilson-Stewart : Stewart, W. Times, d.p., 5 Feb., 1876.
Wilson-Todd : Wilson, W. H. and J. M. R. 14 Aug , 1855 (3178)
Wilson-Thorbou · Wilson, C. A , formerly of Guernsey, now of Bishopsgate Street Within, London, gent. Times, d p , 21 Nov , 22 Nov, 1883.
Wiltshire : Rowland, E., of 17, Grove Road, N. Brixton, Surrey, spinster Times. d.p , 30 Oct., 1889
· Rowland, W. S., of 17, Grove Road, Brixton, Surrey Times, d p , 26 Nov , 1889
Wilym-Jones : Jones Rev. J., of Bwlch Gwyr Vicarage, Denbigh. M A. Times, d.p., 24 Aug., 1888.
Winchcombe *see* Clifford
Winckler *see* Von Winckler.
Winder *see* Lyon-Winder.
„ Corbett-Winder.
Windebank *see* Barber.
Windeck *see* Schapira Windeck
Windham : Lukin, W 28 April, 1824 (700)
· Smijth-Windham, A 23 June. 1888 (3556)
: Smijth-Windham, W. G 12 Nov , 1861 (4515).
see Smijth-Windham.
Windle Pilkington : Pilkington, W. Times, 22 Aug , 1867.
Windsor *see* Smith-Windsor
Windsor-Aubrey : Windsor, H. G 13 April, 1847 (1374).
Window Morisset Morisset Window, H , of Porto Grande, St. Vincente. Port Times, d p., 6 Jan , 1886.
Windsor-Clive : Clive, H. (Baroness Windsor) 8 Nov., 1855 (4184).
Winfield · Higgin, E , of Troston Lodge, nr Bury St Edmunds, gent Times, d.p., 30 Sept., 1880.
Winfield-Roll : Roll, G. W., of 33, Fentiman Road, Clapham Road, London, gent Times. 25 Oct . 1886
Wing *see* Staunton-Wing
Wingate *see* Fenton-Wingate.
Wingate-Saul : Saul, W. W., of Fenton-Cauthorne House, Lancs., M D. Times, d p , 20 July, 1891.
Wingfield *see* Baker.
„ Digby-Wingfield.
Wingfield-Digby : Wingfield, G D. W., 2 July, 1856 (D G 761)

Wingfield-Stratford : Wingfield, Hon. J. 23 Dec., 1803 (5).
Winn : Williamson, J. 17 March, 1815 (509)
Winne *see* Griffith-Winne
Winnington-Ingram : Winnington, E. 8 July, 1817 (1621)
Winsloe *see* Phillipps.
Winslow *see* Forbes Winslow
Winsor *see* Benyon Winsor
Winston : Bown, J. 29 April, 1795 (392)
       : Sandford, B. 53rd Geo. III , 1813
Winstone *see* Davis-Winstone.
Winter : Cason, W., of Mileham, Norfolk, farmer and cattle
           dealer. Times, d p , 2 Oct , 1891
       see Sanderson
Winter-Irving : Winter, W. I. 24 Jan., 1889 (668)
Winterbottom *see* Shepley
       ,, Wynter
Winton-Robertson : Robertson. R., of 244, Cowbridge Road,
       Canton. Cardiff. Times, d.p., 28 July, 1891
Wiseman Clarke : Clarke, S. M , Lieut.-Col H M. 73rd Perth-
       shire Reg Times, 21 Oct , 1873.
Wisheart *see* Baillie-Cochrane-Wisheart
Witham : Silvertop, H. 16 Nov., 1802 (1205).
       see Sutcliffe-Witham
Witham-Wignall : Witham, J. W. 13 Feb, 1892 (1107)
Wither · Bigg, L. 5 Dec , 1789 (757).
Withers *see* Mitchell-Withers
Witkowski *see* Witting
Witt *see* de Witt
Witting : Witkowski, S. C. and M. C., both of Gresham House,
       Old Broad Street, London, merchants Times, d.p., 1
       May, 1875
Witts *see* Steere
Wolf *see* Birch-Wolfe
Wolfe *see* Ward
Wolfenden, Geo. : King, Chas (being an assumed name to
       resume original), of Exeter, land surveyor Times, 9
       June, 1873.
Wolferstan : Pipe, S. 5 June, 1776 (11672)
Wolley *see* Phillips-Wolley
       ,, Copley.
       : Hurt, J F. T. 25 Sept. 1827 (2097).
       see Oldnall-Wolley
Wolley Dod · Wolley, C. 8 April, 1868 (2220)
Wolrige *see* Gordon-Wolrige
Wolrige Gordon : Gordon-Wolrige, Henry. previously Perkins.
       Lyon Register, Vol. IX., 17 March, 1873.
Wolryche-Whitmore : Laing. F. H. 26 Nov., 1864 (6373).

Wolryche Stansfield *see* Stansfield.
Wolseley-Jenkins : Jenkins, C B. H. 15 Nov., 1894 (6506)
Wolstenholme : Breton, W 26 April, 1806 (570).
Wombwell *see* Orby-Wombwell.
Wontner *see* Hill-Wontner.
Wontner-Smith Smith, L., M , G M , J W, and W. C., all of
    13, Aubert Park, Highbury, Middlesex Times, d p., 16
    March 1890
Wood *see* Bateson Wood.
    Bolesworth, C , of Leicester Times, d p., 30 Dec, 1879.
    : Carey, C , of 9, Barnsbury Road, Islington, Middlesex,
        surgeon and apothecary Times, d p., 11 April,
        1870
    see Carter-Wood.
    „ Davies.
    „ Edwards-Wood.
    : Hipwell, J., farmer, of Welford, Northampton. Times,
        d p , 30 June, 1866
    : Howarth, Margt., late of Anerley, Surrey, now of 15,
        Hodge Lane, Prestwich, Lancs., gentlewoman.
        Times, d p., 16 Nov., 1891
    see Laud du Boys.
    „ Lee-Wood.
    : Lockwood, W. M. 9 June, 1838 (1341)
    see Lockwood
    „ Moore
    : Parrott 8 Nov., 1850 (2946).
    see Pendarves
    „ Searles-Wood.
    : Skelton, W., of Brampton, Cumberland, Inland Rev.
        Officer Times, d.p , 1 Dec, 1888
    see Shuckburgh
    „ Stuckey.
    : Walker, T 25 April, 1817 (1132).
    see Watson
    „ Williams
    „ Woodd
Wood-Acton : Wood, A 4 July, 1874 (3462)
Wood-Besly : Wood, E H 23 Aug , 1890 (4831)
Wood-Craster Wood. T. 8 May, 1838 (1112)
Wood-Davison : Wood, T. 16 June, 1818 (1153).
Wood Macdonald Wood, L M , of Home Villa, Queen's Park,
    Brighton, spinster. Times. 20 June. 1891
Wood-Martin Wood, A (widow) 28 Aug , 15 Sept., 1874
    (D.G 553).
Wood-Ryder : Wood, A R 30 Dec., 1875 (D.G 2 and 858)
Woodall-Woodhall : Woodhall. G F G Times, d.p , 6 June.
    1896

Woodbridge : Fellows, M 9 March, 1824 (395)
    see Pindar
Woodcock see Croft
    ,, Little.
Woodd · Wood, J., of 22, Upper Woburn Place, widow, to resume family surname of late husband's ancestors Times, 8 Feb., 1881
  : Wood, B. H., J. M., and A. A., all of 22 Upper Woburn Place, London, to resume ancestral surname of Woodd Times, 8 Feb., 1881
    Wood, W N., of Ontario, Canada, gent., descendant of Alexr. Woodd, of Salop, Eng., esq Times, 29 March, 1883
  : Wood, P C., of 79, Marquess Road, Canonbury, London, to resume family name Woodd Times. 23 Oct., 1896.
Woodforde : Ffooks, W., M.A., barrister-at-law Times, d p, 26 Oct, 1871
Woodhall see Woodall-Woodhall
Woodham-Kingsmill : Woodham, J 3 June, 1824 (931)
Woodham see Nash-Woodham
Woodhead Schenck, J W R., of Stretford Road. Old Trafford, Lancs, and of Trinity Hall. Cambs., gent Times, d p., 2 Jan., 1892.
Woodhouse see Beldams-Johns.
    ,, Gordon-Woodhouse
Woodman-Hastings · Woodman, C J., of Cornwell, Oxford, spinster. Times, 31 Oct, 1867.
           Woodman, W H. formerly of Canon Frome, Hereford, now of Maugersbury Manor, Gloucester, esq Times, 31 Oct, 1867
Woodroffe Billinghurst, W 2 Oct., 1790 (599).
    : Billinghurst, G. 17 Sept, 1824 (1536)
Woodrouffe-Smith Woodrouffe, T 12 April. 1785 (177).
Woodrow see Cremer.
Woods Snooke, M. G., Fellow and late Assistant Tutor of Trinity College, Cambridge, and of Lincoln's Inn Times, 16 Feb, 1864
    see Snooke Woods.
Woodward Andrews A. 13 Oct, 1820 (1997 and 2014)
         Andrews R. 9 July, 1796 (653)
         Atkins, L 22 Jan., 1853 (201)
    see Lee-Warner.
Woodyeare Elwin, F J. 26 June, 1812 (1258).
Woodwright see Lucas
Woolby see Balls Woolby.

Woolcock *see* Pye.
Woolcombe-Adams : Woolcombe, E. 29 April, 1893 (2686).
Woolley-Hart : Isaac, A. B., of 14, Devonshire Place, Middlesex. Times, d p., 9 Feb., 1894.
Woolloton *see* Gardner-Woolloton.
Woolsey *see* Packer.
Worge : Jenner, T. 8th Geo. III., 1768.
Workman : MacNaghten, Sir F. 11 March, 1823 (394).
Wormal, Robert O. · Wormal, O., of Alford, Lincoln. bank manager. Times, 14 Dec., 1888
Wormald : Armitage, H. W. 20 Sept., 1871 (4267)
· Wormald-Mason, J., now residing at Kentish Town, Middlesex, gent., 4th s. of John, late of Cookridge Hall, York, esq. Times, d p., 7 Jan., 1870.
Wormald-Wormald : Wormald. Harry W., of Sawley Hall, Ripon, and Cookridge Hall, near Leeds, York, and of the Union Club, Brighton, Sussex. 20 April. 1882.
: Wormald. H. W., of Yorks. and of Union Club, Brighton, Sussex. esq. Times, 24 April, 1882.
Worrall *see* Rooke.
Worsley *see* Fleming.
: Lees, J. 31 Jan., 1775 (11531).
see Pennyman.
,, Tindal-Carill-Worsley.
Worsley-Benison : Worsley, H. 7 March, 1837 (612).
Worsley-Taylor : Worsley, H. W. 30 Nov., 1881 (6605).
Wort *see* Wortley.
Worthington *see* Bayley-Worthington.
: Bromfield, S W. 9 March, 1883 (1385).
: Pistor, J. 23 May, 1826 (1221).
Worthington-Wright : Worthington, W. W. 28 Dec., 1847 (1)
Wortley : Stuart, Hon. J. A. 17 Jan., 1795 (43).
see Montague-Stuart-Wortley-Mackenzie.
· Wort J., chymical manufr., of Euston Road, Midx Times, d.p., 8 Nov., 1877.
Wray : Atkinson. G. D.G., 20 Oct., 1809.
Wren : Uren, G G. Times. d.p., 13 June, 1896.
Wren-Hoskyns Hoskyns, C. 15 April. 1837 (1027).
Wrigglesworth *see* Mills.
Wright *see* Atkyins-Wright.
,. Barton-Wright.
,, Burton-Phillipson.
., Collier-Wright.
., Cory-Wright.
.. Despard.

Wright *see* Howell.
  „ Ingilby.
  „ Lawson.
  : Luard, P. 14 May, 1796 (463)
  : Ord, R. 20 July, 1814 (1535)
  see Osmaston.
  · Street, J F., D., and J C 8 March, 1865 (1498)
  : Trice, T 8 June, 1818 (1075)
  · Turner, S W. 19 May, 1863 (2632)
  see Tylden-Wright.
  „ Verney.
  „ Warren
  „ Wilson.
  „ Worthington-Wright.
Wright-Anderson : Wright, E. 26 Nov., 1835 (2255).
Wright Armstrong : Armstrong, W. J. and F. E. 20 Feb., 1868 (1364)
Wright-Biddulph Wright, A. G. 11 Jan. 1836 (79)
Wright Bruce Bruce, Sir F. W. A. 1 Feb., 1867 (160).
Wright-Ingle Ingle, G W., of St. Neot's, Hunts., esq. Times, 8 March, 1881
Wright-Nooth : Wright, G. W. W., of Miascourt, Dulwich Road, Herne Hill, Surrey. Times, d p., 1 Jan., 7 Jan., 1879
Wright-Wilson Wilson, Sir H. 10 Dec., 1814 (2487)
Wrighte *see* Powlett-Wright.
  ., Benyon-de Beauvoir.
Wrighte-Wyndham Wyndham, Maria A 26 Nov., 1830 (2518).
Wrightson *see* Battie-Wrightson
Wrixon *see* Becher.
Wroughton : Montagu, G. W 12 April, 1826 (878).
Wyatt Goode, T. 14 March, 1814 (650).
  : Penfold, H. 18 Nov., 1839 (2276)
  see Davies
Wyatt-Edgell *see* Verney-Cave.
      : Wyatt, E 22 Oct., 1813 (2117)
Wyatt-Smith : Smith, F. of 316, Goldhawk Road, Shepherd's Bush, Middlesex 1 Nov., 1878
Wybergh *see* Lawson
      · Wiber, F. L., of Fenchurch Street and Woburn Place, Middlesex Times, 7 Feb., 1876
Wybrants *see* Battersby-Wybrants
      ., Geale-Wybrants
      : Higginbotham, C W, of Rathmines, co. Dublin Times, 12 Jan., 1900.
      see Middleton-Wybrants.
      „ Phipson-Wybrants
Wyeth *see* Taylor.

Wygram *see* FitzWygram.
Wyke-Smith : Smith, W., L.R.C.P., M.R.C.S., of Islip, Oxon. Times, 26 Jan., 1871.
Wykeham-Fiennes *see* Twisleton.
Wykeham *see* Twisleton-Wykeham-Fiennes.
Wykeham-Musgrave : Wykeham, A. W and G. 11 July, 1876 (4595).
Wykeham-Martin *see* Cornwallis.
            : Wykeham, F. 18 Oct., 1821 (2072).
Wykes-Finch : Finch, Wm. Revd Times, d.p., 11 May, 1896.
Wylde *see* Browne.
    „ Fewtrell-Wyde.
    „ Wilde.
Wyley, James H. : Wyley, H., formerly of Coventry, now of High Onn, Staffs., land agent and valuer. Times, d.p., 1 April, 1880.
Wylie *see* Adams-Wylie.
Wynch *see* St. Maur-Wynch.
Wyndham *see* Bouverie-Campbell-Wyndham.
      „ Campbell-Wyndham.
      „ Edwin.
      „ Pleydell-Bouverie-Campbell-Wyndham.
      · Thorne-George, A. M. E. Times, 11 Jan., 1890
      see Wrighte-Wyndham.
      · Wyndham-Ihve. 21 Jan., 1839 (142)
Wyndham-Quin : Quin, Hon. W. H. 7 April, 1815 (651).
Wynn-Bellasyse : Wynn, T. E. 3 Jan., 1803 (114).
Wynne . Cumming, B. W. 17 Jan., 1843 (160).
      · Fletcher, L 16 March, 1836 (515).
      : Fletcher, T. H. 31 Aug., 1864 (4415).
      see Griffith-Winne.
      „ Holland Wynne.
      „ Miles-Wynne.
Wynne-Aubrey : Wynne, G. 17 April, 1813 (773).
Wynne-Finch · Griffiths-Wynne, C. 7 Aug., 1863 (3946).
Wynne-Owen : Owen, Jane, of 7, Warrior Gardens, St. Leonards-on-Sea Times, 15 Aug., 1892.
Wynne-Pendarvis : Stackhouse, E. W. 15 May, 1815 (924).
Wynter : Mammatt, A. 6 Dec., 1802 (1293).
       : Winterbottom, D., of Fulham Times, d.p., 23 June, 1894.
Wytt *see* de Hyde Wytt.
Wyrley Birch : Birch, W., late of Norfolk now of Shrewsbury, Salop, esq. Times, d.p., 3 Feb., 1888.

Y

Yalden : Lambden, G   19 June, 1781 (12199).
        · Lambden, M   19 June, 1781 (12199)
Yale   Jones-Parry, W P   30 May, 1823 (1075)
        Jones-Parry, W.   24 Aug., 1867 (4823).
Yapp *see* Chapman
    Chapman, S. A   1 Oct., 1838 (2108)
    see Chapman-Yapp
Yarborough *see* Cooke-Yarborough
Yarburgh   Greame, Y.   25 Sept., 1852 (2574)
        : Lloyd, G J   25 April, 1857 (1536)
Yarde-Buller   Buller-Yarde-Buller, J (Baron Churston)   W, 6 March, 1860 (D G 359).
    see Buller-Yarde-Buller
Yate *see* Peacock-Yate
Yate-Sprott . Yate, S   9 Jan., 1801 (69)
Yates *see* Leigh
    „ Park-Yates
    „ Shaw-Yates.
    „ Thompson-Yates
    Wardell, H. Y.   Times, d p , 1 June, 1896.
Yates-Southgate : Yates, C. and A , of Esquimalt House, Chiswick   Times, d p , 18 July, 1895.
Yeates   Michaelson, R H M   31 May, 1837 (1406)
    : Richards, J   31 May, 1837 (1406).
Yeatman-Biggs   Yeatman, A G   2 Jan., 1877 (169)
Yeldham-Richard   Yeldham   5 May, 1792 (273)
Yelverton : Gould, Rt. Hon Lord Grey of Ruthyn.   25 Feb., 1800 (186)
    Henry. H. R., and Barbara (Baroness Grey de Ruthyn) his wife. W., 3 Jan., 1849 (D G 30)
    : Henry, H. R   2 Jan., 1849 (73).
Yerburgh *see* Wardell-Yerburgh.
Yeulett *see* Stubington.
Yockney *see* Hansard.
York   Sheepshanks, W   23 July, 1796 (743).
Yorke *see* Dallas-Yorke
Young *see* Anderson
    „ Brooke.
    : Jarvis, J   3 June, 1805 (749).
    see Kettle-Young
    : Latour, W F. J , of Hexton. Hertford formerly Capt H M Grenadier Guards   Times, d p , 7 April, 1870.

Young *see* Lewis.
    Sir John *see* Lisgar (Baron).
    see Reynolds.
    ,, White-Young.
Young-Hughes: Hughes, T., of St. David's College, Lampeter. 22 Sept, 1888
Young-Jamieson   Young, J.   14 April, 1848 (1452).
Young-Leslie *see* Farquharson
Younghusband *see* Palmer.
Young-Scott of Redford . Young, John   Lyon Register, Vol. X., 18 Jan., 1878.

Z

Zacharoff Gortzacoff   Zacharoff, Z. B., of 41, Threadneedle St., London, merchant and interpreter.   Times, 11 March, 1873.
von Zedlitz *see* Angern.
Ziegenbein *see* Liebenrood
Zimmermann Barbaro   Barbaro, C E , of S. Mary's Church, Devon, and of Malta, gent.   Times, 5 Feb., 1878
Zwilchenbart *see* Erskine.

CPSIA information can be obtained
at www.ICGtesting.com
Printed in the USA
BVHW042240131121
621597BV00008BA/504